T0214073

Lecture Notes in Computer Science   12810

More information about this subseries at http://www.springer.com/series/7407

Tomasz Jurdziński · Stefan Schmid (Eds.)

Structural Information and Communication Complexity

28th International Colloquium, SIROCCO 2021
Wrocław, Poland, June 28 – July 1, 2021
Proceedings

 Springer

Editors
Tomasz Jurdziński (ID)
Institute of Computer Science
University of Wrocław
Wrocław, Poland

Stefan Schmid (ID)
University of Vienna
Vienna, Austria

ISSN 0302-9743   ISSN 1611-3349   (electronic)
Lecture Notes in Computer Science
ISBN 978-3-030-79526-9   ISBN 978-3-030-79527-6   (eBook)
https://doi.org/10.1007/978-3-030-79527-6

LNCS Sublibrary: SL1 – Theoretical Computer Science and General Issues

This Springer imprint is published by the registered company Springer Nature Switzerland AG
The registered company address is: Gewerbestrasse 11, 6330 Cham, Switzerland

Preface

The papers in this volume were presented at the 28th International Colloquium on Structural Information and Communication Complexity (SIROCCO 2021), which was planned to be held during June 28 – July 1, 2021, in Wrocław, Poland. However, due to the COVID-19 pandemic, the conference took place online, as in the previous year.

SIROCCO is devoted to the study of the interplay between structural knowledge, communication, and computing in decentralized systems of multiple communicating entities. Special emphasis is given to innovative approaches leading to better understanding of the relationship between computing and communication.

This year, for the first time, we moved the submission deadline significantly earlier, to 4 December, 2020, (usually the deadline is around March), while keeping the usual conference date. We are happy that because of, or despite, this change we could attract a large number of submissions compared to previous years. In total we received 48 submissions, from which we accepted 20, i.e., 42%.

This volume also includes abstracts of the keynote presentations and one invited paper from a keynote speaker. The paper "Superfast Coloring in CONGEST via Efficient Color Sampling" by Magnús M. Halldórsson and Alexandre Nolin received the Best Paper Award, and "New Approximation Algorithms for the Heterogeneous Weighted Delivery Problem" by Davide Bilò, Luciano Gualà, Stefano Leucci, Guido Proietti, and Mirko Rossi won the Best Student Paper Award.

We would like to thank the authors who submitted their work to SIROCCO this year and the Program Committee members and subreviewers for their valuable and insightful reviews and comments. We would also like to thank the keynote speakers, Rotem Oshman (Tel Aviv University, Israel), Dan Alistarh (IST, Austria), and Kenneth Cheung (NASA, USA), for their excellent talks, and Friedhelm Meyer auf der Heide for his featured talk as the recipient of the 2021 SIROCCO Prize for Innovation in Distributed Computing. The SIROCCO Steering Committee, chaired by Magnús M. Halldórsson, provided help and guidance throughout the process. The EasyChair system was used to handle the submission of papers and to manage the review process. Without all of these people it would not have been possible to come up with these proceedings and the great conference program.

June 2021

Tomasz Jurdziński
Stefan Schmid

Laudatio

2021 SIROCCO Prize for Innovation in Distributed Computing

It is a pleasure to award the 2021 SIROCCO Prize for Innovation in Distributed Computing to Friedhelm Meyer auf der Heide. Friedhelm has been an active contributor to the field of Distributed Computing since its very beginning, with pioneering contributions to online scheduling problems, load balancing, distributed data structures, hashing, network routing, mobile facility location, and distributed data streams. Not only has he produced excellent research on distributed computing but he has also inspired and mentored several young researchers, some of whom are now well established scientists in this field. His numerous research contributions include seven articles in SIROCCO and a keynote lecture.

The prize is awarded for his contributions to **continuous strategies for swarms of mobile robots**. The decentralized coordination of large teams of mobile robots has been a key research theme is this community, but primarily with the simplifying assumption that robots act only at discrete times. This discrete time model and its variations have been canonical in the research on distributed mobile robotics. Friedhelm advocated the unorthodox model of *continuous protocols* [8] where robots observe their surroundings and execute the protocol continuously while they are moving. Such a model requires a completely different set of tools for analyzing robot protocols and proving their correctness and efficiency. This model was first presented in the SIROCCO 2010 paper [1], which considers continuous strategies for line formation by mobile robots with limited vision. Subsequent papers addressed the fundamental problem of gathering and its other variants [4, 6, 7] in the same model, thus establishing the utility of this new model.

Another important contribution of Friedhelm is the introduction of new techniques for analyzing well-known algorithms for mobile robots which, among other results, provided an asymptotically optimal time bound for the classical convergence algorithm [3] and a tight bound for the first known gathering algorithm in the limited visibility model [2]. Yet another novel contribution of Friedhelm is the consideration of energy-efficient strategies for mobile robot formation problems in the continuous plane [5].

The model proposed and studied in detail by Friedhelm and his coauthors has two key features: limited visibility of robots and continuous motion, which brings it closer to the research performed by the robotics community as well as control theory researchers, thus bridging the gap between three different communities of researchers who work on mobile robots. With his coauthors, Friedhelm is already extending his work to the three dimensional case, presenting the first gathering algorithm for robots moving continuously in the 3D space in an article [9] that received the Best Student

Paper Award at SIROCCO 2020. We believe Friedhelm's contributions will continue to inspire young researchers to work in this emerging area of distributed computing.

The 2021 Award committee[1]

Keren Censor-Hillel	Technion, Israel
Shantanu Das	Aix-Marseille Université, France
Michele Flammini	Gran Sasso Science Institute, Italy
Magnús M. Halldórsson (Chair)	Reykjavik University, Iceland
Zvi Lotker	Ben Gurion University, Israel
Boaz Patt-Shamir	Tel Aviv University, Israel
Sébastien Tixeuil	Sorbonne Université, France

Selected Publications Related to Friedhelm Meyer auf der Heide's Contribution:

1. B. Degener, B. Kempkes, P. Kling, F. Meyer auf der Heide, A Continuous, Local Strategy for Constructing a Short Chain of Mobile Robots. Proc. SIROCCO 2010: 168–182.
2. B. Degener, B. Kempkes, T. Langner, F. Meyer auf der Heide, P. Pietrzyk, R. Wattenhofer, A tight runtime bound for synchronous gathering of autonomous robots with limited visibility. Proc. SPAA 2011: 139–148.
3. A. Cord-Landwehr, B. Degener, M. Fischer, M. Hüllmann, B. Kempkes, A. Klaas, P. Kling, S. Kurras, M. Märtens, F. Meyer auf der Heide, C. Raupach, K. Swierkot, D. Warner, C. Weddemann, D. Wonisch, A New Approach for Analyzing Convergence Algorithms for Mobile Robots. Proc. ICAL P(2) 2011: 650–661.
4. B. Kempkes, P. Kling, F. Meyer auf der Heide, Optimal and Competitive runtime bounds for continuous, local gathering of mobile robots. Proc. SPAA 2012: 18–26.
5. P. Brandes, B. Degener, B. Kempkes, F. Meyer auf der Heide, Energy-efficient Strategies for Building Short Chains of Mobile Robots Locally. Theoretical Computer Science, 509: 97–112 (2013).
6. B. Degener, B. Kempkes, P. Kling, F. Meyer auf der Heide, Linear and Competitive Strategies for Continuous Robot Formation Problems. ACM Transactions on Parallel Computing, 2(1): 2:1–2:18 (2015).
7. S. Li, C. Markarian, F. Meyer auf der Heide, P. Podlipyan, A Continuous Strategy for Collisionless Gathering. Proc. ALGOSENSORS 2017: 182–197.
8. P. Kling, F. Meyer auf der Heide, Continuous Protocols for Swarm Robotics. Distributed Computing by Mobile Entities, Current Research in Moving and Computing, 317–334 (2019).
9. M. Braun, J. Castenow, F. Meyer auf der Heide, Local Gathering of Mobile Robots in Three Dimensions. Proc. SIROCCO 2020: 63–79.

---

[1] We wish to thank the nominator for the nomination and for contributing to this text.

Organization

Program Committee Chairs

Tomasz Jurdziński   University of Wrocław, Poland
Stefan Schmid   University of Vienna, Austria

Program Committee

Ittai Abraham	VMware Research, Israel
Petra Berenbrink	University of Hamburg, Germany
Marcin Bieńkowski	University of Wrocław, Poland
Sebastian Brandt	ETH Zurich, Switzerland
Shantanu Das	Aix-Marseille University, France
Sándor Fekete	TU Braunschweig, Germany
Antonio Fernandez Anta	IMDEA Networks Institute, Spain
Magnús M. Halldórsson	Reykjavik University, Iceland
Taisuke Izumi	Osaka University, Japan
Tomasz Jurdzinski	University of Wrocław, Poland
Christoph Lenzen	MPI for Informatics, Germany
Toshimitsu Masuzawa	Osaka University, Japan
Friedhelm Meyer Auf der Heide	Heinz Nixdorf Institute and University of Paderborn, Germany
Stefan Neumann	University of Vienna, Austria
Rotem Oshman	Tel Aviv University, Israel
Boaz Patt-Shamir	Tel Aviv University, Israel
Yvonne-Anne Pignolet	DFINITY, Switzerland
Maria Potop-Butucaru	Sorbonne Université and LIP6, France
Andrea Richa	Arizona State University, USA
Peter Robinson	City University of Hong Kong, Hong Kong
Christian Scheideler	University of Paderborn, Germany
Stefan Schmid	University of Vienna, Austria
Sebastien Tixeuil	Universite Pierre et Marie Curie, France
Jara Uitto	Aalto University, Finland
Przemysław Uznański	University of Wrocław, Poland
André van Renssen	The University of Sydney, Australia

Steering Committee

Keren Censor-Hillel	Technion, Israel
Michele Flammini	Gran Sasso Science Institute, Italy
Pierre Fraigniaud	Université de Paris and CNRS, France

Magnús M. Halldórsson (Chair)	Reykjavik University, Iceland
Zvi Lotker	Ben-Gurion University, Israel
Andrea Richa	Arizona State University, USA
Christian Scheideler	Paderborn University, Germany
Boaz Patt-Shamir	Tel Aviv University, Israel

Organizing Committee

Marcin Bieńkowski	University of Wrocław, Poland
Adam Gańczorz	University of Wrocław, Poland
Paweł Garncarek	University of Wrocław, Poland
Tomasz Jurdziński	University of Wrocław, Poland
Artur Kraska	University of Wrocław, Poland
Aleksander Łukasiewicz	University of Wrocław, Poland
Przemysław Uznański	University of Wrocław, Poland

Additional Reviewers

Almethen, Abdullah
Altisen, Karine
Brankovic, Milutin
Bu, Gewu
Bund, Johannes
Böhm, Martin
Cambus, Mélanie
Castenow, Jannik
Chalopin, Jérémie
Connor, Matthew
Daymude, Joshua
Dereniowski, Dariusz
Di Luna, Giuseppe Antonio
Dobrev, Stefan
Dong, Rongcheng
Eades, Patrick
Feldmann, Michael
Fischer, Orr
Függer, Matthias
Götte, Thorsten
Hanckowiak, Michal

Harbig, Jonas
Hinnenthal, Kristian
Keldenich, Phillip
Knollmann, Till
Kraska, Artur
Labourel, Arnaud
Maack, Marten
Maus, Yannic
Miller, Avery
Molla, Anisur Rahaman
Navarra, Alfredo
Ost, Wolfgang
Padalkin, Andreas
Portmann, Julian
Sauerwald, Thomas
Saulpic, David
Sha, Yuan
Skretas, George
Srinivas, Shreyas
Theofilatos, Michail
Wiederhake, Ben

Abstracts of Invited Talks

Collecting Coupons is Faster with Friends

Dan Alistarh and Peter Davies

Institute of Science and Technology Austria (IST Austria), Am Campus 1, 3400
Klosterneuburg, Austria
{dan.alistarh,peter.davies}@ist.ac.at

Abstract. In this note, we introduce a distributed twist on the classic coupon
collector problem: a set of m collectors wish to each obtain a set of n coupons;
for this, they can each sample coupons uniformly at random, but can also meet
in pairwise interactions, during which they can exchange coupons. By doing so,
they hope to reduce the number of coupons that must be sampled by each
collector in order to obtain a full set. This extension is natural when considering
real-world manifestations of the coupon collector phenomenon, and has been
remarked upon and studied empirically (Hayes and Hannigan 2006, Ahmad
et al. 2014, Delmarcelle 2019).

We provide the first theoretical analysis for such a scenario. We find that
"coupon collecting with friends" can indeed significantly reduce the number of
coupons each collector must sample, and raises interesting connections to the
more traditional variants of the problem. While our analysis is in most cases
asymptotically tight, there are several open questions raised, regarding finer-
grained analysis of both "coupon collecting with friends," and of a long-studied
variant of the original problem in which a collector requires multiple full sets of
coupons.

Keywords: Coupon collector problem · Population protocols · Probability

Structure Structuring Structures

Kenneth C. Cheung📇

NASA Ames Research Center, Moffett Field CA 94035, USA
kenny@nasa.gov
https://www.nasa.gov/centers/ames/cct/about/bios/
kennycheung

Abstract. We consider programmable materials as systems with the ability to form versatile structures as similar to the ability of a digital image to approximate any image, given high enough resolution, with a very simple set of discrete components. Instead of colors, we can tune effective shape and mechanical behavior (instead of pixels, we refer to building blocks as voxels, for volumetric pixels). Modular reconfigurable structures have been appreciated throughout technological history. A key philosophical idea behind programmable materials is that they can be engineered to maintain a fixed precision at essentially arbitrary scale, achieved by careful design of connections that display symmetric error distributions [4], allowing for tolerances that do not increase with system size. This principle is well exercised in the scaling robustness of digital communication and computation systems, which rely on well-engineered encoding, error detection, and correction for systems composed of many similar discrete information building blocks [5]. Can we formulate a general mathematical theory of structured fabrication of physical products? An argument for the timeliness of this question (and revisiting prior versions thereof) is given by the existence of examples of physical modular structural systems that no longer present a mechanical performance compromise relative to conventionally manufactured hardware. These 'metamaterials' are possible because assembly allows production of almost any geometry with almost any material [2], and with progress in our ability to characterize the effect of geometry on the whole of material mechanical properties [1]. The most significant benefit might be in extended material life-cycles and corresponding reductions in energy use [3].

Keywords: Programmable materials · Fabrication · Metamaterials

References

1. Ashby, M.F., Gibson, L.J.: Cellular Solids: Structure and Properties, pp. 175–231. Press Syndicate of the University of Cambridge, Cambridge (1997)
2. Cheung, K.C., Gershenfeld, N.: Reversibly assembled cellular composite materials. Science **341**(6151), 1219–1221 (2013). https://doi.org/10.1126/science.1240889. https://science.sciencemag.org/content/341/6151/1219

Supported by NASA STMD Game Changing Development Program.

3. Gregg, C.E., Jenett, B., Cheung, K.C.: Assembled, modular hardware architectures-what price reconfigurability? In: 2019 IEEE Aerospace Conference, pp. 1–10. IEEE (2019)
4. Gregg, C.E., Kim, J.H., Cheung, K.C.: Ultra-light and scalable composite lattice materials. Adv. Eng. Materials **20**(9), 1800213 (2018)
5. Shannon, C.E.: A mathematical theory of communication. Bell Syst. Techn. J. **27**(3), 379–423 (1948)

Distributed Zero-Knowledge Proofs

Rotem Oshman

Computer Science Department, Tel Aviv University

Abstract. Zero-knowledge proofs are one of the most influential concepts in theoretical computer science. In the seminal definition due to Goldwasser, Micali and Rackoff dating back to the 80's, a computationally-bounded verifier interacts with a powerful but untrusted prover, with the goal of becoming convinced that the input is in some language. In addition to the usual requirements of completeness and soundness, in a zero-knowledge proof, we protect the prover's knowledge: assuming the prover is honest, anything that the verifier can deduce after interacting with the prover, it could have deduced by itself. Zero-knowledge proofs have found many applications within theoretical computer science and beyond, e.g., in cryptography, client-cloud computing, blockchains and cryptocurrencies, electronic voting and auctions, and in the financial industry.

In this talk I will describe recent work on extending the notion of zero-knowledge proofs to distributed networks, where a network of verifiers interacts with an untrusted prover to decide some distributed language. The prover is assumed to know the entire network graph, as well as any input that the nodes may possess, and, as in the centralized setting, the protocol we design should protect this knowledge. Building on the recent introduction of distributed interactive proofs, we define distributed zero-knowledge proofs and construct such proofs for the 3-coloring problem and for other fundamental problems.

Joint work with Aviv Bick and Gillat Kol.

Contents

Keynote Talk

Collecting Coupons is Faster with Friends

Dan Alistarh$^{(\boxtimes)}$ and Peter Davies

Institute of Science and Technology Austria (IST Austria), Am Campus 1,
3400 Klosterneuburg, Austria
{dan.alistarh,peter.davies}@ist.ac.at

Abstract. In this note, we introduce a distributed twist on the classic coupon collector problem: a set of m collectors wish to each obtain a set of n coupons; for this, they can each sample coupons uniformly at random, but can also meet in pairwise interactions, during which they can exchange coupons. By doing so, they hope to reduce the number of coupons that must be sampled by each collector in order to obtain a full set. This extension is natural when considering real-world manifestations of the coupon collector phenomenon, and has been remarked upon and studied empirically (Hayes and Hannigan 2006, Ahmad et al. 2014, Delmarcelle 2019).

We provide the first theoretical analysis for such a scenario. We find that "coupon collecting with friends" can indeed significantly reduce the number of coupons each collector must sample, and raises interesting connections to the more traditional variants of the problem. While our analysis is in most cases asymptotically tight, there are several open questions raised, regarding finer-grained analysis of both "coupon collecting with friends," and of a long-studied variant of the original problem in which a collector requires multiple full sets of coupons.

Keywords: Coupon collector problem · Population protocols · Probability

1 Introduction

The coupon collector problem is a classic exercise in probability theory, appearing in standard textbooks such as those of Feller [5] and Motwani and Raghavan [7]. It is often introduced with a story along the lines of the following: a cereal company runs a promotion giving away a toy (the "coupon") in each box of cereal sold. The toys are chosen uniformly at random from some finite set of different types. A child wishes to collect the full set of toys, and our task is to analyze the number of cereal boxes her parents must purchase to achieve this. This number is, of course, a random variable, and while elementary bounds on it are quite straightforward, a tighter analysis requires more sophisticated techniques (see, e.g., [4]).

A modern real-world example of this phenomenon is the World Cup sticker album [6]. Collectors purchase sealed packs of stickers of football players, and

© Springer Nature Switzerland AG 2021
T. Jurdziński and S. Schmid (Eds.): SIROCCO 2021, LNCS 12810, pp. 3–12, 2021.
https://doi.org/10.1007/978-3-030-79527-6_1

aim to collect one of each in order to fill all the slots in their album. Completing the sticker album has proven a very popular activity among (mostly, but by no means exclusively) young football fans every four years, and has highlighted an aspect which is absent from the classical analysis of the coupon collector's problem: one can achieve a full collection much faster by swapping duplicate coupons with friends who are also collecting. This has been noted previously and studied empirically, specifically for the World Cup sticker album [1,2,6], but we are not aware of any prior theoretical analysis for such a setting in general.

Of course, for theoretical analysis, one must first define a model specifying how swapping of coupons is permitted. If all collectors are allowed to swap freely, then the problem is equivalent to a variant which *has* seen prior theoretical study: that in which $m > 1$ full sets of coupons must be completed by a single collector. This variant was studied by Newman and Shepp [8] and Erdös and Rényi [4]. In more recent works (e.g., [3] and the references therein), problem settings of this sort are often referred to as "coupon collector with *siblings:*" the accompanying story is that there is a single collector, but she has a succession of younger siblings to whom she gives duplicate coupons upon receiving them. One can then ask long it takes for the mth sibling to complete his collection. Specifically, Newman and Shepp [8] showed that the number of coupons needed to complete m full sets is $n(\log n + (m-1) \log \log n + O(1))$ in expectation. Erdös and Rényi [4] provided concentration bounds around this expectation, and specified the constant in the linear term. However, it is important to note that this bound holds *only when m is a constant*; as Erdös and Rényi themselves note, "It is an interesting problem to investigate the limiting distribution of $v_m(n)$ when m increases together with n, but we can not go into this question here." Surprisingly, to our knowledge, this open problem has never been addressed, and while we give an asymptotic analysis here, it remains an open question to extend the more fine-grained bounds of Newman and Shepp, and Erdös and Rényi to the case where m also tends to infinity.

Our primary focus is a *distributed* generalization: when completing, for example, the World Cup sticker album, collectors generally do not, to the authors' knowledge, deliberately congregate in large groups in order to exchange stickers in an organized fashion. Instead, we would expect that exchanges are usually ad-hoc, and made between individual pairs of collectors. So, we will abstract such behavior using a "population protocol"-style model of random pairwise interactions: in each round, an independent, uniformly random pair of collectors will meet, and can swap coupons between them as they wish. We then aim to analyze the trade-off between the number of coupons that each collector must sample, and the number of interactions required, in order for all collectors to obtain full collections. We call this problem "coupon collecting with friends."

1.1   The Formal Problem Setting

A set M of m collectors each wish to obtain a full collection of n distinct coupons. For this, they will operate in sequences of *collection* (sampling) and *exchanging* (interaction) phases:

1. A collection phase, in which each collector independently and uniformly samples, with replacement, r_c coupons from $[n]$.
2. An exchanging phase, in which r_e sequential interactions between independent, uniformly random pairs of collectors occur. An interacting pair of collectors can choose to exchange coupons however they wish.

We are interested in the trade-off between the numbers of collection rounds and exchanging rounds (r_c and r_e) that are required for each of the m agents to obtain a full collection of n distinct coupons.

1.2   Preliminaries

In the following, we denote $\ln x := \log_e x$ and $\log x := \log_2 x$. We make frequent use of the well-known inequalities $1 - x \le e^{-x}$ for $x \in \mathbb{R}$ and $1 - x \ge 4^{-x}$ for $x \in [0, \frac{1}{2}]$, and the Chernoff bound in the following standard form:

Lemma 1 (Chernoff bound). *Suppose $Z_1, \ldots, Z_t$ are independent random variables taking values in $\{0, 1\}$. Let Z denote their sum and let $\mu = \mathbf{E}[Z]$ denote the sum's expected value. Then for any $\delta \in [0, 1]$,*

$$\mathbf{Pr}[Z \le (1 - \delta)\mu] \le e^{-\frac{\delta^2 \mu}{2}} .$$

2   What Happens with No Exchanges?

We first look at the most "standard" variant of the trade-off: when $r_e = 0$, i.e., no exchanges are allowed. In this case, the problem is simply m separate instances of the standard coupon collector problem, since each collector must independently collect a full set without help from the other collectors.

It has long been known [4,8] that the number of samples needed for a single collector to obtain a full set is $n \ln n \pm O(n)$ with probability $1 - \varepsilon$, where $\varepsilon > 0$ is any positive constant. To be precise, we use the following statement as phrased by Motwani and Raghavan:

Statement 1 ([7], corollary to Theorem 3.8, Section 3.6.3). *For any real constant c, we have*

$$\lim_{n \to \infty} \mathbf{Pr}[X \le n(\ln n - c)] = e^{-e^c}$$

and

$$\lim_{n \to \infty} \mathbf{Pr}[X \ge n(\ln n + c)] = 1 - e^{-e^{-c}} .$$

(Here X is the random variable denoting the number of required samples.) The statement implies that the probability of failure for a single collector after $n \ln n + \omega(n)$ samples tends to 0 as n tends to infinity. However, this is not quite sufficient for us: we require m independent instances to all succeed, so we need the probability of failure for each collector to be less than $1/m$, and we do not treat m as a constant. So, we need to know how *fast* the failure probability tends to 0.

We give the following straightforward asymptotic upper and lower bounds for the problem (for $n > 1$; for $n = 1$, exactly 1 collection round is clearly necessary and sufficient).

Lemma 2. *If $r_e = 0$, then $r_c = O(n \log mn)$ is sufficient to succeed with probability $1 - (mn)^{-1}$.*

Proof. Let $r_c = 2n \ln mn$. Fix a particular collector v and coupon α. The probability that v does not collect a copy of α is at most $\left(1 - \frac{1}{n}\right)^{2n \ln mn} \le e^{-\frac{2n \ln mn}{n}} = (mn)^{-2}$. By a union bound over all coupons and collectors, the probability that any collector does not receive a copy of any coupon is at most $mn \cdot (mn)^{-2} = (mn)^{-1}$. $\qquad\blacksquare$

Lemma 3. *For $n > 1$, if $r_e = 0$, then $r_c = \Omega(n \log mn)$ is necessary to succeed with any positive constant probability.*

Proof. By Statement 1, even a single collector must perform $\Omega(n \log n)$ samples to collect all n coupons with any constant probability. We now show that $\Omega(n \log m)$ samples per collector are required for all m collectors to be successful. The lower bound is then $\Omega(\max\{n \log m, n \log n\}) = \Omega(n \log mn)$.

Fix a particular coupon α, and let $r_c \le \frac{1}{4}n \log m$. The probability that a particular collector v does not receive a copy of α is $(1 - \frac{1}{n})^{r_c} \ge 4^{\frac{-r_c}{n}} \ge 4^{\frac{-\log m}{4}} = m^{-\frac{1}{2}}$ (using that $1 - x \ge 4^{-x}$ for $x \in [0, \frac{1}{2}]$).

The events that each collector receives a copy of α are independent. Therefore, the probability that all collectors receive a copy is

$$\mathbf{Pr}\left[\bigcap_{v \in M} \{v \text{ receives a copy of } \alpha\}\right] = \prod_{v \in M} \mathbf{Pr}\left[v \text{ receives a copy of } \alpha\right]$$
$$\le \prod_{v \in M} \left(1 - m^{-\frac{1}{2}}\right)$$
$$= \left(1 - m^{-\frac{1}{2}}\right)^m$$
$$= e^{-m^{-\frac{1}{2}} \cdot m} = e^{-\sqrt{m}}.$$

So, in order to achieve any constant (as $m \to \infty$, which we may assume since this component of the lower bound is only relevant when $m > n$) probability of success, we require $r_c > \frac{1}{4}n \log m$. $\qquad\blacksquare$

3   What Happens with Unlimited Exchanges?

If an unlimited amount of exchanges are allowed, then the problem is equivalent to simply ensuring that m copies of each coupon are sampled between all collectors, since the exchanges will then allow these to eventually be distributed to each collector. As mentioned, for constant m strong bounds are known [4,8], but we are not aware of any prior work for non-constant m.

Again, we can show straighforward matching asymptotic bounds:

Lemma 4. *If* $r_e = \infty$, *then* $r_c = O(n + \frac{n \log n}{m})$ *is sufficient to succeed with probability* $1 - \frac{1}{n}$.

Proof. Let $r_c = 16(n + \frac{n \ln n}{m})$, i.e., $16(mn + n \ln n)$ total samples are taken. Fix a particular coupon α. The expected number of copies of α obtained is $\mu := 16(m + \ln n)$, and each sample is independent. So, by a Chernoff bound (Lemma 1),

$$\mathbf{Pr}\,[\text{fewer than } m \text{ copies of } \alpha \text{ are collected}]$$

$$< \mathbf{Pr}\left[\text{at most } (1 - \frac{1}{2})\mu \text{ copies of } \alpha \text{ are collected}\right]$$

$$\le e^{-\frac{\mu}{8}} \le e^{-\frac{16 \ln n}{8}} \le n^{-2}.$$

Taking a union bound over all coupons, we find that the probability that any coupon does not have at least m copies sampled is at most $\frac{1}{n}$. So, with probability at least $1 - \frac{1}{n}$, every coupon is sampled at least m times, and with unlimited exchanges we can complete every collector's collection.

Lemma 5. *If* $r_e = \infty$, *then* $r_c = \Omega(n + \frac{n \log n}{m})$ *is necessary to succeed with any positive constant probability.*

Proof. A lower bound of $\Omega(n \log n)$ samples follows from the standard coupon collector problem: by Statement 1, with $o(n \log n)$ samples we cannot collect even one copy of all coupons with any constant probability. Furthermore, mn samples are clearly necessary to collect m copies of each of the n coupons. So, we have a lower bound of $\Omega(\max\{mn, n \log n\})$ total samples, i.e. $r_c = \Omega(n + \frac{n \log n}{m})$.

We now see the power of allowing exchanges: with unlimited exchanges between m participants, the amount of samples required per collector reduces from $\Theta(n \log mn)$ to $\Theta(n + \frac{n \log n}{m})$. In particular, collaborating with a small group of $m = O(\log n)$ collectors reduces the required number of samples linearly in m (from $\Theta(n \log n)$ to $\Theta(\frac{n \log n}{m})$), which may be an appealing prospect to collectors of World Cup stickers (or their parents).

4   Minimizing Exchanges for Optimal Collection Rounds

Now we reach the main question of this work: how many exchanging rounds are necessary to ensure completion using the asymptotically optimal amount of collection rounds?

We first prove the following upper bound:

Theorem 2. *If $r_c \geq 36(n + \frac{n \ln n}{m})$, $r_e = O(m \log mn)$ is sufficient to succeed with probability $1 - \frac{1}{mn}$.*

Proof. Fix a coupon α to analyze during the collection phase. We will call collectors that receive fewer than 2 copies of α during the collection phase *bad*, and call them *good* otherwise. Fix also a specific collector v. After r_c collection rounds, v receives, in expectation, $\mu := \frac{r_c}{n}$ copies of α. Every collection round is independent, so by a Chernoff bound, the probability that v is bad is at most:

$$\mathbf{Pr}\left[v \text{ is bad}\right] = \mathbf{Pr}\left[v \text{ receives at most } \left(1 - \frac{\mu - 1}{\mu}\right)\mu \text{ copies of } \alpha\right]$$

$$\leq e^{-\frac{(\mu - 1)^2}{2\mu}} < e^{1 - \frac{\mu}{2}}.$$

Keeping α fixed but unfixing v, we now wish to bound the probability that at least $\frac{m}{3}$ collectors are bad (have fewer than 2 copies of α). We do this by a union bound over all possible sets of $\frac{m}{3}$ collectors (technically $\lceil \frac{m}{3} \rceil$, but we omit the ceiling functions for clarity since the effect is negligible), using that the 'badness' of collectors is independent:

$$\mathbf{Pr}\left[\text{at least } \frac{m}{3} \text{ collectors are bad}\right] = \mathbf{Pr}\left[\bigcup_{\substack{S \subset M \\ |S| = \frac{m}{3}}} \text{all collectors in } S \text{ are bad}\right]$$

$$\leq \sum_{\substack{S \subset M \\ |S| = \frac{m}{3}}} \mathbf{Pr}\left[\text{all collectors in } S \text{ are bad}\right]$$

$$\leq \binom{m}{\frac{m}{3}}\left(e^{1 - \frac{\mu}{2}}\right)^{\frac{m}{3}}$$

$$\leq (3e)^{\frac{m}{3}} e^{(1 - \frac{\mu}{2})\frac{m}{3}}$$

$$= e^{-(\frac{\mu}{2} - 2 - \ln 3)\frac{m}{3}}.$$

In the penultimate line here we used the inequality $\binom{a}{b} \leq \left(\frac{ae}{b}\right)^b$. Since $\mu = \frac{r_c}{n} \geq 36$, we have $\frac{\mu}{2} - 2 - \ln 3 > \frac{\mu}{3}$. So,

$$\mathbf{Pr}\left[\text{at least } \frac{m}{3} \text{ collectors are bad}\right] < e^{-\frac{\mu}{3} \cdot \frac{m}{3}} = e^{-\frac{r_c m}{9n}} \leq e^{-4(m + \ln n)}.$$

Taking a union bound over all coupons, we have that for all coupons there are fewer than $\frac{m}{3}$ bad collectors with probability at least $1 - ne^{-4(m + \ln n)} = 1 - e^{-4m - 3 \ln n}$. We call this event a *successful collection phase*.

We now describe the exchanging phase. Let $r_e = 6m \ln mn$. We will use the following simple swapping rule: whenever a collector with at least two copies of some coupon α interacts with a collector with 0 copies of that coupon, it will give one of its copies.

A crucial observation is that for a coupon α which has fewer than $\frac{m}{3}$ bad collectors after the collection phase, there will always be at least $\frac{m}{3}$ collectors with at least two copies throughout the exchanging phase. This is because every time a *good* collector gives away a copy (possibly dropping to 1 copy itself), a collector with 0 copies goes up to 1 copy. Since there are at most $\frac{m}{3}$ collectors with 0 copies to begin with (and collectors never drop down to 0 copies), this can occur at most $\frac{m}{3}$ times, leaving at least $\frac{m}{3}$ collectors with multiple copies.

To analyze the exchanging phase, we fix a particular interaction, a particular coupon α which is not yet held by all collectors, and a particular collector v which currently has 0 copies of α. By the above observation, with probability at least $2 \cdot \frac{1}{m} \cdot \frac{1}{3} = \frac{2}{3m}$, the interaction pairs v with a collector who has at least 2 copies of α, and so v receives a copy.

There are initially (trivially) at most mn such pairs (α, v) where v holds 0 copies of α. Conditioning on a successful collection phase, each of these pairs is removed in each iteration with probability at least $\frac{2}{3m}$. For a fixed pair, these probabilities hold independently over all iterations. So the probability of a particular pair (α, v) remaining over the entire exchanging phase (i.e., for v to still hold no copy of α upon completion) is at most

$$\left(1 - \frac{2}{3m}\right)^{6m \ln mn} \le e^{-3 \ln mn} = (mn)^{-3}.$$

Taking a union bound over all such pairs, the probability that any pair remains is at most $(mn)^{-2}$. Finally, taking another union bound to remove the conditioning on a successful collection phase, the probability of successfully completing all collections is at least $1 - e^{-4m-3 \ln n} - (mn)^{-2} \ge 1 - \frac{1}{mn}$.

We next give a pair of lower bounds, which when combined will match the asymptotic expression for r_e from Theorem 2.

Lemma 6. *If $r_c \le \frac{1}{4} n \ln n$, then $r_e = \Omega(m \log n)$ is necessary to succeed with probability $1 - \frac{1}{n}$.*

Proof. Fix a collector v. By Statement 1, since $r_c = n \log n - \omega(n)$, the probability that v receives a full set of coupons during the collection phase is $o(1)$. Denote this probability q. To succeed overall with probability $1 - \frac{1}{n}$, there must be some case in which v does not receive a full collection during the collection phase, but gains it during the exchanging phase with probability at least $1 - \frac{2}{n}$ (over the randomness in the exchanging phase only), since otherwise the total probability of v having a full collection is at most $q + (1-q)(1 - \frac{2}{n}) = 1 - \frac{2}{n} + \frac{o(1)}{n} < 1 - \frac{1}{n}$ (for sufficiently large n).

If $r_e \le \frac{1}{8} m \log n$, and for $m \ge 4$, the probability that v is not involved in *any* interactions is at least

$$\left(1 - \frac{2}{m}\right)^{r_e} \ge 4^{-\frac{2}{m} r_e} \ge 4^{-\frac{1}{4} \log n} = n^{-\frac{1}{2}} .$$

In this case v cannot obtain a full collection of coupons if it did not have one after the collection phase. So, the probability of success if v did not gain a full collection during the collection phase is at most $1 - n^{-\frac{1}{2}} < 1 - \frac{2}{n}$, which means that the total success probability is less than $1 - \frac{1}{n}$.

For the remaining case $m < 4$, we again apply Statement 1, which implies that the probability of collecting a single full collection with $n \ln n - \omega(n)$ samples is $o(1)$. In total, over the $m < 4$ collectors, we are taking at most $\frac{3}{4} n \ln n = n \ln n - \omega(n)$ samples during the collection phase. So, with probability $1 - o(1)$, there is some coupon for which no collector has a copy, in which case we cannot hope to be successful even with $r_e = \infty$. Thus, our overall success probability is $o(1)$.

Lemma 7. *If $r_c = n \ln n - \omega(n)$, then $r_e = \Omega(m \log m)$ is necessary to succeed with any positive constant probability.*

Proof. By Statement 1, for $r_c = n \log n - \omega(n)$, the probability that a particular collector v receives a full set of coupons during the collection phase is $o(1)$. The expected number of collectors receiving full sets is therefore $o(m)$. By Markov's inequality, the probability that at least $\frac{m}{2}$ collectors receive full sets at most $o(1)$. With probability $1 - o(1)$, therefore, there are at least $\frac{m}{2}$ collectors without full sets. We call this event an *unsuccessful collection phase*.

To fill each collector's collection overall with any positive constant probability $\varepsilon > 0$, there must be at least one instance with an unsuccessful collection phase on which we do so with probability at least $\frac{\varepsilon}{2}$ (over the randomness of the exchanging phase), since otherwise the total success probability would be at most $\frac{\varepsilon}{2} + o(1)$. We will now show that this requires $r_e = \Omega(m \log m)$ exchanging rounds.

Assume that we have an unsuccessful collection phase, and a set S of $\frac{m}{2}$ collectors without full sets (again omitting ceiling functions for clarity). Fixing some $v \in S$, the probability that each interaction involves v is $\frac{2}{m}$. Furthermore, it is at most $\frac{4}{m}$ independently of the behavior of all other $u \in S$ (the worst case is that all other $u \in S$ are not involved in the interaction, in which case v is involved with probability $\frac{2}{\frac{m}{2}+1} < \frac{4}{m}$).

If $r_e \leq \frac{1}{16} m \log m$, and for $m \geq 8$, the probability that v is not involved in *any* interactions is at least

$$\left(1 - \frac{4}{m}\right)^{r_e} \geq 4^{-\frac{4}{m} r_e} \geq 4^{-\frac{1}{4} \log m} = m^{-\frac{1}{2}} \ ,$$

independently of the other $u \in S$. Then, the probability that all collectors in S are involved in at least one interaction is at most

$$\left(1 - m^{-\frac{1}{2}}\right)^{|S|} \leq e^{-m^{-\frac{1}{2}} \frac{m}{2}} = e^{-\frac{\sqrt{m}}{2}} = o(1).$$

That is, with probability $1 - o(1)$, at least one collector v in S is not involved in any interactions. In this case v cannot obtain a full collection of coupons: by definition of S its collection is incomplete after the collection phase, and it has no interactions in which to gain new coupons in the exchanging phase. So, we have a total success probability of $o(1)$.

The above analysis assumes that $m \to \infty$; the case $m = O(1)$ is trivial, since by Statement 1, with probability $1 - o(1)$ we have not completed all collections during the collection phase, and so require at least $1 = \Omega(m \log m)$ exchanging rounds.

Combining Lemmas 6 and 7 yields the following theorem:

Theorem 3. *If $r_c \leq \frac{1}{4} n \ln n$, then $r_e = \Omega(m \log mn)$ is necessary to succeed with probability $1 - \frac{1}{n}$.*

Proof. By Lemmas 6 and 7, we require $r_e = \Omega(\max\{m \log m, m \log n\}) = \Omega(m \log mn)$.

We make some observations about the bounds we have shown in Theorems 2 and 3. We now know that $\Theta(m \log mn)$ interactions suffice to achieve an asymptotically optimal number of collection rounds, and are necessary to asymptotically improve over the number of samples needed for the standard single-collector case. If one requires a high probability of success in n (i.e. probability at most $\frac{1}{n}$ of failure), these bounds are tight. However, they leave open the possibility of using fewer interactions to achieve a lower (but still at least a positive constant) success probability. In this regime, Lemma 6 does not apply, so we have only that $O(m \log mn)$ interactions suffice by Theorem 2, and that $\Omega(m \log m)$ are necessary by Lemma 7. We conjecture that it is the upper bound that is tight, and the lower bound that could be improved:

Conjecture 1. If $r_c = O(n + \frac{n \ln n}{m})$, then $r_e = \Omega(m \log mn)$ is necessary to succeed with any positive constant probability.

The reason for this conjecture is that the current lower bound does not take into account the difficulty for collectors with incomplete collections to obtain *multiple* coupons during the exchanging phase; it uses only the hardness of ensuring a single interaction. Since most collectors will have $\Theta(n)$ coupons missing after the collection phase, we would expect that collectors will require some number of interactions depending on n in order to complete their collections. However, since the events of a collector gaining two different coupons from an interaction are not independent, this would require more sophisticated techniques to analyze.

5   Conclusions and Open Problems

Our aim in this paper has been to introduce the study of what we argue is a natural distributed variant of the coupon collector problem: collection by a group of collectors which can meet, in random pairwise fashion, to exchange coupons. As mentioned, there is one gap in the asymptotic analysis we provide: whether $o(m \log mn)$ exchanges can suffice for the asymptotic optimum of $\Theta(n + \frac{n \ln n}{m})$ collection rounds, under a weaker success guarantee (than high probability in n).

Generally, most of the prior work on the standard coupon collector problem has been on finer-grained analysis, pinning down the exact terms in the number of samples required, and one could ask whether we can do the same here. Such a focus would change the problem significantly: in particular, the approach of Theorem 2 (ensuring that a constant fraction of collectors always hold multiple copies of each coupon) would not work if the number of samples was "only just" sufficient, and one would need to find a different way to analyze the exchanging phase.

Surprisingly, the situation is still not fully understood, even for the more "traditional" case, corresponding to $r_c = \infty$, when m tends to infinity alongside n. We therefore close by reiterating the open question posed by Erdös and Rényi, and ask how the coupon collector problem behaves when a non-constant number of full collections are required.

Acknowledgements. Peter Davies is supported by the European Union's Horizon 2020 research and innovation programme under the Marie Skłodowska-Curie grant agreement No. 754411.

References

1. Ahmad, N., Sinha, S., Gnegel, F., Boushehri, S.S., Chakaroglu, A.E., Mensah, E.K.: The coupon collector's problem and generalizations. University of Hamburg, Hamburg (2014)
2. Delmarcelle, O.: The Panini collector' s problem: optimal strategy and trading analysis, Master thesis (2019)
3. Doumas, A.V., Papanicolaou, V.G.: The siblings of the coupon collector. Theor. Probab. Appl. **62**(3), 444–470 (2018)
4. Erdös, P., Rényi, A.: On a classical problem of probability theory. Publ. Math. Inst. Hung. Acad. Sci. Ser. A 6, 215–220 (1961)
5. Feller, W.: An Introduction to Probability Theory and Its Applications, Wiley, London (1957)
6. Hayes, K., Hannigan, A.: Trading coupons: completing the world cup football sticker album. Significance **3**(3), 142–144 (2006)
7. Motwani, R., Raghavan, P.: Randomized Algorithms, Cambridge University Press, New York (1995)
8. Newman, D.J., Shepp, L.: The double Dixie cup problem. Am. Math. Monthly **67**(1), 58–61 (1960)

Distributed Graph Algorithms

Distributed Algorithms for Fractional Coloring

Nicolas Bousquet[1] , Louis Esperet[2(✉)] , and François Pirot[2]

[1] Laboratoire LIRIS (UMR 5205), CNRS, Université Claude Bernard Lyon 1,
Lyon, France
`nicolas.bousquet@univ-lyon1.fr`
[2] Laboratoire G-SCOP, CNRS, Univ. Grenoble Alpes, Grenoble, France
{`louis.esperet,francois.pirot`}`@grenoble-inp.fr`

Abstract. In this paper we study fractional coloring from the angle of distributed computing. Fractional coloring is the linear relaxation of the classical notion of coloring, and has many applications, in particular in scheduling. It was proved by Hasemann, Hirvonen, Rybicki and Suomela [19] that for every real $\alpha > 1$ and integer Δ, a fractional coloring of total weight at most $\alpha(\Delta + 1)$ can be obtained deterministically in a single round in graphs of maximum degree Δ, in the LOCAL model of computation. However, a major issue of this result is that the output of each vertex has unbounded size. Here we prove that even if we impose the more realistic assumption that the output of each vertex has constant size, we can find fractional colorings of total weight arbitrarily close to known tight bounds for the fractional chromatic number in several cases of interest. More precisely, we show that for any fixed $\varepsilon > 0$ and Δ, a fractional coloring of total weight at most $\Delta + \varepsilon$ can be found in $O(\log^* n)$ rounds in graphs of maximum degree Δ with no $K_{\Delta+1}$, while finding a fractional coloring of total weight at most Δ in this case requires $\Omega(\log \log n)$ rounds for randomized algorithms and $\Omega(\log n)$ rounds for deterministic algorithms. We also show how to obtain fractional colorings of total weight at most $2 + \varepsilon$ in grids of any fixed dimension, for any $\varepsilon > 0$, in $O(\log^* n)$ rounds. Finally, we prove that in sparse graphs of large girth from any proper minor-closed family we can find a fractional coloring of total weight at most $2 + \varepsilon$, for any $\varepsilon > 0$, in $O(\log n)$ rounds.

Keywords: Fractional coloring · Graph coloring · Distributed algorithms

1 Introduction

A *(proper)* kA *-coloring* of a graph G is an assignment of colors to the vertices of G, such that adjacent vertices receive different colors. This is the same as a

N. Bousquet, L. Esperet and F. Pirot are supported by ANR Projects GAT (ANR-16-CE40-0009-01) and GrR (ANR-18-CE40-0032).

T. Jurdziński and S. Schmid (Eds.): SIROCCO 2021, LNCS 12810, pp. 15–30, 2021.
https://doi.org/10.1007/978-3-030-79527-6_2

partition of the vertices of G into (or covering of the vertices of G by) k independent sets. This has many applications in physical networks; for instance most scheduling problems can be expressed by a coloring problem in the underlying graph. When the resources at play inside the network are fractionable, it is more relevant to consider the linear relaxation of this problem, where one wants to assign weights $x_S \in [0, 1]$ to the independent sets S of G, so that for each vertex v of G, the sum of the weights x_S of the independent sets S containing v is at least 1, and the objective is to minimize the sum of the weights x_S. The solution of this linear program is the *fractional chromatic number* of G, denoted by $\chi_f(G)$. The definition shows that χ_f is rational and that $\omega(G) \leqslant \chi_f(G) \leqslant \chi(G)$ for any graph G where $\omega(G)$ denotes the clique number of G (maximum size of a set of pairwise adjacent vertices), and $\chi(G)$ denotes the usual chromatic number (minimum k such that G admits a proper k-coloring). A polyhedral definition of χ_f, which is not difficult to derive from the definition above, is that $\chi_f(G)$ is the minimum x such that there is a probability distribution on the independent sets of G, such that each vertex appears in a random independent set (drawn from this probability distribution) with probability at least $\frac{1}{x}$.

In this paper, we study fractional coloring from the angle of distributed algorithms. In this context, each vertex outputs its "part" of the solution, and in a Locally Checkable Labelling (whose precise definition will be given in Sect. 2) this part should be of constant size. For instance, in a distributed algorithm for proper k-coloring of G, each vertex can output its color (an integer in $[k] = \{1, \ldots, k\}$), and in a distributed algorithm for maximal independent set, each vertex can output a bit saying whether it belongs to the independent set. In both cases the fact that the solution is correct can then be checked locally, in the sense that adjacent vertices only need to compare their outputs, and if there is no local conflict then the global solution is correct. For more details about the distributed aspects of graph coloring, the reader is referred to the book [4].

Looking back at the polyhedral definition of fractional coloring introduced above, a first possibility would be to design a randomized distributed algorithm producing a (random) independent set, in which each vertex has a large probability to be selected (in this case, the output of each vertex is a single bit, telling whether it belongs to the chosen independent set). A classical algorithm in this vein is the following [1,6]: Each vertex is assigned a random identifier, and joins the independent set if its identifier is smaller than that of all its neighbors. This clearly produces an independent set, and it is not difficult to prove that each vertex v is selected with probability at least $\frac{1}{d(v)+1}$, so in particular this 1-round randomized algorithm witnesses the fact that the fractional chromatic number of graphs of maximum degree Δ is at most $\Delta + 1$. Note that *factor-of-IID* algorithms for independent sets introduced in the past years are of this form (see for instance [14,15]). This leaves the question of how to produce a *deterministic* distributed algorithm for fractional coloring. Recall that a fractional coloring is a distribution of independent sets, so the first issue is to decide what the output of the algorithm should be in order to be locally checkable. A solution explored in [19] is to assign to each independent set S of G an interval $I_S \subset \mathbb{R}$ of length

x_S (or a finite union of intervals of total length x_S), where x_S is the weight defined above in the linear programming definition of fractional coloring, such that all I_S are pairwise disjoint. The output of each vertex v is then the union of all subsets $I_S \subset \mathbb{R}$ such that $v \in S$. Each vertex can check that its output (which is a finite union of intervals) has total length at least 1, and pairs of adjacent vertices can check that their outputs are disjoint, so the fact that this is a fractional coloring can be checked locally. If the set of identifiers of the vertices of G is known to all the vertices in advance (for instance if there are n vertices and the identifiers are $\{1, \ldots, n\}$), then by enumerating all permutations of the identifiers in some canonical order, it is not difficult to transform the 1-round randomized algorithm described above into a 1-round deterministic algorithm producing such an output and with total weight at most $\Delta + 1$ (by running it for all permutations and aggregating all the solutions). The main result of [19] is a 1-round deterministic algorithm producing such an output and with total weight at most $\alpha(\Delta + 1)$ (for any $\alpha > 1$), when the set of identifiers is not known in advance. As observed in [19], the unbounded size of the output implies that this algorithm is unusable in practice. In this paper, we explore a different way to design deterministic distributed algorithms producing fractional colorings of small total weight.

Given two integers $p \geqslant q \geqslant 1$, a $(p:q)$-*coloring* of a graph G is an assignment of q-element subsets of $[p]$ to the vertices of G, such that the sets assigned to any two adjacent vertices are disjoint. An alternative view is that a $(p:q)$-coloring of G is precisely a homomorphism from G to the *Kneser graph* KG (p, q), which is the graph whose vertices are the q-element subsets of $[p]$, and in which two vertices are adjacent if the corresponding subsets of $[p]$ are disjoint. The *weight* of a $(p:q)$-coloring c is $w(c) = p/q$.

The fractional chromatic number $\chi_f(G)$ can be equivalently defined as the infimum of $\{\frac{p}{q} \mid G$ has a $(p:q)$-coloring$\}$ [25] (as before, it can be proved that this infimum is indeed a minimum). Observe that a $(p:1)$-coloring is a (proper) p-coloring. It is well known that the Kneser graph KG (p, q) has fractional chromatic number $\frac{p}{q}$, while Lovász famously proved [22] that its chromatic number is $p - 2q + 2$ using topological methods. This shows in particular that $\chi_f(G)$ and $\chi(G)$ can be arbitrarily far apart.

This definition of the fractional chromatic number gives a natural way to produce distributed fractional colorings, while keeping the output of each vertex bounded. It suffices to fix the integer $q \geqslant 1$, and ask for the smallest integer p such that G has a $(p:q)$-coloring c; then the output of each vertex is the sequence of its q colors from $[p]$, which can be encoded in a bit-string with at most $q \log p = q(\log q + \log w(c))$ bits (in the remainder of the paper, the *output size* always refers to the number of bits in this string, and log stands for the binary logarithm). The requirement that the output of each vertex has bounded size is quite constraining in the case of fractional colourings, since in general the smallest integers p and q such that $\chi_f(G) = \frac{p}{q}$ can be exponential in $|V(G)|$ [16].

In addition to the classical applications of fractional coloring in scheduling (see [19]), there is another more theoretical motivation for studying this problem (or the relaxation above where q is fixed). In n-vertex graphs of maximum degree Δ (which is assumed to be a constant), a coloring with $\Delta + 1$ colors can be found in $O(\log^* n)$ rounds [18,21] in the LOCAL model of computation (which will be introduced formally below). On the other hand, Brooks' Theorem says that if $\Delta \geqslant 3$, any graph of maximum degree Δ with no clique $K_{\Delta+1}$ is Δ-colorable [10], and finding such a coloring has proved to be an interesting problem of *intermediate* complexity in distributed computing. It was proved that the round complexity for computing such a coloring is $\Omega(\log \log n)$ for randomized algorithms [9] and $\Omega(\log n)$ for deterministic algorithms [11] (see also [7]). Thus a large complexity gap appears between Δ and $\Delta+1$ colors, and since the values are integral it is all that can be said about this problem. However, if the number of colors is real, or rational, the precise location of the complexity threshold in the interval $[\Delta, \Delta + 1]$ can be investigated. In Sect. 3, we will show that for fractional coloring, the complexity threshold is arbitrarily close to Δ; namely finding a fractional Δ-coloring is as difficult as finding a Δ-coloring, but for any fixed $\varepsilon > 0$ and Δ, a fractional $(\Delta + \varepsilon)$-coloring with output size of $O\left(\frac{1}{\varepsilon} \log \frac{\Delta}{\varepsilon}\right)$ bits per vertex can be found in $O_\varepsilon(\log^* n)$ rounds in graphs of maximum degree Δ with no $K_{\Delta+1}$. Here, the subscript ε in the big-O notation indicates that the implicit multiplicative constant depends on ε.

Theorem 1. *For any integer $q \geqslant 1$, and any n-vertex graph G of maximum degree $\Delta \geqslant 3$, without $K_{\Delta+1}$, a $(q\Delta + 1 : q)$-coloring of G can be computed in $O(q^3 \Delta^{2q} + q \log^* n)$ rounds deterministically in the LOCAL model.*

There are other similar complexity thresholds in distributed graph coloring. For instance, it was proved that D-dimensional grids[1] can be colored with 4 colors in $O(\log^* n)$ rounds, while computing a 3-coloring in a 2-dimensional $n \times n$-grid takes $\Omega(n)$ rounds [8] (see also [20] for related results). For (almost) vertex-transitive graphs like grids finding minimum fractional colorings is essentially equivalent to finding maximum independent sets, and simple local randomized algorithms approaching the optimal independent set in grids can be used to produce fractional $(2 + \varepsilon)$-colorings with small output (see for instance [15]). In Sect. 4, we will show that for any fixed $\varepsilon > 0$ and $D \geqslant 1$, a fractional $(2 + \varepsilon)$-coloring of the D-dimensional grid $G(n, D)$ of dimension $n \times \cdots \times n$ with output size of $O(\frac{6^D}{\varepsilon} \log(\frac{6^D}{\varepsilon}))$ bits per vertex can be computed *deterministically* in $O_{\varepsilon,D}(\log^* n)$ rounds, while it can be easily observed that finding a $(2q : q)$-coloring takes $\Omega(n)$ rounds (even if $D = 1$, i.e., when the graph is a path).

Theorem 2. *For every integers $D \geqslant 1$ and $q \geqslant 1$, a $(2q + 4 \cdot 6^D : q)$-coloring of the D-dimensional grid $G(n, D)$ can be found in $O(D\ell(2\ell)^D + D\ell \log^* n)$ rounds deterministically in the LOCAL model, where $\ell = q + 2 \cdot 6^D$.*

---

[1] We note that these results are proved for toroidal grids with a consistent orientation, while Theorem 2 considers classical, non-oriented grids.

The last observation implies in particular that $(2q:q)$-coloring trees takes $\Omega(n)$ rounds. On the other hand, trees can be colored with 3 colors in $O(\log n)$ rounds and this is best possible (even with 3 replaced by an arbitrary number of colors) [18,21]. The *maximum average degree* of a graph G, denoted by $\mathrm{mad}(G)$, is the maximum of the average degrees of all the subgraphs H of G. In Sect. 5 we prove that, for every $\varepsilon > 0$, graphs of maximum average degree at most $2 + \varepsilon/40$ and large girth can be $(2 + \varepsilon)$-colored in $O_\varepsilon(\log n)$ rounds with output size of $O(\frac{1}{\varepsilon} \log \frac{1}{\varepsilon})$ bits per vertex.

Theorem 3. *Let G be an n-vertex graph with girth at least $2q+2$, and $\mathrm{mad}(G) \leqslant 2 + \frac{1}{40q}$, for some fixed $q \geqslant 1$. Then a $(2q+1:q)$-coloring of G can be computed deterministically in $O(q \log n + q^2)$ rounds in the LOCAL model.*

This implies that trees, and more generally graphs of sufficiently large girth from any minor-closed class can be $(2 + \varepsilon)$-colored in $O(\log n)$ rounds, for any $\varepsilon > 0$. Note that the assumption that the girth is large cannot be avoided, as a cycle of length $2q - 1$ has fractional chromatic number equal to $2 + \frac{1}{q-1} > 2 + \frac{1}{q}$.

We conjecture that more generally, graphs of girth $\Omega(q)$ and maximum average degree $k + O(1/q)$ (where $k \geqslant 2$ and q are integers) have a $(kq+1:q)$-coloring that can be computed efficiently by a deterministic algorithm in the LOCAL model (the fact that such a coloring exists is a simple consequence of [24] but the proof there uses flows and does not seem to be efficiently implementable in the LOCAL model).

2   The LOCAL Model of Computation

All our results are proved in the LOCAL model, introduced by Linial [21]. We consider a network, in the form of an n-vertex graph G whose vertices have unbounded computational power, and whose edges are communication links between the corresponding vertices. We are given a combinatorial problem that we need to solve in the graph G. In the case of deterministic algorithms, each vertex of G starts with an arbitrary unique identifier (an integer between 1 and n^c, for some constant $c \geqslant 1$, such that all integers assigned to the vertices are distinct). For randomized algorithms, each vertex starts instead with a collection of (private) random bits. The vertices then exchange messages (of unbounded size) with their neighbors in synchronous rounds, and after a fixed number of rounds (the *round complexity of the algorithm*), each vertex outputs its local "part" of the global solution of the problem. This could for instance be the color of the vertex in a proper k-coloring. In Locally Checkable Labelling (LCL) problems, this output has to be of constant size, and should be checkable locally, in the sense that the solution is correct globally if and only if it is correct in all neighborhoods of some (constant) radius. LCL problems include problems like k-coloring (with constant k), or maximal independent set, but not maximum independent set (for instance), and are central in the field of distributed algorithms.

It turns out that with the assumption that messages have unbounded size, vertices can just send to their neighbors at each round all the information that they have received so far, and in t rounds each vertex v "knows" its neighborhood $B_t(v)$ at distance t (the set of all vertices at distance at most t from v). More specifically v knows the labelled subgraph of G induced by $B_t(v)$ (where the labels are the identifiers of the vertices), and nothing more, and the output of v is based solely on this information.

The goal is to minimize the round complexity. Since in t rounds each vertex sees its neighborhood at distance t, after a number of rounds equal to the diameter of G, each vertex sees the entire graph. Since each vertex has unbounded computational power, a distinguished vertex (the vertex with the smallest identifier, say) can compute an optimal solution of the problem and communicate this solution to all the vertices of the graph. This shows that any problem can be solved in a number of rounds equal to the diameter of the graph, which is at most n when G is connected. The goal is to obtain algorithms that are significantly more efficient, i.e., of round complexity $O(\log n)$, or even $O(\log^* n)$, where $\log^* n$ is the number of times we have to iterate the logarithm, starting with n, to reach a value in $(0, 1]$.

3   Maximum Degree

In this section we will need the following consequence of a result of Aubry, Godin and Togni [2, Corollary 8] (see also [13]).

Theorem 4 ([2]). *Let $q \geqslant 1$ be an integer and let $P = v_1, v_2, \ldots, v_{2q+1}$ be a path. Assume that for $i \in \{1, 2q + 1\}$ the vertex v_i has a list $L(v_i)$ of at least $q + 1$ colors, and for any $2 \leqslant i \leqslant 2q$, v_i has a list $L(v_i)$ of at least $2q + 1$ colors. Then each vertex v_i of P can be assigned a subset $S_i \subseteq L(v_i)$ of q colors, so that adjacent vertices are assigned disjoint sets.*

In a graph G, we say that a path P is an *induced path* if the subgraph of G induced by $V(P)$, the vertex set of P, is a path. The *length* of a path is its number of vertices. Note that shortest paths are induced paths, and in particular every connected graph that has no induced path of length k has diameter at most $k - 2$.

We are now ready to prove Theorem 1, which we restate here for the convenience of the reader.

Theorem 1. *For any integer $q \geqslant 1$, and any n-vertex graph G of maximum degree $\Delta \geqslant 3$, without $K_{\Delta+1}$, a $(q\Delta + 1 : q)$-coloring of G can be computed in $O(q^3 \Delta^{2q} + q \log^* n)$ rounds deterministically in the LOCAL model.*

Proof. The first step is to construct the graph H_1, whose nodes are all the induced paths of length $2q + 1$ in G, with an edge between two nodes of H_1 if the corresponding paths in G share at least one vertex. So H_1 can be seen as the intersection graph of the induced paths of length $2q + 1$ of G. Note that any communication in H_1 can be emulated in G, by incurring a multiplicative factor of $O(q)$ on the round complexity. Note that H_1 has at most $n \cdot \Delta^{2q}$

vertices and maximum degree $O(q^2\Delta^{2q})$ (given a path P, one has $O(q^2)$ possible choices for the position of the intersection vertex x on P and on an intersecting path, then at most Δ^{2q} possible ways of extending x into such an intersecting path). It follows that a maximal independent set S_1 in H_1 can be computed in $O(\Delta(H_1) + \log^*(|V(H_1)|)) = O(q^2\Delta^{2q} + \log^*(\Delta^{2q}n)) = O(q^2\Delta^{2q} + \log^* n)$ rounds in G_1 [5], and thus in $O(q^3\Delta^{2q} + q\log^* n)$ rounds in G.

Observe that the set S_1 corresponds to a set of vertex-disjoint induced paths of length $2q + 1$ in G. Let $\mathcal{P} = \bigcup_{P \in S_1} V(P)$. By maximality of S_1, the graph $G - \mathcal{P}$ has no induced path of length $2q + 1$, and in particular each connected component C of $G - \mathcal{P}$ has diameter at most $2q - 1$. Each such component C has indeed a $(q\Delta + 1 : q)$-coloring c (since C, as a subgraph of G, is Δ-colorable, by Brooks' theorem), which can be computed in $O(q)$ rounds. Our next step is to extend this coloring c of $G - \mathcal{P}$ to $\mathcal{P}$. To this end, define a graph H_2 whose nodes are the elements of S_1, in which two nodes are adjacent if the two corresponding paths are adjacent in G (i.e., some edge of G has a vertex in each of these two paths). Observe that H_2 has at most n nodes and maximum degree $O(q\Delta)$. So a proper coloring c_2 of H_2 with $t = O(q\Delta)$ colors $1, 2, \ldots, t$ can be found in $O(q\Delta + \log^* n)$ rounds in H_2 [5] (and thus in $O(q^2\Delta + q\log^* n)$ rounds in G). For each color i, consider the paths of $\mathcal{P}$ of color i in c_2. We extend the current partial coloring of G to these paths (which are pairwise non-adjacent by definition) using Theorem 4. For each of these paths, each vertex starts with $q\Delta + 1$ available colors and the coloring of the neighborhood of this path forbids at most $q(\Delta - 2)$ colors for each internal vertex of the path, and at most $q(\Delta - 1)$ colors for each endpoint of the path. Thus each internal vertex of a path of $\mathcal{P}$ has a list of $2q + 1$ colors and each endpoint has a list of $q + 1$ colors, as required for the application of Theorem 4. The extension thus takes $t = O(q\Delta)$ steps, each taking $O(q)$ rounds, and thus the final round complexity is $O(q^3\Delta^{2q} + q\log^* n)$. $\square$

We now prove that finding a $(q\Delta : q)$-coloring is significantly harder. We will use a reduction from the *sinkless orientation* problem: given a bipartite n-vertex Δ-regular graph G, with $\Delta \geqslant 3$ we have to find an orientation of the edges of G so that each vertex has at least one outgoing edge. It was proved that in the LOCAL model this takes $\Omega(\log\log n)$ rounds for a randomized algorithm [9] (see also [11]) and $\Omega(\log n)$ for a deterministic algorithm [11] (see also [7]). Note that the results in [9] and [7] are proved for $\Delta = 3$, while the results of [11] are proved for any $\Delta \geqslant 3$.

Theorem 5. *For any integers $\Delta \geqslant 3$ and $q \geqslant 1$, obtaining a $(q\Delta : q)$-coloring of an n-vertex Δ-regular graph with no $K_{\Delta+1}$ takes $\Omega(\log\log n)$ rounds for a randomized algorithm and $\Omega(\log n)$ rounds for a deterministic algorithm in the LOCAL model.*

Proof. Let $\mathcal{A}$ be a distributed algorithm which returns a $(q\Delta : q)$-coloring of any n-vertex Δ-regular graph G with no $K_{\Delta+1}$ within $f(n)$ rounds, for every integer $q \geqslant 1$. Note that such an algorithm exists with $f(n) \leqslant n$, since by Brook's

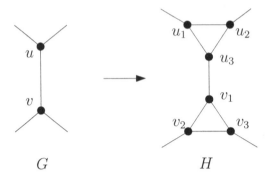

Fig. 1. The construction of H from G in the proof of Theorem 5, for $\Delta = 3$.

theorem G is Δ-colorable, and we obtain a $(q\Delta : q)$-coloring of G by exploding each color into q copies in a Δ-coloring of G (that we find for free once each node has a complete knowledge of the graph G within n rounds).

Consider a bipartite Δ-regular n-vertex graph G, in which we want to compute a sinkless orientation. Let H be the Δn-vertex Δ-regular graph obtained from G by replacing each vertex v by a clique $v_1, v_2, \ldots, v_\Delta$ on Δ vertices (see Fig. 1). Note that H does not contain any copy of $K_{\Delta+1}$. We now apply the algorithm $\mathcal{A}$ on H in order to compute a $(q\Delta : q)$-coloring c of H. Note that each copy of K_Δ in H uses all $q\Delta$ colors, and thus the set S of vertices of H whose set of colors in c contains the color 1 intersects each copy $v_1, \ldots, v_\Delta$ of K_Δ in H in a single vertex (say v_1, up to renaming of the vertices of H). Let e_v be the edge of H that contains v_1, but is disjoint from $v_2, \ldots, v_\Delta$. Then for every vertex v of G we orient e_v from v to the other endpoint of e_v in H. Note that this gives a partial orientation of H (an edge cannot be oriented in both directions, since otherwise the two endpoints contain color 1, which is a contradiction), which can be transferred to a partial orientation of G by contracting each clique $v_1, \ldots, v_\Delta$ back to the vertex v. Since S intersects each copy of K_Δ in H, the resulting partial orientation of G is sinkless, as desired.

We have described a distributed algorithm which returns a sinkless orientation of any bipartite Δ-regular graph n-vertex graph within $f(\Delta n)$ rounds, hence $f(n) = \Omega\left(\log \frac{n}{\Delta}\right)$ if $\mathcal{A}$ is deterministic, or $f(n) = \Omega\left(\log \log \frac{n}{\Delta}\right)$ if $\mathcal{A}$ is randomized. $\qquad\square$

A natural question is whether one can find another description of fractional coloring with bounded size certificates for which the existence of a fractional coloring of total weight Δ can be determined faster. The existence of such a fractional coloring implies the existence of an independent set of weight at least $\frac{1}{\Delta}$ in G. It can be observed that the same proof as that of Theorem 5, shows that finding such an independent set in a graph of maximum Δ with no $K_{\Delta+1}$ is as hard as finding a sinkless orientation.

4   Coloring the Grid

Let $G(n, D)$ be the D-dimensional grid with vertex set $[n]^D$, i.e., two distinct vertices $x = (x_1, \ldots, x_D)$ and $y = (y_1, \ldots, y_D)$ in $[n]^D$ are adjacent in $G(n, D)$ if and only if $d_1(x, y) = \sum_{i=1}^{D} |x_i - y_i| = 1$ (where d_1 denotes the usual taxicab distance). We assume that all the vertices know their identifier (but do not have access to their own coordinates in the grid). We note that our results do not assume any knowledge of directions in the grid (i.e., a consistent orientation of edges, such as South→North and West→East in 2 dimensions), in contrast with the results of [8].

Note that the distance between vertices in the grid coincides with the taxicab distance d_1 in $\mathbb{R}^D$. In this section it will be convenient to work instead with the Chebyshev distance $d_\infty(x, y) = \max_{1 \leqslant i \leqslant n} |x_i - y_i|$, since balls with respect to d_∞ are grids themselves, as well as their (possibly empty) pairwise intersections. We observe that any communication between two nodes at distance d_∞ at most ℓ can be emulated within $D \cdot \ell$ rounds, hence working with d_∞ rather than with d_1 does not have a significant impact in terms of round complexity. In the remainder of this section, all distances refer to the d_∞-distance.

We now prove Theorem 2, restated here for convenience.

Theorem 2. *For every integers $D \geqslant 1$ and $q \geqslant 1$, a $(2q + 4 \cdot 6^D : q)$-coloring of the D-dimensional grid $G(n, D)$ can be found in $O(D\ell(2\ell)^D + D\ell \log^* n)$ rounds deterministically in the LOCAL model, where $\ell = q + 2 \cdot 6^D$.*

Proof. Let $G = G(n, D)$ and $\ell = q + 2 \cdot 6^D$. We assume that $n \geqslant 2\ell$, for otherwise G has diameter (with respect to d_∞) at most $O(\ell)$ and a desired coloring can be found in $O(D\ell)$ rounds. We start by finding an inclusionwise maximal independent set I of $G^{[\ell]}$, the graph obtained from G by linking each pair of vertices at (d_∞-)distance at most ℓ from each other, which are therefore linked by a path of length at most $D\ell$ in G. Note that the maximum degree of $G^{[\ell]}$ corresponds to the maximum size of a ball of radius ℓ in a D-dimensional grid, that is at most $(2\ell + 1)^D$; therefore I can be constructed in $O((2\ell + 1)^D + \log^* n)$ rounds in $G^{[\ell]}$ [5], and this can be emulated in $O(D\ell(2\ell)^D + D\ell \log^* n)$ rounds in G.

A given vertex x of the grid can find the list L_x of vertices of coordinates $x + \mathbf{e}$ for every $\mathbf{e} \in \{-1, 1\}^D$ within D rounds (although x is not aware of the absolute directions in the grid corresponding to each of these vertices). This can be done with the following procedure. Given a vertex $y \in V(G)$, we say that a vertex $z \in V(G)$ is a 1-neighbour of y if $N(z)$ contains y, and for every $2 \leqslant i \leqslant D$ we say that z is an i-neighbour of y if $N(z)$ contains at least two $(i-1)$-neighbours of y. Then L_x is the list of vertices $y \in V(G)$ such that x is a D-neighbour of y, and this list can be found within D rounds. Given x and $y = x + \mathbf{e} \in L_x$, finding $z = x + 2\mathbf{e}$ can be done in $2D$ rounds, since z is the vertex in L_y furthest away from x with respect to the d_1-distance in G (and more generally $x + i\mathbf{e}$ can be found in iD rounds).

The next step of the coloring procedure is as follows. Every vertex $x \in I$ chooses a direction $\mathbf{e}_x \in \{-1, 1\}^D$ in such a way that $x[i] := x + i \cdot \mathbf{e}_x \in [n]^D$ is well-defined for every $i \leqslant \ell$ (this is possible since $n \geqslant 2\ell$, and such a direction can be chosen in $\ell \cdot D$ rounds).

For any $x \in I$ and $1 \leqslant i \leqslant \ell$, we define a set $B(x, i)$ as follows. Each vertex y considers the vertex $x \in I$ of smallest identifier such that $d_\infty(y, x[i]) \leqslant 2\ell$ and joins the set $B(x, i)$. Equivalently, $B(x, i)$ is the ball of center $x[i]$ and radius 2ℓ, in which we remove all vertices at distance at most 2ℓ from $x'[i]$ for some $x' \in I$ of smaller identifier than that of x. We also let $\widetilde{B}(x, i)$ be obtained from $B(x, i)$ after removing all vertices at distance exactly 2ℓ from $x[i]$. When some vertex v is in $B(x, i) \setminus \widetilde{B}(x, i)$, we say that v is a *boundary vertex for* $x[i]$. An example of such a partition of the grid is depicted in Fig. 2.

Each vertex $v \in V(G)$ is at distance at most ℓ from at least one vertex $x \in I$ by maximality of I, and therefore at distance at most 2ℓ from $x[i]$ for every $i \leqslant \ell$. It follows that for every fixed $1 \leqslant i \leqslant \ell$, the collection of the sets $B(x, i)$ over all $x \in I$ forms a partition of $V(G)$.

We now show that for each i, no two distinct sets $\widetilde{B}(x, i)$ and $\widetilde{B}(y, i)$ (with $x, y \in I$) are connected by an edge. Indeed, assume for the sake of contradiction that there is an edge uv with $u \in \widetilde{B}(x, i)$ and $v \in \widetilde{B}(y, i)$, for two distinct vertices x and y in I with $\mathrm{ID}(x) < \mathrm{ID}(y)$, where $\mathrm{ID}(x)$ denotes the identifier of x. Then $d_\infty(x, u) \leqslant 2\ell - 1$ and thus $d_\infty(x, v) \leqslant 2\ell$ which contradicts the fact that $v \notin B(x, i)$ since $\mathrm{ID}(x) < \mathrm{ID}(y)$. This shows that no two distinct sets $\widetilde{B}(x, i)$ and $\widetilde{B}(y, i)$ (with $x, y \in I$) are connected by an edge, as desired. This implies that all the components of the subgraph G_i of G induced by $\bigcup_{x \in I} \widetilde{B}(x, i)$ (which is bipartite) have diameter $O(\ell)$, and in particular for every $1 \leqslant i \leqslant \ell$, we can find a proper 2-coloring c_i of G_i with colors in $\{2i - 1, 2i\}$ within $O(\ell)$ rounds. We now show that the union of these colorings over all $i \leqslant \ell$ yields a $(2q + 4 \cdot 6^D : q)$-coloring c of G.

The total number of colors is $2\ell = 2q + 4 \cdot 6^D$, so it remains to show that each vertex $v \in V(G)$ is assigned at least q colors in c. This is equivalent to showing that each vertex $v \in V(G)$ is a boundary vertex for $x[i]$ for at most $2 \cdot 6^D$ different combinations of x and i. If v is a boundary vertex for $x[i]$, then $x[i]$ lies on the boundary of the ball B_v of center v and radius 2ℓ. Note that every line intersects the boundary of a convex polytope in at most two points or in a segment, and in the latter case the line is contained in the hyperplane defining a facet. Since we have chosen the directions $\mathbf{e}_x \in \{-1, 1\}^D$ while balls in d_∞ are grids (bounded by axis-parallel hyperplanes), this shows that for every vertex $x \in I$, the set of vertices $\{x[i] : 1 \leqslant i \leqslant \ell\}$ intersects the boundary of B_v at most twice, and if the intersection is non-empty then x is at distance at most 3ℓ from v. For a fixed vertex v there can be at most 6^D vertices in $N_{G^{[3\ell]}}(v) \cap I$. To see this, for every $(i_1, \ldots, i_D) \in \{-3, -2, \ldots, 2\}^D$, we let $S_{(i_1, \ldots, i_D)}$ be the set of vertices $y \in V(G)$ of coordinates $(y_1, \ldots, y_D)$ satisfying $v_j + i_j \cdot \ell \leqslant y_j \leqslant v_j + (i_j + 1) \cdot \ell$ for every $1 \leqslant j \leqslant D$. It is straightforward to see that the diameter of $S_{(i_1, \ldots, i_D)}$ is ℓ, so it contains at most 1 element of I. Since moreover the collection $(S_{(i_1, \ldots, i_D)})$ covers $N_{G^{[3\ell]}}(v)$, the results follows, which concludes the proof.   □

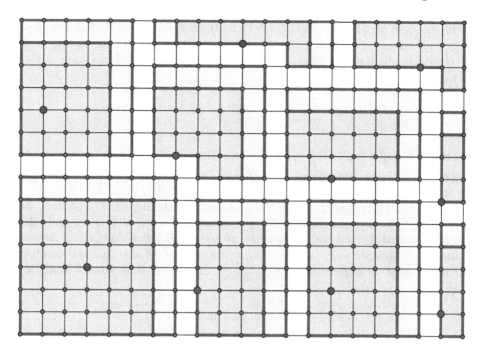

Fig. 2. An example of the partition of the 2-dimensional grid into the sets $B(x,i)$; here $2\ell = 4$, and the labels of the vertices are increasing according to the lexicographical ordering of the coordinates. The regions containing the boundary vertices are lighter; the vertices $x[i]$ (for $x \in I$) are colored in red. (Color figure online)

5   Sparse Graphs

The *average degree* of a graph $G = (V, E)$, denoted by $\mathrm{ad}(G)$, is defined as the average of the degrees of the vertices of G (it is equal to 0 if V is empty and to $2|E|/|V|$ otherwise).

In this section we are interested in graphs of average degree at most $2 + \varepsilon$, for some small $\varepsilon > 0$, and with no connected component isomorphic to a short cycle (later we will need the stronger property that all cycles in the graph are large). We first prove that they contain a linear number of vertices that are either of degree at most 1 or belong to long chains of vertices of degree 2, and such a set can be found efficiently. Note that the condition that no connected component is isomorphic to a short cycle is necessary (a disjoint union of short cycles has average degree 2 but no vertex of degree 1 and no long chain of vertices of degree 2).

Lemma 1. *Let G be an n-vertex graph with $\mathrm{ad}(G) \leqslant 2 + \frac{1}{40q}$ and without component isomorphic to a cycle of length less than $2q + 2$, for some $q \geqslant 1$. Let S be the set of vertices of degree at most 1 in G, and let P be the set of vertices belonging to a path consisting of at least $2q + 1$ vertices, all of degree 2 in G (in particular each vertex of P has degree 2 in G). Then $|S \cup P| \geqslant \frac{1}{40q} n$.*

Proof. Let $\varepsilon = \frac{1}{40q}$. For $i = 0, 1, 2$, let V_i be the set of vertices of degree i, and let V_3^+ be the set of vertices of degree at least 3. We denote by n_0, n_1, n_2, and n_3^+ the cardinality of these four sets. Since G has average degree at most $2 + \varepsilon$, we have

$$n_1 + 2n_2 + 3n_3^+ \leqslant n_1 + 2n_2 + \sum_{v \in V_3^+} d_G(v) \leqslant (2 + \varepsilon)(n_0 + n_1 + n_2 + n_3^+),$$

and thus $n_3^+ \leqslant \frac{2+\varepsilon}{1-\varepsilon} \cdot n_0 + \frac{1+\varepsilon}{1-\varepsilon} \cdot n_1 + \frac{\varepsilon}{1-\varepsilon} \cdot n_2 \leqslant \frac{5}{2} n_0 + \frac{3}{2} n_1 + \frac{3}{2}\varepsilon n_2$ (since $\varepsilon \leqslant \frac{1}{8}$).

Let H be the multigraph obtained from G by removing all connected components isomorphic to a cycle, and then replacing each maximal path of vertices of degree 2 in G by a single edge (i.e., for each maximal path P in which all internal vertices have degree 2 in G, we delete these internal vertices and add an edge between the two endpoints of P). Note that H has no vertices of degree 2, and it contains precisely $n_0 + n_1 + n_3^+$ vertices. Observe also that the number m_H of edges of H is precisely $\frac{1}{2} \sum_{v \in V_0 \cup V_1 \cup V_3^+} d_G(v)$. It thus follows from the inequalities above that

$$\begin{aligned}
m_H &\leqslant \tfrac{1}{2}(2 + \varepsilon)(n_0 + n_1 + n_3^+) - n_2 \\
&= (1 + \tfrac{\varepsilon}{2})(n_0 + n_1 + n_3^+) + \tfrac{\varepsilon}{2} \cdot n_2 \\
&\leqslant \tfrac{5}{4} n_0 + \tfrac{5}{4} n_1 + \tfrac{5}{4}(\tfrac{5}{2} n_0 + \tfrac{3}{2} n_1 + \tfrac{3}{2}\varepsilon n_2) + \tfrac{\varepsilon}{2} \cdot n_2. \\
&\leqslant 5(n_0 + n_1) + 3\varepsilon n_2.
\end{aligned}$$

We now set $S = V_0 \cup V_1$. Thus, if $|S| = n_0 + n_1 \geqslant \frac{1}{40q} n = \varepsilon n$ we have sets S and $P = \emptyset$ satisfying all required properties. Hence, we can assume in the remainder of the proof that

$$\begin{aligned}
n_0 + n_1 \leqslant \varepsilon n &\leqslant \varepsilon (n_0 + n_1 + n_2 + n_3^+) \\
&\leqslant \varepsilon (n_0 + n_1 + n_2 + \tfrac{5}{2}(n_0 + n_1) + \tfrac{3}{2}\varepsilon n_2) \\
&\leqslant (n_0 + n_1)\tfrac{7}{2}\varepsilon + n_2\varepsilon(1 + \tfrac{3}{2}\varepsilon) \\
&\leqslant (n_0 + n_1)\tfrac{7}{2}\varepsilon + 2n_2\varepsilon
\end{aligned}$$

It follows that

$$n_0 + n_1 \leqslant \frac{1}{1 - \frac{7}{2}\varepsilon} \cdot 2n_2\varepsilon \leqslant 3\varepsilon n_2,$$

since $\varepsilon \leqslant \frac{1}{12}$. This implies that $n_3^+ \leqslant 9\varepsilon n_2$ since otherwise the average degree would be larger than $(2 + \varepsilon)$. Consequently, we obtain $n \leqslant (1 + 12\varepsilon) n_2$, and $m_H \leqslant 18\varepsilon n_2$.

In G, remove all the vertices of degree at most 1 and at least 3. We are left with m_H (possibly empty) paths $P_1, P_2, \ldots, P_{m_H}$ of vertices of degree 2 in G, each corresponding to an edge of H (each edge of H is either a path in G of vertices of degree two, or a real edge of G in which case the corresponding path is empty), plus a certain number of cycles (consisting of vertices of degree 2 in G). Since G has no connected component isomorphic to a cycle of length less than $2q + 2$, each vertex of such a cycle is included in a path consisting of at least $2q + 1$ vertices of degree 2 in G, so all these vertices can be added to the set P. We also add to P all the paths P_i ($1 \leqslant i \leqslant m_H$) containing at least $2q + 1$ vertices. As a consequence, the set P contains all the vertices of degree 2 in G, except those which only belong to paths P_i of at most $2q$ vertices. So we have $|P| \geqslant n_2 - 2qm_H$. By the inequalities above, we have

$$n_2 - 2qm_H \geqslant n_2(1 - 18\varepsilon \cdot 2q) \geqslant \frac{1 - 2 \cdot 18\varepsilon q}{1 + 12\varepsilon} \cdot n \geqslant \frac{n}{40},$$

where the last inequality follows from $\varepsilon = \frac{1}{40q}$. Since $\frac{n}{40} \geqslant \varepsilon n$, the set P contains at least εn vertices, as desired. $\square$

The *girth* of a graph G is the length of a shortest cycle in G (if the graph is acyclic we set its girth to $+\infty$). We recall that the *maximum average degree* of a graph G, denoted by $\mathrm{mad}(G)$, is the maximum of the average degrees of the subgraphs of G. We now explain how to apply Lemma 1 to design a distributed algorithm for $(2q + 1 : q)$-coloring. Note that Theorem 3, which we restate below for convenience, requires that the *maximum* average degree of G is close to 2 and the girth is at least $2q + 2$, while the previous result only required that the average degree is close to 2, and there is no component isomorphic to a cycle of length less than $2q + 2$. As observed by a reviewer, there are similarities between our approach and the *rake and compress* technique of Miller and Reif [23] (see also [3] and [12] for distributed algorithms in trees using this technique).

Theorem 3. *Let G be an n-vertex graph with girth at least $2q+2$, and $\mathrm{mad}(G) \leqslant 2 + \frac{1}{40q}$, for some fixed $q \geqslant 1$. Then a $(2q + 1 : q)$-coloring of G can be computed deterministically in $O(q \log n + q^2)$ rounds in the LOCAL model.*

Proof. The algorithm proceeds similarly as in [18]. We set $G_0 := G$ and for $i = 1$ to $\ell = O(\log n)$ we define $S_{i-1} \cup P_{i-1}$ as the set of vertices of degree at most 2 given by applying Lemma 1 to G_{i-1} (which has average degree at most $2 + \frac{1}{40q}$ since $\mathrm{mad}(G) \leqslant 2 + \frac{1}{40q}$), and set $G_i := G_{i-1} - (S_{i-1} \cup P_{i-1})$. Note that each $S_i \cup P_i$ consists of a set of vertices of $V(G_i)$ of size at least $\frac{1}{40q}|V(G_i)|$, and in particular we can choose $\ell = O(\log n)$ such that G_ℓ is empty. Note that the induced subgraph $G[S_i \cup P_i] = G_i[S_i \cup P_i]$ consists of isolated vertices and edges, paths consisting of at least $2q + 1$ vertices, all of degree 2 in G_i, and cycles consisting of at least $2q + 2$ vertices, all of degree 2 in G_i.

Note that each $S_i \cup P_i$ can be computed in $O(q)$ rounds (each vertex only needs to look at its neighborhood at distance at most $2q+1$), and thus the decomposition of G into $S_1, P_1, \ldots, S_\ell, P_\ell$ (and the sequence of graphs $G_1, \ldots, G_\ell$) can be computed in $O(q \log n)$ rounds.

For each $1 \leqslant i \leqslant \ell$, *in parallel*, compute a maximal set I_i of vertices at pairwise distance at least $2q + 1$ in $G[S_i \cup P_i]$. Recall that the vertices of S_i have degree at most 1 in G_i, so they induce isolated vertices or isolated edges in G_i (and G), while P_i induces a disjoint union of cycles of length at least $2q + 2$ and paths of at least $2q + 1$ vertices, each consisting only of vertices of degree 2 in G_i.

In particular, by maximality of I_i, the set $P_i - I_i$ induces a collection of disjoint (and pairwise non-adjacent) paths of at least $2q + 1$ and at most $4q + 2$ vertices (except the first and last segment of each path of P_i, which might contain fewer vertices). For each path of P_i, discard from I_i the first and last vertex of I_i in the path (these two vertices might coincide if a path of P_i contains a single vertex of I_i), and call I_i' the resulting subset of I_i (note that each vertex $x \in I_i$ can check in $O(q)$ rounds if it belongs to I_i' by inspecting the lengths of the two subpaths of vertices of degree 2 adjacent to x, if any of them is smaller than $2q + 1$ then $x \in I_i'$). By maximality of I_i and the definition of I_i', the set $P_i - I_i'$ induces a collection of disjoint (and pairwise non-adjacent) paths of length at least $2q + 1$ and at most $8q + 2$. Note that each graph $G[S_i \cup P_i]$ has maximum degree at most 2, so a maximal set I_i of vertices at pairwise distance at least $2q + 1$ can be computed in $O(q + \log^* n)$ rounds in the $(2q + 1)$-th power of $G[S_i \cup P_i]$ [5], and thus in $O(q^2 + q \log^* n)$ rounds in G. Since the computation of the sets I_i is made in parallel in each $G[S_i \cup P_i]$, this step takes $O(q^2 + \log^* n)$ rounds.

We now color each $S_i \cup P_i$ in reverse order, i.e., from $i = \ell - 1$ to 0. For the components induced by S_i this can be done greedily, since the vertices have degree at most 1 in G_i, they have at most one colored neighbor and thus at most q forbidden colors (and at least $q + 1$ available colors). For the components induced by P_i, we start by coloring I_i' arbitrarily, and then extend the coloring greedily to $P_i - I_i'$ until each path of uncolored vertices has size precisely $2q + 1$ (this can be done in $O(q)$ rounds). We then use Theorem 4 (each endpoint of an uncolored path has a list of at least $2q + 1 - q \geqslant q + 1$ available colors). Each coloring extension takes $O(q)$ rounds, so overall this part takes $O(q \log n)$ rounds. It follows that the overall round complexity is $O(q^2 + q \log n)$, as desired. □

This immediately implies the following.

Corollary 1. *Let G be an n-vertex tree. Then for any fixed $q \geqslant 1$, a $(2q + 1 : q)$-coloring of G can be computed in $O(q \log n + q^2)$ rounds.*

Note that given any $(2q + 1 : q)$-coloring, we can deduce a $(q + 2)$-coloring in a single round (each vertex chooses the smallest color in its set of q colors given by the $(2q + 1 : q)$-coloring), while coloring trees with a constant number of colors takes $\Omega(\log n)$ rounds [21], so the round complexity in Corollary 1 is best possible.

For $k \geqslant 1$, a graph G is k-*path-degenerate* if any non-empty subgraph H of G contains a vertex of degree at most 1, or a path consisting of k vertices of degree 2 in H.

Lemma 2. *If G is k-path-degenerate, then $\mathrm{mad}(G) \leqslant 2 + \frac{2}{k}$.*

Proof. Let H be a subgraph of G. Let n and m be the number of vertices and edges of H. We prove that $\mathrm{ad}(H) = 2m/n \leqslant 2 + \frac{2}{k}$ by induction on n. If H is empty, then the result is trivial, so assume that $n \geqslant 1$. Since G is k-path-degenerate, H contains a vertex of degree at most 1 or a path of k vertices of degree 2 in H. Assume first that H contains a vertex v of degree at most 1. Then $H - v$ contains $n - 1$ vertices and at least $m - 1$ edges, and thus by induction $2 + \frac{2}{k} \geqslant \text{ad}(H - v) \geqslant \frac{2m-2}{n-1}$. It follows that $2m \leqslant (n-1)(2 + \frac{2}{k}) + 2 \leqslant n(2 + \frac{2}{k})$, and thus $\text{ad}(H) \leqslant 2 + \frac{2}{k}$, as desired. Assume now that H contains a path P of k vertices of degree 2 in H. Then $H - P$ contains $n - k$ vertices and $m - k - 1$ edges, and by induction $2 + \frac{2}{k} \geqslant \text{ad}(H - P) = \frac{2m-2k-2}{n-k}$. It follows that $2m \leqslant (n - k)(2 + \frac{2}{k}) + 2k + 2 \leqslant n(2 + \frac{2}{k})$, thus $\text{ad}(H) \leqslant 2 + \frac{2}{k}$, as desired. □

It was proved by Gallucio, Goddyn, and Hell [17] that if $\mathcal{C}$ is a proper minor-closed class, or a class closed under taking topological minors, then for any $k \geqslant 1$ there is a girth $g(k)$ such that any graph $G \in \mathcal{C}$ with girth at least $g(k)$ is k-path-degenerate. Using Lemma 2 and Theorem 3, this immediately implies the following.

Corollary 2. *For any integer $q \geqslant 1$ and any proper class $\mathcal{C}$ that is closed under taking minors or topological minors, there is an integer g such that any n-vertex graph $G \in \mathcal{C}$ of girth at least g can be $(2q + 1 : q)$-colored in $O(\log n)$ rounds.*

Acknowledgement. We thank the anonymous reviewers for their detailed comments and suggestions.

References

1. Alon, N., Spencer, J.H.: The Probabilistic Method. John Wiley & Sons, New York (2004)
2. Aubry, Y., Godin, J.-C., Togni, O.: Every triangle-free induced subgraph of the triangular lattice is $(5m, 2m)$-choosable. Discrete Appl. Math. **166**, 51–58 (2014)
3. Balliu, A., et al. : Classification of distributed binary labeling problems. In: Proceedings of the 34th International Symposium on Distributed Computing (DISC) (2020)
4. Barenboim, L., Elkin, M.: Distributed graph coloring: fundamentals and recent developments. Synth. Lect. Distrib. Comput. Theor. **4**(1), 1–171 (2013)
5. Barenboim, L., Elkin, M., Kuhn, F.: Distributed $(\Delta + 1)$-coloring in linear (in Δ) time. SIAM J. Comput. **43**(1), 72–95 (2014)
6. Boppana, R.B., Halldórsson, M.M., Rawitz, D.: Simple and local independent set approximation. In: Lotker, Z., Patt-Shamir, B. (eds.) SIROCCO 2018. LNCS, vol. 11085, pp. 88–101. Springer, Cham (2018). https://doi.org/10.1007/978-3-030-01325-7_12
7. Brandt, S.: An automatic speedup theorem for distributed problems. In: Proceedings of the ACM Symposium on Principles of Distributed Computing (PODC), pp. 379–388 (2019)
8. Brandt, S., et al.: LCL problems on grids. In: Proceedings of the ACM Symposium on Principles of Distributed Computing (PODC) (2017)
9. Brandt, S., et al.: A lower bound for the distributed Lovász local lemma. In: Proceedings of the 48th ACM Symposium on Theory of Computing (STOC), pp. 479–488 (2016)

10. Brooks, R.L.: On colouring the nodes of a network. Math. Proc. Camb. Philos. Soc. **37**(2), 194–197 (1941)
11. Chang, Y.-J., Kopelowitz, T., Pettie, S.: An exponential separation between randomized and deterministic complexity in the LOCAL model. SIAM J. Comput. **48**(1), 122–143 (2019)
12. Chang, Y.-J., Pettie, S.: A time hierarchy theorem for the LOCAL model. SIAM J. Comput. **48**(1), 33–69 (2019)
13. Cropper, M.M., Goldwasser, J.L., Hilton, A.J.W., Hoffman, D.G., Johnson, P.D.: Extending the disjoint-representatives theorems of Hall, Halmos, and Vaughan to list-multicolorings of graphs. J. Graph Theor. **33**(4), 199–219 (2000)
14. Csóka, E., Gerencsér, B., Harangi, V., Virág, B.: Invariant gaussian processes and independent sets on regular graphs of large girth. Rand. Struct. Algorith. **47**, 284–303 (2015)
15. Csóka, E., Harangi, V., Virág, B.: Entropy and expansion. Ann. Inst. Henri Poincaré Probab. Stat. **56**(4), 2428–2444 (2020)
16. Fisher, D.: Fractional colorings with large denominators. J. Graph Theor **20**(4), 403–409 (1995)
17. Galluccio, A., Goddyn, L.A., Hell, P.: High-girth graphs avoiding a minor are nearly bipartite. J. Combin. Theor. Ser. B **83**(1), 1–14 (2001)
18. Goldberg, A., Plotkin, S., Shannon, G.: Parallel symmetry-breaking in sparse graphs. SIAM J. Discrete Math. **1**(4), 434–446 (1988)
19. Hasemann, H., Hirvonen, J., Rybicki, J., Suomela, J.: Deterministic local algorithms, unique identifiers, and fractional graph colouring. Theoret. Comput. Sci. **610**, 204–217 (2016)
20. Holroyd, A.E., Schramm, O., Wilson, D.B.: Finitary coloring. Ann. Probab. **45**(5), 2867–2898 (2017)
21. Linial, N.: Locality in distributed graph algorithms. SIAM J. Comput. **21**, 193–201 (1992)
22. Lovász, L.: Kneser's conjecture, chromatic number, and homotopy. J. Comb. Theor Ser. A **25**(3), 319–324 (1978)
23. Miller, G.L., Reif, J.H.: Parallel tree contraction-Part I: fundamentals. Adv. Comput. Res. **5**, 47–72 (1989)
24. Nadara, W., Smulewicz, M.: Decreasing the maximum average degree by deleting an independent set or a d-degenerate subgraph. arXiv e-print arXiv:1909.10701 (2019)
25. Scheinerman, E.R., Ullman, D.H.: Fractional Graph Theory: A Rational Approach to the Theory of Graphs, Dover Publications, Minola(2013)

Distributed Graph Problems Through an Automata-Theoretic Lens

Yi-Jun Chang[1], Jan Studený[2($\boxtimes$)], and Jukka Suomela[2]

[1] ETH Zürich, Zürich, Switzerland
[2] Aalto University, Espoo, Finland
`jan.studeny@aalto.fi`

Abstract. The *locality* of a graph problem is the smallest distance T such that each node can choose its own part of the solution based on its radius-T neighborhood. In many settings, a graph problem can be solved efficiently with a distributed or parallel algorithm if and only if it has a small locality. In this work we seek to *automate* the study of solvability and locality: given the description of a graph problem Π, we would like to determine if Π is solvable and what is the asymptotic locality of Π as a function of the size of the graph. Put otherwise, we seek to automatically *synthesize* efficient distributed and parallel algorithms for solving Π. We focus on *locally checkable* graph problems; these are problems in which a solution is globally feasible if it looks feasible in all constant-radius neighborhoods. Prior work on such problems has brought primarily bad news: questions related to locality are undecidable in general, and even if we focus on the case of *labeled* paths and cycles, determining locality is PSPACE-hard (Balliu et al. PODC 2019). We complement prior negative results with efficient algorithms for the cases of *unlabeled* paths and cycles and, as an extension, for rooted trees. We study locally checkable graph problems from an automata-theoretic perspective by representing a locally checkable problem Π as a *nondeterministic finite automaton* $\mathcal{M}$ over a *unary alphabet*. We identify polynomial-time-computable properties of the automaton $\mathcal{M}$ that near-completely capture the solvability and locality of Π in cycles and paths, with the exception of one specific case that is co-NP-complete.

1 Introduction

In this work, our goal is to *automate* the design of efficient distributed and parallel algorithms for solving graph problems, as far as possible. In the full generality, such tasks are undecidable: for example, given a Turing machine M, we can easily construct a graph problem Π such that there is an efficient distributed algorithm for solving Π if and only if M halts [27]. Nevertheless, we are bringing here good news.

We focus on so-called *locally checkable* graph problems in *paths, cycles, and rooted trees*, and we show that in many cases, the task of designing efficient distributed or parallel algorithms for such problems can be automated, not only in principle but also in practice.

© Springer Nature Switzerland AG 2021
T. Jurdziński and S. Schmid (Eds.): SIROCCO 2021, LNCS 12810, pp. 31–49, 2021.
https://doi.org/10.1007/978-3-030-79527-6_3

We study the *locality* of graph problems from an *automata-theoretic perspective*. To introduce the concrete research questions that we study, we first define one specific model of distributed computing, the LOCAL model—through this model we can define the fundamental concept of locality. However, as we will discuss in Sect. 1, our results are directly applicable in many other synchronous models of distributed and parallel computing as well.

Background: Locality and Round Complexity in Distributed Computing. In classical centralized sequential computing, a particularly successful idea has been the comparison of deterministic and nondeterministic models of computing. The question of P vs. NP is a prime example: given a problem in which solutions are easy to verify, is it also easy to solve?

In distributed computing a key computational resource is locality, and hence the distributed analogue of this idea can be phrased as follows: given a problem in which solutions can be verified locally, can it also be solved locally?

This question is formalized in the study of so-called *locally checkable labeling* (LCL) problems in the LOCAL model of distributed computing. LCL problems are graph problems in which solutions are *labelings* of nodes and/or edges that can be *verified locally*: if a solution looks feasible in all constant-radius neighborhoods, then it is also globally feasible [27]. A simple example of an LCL problem is proper 3-coloring of a graph: if a labeling of the nodes looks like a proper 3-coloring in the radius-1 neighborhood of each node, then it is by definition a feasible solution.

In the LOCAL model of computing [25,28], we assume that the nodes of the input graph are equipped with unique identifiers from $\{1, 2, \ldots, \text{poly}(n)\}$, where n is the number of nodes. A distributed algorithm with a time complexity $T(n)$ is then a function that maps the radius-$T(n)$ neighborhood of each node into its local output. The local output of a node is its own part of the solution, e.g., its own color in the graph coloring problem. Here we say that the algorithm has locality T; the locality of a problem is the smallest T such that there is an algorithm for solving it with locality T.

If we interpret the input graph as a computer network, with nodes as computers and edges as communication links, then in T synchronous communication rounds all nodes can gather full information about their radius-T neighborhood. Hence time (number of communication rounds) and distance (how far one needs to see) are interchangeable in the LOCAL model. In what follows, we will primarily use the term *round complexity*.

Prior Work: The Complexity Landscape of LCL Problems. Now we have a natural distributed analog of the classical P vs. NP question: given an LCL problem, what is its round complexity in the LOCAL model? This is a question that was already introduced by Naor and Stockmeyer in 1995 [27], but the systematic study of the complexity landscape of LCL questions was started only very recently, around 2016 [4–6,8,9,12,13,19,21,22,30].

By now we have got a relatively complete understanding of *possible complexity classes*: to give a simple example, if we look at deterministic algorithms in the LOCAL model, there are LCL problems with complexity $\Theta(\log^* n)$, and there are also LCL problems with complexity $\Theta(\log n)$, but it can be shown that there is no LCL problem with complexity between $\omega(\log^* n)$ and $o(\log n)$ [8,12].

However, much less is known about *how to decide the complexity* of a given LCL problem. Many such questions are undecidable in general, and undecidability holds already in relatively simple settings such as LCLs on 2-dimensional grids and tori [9,27]. We will zoom into graph classes in which no such obstacle exists.

Our Focus: Cycles, Paths, and Rooted Trees. Throughout this work, our main focus will be on paths and cycles. This may at first seem highly restrictive, but as we will show in the full version [14], once we understand LCL problems in paths and cycles, through reductions we will also gain understanding on so-called edge-checkable problems in rooted trees.

In cycles and paths, there are only three possible round complexities: $O(1)$, $\Theta(\log^* n)$, or $\Theta(n)$ [1]. Randomness does not help in cycles and paths—this is a major difference in comparison with trees, in which there are LCL problems in which randomness helps exponentially [7,12,29].

If our input is a *labeled* path or cycle, the round complexity is known to be decidable, but unfortunately it is at least PSPACE-hard [1]. On the other hand, the round complexity of LCLs on *unlabeled directed cycles* has a simple graph-theoretic characterization [9].

However, many questions are left open by prior work, and these are the questions that we will resolve in this work:

- What happens in *undirected* cycles?
- What happens if we study *paths* instead of cycles?
- Can we also characterize the *existence* of a solution for all graphs in a graph class?

To illustrate these questions, consider the following problems that can be expressed as LCLs:

- Π_{2col}: finding a proper 2-coloring,
- Π_{orient}: finding a globally consistent orientation (i.e., an orientation of edges such that it does not contain a node with two incoming or outgoing edges).

The round complexity of Π_{2col} is $\Theta(n)$ both in cycles and paths, regardless of whether they are directed or undirected, while the complexity of Π_{orient} is $\Theta(n)$ in the undirected setting but it becomes $O(1)$ in the directed setting. Problems Π_{2col} and Π_{orient} are always solvable on paths, and Π_{orient} is always solvable on cycles, but if we have an odd cycle, then a solution to Π_{2col} does not exist. In particular, for Π_{2col} there are infinitely many solvable instances and infinitely many unsolvable instances. Our goal in this work is to develop a framework that enables us to make these kind of observations automatically for any given LCL problem.

LCLs as Nondeterministic Automata over a Unary Alphabet. In this work we study the solvability and the round complexity of LCL problems from an automata-theoretic perspective. Specifically, we generalize the graph-theoretic characterization for LCL problems on unlabeled directed cycles in [9] to all paths and cycles, directed and undirected, and identify a connection between such a characterization and automata theory.

This connection allows us to leverage prior work on automata theory. For example, as we will later see in this work, the co-NP-completeness of the universality problem for nondeterministic finite automata [31] allows us to deduce the NP-hardness for distinguishing between zero and infinitely many unsolvable instances for LCL problems on paths.

We would like to emphasize that there are many ways to interpret LCLs as automata—and the approach that might seem most natural does not make it possible to directly leverage prior work on automata theory. We will later see that the approach we take enables us to identify direct connections between distributed computational complexity and automata theory.

Let us first briefly describe the "obvious" encoding and show why it does not achieve what we want: A labeling of a directed path with symbols from some alphabet Σ can be interpreted as a string. Then a locally checkable problem can be interpreted as a regular language over alphabet Σ. We can then represent an LCL problem Π as a finite automaton $\mathcal{M}$ such that $\mathcal{M}$ accepts a string $x \in \Sigma^*$ if and only if a directed path labeled with x is a feasible solution to Π.

However, such an interpretation does *not* seem to lead to a useful theory of LCL problems. To see one challenge, consider these problems on paths:

- Π_{2col}: finding a proper 2-coloring,
- Π_{3col}: finding a proper 3-coloring.

These are fundamentally different problems from the perspective of LCLs in the LOCAL model: problem Π_{2col} requires $\Theta(n)$ rounds while problem Π_{3col} is solvable in $\Theta(\log^* n)$ rounds [15]. However, if we consider analogous automata $\mathcal{M}_{2col}$ and $\mathcal{M}_{3col}$ that recognize these solutions, it is not easy to identify a classical automata-theoretic concept that would separate these cases.

Instead of identifying the *alphabet* of the automaton with the set of labels in the LCL, it turns out to be a better idea to have a *unary* alphabet and identify the *set of states* of the automaton with the set of labels. In brief, the perspective that we take throughout this work is as follows (this is a simplified version of the idea):

Assume Π is an LCL problem in which the set of output labels is Γ. We interpret Π as a *nondeterministic finite automaton* $\mathcal{M}_\Pi$ over the *unary alphabet* $\Sigma = \{o\}$ such that the set of states of $\mathcal{M}_\Pi$ is Γ.

At first this approach may seem counterintuitive. But as we will see in this work, it enables us to connect classical automata-theoretic concepts to properties of LCLs this way.

To give one nontrivial example, consider the question of whether a given LCL problem Π can be solved in $O(\log^* n)$ rounds. With the above interpretation, this turns out to be directly connected to the existence of *synchronizing words* [10,17], in the following nondeterministic sense: we say that w is a synchronizing word for an NFA $\mathcal{M}$ that takes $\mathcal{M}$ into state t if, given any starting state $s \in Q$ there is a sequence of state transitions that takes $\mathcal{M}$ to state t when it processes w. Such a sequence w is known as the *D3-directing word* introduced in [24] and further studied in [16,20,23,26]. We will show that the following holds (up to some minor technicalities):

> An LCL on directed paths and cycles has a round complexity of $O(\log^* n)$ if and only if a strongly connected component of the corresponding NFA $\mathcal{M}$ over the unary alphabet has a D3-directing word.

Moreover, we will show that for the unary alphabet, the existence of such a word can be decided in *polynomial time* in the size of the NFA $\mathcal{M}$, or equivalently, in the size of the description of the LCL Π. In contrast, when the size of the alphabet is at least two, the problem of deciding the existence of a D3-directing word is known to be PSPACE-hard [26].

We would like to emphasize that this connection between LCL problems and automata theory is not inherent to unlabeled paths and cycles. For example, *tree automata* can be used to encode LCL problems on bounded-degree trees, and to encode LCL problems with input labels Σ, it suffices to consider automata over the alphabet Σ. Whether such a connection beyond unlabeled paths and cycles can lead to new results is an interesting future work direction.

Contributions. We study LCL problems in unlabeled cycles and paths, both with and without consistent orientation. For each of these settings, we show how to answer the following questions in a mechanical manner, for any given LCL problem Π:

- How many unsolvable instances there are (none, finitely, or infinitely many)?
- How many solvable instances there are (none, finitely, or infinitely many)?
- What is the round complexity of Π for solvable instances ($O(1)$, $\Theta(\log^* n)$, or $\Theta(n)$)?

We show that all such questions are not only decidable but they are in NP or co-NP, and almost all such questions are in P, with the exception of a couple of specific questions that are NP-complete or co-NP-complete. We also give a complete classification of all possible case combinations—for example, we show that if there are infinitely many unsolvable instances, then the complexity of the problem for solvable instances cannot be $\Theta(\log^* n)$.

We give a uniform automata-theoretic formalism that enables us to study such questions, and that makes it possible to leverage prior work on automata

Table 1. Classification of LCL problems in cycles and paths. This table defines 11 types, labeled with A–K, based on six properties (Definitions 3, 6–10); see Fig. 3 for examples of problems of each type. For each problem type, we show what is the number of solvable instances, the number of unsolvable instances, and the distributed round complexity for both directed and undirected paths and cycles. The cases marked with "×" refer to problems that are not well-defined or that are never solvable. For the cases labeled with "?" deciding the number of unsolvable instances is NP-complete (or co-NP-complete depending on the way one defines the decision problem). However, for all other cases the type directly determines both solvability, and all these cases are also decidable in polynomial time. The correctness of this classification is proved in the full version [14].

Type	A	B	C	D	E	F	G	H	I	J	K
Def. 3: symmetric problem	yes	yes	yes	no	yes	yes	no	yes	no	yes	no
Def. 6: repeatable state	yes	yes	yes	yes	yes	yes	yes	yes	yes	no	no
Def. 7: flexible state [9]	yes	yes	yes	yes	yes	yes	yes	no	no	no	no
Def. 8: loop [9]	yes	yes	yes	yes	no	no	no	no	no	no	no
Def. 9: mirror-flexible state	yes	yes	no	—	yes	no	—	no	—	no	—
Def. 10: mirror-flexible loop	yes	no	no	—	no	no	—	no	—	no	—

Num. of instances: $0 = $ zero $< = $ finite $\infty = $ infinite $? = $ NP-complete to decide

	A	B	C	D	E	F	G	H	I	J	K
· solvable cycles	∞	∞	∞	∞	∞	∞	∞	∞	∞	0	0
· solvable paths	∞	∞	∞	∞	∞	∞	∞	∞	∞	$<$	$<$
· unsolvable cycles	0	0	0	0	$<$	$<$	$<$	∞	∞	∞	∞
· unsolvable paths	$<$	$<$	$<$	$<$	$<$	$<$	$<$	$?$	$?$	∞	∞

Round complexity: $\square = O(1)$ $\boxplus = \Theta(\log^* n)$ $\blacksquare = \Theta(n)$ $\times = $ N/A

	A	B	C	D	E	F	G	H	I	J	K
· directed cycles [9]	$\square$	$\square$	$\square$	$\square$	$\boxplus$	$\boxplus$	$\boxplus$	$\blacksquare$	$\blacksquare$	$\times$	$\times$
· directed paths	$\square$	$\square$	$\square$	$\square$	$\boxplus$	$\boxplus$	$\boxplus$	$\blacksquare$	$\blacksquare$	$\square$	$\square$
· undirected cycles	$\square$	$\boxplus$	$\blacksquare$	$\times$	$\boxplus$	$\blacksquare$	$\times$	$\blacksquare$	$\times$	$\times$	$\times$
· undirected paths	$\square$	$\boxplus$	$\blacksquare$	$\times$	$\boxplus$	$\blacksquare$	$\times$	$\blacksquare$	$\times$	$\square$	$\times$

theory. We also develop new efficient algorithms for some automata-theoretic questions that to our knowledge have not been studied before.

Finally, we show that our results can be used to analyze also a family of LCL problems in rooted trees. This demonstrates that the automata-theoretic framework considered here is applicable also beyond the seemingly restrictive case of cycles and paths.

Our main result—the complete classification of the solvability and distributed round complexity of all LCL problems in undirected and directed cycles and paths is presented in Table 1.

Extensions to Other Models of Distributed and Parallel Computing.
While we use the LOCAL model of distributed computing throughout this work,
our results are directly applicable also in many other models of distributed and
parallel computing.

In distributed computing we usually assume that the input graph represents
the communication network; each node is a computer, each edge is a communication link, and the nodes can communicate by passing messages to each other.
However, in parallel computing we usually take a very different perspective: we
assume that the input graph is stored as a linked data structure somewhere in
the shared memory, and we have multiple processors that can access the memory. In such a setting, directed paths and rooted trees are particularly relevant
families of input, as they correspond to linked lists and tree data structures.

While the settings are superficially different, our *upper bounds* apply directly
in all such settings. All of our distributed algorithms are based on the observation
that there are two canonical problems: *distance-k anchoring* (Definition 11) and
distance-k orientation (Definition 12). Both of the canonical problems can be
solved in the message-passing setting with small messages and with little local
memory. Furthermore, when we look at rooted trees (see the full version [14]),
our algorithms are "one-sided": each node only needs to receive information from
its parent. It follows that our algorithms work also e.g. in the CONGEST model
[28] of distributed computing, and they can be efficiently simulated e.g. in the
classic PRAM model, as well as various modern models of massively parallel
computing.

Our *lower bounds* are also broadly applicable, as they hold in the LOCAL
model, which is a very strong model of distributed computing (unbounded message size; unlimited local storage; unbounded local computation; nodes can talk
to all of their neighbors in parallel). In particular, the lower bounds trivially
hold also the CONGEST model. Adapting the lower bounds to shared-memory
models takes more effort, but it is also possible—see Fich and Ramachandran
[18] for an example of how to turn $\Omega(\log^* n)$ lower bounds for the LOCAL model
into $\Omega(\log \log^* n)$ lower bounds for variants of the PRAM model.

Comparison with Prior Work. In comparison with [1,9,12,13,27], our work
gives a more fine-grained perspective: instead of merely discussing decidability,
we explore the question of which of the decision problems are in P, NP, and
co-NP.

In comparison with the discussion of directed cycles in [9], our work studies a
much broader range of settings. Previously, it was not expected that the simple
characterization of LCLs on directed cycles could be extended in a straightforward manner to paths or undirected cycles. For example, we can define an infinite
family of orientation problems that can be solved in undirected cycles in $O(1)$
rounds but that require a nontrivial algorithm; such problems do not exist in
directed cycles, as $O(1)$-round solvability implies trivial 0-round solvability.

Furthermore, we study the graph-theoretic question of the existence of a
solution in addition to the algorithmic question of the complexity of finding a

solution, and relate solvability with complexity in a systematic manner; we are not aware of prior work that would do the same in the context of LCLs in the LOCAL model.

Our work also takes the first steps towards an effective (i.e., polynomial-time computable) characterization of LCL problems in trees, by showing how to characterize so-called edge-checkable problems in rooted trees.

For general LCL problems on bounded-degree trees, previous work [4,11,13] showed that it is decidable to distinguish between the complexity pairs $O(\log n)$ $- n^{\Omega(1)}$ and $O(n^{1/(k+1)}) - \Omega(n^{1/k})$ for any constant $k \geq 1$. These algorithms are not efficient, as these are EXPTIME-hard problems [13].

The previous work [1,4,11,13] studying the complexity landscape of LCL problems on paths, cycles, and bounded-degree trees *with input labels* uses a different connection to automata theory. In their proofs, they classified paths and trees into a finite number of classes satisfying certain properties using the *pumping lemma* for regular languages.

2   Representation of LCLs as Automata

To reiterate, LCL problems [27], broadly speaking, are problems in which the task is to label nodes and/or edges with labels from a constant-size alphabet (denoted by Γ), subject to local constraints. That is, a solution is globally feasible if it looks good in all radius-r neighborhoods for some constant r. In this section we will develop a way to represent all LCL problems on paths and cycles as nondeterministic automata.

In this paper, we consider as input graphs only paths and cycles that are either undirected (undirected case) or the edges are consistently oriented (directed case). We say that a cycle or a path has *consistently oriented edges* if it does not contain a node with two incoming or outgoing edges.

2.1   Formalizing LCLs as Node-Edge-Checkable Problems

LCL problems can be specified in many different forms, and we have to be able to capture, among others, problems of the following forms:

- The problem may ask for a labeling of nodes, a labeling of edges, a labeling of the endpoints of the edges, an orientation of the edges, or any combination of these.
- The input graph can be a path or a cycle.
- The input graph may be directed or undirected.

As discussed in the recent papers [2,3], a rather elegant way to capture all LCL problems is the following approach: We imagine that we have split every edge into two *half-edges*, which are also called *ports*. The labeling refers only to the ports.

More formally, a *port* or a *half-edge* p is a pair (e, v) consisting of an edge e and a node $v \in e$ incident to e. Let P be the set of all ports. A *labeling* is a function $\lambda \colon P \to \Gamma$ from ports to labels from some alphabet Γ.

It is easy to see that we can represent LCL problems of different flavors in this formalism, for example:

- If the task is to label nodes, we require all ports incident to a node to be labeled by the same label, so that the label of a node is well-defined.
- If the task is to label edges, we require that both half-edges of each edge have the same label, so that the label of an edge is well-defined.
- If the task is to find an orientation, we can use e.g. symbols H (head) and T (tail) and require that for each edge exactly one half is labeled with H and the other half is labeled with T, so that the orientation of each edge is well-defined.

Moreover, the constraints for node-edge-checkable problems will be divided into *node constraints* and *edge constraints*. Node constraints consider only incident port labels of a node and edge constraints consider only incident port labels of an edge.

We will now formally define an LCL problem in the node-edge-checkable formalism. Let us first consider the case of directed cycles or paths. By assumption, a directed cycle or a directed path is consistently oriented. For each edge, one port is a *tail port* and the other port is a *head port*. Furthermore, for each degree-2 node, there is also exactly one head port and exactly one tail port incident to it.

Definition 1 (LCL problem). *An* LCL *problem Π in the node-edge-checkable formalism on cycles or paths is a tuple $\Pi = (\Gamma, \mathcal{C}_{edge}, \mathcal{C}_{node}, \mathcal{C}_{start}, \mathcal{C}_{end})$ consisting of*

- *a finite set Γ of output labels,*
- *an edge constraint $\mathcal{C}_{edge} \subseteq \Gamma \times \Gamma$,*
- *a node constraint $\mathcal{C}_{node} \subseteq \Gamma \times \Gamma$, and*
- *start and end constraints $\mathcal{C}_{start} \subseteq \Gamma$ and $\mathcal{C}_{end} \subseteq \Gamma$.*

Definition 2 (solution on directed cycles or paths). *Let G be a directed cycle or a directed path, and let Π be an* LCL *problem, and let $\lambda \colon P \to \Gamma$ be a labeling of G. We say that λ is a* solution *to Π if the following holds:*

- *For each edge e, if p is the tail port and q is the head port of e, then $(\lambda(p), \lambda(q)) \in \mathcal{C}_{edge}$.*
- *For each degree-2 node v, if p is the head port and q is the tail port of v, then $(\lambda(p), \lambda(q)) \in \mathcal{C}_{node}$.*
- *For each degree-1 node v with only one tail port p, we have $\lambda(p) \in \mathcal{C}_{start}$.*
- *For each degree-1 node v with only one head port p, we have $\lambda(p) \in \mathcal{C}_{end}$.*

Informally, when we follow the labeling in the positive direction along the directed path, we will first see a label from $\mathcal{C}_{start}$, then each edge is labeled with a pair from $\mathcal{C}_{edge}$, each internal node is labeled with a pair from $\mathcal{C}_{node}$, and the final label along the path is $\mathcal{C}_{end}$.

Next we consider the case of undirected cycles or paths.

Definition 3 (symmetric LCL problems). *We say that an* LCL *problem* $\Pi = (\Gamma, \mathcal{C}_{\mathsf{edge}}, \mathcal{C}_{\mathsf{node}}, \mathcal{C}_{\mathsf{start}}, \mathcal{C}_{\mathsf{end}})$ *is* symmetric *if* $\mathcal{C}_{\mathsf{edge}}$ *and* $\mathcal{C}_{\mathsf{node}}$ *are symmetric relations and* $\mathcal{C}_{\mathsf{start}} = \mathcal{C}_{\mathsf{end}}$. *Otherwise the problem is* asymmetric.

As in the undirected case, we cannot consistently distinguish ports, hence we can only solve and define solution for symmetric LCL problems.

Definition 4 (solution on undirected cycles or paths). *Let G be an undirected cycle or an undirected path, and let Π be a symmetric* LCL *problem, and let $\lambda: P \to \Gamma$ be a labeling of G. We say that λ is a* solution *to Π if the following holds:*

- *For each edge e, if the ports of e are p and q, then $(\lambda(p), \lambda(q)) \in \mathcal{C}_{\mathsf{edge}}$.*
- *For each degree-2 node v, if the ports incident to v are p and q, then $(\lambda(p), \lambda(q)) \in \mathcal{C}_{\mathsf{node}}$.*
- *For each degree-1 node v, if the port incident to v is p, then $\lambda(p) \in \mathcal{C}_{\mathsf{start}} = \mathcal{C}_{\mathsf{end}}$.*

Recall that in symmetric problems $\mathcal{C}_{\mathsf{edge}}$ and $\mathcal{C}_{\mathsf{node}}$ are symmetric, so the above formulation is well-defined. When we study the case of cycles, we can set $\mathcal{C}_{\mathsf{start}} = \mathcal{C}_{\mathsf{end}} = \emptyset$. For brevity, in what follows, we will usually write the pair (a, b) simply as ab.

It is usually fairly easy to encode any given LCL problem in a natural manner in this formalism—see Fig. 1 for examples. In the figure, *maximal matching* serves as an example of a problem in which the natural encoding of indicating which edges are part of the matching does not work (it does not capture maximality) but with one additional label we can precisely define a problem that is equivalent to maximal matchings.

In general, if we have any LCL problem Π (in which the problem description can refer to radius-r neighborhoods for some constant r), we can define an equivalent problem Π' that can be represented in the node-edge-checkable formalism, modulo constant-time preprocessing and postprocessing. In brief, one label in the new problem Π' corresponds to the labeling of a subpath of length $\Theta(r)$ in Π. Now given a solution of Π, one can construct a solution of Π' in $O(r)$ rounds, and given a solution of Π', one can construct a solution of Π in zero rounds. Moreover, Π' can be specified in the node-edge-checkable formalism. We will give the details in the full version [14]. From now on, all LCL problems considered are by default problems defined using the node-edge-checkable formalism.

2.2 Turning Node-Edge-Checkable Problems into Automata

Now consider an LCL problem Π that is specified in the node-edge-checkable formalism. Construct a nondeterministic finite automaton $\mathcal{M}_\Pi$ as follows; see Figs. 1 and 2 for examples.

- The set of states is $\mathcal{C}_{\text{edge}}$.
- There is a transition from (a, b) to (c, d) whenever $(b, c) \in \mathcal{C}_{\text{node}}$.
- $(a, b) \in \mathcal{C}_{\text{edge}}$ is a starting state whenever $a \in \mathcal{C}_{\text{start}}$.
- $(a, b) \in \mathcal{C}_{\text{edge}}$ is an accepting state whenever $b \in \mathcal{C}_{\text{end}}$.

We will interpret $\mathcal{M}_\Pi$ as an NFA over the unary alphabet $\Sigma = \{o\}$. Note that there can be multiple starting states; the automaton can choose the starting state nondeterministically. We remark that in case of cycles, the sets $\mathcal{C}_{\text{start}}$ and $\mathcal{C}_{\text{end}}$ are empty which transforms an NFA into a nondeterministic semiautomaton

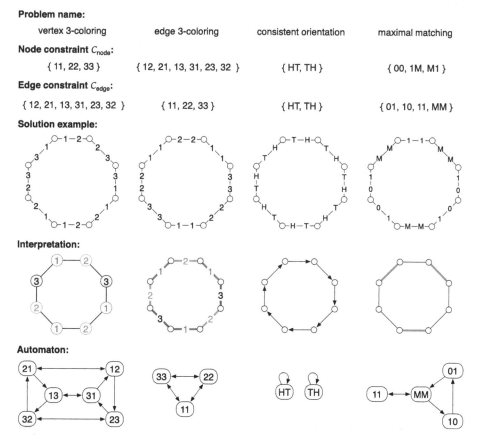

Fig. 1. Examples of how to encode LCL problems in the node-edge-checkable formalism, and how to represent the problem as an automaton. Here the problems are symmetric, so they are well-specified also on undirected cycles. For maximal matching, ports incident to matched nodes are labeled with "1" and "M", ports incident to unmatched nodes are labeled with "0", and the edge constraints ensure that there are no unmatched nodes adjacent to each other.

(i.e., an automation having no starting or accepting states). In the following part we will see how to view the constructed automata.

We define the following concepts:

Definition 5 (generating paths and cycles). *Automaton $\mathcal{M}$ can generate the cycle $(x_1, x_2, \ldots, x_m)$ if each x_i is a state of $\mathcal{M}$, there is a state transition from x_i to x_{i+1} for each $i < m$, and there is a state transition from x_m to x_1.*

Automaton $\mathcal{M}$ can generate the path $(x_1, x_2, \ldots, x_m)$ if each x_i is a state of $\mathcal{M}$, x_1 is a starting state, x_m is an accepting state, and there is a state transition from x_i to x_{i+1} for each $i < m$.

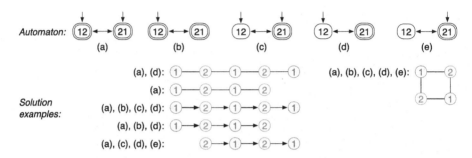

Fig. 2. Five variants of the node 2-coloring problem. Each variant has different allowed colors for the endpoints, hence also different starting and accepting states. Here (a) and (d) are the only problems that are symmetric; therefore problems (b), (c), and (e) are not meaningful on undirected paths.

Note that $\mathcal{M}$ can generate cycles even if there are no starting states or accepting states.

Example 1. Consider the state machines in Fig. 1. The state machine for consistent orientation can generate the following cycles:

$$(HT),\ (TH),\ (HT, HT),\ (TH, TH),\ (HT, HT, HT),\ (TH, TH, TH),\ \ldots$$

The state machine for maximal matching can generate the following cycles:

$$(11, MM),\ (MM, 11),\ (10, 01, MM),\ (01, MM, 10),\ (MM, 10, 01),$$
$$(11, MM, 11, MM),\ (MM, 11, MM, 11),\ \ldots$$

Remark 1. If we start with a symmetric problem, the automaton will be *mirror-symmetric* in the following sense: there is a state transition $(a, b) \to (c, d)$ if and only if there is a state transition $(d, c) \to (b, a)$, and the automaton can generate $(x_1 y_1, \ldots, x_m y_m)$ if and only if it can generate $(y_m x_m, \ldots, y_1 x_1)$. All automata in Fig. 1 have this property, while in Fig. 2 only automata (a) and (d) are mirror-symmetric.

Automata Capture Node-Edge-Checkable Problems. These observations follow directly from the definitions:

- Let Π be a symmetric or asymmetric problem. Automaton $\mathcal{M}_\Pi$ can generate a cycle $(x_1, x_2, \ldots, x_m)$ if and only if the following is a feasible solution for problem Π: Take a *directed* cycle with m nodes and m edges and walk along the cycle in the positive direction, starting at an arbitrary edge. Label the ports of the first edge with x_1, the ports of the second edge with x_2, etc.
- Let Π be a symmetric problem. Automaton $\mathcal{M}_\Pi$ can generate a cycle $(x_1, x_2, \ldots, x_m)$ if and only if the following is a feasible solution for problem Π: Take an *undirected* cycle with m nodes and m edges and walk the cycle in some consistent direction, starting at an arbitrary edge. Label the ports of the first edge with x_1, the ports of the second edge with x_2, etc.
- We can make analogous observations also related to directed and undirected paths; see the full version [14] for details.

Hence, for example, the question of whether a given problem Π is solvable in a path of length m is equivalent to the question of whether $\mathcal{M}_\Pi$ accepts the string o^m. Similarly, the question of whether Π is solvable in a cycle of length m is equivalent to the question of whether there is a state q such that $\mathcal{M}_\Pi$ can return to state q after processing o^m.

However, the key question is what can be said about the complexity of solving Π in a distributed setting. As we will see, this is also captured in the structural properties of $\mathcal{M}_\Pi$.

3   Classification of All LCL Problems on Cycles

Consider a problem Π and its corresponding automation $\mathcal{M}_\Pi$. We introduce the following definitions; see Fig. 3 for examples.

To clarify, for states ab, cd in $\mathcal{M}_\Pi$, a walk from ab to cd (denoted by $ab \rightsquigarrow cd$) is a sequence of state transitions starting at state ab and ending at state cd.

Definition 6 (repeatable state). *State $ab \in \mathcal{C}_{\mathsf{edge}}$ is repeatable if there is a walk $ab \rightsquigarrow ab$ in $\mathcal{M}_\Pi$.*

Definition 7. (flexible state [9]). *State $ab \in \mathcal{C}_{\mathsf{edge}}$ is flexible with flexibility K if for all $k \geq K$ there is a walk $ab \rightsquigarrow ab$ of length exactly k in $\mathcal{M}_\Pi$.*

Definition 8 (loop). *State $ab \in \mathcal{C}_{\mathsf{edge}}$ is a loop if there is a state transition $ab \rightarrow ab$ in $\mathcal{M}_\Pi$.*

Observe that each defined property of a state is a proper strengthening of the previous property (i.e. each loop is a flexible state and each flexible state is a repeatable state).

For a symmetric problem Π we also define:

Definition 9 (mirror-flexible state). *State $ab \in \mathcal{C}_{\mathsf{edge}}$ is mirror-flexible with flexibility K if for all $k \geq K$ there are walks $ab \rightsquigarrow ab$, $ab \rightsquigarrow ba$, $ba \rightsquigarrow ab$, and $ba \rightsquigarrow ba$ of length exactly k in $\mathcal{M}_\Pi$.*

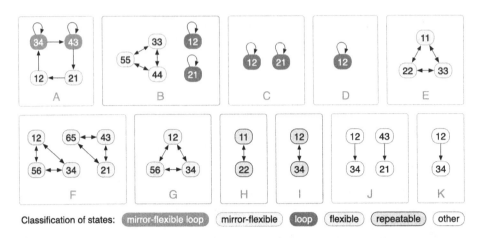

Fig. 3. Examples of LCL problems of each type (type A–K in Table 1) represented as automata, together with a classification of their states using Definitions 6–10. The states are colored only by the most restrictive property. Here is a brief description of each sample problem: **A:** orient the edges so that each consistently oriented fragment consists of at least two edges, one with the label pair 12 and at least one with the label pair 34. **B:** either find a consistent orientation (encoded with labels 1–2) or find a proper 3-coloring of the edges (encoded with labels 3–5). **C:** consistent orientation. **D:** orientation in the positive direction. **E:** edge 3-coloring. **F:** consistent orientation together with an edge 3-coloring. **G:** orientation in the positive direction together with an edge 3-coloring. **H:** edge 2-coloring. **I:** orientation in the positive direction together with an edge 2-coloring. **J–K:** problems only solvable on paths of length at most 2 (assuming appropriate starting and accepting states).

Definition 10 (mirror-flexible loop). *State $ab \in \mathcal{C}_{\mathsf{edge}}$ is a mirror-flexible loop with flexibility K if ab is a mirror-flexible state with flexibility K and ab is also a loop.*

Note that if ab is mirror-flexible loop, then so is ba, as the problem is symmetric.

3.1   Flexibility and Synchronizing Words

Flexibility is a key concept that we will use in our characterization of LCL problems. We will now connect it to the automata-theoretic concept of synchronizing words.

First, let us make a simple observation that allows us to study automata by their strongly connected components:

Lemma 1. *Let $\mathcal{M}'$ be a strongly connected component of automaton $\mathcal{M}_\Pi$, and let q be a state in $\mathcal{M}'$. Then q is flexible in $\mathcal{M}_\Pi$ if and only if q is flexible in $\mathcal{M}'$.*

Proof. A walk from q back to q in $\mathcal{M}_\Pi$ cannot leave $\mathcal{M}'$.

Recall that a word w is called *D3-directing word* [24] for NFA $\mathcal{M}$ if there is a state t such that starting with any state s of $\mathcal{M}$ there is a sequence of state transitions that takes $\mathcal{M}$ to state t when it processes w. We show that this specific notion of a nondeterministic synchronizing word is, in essence, equivalent to the concept of flexibility:

Lemma 2. *Consider a strongly connected component $\mathcal{M}'$ of some automaton $\mathcal{M}_\Pi$. The following statements are equivalent:*

1. *There is a flexible state in $\mathcal{M}'$.*
2. *All states of $\mathcal{M}'$ are flexible.*
3. *There is a D3-directing word for $\mathcal{M}'$.*

Proof. (1) $\implies$ (2): Assume that state q has flexibility K. Let x be another state in $\mathcal{M}'$. As it is in the same connected component, there is some r such that we can walk from x to q and back in r steps. Therefore for any $k \geq K$ we can walk from x back to x in $k + r$ steps by following the route $x \rightsquigarrow q \rightsquigarrow q \rightsquigarrow x$. Hence x is a flexible state with flexibility at most $K + r$.

(2) $\implies$ (3): Assume that state q has flexibility K, and there is a walk of length at most r from any state x to state q. Then we can walk from any state x to q in exactly $r + K$ steps: first in $r' \leq r$ steps we can reach q and then in $K + r - r' \geq K$ steps we can walk from q back to itself. Hence $w = o^{K+r}$ is a D3-directing word for automaton $\mathcal{M}'$ that takes it from any state to state q.

(3) $\implies$ (1): Assume that there is some D3-directing word $w = o^K$ that can take one from any state of $\mathcal{M}'$ to state q in exactly K steps. Then we can also walk from q to itself in k steps for any $k \geq K$: first take $k - K$ steps arbitrarily inside $\mathcal{M}'$, and then walk back to q in exactly K steps. $\square$

Hence, in what follows, we can freely use any of the above perspectives when reasoning about the distributed complexity of LCL problems. Mirror-flexibility can be then seen as a mirror-symmetric extension of D3-directing words.

There is also a natural connection between flexibility and *Markov chains*. Automaton $\mathcal{M}_\Pi$ over the unary alphabet can be viewed as the diagram of a Markov Chain for unknown probabilities of the transitions. If we assume that every edge will have a non-zero probability, then a strongly connected component of the automaton is an *irreducible* Markov chain, and in such a component the notion of flexibility coincides with the notion of *aperiodicity*.

3.2   Results

Our main result is the classification presented in Table 1; see also Fig. 3 for some examples of problems in each class. What was already well-known by prior work [1,13] is that there are only three possible complexities: $O(1)$, $\Theta(\log^* n)$, and $\Theta(n)$. However, our work gives the first concise classification of exactly which problems belong to which complexity class. In the full version [14] we show that our classification of locally checkable problems on cycles or paths into types A–K, defined by properties of the automaton, is correct and complete.

The entire classification *can be computed efficiently*. In particular, for all of the defined properties (repeatable states, flexible states, loops, mirror-flexible states and mirror-flexible loops) a polynomial-time algorithm can determine if an automaton contains a state with such a property. The non-trivial cases here are flexibility and mirror-flexibility; we present the proofs in the full version [14].

The role of mirror-flexibility. Consider the following problem that we call *distance-k anchoring*; here the selected edges are called *anchors*:

Definition 11. *A distance-k anchoring is a maximal subset of edges that splits the cycle in fragments of length at least $k - 1$.*

This problem can be solved in $O(\log^* n)$ rounds (e.g. by applying maximal independent set algorithms in the kth power of the line graph of the input graph). Now consider an LCL problem Π that has a flexible state q with flexibility k. It is known by prior work [9] that we can now solve Π on directed cycles in $O(\log^* n)$ rounds, as follows: Solve distance-k anchoring and label the anchor edges with the label pair of state q. As state q is flexible, we can walk along the cycle from one anchor to another, and find a way to fill in the fragment between two anchors with a feasible label sequence.

Mirror-flexibility plays a similar role for undirected cycles: the key difference is that the anchor edges cannot be consistently oriented, and hence we need to be able to also fill a gap between state $q = ab$ and its mirror $q' = ba$, in any order. It is easy to see that mirror-flexibility then implies $O(\log^* n)$-round solvability—what is more surprising is that the converse also holds: $O(\log^* n)$-round solvability necessarily implies the existence of a mirror-flexible state.

A new canonical problem for constant-time solvability. One of the new conceptual contributions of this work is related to the following problem, which we call *distance-k orientation*:

Definition 12. *A distance-k orientation is an orientation in which each consistently oriented fragment has a length at least k.*

The problem is trivial to solve in directed cycles in 0 rounds, but the case of undirected cycles is not equally simple. However, with some thought, one can see that the problem can be solved in $O(1)$ rounds also on undirected cycles [13]. This shows that there are infinite families of nontrivial $O(1)$-time solvable problems, and hence it seems at first challenging to concisely and efficiently characterize all such problems. However, as we will see in the full version [14], distance-k orientation can be seen as the *canonical $O(1)$-time solvable problem* on undirected cycles. We show that any problem Π that is $O(1)$-time solvable on undirected cycles has to be of type A (see Table 1), and any such problem can be solved in two steps: first find a distance-k orientation for some constant k that only depends on the structure of $\mathcal{M}_\Pi$, and then map the distance-k orientation to a feasible solution of Π.

We summarize the key new observations related to undirected cycles as follows:

$$\Theta(1) \text{ rounds } \iff \text{ mirror-flexible loop}$$
$$\iff \text{ solvable with distance-}k \text{ orientation}$$

$$\Theta(\log^* n) \text{ rounds } \iff \text{ mirror-flexible state}$$
$$\iff \text{ solvable with distance-}k \text{ anchoring}$$

4   Classification of All LCL Problems on Paths

We present the classification of all LCL problems on paths in Table 1. The detailed proofs of the correctness of the classification, as well as discussion on the key properties are presented in the full version [14].

Acknowledgments. We would like to thank Alkida Balliu, Sebastian Brandt, Laurent Feuilloley, Juho Hirvonen, Yannic Maus, Dennis Olivetti, Aleksandr Tereshchenko, Jara Uitto, and all participants of the Helsinki February Workshop 2018 on Theory of Distributed Computing for discussions related to the decidability of LCLs on trees. We would also like to thank the anonymous reviewers of previous versions of this works for their helpful comments and feedback.

Yi-Jun Chang was supported by Dr. Max Rössler, by the Walter Haefner Foundation, and by the ETH Zürich Foundation.

References

1. Balliu, A., Brandt, S., Chang, Y.J., Olivetti, D., Rabie, M., Suomela, J.: The distributed complexity of locally checkable problems on paths is decidable. In: PODC 2019 (2019). https://doi.org/10.1145/3293611.3331606
2. Balliu, A., et al.: Classification of distributed binary labeling problems. In: DISC 2020 (2020)
3. Balliu, A., Brandt, S., Hirvonen, J., Olivetti, D., Rabie, M., Suomela, J.: Lower bounds for maximal matchings and maximal independent sets. FOCS **2019**, 481–497 (2019). https://doi.org/10.1109/FOCS.2019.00037
4. Balliu, A., Brandt, S., Olivetti, D., Suomela, J.: Almost global problems in the LOCAL model. In: DISC 2018 (2018). https://doi.org/10.4230/LIPIcs.DISC.2018.9
5. Balliu, A., Brandt, S., Olivetti, D., Suomela, J.: How much does randomness help with locally checkable problems? In: PODC 2020 (2020). https://doi.org/10.1145/3382734.3405715
6. Balliu, A., Hirvonen, J., Korhonen, J.H., Lempiäinen, T., Olivetti, D., Suomela, J.: New classes of distributed time complexity. In: STOC 2018 (2018). https://doi.org/10.1145/3188745.3188860
7. Barenboim, L., Elkin, M., Pettie, S., Schneider, J.: The locality of distributed symmetry breaking. J. ACM **63**(3), 20 (2016)
8. Brandt, S., et al.: A lower bound for the distributed Lovász local lemma. In: STOC 2016 (2016). https://doi.org/10.1145/2897518.2897570

9. Brandt, S., et al.: LCL problems on grids. In: PODC **2017**, (2017). https://doi.org/10.1145/3087801.3087833
10. Černý, J.: Poznámka k homogénnym experimentom s konečnými automatmi. Matematicko-fyzikálny časopis **14**(3), 208–216 (1964), http://dml.cz/dmlcz/126647
11. Chang, Y.J.: The complexity landscape of distributed locally checkable problems on trees. In: DISC 2020 (2020). https://doi.org/10.4230/LIPIcs.DISC.2020.18
12. Chang, Y.J., Kopelowitz, T., Pettie, S.: An exponential separation between randomized and deterministic complexity in the local model. SIAM J. Comput. **48**(1), 122–143 (2019). https://doi.org/10.1137/17M1117537
13. Chang, Y.J., Pettie, S.: A time hierarchy theorem for the LOCAL model. SIAM J. Comput. **48**(1), 33–69 (2019). https://doi.org/10.1137/17M1157957
14. Chang, Y.J., Studený, J., Suomela, J.: Distributed graph problems through an automata-theoretic lens (2020), https://arxiv.org/abs/2002.07659
15. Cole, R., Vishkin, U.: Deterministic coin tossing with applications to optimal parallel list ranking. Inf. Control **70**(1), 32–53 (1986). https://doi.org/10.1016/S0019-9958(86)80023-7
16. Don, H., Zantema, H.: Synchronizing non-deterministic finite automata. J. Automat. Lang. Comb. **23**(4), 307–328 (2018)
17. Eppstein, D.: Reset sequences for monotonic automata. SIAM J. Comput. **19**(3), 500–510 (1990). https://doi.org/10.1137/0219033
18. Fich, F.E., Ramachandran, V.: Lower bounds for parallel computation on linked structures. In: SPAA 1990 (1990). https://doi.org/10.1145/97444.97676
19. Fischer, M., Ghaffari, M.: Sublogarithmic distributed algorithms for Lovász local lemma, and the complexity hierarchy. In: DISC 2017 (2017). https://doi.org/10.4230/LIPIcs.DISC.2017.18
20. Gazdag, Z., Iván, S., Nagy-György, J.: Improved upper bounds on synchronizing nondeterministic automata. Inf. Proces. Lett. **109**(17), 986–990 (2009). https://doi.org/10.1016/j.ipl.2009.05.007
21. Ghaffari, M., Harris, D.G., Kuhn, F.: On derandomizing local distributed algorithms. In: FOCS 2018 (2018). https://doi.org/10.1109/FOCS.2018.00069
22. Ghaffari, M., Su, H.H.: Distributed degree splitting, edge coloring, and orientations. In: SODA 2017 (2017). https://doi.org/10.1137/1.9781611974782.166
23. Imreh, B., Ito, M.: On regular languages determined by nondeterministic directable automata. Acta Cybernet. **17**(1), 1–10 (2005)
24. Imreh, B., Steinby, M.: Directable nondeterministic automata. Acta Cybernetica **14**(1), 105–115 (1999)
25. Linial, N.: Locality in distributed graph algorithms. SIAM J. Comput. **21**(1), 193–201 (1992). https://doi.org/10.1137/0221015
26. Martyugin, P.: Computational complexity of certain problems related to carefully synchronizing words for partial automata and directing words for nondeterministic automata. Theor. Comput. Syst. **54**(2), 293–304 (2013). https://doi.org/10.1007/s00224-013-9516-6
27. Naor, M., Stockmeyer, L.: What can be computed locally? SIAM J. Comput. **24**(6), 1259–1277 (1995). https://doi.org/10.1137/S0097539793254571
28. Peleg, D.: Distributed Computing: A Locality-Sensitive Approach. SIAM (2000). https://doi.org/10.1137/1.9780898719772

29. Pettie, S., Su, H.H.: Distributed algorithms for coloring triangle-free graphs. Inf. Comput. **243**, 263–280 (2015)
30. Rozhoň, V., Ghaffari, M.: Polylogarithmic-time deterministic networkdecomposition and distributed derandomization. In: STOC 2020 (2020). https://doi.org/10.1145/3357713.3384298
31. Stockmeyer, L.J., Meyer, A.R.: Word problems requiring exponential time. In: STOC 1973 (1973). https://doi.org/10.1145/800125.804029

Near-Optimal Scheduling in the Congested Clique

Keren Censor-Hillel⬤, Yannic Maus⬤, and Volodymyr Polosukhin[(✉)]⬤

Technion, Haifa, Israel
{ckeren,yannic.maus,po}@cs.technion.ac.il

Abstract. This paper provides three nearly-optimal algorithms for scheduling t jobs in the CLIQUE model. First, we present a deterministic scheduling algorithm that runs in $O(\mathsf{GlobalCongestion} + \mathsf{dilation})$ rounds for jobs that are sufficiently efficient in terms of their memory. The dilation is the maximum round complexity of any of the given jobs, and the GlobalCongestion is the total number of messages in all jobs divided by the per-round bandwidth of n^2 of the CLIQUE model. Both are inherent lower bounds for any scheduling algorithm.

Then, we present a randomized scheduling algorithm which runs t jobs in $O(\mathsf{GlobalCongestion} + \mathsf{dilation} \cdot \log n + t)$ rounds and only requires that inputs and outputs do not exceed $O(n \log n)$ bits per node, which is met by, e.g., almost all graph problems. Lastly, we adjust the *random-delay-based* scheduling algorithm [Ghaffari, PODC'15] from the CONGEST model and obtain an algorithm that schedules any t jobs in $O(t/n + \mathsf{LocalCongestion} + \mathsf{dilation} \cdot \log n)$ rounds, where the LocalCongestion relates to the congestion at a single node of the CLIQUE. We compare this algorithm to the previous approaches and show their benefit.

We schedule the set of jobs on-the-fly, without a priori knowledge of its parameters or the communication patterns of the jobs. In light of the inherent lower bounds, all of our algorithms are nearly-optimal.

We exemplify the power of our algorithms by analyzing the message complexity of the state-of-the-art MIS protocol [Ghaffari, Gouleakis, Konrad, Mitrovic and Rubinfeld, PODC'18], and we show that we can solve t instances of MIS in $O(t + \log \log \Delta \log n)$ rounds, that is, in $O(1)$ amortized time, for $t \geq \log \log \Delta \log n$.

Keywords: Distributed algorithms · Congested clique · Scheduling · Maximal independent set

1 Introduction

Motivated by the ever-growing number of frameworks for parallel computations, we address the complexity of executing multiple jobs in such settings. Such

Full version of the paper available under https://arxiv.org/abs/2102.07221 [4].

T. Jurdziński and S. Schmid (Eds.): SIROCCO 2021, LNCS 12810, pp. 50–67, 2021.
https://doi.org/10.1007/978-3-030-79527-6_4

frameworks, e.g., MapReduce [20], typically need to execute a long queue of jobs. A fundamental goal of such systems is to schedule many jobs in parallel, for utilizing as much of the computational power of the system as possible. Ideally, this is done by the system in a black-box manner, without the need to modify the jobs and, more importantly, without the need to know their properties and specifically their communication patterns beforehand.

In their seminal work, Leighton, Maggs, and Rao [23] studied the special case where each of the to-be-scheduled jobs is a routing protocol that routes a packet through a network along a given path. The goal in their work is to schedule t jobs such that the *length* of the schedule, i.e., the overall runtime until all t packets have reached their destination, is minimized. They showed that there exists an optimal packet-routing schedule of length $O(\text{congestion}+\text{dilation})$, where congestion is the maximum number of packets that need to be routed over a single edge of the network and dilation is the maximum length of a path that a packet needs to travel. Clearly, both parameters are lower bounds on the length of any schedule, implying that the above schedule is asymptotically optimal. Further, Leighton, Maggs, and Rao [23] showed that assigning a random delay to each packet gives a schedule of length $O(\text{congestion}+\text{dilation}\cdot\log{(t\cdot\text{dilation})})$.

In his beautiful work, Ghaffari [10] raised the question of running multiple jobs in the distributed CONGEST model on n nodes. Applying the random delays method [23], he showed a randomized algorithm which after $O(\text{dilation}\cdot\log^2 n)$ rounds of pre-computation, runs a given a set of jobs in $O(\text{congestion}+\text{dilation}\cdot\log n)$ rounds. Here, in a similar spirit to [23], congestion is the maximum number of messages that need to be sent over a single edge and dilation is the maximum round complexity of all jobs. Further, Ghaffari [10] showed that this is nearly optimal, by constructing an instance which requires $\Omega(\text{congestion} + \text{dilation}\cdot\log n/\log\log n)$ rounds to schedule.

In this paper, we address the t-scheduling problem in the (CONGESTED) CLIQUE model [25], in which each of n machines can send $O(\log n)$-bit messages to any other machine in each round. Our goal is thus to devise scheduling algorithms that run t jobs in a black-box manner, such that they complete in a number of rounds that beats the trivial solution of simply running the jobs sequentially one after the other, and, ideally, reaches inherent lower bounds that we discuss later. We emphasize that we schedule all jobs' actions *on-the-fly* during their execution. Throughout the paper, we use the terminology that a job is a *protocol* that n *nodes*, $v_0, \dots, v_{n-1}$, need to run on some input, and we use the notion of an *algorithm* for the scheduling procedure that the n *machines*, $p_0, \dots, p_{n-1}$, execute. Each machine p_i is given the inputs of the nodes v_i^j for all jobs j, and the machines run an algorithm which simulates the protocols of their assigned nodes.

Our contributions are three algorithms for scheduling t jobs in the CLIQUE model, which exhibit trade-offs based on the parameters of dilation, LocalCongestion, and GlobalCongestion of the set of jobs, which we formally define below. Our scheduling algorithms complete within round complexities that are nearly optimal w.r.t. the appropriate parameters.

1.1   Our Contributions

No scheduling algorithm can beat the dilation of the set of jobs, which is the maximum runtime of a job in the set, had this job been executed standalone. Similarly, another natural lower bound is given by the GlobalCongestion, which is the total number of messages that all nodes in all jobs send over all rounds, normalized by the n^2 per-round-bandwidth of the CLIQUE model (for simplicity, this considers the possibility that a machine sends a message to itself). The main goal is thus to get as close as possible to these parameters.

As a toy example, consider a set of jobs in which each completes within a single round. Intuitively, if the total number of messages that need to be sent by all nodes in all jobs is at most n^2, then one could hope to squeeze all of these jobs into a single round of the CLIQUE model, as n^2 is the available bandwidth per round. The main hurdle in a straightforward argument as above, lies in the fact that a machine cannot send more than n messages in a round. Thus, although we are promised that in total there no more than n^2 messages, it might be that a machine is required to send/receive $\omega(n)$ messages because the heaviest-loaded nodes of multiple jobs might be located on the same machine.

This implies that a naïve scheduling, in which each machine simulates the nodes that are located at it, is more expensive than our single-round goal scheduling, as some messages must wait for later rounds. In the general case, these issues become more severe, as the jobs may originally require more than a single round, and it could be that each round displays an imbalance in a different set of nodes and machines.

The key ingredient in the first two scheduling algorithms that we present is hence to *rebalance* the nodes among the machines, for the sake of a more efficient simulation that deals with the possible imbalance, which also may vary from round to round. The third scheduling algorithm we present is inspired by the random-delay approach of [10,23]. In what follows, we present the guarantees that are obtained by our three scheduling algorithms, and discuss the trade-offs that they exhibit.

Deterministic Scheduling. A crucial factor in the complexity of rebalancing the nodes among the machines is the amount of information that needs to be passed from one machine to another in order for the latter to take over the simulation of a node. To this end, we define an *M-memory efficient* job as a job where for each node, its state can be encoded in $M \log n$ bits, and that the number of messages it needs to receive in this round can be inferred from its state. In Sect. 3, we obtain the following deterministic algorithm for scheduling t jobs that are M-memory efficient.

Theorem 3. *There is a deterministic algorithm that schedules $t = \text{poly } n$ jobs that are M-memory efficient in $O(\mathsf{GlobalCongestion} + \lceil M \cdot t/n \rceil \cdot \mathsf{dilation})$ rounds.*

At a very high level, in the algorithm for Theorem 3, the machines rebalance nodes in each round by sending the states of nodes. The main technical effort is that the reassignment needs to be computed by the machines *on-the-fly*, and we show how to do so in a fast way.

Notice that for the case that $M \cdot t = O(n)$, the round complexity we get from Theorem 3 is $O(\mathsf{GlobalCongestion} + \mathsf{dilation})$, which is *optimal*. Another crucial point is that our algorithm does not require the knowledge of either the GlobalCongestion or the dilation of the set of jobs.

Randomized Scheduling. If we are given a set of jobs that are not memory efficient for a reasonable value of M, it may be too expensive to rebalance the nodes among the machines in every simulated round. However, if the input of each node is not too large, we can randomly shuffle the nodes at the beginning of the simulation, and if the output is also not too large then we can efficiently unshuffle, and reach the original assignment.

To capture this, we say that a job is *I/O efficient* if its input and output can be encoded within $O(n \log n)$ bits. Notice that most graph-related problems are I/O efficient, e.g., MST [15,16,19,22,25,26], MIS [5,11,12], Minimum Cut [13,14], as well as many algebraic problems [3,9]. An example of a graph problem that is not I/O efficient is *k-clique listing*, in which all nodes together have to explicitly output *all* k-cliques in the input graph [2,6,8,18,27] which can be as many as $\Omega(n^k)$, thus necessitating large outputs. While the k-clique listing problem is not *output efficient*, it is *input efficient*, and as it does not require a specific node to output a specific clique, one could also run several instances of the problem by omitting the output unshuffling step of our scheduling algorithm.

The following randomized algorithm schedules t I/O efficient jobs.

Theorem 4. *There is a randomized algorithm in the* CLIQUE *model that schedules* $t =$ poly n *jobs that are I/O efficient in* $O(t + \mathsf{GlobalCongestion} + \mathsf{dilation} \cdot \log n)$ *rounds, w.h.p.*[1]

As the deterministic scheduling algorithm (Theorem 3), the scheduling algorithm of Theorem 4 requires neither the knowledge of GlobalCongestion nor the knowledge of dilation.

Both of our scheduling algorithms for Theorem 3 and Theorem 4 have the machines possibly simulate the execution of nodes that are not originally assigned to them. We stress that any black-box scheduling algorithm in which each machine only simulates the nodes that are originally assigned to it must inherently suffer from another type of congestion as a lower bound on its round complexity, namely, the maximum number of messages that all nodes assigned to a single machine have to send or receive, normalized by the bandwidth n that each machine has per round. We call this the LocalCongestion of a set of jobs. We obtain the following *random-delay-based* algorithm for scheduling any t jobs, without reassigning nodes.

---

[1] An event occurs *w.h.p.* (*with high probability*) if for an arbitrary constant $c \geq 1$, the probability that the event occurs is at least $1 - n^{-c}$, where n is the number of machines. All our results can be adapted to any constant c at the cost of increasing the runtime by a constant factor.

Theorem 5 *(Simplified). There is a randomized algorithm in the* CLIQUE *model that schedules* $t = \text{poly } n$ *jobs in* $O(t/n + \text{LocalCongestion} + \text{dilation} \cdot \log n)$ *rounds w.h.p.*

The stated complexity in the above simplified version of Theorem 5 requires the knowledge of the LocalCongestion, but this can be eliminated using a standard doubling approach, at the cost of a logarithmic multiplicative factor (see precise statement in Sect. 4).

The random-delay algorithm which gives Theorem 5 is suboptimal for a set of jobs which have a single machine with heavily-loaded nodes assigned to it, since in this case it does not exploit the entire bandwidth of the CLIQUE model. For example, for a problem with inputs of at most $O(n \log n)$ bits per node, a protocol in which a fixed leader learns the entire input takes $O(n)$ rounds, where on each round each node sends one message to the leader, who receives n messages. For n such jobs, the GlobalCongestion is n, while the LocalCongestion is n^2. In such a setting, our random-shuffling algorithm from Theorem 4 outperforms the random-delay algorithm from Theorem 5. One may suggest to replace the fixed leader by a randomly or more carefully chosen leader. However, this trick might be more complicated in the general case: suppose now that $n^{0.9}$ nodes need to learn $n^{1.1}$ messages each. For such a set of jobs, it holds that LocalCongestion $= n^{0.1}$, while GlobalCongestion $= 1$. Thus, it is more efficient to run Theorem 4 in this case. Another crucial example in which random-shuffling outperforms random-delays is the maximal independent set protocol that we describe below. Note that our algorithms address these cases in a black-box manner without assuming knowledge of the communication pattern.

Applications. In the full version of the paper [4], we present two applications in order to exemplify our scheduling algorithms. We summarize these applications below and defer a more detailed discussion to the full version and Sect. 5.

A *maximal independent set* (MIS) of a graph $G = (V, E)$ is a set $M \subseteq V$ such that no two nodes in M are adjacent and no node of V can be added to M without violating this condition. The state-of-the-art randomized CLIQUE protocol for solving the MIS problem completes in $O(\log \log \Delta)$ rounds, w.h.p., where Δ is the maximum degree of the graph [12]. We analyze the message complexity of this protocol, and show that it does not utilize the entire bandwidth. Thus, we can schedule multiple MIS jobs efficiently using our random shuffling scheduling algorithm from Theorem 4, and we obtain the following theorem.

Theorem 1 (Multiple MIS instances). *There is a randomized algorithm in the* CLIQUE *model which solves* $t = \text{poly } n$ *instances of MIS in* $O(t + \log \log \Delta \log n)$ *rounds, w.h.p.*

Another application that exemplifies our scheduling algorithms is a variant of the *pointer jumping* problem, which is a widespread algorithmic technique [17]. In the P-pointer jumping problem, each node has a permutation on P elements. A fixed node has a value *pointer* p and should learn the result of applying these permutations one after another on p. Pointer jumping can be solved by an $O(\log n)$-round protocol in the CLIQUE model by learning the composition of all permutations. We observe that this protocol does not utilize the entire bandwidth and leverage this for obtaining an algorithm that executes multiple instances of this protocol efficiently.

Theorem 2 (Pointer Jumping). *For $P \leq n$, there are algorithms in the CLIQUE model that solve $t =$ poly n instances of the P-pointer jumping problem deterministically in $O(\lceil P \cdot t/n \rceil \cdot \log n)$, and randomized in $O(t + \log^2 n)$ rounds, w.h.p.*

We obtain the deterministic result using our scheduling algorithm and the randomized result using our random-shuffling scheduling algorithm in the full version of the paper. The proposed simple $O(\log n)$ round pointer jumping protocol also serves as an example where scheduling jobs via the random-shuffling approach of Theorem 4 is significantly better than the random-delay based approach of Theorem 5. For more details we refer to the full version of the paper.

In Sect. 5 we discuss the amortized versions of these results, and present a small example of a set of jobs that can be scheduled with $o(1)$-amortized complexity. In light of the growing number of $O(1)$-round CLIQUE-protocols, e.g., [7, 14, 26], we propose the amortized complexity of solving many instances of a problem in parallel, as a valuable measure for the efficiency in future research.

1.2 Related Work

Many graph problems are studied in the CLIQUE model. There are fast protocols for the CLIQUE model for distance computations [3, 9], minimum spanning tree (MST) [15, 22, 25, 26], MIS [5, 11, 12], and more.

To the best of our knowledge, there are no previous works that study the scheduling of jobs in the CLIQUE model. In the past, it has been shown that running multiple instances of *the same* protocol on different inputs can result in fast algorithms for some complex problems. We survey some of these. Hegeman et al. [16] reduce the MST problem to multiple smaller instances of graph connectivity, breaking below the long-standing upper bound of $O(\log \log n)$ by Lotker et al. [25]. Further variants and improvements on the MST problem [15, 19, 22, 26] all invoke multiple instances of sparser problems. This line of work culminated in the deterministic $O(1)$-round algorithm of Nowicki [26].

In [13], Ghaffari and Nowicki show a randomized algorithm which solves $O(n^{1-\epsilon})$ many instances of the MST problem in $O(\epsilon^{-1})$ rounds. This is used for finding the minimum cut of a graph. The state-of-the-art $O(1)$-round algorithm for the minimum cut problem, by Ghaffari et al. [14], runs $\Theta(\log n)$ instances of connected components as a subroutine. The complexity of computing multiple matrix multiplications in parallel was explored by Le Gall [9] and was used in the same paper to solve the *all-pairs-shortest-path problem*.

The notion of LocalCongestion is similar to the notion of Communication Degree Complexity [21]. The difference lies in the fact that the latter is an upper bound on the number of messages sent or received by any node on *any round*, while LocalCongestion is an upper bound on the *total* number of messages sent or received by any node *over all* rounds.

2 Preliminaries

The CLIQUE *Model.* In the (CONGESTED) CLIQUE model, n machines $p_0, \ldots, p_{n-1}$ communicate with each other in synchronous rounds in an all-to-all fashion. In each round, any pair of machines can exchange $O(\log n)$ bits. There is usually no constraint neither on the size of the *local memory* nor on the time complexity of the *local computations*. Besides the local memory, each machine has a *read-only input buffer* and a *write-only output buffer*, as well as *read/write incoming- and outgoing- message buffers*.

Routing in the CLIQUE *Model.* Lenzen's routing scheme [24] says that a set of messages can be routed in the CLIQUE model within $O(1)$ rounds, given that each machine sends and receives at most $O(n)$ messages. We formally state it here in its generalized version, which addresses the case of more than a linear number of messages. In the generalized version, each machine p_i holds a set of messages $M_i = \bigcup_{i' \in [n]} M_i^{i'}$, where $M_i^{i'}$ is a set of messages with the destination $p_{i'}$. The claim follows by having each node chop its set of messages M_i into chunks of n messages, each of which containing $|M_i^{i'}| n / X$ messages for each $i' \in [n]$, and applying the original routing scheme X/n times. The routing scheme could be adapted to preserve the message complexity in the following way.[2] Let $Y = \sum_{i \in [n]} |M_i| \leq n^2$ be the total number of messages. First, compute a global numbering of messages and the total number of messages Y. Then, send $O(\lceil \sqrt{Y} \rceil)$ messages to each one of the first $O(\lceil \sqrt{Y} \rceil)$ machines via intermediate nodes based on the numbering. Sort messages by the destination in the using Lenzen's sorting algorithm [24] over $O(\lceil \sqrt{Y} \rceil)$-clique. Finally, deliver the messages to their destinations via intermediate nodes based on the indices of messages in the sorted sequence. The round complexity of the algorithm is $O(1)$ and the message complexity of the algorithm in $O(Y + \lceil \sqrt{Y} \rceil \cdot \lceil \sqrt{Y} \rceil) = O(Y)$.

Claim 1 (Lenzen's Routing Scheme). *Let X be a globally known value and let $\mathcal{P}$ be the property that $|M_i| \leq X$ for all $i \in [n]$ and $\sum_{i \in [n]} |M_i^{i'}| \leq X$ for all $i' \in [n]$. There is an algorithm in the CLIQUE model which completes in $O(\lceil X/n \rceil)$ rounds and $O(\sum_{i \in [n]} M_i)$ messages, and delivers all messages if $\mathcal{P}$ holds, or indicates that it does not hold.*

Protocols and Jobs. A *protocol* is run on an *input*, that is provided in a distributed manner in the *read-only input buffer* of each machine. The *complexity* of a protocol is the number of synchronous rounds until each machine has finished writing its output to its *write-only output buffer*.

---

[2] We thank an anonymous reviewer for pointing this out.

A *job* is an instance of a protocol together with a given input and a job is *finished* when each machine has written its output. We generally assume that each job finishes in $O(\text{poly } n)$ rounds.

For our purposes of fast scheduling, we need to specify the internals of each synchronous round. We follow the standard description, which is usually omitted and simply referred to as a 'round'. We require that for each machine, the input and output buffers are only accessed in the first and last rounds of the protocol on that machine, respectively. In particular, this means that any further access to the input requires storing it in the local memory. Accessing the incoming- and outgoing-message buffers is not restricted to certain rounds. Each synchronous round of a protocol consists of 3 steps, in the following order.

- **Receiving Step:** Read from incoming-message buffer (or from input buffer if this is the first round), possibly modifying the local memory.
- **Computation Step:** Possibly modify local memory.
- **Sending Step:** Write to outgoing-message buffer, (or to output buffer if this is the last round), possibly modifying the local memory.

After these 3 phases, all messages written in outgoing-message buffers are delivered into the incoming-message buffers of their targets.

The Scheduling Problem. In the *t-scheduling problem* (or simply a scheduling problem, if t is clear from the context) the objective is to execute t jobs. Since our goal is to do this in an efficient manner, we wish to allow a machine to simulate a computation that originally should take place in a different machine, in a naïve execution of the t jobs. To this end, we distinguish between the physical machine and the *nodes*, which are the virtual machines that need to execute each job. That is, for each job j we denote by $\{v_{i,j} | i \in [n]\}$ the set of nodes that need to execute job j.

Formally, in the t-scheduling problem, the input for machine p_i is composed of the inputs of all the nodes with identifiers of the form $v_{i,j}$ for each job $j \in [t]$. We also assume that each machine knows the protocol for each of the t jobs. An algorithm *solves the scheduling problem* or *schedules the jobs* when each job has finished writing its output. That is, for deterministic jobs, we require each machine p_i to write the output of nodes $v_{i,j}$ for all $j \in [t]$. For randomized jobs, the machines' output distribution for each job has to be equal to the distribution of outputs in a naïve execution of the job. In the rest of the paper, we refer to the scheduling solution as an *algorithm*, while we use the term *protocol* only for the content of a job.

Notations. Following the widespread conventions, we denote by log the logarithm base 2, and by ln the natural logarithm. Also, we denote $[n] = \{0, 1, \ldots, n-1\}$. We denote by $s_{i,j}^r$ and $t_{i,j}^r$ the number of messages sent and received by $v_{i,j}$ in round r, respectively. If job j terminates before round r, we indicate $s_{i,j}^r = t_{i,j}^r = 0$. We sometimes drop the superscript r, when it is clear from the context. We denote by ℓ_j the round complexity of job j and by $m_j = \sum_{i \in [n], r \in [\ell_j]} s_{i,j}^r = \sum_{i \in [n], r \in [\ell_j]} t_{i,j}^r$ the total number of messages sent or received during the execution of job j, i.e., the message complexity of job j.

Another notation we extensively use is $m^r = \sum_{i\in[n],j\in[t]} s^r_{i,j} = \sum_{i\in[n],j\in[t]} t^r_{i,j}$, which is the number of messages all nodes in all jobs sent or received during round r.

Congestion Parameters. We define the normalized GlobalCongestion as the total number of messages sent by all the jobs divided by n^2, and normalized LocalCongestion as the maximum number of messages send to or received by some node in the entire course of the execution of all jobs divided by n. Formally, dilation $= \max_{j\in[t]} \ell_j$,

$$\text{GlobalCongestion} = \sum_{j\in[t]} m_j = \sum_{i\in[n]}\sum_{j\in[t]}\sum_{r\in[\ell_j]} s^r_{i,j}/n^2 = \sum_{r\in[\text{dilation}]} m^r/n^2,$$

$$\text{LocalCongestion} = \max\left\{\max_{i\in[n]}\sum_{j\in[t]}\sum_{r\in[\ell_j]} s^r_{i,j}/n, \max_{i\in[n]}\sum_{j\in[t]}\sum_{r\in[\ell_j]} t^r_{i,j}/n\right\}.$$

3 Deterministic Scheduling

The objective of this section is to prove the following theorem.

Theorem 3. *There is a deterministic algorithm that schedules $t = \text{poly } n$ jobs that are M-memory efficient in $O(\text{GlobalCongestion} + \lceil M\cdot t/n\rceil \cdot \text{dilation})$ rounds.*

The formal definition of an M-memory efficient job as used in Theorem 3 is as follows.

Definition 1 (M-memory efficient job). *For a given value M, an M-memory efficient job is a job in which for each node v in each round r, the state (local memory) of v at the end of the Computation Step can be encoded in $M\log n$ bits. In addition, there is a function that, given the state of node v after the Computation Step of round r, infers the number of messages it sends and receives on this round.*

Theorem 3 requires that jobs use at most M bits of local memory per machine. Thus, the power of the result is when $M = o(n)$, as otherwise the naïve execution of jobs one after another schedules them in dilation $\cdot\, t$ rounds. In the case that $M\cdot t = O(n)$, the runtime becomes $O(\text{GlobalCongestion} + \text{dilation})$, which is optimal up to a constant factor as, clearly, any schedule for any collection of jobs requires at least $\Omega(\text{GlobalCongestion} + \text{dilation})$ rounds.

To schedule the jobs for Theorem 3, we work in epochs. Each machine p_i first simulates round 0 up to the end of the Computation Step for the nodes $v_{i,j}$, for each $j \in [t]$. This does not require any communication. Then, the epochs are such that for each round r, at the start of epoch r, all nodes in all jobs are at the end of the Computation Step of round r. Clearly, for each simulated node that finishes in round r, the machine does not need to do anything for the part that executes the beginning of round $r+1$. The reason why we execute the protocol in these *shifted* epochs, from Sending Step of round r (including) to Sending Step of round $r + 1$ (excluding), lies in the fact that the bottleneck is the possible imbalance in communication.

Recall that m^r denotes the number of messages all nodes from all jobs send in round r. Since in each round of the CLIQUE model, at most n^2 messages can be exchanged, routing m^r messages cannot be done faster than $\lceil m^r / n^2 \rceil$ rounds. We aim to execute an epoch in this optimal number of $O(\lceil m^r / n^2 \rceil)$ rounds. We start with the simple case and then use it to solve the general case.

The first case is when $m^r \leq 2n^2$. In Lemma 1, we show that in this case, we can route all m^r messages in $O(\lceil M \cdot t/n \rceil)$ rounds. The challenge we encounter is that although $m^r \leq 2n^2$, we are not promised that the messages are balanced across the machines in the following sense. It is possible that some machine p_i, which simulates the nodes $v_{i,j}$, for all jobs $0 \leq j < t$, is required to send significantly more than n messages when summing over all messages that need to be sent by these nodes $v_{i,j}$. We overcome this issue by assigning the simulation of some of these nodes to some other machine $p_{i'}$, which originally has a smaller load of messages to send. The crux that underlies our ability to defer a simulation of a node $v_{i,j}$ to a machine $p_{i'}$ is that the state of the node does not consume too many bits. We show how to compute a well-balanced assignment of nodes to machines in Claim 2. This assignment allows us to execute the epoch in the claimed number of $O(\lceil M \cdot t/n \rceil)$ rounds.

In the general case, we can have $m^r > 2n^2$. We show how to carefully split up the messages that need to be sent into chunks that allow us to use multiple invocations of Lemma 1. This allows us to execute the epoch in the $O(\lceil m^r / n^2 \rceil + M \cdot t/n)$ rounds. As the core of our algorithm is handling the case $m^r \leq 2n^2$, the proof of the general case as well as using these results to prove Theorem 3 is deferred to the full version of the paper. Now, we focus on the case $m^r \leq 2n^2$.

We start with the following notation. An *assignment* of nodes to machines corresponds to a function $\varphi \colon [n] \times [t] \mapsto [n]$, where $\varphi(i, j) = k$ says that the i-th node in job j, i.e., $v_{i,j}$, is assigned to the k-th machine p_k. We sometimes abuse notation and write that $\varphi(v_{i,j}) = p_k$ for $\varphi(i, j) = k$. We call an assignment *balanced*, if the number of nodes assigned to each machine is $O(t)$, i.e., if for each k, it holds that $|\varphi^{-1}(p_k)| = O(t)$. The (balanced) assignment $\varphi(i, j) = i$ is called the *trivial* assignment. The next claim (proof deferred to the full version of the paper) states that nodes can be efficiently reassigned from an initial balanced assignment φ_s to a finial balanced assignment φ_f.

We denote by $S_{i,j,r}$ the state of node $v_{i,j}$ after its Computation Step in round r.

Claim 2 (Distributing the states). *Given are t jobs that are M-memory efficient, and globally known initial and final balanced assignments, φ_s and φ_f, respectively. Assume that for each $i \in [n]$ and $j \in [t]$, machine $\varphi_s(i, j)$ holds the state $S_{i,j,r}$ of node $v_{i,j}$ after its Computation Step in round r. Then, there exists a CLIQUE algorithm which completes in $O(\lceil M \cdot t/n \rceil)$ rounds and moves* *the states according to φ_f, that is, at the end of the algorithm, for each $i \in [n]$ and $j \in [t]$, machine $\varphi_f(i,j)$ holds the state $S_{i,j,r}$ of node $v_{i,j}$.*

Lemma 1 (Scheduling of a round with $m^r \leq 2n^2$ messages). *Given are t jobs that are M-memory efficient, and given is a round number, r, for which $m^r \leq 2n^2$. Assume that for each $i \in [n]$, p_i holds $S_{i,j,r}$ for all $j \in [t]$. Then there exists a deterministic CLIQUE algorithm which completes in $O(\lceil M \cdot t/n \rceil)$ rounds, at the end of which, for each $i \in [n]$, p_i holds $S_{i,j,r+1}$ for all $j \in [t]$.*

The outline of the algorithm is as follows. Each machine partitions its simulated nodes into buckets of contiguous ranges of indices, such that nodes in each bucket send and receive $O(n)$ messages altogether. Thus, the messages of all nodes in the bucket can be sent or received by a single machine.

We show that the number of buckets over all machines is $O(n)$. The machines collectively assign the buckets such that each machine gets $O(1)$ buckets, and they make the assignment globally known. Then, the states $S_{i,j,r}$ are distributed according to the assignment using Claim 2, and each machine executes the Sending Step of round r for each of its newly assigned nodes and all messages get delivered. Then, each machine executes the remainder of the protocol of its newly assigned nodes until after the Computation Step of round $r + 1$. Finally, the states $S_{i,j,r+1}$ for round $r + 1$ are distributed back according to the trivial assignment.

Proof of Lemma 1. We begin with describing the algorithm (see Algorithm 1). Afterwards, we prove the correctness and analyze the round complexity.

Algorithm 1. Simulating a round with $m^r \leq n^2$.

1: Compute the balanced assignment $\varphi \colon [n] \times [t] \mapsto [n]$.
2: Distribute the states according to the assignment φ.
3: Execute the protocol for round r accounting for φ.
4: Distribute the states back according to the trivial assignment.

The Algorithm. We first show how to split nodes into buckets. Then we show how to compute a globally known assignment φ, distribute the nodes according to φ, execute the jobs until after the next Computation Step, and assign nodes back to their initial machines.

Forming Buckets (Locally). Each machine p_i for each $j \in [t]$ uses $S_{i,j,r}$ to locally compute $s_{i,j}$ and $t_{i,j}$, the number of messages each node $v_{i,j}$ sends and receives in round r, respectively. This is possible by the definition of an M-memory efficient job. Let $S_i = \sum_{j=0}^{t-1} s_{i,j}$ and $T_i = \sum_{j=0}^{t-1} t_{i,j}$. Then, each machine p_i (locally and independently) applies [1, Lemma 7] with $k = k_i = \lceil \max\{S_i/n, T_i/n\} \rceil$ to the sequences $(s_{i,j})_{j=0}^{t-1}$ and $(t_{i,j})_{j=0}^{t-1}$, to split its nodes into k_i buckets $B_{i,0}, \ldots, B_{i,k_i-1}$ of continuous ranges of jobs' indices. Invoking the lemma with $s = n \geq s_{i,j}$, $t = n \geq t_{i,j}$, $S = S_i$, and $T = T_i$, implies that for each $i \in [n]$

and $i' \in [k_i]$, the nodes inside each bucket $B_{i,i'}$ want to send/receive at most $4n$ messages, i.e.,

$$\sum_{j \in B_{i,i'}} s_{i,j} \leq 2 \left(\frac{S}{k} + s \right) \leq 2 \left(\frac{S_i}{(S_i/s)} + s \right) = 4s = 4n, \text{ and}$$

$$\sum_{j \in B_{i,i'}} t_{i,j} \leq 2 \left(\frac{T}{k} + t \right) \leq 2 \left(\frac{T_i}{(T_i/t)} + t \right) = 4t = 4n.$$

Computing the Assignment φ. We first define the assignment φ and then show how it becomes globally known. Recall that the buckets of machine p_i are numbered from 0 to $k_i - 1$ and define the following value for $i \in [n]$ and $i' \in [k_i]$:

$$f(i, i') = \left\lfloor \left(i' + \sum_{i'' < i} k_{i''} \right) / 5 \right\rfloor.$$

Then, we define the assignment φ to assign all nodes in bucket $B_{i,i'}$ to machine $p_{f(i,i')}$. Notice that this is a valid assignment because with $\sum_i S_i \leq 2n^2$ and $\sum_i T_i \leq 2n^2$ (due to $m^r \leq 2n^2$) we obtain

$$f(i, i') < \sum_{0 \leq i < n} \frac{k_i}{5} = \frac{1}{5} \sum_i \lceil \max \{ \frac{S_i}{n}, \frac{T_i}{n} \} \rceil$$

$$\leq \frac{1}{5} \sum_i \left(\frac{S_i}{n} + \frac{T_i}{n} + 1 \right) \leq \frac{1}{5} \cdot 5n = n.$$

Here, the first inequality follows from $i' < k_{i'}$. Also, notice that each machine receives at most 5 different buckets because at most five pairs (i, i') are mapped to the same index by f.

Now, we want to make the assignment φ globally known to all machines. To this end, each machine p_i broadcasts the number of its buckets, k_i. Thus, machine p_i can compute $f(i, i')$ for each of its buckets $B_{i,i'}$. Then, for all $i' \in [k_i]$, machine p_i informs machine $p_{f(i,i')}$ about the smallest and the largest job number of a node in bucket $B_{i,i'}$. As the buckets $B_{i,1}, \ldots, B_{i,k_i}$ are ordered (increasingly) by the jobs' indices for all $i \in [n]$, this information is sufficient for each machine to deduce which nodes are assigned to it in φ. In the last step, each machine broadcasts the messages that it has received, i.e., machine $p_{f(i,i')}$ broadcasts the smallest and largest job index of bucket $B_{i,i'}$ together with the index i, and each machine can deduce the full assignment φ.

Executing Round $r + 1$. We now use Claim 2 to distribute the states $S_{i,j,r}$ from the trivial initial assignment $\varphi_s(i, j) = i$ to the globally known final assignment $\varphi_f = \varphi$. Then, each machine executes the Sending Step of round r for each of its newly assigned nodes, where a message from $v_{i,j}$ to $v_{i',j}$ is sent from $p_{\varphi(i,j)}$ to $p_{\varphi(i',j)}$. This is possible since φ is globally known. Then, each machine executes the remainder of the protocol of its newly assigned nodes until after the

Computation Step of round $r + 1$. Finally, the obtained states $S_{i,j,r+1}$ for round $r + 1$ are re-distributed according to the trivial assignment by using Claim 2 once more, with $\varphi_s = \varphi$ and $\varphi_f(i,j) = i$.

Correctness. For each $i \in [n]$ and $j \in [t]$ the machine $p_{f(i,j)}$ receives the state $S_{i,j,r}$ and executes the Sending Step of round r, the Receiving Step of round $r + 1$, and the Computation Step of round $r + 1$ for node $v_{i,j}$. Thus, afterwards it holds the state $S_{i,j,r+1}$. Since this state is then sent back to p_i, the correctness follows.

Round Complexity. The partitioning of each machine's nodes into buckets is done locally without communication. Broadcasting the number of buckets (the value of k_i) can be done in a single round. We next reason about the time complexity that is required to make the assignment φ globally known. The computation of $f(i, i')$ is done locally. Informing machine $p_{f(i,i')}$ about the smallest and largest job in the bucket $B_{i,i'}$ requires for each machine p_i to send at most t messages and to receive at most 5 messages. Thus, by $\lceil t/n \rceil$ invocations of Claim 1, this step completes in $O(\lceil t/n \rceil)$ rounds. Since each machine p_i is assigned at most 5 buckets, and for each bucket $B_{i',j}$ it broadcasts a constant number of elements (smallest and largest job index in it together with the identifier i'), this step completes in $O(1)$ rounds.

The runtime is hence dominated by distributing the states via Claim 2, which takes $O(\lceil M \cdot t/n \rceil)$ rounds. All nodes in a bucket send/receive at most $4n$ messages in total and each machine executes the sending/receiving phase for at most 5 buckets, and thus these steps are done in $O(1)$ rounds by Claim 1. □

4 Randomized Scheduling

In this section we show and compare the two approaches for randomized scheduling: random shuffling (Sect. 4.1) and random delaying (Sect. 4.2). In contrast to Theorem 3, the results in this section do not require the jobs to be memory efficient.

4.1 Scheduling Through Random Shuffling

In this subsection we use random shuffling to schedule I/O efficient jobs and we obtain the following theorem.

Theorem 4. *There is a randomized algorithm in the* CLIQUE *model that schedules* $t =$ poly n *jobs that are I/O efficient in* $O(t +$ GlobalCongestion $+$ dilation $\cdot \log n)$ *rounds, w.h.p.*

The definition of an I/O efficient job as used in Theorem 4 is as follows.

Definition 2 (I/O efficient job). *An I/O efficient job is a job where each node receives and produces at most* $O(n \log n)$ *bits of input and output.*

Algorithm. The high level overview of the algorithm for Theorem 4 (see Algorithm 2) consists of three steps: `Input Shuffling`, `Execution`, and `Output Unshuffling`.

Algorithm 2. Scheduling of I/O efficient job.

1: `Input Shuffling`
2: `Execution`: Run dilation many phases, where in phase r each machine p_i runs the protocol for its nodes $\{v_{\pi_j^{-1}(i),j} \mid j \in [t]\}$, and messages are routed via Claim 1.
3: `Output Unshuffling`

`Input Shuffling`: We iterate sequentially through the jobs. For each job, a leader machine, say, p_0, generates a random uniform permutation $\pi_j \colon [n] \mapsto [n]$. The permutation becomes globally known within two rounds by having p_0 send $\pi_j(i)$ to each p_i and then each p_i broadcasts $\pi_j(i)$ to all machines. In the last round of this subroutine, each machine p_i sends the input of $v_{i,j}$ to machine $p_{\pi_j(i)}$. A single round is sufficient because the job is I/O efficient. Thus, at the end, machine p_i holds the state of the nodes $v_{\pi_j^{-1}(i),j}$ for all $j \in [t]$. We call this subroutine `Input Shuffling`.

`Execution`: In dilation many phases we progress each job by one round. That is, each machine p_i performs all actions of the nodes that it holds, which are $v_{\pi_j^{-1}(i),j}$ for all $j \in [t]$. In order to use Claim 1 efficiently for each phase r, the machines need to compute a bound on the number of messages that any of them sends or receives in phase r. To this end, the machines jointly compute the value of $m^r = \sum_{j \in [t]} \sum_{i \in [n]} s_{i,j}^r$, where $s_{i,j}^r$ is the number of messages that node $v_{i,j}$ sends in round r. They do this by having each machine p_i send $\sum_{j \in [t]} s_{\pi_j^{-1}(i),j}^r$ to a leader machine, say, p_0, which then sums these values and broadcasts their sum m^r. That is, m^r is the total number of messages sent by all nodes in all jobs in round r, and we show that for each $i \in [n]$, $O(m^r/n + n \log n)$ is a bound on $\sum_{j \in [t]} s_{\pi_j^{-1}(i),j}^r$ ($\sum_{j \in [t]} t_{\pi_j^{-1}(i),j}^r$), which is the number of messages that machine p_i has to send (receive) in phase r, to be used when invoking Claim 1.

`Output Unshuffling`: At the end, after each machine executes the protocols until they finish, we use a single round of communication for each job to unshuffle the outputs according to π_j^{-1}. At the end of this `Output Unshuffling` subroutine, machine p_i holds the output $v_{i,j}$ for all $j \in [t]$. This finishes the description of the algorithm.

In the following lemma, we bound the number of messages that each machine has to send/receive in one phase by $X = O(m^r/n + n \cdot \log n)$. Its proof is deferred to the full version of the paper.

Lemma 2. *Consider t jobs and a set of permutations $\{\pi_j\}_{j \in [t]}$ generated uniformly at random and let $S = \max_{i \in [n]} \sum_{j \in [t]} s_{\pi_j^{-1}(i),j}^r$ and $R =*

$\max_{i \in [n]} \sum_{j \in [t]} t^r_{\pi_j^{-1}(i),j}$. *Then, w.h.p., it holds that* $X = \max\{S, R\} = O(m^r/n + n \log n)$, *where* $m^r = \sum_{i \in [n]} \sum_{j \in [t]} s^r_{i,j}$.

With an upper bound at hand, on the number of messages that each machine sends or receives in phase r, we can prove that Algorithm 2 satisfies the statement of Theorem 4.

Proof of Theorem 4. We prove the correctness and bound the runtime of the presented algorithm (see Algorithm 2).

Correctness: After the `Input Shuffling` subroutine (Algorithm 2), the input for node $v_{i,j}$ is stored on machine $p_{\pi_j(i)}$. For each phase $r \in [\text{dilation}]$, we invoke Claim 1 with the computed value X, which is w.h.p. a bound the number of messages that each machine sends or receives. Thus, w.h.p. this invocation succeeds. Since dilation $= O(n)$, a union bound over all phases gives that at the end of the `Execution` subroutine, each machine p_i holds the outputs of all nodes $v_{\pi^{-1}(i),j}$ for each $j \in [t]$. After `Output Unshuffling`, machine p_i holds the output for node $v_{i,j}$ for each job $j \in [t]$.

Round Complexity: The initial `Input Shuffling` (Algorithm 2) and the `Output Unshuffling` at the end of the algorithm (Algorithm 2) complete with t rounds each. For each phase r in the `Execution` part of the algorithm, computing m^r is done in 2 rounds. By Lemma 2, $X = O(m^r/n + n \log n)$ is a bound on $\sum_{j \in [t]} s^r_{\pi^{-1}(i),j}$ and $\sum_{j \in [t]} t^r_{\pi^{-1}(i),j}$, which are the number of messages that machine p_i sends and receives in phase r, respectively, for all $i \in [n]$. Thus, invoking Claim 1 completes in $O(m^r/n^2 + \log n)$ rounds, w.h.p. Thus, the overall round complexity of the algorithm is

$$O(t + \sum_{r \in [\text{dilation}]} (m^r/n^2 + \log n)) = O(t + \sum_{j \in [t]} m_j/n^2 + \text{dilation} \cdot \log n)$$

$$= O(t + \text{GlobalCongestion} + \text{dilation} \cdot \log n). \qquad \square$$

4.2 Scheduling Through Random Delays

In this subsection we show how to use random delays approach introduced in [23] to schedule jobs.

Theorem 5. *There is a randomized algorithm in the* CLIQUE *model, which schedules* t *jobs* $O(\text{LocalCongestion} + \text{dilation} \cdot \log n + t/n)$ *rounds, w.h.p., given an upper bound on the value of* LocalCongestion, *and in* $O(\text{LocalCongestion} + \log \text{LocalCongestion} \cdot (\text{dilation} \cdot \log n + t/n))$ *rounds, w.h.p., if such a bound is not known.*

We next sketch the algorithm and the crucial proof step; the formal proof is deferred to Sect. 4.2. In the algorithm, job $j \in [t]$ is executed with a delay D_j that is chosen uniformly at random from $[D]$, where $D = \lfloor \text{LocalCongestion}/ \ln n \rfloor$.

In the crucial step of the proof, we use a Hoeffding Bound to show that this random delay implies that each node has to send and receive at most $X = O(\mathsf{LocalCongestion} \cdot n/D)$ messages per round in all jobs combined. The claim then follows by routing all messages of a single round with Lenzen's routing scheme (Claim 1). This approach uses that all nodes know a bound on $\mathsf{LocalCongestion}$, which can be removed at the cost of a logarithmic factor with a standard *doubling*-technique.

5 Discussion

Our results suggest that the amortized complexity, i.e., the runtime of solving many instances of a problem divided by the number of instances, is a valuable measure for the efficiency of protocols in the CLIQUE model. Our interest in obtaining protocols with fast amortized complexities stems from the growing number of problems which admit $O(1)$-round CLIQUE-protocols, e.g., [7,14,26], whose amortized complexity could potentially be shown to go below constant, as well as from problems that are still not known to have a constant worst-case complexity. We now elaborate on this viewpoint.

We give MIS as an example of a problem which can be solved with a good amortized complexity. The best known protocol [12] requires $O(\log \log \Delta)$ rounds. In the full version of the paper we show how to run $t = \mathrm{poly}\, n$ instances of MIS in $O(t + \log \log \Delta \log n)$ rounds. For $t = \Omega(\log \log \Delta \log n)$, the second part of the complexity "amortizes out" and we obtain that we run t instances of the MIS problem in $O(t)$ rounds. Basically, we show that the amortized complexity of the MIS problem is $O(1)$ rounds.

Note that the amortized complexity should not be optimized isolated from other measures. For example, consider the trivial $O(n)$-round protocol for pointer jumping, in which in the i-th round, the i-th node applies its permutation to the *current pointer* and sends the result to the next node. It requires only $O(n)$ messages. Thus, it is trivial to run $t \leq n^2$ instances of this pointer jumping protocol in only $O(n)$ rounds, leading to an amortized complexity of $O(1/n) = o(1)$. However, the *latency* of this algorithm is an unacceptable $O(n)$ rounds. Instead, in the full version of the paper we show that the pointer jumping problem has an acceptable amortized complexity of $O(1)$ rounds and a small latency of $O(\log^2 n)$ rounds.

For certain protocols, Theorem 3 might even yield $o(1)$ amortized complexity. For example, consider a job in which it is required to compute the $\sqrt{n}$-bin histogram of some given data. In the trivial 2-round protocol, each node locally builds a histogram of its input and sends the number of elements in its i-th bin to v_i. For all $i \in [\sqrt{n}]$, node v_i sums the received values and broadcasts the result. Clearly, such an algorithm is $O(\sqrt{n})$-memory efficient and uses $O(n\sqrt{n})$ messages. Our algorithm from Theorem 3 executes t instances of this protocol in $O(\lceil t/\sqrt{n} \rceil)$ rounds. Whenever $t = o(\sqrt{n})$, this gives an $o(1)$ amortized round complexity with constant latency.

The reader may notice that for some sets of jobs, it may be that some ad-hoc routing could be developed for efficient scheduling. We emphasize that, in contrast, the power of our algorithms is that they *do not* require tailoring the protocols for the sake of scheduling them within a given set of jobs. This is pivotal for obtaining a general framework, because knowing in advance the setting in which a protocol would be executed is an unreasonable assumption that we do not wish to make.

Acknowledgments. This project has received funding from the European Union's Horizon 2020 research and innovation programme under grant agreement no. 755839-ERC-BANDWIDTH.

References

1. Censor-Hillel, K., Dory, M., Korhonen, J.H., Leitersdorf, D.: Fast approximate shortest paths in the congested clique. In: Proceedings of the ACM Symposium on Principles of Distributed Computing (PODC), pp. 74–83 (2019). https://doi.org/10.1145/3293611.3331633
2. Censor-Hillel, K., Gall, F.L., Leitersdorf, D.: On distributed listing of cliques. In: Proceedings of the ACM Symposium on Principles of Distributed Computing (PODC), pp. 474–482 (2020). https://doi.org/10.1145/3382734.3405742
3. Censor-Hillel, K., Kaski, P., Korhonen, J.H., Lenzen, C., Paz, A., Suomela, J.: Algebraic methods in the congested clique. Distrib. Comput. **32**(6), 461–478 (2016). https://doi.org/10.1007/s00446-016-0270-2
4. Censor-Hillel, K., Maus, Y., Polosukhin, V.: Near-optimal scheduling in the congested clique (2021). arXiv:2102.07221
5. Censor-Hillel, K., Parter, M., Schwartzman, G.: Derandomizing local distributed algorithms under bandwidth restrictions. Distributed Comput. **33**(3–4), 349–366 (2020). https://doi.org/10.1007/s00446-020-00376-1
6. Chang, Y., Pettie, S., Zhang, H.: Distributed triangle detection via expander decomposition. In: Proceedings of the ACM-SIAM Symposium on Discrete Algorithms (SODA), pp. 821–840 (2019). https://doi.org/10.1137/1.9781611975482.51
7. Czumaj, A., Davies, P., Parter, M.: Simple, deterministic, constant-round coloring in the congested clique. In: Proceedings of the ACM Symposium on Principles of Distributed Computing (PODC), pp. 309–318 (2020). https://doi.org/10.1145/3382734.3405751
8. Dolev, D., Lenzen, C., Peled, S.: "Tri, tri again": finding triangles and small subgraphs in a distributed setting. In: Aguilera, M.K. (ed.) DISC 2012. LNCS, vol. 7611, pp. 195–209. Springer, Heidelberg (2012). https://doi.org/10.1007/978-3-642-33651-5_14
9. Le Gall, F.: Further algebraic algorithms in the congested clique model and applications to graph-theoretic problems. In: Gavoille, C., Ilcinkas, D. (eds.) DISC 2016. LNCS, vol. 9888, pp. 57–70. Springer, Heidelberg (2016). https://doi.org/10.1007/978-3-662-53426-7_5
10. Ghaffari, M.: Near-optimal scheduling of distributed algorithms. In: Proceedings of the ACM Symposium on Principles of Distributed Computing (PODC), pp. 3–12 (2015). https://doi.org/10.1145/2767386.2767417
11. Ghaffari, M.: Distributed MIS via all-to-all communication. In: Proceedings of the ACM Symposium on Principles of Distributed Computing (PODC), pp. 141–149 (2017). https://doi.org/10.4230/LIPIcs.ICALP.2019.142
12. Ghaffari, M., Gouleakis, T., Konrad, C., Mitrovic, S., Rubinfeld, R.: Improved massively parallel computation algorithms for MIS, matching, and vertex cover. In: Proceedings of the ACM Symposium on Principles of Distributed Computing (PODC), pp. 129–138 (2018). https://doi.org/10.1145/3212734.3212743

13. Ghaffari, M., Nowicki, K.: Congested clique algorithms for the minimum cut problem. In: Proceedings of the ACM Symposium on Principles of Distributed Computing (PODC), pp. 357–366 (2018)
14. Ghaffari, M., Nowicki, K., Thorup, M.: Faster algorithms for edge connectivity via random 2-out contractions. In: Proceedings of the ACM-SIAM Symposium on Discrete Algorithms (SODA), pp. 1260–1279 (2020). https://doi.org/10.1137/1.9781611975994.77
15. Ghaffari, M., Parter, M.: MST in log-star rounds of congested clique. In: Proceedings of the ACM Symposium on Principles of Distributed Computing (PODC), pp. 19–28 (2016). https://doi.org/10.1145/2933057.2933103
16. Hegeman, J.W., Pandurangan, G., Pemmaraju, S.V., Sardeshmukh, V.B., Scquizzato, M.: Toward optimal bounds in the congested clique: graph connectivity and MST. In: Proceedings of the ACM Symposium on Principles of Distributed Computing (PODC), pp. 91–100 (2015). https://doi.org/10.1145/2767386.2767434
17. Hirschberg, D.S.: Parallel algorithms for the transitive closure and the connected component problems. In: Proceedings of the ACM Symposium on Theory of Computing (STOC), pp. 55–57 (1976). https://doi.org/10.1145/800113.803631
18. Izumi, T., Gall, F.L.: Triangle finding and listing in CONGEST networks. In: Proceedings of the ACM Symposium on Principles of Distributed Computing (PODC), pp. 381–389 (2017). https://doi.org/10.1145/3087801.3087811
19. Jurdzinski, T., Nowicki, K.: MST in $O(1)$ rounds of congested clique. In: Proceedings of the ACM-SIAM Symposium on Discrete Algorithms (SODA), pp. 2620–2632 (2018). https://doi.org/10.1137/1.9781611975031.167
20. Karloff, H.J., Suri, S., Vassilvitskii, S.: A model of computation for MapReduce. In: Proceedings of the ACM-SIAM Symposium on Discrete Algorithms (SODA), pp. 938–948 (2010). https://doi.org/10.1137/1.9781611973075.76
21. Klauck, H., Nanongkai, D., Pandurangan, G., Robinson, P.: Distributed computation of large-scale graph problems. In: Proceedings of the ACM-SIAM Symposium on Discrete Algorithms (SODA), pp. 391–410 (2015). https://doi.org/10.1137/1.9781611973730.28
22. Korhonen, J.H.: Deterministic MST sparsification in the congested clique (2016). arXiv:1605.02022
23. Leighton, F.T., Maggs, B.M., Rao, S.: Packet routing and job-shop scheduling in $O(\text{congestion} + \text{dilation})$ steps. Combinatorica 14(2), 167–186 (1994). https://doi.org/10.1007/BF01215349
24. Lenzen, C.: Optimal deterministic routing and sorting on the congested clique. In: Proceedings of the ACM Symposium on Principles of Distributed Computing (PODC), pp. 42–50 (2013). https://doi.org/10.1145/2484239.2501983
25. Lotker, Z., Patt-Shamir, B., Pavlov, E., Peleg, D.: Minimum-weight spanning tree construction in $O(\log \log n)$ communication rounds. SIAM J. Comput. 35(1), 120–131 (2005). https://doi.org/10.1137/S0097539704441848
26. Nowicki, K.: A deterministic algorithm for the MST problem in constant rounds of congested clique. In: Proceedings of the ACM Symposium on Theory of Computing (STOC) (2021). arXiv:1912.04239
27. Pandurangan, G., Robinson, P., Scquizzato, M.: On the distributed complexity of large-scale graph computations. In: Proceedings of the ACM Symposium on Parallelism in Algorithms and Architecture (SPAA), pp. 405–414 (2018). https://doi.org/10.1145/3210377.3210409

Superfast Coloring in CONGEST via Efficient Color Sampling

Magnús M. Halldórsson and Alexandre Nolin[✉]

ICE-TCS, Department of Computer Science, Reykjavik University, Reykjavik, Iceland
{mmh,alexandren}@ru.is

Abstract. We present a procedure for efficiently sampling colors in the CONGEST model. It allows nodes whose number of colors exceeds their number of neighbors by a constant fraction to sample up to $\Theta(\log n)$ semi-random colors unused by their neighbors in $O(1)$ rounds, even in the distance-2 setting. This yields algorithms with $O(\log^* \Delta)$ complexity for different edge-coloring, vertex coloring, and distance-2 coloring problems, matching the best possible. In particular, we obtain an $O(\log^* \Delta)$-round CONGEST algorithm for $(1+\epsilon)\Delta$-edge coloring when $\Delta \geq \log^{1+1/\log^* n} n$, and a poly$(\log \log n)$-round algorithm for $(2\Delta - 1)$-edge coloring in general. The sampling procedure is inspired by a seminal result of Newman in communication complexity.

1 Introduction

The two primary models of locality, LOCAL and CONGEST, share most of the same features: the nodes are connected in the form of an undirected graph, time proceeds in synchronous rounds, and in each round, each node can exchange different messages with each of its neighbors. The difference is that the messages can be of arbitrary size in LOCAL, but only logarithmic in CONGEST. A question of major current interest is to what extent message sizes matter in order to achieve fast execution.

Random sampling is an important and powerful principle with extensive applications to distributed algorithms. In its basic form, the nodes of the network compute their random samples and share it with their neighbors in order to reach collaborative decisions. When the samples are too large to fit in a single CONGEST message, then the LOCAL model seems to have a clear advantage. The goal of this work is to overcome this handicap and derive equally efficient CONGEST algorithms, particularly in the context of coloring problems.

Graph coloring is one of the most fundamental topics in distributed computing. In fact, it was the subject of the first work on distributed graph algorithms by Linial [18]. The task is to either color the *vertices* or the *edges* of the underlying communication graph G so that adjacent vertices/edges receive different colors. The most basic distributed coloring question is to match what is achieved by a

Partially supported by Icelandic Research Fund grant 174484-051.

T. Jurdziński and S. Schmid (Eds.): SIROCCO 2021, LNCS 12810, pp. 68–83, 2021.
https://doi.org/10.1007/978-3-030-79527-6_5

simple centralized algorithm that colors the vertices/edges in an arbitrary order. Thus, our primary focus is on the $(\Delta + 1)$-vertex coloring and the $(2\Delta - 1)$-edge coloring problems, where Δ is the maximum degree of G.

Randomized distributed coloring algorithms are generally based on sampling colors from the appropriate domain. The classical and early algorithms for vertex coloring, e.g. [1,16], involve sampling individual colors and operate therefore equally well in CONGEST. The more recent fast coloring algorithms, both for vertex [2,6,14,24] and edge coloring [6], all involve a technique of Schneider and Wattenhofer [24] that uses samples of up to logarithmic number of colors. In fact, there are no published sublogarithmic algorithms (in n or Δ) for these coloring problems in CONGEST, while there are now poly$(\log \log n)$-round algorithms [2,6,8] in LOCAL. A case in point is the $(2\Delta - 1)$-edge coloring problem when $\Delta = \log^{1+\Omega(1)} n$, which can be solved in only $O(\log^* n)$ LOCAL rounds [6]. The bottleneck in CONGEST is the sampling size of the Schneider-Wattenhofer protocol.

We present here a technique for sampling a logarithmic number of colors and communicating them in only $O(1)$ CONGEST rounds. It allows us to match in CONGEST the best complexity known in LOCAL for a number of coloring problems where the nodes/edges to be colored have a large *slack*: the number of colors available exceeds by a constant fraction the number of neighbors. We particularly apply the technique to settings where the maximum degree Δ is superlogarithmic (we shall assume $\Delta = \Omega(\log^{1+1/\log^* n} n)$).

The sampling technique is best viewed as making random choices with a limited amount of randomness. This is achieved by showing that sampling within an appropriate subfamily of all color samples can retain some of the useful statistical properties of a fully random sample. It is inspired by Newman's theorem in communication complexity [19], where dependence on shared randomness is removed through a similar argument.

We obtain a superfast $O(\log^* \Delta)$-round algorithm for $(2\Delta - 1)$-edge coloring when $\Delta = \Omega(\log^{1+1/\log^* n} n)$. Independent of Δ, we obtain a poly$(\log \log n)$-round algorithm. This shows that coloring need not be any slower in CONGEST than in LOCAL.

We also obtain similar results for vertex coloring, for the same values of Δ ($\Delta = \Omega(\log^{1+1/\log^* n} n)$). We obtain an $O(\log^* \Delta)$-round algorithm for $(1 + \epsilon)\Delta$-coloring, for any $\epsilon > 0$. For graphs that are locally sparse (see Sect. 2 for definition), this gives a $(\Delta + 1)$-coloring in the same time complexity. Matching results also hold for the *distance-2* coloring problem, where nodes within distance 2 must receive different colors.

1.1 Related Work

The literature on distributed coloring is vast and we limit this discussion to work that is directly relevant to ours, primarily randomized algorithms.

An edge coloring of a graph G corresponds to a vertex coloring of its line graph, whose maximum degree is $2\Delta(G) - 2$. Therefore, LOCAL algorithms for

$(\Delta + 1)$-vertex coloring yield $(2\Delta - 1)$-edge coloring in the same time. Since line graphs have a special structure, edge coloring often allows for either faster algorithms or fewer number of colors. For CONGEST, the situation is different: Because of capacity restrictions, no single node can expect to learn the colors of all edges adjacent to a given edge. In fact, there are no published results on efficient edge-coloring algorithms in CONGEST, to the best of our knowledge[1].

A classical simple (probably folklore) algorithm for vertex coloring is for each vertex to pick in each round a color uniformly at random from its *current palette*, the colors that are not used on neighbors. Each node can be shown to become colored in each round with constant probability and thus this procedure completes in $O(\log n)$ rounds, w.h.p. [16]. In fact, each round of this procedure reduces w.h.p. the *uncolored degree* of each vertex by a constant factor, as long as the degree is $\Omega(\log n)$ [1]. Within $O(\log \Delta)$ rounds, the maximum uncolored degree of each node is logarithmic. This algorithm works also in CONGEST for node coloring, and as well for edge coloring in LOCAL, but not for edge coloring in CONGEST, as it is not clear how to randomly select a color from an edge's palette in this setting.

Color sampling algorithms along a similar vein have also been studied for edge coloring [3,10,20], all running in $O(\log n)$ LOCAL rounds in general. Panconesi and Srinivasan [20] showed that one of the most basic algorithms finds a $(1.6\Delta + \log^{2+\Omega(1)} n)$-edge coloring. Grable and Panconesi [10] showed that $O(\log \log n)$ rounds suffice when $\Delta = n^{\Omega(1/\log \log n)}$. Dubhashi, Grable and Panconesi [3] proposed an algorithm based on the Rödl nibble technique, where only a subset of the edges try a color in each round, and showed that it finds a $(1 + \epsilon)\Delta$-edge coloring, when $\Delta = \omega(\log n)$.

Sublogarithmic round vertex coloring algorithms have two phases, where the first phase is completed once the *uncolored degree* of the nodes is low (logarithmic or polylogarithmic). Barenboim et al. [1] showed that within $O(\log \log n)$ additional rounds, the graph is *shattered*: each connected component (induced by the uncolored nodes) is of polylogarithmic size. The default approach is then to apply fast deterministic algorithms. With recent progress on network decomposition [8,23], as well as fast deterministic coloring algorithms [9], the low degree case can now be solved in poly$(\log \log n)$ rounds.

Recent years have seen fast LOCAL coloring algorithms that run in sublogarithmic time. These methods depend crucially on a random sampling method of Schneider and Wattenhofer [24] where each node picks as many as $\log n$ colors at a time. The method works when each node has large *slack*; i.e., when the number of colors in the node's palette is a constant fraction larger than the number of neighbors (competing for those colors). This holds in particular when computing a $(1 + \epsilon)\Delta$-coloring, for some $\epsilon > 0$, which they achieve in $O(\log^* \Delta)$ rounds, when $\Delta \geq \log^{1+\Omega(1)} n$.

---

[1] Fischer, Ghaffari and Kuhn [7] suggest in a footnote that their edge coloring algorithms, described and proven in LOCAL, actually work in CONGEST. It does not hold for their randomized edge-coloring result, which applies the algorithm of [6].

In the $(\Delta+1)$-node coloring and $(2\Delta-1)$-edge coloring problems, the nodes do not have any slack *a priori*. It turns out that such slack can sometimes be generated by a single round of color guessing. Suppose the graph is triangle free, or more generally, *locally sparse*, meaning that the induced subgraph of each node has many non-adjacent pairs of nodes. Then, when each node tries random color, each pair of non-adjacent common neighbors of v has a fair chance of being colored with the same color, which leads to an increase in the slack of v. As shown by Elkin et al. [6] (with a longer history in graph theory, tracing back at least to Reed [22]), locally sparse graphs will have slack $\Omega(\Delta)$ after this single color sampling round. Line graphs are locally sparse graphs, and thus we obtain this way a $O(\log^* \Delta)$-round algorithm for $(2\Delta-1)$-edge coloring [6], for $\Delta \geq \Delta^{1+\Omega(1)}$. They further obtain a $(1+\epsilon)\Delta$-edge list coloring in the same time frame, using the nibble technique of [20].

This fast coloring of locally sparse graphs is also useful in $(\Delta+1)$-vertex coloring. Both the first sublogarithmic round algorithm of Harris, Schneider, Su [14] and the current fastest algorithm of Chang et al. [2] partition the graph into a sparse and a dense part, and use a variation of the method of [24] to color the sparse part.

A *distance-2 coloring* is a vertex coloring such that nodes within distance at most 2 receive different colors. This problem in CONGEST shares a key property with edge coloring: nodes cannot obtain a full knowledge of their available palette, but they can try a color by asking their neighbors. A recent (Δ^2+1)-distance-2 coloring algorithm of [11] that runs in $O(\log \Delta) + \text{poly}(\log \log n)$ CONGEST rounds can be used to compute $(2\Delta-1)$-edge colorings in the same time complexity.

2   Intuition and Preliminaries

Existing $O(\log^* \Delta)$ algorithms for the different coloring problems in LOCAL such as those by Schneider and Wattenhofer [24] all involve sampling several colors in a single round. In such algorithms, the nodes try colors in a way that guarantees each color an independent, $\Omega(1)$ probability of success. While this probability of success is a given when nodes try a single color, trying several colors simultaneously could create more conflicts between colors and reduce the probability of success of any given one.

This issue is usually solved using *slack*, the difference between the number of colors unused by the neighbors of a node and how many of its neighbors are still uncolored. Slack is a given when we allow more colors than each node has neighbors, and is otherwise easily generated in a locally sparse graph.

If the nodes are all able to try $\Theta(\log n)$ colors in $O(1)$ rounds, and all colors have an independent, $\Omega(1)$ probability of success, $O(1)$ rounds suffice to color all nodes w.h.p. However, this is usually not immediately possible, unless all nodes have a large amount of slack from the beginning. The $O(\log^* n)$ algorithms work through increasing the ratio of slack to uncolored degree, trying more and more colors as this ratio increases, allowing nodes to try $\Theta(\log n)$ colors each with constant probability over the course of $O(\log^* n)$ rounds. The speed comes from the fact that slack never decreases but the uncolored degree of the edges decreases with exponentially increasing speed as the nodes try more and more colors.

However, sending $\Theta(\log n)$ arbitrary colors requires $\Theta(\log n \cdot \log \Delta)$ bits, i.e., a minimum of $\Theta(\log \Delta)$ CONGEST rounds. Our algorithms will also involve having each node try up to $\Theta(\log n)$ colors, but without transmitting $\Theta(\log n)$ arbitrary colors.

2.1   Sampling Colors with Shared Randomness

While $\Theta(\log n \cdot \log \Delta)$ bits are needed to describe an arbitrary choice of $\Theta(\log n)$ colors in a color space of size $\Theta(\Delta)$, being able to describe any choice of $\Theta(\log n)$ colors can be unnecessary. To get intuition about this, consider the setting where all nodes have access to a shared source of randomness.

With a shared source of randomness, instead of sending $\log \Delta$ bits to specify a color, a node can interpret blocks of $\log \Delta$ bits in the source as colors and send the index of one of them. If each random color has a chance $\geq p$ of having the properties needed to be tried, the index of the first satisfactory color will only take $O(\log(1/p))$ bits to communicate. The nodes can also use $O(\log n)$ bits to indicate which of the first $O(\log n)$ colors in the random source they try. This technique allows the edges to sample $\Theta(p \log n)$ colors in a single round of CONGEST. The choices made by nodes are made independent by having the nodes use disjoint parts of the shared randomness (for example, each node might only use the bits at indices equal to its ID modulo n). This type of saving in the communication based on a shared source of randomness appears in several places in communication complexity, in particular in [15] where it is used with the Disjointness problem, and in the folklore protocol for Equality (e.g., Example 3.13 in [17]).

It is crucial in the above argument that all nodes have access to a shared source of randomness, as messages making references to the shared randomness lose their meaning without it. Our goal will now be to remove this need for a shared source of randomness, taking inspiration from Newman's Theorem in communication complexity [19] (Theorem 3.14 in [17], Theorem 3.5 in [21]). It is not an application of it, however, as contrary to the 2-party communication complexity setting, distributing a common random seed to all parties would require many rounds in our context, and the success of any node trying one or more colors is interrelated with the random choices of up to $\Delta + 1$ parties. Our contribution is best understood as replacing a fully random sample of colors by a pseudorandom one with appropriate statistical guarantees, whose proof of existence resembles the proof of Newman's Theorem. We do so in Sect. 3, and give multiple applications of this result in subsequent sections.

2.2   Tools and Notation

Our results rely heavily on the existence of a family of sets with the right properties, whose existence we prove by a probabilistic argument. We make frequent use of the Chernoff-Hoeffding bounds in this proof, as well as in other parts of the paper. We use a version of the bounds that holds for *negatively associated* random variables.

Definition 1 (Negative association). *The random variables $X_1, \ldots, X_n$ are said to be negatively associated if for all disjoint subsets $I, J \subseteq [n]$ and all non-decreasing functions f and g,*

$$\mathbb{E}[f(X_i, i \in I) \cdot g(X_j, j \in J)] \leq \mathbb{E}[f(X_i, i \in I)] \cdot \mathbb{E}[g(X_j, j \in J)]$$

Lemma 1 (Chernoff-Hoeffding bounds). *Let $X_1, \ldots, X_n$ be n negatively associated random variables in $[0, 1]$, $X := \sum_{i=1}^{n} X_i$ their sum, and let the expectation of X satisfy $\mu_L \leq \mathbb{E}[X] \leq \mu_H$. For $0 < \epsilon < 1$:*

$$\Pr[X > (1 + \epsilon)\mu_H] \leq e^{-\epsilon^2 \mu_H / 3}, \qquad \Pr[X < (1 - \epsilon)\mu_L] \leq e^{-\epsilon^2 \mu_L / 2}.$$

Negative association is a somewhat complicated-looking property but the property holds in simple scenarios. In particular it holds for balls and bins experiments [4,5], such as when the random variables $X_1, \ldots, X_n$ correspond to sampling k elements out of n (i.e., when the random variables satisfy $\Pr[X_i = v_i, \forall i \in [n]] = 1/\binom{n}{k}$ for all $v \in \{0, 1\}^n, \|v\|_1 = k$). It also encompasses the usual setting where $X_1, \ldots, X_n$ are independent.

For ease of notation, we use the following shorthands: $[a, b]k$ for the interval $[a \cdot k, b \cdot k]$, $[a..b]$ for the set $\{a, \ldots, b\}$, and $[k]$ for the set $\{1, \ldots, k\}$.

Throughout the paper we describe algorithms that try an increasing number of colors in a single round. This increase is much faster than exponential and we use Knuth's up-arrow notation to denote it. In fact, the increase is as fast as the inverse of $\log^*$, which already gives a sense of why our algorithms run in $O(\log^* n)$ rounds.

Definition 2 (Knuth's up-arrow notation for tetration). *For $a \in \mathbb{R}, b \in \mathbb{N}$, $a \uparrow\uparrow b$ represents the* tetration *or* iterated exponentiation *of a by b, defined as:*

$$a \uparrow\uparrow 0 = 1, \qquad and \qquad a \uparrow\uparrow b = a^{a \uparrow\uparrow (b-1)} \text{ when } b > 0.$$

Throughout the paper, as we work on a graph $G(V, E)$ of vertices V and edges E, we denote by n the number of vertices and by Δ the maximum degree of the graph. The degree of a vertex is denoted by $d(v)$, its uncolored degree (how many of its neighbors are uncolored) by $d^*(v)$. The sparsity of v (Definition 3) is denoted by $\zeta(v)$, the palette of v (the set of colors not yet used by one of v's neighbors) by ψ_v, and its slack $s(v)$ is defined as $s(v) = |\psi_v| - d^*(v)$. Whenever we consider an edge-coloring problem, we will often work on the line graph and add an L subscript to indicate that we consider the same quantities but on $L(G)$: the maximum degree of this graph is $\Delta_L = 2\Delta - 1$, the degree of an edge is denoted by $d_L(e)$, and so on.

Definition 3 (Sparsity). *Let v be a node in the graph $G(V, E)$ of maximum degree Δ, and let $E[N(v)]$ the set of edges between nodes of v's neighborhood $N(v)$. The sparsity of v is defined as:*

$$\zeta(v) = \frac{1}{\Delta} \cdot \left(\binom{\Delta}{2} - |E[N(v)]| \right)$$

The sparsity is a measure of how many edges are missing out of all the edges that could exist in the neighborhood of a node. As immediate property, $\zeta(v)$ is a rational number in the range $[0, (\Delta - 1)/2]$. A value close to 0 indicates a very dense neighborhood (in particular $\zeta(v) = 0$ iff $\{v\} \cup N(v)$ forms a $(\Delta+1)$-clique) while a value close to $(\Delta - 1)/2$ indicates the opposite, that v's neighborhood is sparse (at the extreme, $\zeta(v) = (\Delta - 1)/2$ iff no two neighbors of v are connected to one another). A graph is said to be $(1 - \epsilon)$-*locally sparse* iff its vertices are all of sparsity at least $\epsilon \Delta$. A vertex v of sparsity ζ is equivalently said to be ζ-sparse.

Sparsity is of interest here for two reasons: first, because we know from a result of [6] that nodes receive slack proportional to their sparsity w.h.p. in just one round of all nodes trying a random color if $\zeta(v) \in \Omega(\log n)$ (Proposition 1), and second because the line graph is sparse by construction (Proposition 2).

Proposition 1 ([6], Lemma 3.1). *Let v be a vertex of sparsity ζ and let Z be the slack of v after trying a single random color. Then,*

$$\Pr[Z \leq \zeta/(4e^3)] \leq e^{-\Omega(\zeta)}.$$

Proposition 2. *A node e of the line graph $L(G)$ (i.e., an edge of G) has degree $d_L(e)$ at most $\Delta_L = 2(\Delta - 1)$, and the number of edges in its neighborhood $E_{L(G)}[N(e) \setminus \{e\}]$ is at most $(\Delta - 1)^2$, meaning e is $(\Delta - 2)/2$-sparse, i.e., $(\Delta_L - 2)/4$-sparse.*

3 Efficient Color Sampling with Representative Sets

We now introduce the tool that will allow us to sample and communicate $\Theta(\log n)$ colors in $O(1)$ CONGEST rounds with the right probabilistic guarantees. Let s be the number of elements we sample and k the size of the universe to be sampled from. If we wanted to be able to sample any subset of $[k]$ of size s, we would need $\log \binom{k}{s}$ bits to communicate our choice of subset. But our goal is to communicate less than this amount, so we instead consider a family of s-sized subsets of $[k]$ such that picking one of those subsets at random has some of the probabilistic properties of sampling an s-sized subset of $[k]$ uniformly at random. The family is much smaller that the set of all possible s-sized subsets of $[k]$, which allows us to communicate a member of it in much less than $\log \binom{k}{s}$ bits. We call the family of subsets a *representative family*, made of *representative sets*, and the probabilistic properties we maintain are essentially that:

- Every element of $[k]$ is present in about the same number of sets.
- For any large enough subset T of $[k]$, a random representative set intersects T in about as many elements as a fully random s-sized set.

Crucially, the second property holds for a large enough arbitrary T, so we will be able to apply it even as T is dependent on the choices of other nodes in the graph as long as the representative set is picked independently from T. T will typically be the palette of a node or edge, or the set of colors not tried by any neighbors of a node or edge. Maintaining these two properties is enough to efficiently adapt many LOCAL algorithms that rely on communicating large subsets of colors to the CONGEST setting.

Definition 4 (Representative sets). *Let U be a universe of size k. A family $\mathcal{F} = \{S_1, \ldots, S_t\}$ of s-sized sets is said to be an (α, δ, ν)-representative family iff:*

$$\forall T \subseteq U, |T| \geq \delta k : \quad \Pr_{i \in [t]} \left[\frac{|S_i \cap T|}{|S_i|} \in [1 - \alpha, 1 + \alpha] \frac{|T|}{k} \right] \geq (1 - \nu), \quad (1)$$

$$\forall T \subseteq U, |T| < \delta k : \quad \Pr_{i \in [t]} \left[\frac{|S_i \cap T|}{|S_i|} \leq (1 + \alpha)\delta \right] \geq (1 - \nu), \quad (2)$$

$$\forall u \in U : \quad \Pr_{i \in [t]} [u \in S_i] \in [1 - \alpha, 1 + \alpha] \frac{s \cdot t}{k}. \quad (3)$$

We show in Lemma 2 that such families exist for some appropriate choices of parameters. The proof of this result, which relies on the probabilistic method, takes direct inspiration from Newman's Theorem [19].

Lemma 2 (Representative sets exist). *Let U be a universe of size k. For any $\alpha, \delta, \nu > 0$, there exists an (α, δ, ν)-representative family $(S_i)_{i \in [t]}$ of $t \in O(k/\nu + k \log(k))$ subsets, each of size $s \in O(\alpha^{-2}\delta^{-1} \log(1/\nu))$.*

Proof. Our proof is probabilistic: we show that Eqs. 1, 2 and 3 all hold with non-zero probability when picking sets at random. We first study the probability that Eqs. 1 and 2 hold, and then the probability that Eq. 3 holds.

Consider any set $T \subseteq U$ of size $\geq \delta k$. Pick a random set $S \subseteq U$ of size s. The intersection of S and T has expected size $\mathbb{E}_S[|S \cap T|] = \frac{|T|}{k}s$. Let us say that S has an *unusual* intersection with T if its size is outside the $[1 - \alpha, 1 + \alpha]\frac{|T|}{k}s$ range. By Chernoff with negative dependence,

$$\Pr_S \left[|S \cap T| \notin [1 - \alpha, 1 + \alpha] \frac{|T|}{k} s \right] \leq 2e^{-s\alpha^2 \frac{|T|}{3k}} \leq 2e^{-\frac{\alpha^2 \delta}{3} s}.$$

This last quantity also bounds the probability that $|S \cap T| > (1 + \alpha)\delta s$ when $|T| < \delta k$, which we also consider as an unusual intersection.

Pick t sets $S_1, \ldots, S_t$ of size s at random independently from each other, let X_i be the event that the ith set S_i unusually intersects T. By Chernoff, the probability that more than $4t \cdot \exp\left(-\frac{\alpha^2 \delta}{3} s\right)$ of the sets unusually intersect T is:

$$\Pr_{S_1 \ldots S_t}\left[\sum_i X_i > 4t \cdot e^{-\frac{\alpha^2 \delta}{3} s}\right] \leq e^{-\frac{t}{3} \cdot \exp\left(-\frac{\alpha^2 \delta}{3} s\right)}$$

There are less than 2^k subsets of U. Therefore, the probability that there exists a set T such that out of the t sampled sets $S_1 \ldots S_t$, more than $4t \cdot \exp\left(-\frac{\alpha^2 \delta}{3} s\right)$ have an unusual intersection with T, is at most:

$$2^k \cdot e^{-\frac{t}{3} \cdot \exp\left(-\frac{\alpha^2 \delta}{3} s\right)} = \exp\left(k \cdot \ln(2) - \frac{t}{3} \cdot \exp\left(-\frac{\alpha^2 \delta}{3} s\right)\right)$$

This last quantity is an upper bound on the probability that one of Eqs. 1 and 2 does not hold. Let us now similarly bound the probability that Eq. 3 does not hold.

For any $u \in U$, the probability that a random s-sized subset of U contains u is s/k. Let X_i be the event that our i^{th} random set S_i contains u, we have:

$$\Pr_{S_1 \ldots S_t}\left[\sum_i X_i \notin [1 - \alpha, 1 + \alpha]\frac{s \cdot t}{k}\right] \leq 2e^{-\alpha^2 \frac{s \cdot t}{3k}}$$

Therefore the probability that Eq. 3 does not hold, i.e., that there exists an under- or over-represented element $u \in U$ in our t randomly picked sets, is less than $2k \cdot e^{-\alpha^2 \frac{s \cdot t}{3k}}$. The probability that one of Eqs. 1, 2, and 3 does not hold is at most:

$$\exp\left(k \cdot \ln(2) - \frac{t}{3} \cdot \exp\left(-\frac{\alpha^2 \delta}{3} s\right)\right) + \exp\left(\ln(2k) - \alpha^2 \frac{s \cdot t}{3k}\right)$$

We now pick the right values for s and t such that: first, this last probability is less than 1 and, therefore, a family with all the above properties exist; second, the fraction of sets S_i with the wrong intersection is less than ν for all T.

The fraction of bad sets is guaranteed to be less than ν if $4 \cdot e^{-\frac{\alpha^2 \delta}{3} s} \leq \nu$, which is achieved with $s \geq \ln(4/\nu) \cdot \frac{3}{\alpha^2 \delta}$. We take s to be this last value rounded up, i.e., we have $s \in O(\alpha^{-2}\delta^{-1} \log(1/\nu))$. For t, we pick it satisfying $t > 3(k \cdot \ln(2) + 1) \cdot \exp\left(\frac{\alpha^2 \delta}{3} s\right)$ and $t > \frac{3k \cdot (\ln(2k) + 1)}{\alpha^2 \cdot s}$, that is, we can pick t of order $\Theta(k/\nu + k\log(k))$ and satisfy all properties with non-zero probability, implying the existence of the desired representative family.

4 $(1 + \epsilon)\Delta$-Vertex Coloring

We first apply our techniques to the relatively simple $(1 + \epsilon)\Delta$-vertex coloring problem. The arguments deployed here for this setting are core to all our results. Our main result in this section is Theorem 1:

Theorem 1. *Suppose* $\Delta \in \Omega(\log^{1+1/\log^* n} n)$. *There is a* CONGEST *algorithm that solves the* $(1 + \epsilon)\Delta$-*vertex coloring problem w.h.p. in* $O(\log^* n)$ *rounds.*

Throughout this section, let us assume that all nodes know a common representative family $(S_i)_{i \in [t]}$ with parameters $\alpha = 1/2$, $\delta = \frac{\epsilon}{4(1+\epsilon)}$, and $\nu = n^{-3}$ over the color space $U = [(1+\epsilon)\Delta]$. The nodes may, for example, all compute the lexicographically first (α, δ, ν)-representative family over U guaranteed by Lemma 2, with $t \in O(\Delta \cdot n^3)$ and $s \in O(\log n)$, at the very beginning of the algorithm.

We leverage this representative family in a procedure we call MULTITRIALS, where nodes can try up to $\Theta(\log n)$ colors in a round. The trade-off is that the colors they try are not fully random but picked from a representative set. We show that this does not matter in this application.

Algorithm 1. Procedure MULTITRIALS(x) (vertex coloring version)

1. v picks $i_v \in [t]$ uniformly at random and chooses a subset X_v of x colors uniformly at random in $S_{i_v} \cap \psi_v$. These are the colors v tries. v describes X_v to its neighbors in $O(1)$ rounds by sending i_v and $(\delta_{[c \in X_v]})_{c \in S_{i_v}}$ in $\log(t) + s \in O(\log n)$ bits.
2. If v tried a color that none of its neighbors tried, v adopts one such color and informs its neighbors of it.

Using MULTITRIALS with an increasing number of colors, we immediately get an $O(\log^* n)$ algorithm for the $(1 + \epsilon)\Delta$-coloring problem (Algorithm 2).

Algorithm 2. Algorithm for $(1 + \epsilon)\Delta$-vertex coloring (large Δ)

1. Nodes compute a common (α, δ, ν)-representative family over $[(1+\epsilon)\Delta]$ guaranteed by Lemma 2.
2. For $i \in [0.. \log^* n]$, for $O(1)$ rounds, each uncolored node runs MULTITRIALS($2 \uparrow\uparrow i$).
3. For $i \in [0.. \log^* n]$, each uncolored node runs MULTITRIALS$\left(\frac{\epsilon\Delta \cdot \log^{i/\log^* n} n}{2(1+\epsilon)C_c \log n} \right)$ $O(1)$ times.

To show that Algorithm 2 works, we first show that MULTITRIALS, under the right circumstances, is very efficient at coloring nodes (Lemma 3). In fact, given the right ratio between slack and uncolored degree, as the nodes try multiple colors, they get colored as if each color tried succeeded independently with constant probability.

Lemma 3. *Suppose a node v has slack $s(v) \geq \epsilon\Delta$ and $d^*(v)$ uncolored neighbors. Suppose $x \leq \frac{\epsilon}{2(1+\epsilon)}\Delta$. If $x \leq s(v)/2d^*(v)$, then conditioned on an event of high probability $\geq 1 - 2\nu$, an execution of MULTITRIALS(x) colors v with probability at least $1 - 2^{-x/4}$, even conditioned on any particular combination of random choices from the other nodes.*

Proof. Consider the representative set S_{i_v} randomly picked by v in the commonly known representative family of parameters $\alpha = 1/2$, $\delta = \frac{\epsilon}{4(1+\epsilon)}$, and $\nu = n^{-3}$. We know that S_{i_v} intersects any set of colors $T \subseteq [(1+\epsilon)\Delta]$ of size at least $\delta(1+\epsilon)\Delta$ in $[1/2, 3/2]\frac{|T|}{(1+\epsilon)\Delta}|S_{i_v}| \geq \frac{\delta}{2}|S_{i_v}|$ positions w.h.p.

Let us apply this with ψ_v, the set of colors not currently used by neighbors of v, and T_{good}, the set of colors that are neither already used nor tried in this round by nodes adjacent to v.

Clearly, $T_{\text{good}} \subseteq \psi_v$, $|\psi_v| = s(v)+d^*(v)$, and $|T_{\text{good}}| \geq s(v)+d^*(v)-x\cdot d^*(v) \geq (s(v)+d^*(v))/2 = |\psi_v|/2$. Both sets are of size at least $\delta(1+\epsilon)\Delta$, therefore w.h.p. $|S_{i_v} \cap T_{\text{good}}| \geq \frac{1}{2}|S_{i_v}| \cdot \frac{|T_{\text{good}}|}{(1+\epsilon)\Delta} \geq \frac{1}{4}|S_{i_v}| \cdot \frac{|\psi_v|}{(1+\epsilon)\Delta} \geq \frac{1}{6}|S_{i_v} \cap \psi_v|$.

Therefore, assuming that the above holds and that there are at least x colors in $S_{i_v} \cap \psi_v$, when v picks x random colors in $S_{i_v} \cap \psi_v$, the colors picked each have a chance at least $1/6$ of being in T_{good}. The probability that none of them succeeds is at most $(5/6)^x \leq 2^{-x/4}$. The event that S_{i_v} does not have an intersections of unusual size with either ψ_v or T_{good} has probability at least $1 - 2\nu$.

The second part of the argument consists of showing that the ratio of slack to uncolored degree increases as Algorithm 2 uses MULTITRIALS with an increasing number of colors. Lemma 4 helps guarantee that the repeated use of MULTITRIALS leaves all uncolored nodes with an uncolored degree at most $C_c \log n$ for some constant C_c.

Lemma 4. *Suppose the nodes all satisfy $d^*(v) \leq s(v)/(2 \cdot 2 \uparrow\uparrow i)$, with $s(v)/(2 \cdot 2 \uparrow\uparrow i) \geq C_c \log n$. Then after $O(1)$ rounds of MULTITRIALS($2 \uparrow\uparrow i$), w.h.p., they all satisfy $d^*(v) \leq \max(s(v)/(2 \cdot 2 \uparrow\uparrow (i + 1)), C_c \log n)$.*

Proof. Let v be a node of uncolored degree at least $C_c \log n$ (if not, it already satisfies the desired end property).

By Lemma 3, each uncolored neighbor of v stays uncolored with probability at most $2^{-(2\uparrow\uparrow i)/4}$. By a Chernoff bound, C_c being large enough, at most $2^{1/4} \cdot 2^{-(2\uparrow\uparrow i)/4} \cdot d^*(v)$ neighbors of v stay uncolored w.h.p.

Let us repeat this process for 4 rounds. If at any point the uncolored degree drops below $C_c \log n$, we reached the desired property, and the argument is over. Otherwise, we can apply the Chernoff bound for all 4 rounds and get that at most $2 \cdot 2^{-(2\uparrow\uparrow i)} \cdot d^*(v) = 2 \cdot \frac{1}{2\uparrow\uparrow(i+1)} \cdot d^*(v)$ neighbors of v stay uncolored, so the new uncolored degree of v satisfies:

$$d^*(v) \leq 2 \cdot \frac{1}{2 \uparrow\uparrow (i+1)} \cdot \frac{s(v)}{2 \cdot 2 \uparrow\uparrow i} \leq \frac{s(v)}{2 \cdot 2 \uparrow\uparrow (i+1)}.$$

Lemma 5. *Suppose the nodes all satisfy $d^*(v) \leq C_c \log^{1-i/\log^* n} n$. Then after $O(1)$ rounds of MULTITRIALS$\left(\frac{\epsilon\Delta \cdot \log^{i/\log^* n} n}{2(1+\epsilon)C_c \log n}\right)$, w.h.p., they all satisfy $d^*(v) \leq C_c \log^{1-(i+1)/\log^* n} n$.*

Proof. Let $x = \frac{\epsilon\Delta \cdot \log^{i/\log^* n} n}{2(1+\epsilon)C_c \log n}$ denote the number of colors tried in our application of MULTITRIALS. For each uncolored node v we have $x \leq s(v)/2d^*(v)$. By

Lemma 3, conditioned on a high probability event, each uncolored node stays uncolored with probability at most $2^{-x/4}$, regardless of the random choices of other nodes. We set $q = C_c \log^{1-(i+1)/\log^* n} n$. Since $\Delta \geq \log^{1+1/\log^* n} n$ and $x \geq \frac{\epsilon}{2(1+\epsilon)C_c} \log^{(i+1)/\log^* n} n$, we have $q \cdot x \in \Omega(\log n)$.

Consider q neighbors of a node v, $\Theta(1)$ runs of MULTITRIALS(x) leave them all uncolored with probability at most $2^{-\Omega(q \cdot x)}$. The probability that a set of q neighbors stays uncolored is bounded by $d^*(v)^q \cdot 2^{-\Omega(q \cdot x)} = 2^{-\Omega(q \cdot (x - \log \log n))} = 2^{-\Omega(\log n)}$. So, w.h.p., less than q neighbors of v stay uncolored.

With Lemmas 3 to 5 proved, we only need a few additional arguments to complete the proof of Theorem 1.

Proof (Proof of Theorem 1). Step 2. of Algorithm 2 with $i = 0$ creates a situation where the hypotheses of Lemma 4 hold for $i = 1$. The repeated application of Lemma 4 guarantees that, w.h.p., all nodes are either colored or have uncolored degree $\leq C_c \log n$.

In Step 3., all nodes start with uncolored degree at most $C_c \log n$ and slack at least $\epsilon \Delta$, thus fitting the hypotheses of Lemma 5. Its repeated application yields that after the first $\log^* n - 1$ first phases of this step, each node is either already colored or tries $\Omega(\log n)$ colors in each run of MULTITRIALS, which colors all remaining nodes w.h.p.

Lower Δ and Concluding Remarks: When $\Delta \in O(\log^{1+1/\log^* n} n)$, a simple use of the shattering technique [1] together with the recent deterministic algorithm of [9] (using $O(\log^2 \mathcal{C} \log n)$ rounds with $O(\log \mathcal{C})$ bits to compute a degree+1 list-coloring of a n-vertex graph whose lists are subsets of $[\mathcal{C}]$) is enough to solve the problem in $O(\log^3 \log n)$ CONGEST rounds, which combined with our previous $O(\log^*(n))$ algorithm for $\Delta \in O(\log^{1+1/\log^* n} n)$ means there exists an algorithm for all Δ that solves the $(1 + \epsilon)\Delta$ coloring problem in $O(\log^3 \log n)$ CONGEST rounds w.h.p.

Theorem 2. *There is a CONGEST algorithm that solves the $(1 + \epsilon)\Delta$-vertex coloring problem in $O(\log^3 \log n)$ rounds w.h.p.*

5   Edge Coloring

Moving on to the more complicated setting of edge-coloring, we will see that most of what we proved in the previous section is easily adapted to the edge-coloring setting. We first convert the $(1 + \epsilon)\Delta$-vertex coloring result to a $(2 + \epsilon)\Delta$-edge coloring and then sketch how to obtain superfast algorithms for only $(2\Delta - 1)$ and $(1+\epsilon)\Delta$ colors, with the details deferred to the full version of the paper [13].

5.1 $(2 + \epsilon)\Delta$-Edge Coloring

Theorem 3. *Suppose $\Delta \in O(\log^{1+1/\log^* n} n)$. There is a CONGEST algorithm that solves the $(2 + \epsilon)\Delta$-edge coloring problem w.h.p. in $O(\log^* n)$ rounds.*

To prove Theorem 3, the most crucial observation is that the elements of the graph trying to color themselves no longer know their palette. In the edge-coloring setting, each of the two endpoints of an edge e only has a partial view of which colors are used by e's neighbors. Communicating the list of colors used at one endpoint of e to the other endpoint is impractical, as it could require up to $\Theta(\Delta \log \Delta)$ bits. To circumvent this, we introduce a procedure (PALETTESAMPLING) for the two endpoints of an edge e to efficiently sample colors in ψ_e, the palette of e, again using representative sets. The MULTITRIALS procedure is then easily adapted to the edge-setting by making it use PALETTE-SAMPLING, and the same algorithm as the one we had in the node setting works here, simply swapping its basic building block procedure for an edge-adapted variant.

As before (but with a different color space) let us assume throughout this section that all nodes know a common representative family $(S_i)_{i \in [t]}$ with parameters $\alpha = 1/2$, $\delta = \frac{\epsilon}{4(1+\epsilon)}$, and $\nu = n^{-3}$ over the color space $U = [(2+\epsilon)\Delta]$.

For each edge e, let us denote by v_e and v'_e its two endpoints, with v_e the one of higher ID. Let us denote by ψ_e the *palette* of e, the set of colors unused by e's neighboring edges, and for a node u let ψ_u be the set of colors unused by edges around u. For an uncolored edge e, $\psi_e = \psi_{v_e} \cap \psi_{v'_e}$.

Algorithm 3. Procedure PALETTESAMPLING (edge-coloring version)

---

1. v_e picks $i_e \in [t]$ uniformly at random and sends i_e to v'_e in $O(\log(t)/\log(n)) = O(1)$ rounds.
2. v'_e replies with s bits describing $S_{i_e} \cap \psi_{v'_e}$ in $O(1)$ rounds.
3. v_e sends s bits to v'_e describing $S_{i_e} \cap \psi_{v_e}$ in $O(1)$ rounds.

Proposition 3. *Suppose e's palette ψ_e satisfies $|\psi_e| \geq \delta \cdot (2+\epsilon)\Delta$. Then v_e and v'_e find $[1 - \alpha, 1 + \alpha] \cdot s \cdot |\psi_e|/(2+\epsilon)\Delta$ colors in e's palette in an execution of* PALETTESAMPLING *w.h.p.*

Proof. The result follows directly from Eq. 1 in the definition of representative sets (Definition 4). ∎

PALETTESAMPLING leverages that sending a random color for the other endpoint to reject or approve requires much less communication than learning which colors are used at the other endpoint. The representative sets and the slack at the edges' disposal further allow us to sample not just $\Theta(\log n/\log \Delta)$ colors (represented in $\log \Delta$ bits each) in $O(1)$ rounds but $\Theta(\log n)$ colors by sampling pseudo-independent colors.

Algorithm 4. Procedure MULTITRIALS(x) (edge-coloring version)

---

1. v_e and v'_e execute PALETTESAMPLING. Let S_{i_e} be the randomly picked representative set.
2. v_e picks a subset X_e of x colors uniformly at random in $S_{i_e} \cap \psi_e$ and sends s bits to v'_e to describe it. These are the colors e tries.
   At this point, each node u knows which colors are tried by all its incident edges.
3. Each v_e describes to v'_e which of the x colors tried by e were not tried by any other edge adjacent to v_e in $O(1)$ rounds, and reciprocally.
4. If e tried a color that no edge adjacent to e tried, v_e picks an arbitrary such color, sends it to v'_e, and e adopts this color.

An execution of MULTITRIALS maintains the invariant that each node knows which colors are used by edges incident to it. As before, the representative sets guarantee that for any uncolored edge e, whatever colors other edges adjacent to e are trying, the chosen representative set S_{i_e} has a large intersection with the set of unused and untried colors, as long as this set represents a constant fraction of the color space (which slack and a good choice of x guarantee).

Algorithm 5. Algorithm for $(2+\epsilon)\Delta$-edge coloring (large Δ)

---

1. Nodes send their ID to their neighbors.
2. Nodes compute a common (α, δ, ν)-representative family over $[(2+\epsilon)\Delta]$.
3. For $i \in [0..\log^* n]$, for $O(1)$ rounds, each uncolored edge runs MULTITRIALS($2 \uparrow\uparrow i$).
4. For $i \in [0..\log^* n]$, for $O(1)$ rounds, each uncolored edge runs MULTITRIALS$\left(\frac{\epsilon \Delta \cdot \log^{i/\log^* n} n}{2(2+\epsilon)C_c \log n} \right)$.

Algorithm 5 is exactly the same algorithm as Algorithm 2 in which we have swapped the node version of MULTITRIALS for its edge-variant, which makes for a straightforward proof.

Proof (Proof of Theorem 3). The edge-coloring version of MULTITRIALS has the same properties as its vertex-coloring counterpart. More precisely, Lemmas 3 and 4 still hold (with the line graph $L(G)$ instead of G and edges instead of nodes), and we can simply refer to the Proof of Theorem 1 for the details of how all edges get colored w.h.p. by Algorithm 5.

Table 1. Summary of our results. $\log^{(c)}$ is the c-iterated logarithm, c and c' are constants. Note that $(2+\epsilon)\Delta > (2\Delta-1) > (1+\epsilon)\Delta$. Proposition 1 implies similar results for vertex-coloring using less colors on locally sparse graphs for large Δ.

Degree	Tasks	Complexity in CONGEST
$\Delta = \Omega(\log^{1+1/\log^* n} n)$	$(1+\epsilon)\Delta$-vertex coloring	$O(\log^* n)$
	$(1+\epsilon)\Delta$-edge coloring	
$\Delta = O(\log^{1+1/\log^* n} n)$	$(1+\epsilon)\Delta$-vertex coloring	$O(\log^3 \log n)$
	$(2\Delta-1)$-edge coloring	$O(\log^4 \log n)$
$\Delta = \Omega(\sqrt{\log^{1+1/\log^* n} n})$	$(1+\epsilon)\Delta^2$-vertex distance-2 coloring	$O(\log^* n)$
$\Delta = O(\sqrt{\log^{1+1/\log^* n} n})$		$O(\log^4 \log n)$
$\Delta = \Omega(\log^{1+1/c'} n)$	$\Delta \log^{(c)}$-vertex coloring	$O(1)$
	$\Delta \log^{(c)}$-edge coloring	
$\Delta = \Omega(\sqrt{\log^{1+1/c'} n})$	$\Delta^2 \log^{(c)} n$-vertex distance-2 coloring	

5.2 $(2\Delta-1)$-Edge and $(1+\epsilon)\Delta$-Edge Coloring

A few extra steps prior to using our algorithm for $(2+\epsilon)\Delta$-edge coloring suffice to reduce the number of colors to $(2\Delta-1)$ and even $(1+\epsilon)\Delta$ at no cost in complexity, for $\Delta \in \Omega(\log^{1+1/\log^* n} n)$. The $(2\Delta-1)$ result only relies on Propositions 1 and 2 to generate slack, and the $(1+\epsilon)\Delta$ result uses a technique presented in [3] to significantly reduce the live degree of the graph with few colors. We also obtain results for lower values of Δ using shattering and the deterministic algorithm of [9] for vertex coloring.

6   Conclusions

We have presented a new technique, inspired by communication complexity, for speeding up CONGEST algorithms. We have applied it to a range of coloring problems, but it would be interesting to see it used more widely, possibly with extensions.

All our results are summarized in Table 1. For related proofs and details absent here, we refer readers to the full version of the paper [13].

References

1. Barenboim, L., Elkin, M., Pettie, S., Schneider, J.: The locality of distributed symmetry breaking. J. ACM **63**(3), 20:1–20:45 (2016)
2. Chang, Y.J., Li, W., Pettie, S.: Distributed $(\Delta+1)$-coloring via ultrafast graph shattering. SIAM J. Comput. **49**(3), 497–539 (2020)
3. Dubhashi, D., Grable, D.A., Panconesi, A.: Near-optimal, distributed edge colouring via the nibble method. Theoret. Comput. Sci. **203**(2), 225–252 (1998)

4. Dubhashi, D.P., Panconesi, A.: Concentration of Measure for the Analysis of Randomized Algorithms, Cambridge University Press, New York (2009)
5. Dubhashi, D.P., Ranjan, D.: Balls and bins: a study in negative dependence. Rand. Struct. Algorith. **13**(2), 99–124 (1998)
6. Elkin, M., Pettie, S., Su, H.H.: $(2\Delta - 1)$-edge-coloring is much easier than maximal matching in the distributed setting. In: Proceedings of the ACM-SIAM Symposium on Discrete Algorithms (SODA), pp. 355–370 (2015)
7. Fischer, M., Ghaffari, M., Kuhn, F.: Deterministic distributed edge-coloring via hypergraph maximal matching. In: Proceedings of the IEEE Symposium on Foundations of Computer Science (FOCS), pp. 180–191 (2017)
8. Ghaffari, M., Grunau, C., Rozhoň, V.: Improved deterministic network decomposition. In: Proceedings of the ACM-SIAM Symposium on Discrete Algorithms (SODA) (2021)
9. Ghaffari, M., Kuhn, F.: Deterministic distributed vertex coloring: simpler, faster, and without network decomposition. CoRR abs/2011.04511 (2020)
10. Grable, D.A., Panconesi, A.: Nearly optimal distributed edge coloring in $O(\log \log n)$ rounds. Rand. Struc. Algorith. **10**(3), 385–405 (1997)
11. Halldórsson, M.M., Kuhn, F., Maus, Y., Nolin, A.: Coloring fast without learning your neighbors' colors. CoRR abs/2008.04303 (2020), (full version of [12])
12. Halldórsson, M.M., Kuhn, F., Maus, Y., Nolin, A.: Coloring fast without learning your neighbors' colors. In: Proceedings of the International Symposium on Distributed Computing (DISC), pp. 39:1–39:17 (2020)
13. Halldórsson, M.M., Nolin, A.: Superfast coloring in CONGEST via efficient color sampling. CoRR abs/2102.04546 (2021), (full version of this paper)
14. Harris, D.G., Schneider, J., Su, H.H.: Distributed $(\Delta + 1)$-coloring in sub logarithmic rounds. In: Proceeding of the ACM SIGACT Symposium on Theory of Computing (STOC), pp. 465–478 (2016)
15. Håstad, J., Wigderson, A.: The randomized communication complexity of set disjointness. Theor. Compu. **3**(11), 211–219 (2007)
16. Johansson, Ö.: Simple distributed $\Delta + 1$-coloring of graphs. Inf. Process. Lett. **70**(5), 229–232 (1999)
17. Kushilevitz, E., Nisan, N.: Communication complexity. Cambridge University Press, New York (1997)
18. Linial, N.: Locality in distributed graph algorithms. SIAM J. Comput. **21**(1), 193–201 (1992)
19. Newman, I.: Private vs. common random bits in communication complexity. Inf. Process. Lett. **39**(2), 67–71 (1991)
20. Panconesi, A., Srinivasan, A.: Randomized distributed edge coloring via an extension of the Chernoff-Hoeffding bounds. SIAM J. Comput. **26**(2), 350–368 (1997)
21. Rao, A., Yehudayoff, A.: Communication Complexity: and Applications. Cambridge University Press, New York (2020)
22. Reed, B.A.: ω, Δ, and χ. J. Graph Theor. **27**(4), 177–212 (1998)
23. Rozhoň, V., Ghaffari, M.: Polylogarithmic-time deterministic network decomposition and distributed derandomization. In: Proceedings of the ACM SIGACT Symposium on Theory of Computing (STOC), pp. 350–363 (2020)
24. Schneider, J., Wattenhofer, R.: A new technique for distributed symmetry breaking. In: Proceedings of the ACM Symposium Principles of Distributed Computing (PODC), pp. 257–266 (2010)

Concurrency, Consensus and Dynamics

Wait-Free Approximate Agreement
on Graphs

Dan Alistarh[1], Faith Ellen[2], and Joel Rybicki[1(✉)]

[1] IST Austria, Klosterneuburg, Austria
{dan.alistarh,joel.rybicki}@ist.ac.at
[2] University of Toronto, Toronto, Canada
faith@cs.toronto.edu

Abstract. Approximate agreement is one of the few variants of consensus that can be solved in a wait-free manner in asynchronous systems where processes communicate by reading and writing to shared memory. In this work, we consider a natural generalisation of approximate agreement on arbitrary undirected connected graphs. Each process is given a vertex of the graph as input and, if non-faulty, must output a vertex such that

- all the outputs are within distance 1 of one another, and
- each output value lies on a shortest path between two input values.

From prior work, it is known that there is no wait-free algorithm among $n \geq 3$ processes for this problem on any cycle of length $c \geq 4$, by reduction from 2-set agreement (Castañeda et al. 2018).

In this work, we investigate the solvability and complexity of this task on general graphs. We give a new, direct proof of the impossibility of approximate agreement on cycles of length $c \geq 4$, via a generalisation of Sperner's Lemma to convex polygons. We also extend the reduction from 2-set agreement to a larger class of graphs, showing that approximate agreement on these graphs is unsolvable. On the positive side, we present a wait-free algorithm for a class of graphs that properly contains the class of chordal graphs.

Keywords: Approximate agreement · Wait-free · Extension-based proofs

1 Introduction

Understanding the solvability and complexity of coordination tasks is one of the key questions in distributed computing. The difficulty of coordination often

This project has received funding from the European Research Council (ERC) under the European Union's Horizon 2020 research and innovation programme (grant agreement No. 805223 ScaleML) and under the Marie Skłodowska-Curie grant agreement No. 840605 and from the Natural Science and Engineering Research Council of Canada grant RGPIN-2020-04178.

T. Jurdziński and S. Schmid (Eds.): SIROCCO 2021, LNCS 12810, pp. 87–105, 2021.
https://doi.org/10.1007/978-3-030-79527-6_6

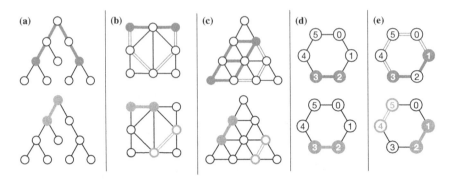

Fig. 1. Examples of approximate agreement with $n = 2$ processes. In the top row, blue nodes are input values for a particular instance. Solid blue edges denote edges on *shortest* paths, and blue double lines denote the additional edges that are also on some *minimal* path connecting input nodes. Solid and non-solid orange nodes denote outputs that satisfy the shortest path and minimal path validity constraints, respectively. (a) Agreement on a tree. All minimal paths are also shortest paths. (b) Agreement on a chordal graph. (c) Agreement on a non-chordal bridged graph. (d)–(e) Instances of 6-cycle agreement. (Color figure online)

arises from *uncertainty*: processes have limited knowledge about each other's inputs, the relative speed of computation and communication between processes can vary, and processes may fail during computation.

Tasks which require perfect agreement, such as *consensus* [36], are typically hard to solve: Fischer, Lynch, and Paterson [25] proved that consensus cannot be reached in asynchronous message-passing systems if even one process may crash. Later, this was extended to shared memory systems where processes communicate using shared registers [13,32].

While perfect agreement is not needed for many applications, it is known that agreeing on at most $k > 1$ different values is still hard: There exists no algorithm for k-set agreement that tolerates k crash faults in the asynchronous setting for $n > k$ processes [9,30,37]. In contrast, approximate agreement – agreeing on values that are sufficiently close to one another – can be considerably easier [8,18,22,23,34,38].

1.1   Graphical Approximate Agreement

In this work, we study solvability and complexity of approximate agreement when the set of input and output values reside on a graph. Consider a distributed system with n processes and let $G = (V, E)$ be a connected graph. The graph G is not necessarily related to the communication topology of the distributed system, but it is assumed to be known by all processes. In approximate agreement on G, each process p_i is given a node $x_i \in V$ as input and has to output a node $y_i \in V$ subject to the following constraints:

- agreement: every two output values are adjacent in G, and
- validity: each output value lies on a shortest path between two input values.

Note that the output values form a clique. Figure 1(a) gives an example of graphical approximate agreement on a tree. Prior work has mostly focused on the cases when G is a path [8,18,22,23,38], a graph whose clique graph is a tree [3], or a chordal graph [35], i.e., a graph that contains no induced cycle of length greater than three.

Approximate Agreement on a Path. The special case when G is a path is well-understood. This case is typically studied in the continuous setting, where the values reside on the real line and the goal is to output values within distance $\varepsilon > 0$ of each other. A discrete version of the problem can be obtained by considering integer-valued inputs and outputs and taking $\varepsilon = 1$. In the shared-memory setting, Attiya, Lynch, and Shavit [8] showed that the step complexity of wait-free solutions using single-writer registers is $\Theta(\log n)$. Using multi-writer registers, Schenk [38] established that the step complexity of obtaining agreement is $O(\log D)$, where D is the maximum distance between two input values.

In asynchronous message-passing systems, Dolev, Lynch, Pinter, Stark and Weihl [18] showed that approximate agreement can be solved with $f < n/5$ Byzantine faults. This was improved by Abraham, Amit, and Dolev [1] to allow $f < n/3$ Byzantine faults, matching a lower bound by Fischer, Lynch, and Merritt [24]. Efficient algorithms tolerating more benign faults in the synchronous and asynchronous message-passing settings were given by Fekete [22,23].

Approximate Agreement Under Minimal Path Validity. Rybicki and Nowak [35] studied approximate agreement on chordal graphs under a different validity condition, where output values have to lie on a *minimal* path between any two input values. A path in G is *minimal* if no two non-consecutive nodes in the path are connected by an edge, i.e. if $v_0, \ldots, v_k$ is a minimal path and $0 \leq i < j-1 \leq k-1$, then $\{v_i, v_j\} \notin E$. This validity condition is weaker, since every shortest path between two nodes is a minimal path, but the converse is not true. Figures 1(b)–(c) illustrate the difference between minimal and shortest paths. If G is chordal, then there exists an algorithm tolerating f *Byzantine* faults in the asynchronous message-passing model for $n > (\omega(G) + 1)f$ processes, where $\omega(G)$ is the size of the largest clique in G [35].

Approximate Gathering on Graphs. Alcántara, Castañeda, Flores-Peñaloza, and Rajsbaum [3] investigated approximate agreement with the following weaker *clique gathering* validity condition: if all inputs values are adjacent, then each output value has to be one of the input values. Their validity condition arises from considering an approximate gathering problem for robots on a graph. This condition is weaker than shortest path and minimal path validity: for example, in the instances given in Figs. 1(b)–(e), any set of outputs that lie on a clique would satisfy clique gathering validity.

They showed that this problem is solvable in a wait-free manner on graphs whose clique graphs are trees and on graphs of radius one (i.e., graphs with a

Table 1. Algorithms for asynchronous approximate agreement on graphs.

Graph class	Validity condition	Fault model	Reference
Clique graph is a tree	Clique gathering	Wait-free	[3]
Radius one		Wait-free	[3]
Chordal	Minimal paths	Byzantine, $n > (\omega + 1)f$	[35]
Paths	Shortest paths	Wait-free	[8,38]
Paths		Byzantine, $n > 3f$	[1]
Nicely bridged or radius one		Wait-free	**This work**
Any		1-resilient	**This work**

dominating set of size one). A clique graph $K(G)$ of G is the graph where vertices of $K(G)$ are the maximal cliques of G and two vertices of $K(G)$ are adjacent if they correspond to cliques with a common vertex. Note that there are chordal graphs whose clique graphs are not trees; for example, see Fig. 1(b).

Approximate Agreement on Cycles. When G is a cycle of length c, approximate agreement under minimal path validity and clique gathering validity are the same problem. We refer to this special case as *c-cycle agreement*. When $c = 3$, the problem is trivial, since each process can output its input.

Castañeda, Rajsbaum, and Roy [12] showed that 2-set agreement reduces to c-cycle agreement, for $c \geq 4$. This implies that there is no algorithm for approximate agreement on c-cycles (under both minimal and shortest path validity) for $c \geq 4$ that tolerates 2 crash faults in in asynchronous shared memory systems consisting of registers. Hence, approximate agreement on cycles of length at least 4 is harder than on paths and chordal graphs.

1.2   Contributions

In this work, we establish additional positive and negative results on the solvability and complexity of graphical approximate agreement.

Positive Results. We present a wait-free asynchronous algorithm for $n \geq 2$ processes that solves approximate agreement on a large subclass of bridged graphs, and on any radius one graph. A *bridged graph* is a graph in which each of its cycles of length at least 4 contains 2 vertices that are connected by a shorter path than either path in the cycle connecting them [20,21]. All chordal graphs are bridged, but the converse is not necessarily true; for an example, see Fig. 1(c).

Our algorithm solves the graphical approximate agreement problem on all chordal graphs and a large class of non-chordal graphs of arbitrary large radius. This includes graphs of radius one and graphs whose clique graphs are trees. Thus, our algorithm handles all graphs handled by previous algorithms, while guaranteeing a stronger validity condition. See Table 1 for a comparison.

In addition, we give a 1-resilient asynchronous algorithm for graphical approximate agreement using only registers on *any* connected graph for $n \geq 2$ processes. Note that, when $n = 2$, this algorithm is wait-free. In the full version [6], we also present an f-resilient synchronous algorithm for the fully-connected message-passing model with $n > f$ processes. The algorithm solves approximate agreement on any connected graph G in $\lfloor f/2 \rfloor + \lceil \log_2 \text{diam}(G) \rceil + 1$ rounds, where $\text{diam}(G)$ is the diameter of G.

Negative Results. We provide a new, direct proof of the impossibility of approximate agreement on cycles of length $c \geq 4$. It uses a generalisation of Sperner's Lemma to convex polygons. It follows from known simulation techniques [11,27] that there is no 2-resilient asynchronous algorithm using registers and any f-resilient synchronous algorithm requires at least $\lfloor f/2 \rfloor + 1$ rounds for $n > f$ processes. Furthermore, we present a simplified version of the existing reduction from k-set agreement to cycle agreement and use it to extend the impossibility of graphical approximate agreement to a larger class of graphs.

Extension-Based Proofs. In the full version [6], we show that extension-based proofs [4], such as valency arguments, are not powerful enough to show the impossibility of 4-cycle agreement in the non-uniform iterated snapshot model. Note that this result does not follow from the fact that there are no extension-based proofs of the impossibility of 2-set agreement in the non-uniform iterated snapshot model [5], even though there is a reduction from 2-set agreement to c-cycle agreement for $c \geq 4$.

2 Related Work

Multidimensional Approximate Agreement. Mendes, Herlihy, Vaidya and Garg [33] generalised approximate agreement to the multidimensional setting, where the input values are points in m-dimensional Euclidean space $\mathbb{R}^m$, for $m > 0$. In the multidimensional approximate agreement problem, the output values should be within distance $\varepsilon > 0$ of one another and be contained in the convex hull of the input values of the non-faulty processes. When $m = 1$, this is approximate agreement on a line. Multidimensional approximate agreement on $\mathbb{R}^m$ is solvable with f Byzantine faults in the asynchronous completely-connected message-passing setting if and only if $n > (m+2)f$ [33]. In the synchronous setting, the problem is solvable if and only if $n > \max\{3f, (m+1)f\}$. Recently, Függer and Nowak [26] established asymptotically tight convergence rates for multidimensional approximate agreement by removing the dependence on the dimension m of the space.

Unlike approximate agreement on the real line, it is not straightforward to obtain a discrete version of multidimensional approximate agreement when $m \geq 2$. For example, in the two-dimensional integer lattice $\mathbb{Z}^2 \subseteq \mathbb{R}^2$, one can find a pair of points arbitrarily far apart such that they are the only integral points in their convex hull. In this case, solving approximate agreement is the same as solving consensus. More generally, Herlihy and Shavit [29] showed that approximate agreement in a multidimensional setting with Euclidean convex hulls cannot be solved in a wait-free manner when processes communicate using registers if the space of values has holes of size ε. Since the Euclidean convex hull of two antipodal points around the hole consists of only the two points, outputting values within distance ε of one another in this convex hull would amount to solving consensus.

Barycentric agreement [28] is a multidimensional problem that can be solved wait-free manner: processes are given inputs that lie on a simplex σ of a simplicial complex and must output values that are on a simplex of the barycentric subdivision of σ. This problem can be solved, for example, using m-dimensional approximate agreement [34].

Approximate Robot Gathering in Graphs. Robot gathering problems have been studied in the continuous setting [2,15], but we focus on the discrete setting, where n robots reside on nodes in a graph G. The inputs represent the initial positions of the robots, the outputs represent the final positions of the robots, and the goal is that the outputs are close to one another.

Exact gathering of asynchronous robots, where the goal is to get all robots to the same vertex, has been studied extensively in various models. See a recent survey of Cicerone, Di Stefano, and Navarra [14]. Castañeda, Rajsbaum, and Roy [12] and Alcántara, Castañeda, Flores-Peñaloza, and Rajsbaum [3] studied several variants of approximate gathering of asynchronous robots moving on a graph that communicate via snapshots. In *edge gathering* [3, Definition 4], agreement is satisfied if all outputs belong to the same edge. Validity requires that (i) if all inputs values are the same, then the output values are the same as the input values, and (ii) if all inputs belong to the same edge, then the output values also belong to this edge. The *1-gathering* task [3, Definition 5] is a relaxation of edge gathering, where agreement is satisfied if the output values form a clique, and validity requires that the output values must be a subset of the input values if the input values form a clique.

Note that neither edge gathering or 1-gathering solve graphical approximate agreement, as the validity constraint of graphical approximate agreement is stronger: each output value has to lie on some shortest path between two input values. The difference is best illustrated by the simple case of a path, where approximate agreement requires that the outputs always lie between the minimal and maximal input values, while edge gathering and 1-gathering do not have this requirement.

Edge gathering is solvable if and only if G is a tree [3]. On cliques, edge gathering is the same as the 2-set agreement task, whereas 1-gathering and graphical approximate agreement are trivial. For 1-gathering, Alcántara et al. [3] gave an algorithm for trees, which can also be used to solve 1-gathering on any graph whose clique graph is a tree.

When the graph G is a cycle of length $c \geq 4$, edge gathering and 1-gathering are the same as c-cycle agreement. Castañeda et al. [12] and Alcántara et al. [3] gave a clever reduction showing that this problem is as hard as 2-set agreement for $n = 3$ processes. In Sect. 4, we give a direct proof of this result. Moreover, in Sect. 6, we simplify and adapt the reduction from 2-set agreement to prove that wait-free graphical approximate agreement is impossible on a much larger class of graphs.

3 Models

We consider distributed systems with n processes, where at most f processes may fail by crashing. In particular, we focus on the setting where processes communicate using atomic snapshot objects, which can be implemented from registers. We also consider the synchronous message-passing model under fully-connected communication topologies.

Asynchronous Shared Memory Models. In the *f-resilient non-uniform iterated snapshot* (f-NIS) model, n processes, $p_0, \ldots, p_{n-1}$, communicate using an infinite sequence, $S_1, S_2, \ldots$, of shared *single-writer atomic snapshot* objects. A *single-writer atomic snapshot* object has n components, each of which has initial value $-$. It supports two atomic operations, update and scan. An update(x) by process p_i changes the value of component i to $x \neq -$. A scan returns the value of each component.

Each process performs an update on a snapshot object, starting with S_1, and then repeatedly performs scans of this object until at most f components have value $-$. (Note that, if $f = n - 1$, then one scan of the snapshot object suffices, since the process has already performed an update on its own component.) Next, it updates its state and applies a function, Δ, to its new state to determine whether it should output a value. If the value of Δ is not $\perp$, then p_i outputs this value and terminates. If the value of Δ is $\perp$, then, at its next step, it updates the next snapshot object in the sequence with a value determined by its new state.

Note that it suffices to consider schedules where all accesses to each snapshot object occur before any accesses to the next snapshot object in the sequence. This is because if process p_j performs its update of a particular snapshot object after process p_i performs its scans to this object, then it is indistinguishable to both processes how much later this occurs.

A *configuration* consists of the contents of each shared object and the state of each process. From any configuration C, a *scheduler* decides the order in which the processes take steps. The sequence of processes selected by the scheduler is called a *schedule from* C. Given a finite schedule α from C, we use $C\alpha$ to denote the resulting configuration. An algorithm is *wait-free* if there is no infinite schedule from any initial configuration.

The *non-uniform iterated immediate snapshot* (NIIS) model, introduced by Hoest and Shavit [31], is like a full-information $(n - 1)$-NIS model, except that the scheduler is restricted in how it can schedule processes: It repeatedly selects a set of processes that are all poised to perform updates on the same snapshot object. Each of the processes in the set performs its update. Then, each of these processes performs one scan of this snapshot object. Note that, since each process performs an update to a snapshot object before performing a scan, the scan will return a vector containing at most $n - 1$ components with value $-$. Initially, the state of process p_i consists of its identifier, i, and its input. When it performs an update, the value it uses is its current state. After performing a scan, its new state consists of i and the result of the scan.

Each initial configuration in the NIIS model or f-NIS model corresponds to a *simplex* (or an n-vertex clique) containing one vertex for each process, which specifies its input. The collection of all such simplexes is called the *input complex* (or *input graph*). Likewise, for any algorithm, each reachable terminal configuration corresponds to a simplex (or n-vertex clique) containing one vertex for each process, which specifies its state, including the value it outputs. The collection of all such simplexes (or n-vertex cliques) is called the *protocol complex* (or *protocol graph*). We may assume that the sets of possible states of different processes are disjoint. There is an edge between two vertices if they represent the states of different processes and there is a reachable configuration containing both these states.

A nice feature of the NIIS model is that the protocol complex of any wait-free algorithm can be obtained from the input complex by performing a finite number of *non-uniform chromatic subdivisions* of simplexes. In the special case when there are $n = 3$ processes, each simplex is a triangle and the non-uniform chromatic subdivision of a simplex is a triangulation of the simplex. Likewise, in the $(n - 1)$-NIS model, Alistarh, Aspnes, Ellen, Gelashvili, and Zhu [5] have shown that the protocol graph of any wait-free, full-information algorithm can be obtained from the input graph by performing a finite number of *subdivisions* of n-vertex cliques. For deterministic, wait-free computation, both the NIIS model and the $(n - 1)$-NIS model are equivalent to the asynchronous shared memory model in which processes communicate using shared registers (which support only read and write) [10].

The Synchronous Message-Passing Model. In the synchronous message-passing model, there is no uncertainty regarding the relative speeds of processes. A computation is divided into synchronous rounds. In each round, each process sends its entire state to every other process. Any message sent by a non-faulty process in round r is guaranteed to arrive at its destination before the end of round r. A synchronous algorithm is an f-resilient solution to a task using T rounds if all non-crashed processes decide on an output value by the end of round T in any execution with at most f crashes.

4 Impossibility of Asynchronous Wait-Free Cycle Agreement

In this section, we give a proof of the following result.

Theorem 1. *For $c \geq 4$, there is no wait-free algorithm for the c-cycle agreement problem among $n \geq 3$ processes in the NIIS model.*

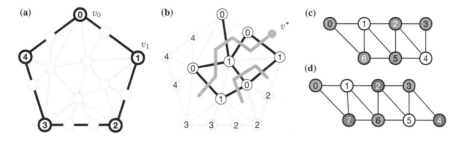

Fig. 2. (a) A triangulation T of a pentagon. (b) A Sperner labelling of T with the edges of the graph G' superimposed in orange. (c) The subcomplex $\mathbb{H}$ for $c = 7$. (d) The subcomplex $\mathbb{H}$ for $c = 8$. (Color figure online)

Our proof relies on a slight generalisation of Sperner's lemma to convex polygons, originally shown by Atanassov [7] and generalised to convex polytopes of any dimension by de Loera, Peterson, and Su [16]. However, for us, a special case in the two-dimensional setting suffices.

Let H be a polygon with c vertices and let T be a triangulation of H. A *Sperner labelling* of T is a function from the vertices of T to the set $\{0, \ldots, c - 1\}$ such that each vertex of H gets a different label and each vertex on the boundary of T between two vertices of H gets the same label as one of those two vertices. Please see Figs. 2(a) and (b).

Lemma 1. *Let H be a convex polygon with c vertices. Any Sperner labelling of a triangulation of H has a triangle whose vertices have three different labels.*

Proof. Let T be a triangulation of H and consider any Sperner labelling of T. Without loss of generality, suppose there are two adjacent vertices v_0 and v_1 of H labelled with 0 and 1, respectively. Consider the graph $G' = (V' \cup \{v^*\}, E')$, where V' is the set of triangles of T. There is an edge in E' between triangles τ and τ' if and only if they have exactly two vertices in common, one of which is labelled 0 and the other of which is labelled 1. There is an edge in E' between v^* and triangle τ if and only if two of the vertices of τ lie on the boundary of T between v_0 and v_1 and they have different labels. This is illustrated in Fig. 2(b).

Each of the nodes of T on the boundary between v_0 and v_1 is labelled by 0 or 1. The labels of the nodes on this path change an odd number of times, since v_0 and v_1 have different labels. Thus, there are an odd number of edges on the boundary whose endpoints are labelled 0 and 1, so v^* has odd degree. If a triangle has two nodes labelled 0 and one node labelled 1 or vice versa, it has degree 2 in G'. If a triangle has one node labelled 0, one node labelled 1, and one node with some other label, it has degree 1 in G'. Otherwise, it has degree 0 in G'.

The handshaking lemma [19] says that any finite graph contains an even number of nodes with odd degree. Since v^* has odd degree, there exists a triangle $\tau \in V$ with odd degree. The vertices of this triangle have three different labels.

Proof of Theorem 1. Let $\mathbb{H}$ denote the part of the input complex for c-cycle agreement among 3 processes p_0, p_1, and p_2, consisting of the simplexes corresponding to the following $c - 2$ input configurations:

- p_0 has input $3a$, p_1 has input $3a + 1$, and p_2 has input $c - 3a - 1$, for $0 \leq a \leq \lfloor (c - 3)/6 \rfloor$.
- p_1 has input $3a + 1$, p_2 has input $c - 3a - 1$, and p_0 has input $c - 3a - 2$, for $0 \leq a \leq \lfloor (c - 4)/6 \rfloor$.
- p_1 has input $3a + 1$, p_2 has input $3a + 2$, and p_0 has input $c - 3a - 2$, for $0 \leq a \leq \lfloor (c - 5)/6 \rfloor$.
- p_2 has input $3a + 2$, p_0 has input $c - 3a - 2$, and p_1 has input $c - 3a - 3$, for $0 \leq a \leq \lfloor (c - 6)/6 \rfloor$.
- p_2 has input $3a + 2$, p_0 has input $3a + 3$, and p_1 has input $c - 3a - 3$, for $0 \leq a \leq \lfloor (c - 7)/6 \rfloor$.
- p_0 has input $3a + 3$, p_1 has input $c - 3a - 3$, and p_2 has input $c - 3a - 4$, for $0 \leq a \leq \lfloor (c - 8)/6 \rfloor$.

Note that $\mathbb{H}$ contains c vertices, one for each possible input value. The cases $c = 7$ and $c = 8$ are illustrated in Figs. 2(c) and (d). The processes p_0, p_1, and p_2 are denoted by the colours red, white, and blue, respectively. The border of $\mathbb{H}$ is a polygon H with c vertices.

Consider any wait-free algorithm for 3 processes in the NIIS model. Let $\mathbb{S}$ denote its protocol complex. It is finite, since the algorithm is wait-free. Let $\mathbb{T}$ denote the subcomplex of $\mathbb{S}$ consisting of all terminal configurations reachable from configurations in $\mathbb{H}$, where each vertex is labelled with the output value it contains. The vertices and edges of $\mathbb{T}$ form a triangulation T of H. For each input value $x \in \{0, \ldots, c - 1\}$, there is a vertex v_x on the boundary of $\mathbb{T}$ that corresponds to the solo execution by some process p_i with input x. If it is not labelled by the value x, then the algorithm does not solve c-cycle agreement. The edges on the border of $\mathbb{T}$ between v_x and $v_{x'}$, where $x' = (x + 1) \bmod c$, correspond to executions by only two processes, one with input x and the other with input x'. If the endpoints of all such edges are not labelled by x or x', the algorithm does not solve c-cycle agreement. Label each vertex of T with the label of the corresponding vertex in $\mathbb{T}$. If the algorithm is correct, then this is a Sperner labelling. By Lemma 1, the triangulation T contains a triangle whose vertices have three different labels. The corresponding configuration is the result of an execution in which the three processes output different values, so the algorithm cannot be solving c-cycle agreement among three processes.

Since all but three processes can crash before taking any steps, any algorithm that solves c-cycle agreement among $n \geq 3$ processes is also an algorithm that solves c-cycle agreement among 3 processes. Therefore no such algorithm exists. $\qed$

5   Impossibility of Extension-Based Proofs

Extension-based proofs were introduced by Alistarh, Aspnes, Ellen, Gelashvili and Zhu [4] to model inductive impossibility arguments, such as the valency-based impossibility of consensus in asynchronous message-passing systems by

Fisher, Lynch and Paterson [25]. These are in contrast to the combinatorial arguments used to show the impossibility of set agreement [9,30,37]. It is known that extension-based proofs cannot be used to prove the impossibility of $(n-1)$-set agreement among $n > 2$ processes in the NIIS model [4] or in the $(n-1)$-NIS model [5].

In the full version of the paper [6], we show that extension-based proofs cannot be used to prove Theorem 1 in the $(n-1)$-NIS model. This is the first application of the extension-based proof framework to a task other than set agreement. We emphasize that this result does not follow directly via reduction from the result for k-set agreement. The main source of novelty in our argument is in carefully extending their adversarial algorithm to the c-cycle agreement task.

Theorem 2. *There is no extension-based proof of the impossibility of a wait-free algorithm solving 4-cycle agreement for $n \geq 3$ processes in the $(n-1)$-NIS model.*

6   Impossibility Results via Reductions

In this section, we show that the impossibility of wait-free cycle agreement implies the impossibility of 2-resilient cycle agreement in the asynchronous shared memory model (where processes communicate by reading from and writing to registers) and a lower bound on the round complexity of cycle agreement in the synchronous message passing model. Finally, we show that approximate agreement is impossible on graphs that admit a certain labelling of the vertices.

There Exists no 2-Resilient Asynchronous Algorithm. A task is *colourless* if the input of any process may be the input of any other process, the output of any process may be the output of any other process, and the specifications of valid outputs only depend on the set of inputs of the processes. Cycle agreement is an example of a colourless task. The BG simulation technique [11] shows that the impossibility of wait-free algorithms for a colourless task for $n \geq 3$ processes implies the impossibility of 2-resilient algorithms for that task.

Theorem 3. *[11] If there exists a k-resilient asynchronous algorithm for $n > k$ processes that solves a colourless task, then there is a wait-free asynchronous algorithm for $(k+1)$ processes that solves the task.*

Together with Theorem 1, the BG simulation immediately implies that there is no 2-resilient asynchronous algorithm for the cycle agreement problem.

Corollary 1. *For any $n \geq 3$ and $c \geq 4$, there is no 2-resilient asynchronous algorithm that solves c-cycle agreement.*

Time Lower Bounds for Synchronous Algorithms. We can now lift the impossibility results to time lower bounds for the synchronous model using the round-by-round simulation by Gafni [27], who showed the following.

Theorem 4. *[27] Let $0 < k < f < n$ be such that $n - k - f > 0$. Fix $T \leq f/k$. Suppose there exists a synchronous f-resilient algorithm for n nodes that solves a colourless task in T rounds. Then there exists a k-resilient asynchronous algorithm that solves the task.*

Applying Corollary 1 and Theorem 4, we obtain a time lower bound for synchronous algorithms.

Corollary 2. *For any $n > f \geq 0$, any f-resilient synchronous message-passing algorithm for c-cycle agreement requires at least $\lfloor f/2 \rfloor + 1$ rounds.*

Graphs on Which Approximate Agreement is Impossible. We now show that approximate agreement is hard on graphs that admit a certain labelling of its vertices. We do so by a reduction from 2-set agreement among $n \geq 3$ processes. In this problem, each process has an input value in $\{0, 1, 2\}$ and, if it does not crash, it must output one of the inputs such that at most two different values are output.

A labelling $\ell \colon V \to \{0, 1, 2\}$ of the vertices of a graph $G = (V, E)$ is a *lower bound labelling* if the following conditions hold:

1. G contains no triangle with three different labels and
2. G contains a cycle C in which exactly one vertex has label 1 and its two neighbours in C have labels 0 and 2.

It is easy to check that any cycle of length $c \geq 4$ admits a lower bound labelling: pick three consecutive vertices, label them with $0, 1, 2$, and label all other vertices with 2. A wheel graph, which consists of a cycle and one central vertex that is a neighbour of all vertices in the cycle, does not admit a lower bound labelling. On the other hand, if one edge adjacent to the central vertex is removed, the resulting graph does admit a lower bound labelling: label the other endpoint of the removed edge with 1, label one of its neighbours with 0, and label all other vertices with 2.

Theorem 5. *Suppose G is a graph that admits a lower bound labelling. Then there is no wait-free algorithm among $n \geq 3$ processes that solves graphical approximate agreement on G.*

Proof. Consider a lower bound labelling ℓ of G. Let C be a cycle in G that contains exactly one vertex, v_1, with label 1, a neighbour v_0 of v_1 with label 0, and a neighbour v_2 of v_1 with label 2. Let A be a wait-free approximate agreement algorithm on the path $C \setminus \{v_1\}$.

To obtain a contradiction, suppose there is a wait-free algorithm B for graphical approximate agreement on G. The following wait-free algorithm solves 2-set agreement:

- Processes with input value $x \in \{0, 2\}$ run the approximate agreement algorithm A on the path $C \setminus \{v_1\}$ using v_x as input. The vertex each of these processes outputs in A is used as its input for algorithm B.
- Processes with input value 1 use v_1 as their input for algorithm B.
- Each process p_i outputs the label $\ell(y_i)$ of the vertex y_i it outputs in B.

By the agreement property of graphical approximate agreement, the values output in B lie on a clique. The first property of a lower bound labelling implies that the nodes in this clique have at most two distinct labels. Thus, at most two different values are output by the processes.

If there are three distinct input values, then validity is immediately satisfied. If all input values are the same, then all output values are this input value, since this is true for algorithms A and B. It remains to consider instances of set agreement with exactly two input values. First, suppose the inputs for set agreement are in $\{0, 1\}$. All processes with input 0 output v_0 in algorithm A, since v_0 is the only value input to A. Thus, each process uses either v_0 or v_1 as its input to algorithm B. As v_0 and v_1 are adjacent in G, each process outputs one of these two values in B, by validity of graphical approximate agreement. Hence, each process outputs a value in $\{\ell(v_0), \ell(v_1)\} = \{0, 1\}$ for set agreement, satisfying validity. The case $\{1, 2\}$ is symmetric.

Now, suppose that the inputs for set agreement are in $\{0, 2\}$. Then each process uses either v_0 or v_1 as its input to algorithm A. Their outputs in A and, hence their inputs to algorithm B, all lie on some edge $\{u, v\}$ on the path $C \setminus \{v_1\}$. By validity of graphical approximate agreement, each process outputs either u or v in B. From the second property of a lower bound labelling, all values in $C \setminus \{v_1\}$ are labelled with either 0 or 2. Thus, each process outputs 0 or 2 for set agreement, satisfying validity.

7   Upper Bounds for Asynchronous Systems

We conclude with upper bounds for graphical approximate agreement: a 1-resilient algorithm on general graphs and a wait-free algorithm on any nicely bridged graph for $n \geq 2$ processes.

Let $G = (V, E)$ be a connected graph. For any set $U \subseteq V$, the subgraph of G induced by U is the graph $G[U] = (U, F)$, where $F = \{e \in E : e \subseteq U\}$. The distance between two vertices u and v in G is denoted by $d(u, v)$. The *eccentricity* $\epsilon(v)$ of a node $v \in V$ is $\max\{d(u, v) : u \in V\}$. The *diameter* of G is $\mathrm{diam}(G) = \max\{\epsilon(v) : v \in V\}$ and the *radius* $\mathrm{rad}(G)$ of G is $\min\{\epsilon(v) : v \in V\}$. For any nonempty set $U \subseteq V$, let $D(U) = \max\{d(u, v) : u, v \in U\}$. In particular, $\mathrm{diam}(G) = D(V)$.

7.1   A 1-Resilient Algorithm for General Graphs

The intuitive idea for solving approximate agreement on G, assuming at most one process crashes, is simple: First use 2-set agreement to reduce the number of input values to at most 2. Then run approximate agreement on a path whose endpoints are these input values, which takes $\lceil \log_2 \text{diam}(G) \rceil$ steps.

There is an easy 1-resilient algorithm for 2-set agreement. However, the second step is not immediate, as there may be many paths of G on which the approximate agreement algorithm could be run. However, since all processes know the graph G, we can avoid this difficulty by fixing in advance a shortest path between every pair of vertices. The rest of this section is dedicated to the following result.

Theorem 6. *Let $G = (V, E)$ be a connected graph. Then for all $n \geq 2$, there exists a 1-resilient algorithm which solves approximate agreement on G.*

Solving 2-Set Agreement. Fix a total order on V. For any nonempty subset $X \subseteq V$, let $\min(X)$ be the smallest element of X under this order. Let $x_i(0) \in V$ be the input of process p_i and let $T = \lceil \log_2 \text{diam}(G) \rceil$. We will use a single-writer atomic snapshot object, S_0, whose components are initialised with the special value $-$. Each process p_i:

- performs **update** on component i of the snapshot object S_0, setting it to the value $x_i(0)$,
- repeatedly performs **scan** on the snapshot object S_0 until at least $n - 1$ components have values other than $-$,
- lets $X_i(0)$ be the *set* of vertices returned by its last **scan**, and
- lets $x_i(1) = \min(X_i(0))$.

Approximate Agreement on a Path. For any two vertices $u, v \in V$, fix a shortest path between u and v in G and let $g(u, v)$ be a fixed node in the center of this path. Then $d(u, g(u, v)), d(v, g(u, v)) \leq \lceil d(u, v)/2 \rceil$. For any nonempty set $X \subseteq V$ of size at most two, define $\psi(X) = u$ if $X = \{u\}$ and $\psi(X) = g(u, v)$ if $X = \{u, v\}$. We will use a sequence $S_1, \ldots, S_T$ of single-writer atomic snapshot objects, whose components are initialised with the special value $-$. For $1 \leq t \leq T$, each process p_i:

- performs **update** on component i of the snapshot object S_t, setting it to the vertex $x_i(t)$,
- repeatedly performs **scan** on the snapshot object S_t until at least $n - 1$ components have values other than $-$,
- lets $X_i(t)$ be the *set* of vertices returned by its last **scan**, and
- lets $x_i(t + 1) = \psi(X_i(t))$.

The output of process p_i is the value $x_i(T + 1)$.

Correctness. Let $0 \leq t \leq T$. If process p_i crashes before computing $X_i(t)$, we define $X_i(t)$ to be the empty set. Observe that each process p_i first performs **update** on S_t with $x_i(t)$ before performing **scan** on S_t. Thus, if p_i computes $X_i(t)$, then $X_i(t)$ is nonempty.

Each component of S_t is **updated** at most once. Since **scan** is an atomic operation, the set of vertices returned in a **scan** is a subset of the set of vertices returned in any later scan. Therefore, $X_i(t) \subseteq X_j(t)$ or $X_j(t) \subseteq X_i(t)$ for any i and j. Each process continues performing scan until it crashes or S_t contains at most one $-$. Thus $\{X_j(t) : 0 \leq j \leq n-1\}$ contains at most two nonempty sets. Since $x_j(t+1)$ is a function of $X_j(t)$, it follows that $\{x_j(t+1) : X_j(t) \neq \emptyset\}$ contains at most two different vertices. These are the only values that are used to update components of S_{t+1}, so $X_i(t+1) \subseteq \{x_j(t+1) : X_j(t) \neq \emptyset\}$. Hence, $|X_i(t+1)| \leq 2$ and, if $X_i(t+1) \neq \emptyset$, then $x_i(t+2) = \psi(X_i(t+1))$ is defined.

Let $X(t) = \bigcup\{X_i(t) : 0 \leq i < n\}$. We use $X(T+1)$ to denote the set of output values. Note that $X(t) \subseteq V$ for $0 \leq t \leq T+1$ and $X(0)$ is a subset of the input values. If $t \geq 1$, then $X(t) \subseteq \{x_j(t) : X_j(t-1) \neq \emptyset\}$, so $|X(t)| \leq 2$.

Lemma 2. *Let* $1 \leq t \leq T$. *Then* $D(X(t+1)) \leq \lceil D(X(t))/2 \rceil$.

Proof. If $X_i(t) = X(t)$ for every nonempty set $X_i(t)$, then $x_i(t+1) = \psi(X(t))$. Hence $X(t+1)$ will contain only one vertex and $D(X(t+1)) = 0$. Otherwise, $X_i(t)$ is a nonempty, proper subset of $X(t)$ for some $0 \leq i < n$. Recall that $|X(t)| \leq 2$, so $X_i(t) = \{u\}$ and $X(t) = \{u, v\}$ for some vertices $u \neq v$. Since $X_j(t) \subseteq X_i(t)$ or $X_i(t) \subseteq X_j(t)$ for all $0 \leq j < n$, it follows that every nonempty set $X_j(t)$ is either equal to $\{u\}$ or $\{u, v\}$ and $x_j(t+1)$ is either equal to $\psi(\{u\}) = u$ or $\psi(\{u, v\}) = g(u, v)$. By definition of g, we have that $d(u, g(u, v)) \leq \lceil d(u, v)/2 \rceil$. Since $X(t+1) \subseteq \{u, g(u, v)\}$, it follows that $D(X(t+1)) \leq \lceil D(X(t))/2 \rceil$. $\qquad\qquad\blacksquare$

Proof of Theorem 6. We verify that the agreement and validity properties of graphical approximate agreement are satisfied. We proceed by induction to show that vertices in $X(t+1)$ lie on some shortest path between the values in $X(t)$ for all $1 \leq t \leq T$. The case $t = 1$ is true because $X(1) \subseteq X(0)$. Suppose the claim holds for some $X(t)$ such that $1 \leq t \leq T$. By definition of g and ψ, all values in $X(t+1)$ lie on some shortest path between the values in $X(t)$. Thus, validity is satisfied. Since $X(1) \subseteq V$, $D(X(1)) \leq \mathrm{diam}(G)$. As $T = \lceil \log_2 \mathrm{diam}(G) \rceil$, Lemma 2 implies that the distance $d(u, v)$ between any two output values $u, v \in X(T+1)$ is $\max\{d(u, v) : u, v \in X(T+1)\} = D(X(T+1)) \leq \lceil \mathrm{diam}(G)/2^T \rceil \leq 1$.

The Synchronous Case. In the full version of the paper [6], we extend the same algorithmic idea to the synchronous message-passing setting under crash faults.

Theorem 7. *Let* G *be a connected graph. For any* $0 \leq f < n$, *there exists an* f-*resilient synchronous message-passing algorithm for* n *processes that solves approximate agreement on* G *in* $\lfloor f/2 \rfloor + \lceil \log_2 \mathrm{diam}(G) \rceil + 1$ *rounds.*

7.2   A Wait-Free Asynchronous Algorithm for Nicely Bridged Graphs

The *center* of G is the set $\{v \in V : \epsilon(v) = \mathrm{rad}(G)\}$ of nodes with minimum eccentricity in G. A graph G is k-*self-centered* if every vertex has eccentricity k. This means that every vertex is in the center of G and $\mathrm{diam}(G) = \mathrm{rad}(G) = k$. A graph is *chordal* if it does not contain any induced cycles of length greater than three. The *3-sun*, also known as the Hajós graph, is obtained from a triangle $\{u, v, w\}$ by subdividing each of its edges and connecting the resulting three vertices $\{x, y, z\}$ to be a clique. This graph is 2-self-centered and chordal.

A set $K \subseteq V$ of nodes is (shortest path) *convex* if, for any $u, v \in K$, all nodes on all shortest paths between u and v are contained in K. For any $U \subseteq V$, the *convex hull* $\langle U \rangle$ of U is the smallest convex superset of U. If $A \subseteq B$, then $\langle A \rangle \subseteq \langle B \rangle$. A vertex v is *simplicial* in the graph G if the neighbours of v in G form a clique.

Bridged and Nicely Bridged Graphs. A subgraph H of G is *isometric* if the distances between any two vertices of H are the same in H and G. A graph is *bridged* if it contains no isometric cycles of length greater than three [20]. All chordal graphs are bridged, but a bridged graph may contain induced cycles of length greater than five. We say that $G = (V, E)$ is *nicely bridged* if any 2-self-centered subgraph $H = G[S]$, induced by a convex set $S \subseteq V$, is chordal.

We now list some useful properties of bridged graphs. Farber proved the following result about the radius and diameter of bridged graphs [20].

Lemma 3. *For any bridged graph G, we have $3 \cdot \mathrm{rad}(G) \leq 2 \cdot \mathrm{diam}(G) + 2$. If G is bridged and does not contain an induced 3-sun as a subgraph, then $2 \cdot \mathrm{rad}(G) \leq \mathrm{diam}(G) + 1$ holds.*

We use the following fact due to Farber and Jamison [21, Theorem 6.5].

Lemma 4. *If $G = (V, E)$ is bridged, then $D(\langle U \rangle) = D(U)$ for any $U \subseteq V$.*

The previous two lemmas can be used to show the following simple result.

Lemma 5. *Suppose G is a bridged graph and $U \subseteq V$ is a nonempty set. Then the induced subgraph $H = G[\langle U \rangle]$ is bridged and satisfies $\mathrm{diam}(H) = D(\langle U \rangle)$.*

The Algorithm. For any nonempty set of vertices $X \subseteq V$, we choose a vertex $\psi(X)$ from the subgraph $H = G[\langle X \rangle]$ induced by $\langle X \rangle$ as follows: If the center of H contains a vertex that is non-simplicial in H, then let $\psi(X)$ be any such vertex. Otherwise, let $\psi(X)$ be any vertex in the center of H. By definition, $\psi(X)$ has minimum eccentricity in H. Since $\psi(X)$ is a vertex in the convex hull of X, it is on some shortest path between two vertices in X.

Let $x_i(0)$ be the input of process p_i and let $T^* = \lceil \log_{3/2} \mathrm{diam}(G) \rceil + 1$. The processes communicate using a sequence $S_0, \ldots, S_T$ of single-writer snapshot objects, where $T = \max\{|V|, T^*\}$. In each iteration $0 \leq t \leq T$, each process p_i

- performs update on component i of the snapshot object S_t, setting it to $x_i(t)$,
- performs scan on the snapshot object S_t,
- defines $X_i(t)$ be the *set* of vertices returned by its scan, and
- sets $x_i(t+1) = \psi(X_i(t))$.

Once p_i has computed $x_i(T+1)$, the process outputs this vertex and terminates.

Sketch of Correctness. As before, if p_i crashes before computing the set $X_i(t)$, we define $X_i(t)$ to be the empty set. We let $X(t) = \bigcup \{X_i(t) : 0 \leq i < n\}$ and use $X(T+1)$ to denote the set of output vertices. We need to show that all the vertices in $X(T+1)$ are contained in a clique. The main challenge is showing that the vertices in $X(t)$ get closer together as t increases. First, we can show using, Lemmas 3–5 that, for $0 \leq t \leq T^*$, if the set of values $X(t)$ does not form a clique, then the diameter of $X(t+1)$ is roughly two thirds the diameter of $X(t)$.

Lemma 6. *Let $0 \leq t \leq T^*$. Then $D(X(t+1)) \leq \frac{2}{3}(D(X(t)) + 1)$.*

We can apply Lemma 6 repeatedly to ensure that we quickly end up in a subgraph with diameter at most two.

Lemma 7. *If $G[\langle X(t) \rangle]$ has radius one, then $X(t+1)$ is a clique.*

Thus, after reaching a subgraph of radius 1, one more iteration suffices. Moreover, the algorithm solves the problem on any (possibly non-bridged) graph of radius 1. If the graph does not contain an induced 3-sun, then the algorithm converges in $T^* + 1$ iterations. However, these two lemmas do not guarantee progress when the convex hull of $X(t)$ has diameter and radius 2.

In bridged graphs, the algorithm converges either to a clique or to a set whose convex hull induces a 2-self-centered subgraph. If G is nicely bridged, i.e., any 2-self-centered convex subgraph is chordal, our algorithm makes progress, because every chordal graph has a simplicial vertex [17]. However, our approach does not work for all bridged graphs, as there are non-chordal 2-self-centered bridged graphs without any simplicial vertices. The details of the proof of the following theorem appear in the full version of this paper [6].

Theorem 8. *For any nicely bridged connected graph G, there is a wait-free algorithm for $n \geq 2$ processes that solves graphical approximate agreement on G.*

References

1. Abraham, I., Amit, Y., Dolev, D.: Optimal resilience asynchronous approximate agreement. In: Higashino, T. (ed.) OPODIS 2004. LNCS, vol. 3544, pp. 229–239. Springer, Heidelberg (2005). https://doi.org/10.1007/11516798_17
2. Agmon, N., Peleg, D.: Fault-tolerant gathering algorithms for autonomous mobile robots. SIAM J. Comput. **36**(1), 56–82 (2006)
3. Alcántara, M., Castañeda, A., Flores-Peñaloza, D., Rajsbaum, S.: The topology of look-compute-move robot wait-free algorithms with hard termination. Distrib. Comput. **32**(3), 235–255 (2018). https://doi.org/10.1007/s00446-018-0345-3
4. Alistarh, D., Aspnes, J., Ellen, F., Gelashvili, R., Zhu, L.: Why extension-based proofs fail. In: Proceedings of the 51st Symposium on Theory of Computing (STOC 2019). ACM (2019)
5. Alistarh, D., Aspnes, J., Ellen, F., Gelashvili, R., Zhu, L.: Brief announcement: why extension-based proofs fail. In: Proceedings of the 39th Symposium on Principles of Distributed Computing (PODC 2020), pp. 54–56. ACM (2020)

6. Alistarh, D., Ellen, F., Rybicki, J.: Wait-free approximate agreement on graphs (2021). https://arxiv.org/abs/2103.08949

7. Atanassov, K.: On Sperner's lemma. Studia Sci. Math. Hungarica **32**, 585–587 (1996)

8. Attiya, H., Lynch, N., Shavit, N.: Are wait-free algorithms fast? J. ACM **41**(4), 725–763 (1994)

9. Borowsky, E., Gafni, E.: Generalized FLP impossibility result for t-resilient asynchronous computations. In: Proceedings of the 25th Symposium on Theory of Computing (STOC 1993), pp. 91–100 (1993)

10. Borowsky, E., Gafni, E.: A simple algorithmically reasoned characterization of wait-free computation. In: Proceedings of the 16th ACM Symposium on Principles of Distributed Computing (PODC 1997), pp. 189–198 (1997)

11. Borowsky, E., Gafni, E., Lynch, N., Rajsbaum, S.: The BG distributed simulation algorithm. Distrib. Comput. **14**(3), 127–146 (2001)

12. Castañeda, A., Rajsbaum, S., Roy, M.: Convergence and covering on graphs for wait-free robots. J. Braz. Comput. Soc. **24**(1), 1–15 (2017). https://doi.org/10.1186/s13173-017-0065-8

13. Chor, B., Israeli, A., Li, M.: On processor coordination using asynchronous hardware. In: Proceedings of the 6th Symposium on Principles of Distributed Computing (PODC 1987), pp. 86–97 (1987)

14. Cicerone, S., Di Stefano, G., Navarra, A.: Asynchronous robots on graphs: gathering. In: Flocchini, P., Prencipe, G., Santoro, N. (eds.) Distributed Computing by Mobile Entities. LNCS, vol. 11340 pp. 184–217. Springer, Cham (2019). https://doi.org/10.1007/978-3-030-11072-7_8

15. Cieliebak, M., Flocchini, P., Prencipe, G., Santoro, N.: Distributed computing by mobile robots: gathering. SIAM J. Comput. **41**(4), 829–879 (2012)

16. De Loera, J.A., Peterson, E., Su, F.E.: A polytopal generalization of Sperner's lemma. J. Comb. Theory, Series A **100**(1), 1–26 (2002)

17. Dirac, G.A.: On rigid circuit graphs. Abhandlungen aus dem Mathematischen Seminar der Universität Hamburg **25**, 71–76 (1961). https://doi.org/10.1007/BF02992776

18. Dolev, D., Lynch, N.A., Pinter, S.S., Stark, E.W., Weihl, W.E.: Reaching approximate agreement in the presence of faults. J. ACM **33**(3), 499–516 (1986)

19. Euler, L.: Solutio problematis ad geometriam situs pertinentis. Commentarii academiae scientiarum Petropolitanae, pp. 128–140 (1741)

20. Farber, M.: On diameters and radii of bridged graphs. Discrete Math. **73**(3), 249–260 (1989)

21. Farber, M., Jamison, R.E.: On local convexity in graphs. Discrete Math. **66**(3), 231–247 (1987)

22. Fekete, A.D.: Asymptotically optimal algorithms for approximate agreement. Distrib. Comput. **4**(1), 9–29 (1990)

23. Fekete, A.D.: Asynchronous approximate agreement. Inf. Comput. **115**(1), 95–124 (1994)

24. Fischer, M.J., Lynch, N.A., Merritt, M.: Easy impossibility proofs for distributed consensus problems. Distrib. Comput. **1**(1), 26–39 (1986)

25. Fischer, M.J., Lynch, N.A., Paterson, M.S.: Impossibility of distributed consensus with one faulty process. J. ACM **32**(2), 374–382 (1985)

26. Függer, M., Nowak, T.: Fast multidimensional asymptotic and approximate consensus. In: Proceedings of the 32nd International Symposium on Distributed Computing (DISC 2018), pp. 27:1–27:16 (2018)

27. Gafni, E.: Round-by-round fault detectors (extended abstract): unifying synchrony and asynchrony. In: Proceedings of the 17th Symposium on Principles of Distributed Computing (PODC 1998), pp. 143–152 (1998)

28. Herlihy, M., Kozlov, D., Rajsbaum, S.: Distributed Computing Through Combinatorial Topology, 1st edn. Morgan Kaufmann, San Francisco (2013)

29. Herlihy, M., Shavit, N.: The asynchronous computability theorem for t-resilient tasks. In: Proceedings of the 25th Symposium on Theory of Computing (STOC 1993), pp. 111–120 (1993)

30. Herlihy, M., Shavit, N.: The topological structure of asynchronous computability. J. ACM **46**(6), 858–923 (1999)

31. Hoest, G., Shavit, N.: Toward a topological characterization of asynchronous complexity. SIAM J. Comput. **36**(2), 457–497 (2006)

32. Loui, M.C., Abu-Amara, H.H.: Memory requirements for agreement among unreliable asynchronous processes. Adv. Comp. Res. **4**(163–183), 31 (1987)

33. Mendes, H., Herlihy, M., Vaidya, N., Garg, V.K.: Multidimensional agreement in Byzantine systems. Distrib. Comput. **28**(6), 423–441 (2014). https://doi.org/10. 1007/s00446-014-0240-5

34. Mendes, H., Tasson, C., Herlihy, M.: Distributed computability in Byzantine asynchronous systems. In: Proceedings of the 46th ACM Symposium on Theory of Computing, pp. 704–713 (2014)

35. Nowak, T., Rybicki, J.: Byzantine approximate agreement on graphs. In: Proceedings of the 33rd International Symposium on Distributed Computing (DISC 2019), vol. 146, pp. 29:1–29:17 (2019)

36. Pease, M.C., Shostak, R.E., Lamport, L.: Reaching agreement in the presence of faults. J. ACM **27**(2), 228–234 (1980)

37. Saks, M., Zaharoglou, F.: Wait-free k-set agreement is impossible: the topology of public knowledge. SIAM J. Comput. **29**(5), 1449–1483 (2000)

38. Schenk, E.: Faster approximate agreement with multi-writer registers. In: Proceedings of the 36th Annual IEEE Symposium on Foundations of Computer Science (FOCS 1995), pp. 714–723 (1995)

Fragmented Objects: Boosting Concurrency of Shared Large Objects

Antonio Fernández Anta[1], Chryssis Georgiou[2], Theophanis Hadjistasi[3], Nicolas Nicolaou[3(✉)], Efstathios Stavrakis[3], and Andria Trigeorgi[2]

[1] IMDEA Networks Institute, Madrid, Spain
`antonio.fernandez@imdea.org`
[2] University of Cyprus, Nicosia, Cyprus
{`chryssis,atrige01`}`@cs.ucy.ac.cy`
[3] Algolysis Ltd., Limassol, Cyprus
{`theo,nicolas,stathis`}`@algolysis.com`

Abstract. This work examines strategies to handle *large* shared data objects in distributed storage systems (DSS), while boosting the number of concurrent accesses, maintaining strong consistency guarantees, and ensuring good operation performance. To this respect, we define the notion of *fragmented objects:* concurrent objects composed of a list of fragments (or *blocks*) that allow operations to manipulate each of their fragments individually. As the fragments belong to the same object, it is not enough that each fragment is linearizable to have useful consistency guarantees in the composed object. Hence, we capture the consistency semantic of the whole object with the notion of *fragmented linearizability*. Then, considering that a variance of linearizability, *coverability*, is more suited for versioned objects like files, we provide an implementation of a distributed file system, called CoBFS, that utilizes coverable fragmented objects (i.e., files). In CoBFS, each file is a linked-list of coverable block objects. Preliminary emulation of CoBFS demonstrates the potential of our approach in boosting the concurrency of strongly consistent large objects.

Keywords: Distributed storage · Large objects · Linearizability · Coverability

1 Introduction

In this paper we deal with the storage and use of shared readable and writable data in unreliable distributed systems. Distributed systems are subject to perturbations, which may include failures (e.g., crashes) of individual computers, or delays in processing or communication. In such settings, large (in size) objects are difficult to handle. Even more challenging is to provide linearizable consistency guarantees to such objects.

Supported by the Cyprus Research and Innovation Foundation under the grant agreement POST-DOC/0916/0090.

T. Jurdziński and S. Schmid (Eds.): SIROCCO 2021, LNCS 12810, pp. 106–126, 2021.
https://doi.org/10.1007/978-3-030-79527-6_7

Researchers usually break large objects into smaller linearizable building blocks, with their composition yielding the complete consistent large object. For example, a linearizable shared R/W memory is composed of a set of linearizable shared R/W objects [3]. By design, those building blocks are usually independent, in the sense that changing the value of one does not affect the operations performed on the others, and that operations on the composed objects are defined in terms of operations invoked on the (smallest possible) building blocks. Operations on individual linearizable registers do not violate the consistency of the larger composed linearizable memory space.

Some large objects, however, cannot be decomposed into independent building blocks. For example, a file object can be divided into *fragments* or *blocks*, so that write operations (which are still issued on the whole file) modify individual fragments. However, the composition of these fragments does not yield a linearizable file object: it is unclear how to order writes on the file when those are applied on different blocks concurrently. At the same time, it is practically inefficient to handle large objects as single objects and use traditional algorithms (like the one in [3]) to distribute it consistently.

Related Work: Attiya, Bar-Noy and Dolev [3], proposed an algorithm, colloquially referred to as ABD, that emulates a distributed shared R/W register in message-passing, crash-prone, asynchronous environments. To ensure availability, the object is replicated among a set of servers and, to provide operation ordering, a logical timestamp is associated with each written value. ABD tolerates replica server crashes, provided a majority of servers do not fail. Write operations involve a single communication round-trip. The writer broadcasts its request to all servers and it terminates once it collects acknowledgments from some majority of servers. A read involves two round-trips. In the first, the reader broadcasts a request to all servers, collects acknowledgments from some majority of servers, and it discovers the maximum timestamp. To ensure that any subsequent read will return a value associated with a timestamp at least as high as the discovered maximum, the reader propagates the value associated with the maximum timestamp to at least a majority of servers before completion, forming the second round-trip. ABD was later extended for the multi-writer/multi-reader model in [20], and its performance was later improved by several works, including [11,13–16]. Those solutions considered small objects, and relied on the dissemination of the object values in each operation, imposing a performance overhead when dealing with large objects.

Fan and Lynch [12] attempted to reduce performance overheads by separating the metadata of large objects from their value. In this way, communication-demanding operations were performed on the metadata, and large objects were transmitted to a limited number of hosts, and only when it was "safe" to do so. Although this work improved the latency of operations, compared to traditional approaches like [3,20], it still required to transmit the entire large object over the network per read and write operation. Moreover, if two concurrent write operations affected different "parts" of the object, only one of them would prevail, despite updates not being directly "conflicting."

Recently, Erasure-Coded (EC) approaches have gained momentum and have proved being extremely effective in saving storage and communication costs, while maintaining strong consistency and fault-tolerance [7,8,10,18,19,22]. EC approaches rely on the division of a shared object into coded blocks and deliver a single block to each data server. While very appealing for handling large objects, they face the challenge of efficiently encoding/decoding data. Despite being subdivided into several fragments, reads and writes are still applied on the entire object value. Therefore, multiple writers cannot work simultaneously on different parts of an object.

Value continuity is important when considering large objects, oftentimes overseen by distributed shared object implementations. In files, for example, a write operation should extend the latest written version of the object, and not overwrite any new value. *Coverability* was introduced in [23] as a consistency guarantee that extends linearizability and concerns versioned objects. An implementation of a coverable (versioned) object was presented, where ABD-like reads return both the version and the value of the object. Writes, on the other hand, attempt to write a "versioned" value on the object. If the reported version is older than the latest, then the write does not take effect and it is converted into a read operation, preventing overwriting a newer version of the object.

Contributions: In this work we set the goal to study and formally define the consistency guarantees we can provide when fragmenting a large R/W object into smaller objects (blocks), so that operations are still issued on the former but are applied on the latter. In particular, the contributions of this paper are as follows:

- We define two types of concurrent objects: (i) the *block* object, and (ii) the *fragmented* object. Blocks are treated as R/W objects, while fragmented objects are defined as lists of block objects (Sect. 3).
- We examine the consistency properties when allowing R/W operations on individual blocks of the fragmented object, in order to enable concurrent modifications. Assuming that each block is linearizable, we define the precise consistency that the fragmented object provides, termed *Fragmented Linearizability* (Sect. 4).
- We provide an algorithm that implements coverable fragmented objects. Then, we use it to build a prototype implementation of a distributed file system, called CoBFS, by representing each file as a linked-list of coverable block objects. CoBFS adopts a modular architecture, separating the object fragmentation process from the shared memory service, which allows to follow different fragmentation strategies and shared memory implementations. We show that CoBFS preserves the validity of the fragmented object and satisfies *fragmented coverability* (Sect. 5).
- We describe an experimental development and deployment of CoBFS on the Emulab testbed [1]. Preliminary results are presented, comparing our proposed algorithm to its non-fragmented counterpart. Results suggest that a fragmented object implementation boosts concurrency while reducing the latency of operations (Sect. 6).

Due to space limitations we refer the reader to [2] for missing proofs in this work.

2   Model

We are concerned with the implementations of highly-available replicated concurrent objects that support a set of operations. The system is a collection of crash-prone, asynchronous processors with unique identifiers (ids) from a totally-ordered set $\mathcal{I}$, composed of two main disjoint sets of processes: (a) a set $\mathcal{C}$ of client processes ids that may perform operations on a replicated object, and (b) a set $\mathcal{S}$ of server processes ids that each holds a replica of the object. Let $\mathcal{I} = \mathcal{C} \cup \mathcal{S}$.

Processors communicate by exchanging messages via asynchronous point-to-point *reliable*[1] channels; messages may be reordered. Any subset of client processes, and up to a minority of servers (less than $|\mathcal{S}|/2$), may crash at any time in an execution.

Executions, Histories and Operations: An *execution* ξ of a distributed algorithm A is an alternating sequence of *states* and *actions* of A reflecting the evolution in real time of the execution. A history H_ξ is the subsequence of the actions in ξ. We say that an operation π is *invoked* (starts) in an execution ξ when the *invocation action* of π appears in H_ξ, and π responds to the environment (ends or completes) when the *response action* appears in H_ξ. An operation is *complete* in ξ when both its invocation and *matching* response actions appear in H_ξ in that order. A history H_ξ is *sequential* if it starts with an invocation action and each invocation is immediately followed by its matching response; otherwise, H_ξ is *concurrent*. Finally, H_ξ is *complete* if every invocation in H_ξ has a matching response in H_ξ (i.e., each operation in ξ is complete). We say that an operation π *precedes in real time* an operation π' (or π' *succeeds in real time* π) in an execution ξ, denoted by $\pi \to \pi'$, if the response of π appears before the invocation of π' in H_ξ. Two operations are *concurrent* if neither precedes the other.

Consistency: We consider *linearizable* [17] R/W objects. A complete history H_ξ is linearizable if there exists some total order on the operations in H_ξ s.t. it respects the real-time order $\to$ of operations, and is consistent with the semantics of operations.

Note that we use read and write in an abstract way: (*i*) write represents any operation that changes the state of the object, and (*ii*) read is any operation that returns that state.

3   Fragmented Objects

A *fragmented object* is a concurrent object (e.g., can be accessed concurrently by multiple processes) that is composed of a finite list of *blocks*. Section 3.1 formally defines the notion of a *block*, and Sect. 3.2 gives the formal definition of a *fragmented object*.

---

[1] Reliability is not necessary for the correctness of the algorithms we present. It is just used for simplicity of presentation.

3.1   Block Object

A *block* b is a concurrent R/W object with a unique identifier from a set $\mathcal{B}$. A block has a value $val(b) \in \Sigma^*$, extracted from an alphabet Σ. For performance reasons it is convenient to bound the block length. Hence, we denote by $\mathcal{B}^\ell \subset \mathcal{B}$, the set that contains bounded length blocks, s.t. $\forall b \in \mathcal{B}^\ell$ the length of $|val(b)| \leq \ell$. We use $|b|$ to denote the length of the value of b when convenient. An *empty block* is a block b whose value is the empty string ε, i.e., $|b| = 0$. Operation create(b, D) is used to introduce a new block $b \in \mathcal{B}^\ell$, initialized with value D, such that $|D| \leq \ell$. Once created, block b supports the following two operations: (i) read$()_b$ that returns the value of the object b, and (ii) write$(D)_b$ that sets the value of the object b to D, where $|D| \leq \ell$.

A block object is linearizable if is satisfies the linearizability properties [17,21] with respect to its create (which acts as a write), read, and write operations. Once created, a block object is an atomic register [21] whose value cannot exceed a predefined length ℓ.

3.2   Fragmented Object

A *fragmented object* f is a concurrent R/W object with a unique identifier from a set $\mathcal{F}$. Essentially, a fragmented object is a *sequence* of blocks from $\mathcal{B}$, with a value $val(f) = \langle b_0, b_1, \ldots, b_n \rangle$, where $b_i \in \mathcal{B}$, for $i \in [0, n]$. Initially, each fragmented object contains an empty block, i.e., $val(f) = \langle b_0 \rangle$ with $val(b_0) = \varepsilon$. We say that f is *valid* and $f \in \mathcal{F}^\ell$ if $\forall b_i \in val(f)$, $b_i \in \mathcal{B}^\ell$. Otherwise, f is *invalid*. Being a R/W object, one would expect that a fragmented object $f \in \mathcal{F}^\ell$, for any ℓ, supports the following operations:

- read$()_f$ returns the list $\langle val(b_0), \ldots, val(b_n) \rangle$, where $val(f) = \langle b_0, b_1, \ldots, b_n \rangle$
- write$(\langle D_0, \ldots, D_n \rangle)_f$, $|D_i| \leq \ell, \forall i \in [0, n]$, sets the value of f to $\langle b_0, \ldots, b_n \rangle$ s.t. $val(b_i) = D_i, \forall i \in [0, n]$.

Having the write operation to modify the values of all blocks in the list may hinder in many cases the concurrency of the object. For instance, consider the following execution ξ. Let $val(f) = \langle b_0, b_1 \rangle$, $val(b_0) = D_0$, $val(b_1) = D_1$, and assume that ξ contains two concurrent writes by two different clients, one attempting to modify block b_0, and the other attempting to modify block b_1: $\pi_1 = $ write$(\langle D_0', D_1 \rangle)_f$ and $\pi_2 = $ write$(\langle D_0, D_1' \rangle)_f$, followed by a read$()_f$. By linearizability, the read will return either the list written in π_1 or in π_2 on f (depending on how the operations are ordered by the linearizability property). However, as blocks are independent objects, it would be expected that both writes could take effect, with π_1 updating the value of b_0 and π_2 updating the value of b_1. To this respect, we redefine the write to only update *one* of the blocks of a fragmented object. Since the update does not manipulate the value of the whole object, which would include also new blocks to be written, it should allow the update of a block b with a value $|D| > \ell$. This essentially leads to the generation of new blocks in the sequence. More formally, the update operation is defined as follows:

– update$(b_i, D)_f$ updates the value of block $b_i \in f$ such that:
  • if $|D| \leq \ell$: sets $val(b_i) = D$;
  • if $|D| > \ell$: partition $D = \{D_0, \ldots, D_k\}$ such that $|D_j| \leq \ell, \forall j \in [0, k]$, set $val(b_i) = D_0$ and create blocks b_i^j, for $j \in [1, k]$ with $val(b_i^j) = D_j$, so that f remains valid.

With the update operation in place, fragmented objects resemble store-collect objects presented in [4]. However, fragmented objects aim to minimize the communication overhead by exchanging individual blocks (in a consistent manner) instead of exchanging the list (view) of block values in each operation. Since the update operation only affects a block in the list of blocks of a fragmented object, it potentially allows for a higher degree of concurrency. It is still unclear what are the consistency guarantees we can provide when allowing concurrent updates on different blocks to take effect. Thus, we will consider that only operations read and update are issued in fragmented objects. Note that the list of blocks of a fragmented object cannot be reduced. The contents of a block can be deleted by invoking an update with an empty value.

Observe that, as a fragmented object is composed of block objects, its operations are implemented by using read, write, and create block operations. The read$()_f$ performs a sequence of read block operations (starting from block b_0 and traversing the list of blocks) to obtain and return the value of the fragmented object. Regarding update operations, if $|D| \leq \ell$, then the update$(b_i, D)_f$ operation performs a write operation on the block b_i as write$(D)_{b_i}$. However, if $|D| > \ell$, then D is partitioned into substrings $D_0, \ldots, D_k$ each of length at most ℓ. The update operation modifies the value of b_i as write$(D_0)_{b_i}$. Then, k new blocks $b_i^1, \ldots, b_i^k$ are created as create$(b_i^j, D_j), \forall j \in [1, k]$, and are inserted in f between b_i and b_{i+1} (or appended at the end if $i = |f|$). The sequential specification of a fragmented object is defined as follows:

Definition 1 (Sequential Specification). *The sequential specification of a fragmented object $f \in \mathcal{F}^\ell$ over the complete sequential history H is defined as follows. Initially $val(f) = \langle b_0 \rangle$ with $val(b_0) = \varepsilon$. If at the invocation action of an operation π in H has $val(f) = \langle b_0, \ldots, b_n \rangle$ and $\forall b_i \in f, val(b_i) = D_i$, and $|D_i| \leq \ell$. Then:*

– *if π is a read$()_f$, then π returns $\langle val(b_0), \ldots, val(b_n) \rangle$. At the response action of π, it still holds that $val(f) = \langle b_0, \ldots, b_n \rangle$ and $\forall b_i \in f, val(b_i) = D_i$.*
– *if π is an update$(b_i, D)_f$ operation, $b_i \in f$, then at the response action of π, $\forall j \neq i, val(b_j) = D_j$, and*
  • *if $|D| \leq \ell$: $val(f) = \langle b_0, \ldots, b_n \rangle$, $val(b_i) = D$;*
  • *if $|D| > \ell$: $val(f) = \langle b_0, \ldots, b_i, b_i^1, \ldots, b_i^k, b_{i+1}, \ldots, b_n \rangle$, such that $val(b_i) = D^0$ and $val(b_i^j) = D^j, \forall j \in [1, k]$, where $D = D^0 | D^1 | \cdots | D^k$ and $|D^j| \leq \ell, \forall j \in [0, k]$.*[2]

---

[2] The operator "|" denotes concatenation. The exact way D is partitioned is left to the implementation.

4   Fragmented Linearizability

A fragmented object is linearizable if it satisfies both the *Liveness* (termination) and *Linearizability* (atomicity) properties [17,21]. A fragmented object implemented by a single linearizable block is trivially linearizable as well. Here, we focus on fragmented objects that may contain a list of multiple linearizable blocks, and consider only read and update operations. As defined, update operations are applied on single blocks, which allows multiple update operations to modify different blocks of the fragmented object concurrently. Termination holds since read and update operations on the fragmented object always complete. It remains to examine the consistency properties.

Linearizability: Let H_ξ be a sequential history of update and read invocations and responses on a fragmented object f. Linearizability [17,21] provides the illusion that the fragmented object is accessed sequentially respecting the real-time order, even when operations are invoked concurrently[3]:

Definition 2 (Linearizability). *A fragmented object f is* linearizable *if, given any complete history H, there exists a permutation σ of all actions in H such that:*

- *σ is a sequential history and follows the sequential specification of f, and*
- *for operations π_1, π_2, if $\pi_1 \rightarrow \pi_2$ in H, then π_1 appears before π_2 in σ.*

Observe, that in order to satisfy Definition 2, the operations must be totally ordered. Let us consider again the sample execution ξ from Sect. 3. Since we decided not to use write operations, the execution changes as follows. Initially, $val(f) = \langle b_0, b_1 \rangle$, $val(b_0) = D_0$, $val(b_1) = D_1$, and then ξ contains two concurrent update operations by two different clients, one attempting to modify the first block, and the other attempting to modify the second block: $\pi_1 = \mathsf{update}(b_0, D_0')_f$ and $\pi_2 = \mathsf{update}(b_1, D_1')_f$ ($|D_0'| \leq \ell$ and $|D_1'| \leq \ell$), followed by a read()$_f$ operation. In this case, since both update operations operate on different blocks, independently of how π_1 and π_2 are ordered in the permutation σ, the read()$_f$ operation will return $\langle D_0', D_1' \rangle$. Therefore, the use of these update operations has increased the concurrency in the fragmented object.

Using linearizable read operations on the entire fragmented object can ensure the linearizability of the fragmented object as can be seen in the example presented in Fig. 1(a). However, providing a linearizable read when the object involves multiple R/W objects (i.e., an atomic snapshot) can be expensive or impact concurrency [9]. Thus, it is cheaper to take advantage of the atomic nature of the individual blocks and invoke one read operation per block in the fragmented object. ***But, what is the consistency guarantee we can provide on the entire fragmented object in this case?*** As seen in the example of Fig. 1(b), two reads concurrent with two update operations may violate linearizability on the entire object. According to the real time ordering of the operations on the individual blocks, block linearizability is preserved if the first

---

[3] Our formal definition of linearizability is adapted from [5].

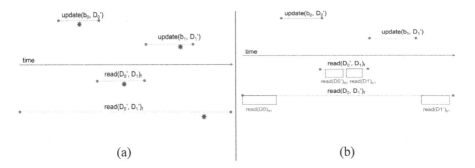

Fig. 1. Executions showing the operations on a fragmented object. Figure (a) shows linearizable reads on the fragmented object (and serialization points), and (b) reads on the fragmented object that are implemented with individual linearizable reads on blocks.

read on the fragmented object should return (D'_0, D_1), while the second read returns (D_0, D'_1). Note that we cannot find a permutation on these concurrent operations that follows the sequential specification of the fragmented object. Thus, the execution in Fig. 1(b) violates linearizability. This leads to the definition of *fragmented linearizability* on the fragmented object, which relying on the fact that *each individual block is linearizable*, it allows executions like the one seen in Fig. 1(b). Essentially, fragmented linearizability captures the consistency one can obtain on a collection of linearizable objects, when these are accessed concurrently and individually, but under the "umbrella" of the collection.

In this respect, we specify each $\mathsf{read}()_f$ operation of a certain process, as a sequence of $\mathsf{read}()_b$ operations on each block $b \in f$ by that process. In particular, a read operation $\mathsf{read}()_f$ that returns $\langle val(b_0), \ldots, val(b_n) \rangle$ is specified by $n+1$ individual read operations $\mathsf{read}()_{b_0}, \ldots, \mathsf{read}()_{b_n}$, that return $val(b_0)$, ..., $val(b_n)$, respectively, where $\mathsf{read}()_{b_0} \to, \ldots, \to \mathsf{read}()_{b_n}$.

Then, given a history H, we denote for an operation π the history H^π which contains the actions extracted from H and performed during π (including its invocation and response actions). Hence, if $val(f)$ is the value returned by $\mathsf{read}()_f$, then $H^{\mathsf{read}()_f}$ contains an invocation and matching response for a $\mathsf{read}()_b$ operation, for each $b \in val(f)$. Then, from H, we can construct a history $H|_f$ that only contains operations on the whole fragmented object. In particular, $H|_f$ is the same as H with the following changes: for each $\mathsf{read}()_f$, if $\langle val(b_0), \ldots, val(b_n) \rangle$ is the value returned by the read operation, then we replace the invocation of $\mathsf{read}()_{b_0}$ operation with the invocation of the $\mathsf{read}()_f$ operation and the response of the $\mathsf{read}()_{b_n}$ block with the response action for the $\mathsf{read}()_f$ operation. Then, we remove from $H|_f$ all the actions in $H^{\mathsf{read}()_f}$.

Definition 3 (Fragmented Linearizability). *Let $f \in \mathcal{F}^\ell$ be a fragmented object, H a complete history on f, and $val(f)_H \subseteq \mathcal{B}$ the value of f at the end of H. Then, f is* fragmented linearizable *if there exists a permutation σ_b over all the actions on b in H, $\forall b \in val(f)_H$, such that:*

- σ_b *is a sequential history that follows the sequential specification of* b^4, *and*
- *for operations* π_1, π_2 *that appear in* $H|_f$ *extracted from* H, *if* $\pi_1 \to \pi_2$ *in* $H|_f$, *then all operations on* b *in* H^{π_1} *appear before any operations on* b *in* H^{π_2} *in* σ_b.

Fragmented linearizability guarantees that all concurrent operations on different blocks prevail, and only concurrent operations on the same blocks are conflicting. Consider two reads r_1 and r_2, s.t. $r_1 \to r_2$; then r_2 must return a supersequence of blocks with respect to the sequence returned by r_1, and that for each block belonging in both sequences, its value returned by r_2 is the same or newer than the one returned by r_1.

5   Implementing Files as Fragmented Coverable Objects

Having laid out the theoretical framework of Fragmented Objects, we now present a prototype implementation of a Distributed File System, we call CoBFS.

When manipulating files it is expected that a value update builds upon the current value of the object. In such cases a writer should be aware of the latest value of the object (i.e., by reading the object) before updating it. In order to maintain this property in our implementation we utilize *coverable linearizable* blocks as presented in [23]. Coverability extends linearizability with the additional guarantee that object writes succeed when associating the written value with the current version of the object. In a different case, a write operation becomes a read operation and returns the latest version and the associated value of the object. Due to space limitations we refer the reader to [23] for the exact coverability properties.

By utilizing coverable blocks, our file system provides *fragmented coverability* as a consistency guarantee. In our prototype implementation we consider each object to be a plain text file, however the underlying theoretical formulation allows for extending this implementation to support any kind of large objects.

File as a Coverable Fragmented Object: Each file is modeled as a fragmented object with its blocks being coverable objects. The file is implemented as a *linked-list of blocks* with the first block being a special block $b_g \in \mathcal{B}$, which we call the *genesis block*, and then each block having a pointer *ptr* to its next block, whereas the last block has a null pointer. Initially each file contains only the genesis block; the genesis block contains special purpose (meta) data. The $val(b)$ of b is set as a tuple, $val(b) = \langle ptr, data \rangle$.

Overview of the Basic Architecure: The basic architecture of CoBFS appears in Fig. 2. CoBFS is composed of two main modules: (*i*) a Fragmentation Module (FM), and (*ii*) a Distributed Shared Memory Module (DSMM). In summary, the FM implements the fragmented object while the DSMM implements an interface to a shared memory service that allows read/write operations

---

[4] The sequential specification of a block is similar to that of a R/W register [21], whose value has bounded length.

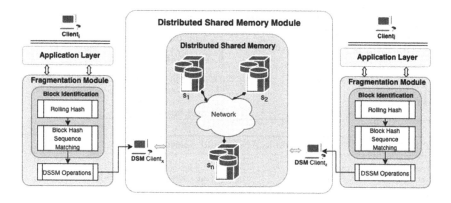

Fig. 2. Basic architecture of CoBFS

on individual block objects. Following this architecture, clients may access the file system through the FM, while the blocks of each file are maintained by servers through the DSMM. The FM uses the DSMM as an external service to write and read blocks to the shared memory. To this respect, CoBFS is flexible enough to utilize any underlying distributed shared object algorithm.

File and Block ID Assignment: A key aspect of our implementation is the unique assignment of ids to both fragmented objects (i.e., files) and individual blocks. A file $f \in \mathcal{F}$ is assigned a pair $\langle cfid, cfseq \rangle \in \mathcal{C} \times \mathbb{N}$, where $cfid \in \mathcal{C}$ is the universally unique identifier of the client that created the file (i.e., the owner) and $cfseq \in \mathbb{N}$ is the client's local sequence number, incremented every time the client creates a new file and ensuring uniqueness of the objects created by the same client.

In turn, a block $b \in \mathcal{B}$ of a file is identified by a triplet $\langle fid, cid, cseq \rangle \in \mathcal{F} \times \mathcal{C} \times \mathbb{N}$, where $fid \in \mathcal{F}$ is the identifier of the file to which the block belongs, $cid \in \mathcal{C}$ is the identifier of the client that created the block (this is not necessarily the owner/creator of the file), and $cseq \in \mathbb{N}$ is the client's local sequence number of blocks that is incremented every time this client creates a block for this file (this ensures the uniqueness of the blocks created by the same client for the same file).

Distributed Shared Memory Module: The DSMM implements a distributed R/W shared memory based on an *optimized coverable variant* of the ABD algorithm, called CoABD [23]. The module exposes three operations for a block b: dsmm-read$_b$, dsmm-write$(v)_b$, and dsmm-create$(v)_b$. The specification of each operation is shown in Algorithm 1. For each block b, the DSMM maintains its latest known version ver_b and its associated value val_b. Upon receipt of a read request for a block b, the DSMM invokes a cvr-read operation on b and returns the value received from that operation.

To reduce the number of blocks transmitted per read, we apply a simple yet very effective optimization (Algorithm 2): a read sends a READ request to all the servers including its local version in the request message. When a server

Algorithm 1. DSM Module: Operations on a coverable block object b at client p

1: **State Variables:**
2: $ver_b \in \mathbb{N}$ initially 0; $val_b \in V$ initially $\perp$;

3: **function** dsmm-read( )$_{b,p}$
4:     $\langle ver_b, val_b \rangle \leftarrow b.\text{cvr-read}()$
5:     **return** val_b
6: **end function**

7: **function** dsmm-create$(val)_{b,p}$
8:     $\langle ver_b, val_b \rangle \leftarrow b.\text{cvr-write}(val, 0)$
9: **end function**

10: **function** dsmm-write$(val)_{b,p}$
11:     $\langle ver_b, val_b \rangle \leftarrow b.\text{cvr-write}(val, ver_b)$
12:     **return** val_b
13: **end function**

Algorithm 2. Optimized coverable ABD (read operation)

1: at each reader r for object b
2: **State Variables:**
3: $tg_b \in \mathbb{N}^+ \times \mathcal{W}$ initially $\langle 0, \perp \rangle$; $val_b \in V$, init. $\perp$;

4: **function** cvr-read( )
5:     send $\langle \text{READ}, ver_b \rangle$ to all servers ▷ Query Phase
6:     **wait until** $\frac{|S|+1}{2}$ reply
7:     $maxP \leftarrow \max(\{\langle tg', v' \rangle\})$
8:     **if** $maxP.tg > tg_b$ **then**
9:         send $(\text{WRITE}, maxP)$ to all servers
                                    ▷ Propagation Phase
10:
11:         **wait until** $\frac{|S|+1}{2}$ servers reply
12:         $\langle tg_b, val_b \rangle \leftarrow maxP$
13:     **end if**
14:     return$(\langle tg_b, val_b \rangle)$
15: **end function**

16: at each server s for object b
17: **State Variables:**
18: $tg_b \in \mathbb{N}^+ \times \mathcal{W}$ initially $\langle 0, \perp \rangle$; $val_b \in V$, init. $\perp$;

19: **function** rcv$(M)_q$ ▷ Reception of a message from q
20:     **if** $M.type \neq \text{READ}$ and $M.tg > tg_b$ **then**
21:         $\langle tg_b, val_b \rangle \leftarrow \langle M.tg, M.v \rangle$
22:     **end if**
23:     **if** $M.type = \text{READ}$ and $M.tg \geq tg_b$ **then**
24:         send$(\langle tg_b, \perp \rangle)$ to q ▷ Reply without content
25:     **else**
26:         send$(\langle tg_b, val_b \rangle)$ to q ▷ Reply with content
27:     **end if**
28: **end function**

---

receives a READ request it replies with both its local tag and block content only if the tag enclosed in the READ request is smaller than its local tag; otherwise it replies with its local tag without the block content. Once the reader receives replies from a majority of servers, it detects the maximum tag among the replies, and checks if it is higher than the local known tag. If it is, then it forwards the tag and its associated block content to a majority of servers; if not then the read operation returns the locally known tag and block content without performing the second phase. While this optimisation makes a little difference on the non-fragmented version of the ABD (under read/write contention), it makes a significant difference in the case of the fragmented objects. For example, if each read is concurrent with a write causing the execution of a second phase, then the read sends the complete file to the servers; in the case of fragmented objects only the fragments that changed by the write will be sent over to the servers, resulting in significant reductions.

The create and write operations invoke cvr-write operations to update the value of the shared block b. Their main difference is that version 0 is used during a create operation to indicate that this is the first time that the block is written. Notice that the write in create will always succeed as it will introduce a new, never before written block, whereas operation write may be converted to a read operation, thus retrieving and returning the latest value of b. We refer the reader to [23] for the implementation of cvr-read and cvr-write, which are simple variants of the corresponding implementations of ABD [3]. We state the following lemma:

Lemma 1. *The DSMM implements R/W coverable block objects.*

Proof (Proof Sketch). When both the read and write operations perform two phases, the correctness of the algorithm is derived from Theorem 10 in [23]. It is easy to see that the optimization does not violate linearizability. The second phase of a read is omitted when all the servers reply with a tag smaller or equal to the local tag of the reader r. Since however, a read propagates its local tag to a majority of servers at every tag update, then every subsequent operation will observe (and return) the latest value of the object to be associated with a tag at least as high as the local tag of r.   □

Fragmentation Module: The FM is the core concept of our implementation. Each client has a FM responsible for (i) fragmenting the file into blocks and identify modified blocks, and (ii) follow a specific strategy to store and retrieve the file blocks from the R/W shared memory. As we show later, the block update strategy followed by FM is necessary in order to preserve the structure of the fragmented object and sufficient to preserve the properties of fragmented coverability. For the file division of the blocks and the identification of the newly created blocks, the FM contains a *Block Identification (BI) module* that utilizes known approaches for data fragmentation and diff extraction.

Block Identification (BI): Given the data D of a file f, the goal of BI is to break D into data blocks $\langle D_0, \ldots, D_n \rangle$, s.t. the size of each D_i is less than a predefined upper bound ℓ. By drawing ideas from the RSYNC (Remote Sync) algorithm [25], given two versions of the same file, say f and f', the BI tries to identify blocks that (a) may exist in f but not in f' (and vice-versa), or (b) they have been changed from f to f'. To achieve these goals BI proceeds in two steps: (1) it fragments D into blocks, using the *Rabin fingerprints* rolling hash algorithm [24], and (2) it compares the hashes of the blocks of the current and the previous version of the file using a string matching algorithm [6] to determine the modified/new data blocks. The role of BI within the architecture of CoBFS and its process flow appears in Fig. 3, while its specification is provided in Algorithm 3. A high-level description of *BI* has as follows:

- **Block Division:** Initially, the BI partitions a given file f into data blocks based on its contents, using *Rabin fingerprints*. This scheme allows to divide f into blocks of at most size ℓ, which are identified by their hashes (fingerprints). When used in two versions of the same file, the scheme guarantees that only the hash of changed blocks (and at most their respective next blocks) will be affected. To this end, any data that may cause a changed block to overflow will yield new blocks.
- **Block Matching:** Given the set of blocks $\langle D_0, \ldots, D_m \rangle$ and associated block hashes $\langle h_0, \ldots, h_m \rangle$ generated by the Rabin fingerprint algorithm, the BI tries to match each hash to a block identifier, based on the block ids produced

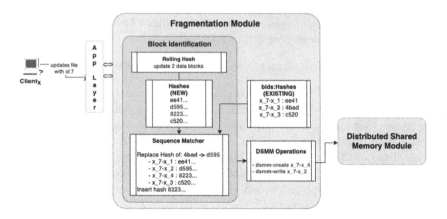

Fig. 3. Example of a writer x writing text at the beginning of the second block of a text file with id $f_{id} = 7$. The hash value of the existing second block "4bad.." is replaced with "d595.." and a new block with hash value "8223.." is inserted immediately after. The block $b_{id} = x\_7\text{-}x\_2$ and the new block $b_{id} = x\_7\text{-}x\_4$ are sent to the DSM.

during the previous division of file f, say $\langle b_0, \ldots, b_n \rangle$. We produce the vector $\langle h(b_0), \ldots, h(b_n) \rangle$ where $h(b_i) = hash(val(b_i).data)$ from the current blocks of f, and using a string matching algorithm [6] we compare the two hash vectors to obtain one of the following statuses for each entry: (i) equal, (ii) modified, (iii) inserted, (iv) deleted.

– **Block Updates:** Based on the hash statuses computed through block matching previously, the blocks of the fragmented object are updated. In particular, in the case of equality, if a $h_i = h(b_j)$ then D_i is identified as the data of block b_j. In case of modification, e.g. $(h(b_j), h_i)$, an update$(b_j, \{D_i\})_{f,p}$ action is then issued to modify the data of b_j to D_i (Lines 10:15). In case new hashes (e.g., $\langle h_i, h_k \rangle$) are inserted after the hash of block b_j (i.e., $h(b_j)$), then the action update$(b_j, \{val(b_j).data, D_i, D_k\})_{f,p}$ is performed to create the new blocks after b_j (Lines 17:22). In our formulation block deletion is treated as a modification that sets an empty data value thus, in our implementation *no blocks are deleted*.

FM Operations: The FM's external signature includes the two main operations of a fragmented object: read$_f$, and update$_f$. Their specifications appear in Algorithm 3.

Read Operation - read()$_{f,p}$: To retrieve the value of a file f, a client p may invoke a read$_{f,p}$ to the fragmented object. Upon receiving, the FM issues a series of reads on file's blocks; starting from the genesis block of f and proceeding to the last block by following the pointers in the linked-list of blocks comprising the file. All the blocks are assembled into one file via the Assemble() function. The reader p issues a read for all the blocks in the file. This is done to ensure the property stated in the following lemma:

Lemma 2. *Let ξ be an execution of COBFS with two reads $\rho_1 = \text{read}_{f,p}$ and $\rho_2 = \text{read}_{f,q}$ from clients p and q on the fragmented object f, s.t. $\rho_1 \rightarrow \rho_2$. If*

Algorithm 3. Fragmentation Module: BI and Operations on a file f at client p

---

1: **State Variables:**
2: H initially $\emptyset$; $\ell \in \mathbb{N}$;
3: $\mathcal{L}_f$ a linked-list of blocks, initially $\langle b_g \rangle$;
4: $bc_f \in \mathbb{N}$ initially 0;

5: **function** fm-block-identify( )$_{f,p}$
6:    $\langle newD, newH \rangle \leftarrow$ RabinFingerprints(f, ℓ)
7:    $curH = hash(\mathcal{L}_f)$
8:       ▷ hashes of the data of the blocks in $\mathcal{L}_f$
9:    $C \leftarrow$ SMatching$(curH, newH)$
10:                                    ▷ blocks modified
11:    **for** $\langle h(b_j), h_k \rangle \in C.mods$ s.t.
12:          $h(b_j) \in curH, h_k \in newH$ **do**
13:       $D \leftarrow \{D_k : D_k \in newD$
14:                  $\wedge h_k = hash(D_k)\}$
15:       fm-update$(b_j, D)_{f,p}$
16:    **end for**
17:                                    ▷ blocks inserted
18:    **for** $\langle h(b_j), S \rangle \in C.inserts$ s.t.
19:          $h(b_j) \in curH, S \subseteq newH$ **do**
20:       $D \leftarrow \{D_i : h_i \in S \wedge D_i \in newD$
21:                  $\wedge h_i = hash(D_i)\}$
22:       fm-update$(b_j, D)_{f,p}$
23:    **end for**
24: **end function**

25: **function** fm-read( )$_{f,p}$
26:    $b \leftarrow val(b_g).ptr$
27:    $\mathcal{L}_f \leftarrow \langle b_g \rangle$ ▷ reset $\mathcal{L}_f$
28:    **while** b *not* NULL **do**
29:       $val(b) \leftarrow$ dsmm-read()$_{b,p}$
30:       $\mathcal{L}_f.insert(val(b))$
31:       $b \leftarrow val(b).ptr$
32:    **end while**
33:    **return** Assemble$(\mathcal{L}_f)$
34: **end function**

35: **function** fm-update$(b, D = \langle D_0, D_1, \ldots,$
     $D_k \rangle)_{f,p}$
36:    **for** $j = k : 1$ **do**
37:       $b_j \leftarrow \langle f, p, bc_f{++} \rangle$ ▷ set block id
38:       $val(b_j).data = D_j$ ▷ set block data
39:       **if** $j < k$ **then**
40:          $val(b_j).ptr = b_{j+1}$ ▷ set block
     ptr
41:       **else**
42:          $val(b_j).ptr = val(b).ptr$
43:                        ▷ point last to b ptr
44:       **end if**
45:       $\mathcal{L}_f.insert(val(b_j))$
46:       dsmm-create$(val(b_j))_{b_j}$
47:    **end for**
48:    $val(b).data = D_0$
49:    **if** $k > 0$ **then**
50:       $val(b).ptr = b_1$ ▷ change b ptr if
     $|D| > 1$
51:    **end if**
52:    dsmm-write$(val(b))_b$
53: **end function**

ρ_1 returns a list of blocks $\mathcal{L}_1$ and ρ_2 a list $\mathcal{L}_2$, then $\forall b_i \in \mathcal{L}_1$, then $b_i \in \mathcal{L}_2$ and $version(b_i)_{\mathcal{L}_1} \leq version(b_i)_{\mathcal{L}_2}$.

Update Operation - update$(b, D)_{f,p}$: Here we expect that the update operation accepts a block id and a set of data blocks (instead of a single data object), since the division is performed by the BI module. Thus, $D = \langle D_0, \ldots, D_k \rangle$, for $k \geq 0$, with the size $|D| = \sum_{i=0}^{k} |D_i|$ and the size of each $|D_i| \leq \ell$ for some maximum block size ℓ. Client p attempts to update the value of a block with identifier b in file f with the data in D. Depending on the size of D the update operation will either perform a write on the block if $k = 0$, or it will create new blocks and update the block pointers in case $k > 0$. Assuming that $val(b).ptr = b'$ then:

- $k = 0$: In this case update, for block b, calls write$(\langle val(b).ptr, D_0 \rangle, \langle p, bseq \rangle)_b$.
- $k > 0$: Given the sequence of chunks $D = \langle D_0, \ldots, D_k \rangle$ the following block operations are performed in this particular order:
    $\rightarrow$ create$(b_k = \langle f, p, bc_p{++} \rangle, \langle b', D_k \rangle, \langle p, 0 \rangle)$ ** Block b_k ptr points to b' **
    $\rightarrow$ ...
    $\rightarrow$ create$(b_1 = \langle f, p, bc_p{++} \rangle, \langle b_2, D_1 \rangle, \langle p, 0 \rangle)$ ** Block b_1 ptr points to b_2 **
    $\rightarrow$ write$(\langle b_1, D_0 \rangle, \langle p, bseq \rangle)_b$ ** Block b ptr points to b_1 **

The challenge here was to insert the list of blocks without causing any concurrent operation to return a divided fragmented object, while also avoiding blocking any ongoing operations. To achieve that, create operations are executed in a reverse order: we first create block b_k pointing to b', and we move backwards until creating b_1 pointing to block b_2. The last operation, write, tries to update the value of block b_0 with value $\langle b_1, D_0 \rangle$. If the last coverable write completes successfully, then all the blocks are inserted in f and the update is *successful*; otherwise none of the blocks appears in f and thus the update is *unsuccessful*. This is captured by the following lemma:

Lemma 3. *In any execution ξ of* CoBFS, *if ξ contains an π =* update$(b, D)_{f,p}$, *then π is successful iff the operation b.cvr-write called within* dsmm-write$(val(b))_{b,p}$, *is successful.*

Lemma 4. *In any execution ξ of* CoBFS, *if a* read$_{f,p}$ *operation returns a list* $\mathcal{L} = \langle b_g, b_1, \ldots, b_n \rangle$ *for a file f, then $val(b_g).prt = b_1$, $val(b_i).ptr = b_{i+1}$, for* $1 \leq i < n - 1$, *and $val(b_n).ptr = \perp$.*

This leads us to the following:

Theorem 1. CoBFS *implements a R/W Fragmented Coverable object.*

Proof. By Lemma 1 every block operation in CoBFS satisfies coverability and together with Lemma 2 it follows that CoBFS implements a coverable fragmented object satisfying the properties presented in Definition 3. Also, the BI ensures that the size of each block is limited under a bound ℓ and Lemma 4 ensures that each operation obtains a connected list of blocks. Thus, CoBFS implements a *valid* fragmented object.

6 Preliminary Evaluation

To further appreciate the proposed approach from an applied point of view, we performed a preliminary evaluation of CoBFS against CoABD. Due to the design of the two algorithms, CoABD will transmit the entire file per read/update operation, while CoBFS will transmit as many blocks as necessary for an update operation, but perform as many reads as the number of blocks during a read operation. The two algorithms use the read optimization of Algorithm 2. Both were implemented and deployed on *Emulab*, [26], a network testbed with tunable and controlled environmental parameters.

Experimental Setup: Across all experiments, three distinct types of distributed nodes are defined and deployed within the emulated network environment as listed below. Communication between the distributed nodes is via point-to-point bidirectional links implemented with a DropTail queue.

– **writer** $w \in W \subseteq C$: a client that dispatches update requests to servers.
– **reader** $r \in R \subseteq C$: a client that dispatches read requests to servers.

– **server** $s \in S$: listens for reader and writer requests and is responsible for maintaining the object replicas according to the underlying protocol they implement.

Performance Metrics: We assess performance using: (i) *operational latency*, and (ii) *the update success ratio*. The operational latency is computed as the sum of communication and computation delays. In the case of CoBFS, computational latency encompasses the time necessary for the FM to fragment a file object and generate the respective hashes for its blocks. The update success ratio is the percentage of update operations that have not been converted to reads (and thus successfully changed the value of the indented object). In the case of CoABD, we compute the percentage of successful updates on the file as a whole over the number of all updates. For CoBFS, we compute the percentage of file updates, where all individual block updates succeed.

Scenarios: Both algorithms are evaluated under the following experimental scenarios:

– **Scalability:** examine performance as the number of service participants increases.
– **File Size:** examine performance when using different initial file sizes.
– **Block Size:** examine performance under different block sizes (CoBFS only).

We use a *stochastic* invocation scheme in which reads are scheduled randomly from the intervals $[1...rInt]$ and updates from $[1...wInt]$, where $rInt, wInt = 4sec$. To perform a fair comparison and to yield valuable observations, the results shown are compiled as averages over five samples per each scenario.

Scalability Experiments: We varied the number of readers $|R|$, the number of writers $|W|$, and the number of servers $|S|$ in the set $\{5, 10, 15, 20, 25, 30, 35, 40, 45, 50\}$. While testing for readers' scalability, the number of writers and servers was kept constant, $|W|, |S| = 10$. Using the same approach, scalability of writers, and in turn of servers, was tested while preserving the two other types of nodes constant (i.e. $|R|, |S| = 10$ and $|R|, |W| = 10$ respectively). In total, each writer performed 20 updates and each reader 20 reads. The size of the initial file used was set to 18 kB, while the maximum, minimum and average block sizes (*Rabin fingerprints* parameters) were set to 64 kB, 2 kB and 8 kB respectively.

File Size Experiments: We varied the f_{size} from 1 MB to 1 GB by doubling the file size in each simulation run. The number of writers, readers and servers was fixed to 5. In total, each writer performed 5 updates and each reader 5 reads. The maximum, minimum and average block sizes were set to 1 MB, 512 kB and 512 kB respectively.

Block Size Experiments: We varied the minimum and average b_{sizes} of CoBFS from 1 kB to 64 kB. The number of writers, readers and servers was fixed to 10. In total, each writer performed 20 updates and each reader 20 reads. The size of the initial file used was set to 18 kB, while the maximum block size was set to 64 kB

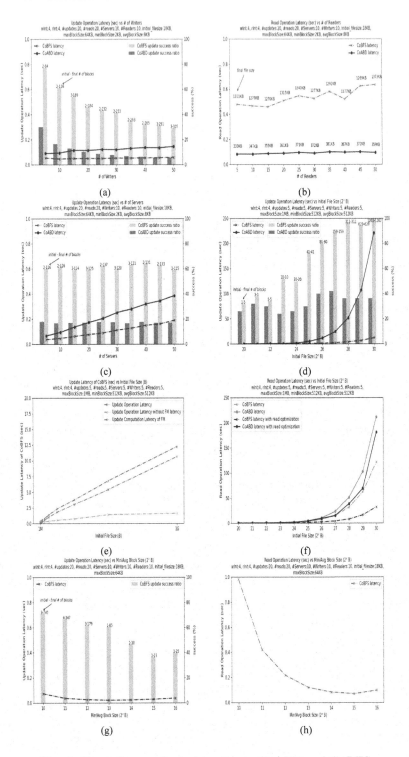

Fig. 4. Simulation results for algorithms CoABD and CoBFS.

Results: Overall, our results suggest that the efficiency of CoBFS is inversely proportional to the number of block operations, rather than the size of the file. This is primarily due to the individual block-processing nature of CoBFS. More in detail:

Scalability: In Figure 4(a), the operational latency of updates in CoBFS remains almost unchanged and smaller than of CoABD. This is because CoABD writer updates a rather small file, while each CoBFS writer updates a subset of blocks which are modified or created. The computational latency of FM in CoBFS is negligible, when compared to the total update operation latency, because of the small file size. In Figure 4(c), we observe that the update operation latency in CoABD increases even more as the number of servers increases. As more updates are successful in CoBFS, reads may transfer more data compared to reads in CoABD, explaining their slower completion as seen in Fig. 4(b). Also, readers send multiple read block requests of small sizes, waiting each time for a reply, while CoABD readers wait for a message containing a small file.

Concurrency: The percentage of successful file updates achieved by CoBFS are significantly higher than those of CoABD. This holds for both cases where the number of writers increased (see Fig. 4(a)) and the number of servers increased (see Fig. 4(c)). This demonstrates the boost of concurrency achieved by CoBFS. In Figure 4(a) we notice that as the number of writers increases (hence, concurrency increases), CoABD suffers greater number of unsuccessful updates, i.e., updates that have become reads per the coverability property. Concurrency is also affected when the number of blocks increases, Fig. 4(d). The probability of two writes to collide on a single block decreases, and thus CoBFS eventually allows all the updates (100%) to succeed. CoABD does not experience any improvement as it always manipulates the file as a whole.

File Size: Figure 4(d) demonstrates that the update operation latency of CoBFS remains at extremely low levels. The main factor that significantly contributes to the slight increase of CoBFS update latency is the FM computation latency, Fig. 4(e). We have set the same parameters for the *Rabin fingerprints* algorithm for all the initial file sizes, which may have favored some file sizes but burdened others. An optimization of the Rabin algorithm or a use of a different algorithm for managing blocks could possibly lead to improved FM computation latency; this is a subject for future work. The CoBFS update communication latency remains almost stable, since it depends primarily on the number and size of update block operations. That is in contrast to the update latency exhibited in CoABD which appears to increase linearly with the file size. This was expected, since as the file size increases, it takes longer latency to update the whole file.

Despite the higher success rate of CoBFS, the read latency of the two algorithms is comparable due to the low number of update operations. The read latencies of the two algorithms with and without the read optimization can be seen in Fig. 4(f). The CoABD read latency increases sharply, even when using the optimized reads. This is in line with our initial hypothesis, as CoABD requires reads to request and propagate the whole file each time a newer version of the file is discovered. Similarly, when read optimization is not used in CoBFS, the latency is close of CoABD. Notice that each read that discovers a new version of the file needs to request and propagate the content of each individual block. On the contrary, read optimization decreases significantly the CoBFS read latency, as reads transmit only the contents of the blocks that have changed.

Block Size: From Figs. 4(g) (h) we can infer that when smaller blocks are used, the update and read latencies reach their highest values. In both cases, small b_{size} results in the generation of larger number of blocks from the division of the initial file. Additionally, as seen in Fig. 4(g), the small b_{size} leads to the generation of more new blocks during update operations, resulting in more update block operations, and hence higher latencies. As the minimum and average b_{sizes} increase, lower number of blocks need to be added when an update is taking place. Unfortunately, smaller number of blocks leads to a lower success rate. Similarly, in Fig. 4(h), smaller block sizes require more read block operations to obtain the file's value. As the minimum and average b_{sizes} increase, lower number of blocks need to be read. Thus, further increase of the minimum and average b_{sizes} forces the decrease of the latencies, reaching a plateau in both graphs. This means that the emulation finds optimal minimum and average b_{sizes} and increasing them does not give better (or worse) latencies.

7   Conclusions

We have introduced the notion of linearizable and coverable fragmented objects and proposed an algorithm that implements coverable fragmented files. It is then used to build CoBFS, a prototype distributed file system in which each file is specified as a linked-list of coverable blocks. CoBFS adopts a modular architecture, separating the object fragmentation process from the shared memory service allowing to follow different fragmentation strategies and shared memory implementations. We showed that it preserves the validity of the fragmented object (file) and satisfies fragmented coverability. The deployment on Emulab serves as a proof of concept implementation. The evaluation demonstrates the potential of our approach in boosting the concurrency and improving the efficiency of R/W operations on strongly consistent large objects.

For future work, we aim to perform a comprehensive experimental evaluation of CoBFS that will go beyond simulations (e.g., full-scale, real-time, cloud-based experimental evaluations) and to further study parameters that may affect the performance of the operations (e.g., file size, block size, etc.), as well as to build optimizations and extensions, in an effort to unlock the full potential of our approach.

References

1. Emulab network testbed. https://www.emulab.net/. Accessed 7 June 2021
2. Fernandez Anta, A., Georgiou, C., Hadjistasi, T., Nicolaou, N., Stavrakis, E., Trigeorgi, A.: Fragmented objects: Boosting concurrency of shared large objects (2021). https://arxiv.org/abs/2102.12786

3. Attiya, H., Bar-Noy, A., Dolev, D.: Sharing memory robustly in message passing systems. J. ACM **42**(1), 124–142 (1996)
4. Attiya, H., Kumari, S., Somani, A., Welch, J.L.: Store-collect in the presence of continuous churn with application to snapshots and lattice agreement (2020)
5. Attiya, H., Welch, J.L.: Sequential consistency versus linearizability. ACM Trans. Comput. Syst. **12**(2), 91–122 (1994)
6. Black, P.: Ratcliff pattern recognition. Dictionary of Algorithms and Data Structures (2021)
7. Cachin, C., Tessaro, S.: Optimal resilience for erasure-coded byzantine distributed storage, pp. 115–124. IEEE Computer Society, Los Alamitos (2006)
8. Cadambe, V.R., Lynch, N.A., Médard, M., Musial, P.M.: A coded shared atomic memory algorithm for message passing architectures. Distrib. Comput. **30**(1), 49–73 (2017)
9. Delporte-Gallet, C., Fauconnier, H., Rajsbaum, S., Raynal, M.: Implementing snapshot objects on top of crash-prone asynchronous message-passing systems. IEEE Trans. Parallel Distrib. Syst. **29**(9), 2033–2045 (2018). https://doi.org/10.1109/TPDS.2018.2809551
10. Dutta, P., Guerraoui, R., Levy, R.R.: Optimistic erasure-coded distributed storage. In: Taubenfeld, G. (ed.) DISC 2008. LNCS, vol. 5218, pp. 182–196. Springer, Heidelberg (2008). https://doi.org/10.1007/978-3-540-87779-0_13
11. Dutta, P., Guerraoui, R., Levy, R.R., Chakraborty, A.: How fast can a distributed atomic read be? In: Proceedings of PODC 2004, pp. 236–245 (2004)
12. Fan, R., Lynch, N.: Efficient replication of large data objects. In: Fich, F.E. (ed.) DISC 2003. LNCS, vol. 2848, pp. 75–91. Springer, Heidelberg (2003). https://doi.org/10.1007/978-3-540-39989-6_6
13. Fernández Anta, A., Hadjistasi, T., Nicolaou, N.: Computationally light "multi-speed" atomic memory. In: Proceedings of OPODIS 2016 (2016)
14. Georgiou, C., Hadjistasi, T., Nicolaou, N., Schwarzmann, A.A.: Unleashing and speeding up readers in atomic object implementations. In: Podelski, A., Taïani, F. (eds.) NETYS 2018. LNCS, vol. 11028, pp. 175–190. Springer, Cham (2019). https://doi.org/10.1007/978-3-030-05529-5_12
15. Georgiou, C., Nicolaou, N., Shvartsman, A.A.: Fault-tolerant semifast implementations of atomic read/write registers. J. Parallel Distrib. Comput. **1**, 62–79 (2009)
16. Hadjistasi, T., Nicolaou, N., Schwarzmann, A.A.: Oh-RAM! one and a half round atomic memory. In: El Abbadi, A., Garbinato, B. (eds.) NETYS 2017. LNCS, vol. 10299, pp. 117–132. Springer, Cham (2017). https://doi.org/10.1007/978-3-319-59647-1_10
17. Herlihy, M.P., Wing, J.M.: Linearizability: a correctness condition for concurrent objects. ACM TOPLAS **12**(3), 463–492 (1990)
18. Konwar, K.M., Prakash, N., Kantor, E., Lynch, N., Médard, M., Schwarzmann, A.A.: Storage-optimized data-atomic algorithms for handling erasures and errors in distributed storage systems. In: Proceedings of IPDPS 2016, pp. 720–729, May 2016
19. Konwar, K.M., Prakash, N., Lynch, N., Médard, M.: RADON: repairable atomic data object in networks. In: The International Conference on Distributed Systems (OPODIS) (2016)
20. Lynch, N., Shvartsman, A.A.: Robust emulation of shared memory using dynamic quorum-acknowledged broadcasts. In: Proceedings of Symposium on Fault-Tolerant Computing (1997)
21. Lynch, N.: Distributed Algorithms. Morgan Kaufmann Publishers, San Francisco (1996)

22. Nicolaou, N., Cadambe, V., Prakash, N., Konwar, K., Medard, M., Lynch, N.: ARES: adaptive, reconfigurable, erasure coded, atomic storage. In: IEEE 39th ICDCS, pp. 2195–2205

23. Nicolaou, N., Fernández Anta, A., Georgiou, C.: Coverability: consistent versioning in asynchronous, fail-prone, message-passing environments. In: Proceedings of IEEE NCA 2016

24. Rabin, M.O.: Fingerprinting by random polynomials. In: Center for Research in Computing Techn., Aiken Computation Laboratory, Univ, pp. 15–18 (1981). http://scholar.google.com/scholar?hl=en&btnG=Search&q=intitle: Fingerprinting+by+Random+Polynomials#0

25. Tridgell, A., Mackerras, P.: The rsync algorithm Andrew Tridgell and Paul Mackerras. Imagine (1996)

26. White, B., et al.: An integrated experimental environment for distributed systems and networks. In: OSDI 2002, pp. 255–270. USENIX Association, Boston, December 2002

Threshold-Based Network Structural Dynamics

Evangelos Kipouridis[1]($\boxtimes$) iD, Paul G. Spirakis[2,3] iD, and Kostas Tsichlas[3] iD

[1] Basic Algorithms Research Copenhagen (BARC), University of Copenhagen, Universitetsparken 1, 2100 Copenhagen, Denmark
kipouridis@di.ku.dk
[2] Department of Computer Science, University of Liverpool, Ashton Street, Liverpool L69 3BX, UK
P.Spirakis@liverpool.ac.uk
[3] Computer Engineering and Informatics Department, University of Patras, Patras, Greece
{spirakis,ktsichlas}@ceid.upatras.gr

Abstract. The interest in dynamic processes on networks is steadily rising in recent years. In this paper, we consider the (α, β)-Thresholded Network Dynamics ((α, β)-Dynamics), where $\alpha \leq \beta$, in which only structural dynamics (dynamics of the network) are allowed, guided by local thresholding rules executed by each node. In particular, in each discrete round t, each pair of nodes u and v that are allowed to communicate by the scheduler, computes a value $\mathcal{E}(u, v)$ (the potential of the pair) as a function of the local structure of the network at round t around the two nodes. If $\mathcal{E}(u, v) < \alpha$ then the link (if it exists) between u and v is removed; if $\alpha \leq \mathcal{E}(u, v) < \beta$ then an existing link among u and v is maintained; if $\beta \leq \mathcal{E}(u, v)$ then a link between u and v is established if not already present.

The microscopic structure of (α, β)-Dynamics appears to be simple, so that we are able to rigorously argue about it, but still flexible, so that we are able to design meaningful microscopic local rules that give rise to interesting macroscopic behaviors. Our goals are the following: a) to investigate the properties of the (α, β)-Thresholded Network Dynamics and b) to show that (α, β)-Dynamics is expressive enough to solve complex problems on networks.

Our contribution in these directions is twofold. We rigorously exhibit the claim about the expressiveness of (α, β)-Dynamics, both by designing a simple protocol that provably computes the k-core of the network as well as by showing that (α, β)-Dynamics are in fact Turing-Complete. Second and most important, we construct general tools for proving stabilization that work for a subclass of (α, β)-Dynamics and prove speed of convergence in a restricted setting.

Keywords: Network dynamics · Stabilization

© Springer Nature Switzerland AG 2021
T. Jurdziński and S. Schmid (Eds.): SIROCCO 2021, LNCS 12810, pp. 127–145, 2021.
https://doi.org/10.1007/978-3-030-79527-6_8

1 Introduction

The interplay between the microscopic and the macroscopic in terms of emergent behavior shows an increasing interest. The most striking examples come from biological systems that seem to form macroscopic structures out of local interactions between simpler structures (e.g., computation of shortest paths by Physarum Polycephalum [23], or of maximal independent sets by the fly's nervous system [1]). The underlying common characteristic of these systems is the emergent behavior at the macroscopic level out of simple local interactions at the microscopic level. This is one of the reasons why in the last years there has been a surge in the analysis and design of elementary and fundamental primitives in distributed systems under restrictive assumptions on the model [9]. In some of these examples, the dynamic processes are purely structural with respect to the network. These examples include network generation models [7,29], community detection [32], "life-like" cellular automata [27], robot motion [25] and go all the way up to fundamental physics as a candidate model for space [30,31]. In view of this recent trend, a stream of work is devoted to the study of such dynamics per se, without a particular application in mind (e.g., [14]). Motivated by such a plethora of examples, we study the stabilization properties of protocols that affect solely the structure of networks.

Henceforth, we will use the term *dynamic network* to represent networks that change due to some process, although in the literature one can find other terms like adaptive networks, time-varying networks, evolving networks and temporal networks that essentially refer to the same general idea of time-dependent networks w.r.t. structure and states. The study of the processes that drive dynamic networks and their resulting properties has been the focus of many different fields but in general one can discern between two distinct viewpoints without excluding overlap: **a) complex systems viewpoint (physics, sociology, ecology, etc.):** the main focus is on modeling (e.g., differential/difference equations, cellular automata, etc. - see [26]) and qualitative analysis (by means of mean field approximations, bifurcation analysis etc.). The main questions here are of qualitative nature and include phase transitions, complexity of system behavior, etc. Rigorous analysis is not usual and simulation is the main tool for providing results. **b) computational viewpoint (mainly computer science and communications):** the main focus is on the computational capabilities (computability/complexity) of dynamic networks in various settings and with different assumptions. The main approach in computer science is based on rigorous proofs while in communications it is based on experimentation.

When designing local rules aiming at some particular global/emergent behavior, it is usually difficult, or at the very least cumbersome, to prove correctness [9]. This is why most studies in complex systems of this sort are based on experimental evidence for their correctness. Thus, it is very important to prove general results about protocols, and not argue about them in a case-by-case fashion. In this paper, we study a dynamic network driven by a simple protocol that is executed by each node in a synchronous manner. The protocol is the same for all nodes and can only affect the structure of the network and not the state of edges or nodes. The locality of the protocol is defined with respect to the available interactions for each node that are defined by a scheduler. We define the (α, β)-Dynamics in Sect. 2 and we also discuss related work. In Sect. 3, we discuss a particular protocol that computes the α-core and the $(\alpha - 1)$-crust [8] of an arbitrary provided network. In Sect. 4 we provide guarantees on the speed of stabilization for a subclass of (α, β)-Dynamics while in Sect. 5 we provide a proof of stabilization for a more general class of such protocols. In this way, we provide general results for (α, β)-Dynamics that may be directly applied elsewhere, e.g., in the case of restricted Network Automata [27]. In Sect. 6 we prove that (α, β)-Dynamics is Turing-Complete. Finally, in Sect. 7 we discuss some extensions of the proposed model and we conclude in Sect. 8.

2   Preliminaries

Assume that an undirected simple network $G^{(0)} = (V, E^{(0)})$ evolves over time (discrete time) based on a set of rules. We represent the network at time t by $G^{(t)} = (V, E^{(t)})$. We denote the *distance* between two nodes u, v in $G^{(t)}$ as $d^{(t)}(u, v)$. Let $n = |V|$, $m^{(t)} = |E^{(t)}|$ and let $N_{G^{(t)}}(u)$ be the set of all neighbors of node u and $d_{G^{(t)}}(u)$ be the *degree* of node u in network $G^{(t)}$. We define $\left|E^{(t)}(u, v)\right|$ to be the number of edges between u and v at time t (either 0 or 1), and more generally $\left|E^{(t)}(U)\right|$ to be the number of edges between nodes in the set $U \subseteq V$ at time t. It follows that $\left|E^{(t)}(N_{G^{(t)}}(u) \cap N_{G^{(t)}}(v))\right|$ is the number of edges between common neighbors of u and v at time t. Let $G^{(t)}[S]$ represent the induced subgraph of the node set $S \subseteq V$ in $G^{(t)}$. The *potential* of a pair of nodes u and v at round t is a function related to this pair and is represented by $\mathcal{E}_{G^{(t)}}^{(t)}(u, v) : G^{(t)}[S] \rightarrow \mathbb{R}$, for some $S \subseteq V$. The domain of the potential is the induced subgraph $G^{(t)}[S]$ defined by the set of nodes S that are at the local structure around nodes u and v. This local structure is defined explicitly by the potential function. In this paper, S consists of all nodes that are within constant distance from u or from v (the constant is 1 throughout the paper, except for Sect. 6 where it is 3). We write $\mathcal{E}^{(t)}(u, v)$ or $\mathcal{E}(u, v)$ when the network and the time we are referring to are clear from the context. An example of such a function defined in [32] that is used to detect communities in networks is the following:

$$\mathcal{E}(u, v) = |N_{G^{(t)}}(u) \cap N_{G^{(t)}}(v)| + |E^{(t)}(u, v)| + |E(N_{G^{(t)}}(u) \cap N_{G^{(t)}}(v))|$$

The potential is equal to the number of common neighbors between u and v plus the number of edges between u and v (0 or 1) plus the number of edges between the common neighbors of u and v.

Finally, let $f : \mathbb{N}^2 \rightarrow \mathbb{R}$ be a continuous function having the following two properties: i) Non-decreasing, that is $f(x, y + \epsilon) \geq f(x, y)$ for $\epsilon > 0$ (similarly $f(x+\epsilon, y) \geq f(x, y)$) and ii) Symmetric, $f(x, y) = f(y, x)$. The second property is related to the fact that we consider undirected networks. We call these functions *proper*.

2.1 (α, β)-Dynamics - Thresholded Network Dynamics

Informally, the (α, β)-Thresholded Network Dynamics ((α, β)-Dynamics henceforth) in its general form is a discrete-time dynamic stateless network of agents $G^{(t)} = (V, E^{(t)})$. It is stateless because the dynamics driven by the protocol depend only on the structure of the network and not on state information stored in each node/edge. The dynamics involve the edges of the network while the set of agents is static. All interactions are pairwise and are defined by a scheduler. For each interaction, the two involved nodes execute a protocol that affects the edge between them. The execution of the protocol and all communication is carried out on the network $G^{(t)}$, while the scheduler is responsible for the determination of the interactions that activate the execution of the protocol between pairs of nodes in $G^{(t)}$.

The protocol is *consistent*, in the sense that it comes to the same decision about the existence of the edge between u and v, both when executed by u and by v. This requires the potential of an arbitrary edge (u, v) to be *computationally symmetric*, in the sense that $\mathcal{E}(u, v)$ is the same when computed in u and in v. The execution evolves in synchronous discrete time rounds. In the following, the edge $e^{(t)}$ is also used as a boolean variable. In particular, when $e^{(t)} = 0$ then $e^{(t)} \notin E^{(t)}$, while $e^{(t)} = 1$ means that $e^{(t)} \in E^{(t)}$. Let α and β be parameters that correspond to a lower and an upper threshold, respectively. Initially, the network $G^{(0)}$ is given as well as the constant thresholds α and β. Formally, (α, β)-Dynamics is a triple $(G^{(0)}, \mathcal{S}, \mathcal{A}(\alpha, \beta))$ defined as follows:

- $G^{(0)} = (V, E^{(0)})$: A network of nodes V and edges $E^{(0)}$ between nodes at time 0. This is the network where the dynamic process concerning the edges is performed. Each node $v \in V$ has a distinct id and maintains a routing table with all its edges.
- $\mathcal{S}$: The scheduler that contains the pairwise interactions between nodes. We represent it by a possibly infinite series of sets of pairwise interactions $C^{(t)}$. Each set $C^{(t)}$ contains the pairwise interactions between nodes activated at time step t in the network $G^{(t)}$. An interaction between nodes u and v, assumes direct communication between u and v irrespective of whether u and v are connected by an edge in $G^{(t)}$. In the following, by slightly abusing notation, we will refer to $C^{(t)}$ as the scheduler for time step t.
- $\mathcal{A}(\alpha, \beta)$: The protocol executed in each round by each node participating in the pairwise interactions defined by the scheduler $C^{(t)}$ in order to update network $G^{(t)}$ to network $G^{(t+1)}$. The (α, β)-Dynamics is defined for the following family of protocols:

    Protocol $\mathcal{A}(\alpha, \beta)$ at node u for a pairwise interaction $(u, v) \in C^{(t)}$:
        Compute the potential $\mathcal{E}(u, v)$.
            1. If $\mathcal{E}(u, v) < \alpha$ then edge $(u, v)^{(t+1)} = 0$.
            2. If $\alpha \leq \mathcal{E}(u, v) < \beta$ then edge $(u, v)^{(t+1)} = (u, v)^{(t)}$.
            3. If $\mathcal{E}(u, v) \geq \beta$ then edge $(u, v)^{(t+1)} = 1$.

The computational capabilities of each node are similar to a LOG-space Turing machine. Each node has two different memories, the input memory as well as the working memory. The input memory contains the local structural information of the network necessary for the computation of the potential function at node u. The potential function reads the input memory and its value is computed by using the working memory. We allow only protocols that require polynomial time w.r.t. the size of the input memory keeping the working memory logarithmic (asymptotically) in size w.r.t. the size of the input memory.

The complexity of the protocol depends solely on the definition of the potential function, since the rest of the protocol are simple threshold comparisons. Similarly to dynamics [9] - although no relevant formal definition exists [10] - we require our protocol to be simple and lightweight and to realize natural, local and elementary rules subject to the constraint that structural dynamics are considered. To this end, we require the potential function to respect the following constraints:

1. The potential function has access to a small constant distance c away from the two interacting nodes.
2. The potential function must be indistinguishable with respect to the nodes - thus not allowing for special nodes (e.g., leaders) [10][1].
3. The potential function must be network-agnostic, in the sense that it is designed without having any access to the topology of $G^{(0)}$.

These restrictions combined with the computational capabilities of nodes do not allow the protocol to use shortcuts for computation in terms of hardwired information in the potential function (node ids) or in terms of replacing large subgraphs by other subgraphs.

In each round, the protocol is executed by the nodes that participate in the pairwise interactions (u, v) determined by the scheduler. A pairwise interaction between nodes u and v requires the computation of the potential between the two nodes and then a decision is made as for the edge between them based on the thresholds α and β. Each round of the computation for node u (symmetrically for v) is divided into the following phases: (1) u sends messages to its local neighborhood (with the exception of v, if edge (u, v) exists) requesting information related to the computation of the potential function, (2) u receives the requested information and stores it in the input memory, (3) u sends its information to v, (4) u receives v's information and stores it in the input memory, (5) u computes the potential using the working memory and (6) it decides as for the edge (u, v) w.r.t. thresholds.

The consistency of the protocol guarantees that the result of its execution is the same for u and v. In accordance to the LOCAL model, there is no restriction on the size of the messages. Finally, direct communication is assumed (in phases (3) and (4)) between the interacting nodes u and v irrespective of the existence of edge (u, v). In the example of the potential function given in Sect. 2, each round executes at u (symmetrically for v) as follows: (1) u sends messages to all its neighbors, (2) u receives messages carrying information about its neighbors and their edges, (3) u sends its gathered information to v, (4) u receives the gathered information from

---

[1] Therefore, we only use identifiers of nodes for analysis purposes.

v, (5) u computes the potential between u and v and (6) it makes a decision about edge (u, v) and appropriately updates its connection information.

(α, β)-Dynamics is stateless, in the sense that the dynamics driven by the algorithm $\mathcal{A}$ consider only the structure of the network. No states that are stored at nodes or edges are considered in the dynamic evolution expressed by (α, β)-Dynamics. Although nodes have memory to store connections to their neighbors that change due to the dynamic process and to store the additional information required for the computation of the potential function, no additional states are used to impose changes in the network. As a result, the network $G^{(t)}$ completely defines the configuration of the system at time t. We say that $G^{(t)}$ *yields* $G^{(t+1)}$, when a transition takes place from $G^{(t)}$ to $G^{(t+1)}$ after time step t, represented as $G^{(t)} \xrightarrow{C^{(t)}} G^{(t+1)}$, which is the result of the $\mathcal{A}$ protocol for all pairwise interactions encoded in $C^{(t)}$. Similarly, we write $G^{(t)} \rightsquigarrow G^{(t')}$, for $t' > t$, if there exists a sequence of transitions $G^{(t)} \xrightarrow{C^{(t)}} G^{(t+1)} \xrightarrow{C^{(t+1)}} \ldots \xrightarrow{C^{(t'-1)}} G^{(t')}$. An *execution* of (α, β)-Dynamics is a finite or infinite sequence of configurations $G^{(0)}, G^{(1)}, G^{(2)}, \ldots$ such that for each t, $G^{(t)}$ yields $G^{(t+1)}$, where $G^{(0)}$ is the initial network.

We say that the algorithm *converges* or *stabilizes* when $\exists t$ such that $\forall t' > t$ it holds that $G^{(t)} = G^{(t')}$, meaning that the network does not change after time t. The *output* of the (α, β)-Dynamics is the network that results after stabilization has been reached. The time complexity of the protocol is the number of steps until stabilization. The time complexity of the protocol heavily depends on $C^{(t)}$. If, for example, there exists a T where for all $t \geq T$ it holds that $C^{(t)}$ is always the null set, then the algorithm stabilizes although it would not stabilize for a different choice of $C^{(t)}$. To avoid stalling, we employ the *weak fairness condition* [2,3] that essentially states that all pairs of nodes interact infinitely often, thus imposing that the scheduler cannot avoid a possible change in the network. In the case of the protocol described in Sect. 3, we will be very careful as to the definition of $C^{(t)}$ w.r.t. time complexity while for our stabilization theorems we either assume a particular $C^{(t)}$ or allow it to be arbitrary. However, in the latter case we do not claim bounds on the time complexity, only eventual stabilization. Note that it is not our goal in this paper to solve the problem of termination detection.

At this point, a discussion on the scheduler $\mathcal{S}$ is necessary. The scheduler $C^{(t)}$ at time t supports parallelism since it is a set of pairwise interactions that has size at most $\binom{n}{2}$. Thus, many pairwise interactions may be activated in each step. For example, consider the case where all $\binom{n}{2}$ possible edges are contained in $C^{(t)}$. This means that simultaneously the potential is computed for all possible pairwise interactions and the edges are updated analogously. In [32], a serialization of this case is used to detect communities in networks. In general, we may assume anything about the scheduler (adversarial, stochastic, etc.). Arguing about an arbitrary set of pairwise interactions for each t is the most general case, since $\mathcal{A}$ can make no assumption at all about the pairwise interactions that will be activated within each round but the fairness condition must be employed in order to argue about stabilization.

On a more technical note, the scheduler has two different but not necessarily mutually exclusive uses. On the one hand, the scheduler models restrictions set by the environment on the interactions (e.g., random interactions in a passive model). On the other hand, it is used as a tool for analysis reasons, to describe the communication links that the protocol $\mathcal{A}$ enforces on $G^{(t)}$ (e.g., when a node communicates with all nodes at distance 2). The scheduler cannot and should not cheat, that is to be used in order to help $\mathcal{A}$ carry out the computation. In this paper, we present some general results w.r.t. the choice of the scheduler. For example, $C^{(t)}$ may be adversarial for all t, satisfying the fairness condition, while our algorithms are still able to stabilize (see Sects. 3 and 5). Although (α, β)-Dynamics may seem to be a rather restricting setting, the freedom in defining the potential and the parameters α and β allow us to have very rich behavior - in fact, we show that (α, β)-Dynamics is Turing-Complete.

2.2 Related Work

The main work on dynamic networks stems either from computer science or from complex systems and is inherently interdisciplinary in nature. In the following, we only highlight results that are directly related to ours (a more extensive discussion can be found in [20]). In computer science, a nice review of the dynamic network domain [22] proposes a partitioning of the current literature into three subareas: Population Protocols [3,4], Powerful Dynamic Distributed Systems (e.g., [24]) and models for Temporal Graphs (e.g., [11]). (α, β)-Dynamics can be compared to Population Protocols, where anonymous agents with only a constant amount of memory available interact with each other and are able to compute functions, like leader election. Their scheduler determines the set of pairs of nodes among which one will be chosen for computation at each time step. The choice is made by a scheduler either arbitrarily (adversarial scheduler) or uniformly at random (uniform random scheduler). The uniform scheduler is used for designing various protocols due to the probabilistic accommodations for analysis it provides. The major differences to our approach are with respect to dynamics and the scheduler. Population protocols study state dynamics while in our case we study stateless structural dynamics. In addition, in our approach, the scheduler consists of a set of pairwise interactions, thus allowing for many computations between pairs of nodes during a time step (parallel time). This parallelism of the scheduler may "artificially" reduce the number of rounds but it can also complicate the protocol leading to interesting research questions. Similarly to population protocols, the notion of dynamics [9,10] that refers to distributed processes that resemble interacting particle systems considers simple and lightweight protocols on states of agents. (α, β)-Dynamics could be cast in such a framework as purely structural dynamics that on the one hand supports simple, uniform and lightweight protocols while on the other hand requires necessarily the communication of structural information between nodes. In the same manner, motivated by population protocols, the Network Constructors model also studies state dynamics that affect the structure of the network resulting in structural dynamics as well, and thus it is much closer to (α, β)-Dynamics.

In [20, 21] the authors study what stable networks can be constructed (like paths, stars, and more complex networks) by a population of finite-automata. Among other complexity related results they also argue that the Network Constructors model is Turing-Complete. Our main differences to the network constructors model are the following:

1. Our motivation comes from the complex systems domain as well, and thus we are more interested in as general as possible convergence/stabilization theorems apart from particular network constructions (like the α-core in our case).
2. They use states for the structural dynamics while in our case the dynamics are stateless. This means that Network Constructors use states that change according to the protocol, which in turn drive the structural changes of the network (coupled dynamics). In our case, we use only the knowledge of the structure of the network to make structural changes.
3. They always start from a null network while we start from an arbitrary one.

In the study of complex systems, one of the tools used for modeling is cellular automata. Cellular automata use simple update rules that give rise to interesting patterns [6, 15]. Structurally Dynamic Cellular Automata (SDCA) that couples the topology with the local site 0/1 value configuration were introduced in [17]. They formalize this notion and move to an experimental qualitative analysis of its behavior for various parameters. They left as an extension (among others) of SDCA purely structural CA models in which there are no value configurations as it holds in the (α, β)-Dynamics studied in this paper. A model for coupling topology with functional dynamics was given in [27], termed Functional Network Automata (FNA), and was used as a model for a biological process. They also defined the restricted Network Automata (rNA), which as (α, β)-Dynamics allows only for stateless structural network dynamics. rNA forces every possible pair of interactions to take place, meaning that for all t it holds that $C^{(t)}$ contains all $\binom{n}{2}$ possible edges of the n nodes. All their results are qualitative and are based on experimentation. By using the machinery built in Sect. 5 we show that for the family of protocols we consider, rNA always stabilizes. To further stimulate the reader as for the need of looking at (α, β)-Dynamics, the author in [25] looked at modular robots as an evolving network with respect only to their topology. The author defined a graph topodynamic, which in fact is a local program common to all modules of the robot, that turns a tree topology to a chain topology conjecturing that stabilization is always achieved but to the best of our knowledge it is still unresolved.

3   Taking the Minimum

As a motivation and exhibition of (α, β)-Dynamics, we first discuss the following interesting example. We define the potential of a pair of nodes u and v as $\mathcal{E}(u, v) = \min\{d_{G^{(t)}}(u), d_{G^{(t)}}(v)\}$, that is the potential is equal to the minimum degree of the two nodes. This potential function respects all constraints described in Sect. 2.1.

It is interesting to notice the similarity of our process, and the process of acquiring the $k - core$ (or complementary the $(k-1) - crust$) of a simple undirected graph [8,28].

Definition 1. *The k-core H of a graph G is the unique maximal subgraph of G such that $\forall u \in H$ it holds that $deg_H(u) \geq k$. All nodes not in H form the $(k-1)$-crust of G.*

The k-core plays an important role in studying the clustering structure of networks [19]. In [8] it was proved that the following process efficiently computes the k-core of a graph:

Lemma 1. *Given a graph G and a number k, one can compute G's k-core by repeatedly deleting all nodes whose degree is less than k.*

The following theorem states that stabilization to the k-core is achieved for an arbitrary scheduler S. Furthermore, the stabilization occurs after $O(m)$ rounds of changes in the network, where m is the number of edges in G. Note that this is not the time complexity of the protocol, since there may be many idle rounds between rounds with changes, depending on the scheduler. The proof of the theorem can be found in the full version of our paper [13].

Theorem 1. *When $\mathcal{E}(u,v) = \min\{d_{G^{(t)}}(u), d_{G^{(t)}}(v)\}$, (α,β)-Dynamics for any value of $\alpha \leq n - 1 < \beta$ and any scheduler S, stabilizes in a network where all isolated nodes form the $(\alpha-1)$-crust and the rest the α-core of $G^{(0)}$ in $O(m)$ rounds where changes happen, where m is the number of edges in $G^{(0)}$.*

A final note concerns the time complexity. Note that the aforementioned theorem does not state anything about the time complexity of the protocol, it just states the maximum number of rounds where a change happens. We can compute the time complexity if we describe the scheduler. If we assume that $\forall t : C^{(t)} = E^{(t)}$, that is the scheduler contains all edges and only those of the $G^{(t)}$ network then the time complexity is $O(n)$. This is because, at each round it is guaranteed that one node will become isolated unless stabilization has been achieved. Similarly, if we assume a uniform scheduler that chooses one pair of nodes uniformly at random in each time step, then the (α,β)-Dynamics stabilizes in $O(mn^2 \log m)$ steps by a simple application of the coupon collector problem on the selection of edges.

4 (α,β)-Dynamics with $\alpha = \beta$ and a Proper Potential Function on the Degrees

We study the (α,β)-Dynamics where the potential is any symmetric non-decreasing function on the degrees of its two endpoints. We prove that in this case (α,β)-Dynamics stabilizes while the time complexity is $O(n)$, assuming that $\alpha = \beta$ and that for all t, $C^{(t)}$ contains all $\binom{n}{2}$ possible pairwise interactions. All proofs can be found in the full version of our paper [13]. More formally, we define the potential of a pair (u, v) to be $\mathcal{E}(u, v) = f(d_{G^{(t)}}(u), d_{G^{(t)}}(v))$, where f is a *proper* (symmetric and non-decreasing in both variables) function. Since f is proper, the potential function is computationally symmetric and thus the protocol is consistent.

For the network $G^{(t)}$, let $R^{(t)}(u, v)$ be an equivalence relation defined on the set of nodes V for time t, such that $(u, v) \in R^{(t)}$ iff $d_{G^{(t)}}(u) = d_{G^{(t)}}(v)$. The equivalence class $R_i^{(t)}$ corresponds to all nodes with degree $d(R_i^{(t)})$, where i is the rank of the degree in decreasing order. Thus the equivalence class $R_1^{(t)}$ contains all nodes with maximum degree in $G^{(t)}$. Assuming that $n = |V|$, the maximum number of equivalence classes is $n - 1$, as the degree can be in the range $[0, n-1]$ and no pair of nodes (u, v) with degrees $d_{G^{(t)}}(u) = 0$ and $d_{G^{(t)}}(v) = n - 1$ can exist. Let $|G^{(t)}|$ be the number of equivalence classes in $G^{(t)}$.

We prove by induction that in this setting, (α, β)-Dynamics always stabilizes in at most $|G^{(0)}| + 1$ steps. To begin with, the clique $\mathcal{K}_n$ as well as the null graph $\overline{\mathcal{K}_n}$ both stabilize in at most one step, for any value of β. The following renormalization lemma describes how the number of equivalence classes is reduced and is crucial to the induction proof.

Lemma 2. *If $d(R_1^{(t)}) = n - 1$, $\forall t \geq c, c \in \mathbb{N}$, and the subgraph $G^{(c)} \setminus R_1^{(c)}$ stabilizes for any value of β and proper function f, then $G^{(c)}$ stabilizes as well. Similarly, if $d(R_{|G^{(t)}|}^{(t)}) = 0$, $\forall t \geq c, c \in \mathbb{N}$, and the subgraph $G^{(c)} \setminus R_{|G^{(c)}|}^{(c)}$ stabilizes for any value of β and proper function f, then $G^{(c)}$ stabilizes as well. The time it takes for $G^{(c)}$ to stabilize is the same as the time it takes for the induced subgraph to stabilize for both cases.*

The following theorem establishes stabilization in linear time.

Theorem 2. *When $\alpha = \beta$, f is proper, $\mathcal{E}(u, v) = f(d_{G^{(t)}}(u), d_{G^{(t)}}(v))$, and the scheduler contains all $\binom{n}{2}$ possible pairwise interactions in each time step, (α, β)-Dynamics with input $G^{(0)}$ stabilizes in at most $|G^{(0)}| + 1$ steps.*

5 (α, β)-Dynamics Stabilization for Arbitrary Scheduler

In this section, we prove stabilization (with no speed bound) for any $\alpha \leq \beta$ in an adversarial setting where the scheduler $\mathcal{S}$ may be completely arbitrary subject to the fairness condition. In addition, we further generalize by changing the definition of potential, from $\mathcal{E}(u, v) = f(d_{G^{(t)}}(u), d_{G^{(t)}}(v))$ to $\mathcal{E}(u, v) = f(g_{G^{(t)}}(u), g_{G^{(t)}}(v))$, for a family of functions $g_G : \mathbb{R}^k \to \mathbb{R}, k \in \mathbb{N}$. We call a function $g_G(u)$ *degree-like* if it only depends on the neighborhood $N_G(u)$ of node u and has the following property: assuming that the neighborhood of node u at time t is $N_{G^{(t)}}(u)$, and the neighborhood of v at time t' is $N_{G^{(t')}}(v)$, and $N_{G^{(t)}}(u) \supseteq N_{G^{(t')}}(v)$, then we require that $g_{G^{(t)}}(u) \geq g_{G^{(t')}}(v)$. The reason we extend the notion of degree is to represent more interesting rules as shown in the toy model of social dynamics of Sect. 7.

The potential function is computationally symmetric since f is proper and g is common for u and v. The protocol in Sect. 4 is a special case of this protocol, where g is the degree of the node, the scheduler contains all $\binom{n}{2}$ possible pairwise interactions at each time step and $\alpha = \beta$. We first need the following definition:

Definition 2. A pair (t, D) is $|D| - Done$ if $t \in \mathbb{N}$, $D \subseteq V$ and $\forall u \in D$ it holds that their neighborhood does not change after time t. That is, $N_{G^{(t')}}(u) = N_{G^{(t)}}(u)$, for $t' \geq t$.

Our stabilization proof repeatedly detects $|D| - Done$ pairs with increasing $|D|$. When $D = V$, all neighborhoods do not change, and thus the process stabilizes.

Lemma 3. If there exists a $|D| - Done$ pair (t, D) at round t with $|D| < |V|$, then $\exists t' > t$ such that at round t' there exists a $(|D| + 1) - Done$ pair (t', D').

Proof. The core idea is to find a time-step t_1 where a node $u \notin D$ maximizes g, as specified in the next paragraph; if u never drops any edge in subsequent time steps, we prove that its neighborhood is stabilized, and we extend D by u; if it drops an edge with a node w, this node w is not able to preserve any other edge, due to the selection of u, and we are able to extend D by w.

More formally, we denote by $t_1 \geq t$ the time-step where there is some node $u \notin D$ such that $g_{G^{(t_1)}}(u) \geq g_{G^{(t_1')}}(v)$, for all $t_1' \geq t_1$ and $v \notin D$. If there are many choices for t_1 and u, we pick any t_1 and u such that u has the highest degree possible. Note that, later in time (say at $t_1' > t_1$), it is entirely possible that u's neighborhood shrinks and thus its g value drops ($g_{G^{(t_1')}}(u) < g_{G^{(t_1)}}(u)$). It is guaranteed that t_1 exists, as there are finitely many graphs with $|V|$ nodes, and finitely many nodes. Thus, there are finitely many values of $g_G(u)$ to appear after time t. Additionally, the fairness condition guarantees that the pairwise interaction between u and v will be eventually activated, for any v.

If u never drops any edge after t_1, then its neighborhood can only grow or stay the same. But if its neighborhood grows, due to the properties of function g, its value will not drop and the degree of u will increase. However, the way we picked u and t_1 does not allow this. We conclude that the neighborhood of u does not change after time t_1, and thus we can extend D by $\{u\}$, that is $(t_1, D \cup \{u\})$ is $(|D| + 1) - Done$. Else, if u drops an edge after t_1, let $t_2 > t_1$ be the first time step that a neighbor w of u in $G^{(t_2-1)}$ is not a neighbor of u in $G^{(t_2)}$. Since u's neighborhood stays the same until $t_2 - 1$, it follows that $g_{G^{(t_1)}}(u) = g_{G^{(t_2-1)}}(u)$. The neighborhood of w does not grow at subsequent time steps, that is $N_{G^{(t_2')}}(w) \supseteq N_{G^{(t_2'+1)}}(w)$, $t_2' \geq t_2 - 1$. To prove this, we show that w never forms a new edge after $t_2 - 1$. Suppose it does at $t_2' + 1$ for the first time. Then w forms an edge with some node $v \notin D$, due to the definition of D. However, we know that $\beta \geq \alpha > f(g_{G^{(t_2-1)}}(u), g_{G^{(t_2-1)}}(w)) = f(g_{G^{(t_1)}}(u), g_{G^{(t_2-1)}}(w)) \geq f(g_{G^{(t_2')}}(v), g_{G^{(t_2')}}(w))$, due to f being non-decreasing, g being degree-like, and the definition of u and t_1. Thus, an edge between v and w cannot be formed.

We conclude that the neighborhood of w can only shrink after time t_2. But there are only finitely many options for the neighborhood of w, and thus there is a time $t_3 \geq t_2$ where the neighborhood of w is the same in all subsequent graphs. Therefore, we can extend D by $\{w\}$, that is $(t_3, D \cup \{w\})$ is $(|D| + 1) - Done$.

Theorem 3. *For $\mathcal{E}(u, v) = f(g_{G^{(t)}}(u), g_{G^{(t)}}(v))$, (α, β)-Dynamics stabilizes for any $\alpha \leq \beta$, proper function f, degree-like function g and arbitrary scheduler $\mathcal{S}$ subject to the fairness condition.*

Proof. It trivially holds that $(0, \emptyset)$ is $0 - Done$. By applying Lemma 3 once, we increase the size of D by 1. Thus, by applying it $|V|$ times, we end up with a $|V| - Done$ pair (t, V). Since all neighborhoods stay the same for all future steps, $G^{(t')} = G^{(t)}$ for all $t' \geq t$.

Theorem 3 can directly prove stabilization of the protocol in Sect. 3.

6   Turing-Completeness

In this section we describe the (α, β)-Dynamics that is able to simulate Rule 110, a one-dimensional Cellular Automaton (CA) that Cook proved to be Turing-Complete [12] (for a discussion on CA and Rule 110, see the appendix of the full version of our paper [13]). Thus, we prove that (α, β)-Dynamics is Turing-Complete as well, meaning that it is computationally universal since it can simulate any Turing machine (or in other terms any algorithm). Due to space restrictions, we only describe our construction; all lemmas and proofs can be found in the full version of our paper [13].

Definition 3. *Rule 110 is a one-dimensional CA. Let $cell^{(t)}(i)$ be the binary value of the i-th cell at time t. If $cell^{(t)}(i) = 0$, then $cell^{(t+1)}(i) = cell^{(t)}(i + 1)$. Else, $cell^{(t+1)}(i)$ is 0 if $cell^{(t)}(i - 1) = cell^{(t)}(i + 1) = 1$, and 1 otherwise.*

Let $CN^{(t)}(u, v) = |N_{G^{(t)}}(u) \cap N_{G^{(t)}}(v)|$ be the number of common neighbors of u and v at time t, and $CE^{(t)}(u, v) = |E(CN^{(t)}(u, v))|$ be the number of edges between the common neighbors of u and v at time t. For the following simulation we assume w.l.o.g. that $\alpha = \beta$ and that the scheduler $\mathcal{S}$ contains all possible $\binom{n}{2}$ interactions, for all time steps. The potential between nodes u and v is defined as follows:

$$\mathcal{E}^{(t)}(u, v) = \begin{cases} \beta + 60 + CE^{(t)}(u, v) - CN^{(t)}(u, v) & \text{if } 66 \leq CN^{(t)}(u, v) + |E^{(t)}(u, v)| \leq 70 \\ \beta + 12 - CE^{(t)}(u, v) & \text{if } CN^{(t)}(u, v) + |E^{(t)}(u, v)| = 71 \\ \beta - |E^{(t)}(u, v)| & \text{if } 40 \leq CN^{(t)}(u, v) \leq 41 \\ \beta - 1 + |E^{(t)}(u, v)| & \text{otherwise} \end{cases}$$

The first 2 branches are the ones that are actually related to Rule 110. The rest of them are only used to ensure technical details, namely that some pairs of nodes always flip the status of their connection (Branch 3), effectively providing us with a clock, and some of them always preserve it (Branch 4).

As required, computing the function only uses a constant number of words in the working memory, which have logarithmic size in bits compared to the input memory (which contains the neighborhoods of u and v), and requires polynomial time in the size of the input memory. For example, to compute $CN^{(t)}(u, v)$, one could iterate over all pairs (u', v') such that $u \in N_{G^{(t)}}(u), v \in N_{G^{(t)}}(v)$, and increment a counter initially set to zero, every time $u' = v'$. Similarly, to compute $CE^{(t)}(u, v)$, one can iterate over quadruples u', u'', v', v'' and increment a counter whenever $u' = v', u'' = v''$ and there exists an edge between u' and u''. Additionally, the potential function only depends on nodes at a constant distance (at most 1) from either u or v, and it is network-agnostic (not assuming access on the topology of $G^{(0)}$). Finally it is computationally symmetric and thus the protocol is consistent.

Informally, our simulation of Rule 110 consists of the following steps. First, we design a primitive cell-gadget (henceforth PCG) that stores binary values, but fails to capture Rule 110 since it doesn't distinguish between the left and the right cell. Then, by making use of the PCG as a building block, we build the main cell-gadget (henceforth CG) that is used to simulate a single cell of the CA. Then, each time step from Rule 110 is simulated using 2 rounds of the (α, β)-Dynamics; on the first round, some $PCGs$ acquire their proper value while on the second round, the rest of the $PCGs$ copy the correct value from the ones that already acquired it. Finally, the two steps are merged into one in order to achieve stabilization of the dynamics when Rule 110 has also stabilized.

For clarity purposes, we slightly abuse notation, and we count the rounds of the (α, β)-Dynamics by multiples of 0.5 instead of 1. Thus, we write that the sequence of configurations is $G^{(0)}, G^{(0.5)}, G^{(1)}...$, where configurations $G^{(t+0.5)}$, for $t \in \mathbb{N}$, are transitional states of the network and have no correspondence with cell states of the CA.

In order to construct the PCG and the CG, we first construct two auxiliary gadgets, the always-on (x, y)-gadget and the flip (x, y)-gadget. The always-on (x, y)-gadget is simply a clique of 22 nodes. 20 of them have no edges to other nodes in the network, while 2 of them (namely x and y) may be connected with other nodes. The flip (x, y)-gadget is basically two always-on (x, y)-gadgets, with nodes x and y being the same for both gadgets, with the exception that the edge between x and y may not exist. See Fig. 1 for both of these gadgets. We later show that, under certain conditions, the edge between x and y always exists in an always-on gadget, and flips its state at each time step, in a flip gadget.

A PCG consists of a pair of nodes (h, l), such that the existence of an edge between them corresponds to value 1 and otherwise it corresponds to value 0, and 60 auxiliary nodes $a_1, \ldots a_{60}$. Furthermore, for each of the 120 pairs of the form (h, a_i) and (l, a_i), there exists a corresponding (h, a_i) and (l, a_i)−flip gadget. When we have two different $PCGs$, say A and B, we write $A(h), A(l), A(a_1), \ldots, A(a_{60})$ for the nodes of A and similarly $B(h), B(l), B(a_1)$, $\ldots, B(a_{60})$ for the nodes of B. We write $A^{(t)}$ to denote the value of A at time t; in other words $A^{(t)} = |E^{(t)}(A(h), A(l))|$.

In order to connect two different $PCGs$ (say A and B) we add 4 always-on gadgets: the always-on $(A(h), B(h))$ gadget, the always-on $(A(h), B(l))$ gadget, the always-on $(A(l), B(h))$ gadget and the always-on $(A(l), B(l))$ gadget, as shown in Fig. 1. Intuitively, this relates $CE^{(t)}(A(h), A(l))$ to the sum of values of the connected $PCGs$.

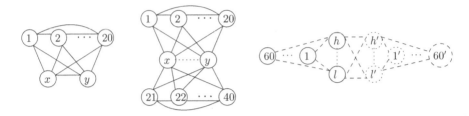

Fig. 1. To the left, we have an always-on (x, y) gadget. In the middle, we have a flip (x, y) gadget; the dotted line between (x, y) denotes that this particular edge may or may not exist. To the right, we have two PCGs. The dashed lines denote flip gadgets, the dotted lines denote that these particular edges may or may not exist. The continuous lines denote always-on gadgets; these 4 always-on gadgets is how we connect PCGs.

The i-th CG that corresponds to the i-th cell (we write $CG(i)$) consists of 4 PCGs, which we identify as $A_1(i)$, $A_2(i)$, $B_1(i)$ and $B_2(i)$. At time $t = 0$, the edge in each flip gadget of $A_1(i)$, $A_2(i)$ exists, while the edge in each flip gadget of $B_1(i)$, $B_2(i)$ does not exist. We connect each $A_j(i)$ with each $B_k(i)$ (4 connections in total, where each connection uses 4 always-on gadgets, as depicted in Fig. 1). In order to connect $CG(i)$ (cell i) with $CG(i + 1)$ (cell $i + 1$) we connect $A_j(i)$ with $A_j(i + 1)$, and $A_j(i)$ with $B_j(i + 1)$. A CG is said to have value 0 if all 4 of its PCGs are set to 0 and 1 if all PCGs are set to 1. We guarantee that no other case can occur in $G^{(t)}$, $t \in \mathbb{N}$, although this is not guaranteed for the intermediate configurations $G^{(t+0.5)}$, $t \in \mathbb{N}$.

To conclude the construction of $G^{(0)}$, each cell of Rule 110 corresponds to a CG in $G^{(0)}$, and neighboring cells have their corresponding CGs connected. Finally, we set the value of its CG (that is the value of its 4 PCGs) equal to the initial value of the corresponding cell.

Using this construction, and by a direct (but quite tedious) case study, we prove that between integer time steps, the only differences in $G^{(t)}$ correspond to the edges defining the values of the CGs. Furthermore, the values of the CGs correspond exactly to the values of the simulated Rule 110 at the same integer time step. Finally, by taking advantage of the locality of our model, we describe a general technique allowing us to skip the intermediate time steps of our current construction, effectively simulating Rule 110. The proof of our final theorem can be found in the full version of our paper [13].

Theorem 4. *The (α, β)-Dynamics is Turing-Complete.*

7   Extensions

We briefly discuss two straightforward extensions of (α, β)-Dynamics and provide related examples. To begin with, we can add static information to nodes/edges (e.g., weights). This information is encoded by the potential function and does not change with time. The degree-like function defined in Sect. 5 can be used to assign a time-independent importance factor (e.g. a known centrality measure in $G^{(0)}$) while letting $g(u)$ be the sum of these factors of nodes in $N_{G^{(t)}}(u)$. To demonstrate it, we provide a small example with a toy model inspired by Structural Balance Theory [16] of networks with friendship and enmity relations [5]. This example is more reminiscent of population dynamics rather than distributed protocols. Assume that the network of agents corresponds to people (nodes) with friendship relations (edges). Each agent v is defined by how nice she is $n(v)$, how extrovert she is $x(v)$ as well as by the set of her enemies $\mathcal{EN}(v)$. We wish to design a model that captures how friendships change in this setting when enemies do not change[2] as well as when friendships are lost in case of very few common friends, while friends are made in the opposite case.

To define the social dynamics we need to define the scheduler and the potential function that essentially describe our toy model. The scheduler captures the interactions between the agents enforced by the model. This toy model is only for the purpose of highlighting our convergence results and we do not claim to realistically capture certain social phenomena. The scheduler is defined as follows: (a) if two agents u and v are enemies then they never become friends (no pairwise interaction between them in $C^{(t)}$, for any t), (b) if two agents u and v are not connected by an edge in $G^{(t)}$ (they are not friends) but their distance is at most the sum of their extrovertedness, then they interact - that is, if at time t it holds that $1 < dist(u, v) \leq x(u) + x(v)$ then there is an edge (u, v) in $C^{(t)}$, (c) if two agents are connected by an edge in $G^{(t)}$, then there is a pairwise interaction between them in $C^{(t)}$ if their number of common friends is $\leq \gamma$. If their common friends are $> \gamma$ then their friendship is strong and it will not be affected at this round, and thus no edge in $C^{(t)}$ is introduced. This concludes the description of the scheduler.

As for the potential function, we define the potential between u and v in $G^{(t)}$ to be $\mathcal{E}(u, v) = (n(u) + \sum_{w \in N(u)} n(w)) + (n(v) + \sum_{w \in N(v)} n(w))$, capturing our intuition that friendships are created or stopped based on how nice the two agents and their neighbors are. This is a computationally symmetric function and thus the protocol is consistent. The function g corresponds to the sum of the niceness of a node plus the niceness of its neighbors and thus it is degree-like. The function f is proper since it is a simple sum between u and v w.r.t. the output of the function g in each node. Thus, (α, β)-Dynamics on this social network stabilizes by Theorem 3 (the proof holds without any modification, even in this somewhat extended version of (α, β)-Dynamics). Theorem 3 also allows us to add any rules w.r.t. the scheduler $\mathcal{S}$ like imposing a maximum number of friends, allowing for additional random connections (to achieve long-range interaction), etc. Similarly, we can change the definition of potential and still prove stabilization as long as the assumptions of Theorem 3 are valid. If these assumptions are violated, as it would be in the case of a potential function that applies to a subset of neighbors (e.g., common neighbors between u and v), then a new analysis is required to prove stabilization, if stabilization can be reached.

---

[2] The permanence of enmity is in fact not exactly compatible with structural balance theory on networks.

Finally, the scheduler allows us to remove the assumption of permanence on enmity by allowing under certain conditions particular pairwise interactions, thus dynamically changing the set $\mathcal{EN}(v)$.

Another straightforward generalization is to allow for general stateless protocols $\mathcal{A}$ targeting at providing algorithmic solutions for specific problems. An example of such a generalization is given below for constructing a spanning star. We show in simple terms the stateless approach when compared to state-dependent approaches for constructing a network (e.g., Network Constructors model [20,21]). In some sense, we already provide such an example of explicit network construction in the case of the α-core. We assume a uniform random scheduler, that is, in our model we assume that in each time step a pairwise interaction is chosen uniformly at random. In [20] they provide a simple protocol that uses states on the nodes, which, starting from the null graph, constructs the spanning star in optimal $\Theta(n^2 \log n)$ expected time. We discuss a protocol $\mathcal{A}$ that computes a spanning star starting from any network. It is reminiscent of the random copying method [18] for generating power law networks. It would be interesting to find out whether hub-and-spoke networks (essentially star networks) can be generated by some similar social process. In this case, the probability of choosing pairwise interactions should be related to the degree of the involved nodes, leading to the definition of a non-uniform random scheduler.

To describe the protocol let u and v be two nodes that interact at time t as determined by the scheduler. If no edge exists between them, an edge (u,v) is added. Assume w.l.o.g. that $d_G^{(t)}(u) > d_G^{(t)}(v)$. Then, the protocol dictates that all edges of v are to be moved to u. In case $d_G^{(t)}(u) = d_G^{(t)}(v) \neq 1$, we break symmetry (symmetry breaking was also needed in [20] by the scheduler) by tossing a fair coin in each node as to which node is going to transfer its neighbors. The nodes communicate the result of their toss and if found equal no change happens in the current round, otherwise we again move all edges from the one node to the other. If $d_G^{(t)}(u) = d_G^{(t)}(v) = 1$ then let x and y be the only neighbors of u and v respectively. If $d_G^{(t)}(x) = d_G^{(t)}(y) = 1$, x and y toss a fair coin and if it happens to be different one of these nodes will be the root of a tree with three leaves. Otherwise, the same process is applied on x and y as in u and v. Note that in this case the degrees of x and y cannot be both equal to 1.

On the positive side, the difference of this protocol to the one given in [20] is that no state dynamics are used and we start from an arbitrary network. However, on the negative side, a pairwise interaction between u and v may affect all nodes up to distance 2 since no states are used that could allow us to move these edges incrementally in future interactions. Correctness is proved based on the observation that in each round when a leaf node has its degree increased then the connected components of the network are reduced, otherwise either a node becomes a leaf or nothing happens due to the symmetry breaking mechanism. Because of this stalling due to symmetry breaking, the time complexity analysis is more involved but we conjecture only by a polylogarithmic factor away from the one in [20] (due to moving the edges). The protocol could be simplified in order to change only the neighborhood of u and v, but the time complexity would increase substantially. To exploit parallel time, we could allow for more interactions per round as long as those are not affecting each other.

8   Conclusion

(α, β)-Dynamics are stateless structural dynamics of a network. The protocol allows for two thresholds that affect the existence of the edges in the pairwise interactions determined by the scheduler at each time step. Since the dynamics are purely structural, the output of the protocol is another network, and thus (α, β)-Dynamics can be considered as a network transformation process. Such a process for example has been used in [32] to detect communities. In fact, the authors wondered whether conditional convergence could be proved. It is a matter of technical details to show that for regular networks one can choose α and β such that the protocol never stabilizes.

For future research, it would be very interesting to look at the notion of parallel time in (α, β)-Dynamics. Another interesting research direction is to see the effect of higher order structural interactions as well as look at how the model is affected when messages are restricted in size (in accordance to the CONGEST model from distributed computing). Finally, inspired by the computation of the α-core in Sect. 3, a very interesting question is to look at more involved problems w.r.t. emergent behavior from simple protocols.

Funding. Evangelos Kipouridis: Received funding from the European Unions Horizon 2020 research and innovation program under the Marie Sklodowska-Curie grant agreement 801199.
Evangelos Kipouridis is also supported by Thorups Investigator Grant 16582, Basic Algorithms Research Copenhagen (BARC), from the VILLUM Foundation.

References

1. Afek, Y., Alon, N., Barad, O., Hornstein, E., Barkai, N., Bar-Joseph, Z.: A biological solution to a fundamental distributed computing problem. Science **331**, 183–5 (2011)
2. Alistarh, D., Gelashvili, R.: Recent algorithmic advances in population protocols. SIGACT News **49**(3), 63–73 (2018)

3. Angluin, D., Aspnes, J., Diamadi, Z., Fischer, M., Peralta, R.: Computation in networks of passively mobile finite-state sensors. Distrib. Comput. **18**(4), 235–253 (2006)
4. Angluin, D., Aspnes, J., Eisenstat, D., Ruppert, E.: The computational power of population protocols. Distrib. Comput. **20**(4), 279–304 (2007)
5. Antal, T., Krapivsky, P., Redner, S.: Social balance on networks: the dynamics of friendship and enmity. Physica D Nonlinear Phenom. **224**(1), 130–136 (2006)
6. Arrighi, P., Dowek, G.: Free fall and cellular automata. Developments in computational models. EPTCS **204**, 1–10 (2015)
7. Barabási, A., Albert, R.: Emergence of scaling in random networks. Science **286**(5439), 509–512 (1999)
8. Batagelj, V., Mrvar, A., Zaveršnik, M.: Partitioning approach to visualization of large graphs. In: Kratochvíyl, J. (ed.) GD 1999. LNCS, vol. 1731, pp. 90–97. Springer, Heidelberg (1999). https://doi.org/10.1007/3-540-46648-7_9
9. Becchetti, L., Clementi, A., Natale, E.: Consensus dynamics: an overview. SIGACT News **51**(1), 58–104 (2020)
10. Becchetti, L., Clementi, A., Natale, E., Pasquale, F., Trevisan, L.: Find your place: simple distributed algorithms for community detection. In: SODA 2017, pp. 940–959 (2017)
11. Casteigts, A., Flocchini, P., Quattrociocchi, W., Santoro, N.: Time-varying graphs and dynamic networks. Int. J. Parallel Emerg. Distrib. Syst. **27**(5), 387–408 (2012)
12. Cook, M.: Universality in elementary cellular automata. Complex Syst. **15**(1), 1–40 (2004)
13. Kipouridis, E., Spirakis, P.G., Tsichals, K.: Threshold-based network structural dynamics. CoRR abs/2103.04955 (2019). http://arxiv.org/abs/2103.04955
14. Gadouleau, M.: On the influence of the interaction graph on a finite dynamical system. Natural Comput. **19**(1), 15–28 (2019). https://doi.org/10.1007/s11047-019-09732-y
15. Gärtner, B., Zehmakan, A.: (Biased) majority rule cellular automata. CoRR abs/1711.10920 (2017)
16. Heider, F.: The Psychology of Interpersonal Relations. John Wiley and Sons, Hoboken (1958)
17. Ilachinski, A.: Structurally dynamic cellular automata. In: Adamatzky, A. (ed.) Cellular Automata. ECSSS, pp. 29–71. Springer, New York (2009). https://doi.org/10.1007/978-1-4939-8700-9_528
18. Kumar, R., Raghavan, P., Rajagopalan, S., Sivakumar, D., Tompkins, A., Upfal, E.: The web as a graph. In: PODS 2000, pp. 1–10 (2000)
19. Malliaros, F.D., Giatsidis, C., Papadopoulos, A.N., Vazirgiannis, M.: The core decomposition of networks: theory, algorithms and applications. VLDB J. **29**(1), 61–92 (2019). https://doi.org/10.1007/s00778-019-00587-4
20. Michail, O., Spirakis, P.G.: Simple and efficient local codes for distributed stable network construction. Distrib. Comput. **29**(3), 207–237 (2015). https://doi.org/10.1007/s00446-015-0257-4
21. Michail, O., Spirakis, P.: Network constructors: a model for programmable matter. In: SOFSEM 2017, pp. 15–34 (2017)
22. Michail, O., Spirakis, P.: Elements of the theory of dynamic networks. Commun. ACM **61**(2), 72 (2018)
23. Nakagaki, T., Yamada, H., Toth, A.: Maze-solving by an amoeboid organism. Nature **407**, 470 (2000)
24. O'Dell, R., Wattenhofer, R.: Information dissemination in highly dynamic graphs. In: DIALM-POMC 2005, pp. 104–110 (2005)

25. Saidani, S.: Self-reconfigurable robots topodynamic. In: Proceedings of the 2004 IEEE International Conference on Robotics and Automation, ICRA, vol. 3, pp. 2883–2887 (2004)
26. Sayama, H., Laramee, C.: Generative network automata: a generalized framework for modeling adaptive network dynamics using graph rewritings. In: Gross, T., Sayama, H. (eds.) Adaptive Networks. UCS, Springer, Heidelberg (2009). https:// doi.org/10.1007/978-3-642-01284-6_15
27. Smith, D., Onnela, J.P., Lee, C., Fricker, M., Johnson, N.: Network automata: coupling structure and function in dynamic networks. Adv. Complex Syst. **14**(03), 317–339 (2011)
28. Szekeres, G., Wilf, H.: An inequality for the chromatic number of a graph. J. Comb. Theory **4**, 1–3 (1968)
29. Watts, D., Strogatz, S.: Collective dynamics of 'small-world' networks. Nature **393**(6684), 440–442 (1998)
30. Wolfram, S.: A New Kind of Science. Wolfram Media Inc., Champaign (2002)
31. Wolfram, S.: A class of models with the potential to represent fundamental physics (2020)
32. Zhang, Y., Wang, J., Wang, Y., Zhou, L.: Parallel community detection on large networks with propinquity dynamics. In: ACM SIGKDD 2009, pp. 997–1006 (2009)

The Epigenetic Consensus Problem

Sabrina Rashid[1], Gadi Taubenfeld[2(✉)], and Ziv Bar-Joseph[3]

[1] Computational Biology Department, Carnegie Mellon University, Pittsburgh, PA, USA
[2] The Interdisciplinary Center, Herzliya, Israel
tgadi@idc.ac.il
[3] Machine Learning Department and Computational Biology Department,
Carnegie Mellon University, Pittsburgh, PA, USA

Abstract. A distributed computing system is a collection of processors that communicate either by reading and writing from shared memory or by sending messages over some communication network. Most prior biologically inspired distributed computing algorithms rely on message passing as the communication model. Here we show that in the process of genome-wide epigenetic modifications, cells utilize their DNA as a shared memory system. We formulate a particular consensus problem, called *the epigenetic consensus problem*, that cells attempt to solve using this shared memory model and then present algorithms, derive expected run time and discuss, analyze and simulate improved methods for solving this problem. Analysis of real biological data indicates that the computational methods indeed reflect aspects of the biological process for genome-wide epigenetic modifications.

1 Introduction

The entire DNA of a single human cell is two meters long, composed of three billion base pairs, and includes about 25,000 genes in it. A gene is a short section of DNA. The purpose of genes are to store information. Most genes contain the information needed to make functional molecules called proteins. Only about one percent of the DNA is made up of protein-coding genes.

The DNA in all the cells of our body is the same, so how can a human (or an organism in general) have different cell types yet one genome? That is, in what sense a neuron is different from a skin cell, given that they both have the same DNA? The answer is that each cell expresses, or turns on, only a fraction of its genes. The rest of the genes are repressed, or turned off. Thus, that set of genes that are expressed in a neuron is different from the set that is expressed in a skin cell.

The expression of some genes (i.e., which genes are on or off) in our body cells are changing all the time. For example, environmental influences, such as a person's diet, stress, and exposure to pollutants, impact gene expression. In this context, *epigenetics* refers to modifications in a cell that do not change the DNA and affect gene activity by activating or deactivating genes. It has been observed that initiating the process of changing the expression of a gene requires many proteins in a cell to coordinate their activates. However, it is not well understood how such coordination is achieved. In this

© Springer Nature Switzerland AG 2021
T. Jurdziński and S. Schmid (Eds.): SIROCCO 2021, LNCS 12810, pp. 146–163, 2021.
https://doi.org/10.1007/978-3-030-79527-6_9

paper, we propose such an explanation by describing an algorithm that each protein is "executing", which achieves the desired observed coordination.

Before we proceed, let us explain the issue of gene expression a bit more. Like virtually all large-scale computing platforms, cellular and molecular systems are mostly distributed, consisting of entities that interact, coordinate, and reach decisions without central control [28]. To date, coordination in such processes was almost always discussed in the context of message passing. Famous examples include neural networks [8] where neurons communicate by passing messages along synapses, cellular decision processes where cells communicate by secreting proteins [2, 36] and protein interaction networks where proteins physically interact to achieve a common goal [43].

While message passing is indeed a useful and dominant method for distributed biological computing, some biological processes utilize another method for coordination. This method is similar to the method of communicating via shared memory, studied intensively in distributed computing, and utilizes modification to the DNA (i.e., leaving marks on the DNA but not changing the DNA itself), which can be sensed (read) by other participating entities. This process is termed *epigenetics* and involves several different groups of proteins, which could largely be divided into three groups: *readers, writers, and erasers* [31].

Epigenetic refers in part to post-translational modifications of the histone proteins on which the DNA is wrapped. Such modifications play an essential role in the regulation of gene expression, and so are themselves highly regulated and consistent across large stretches of the genome [24, 31]. In particular, when switching between cell states (for example, changing gene expression when facing stress or during development), a *coordinated* set of modifications is required such that expression programs that are necessary for these states can be executed.

The DNA is packaged into a small volume to fit into the nucleus of a cell. Stretches of about 170 base pairs (of the DNA) are wrapped around octets of histone proteins to form nucleosomes [11]. These and other DNA-associated proteins make up the *chromatin*. Researchers have been cataloging chromatin proteins and their modifications, to segregate chromatin's complexity into discrete numbers of chromatin states [7]. Chromatin-state mapping promises to reveal many secrets of genome function, how cells inherit acquired states, how chromatin directs functions such as transcription and RNA processing, and how chromatin alterations contribute to disease response and progression.

There are several types of (protein) histone modifiers that regulate transcriptional activity by changing chromatin states. As mentioned, these modifiers can be broadly categorized into three classes: readers, writers, and erasers [31]. As their names suggest, writers can add specific modifications (but cannot erase existing ones), while erasers can remove specific modifications but cannot add others. Readers are the executers, and while their activity is the goal of these modifications, we would not discuss them from now on since their involvement in the process is limited to the outcome, whereas we are focused here on understanding the process of reaching consensus as discussed below.

Several specific types of histone modifiers have been discovered, including acetylation, methylation, phosphorylation, ubiquitination, and so on [31]. While each has its own interpretation, in this paper, we generalize all of them to focus on the interplay between writers and erasers rather than on the specific histone modification type. However, we note that a number of modifiers (including both erasers and writers) were shown to act on the exact same locations [42], which corresponds to a number of different type of processors that may access the same memory location in a shared memory system. Coordination between writers and erasers for these sites is required to maintain a consistent state across the genome.

Although a lot of recent work in the biological literature has focused on histone modifications and the specific proteins that regulate gene expression, to the best of our knowledge, no prior work discussed the issue of global coordination between writers and erasers, which is essential for activation or deactivation of genes. We often see *precisely the same* histone marks (i.e., marks that are left by the writers) for a stretch of DNA (within the same DNA molecule) [24]. However, how such a consensus is reached by the different writers for a particular mark is still not clear. Our goal in this paper is to understand better how such a consensus may be reached.

To this end, we model the histone modifiers as two different types of writer processors and two different types of eraser processors that communicate by accessing a shared memory array (a stretch of DNA), and for such a setting formally define the *epigenetic consensus problem*. We first discuss a simple algorithm for solving the problem and then present a more sophisticated algorithm, that better matches various biological assumptions, and discuss its run time both theoretically and in simulations.

2   Model

We assume a shared memory array with N memory locations, which corresponds to a linear DNA stretch with N total histones that can be modified (N is a large number – and these histones cover hundreds of thousands of DNA bases). Recent biological results indicate that such stretches of DNA, often anchored by CTCF bindings sites, are likely to be jointly modified when switching between cell states [37]. Thus, our focus here is on achieving a consensus assignment for such stretches when cells need to switch between different biological states (i.e., changing gene expression).

Although our processors mimic memory-less proteins, to model some protein's behaviours (such as movement in a given direction), we assume that each processor has only two bits of memory which, for example, prevents it from counting (assuming a bigger memory is biologically unrealistic). While there could be several types of modifications, many of them can co-exist (each changing a different histone residue). For a specific residue most of the modification are restricted to two possible values and so we assume here that only two values can be written to each location of the array, denoted by 0 and 1. Again, following the biological model we allow each processor to be either a writer or an eraser [23].

We assume that two types of writers, 0-writers and 1-writers, are assigned to each DNA stretch. W_0 denotes the number of 0-writers and W_1 denotes the number of 1-writers. Similarly, we have sets of erasers for 0 and for 1, such that 0-erasers can only erase 0 and 1-erasers can only erase 1. Following recent studies [40], we assume that the generation of writers and erasers is similarly regulated and so the number of 0-erasers, $E_0 = W_1$ and the number of 1-erasers, $E_1 = W_0$.

To switch between states (changing gene expression), cells transcribe (generate) new writers and erasers for the modification needed (for example, when changing from 0 to 1). When changing from 0 to 1, the new 1-writers will usually outnumber the existing 0-writers. However, we cannot expect these 0-writers to completely disappear, at least not within the time scales needed for changing the state. Thus, we assume that at any given time, the number of one type of writers is larger than the number of the other type, and the convergence time of our algorithms will depend on this assumption.

Each of the N locations in the shared memory can be in one of three states: Empty (V), 0 or 1. A state transition of a single memory location can occur from V to 0 (1) by a 0 (1) writer and from 0 (1) to V by a 0 (1) eraser. However, a transition from 0 (1) to 1 (0) cannot occur. That is, a 0 state needs to be erased first and only then can be written by a 1-writer. It is assumed that reading a memory location and then possibly updating its value is done as one atomic step. In addition, it is assumed that all locations are initially empty. This assumption is based on studies showing that all marks are completely erased before being rewritten in certain reprogramming events [41]. To address cases where there is no global erasing of markers, in Sect. 9, we relax this assumption and explain how it can be easily removed. More precisely, we show in Sect. 9 that with a tiny change to our algorithm it satisfies the self-stabilization property, that is, starting from any initial assignment of values to the memory locations (i.e., starting from any configuration) the algorithm always produce the desired final result [12, 14].

The shared memory locations are *anonymous*. That is, they do not have names that the processors a priori agreed upon [39]. Each one of the processors (i.e., writers and erasers) starts by accessing a random location in the array. Thereafter, in its next step, a processor may access one of the two locations which are adjacent to the location it has accessed in its previous step. One may view the processors as mobile agents that are moving between locations in the shared array.[1]

The writers and erasers do not have a (global) sense of direction. That is, they do not a priori agree on which side of the array is the left side and which side is the right side. We assume that writers and erasers are *asynchronous*, nothing is assumed about their relative speed. The time efficiency of an asynchronous algorithm is often of crucial importance. However, it is difficult to find the appropriate definition of time complexity, for systems where nothing is assumed about the speed of the processors. Thus, for measuring time, we will assume that a single step of a processor takes at most one time unit.

Assume that a computation is taking place through time and that every step of every processor takes some amount in the interval (0, 1]. That is, there is an upper bound 1 for step time but no lower bound. Thus, for example, if during some period of time, where two processors are taking steps, one processor takes 100 steps while the other takes 5 steps, then the total time that has elapsed is at most 5 time units.

---

[1] In particular, a processor does not have to remember the address (name) of the last memory location it has accessed which will require $log N$ bits of local memory. It only needs to remember one bit which represents the direction in which it is moving. (Recall, that we have assumed that each processor has two bits of local memory.).

Under the assumption that a single step of a processor takes at most one time unit, the time complexity of an algorithm is defined as the maximum number of time units (also called "big steps") that are required for the algorithm to converge (i.e., to terminate) [10,25,33,38]. For the rest of the paper, by a step of the algorithm, we mean a "big step" which takes one time unit and where each correct processor that started participating in the algorithm has taken at least one step. For example, in Sect. 4 we derive the expected number of big steps (i.e., time units) for our consensus algorithm to converge.

3   The Epigenetic Consensus Problem

The *epigenetic consensus problem* is to design an algorithm in which all processors reach an agreement based on their initial opinions. In our context, reaching an agreement is expressed by guaranteeing a consensus outcome of either 0 or 1 for all N memory locations.[2] An epigenetic consensus algorithm is an algorithm that produces such an agreement, assuming only writers and erasers as defined previously.

More formally, the problem is defined as follows. There are a fixed number of W_0 0-writers, W_1 1-writers, E_0 0-erasers, and E_1 1-erasers. Recall that $W_1 = E_0$ and $W_0 = E_1$. Initially, each one of the N memory locations is empty, and upon termination, the value of each location is either 0 or 1. The requirements of the epigenetic consensus problem are that there exists a *decision value* $v \in \{0, 1\}$ such that,

- *Agreement*: With probability 1, the value of each one of the N memory locations is eventually v, and does not change thereafter.
- *Majority*: When there is a strong majority of v-writers, then, with high probability, the final decision value (i.e., the final value of each one of the locations) is v.
- *Validity*: The final value of each location is a value of some writer.

We point out that the first requirement has two parts. The first (the agreement part) is that all N memory locations eventually contain the same value, and the second (the termination part) is that eventually the memory locations do not change their agreed-upon value. In the second requirement, a strong majority of v-writers means that $W_v/W_{1-v} \geq 3$ (recall that $v \in \{0, 1\}$). We use a ratio of 3 to 1 here. However, we note that while recent studies have shown that over-expression of specific writers leads to a change of consensus value, as we assume, the actual ratio in real biological processes has not yet been fully determined [16]. The third requirement ensures that if $W_0 = 0$ then the decision cannot be on the value 0, and similarly if $W_1 = 0$ then the decision cannot be on the value 1. Thus, it precludes a solution that always decides 1 (resp. 0). The consensus problem defined above is also called *binary* consensus as the decision value v is either 0 or 1. A generalization of the problem where the v is taken from a larger set is not considered in this paper.

The consensus problem is a fundamental coordination problem and is at the core of many algorithms for distributed applications. The problem was formally presented in [26,30]. Many (deterministic and randomized) consensus algorithms have been proposed for shared memory systems. Few examples are [1,4,5,21,27,32,35]. Dozens of

---

[2] An agreement on 0 (resp. 1) may correspond to an instruction to deactivate (resp. activate) a specific gene.

papers have been published on solving the consensus problem in various messages passing models. Few examples are [13, 15, 18–20]. For a survey on asynchronous randomized consensus algorithms see [3].

4   Algorithms

4.1   A Naive Algorithm

Before we present our main algorithm, we first discuss a straightforward but non-desirable solution that is easy to analyze. In this solution, the erasers do not participate. Writers compete on writing the leftmost memory location and the value written into that location becomes the final agreed upon value. This is done as follows. Assume v is the written value. The v-writers continue writing v into all the locations. The major downside of this solution is that the probability of ending with the majority value is $p = W_1/(W_0 + W_1)$ (assuming a 1 majority) which is usually very dangerous for cells since there is a constant probability of not reaching the desired state. Furthermore, this solution assumes that all the writers have the same orientation (i.e., they a priori agree on which side is the left side) which is an unacceptable assumption. We present below a much better solution.

4.2   The Epigenetic Consensus Algorithm

While the algorithm above will finish in $\Theta(N)$ steps, as mentioned, it might not lead to the desired outcome. Instead, we propose to rely on recent biological observations that indicate that stretches of consecutive 1's (resp. 0's) are locally extended until they reach other stretches of 1's (resp. 0's) [6]. Based on this, we propose the following algorithm. Let $v \in \{0, 1\}$.

- Each of the writers and erasers starts at a random location. Their direction is also chosen randomly.
- *Rule for a v-writer*: The writer starts moving in the chosen direction. If it sees an empty location, it writes v and moves on to the next location. When a v-writer reaches the end of the stretch, it reverses its direction and continues.
- *Rule for a v-erasers*: The v-eraser starts moving in the chosen direction. When it sees a value v which is preceded by the value $1 - v$, it erases the v. Otherwise, it just moves on. When a v-eraser reaches the end of the stretch, it reverses its direction and continues.

When the values of two consecutive non-empty locations are different, we call that a *collision*. The algorithm will run until all the locations' values are non-empty and until all collisions are resolved. Intuitively, each time there is an empty location after a collision is resolved, assuming $W_1 > W_0$, the probability that the value 1 will be written is higher, and thus the algorithm will eventually converge. Another version of the algorithm we considered, forces a writer to spin (wait) when it notices a collision. Simulations indicate that the spinning version is more efficient than the non-spinning one, but this version is harder to analyze.

5   Analysis: Preliminaries

We prove that the algorithm satisfies the *majority* requirement and compute the expected runtime. We do that by applying known results about biased random walks in one dimension. More precisely, we use the following well-known solution to the *gambler's ruin problem* [17,34].

5.1   The Gambler's Ruin Problem with Ties Allowed

Consider a gambler who at each play of the game has probability p of winning one unit, probability q of losing one unit, and probability r of not winning or losing ($p+q+r = 1$; $0 < p, q < 1$). (In gambling terminology, when $r > 0$ a bet may result in a tie.) Assume successive plays of the game are independent, what is the probability that starting with $0 \le i \le N$ units, the gambler's fortune will reach N before reaching 0.

Lemma 1 (The gambler's ruin lemma [17,34]). *Let f_i denotes the probability that starting with i units, $0 \le i \le N$, the gambler's fortune will eventually reach N. Then, assuming $p \ne q$,*

$$f_i = \frac{1 - (q/p)^i}{1 - (q/p)^N}$$

Lemma 1 is true regardless of the value of r (i.e., regardless of whether ties are allowed or not). As $N \to \infty$, if $p > q$, there is a positive probability that the gambler's fortune will converge to infinity; whereas if $p < q$, then, with probability 1, the gambler will eventually go broke when playing against an infinitely rich adversary. (When $p = q$ and $r = 0$, $f_i = i/N$.) Even though casino gamblers are destined to lose, some of them enjoy the process. Lets figure out how long their game is expected to last.

Lemma 2 (Expected playing time [17]). *Let E_i be the expected number of bets before going home (broke or a winner), starting with i units, $0 \le i \le N$. Then, assuming $p \ne q$,*

$$E_i = \left(\left(\frac{N}{p-q} \right) \left[\frac{1 - (q/p)^i}{1 - (q/p)^N} \right] - \frac{i}{p-q} \right) \left(\frac{1}{p+q} \right)$$

Without ties (i.e., when $r = 0$) the right term equals 1. The expression is much simpler in the following cases. When $p > 1/2$, $r = 0$ and both i and N are large, $E_i \sim (N - i)/(2p - 1)$. This seems to make sense since the gambler is expected to *win* $1p - 1(1 - p) = 2p - 1$ units on every bet and starting with i units, the gambler needs to win additional $N - i$ units. On the other hand, when $p < 1/2$, $r = 0$ and $N - i$ is large, $E_i \sim i/(1 - 2p)$. This seems to make sense since the gambler is expected to *lose* $1(1 - p) + (-1)p = 1 - 2p$ units on every bet and the gambler started with i units. (When $p = q$ and $r = 0$, $E_i = i(N - i)$.)

Finally, the sum of the probabilities that, starting with i units, the gambler's fortune will reach N or the gambler will eventually go broke is known to be 1, so we need not consider the possibility of an unending game. That is, for every $p > 0$, the probability that the game never ends is 0.

5.2 Chernoff Bound

One can encounter many flavors of Chernoff bounds. We will use the following version,

Theorem 1 (Chernoff Bound [22]**).** *Let* $X = \sum_{i=1}^{n} X_i$ *where* $X_i = 1$ *with probability* p_i *and* $X_i = 0$ *with probability* $1 - p_i$, *and all* X_i *are independent. Let* $\mu = E(X) = \sum_{i=1}^{n} p_i$. *Then,*

$$Pr(X \geq (1+\delta)\mu) \leq e^{-\frac{\delta^2}{2+\delta}\mu} \quad for \ all \ \delta > 0$$

5.3 Additional Assumptions About the Model

We state below a few assumptions that capture important aspects of our model, and simplify the analysis of the epigenetic consensus algorithm. Recall that it is assumed that $W_1 = E_0$ and $W_0 = E_1$. The value that is written into an empty memory location depends on the ratio between the 1-writer and 0-writers at that location. In an asynchronous system it is not possible to exactly tell what this ratio is at any given time. However, this ratio is, of course, going to be affected by the overall ratio between the different types of writers. Thus, to abstract away from all the physical details (such as, the time it takes to write, erase, move to the next location, etc.), which may affect the current location of a process, we assume the following,

> Assume that a value (0 or 1) is written at a certain location. The probability that the value written in that location is $v \in \{0,1\}$ is $W_v/(W_0 + W_1)$.

The assumption implies that a value that is written does not depend on past history. Thus, there are no probabilistic dependencies between the values written into different (empty) memory locations. Let X_v be the number of values $v \in \{0,1\}$ that are written into the N memory locations for the first time (i.e., for each location we consider the first value written into it). By definition, $X_v + X_{1-v} = N$. By the assumption above, $E(X_v) = (N \times W_v)/(W_0 + W_1)$.

Given physical space constraints, when resolving a collision on the chromatin, only one value in one of the two adjacent locations participating in the collision can be erased, but not both values. That is, because of their physical size, either a 0-eraser or a 1-eraser may observe a specific collision but not both at the same time. Given this biological observation, from now on we will assume the following,

> An eraser reads two adjacent locations, and possibly erases one of them, in one atomic step. Thus, when a collision is resolved, only one value in one of the two adjacent memory locations participating in the collision can be erased. Furthermore, in case of a collision, the probability that the value erased is $v \in \{0,1\}$ is $E_v/(E_0 + E_1)$.

Thus, there are no dependencies between erasers which attempt to access overlapping (or the same) collisions concurrently. Finally, for simplicity, we assume that before the first value is erased, each one of the N locations is written at least once.

6   Analysis: The Probability of Reaching Agreement on the Majority Value

We prove that the epigenetic algorithm satisfies the *majority* requirement.

Theorem 2 (Satisfying the majority requirement). *Assume $W_1 > W_0$. The probability that the final decision value is 1 is more than*

$$\left(1 - (W_0/W_1)^{4W_0 N/(W_0+W_1)}\right) \times \left(1 - e^{-W_0 N/(3(W_0+W_1))}\right)$$

Corollary 1. *Assume $W_1/W_0 \geq 3$. The probability that the final decision value is 1 is more than*

$$\left(1 - (1/3)^N\right) \times \left(1 - e^{-N/12}\right)$$

Thus, when there is a strong majority of v-writers then, with high probability, the final decision value is v. We prove the theorem by applying the known result about the *Gambler's ruin problem* as captured in Lemma 1, and by using Chernoff bound (i.e., Theorem 1).

For the rest of the section we prove Theorem 2. Let us focus on *update-steps* in which, in an attempt to resolve a collision, a value is erased and then a value is written in the same location. An update-step may result a change in the number of 1's (and hence also of 0's). There are three such types of update-steps which we will name *win*, *lose* and *tie*. A win step is when a collision (of 01 or 10) is changed into 11. A lose step is when a collision (of 01 or 10) is changed into 00. A tie step is when a collision is not changed (a value is erased and then the same value is written). So, the number of 1's increases by one in a win step, it decreases by one in a lose step and it does not change in a tie step.

Recall that $W_1 = E_0$ and $W_0 = E_1$, and the probability of erasing 0 or writing 1 is $W_1/(W_0 + W_1)$. Let P be the probability that the number of 1's increases (and 0's decreases) in an update-step; let Q be the probability that the number of 0's increases (and 1's decreases); and let R be the probability that the number of 1's and 0's does not change. Then,

$$P = \left(\frac{W_1}{W_0 + W_1}\right)^2 \quad ; \quad Q = \left(\frac{W_0}{W_0 + W_1}\right)^2 \quad ; \quad R = 1 - P - Q.$$

Assume that all the memory locations are not empty. Let i denotes the initial number of 1's, after each one of the N locations is written once. Notice that, by definition, the initial number of 0's is $N - i$. The question that we are interested in is, what is the probability that starting with i values of 1 (after each of the locations is written once), the final decision value (i.e., the final value of each one of the N locations) is 1?

This question is identical to the question asked in the gambler's ruin problem that we just analyzed. Going broke is analogous to reaching agreement on 0, where going home winner with a fortune of N is analogous to reaching agreement on 1. Winning one unit with probability p is analogous to a win step with probability P, losing one unit with probability q is analogous to a lose step with probability Q, and not losing or winning with probability r is analogous to a tie step with probability R. Finally, the gambler starting with i units is analogous to assuming that the initial number of 1's is i. Thus, by Lemma 1 we get,

Lemma 3. *Let f_i denote the probability that starting with initially i values of 1, $0 \leq i \leq N$, the final decision value (i.e., the final value of each one of the N locations) is 1. Then, assuming $P \neq Q$,*

$$f_i = \frac{1 - (Q/P)^i}{1 - (Q/P)^N} = \frac{1 - (W_0/W_1)^{2i}}{1 - (W_0/W_1)^{2N}}$$

For the rest of the section, let μ_0 denotes the expected initial number of 0's. Clearly, $\mu_0 = W_0 N/(W_0 + W_1)$. Thus, when assuming that $W_1 > W_0$, we get that $0 \leq 2\mu_0 \leq N$. By Lemma 3,

Lemma 4. *Assume $W_1 > W_0$. The probability that the final decision value is the majority value 1, when starting with at least $2\mu_0$ values of 1, is at least*

$$\frac{1 - (W_0/W_1)^{4\mu_0}}{1 - (W_0/W_1)^{2N}} \geq 1 - (W_0/W_1)^{4\mu_0}$$

The Probability of Starting with at Least $2\mu_0$ Values of 1

In Lemma 4, we computed the probability that the final decision value is the majority value 1, conditioned on starting with at least $2\mu_0$ values of 1. Using Chernoff Bound (Theorem 1), it is possible to compute the probability of starting with at least $2\mu_0$ values of 1.

Lemma 5. *Assume $W_1 > W_0$. Let X_1 be the initial number of 1's. Then,*

$$Pr\left(X_1 \geq 2\mu_0\right) > 1 - e^{-\mu_0/3}$$

Proof. Recall that μ_0 is the expected initial number of 0's ($\mu_0 = W_0 N/(W_0 + W_1)$). Let X_0 be the initial number of 0's. By substituting μ_0 for μ and 1 for δ in Theorem 1 (Chernoff Bound) we get that,

$$Pr\left(X_0 \geq 2\mu_0\right) \leq e^{-\mu_0/3} \tag{1}$$

That is, the probability of starting with at least $2\mu_0$ values of 0 is at most $e^{-\mu_0/3}$, which implies that,

$$Pr\left(X_1 \geq 2\mu_0\right) > 1 - e^{-\mu_0/3} \tag{2}$$

That is, the probability of starting with at least $2\mu_0$ values of 1 is more than $1 - e^{-\mu_0/3}$. □

Putting it all Together

First, in Lemma 4, we computed the probability that the final decision value is the majority value 1, *conditioned* on starting with at least $2\mu_0$ values of 1. Then, in Lemma 5, we computed the probability of starting with at least $2\mu_0$ values of 1. Multiplying these two probabilities gives us the probability that the final decision value is 1. Thus, assuming $W_1 > W_0$, the probability that the final decision value is 1 is more than

$$\left(1 - (W_0/W_1)^{4\mu_0}\right) \times \left(1 - e^{-\mu_0/3}\right)$$

This completes the proof of Theorem 2. □

7 Analysis: Computing the Expected Number of Steps

Recall that it is assumed that $W_1 = E_0$ and $W_0 = E_1$. Next, we compute the expected number of big steps (i.e., time units) needed to until reaching agreement, when executing the epigenetic consensus algorithm. (Time complexity is defined in Sect. 2.)

Theorem 3. *Let T be the number of steps needed to reach agreement (on either 0 or 1). Then, assuming $W_1 > W_0$,*

$$E[T] \leq \frac{2(W_0 + W_1)^4 N^2}{W_1^4 - W_0^4}$$

Corollary 2. *Assuming $W_1/W_0 \geq 3$, $E[T] \leq 6.4N^2$*

Proof. Recall that an *update-steps* is an attempt to resolve a collision, in which a value is erased and then a value is written in the same location. An update-step may result a change in the number of 1's (and hence also of 0's). There are three such types of update-steps which we have named *win*, *lose* and *tie*. A win step, which can happen with probability P, is when a collision is changed into 11. A lose step, which can happen with probability Q, is when a collision is changed into 00. A tie step, which can happen with probability R, is when a collision is not changed. The values of P, Q and R are as in the previous section.

We first focus on computing the expected number of *update-steps* of the epigenetic consensus algorithm. This question is identical to the question about the expected number of steps in the gambler's ruin problem from Sect. 5. As explained in the previous section, going broke is analogous to reaching agreement on 0, where going home winner with a fortune of N is analogous to reaching agreement on 1. Winning one unit with probability p is analogous to a win step with probability P, losing one unit with probability q is analogous to a lose step with probability Q, and not losing or winning with probability r is analogous to a tie step with probability R. Finally, the gambler starting with i units is analogous to assuming that the initial number of 1's is i.

Let U_i be the number of *update-steps* until consensus is reached, starting with initially i values of 1, $0 \leq i \leq N$. By Lemma 2,

$$E[U_i] = \left(\left(\frac{N}{P-Q} \right) \left[\frac{1 - (Q/P)^i}{1 - (Q/P)^N} \right] - \frac{i}{P-Q} \right) \left(\frac{1}{P+Q} \right) \tag{3}$$

The assumption that $W_1 > W_0$ implies that $P > Q$, and thus we can simplify (3) as follows,

$$E[U_i] \leq \left(\frac{N}{P-Q} - \frac{i}{P-Q} \right) \left(\frac{1}{P+Q} \right) = \frac{N-i}{P^2 - Q^2} \tag{4}$$

Since $P = (W_1/(W_0 + W_1))^2$ and $Q = (W_0/(W_0 + W_1))^2$, we get that

$$E[U_i] \leq \frac{(W_0 + W_1)^4 (N - i)}{W_1^4 - W_0^4} \tag{5}$$

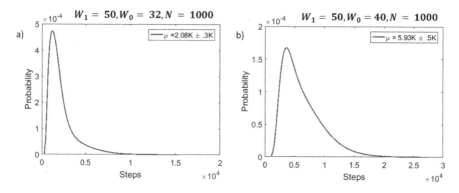

Fig. 1. Distribution of number of steps to reach consensus. Plots summarize 300 random runs of the algorithm. a) low and b) high level of competitions between 1-writers and 0-writers. μ denotes the average time to reach consensus.

Let U be the number of *update-steps* until consensus is reached. Then,

$$E[U] \leq \max_{i \in \{1,\ldots,N-1\}} E[U_i] \leq \frac{(W_0 + W_1)^4 (N-1)}{W_1^4 - W_0^4} \tag{6}$$

So far we have computed, $E[U]$, the expected number of *update-steps* of the epigenetic consensus algorithm. Next, we compute the expected number of (big) steps in general. For update-steps to take place, we need the erasers and writers to arrive at the collision locations. So, for a single update-step, in the worst case, we may need to wait for $N-1$ steps until the eraser arrives and an addition $N-1$ steps until the writer arrives. Thus, for each update-steps, in the worst case, we should count $2N - 2$ additional steps. That is, counting a total of $2N - 1$ steps for each update-step. In addition, in the worst case, we should add N (big) steps for the first writes into the N memory location. Thus, from (6) and as explained above, it follows that

$$E[T] \leq \frac{(W_0 + W_1)^4 (N-1)}{W_1^4 - W_0^4} \times 2(N-1) + N \leq \frac{2(W_0 + W_1)^4 N^2}{W_1^4 - W_0^4} \tag{7}$$

This completes the proof of Theorem 3. □

Remark: The analysis leads to a runtime of $O(N^2)$ steps. However, it assumes a single collision being resolved each time. In practice, we have multiple collisions that can be resolved in parallel. Initially, the number of collisions is a linear function of the number of 0's. If the number of collisions remains a linear function of the number of 0's then in $O(N)$ steps we would resolve $O(N)$ collisions, which would lead to at most $O(N \lg N)$ runtime. Unfortunately, as Fig. 2a) shows based on simulations, this is not the case. The epigenetic consensus algorithm leads to a rapid decrease in the number of collisions while not decreasing the number of 0's at the same rate. This means that long stretches of 0's (and 1's) form, leading to a small number of collisions while still having a large number of 0's. One way to overcome this is to change the algorithm to better mimic what biology does. Specifically, in biology we observe that erasers and writers

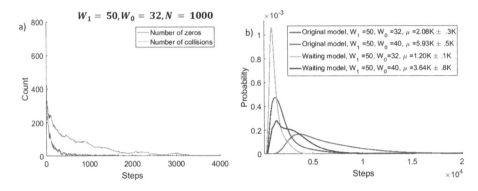

Fig. 2. a) Number of zeros and collisions vs steps in the algorithm. While the initial number of collisions is a linear function of the number of 0's, we observe that towards the end of the algorithm there are very few collisions while the number of 0's remains relatively high. b) Comparison between the proposed original model and a revised model that allows writers to attach themselves with the erasers and the writers wait until a collision is resolved. Here we can see that the waiting version is faster at both competition level compared to the original model.

interact during the establishment of a new state [40]. We hypothesize that an algorithm that utilizes these ideas can indeed lead to a faster runtime as the simulation analysis below shows.

8   Simulations and Analysis of Real Biological Data

We performed simulations of our proposed algorithm at two different levels of competitions between the 1-writers and 0-writers. Figure 1 shows the probability distribution of the number of steps to reach consensus. To simulate high level of competition we used $W_1 = 50, W_0 = 40, p = 0.56$ ($p = W_1/(W_0 + W_1)$). To simulate low level of competition we used $W_1 = 50, W_0 = 32, p = 0.60$. For both cases, $N = 1000$. As expected, at low level of competition consensus is achieved much faster. The average number of steps taken to reach consensus is $2.08K$ compared to $5.93K$ for the high level of competition.

Figure 2(a) shows the change in the number of zeros and collisions as the algorithm progresses towards consensus. As can be seen from the figure, initially the number of collisions is linear in the number of 0's. However, the algorithm proposed leads to a quick drop in the number of collisions while the number of 0's remains fairly high which means that collisions cannot be resolved in parallel. We also simulated an alternative, which allows 1-writers to attach to 0-erasers (forming a writer-eraser complex though not guaranteeing atomicity). As before, erasers continue to scan the DNA until they reach a collision. However, in the revised version erasers wait at the collision site to see what value was written and if the new value leads to another collision they attempt to erase again until the collision is resolved. As mentioned above, if the ratio of erasers from the two types is not 1, it would always converge to a consensus. While we are unable to prove a better worst case runtime for such a method, simulations indicate that

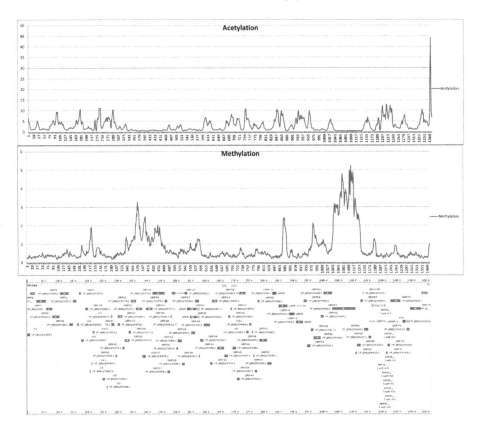

Fig. 3. Different histone modifiers competing for the same residue, Histone 3 Lysine 9 (H3K9). Latent Kaposi Sarcoma-Associated Herpesvirus Genomes (Resolution 250 bp). Two types of histone modifiers are competing to put acetylation and methylation marks on the residue. We can see stretches of regions with only methylation or acetylation marks, showing regional consensus.

it leads to much faster convergence when compared to the epigenetic consensus algorithm (Fig. 2b). Coupled with recent biological observations [29] these results indicate that this method is likely much faster than our current proposed algorithm while still not requiring any memory for the processors.

We have also looked at recent epigenetic data to see if the assumptions we made about increasing stretches using collisions rather than randomly changing location are observed in real data. Figure 3 presents results from a recent study by Gunther *et al.* [24] in which two different types of marks, acetylation and methylation are competing for the same residue H3K9 (and so can be thought of as 0 and 1). As can be seen, and in agreement with our local consensus formulation, there is regional consensus of these marks. The methylation mark is strong in the region that lies between 30K bps to 60K bps and again from 105K bps to 120K bps. The acetylation marks are almost non existent in these regions, demonstrating regional consensus of methylation marks in the DNA and the likely impact of collisions on the establishment of such regions.

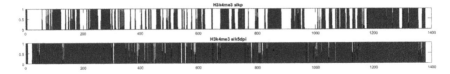

Fig. 4. Increase in histone modification intensity from the initial stage of infection (slkp) to 5 days post infection (5dpi). We can see that the later time point has higher overall consensus of methylation histone mark. (Color figure online)

These consensus states are dynamically regulated in response to stress or for establishing a new state during development. Figure 4 shows results from a temporal study by Gunther *et al.* [24] in which cells are gradually moving towards consensus of trimethylation marks of Histone 3 Lysine 4 (H3K4) residue as a response to Kaposi Sarcoma infection. The blue lines indicate presence of the H3K4me3 mark. The figure presents two time points, the first is at onset of infection (when the virus is applied) while the second one is from a sample 5 days post infection. As can be seen, after 5 days we observe a higher level of consensus than at the onset of infection indicating that collisions continue to be resolved until full consensus is reached. Most likely, in this case, the reason for the increase is the activation of additional modifiers at the later time points which lead to changes in the ratio of 1-writers and 0-writers and erasers. We note that the studies performed to-date are looking at a collection at cells at once and so only report average data. New technologies are enabling us, for the first time, to observe these events at a single cell resolution [9] and we expect that these results will further help us infer the specific algorithms utilized by cell to reach consensus.

9   Discussion

To date, the study of "algorithms in nature" at the molecular and cellular levels, i.e., how collections of molecules and cells process information and solve computational problems, was discussed mainly in the context of networks and message passing [28]. This paper attempts to study biologically inspired distributed computing algorithms in the context of molecular shared memory systems.

We have focused on the process of genome-wide epigenetic modifications in which cells utilize DNA as a shared memory array to establish a new state (i.e., changing gene expression). We formulated the new epigenetic consensus problem that these modifiers need to solve and presented algorithms and their expected run time. We have also discussed and simulated improved methods for solving the problem, which rely on additional recent biological insights. By analyzing real biological data we show that the decisions made in the algorithms we presented, to focus on collisions, indeed reflect experimental results for the establishment of new cell states using epigenetics.

Robustness is a desired property of cellular and molecular systems. That is, they should be able to recover and restore their original state after a disturbance (a transit failure) without any outside intervention. Our epigenetic consensus algorithm is robust, as it can tolerate a limited number of arbitrary memory location (value) changes and processor failures.

Our consensus algorithm is "one-shot," and we would also like to cover the "long-lived" version in which we may switch again possibly many times (i.e., repeated consensus). Also, we assume that all the shared memory locations are initially empty and it would be nice to be able to remove this assumption, especially when a need to establish a new state arises. A tiny change to our algorithm achieves the above desired properties. This is done by assuming that a v-eraser "once in a while" (i.e., at random) unconditionally erase v, even when there is no collision. In such a case, if the ratio between the number of 0-erasers and 1-erasers changes significantly, the decision value will change as well. Thus, with this tiny change (which is biologically justified) the algorithm is self-stabilizing – agreement is reached starting from any configuration (i.e., from any assignment of values to the memory locations).

There are several, possibly faster, variants of our epigenetic consensus algorithm that are theoretically interesting, but require making assumptions that are not acceptable from a biological standpoint. For example, we may assume that each writer is in one of two states: active or inactive. Initially, all writers are active. In an active state, a writer behaves as before (scans and writes in empty locations). In an inactive state, a writer scans the array but never writes. Let k_1 and k_2 be small positive integers. An active (resp. inactive) v-writer becomes inactive (resp. active) if the value in all the last k_1 (resp. k_2) locations it has visited is $1 - v$ (resp. v). Such a solution requires each writer to have a few additional bits of local memory, which is biologically unrealistic.

References

1. Abrahamson, K.: On achieving consensus using a shared memory. In: Proceedings of the 7th ACM Symposium on Principles of Distributed Computing, PODC 1988, pp. 291–302 (1988)
2. Afek, Y., Alon, N., Barad, O., Hornstein, E., Barkai, N., Bar-Joseph, Z.: A biological solution to a fundamental distributed computing problem. Science **331**(6014), 183–185 (2011)
3. Aspnes, J.: Randomized protocols for asynchronous consensus. Distrib. Comput. **16**(2–3), 165–175 (2003). ArXiv version: arXiv:cs.DS/0209014. Accessed 28 May 2018
4. Aspnes, J., Shahand, G., Shah, J.: Wait-free consensus with infinite arrivals. In: Proceedings of the 24th ACM Symposium on Theory of Computing, STOC 2002, pp. 524–533 (2002)
5. Aspnes, J., Herlihy, M.: Fast randomized consensus using shared memory. J. Algorithms **11**(3), 441–461 (1990)
6. Becker, P.B., Workman, J.L.: Nucleosome remodeling and epigenetics. Cold Spring Harb. Perspect Biol. **5**(9), a017905 (2013)
7. Berger, S.L.: The complex language of chromatin regulation during transcription. Nature **447**(7143), 407 (2007)
8. Bishop, C.: Neural Networks for Pattern Recognition. Oxford University Press, New York (1995)
9. Cheung, P., et al.: Single-cell chromatin modification profiling reveals increased epigenetic variations with aging. Cell **173**, 1385–1397 (2018)
10. Cole, R., Zajicek, O.: The APRAM: incorporating asynchrony into the PRAM model. In: SPAA, pp. 169–178 (1989)
11. Diesinger, P.M., Heermann, D.W.: Depletion effects massively change chromatin properties and influence genome folding. Biophys. J. **97**(8), 2146–2153 (2009)
12. Dijkstra, E.W.: Self-stabilizing systems in spite of distributed control. Commun. ACM **17**, 643–644 (1974)

13. Dolev, D., Dwork, C., Stockmeyer, L.: On the minimal synchronism needed for distributed consensus. J. ACM **34**(1), 77–97 (1987)
14. Dolev, S.: Self-Stabilization. The MIT Press, Cambridge (2000)
15. Dwork, C., Lynch, N., Stockmeyer, L.: Consensus in the presence of partial synchrony. J. ACM **35**(2), 288–323 (1988)
16. Cano-Rodriguez, D., et al.: Writing of H3K4Me3 overcomes epigenetic silencing in a sustained but context-dependent manner. Nature Commun. **7**, 12284 (2016)
17. Feller, W.: An Introduction to Probability Theory and Its Applications, vol. 1, 2nd edn. Wiley, Hoboken (1959). 461 pages
18. Fischer, M.J.: The consensus problem in unreliable distributed systems (a brief survey). In: Karpinski, M. (ed.) FCT 1983. LNCS, vol. 158, pp. 127–140. Springer, Heidelberg (1983). https://doi.org/10.1007/3-540-12689-9_99
19. Fischer, M.J., Lynch, N.A., Merritt, M.: Easy impossibility proofs for distributed consensus problems. Distrib. Comput. **1**(1), 26–39 (1986)
20. Fischer, M.J., Lynch, N.A., Paterson, M.S.: Impossibility of distributed consensus with one faulty process. J. ACM **32**(2), 374–382 (1985)
21. Fischer, M.J., Moran, S., Taubenfeld, G.: Space-efficient asynchronous consensus without shared memory initialization. Inf. Process. Lett. **45**(2), 101–105 (1993)
22. Goemans, M.: Chernoff bounds, and some applications (lecture notes), November 2015. http://math.mit.edu/goemans/18310S15/chernoff-notes.pdf. 6 pages
23. Goldberg, A.D., Allis, D.C., Bernstein, E.: Epigenetics: a landscape takes shape. Cell **128**(4), 635–638 (2007)
24. Günther, T., Grundhoff, A.: The epigenetic landscape of latent Kaposi sarcoma-associated herpesvirus genomes. PLoS Pathog. **6**(6), e1000935 (2010)
25. Herlihy, M., Shavit, N.: The Art of Multiprocessor Programming. Morgan Kaufmann Publishers, San Francisco (2008). 508 pages
26. Lamport, L., Shostak, R., Pease, M.: The byzantine generals problem. ACM Trans. Program. Lang. Syst. **4**(3), 382–401 (1982)
27. Loui, M.C., Abu-Amara, H.: Memory requirements for agreement among unreliable asynchronous processes. Adv. Comput. Res. **4**, 163–183 (1987)
28. Navlakha, S., Bar-Joseph, Z.: Distributed information processing in biological and computational systems. Commun. ACM **58**(1), 94–102 (2015)·
29. Panneerdoss, S., et al.: Cross-talk among writers, readers, and erasers of m6a regulates cancer growth and progression. Sci. Adv. **4**(10), eaar8263 (2018)
30. Pease, M., Shostak, R., Lamport, L.: Reaching agreement in the presence of faults. J. ACM **27**(2), 228–234 (1980)
31. Peterson, C.L., Laniel, M.: Histones and histone modifications. Curr. Biol. **14**(14), R546–R551 (2004)
32. Plotkin, S.A.: Sticky bits and universality of consensus. In: Proceedings of the 8th ACM Symposium on Principles of Distributed Computing, pp. 159–175 (1989)
33. Raynal, M.: Concurrent Programming: Algorithms, Principles, and Foundations. Springer, Heidelberg (2013). https://doi.org/10.1007/978-3-642-32027-9. 515 pages
34. Ross, S.M.: Stochastic Processes. Wiley, Hoboken (1983). 309 pages
35. Saks, M., Shavit, N., Woll, H.: Optimal time randomized consensus - making resilient algorithms fast in practice. In: Proceedings of the 2nd ACM-SIAM Symposium on Discrete Algorithms, SODA 1991, pp. 351–362 (1991)
36. Singh, S., et al.: Distributed gradient descent in bacterial food search. In: Proceedings of the 20th Annual International Conference on Research in Computational Molecular Biology (RECOMB) (2016)
37. Tang, Z., et al.: CTCF-mediated human 3D genome architecture reveals chromatin topology for transcription. Cell **163**(7), 1611–1627 (2015)

38. Taubenfeld, G.: Synchronization Algorithms and Concurrent Programming. Pearson/Prentice-Hall, New York (2006). ISBN 0-131-97259-6, 423 pages

39. Taubenfeld, G.: Coordination without prior agreement. In: Proceedings of the ACM Symposium on Principles of Distributed Computing, PODC 2017, pp. 325–334 (2017)

40. Torres, I.O., Fujimori, D.G.: Functional coupling between writers, erasers and readers of histone and DNA methylation. Curr. Opin. Struct. Biol. **35**, 68–75 (2015)

41. von Meyenn, F., Reik, W.: Forget the parents: epigenetic reprogramming in human germ cells. Cell **161**(6), 1248–1251 (2015)

42. Wang, Z., et al.: Combinatorial patterns of histone acetylations and methylations in the human genome. Nat. Genet. **40**(7), 897 (2008)

43. Weigt, M., White, R.A., Szurmant, H., Hoch, J.A., Hwa, T.: Identification of direct residue contacts in protein-protein interaction by message passing. Proc. Natl. Acad. Sci. **106**(1), 67–72 (2009)

Mobile Robots and Agents

New Approximation Algorithms for the Heterogeneous Weighted Delivery Problem

Davide Bilò[1] , Luciano Gualà[2] , Stefano Leucci[3] , Guido Proietti[3,4] ,
and Mirko Rossi[5(✉)]

[1] Department of Humanities and Social Sciences, University of Sassari, Sassari, Italy
davide.bilo@uniss.it
[2] Department of Enterprise Engineering, University of Rome "Tor Vergata",
Rome, Italy
guala@mat.uniroma2.it
[3] Department of Information Engineering, Computer Science and Mathematics,
University of L'Aquila, L'Aquila, Italy
{stefano.leucci,guido.proietti}@univaq.it
[4] Institute for System Analysis and Computer Science "Antonio Ruberti"
(IASI CNR), Rome, Italy
[5] Gran Sasso Science Institute, L'Aquila, Italy
mirko.rossi@gssi.it

Abstract. We study the *heterogeneous weighted delivery* (HWD) problem introduced in [Bärtschi et al., STACS'17] where k heterogeneous mobile agents (e.g., robots, vehicles, etc.), initially positioned on vertices of an n-vertex edge-weighted graph G, have to deliver m messages. Each message is initially placed on a source vertex of G and needs to be delivered to a target vertex of G. Each agent can move along the edges of G and carry at most one message at any time. Each agent has a rate of energy consumption per unit of traveled distance and the goal is that of delivering all messages using the minimum overall amount of energy.

This problem has been shown to be NP-hard even when $k = 1$, and is 4ρ-approximable where ρ is the ratio between the maximum and minimum energy consumption of the agents. In this paper, we provide approximation algorithms with approximation ratios independent of the energy consumption rates. First, we design a polynomial-time 8-approximation algorithm for $k = O(\sqrt{\log n})$, closing a problem left open in [Bärtschi et al., ATMOS'17]. This algorithm can be turned into a $O(k)$-approximation algorithm that always runs in polynomial-time, regardless of the values of k. Then, we show that HWD problem is 36-approximable in polynomial-time when each agent has one of two possible consumption rates. Finally, we design a polynomial-time $\widetilde{O}(\log^3 n)$-approximation algorithm for the general case.

This work was partially funded by the grants "Fondo di Ateneo per la Ricerca 2020" from the University of Sassari, and "ALgorithmic aspects of BLOckchain TECHnology" (E89C20000620005) from the University of Rome "Tor Vergata".

T. Jurdziński and S. Schmid (Eds.): SIROCCO 2021, LNCS 12810, pp. 167–184, 2021.
https://doi.org/10.1007/978-3-030-79527-6_10

Keywords: Message delivery · Energy consumption · Delivery schedules · Shortest-paths · Approximation algorithms

1 Introduction

We study the *heterogeneous weighted delivery* (HWD) problem introduced in [2] where k heterogeneous mobile agents (e.g., robots, vehicles, etc.), initially positioned on vertices of an n-vertex edge-weighted graph G, have to deliver m messages. Each message is initially placed on an individual source vertex of G and needs to be delivered to some individual target vertex of G. Each agent a_i can move along the edges of G and carry at most one message at any time. Messages cannot be duplicated by the agents but they can be picked up and dropped off at any vertex of G. This allows agents to collaboratively deliver messages by exchanging them at intermediate locations. Agent a_i consumes energy at a rate of c_i per unit of traveled distance and the goal is that of delivering all messages using the minimum overall amount of energy.

The above problem finds natural applications in logistics, e.g., transporting large amount of goods using motor lorries and cargo airplanes [4], parcel delivery using a fleet of drones [9], or mission planning using unmanned autonomous vehicles [17].

Among other results, the authors of [2] show that the HWD problem is NP-hard even with a single agent, while it can be solved in polynomial time when a single message needs to be delivered. Moreover, they also design a polynomial-time approximation algorithm achieving an approximation ratio of $4\frac{\max_i c_i}{\min_i c_i}$, which yields a 4-approximation whenever all agents are identical but can be arbitrarily large if the agents' energy consumption rates vary wildly. This can indeed happen since the algorithm actually ignores the agents' energy consumption.

In this paper we are interested in designing approximation algorithms achieving approximation ratios that are *independent of the agents' energy consumption*.

This scenario has been considered in [4] where the authors describe a 2-approximation fixed-parameter (FPT) algorithm with respect to the parameter m, i.e., an algorithm whose time complexity is $O(f(m) \cdot \text{poly}(k, n, m))$, for some (fast-growing) function $f(m)$ depending only on m. This implies a polynomial-time 2-approximation for $m = O(1)$. They leave open the problem of designing polynomial-time $O(1)$-approximations for $m = \omega(1)$ and $k = O(1)$. We deem this scenario as particularly significant as one can reasonably expect the number of agents to be small when compared to the number of messages to be delivered and/or the environment (modelled by the graph G).

We provide the following results:

- An 8-approximation FPT algorithm running in time $O^*\left(2^{\frac{k(k+1)}{2}}\right)$.[1] Notice that our algorithm requires polynomial-time whenever $k = O(\sqrt{\log n})$, thus answering the aforementioned open problem of [4]. We also show how

---

[1] The $O^*(\cdot)$ notation hides polynomial factors in the size of the instance.

the above algorithm can be modified to obtain a polynomial-time $4k^*$-approximation algorithm, where $k^* \leq k$ is the number of agents actually used by any optimal solution.
- Another very natural scenario is when the fleet of agents consists of few *types* of vehicles, i.e., the energy consumption rates belong to a small set of values. Although no constant approximation is known for a general number of types, we show how to design a polynomial-time 36-approximation algorithm for the special case of two types of agents.
- Finally, we design an approximation algorithm for the general HWD problem achieving an approximation ratio of $\widetilde{O}(\log^3 n)$.[2]

1.1   Related Work

As we already mentioned, the HWD problem has been introduced in [2] where the authors address also other related problems like bounding the increase in energy consumption resulting from denying cooperation between agents (i.e., by requiring each message to be carried by exactly one agent).

In [4] the HWD problem is considered in a non-cooperative scenario in which consumption rates are private. In this setting, the goal is that of designing energy-efficient truthful mechanisms. Along the way, the authors develop a 2-approximation FTP algorithm w.r.t. m, with a time complexity of $O^*(e^{2\sqrt{m}} \cdot (m/e)^m)$ and a 3.6-approximation algorithm with time complexity $O^*(k^m)$ for the HWD problem.

A variant of the HWD problem in which the objective is that of optimizing the maximum amount of energy consumed by any agent has been considered in [1,10,11], while the problem in which the total time needed to collaboratively deliver a message need to be minimized is studied in [9]. Hybrid measures that are combinations of both the total energy consumption and the minimum amount of time needed by the agents to deliver all messages (measured w.r.t. the edge weights) have also been studied [3,5].

The setting in which there are locations that need to be visited instead of messages to be delivered can often be modelled as generalizations of the travelling salesman problem. Some examples of such problems have been considered, e.g., in [14–17].

Finally, problems in which we are given an initial configuration of agents on graph that need to be rearranged into some final configuration while minimizing some function of the traveled distance have been studied in [6–8,13].

2   Preliminaries and Notation

We are given an undirected graph $G = (V(G), E(G))$ of n vertices where each edge $e \in E(G)$ has a positive real valued length l_e. There are k agents $a_1 \ldots a_k$ and each agent a_i is located on a vertex $p_i \in V(G)$ and has a real positive

---

[2] The $\widetilde{O}(f(\cdot))$ notation is a shorthand for $O(f(\cdot) \operatorname{poly} \log f(\cdot))$.

weight c_i representing the unitary movement cost incurred by the agent while traversing the graph edges. More precisely, every time agent a_i traverses an edge e it consumes energy equal to $c_i \cdot l_e$. There are m messages that have to be delivered by the agents; message m_j is represented by a pair (s_j, t_j) meaning that the message is initially placed at the source vertex $s_j \in V(G)$ and has to be delivered at the target vertex $t_j \in V(G)$. Each agent can simultaneously carry at most one message, and is allowed to drop-off/pick-up any message on/from any vertex of the graph. We will use $d_G(x, y)$ to denote the distance between vertices x and y in G, i.e., the length of a shortest path from x to y w.r.t. the edge lengths. A schedule is a sequence of moves that every agent performs. There are 3 types of moves allowed:

- agent a_i moves from the vertex where it is located, say u, to vertex v via the edge $(u, v) \in E(G)$;
- agent a_i located at vertex u picks-up message m_j that is also placed on u;
- agent a_i drops-off a message it is carrying on the vertex where it is located.

A schedule is feasible if the following conditions hold:

- every pick-up move of message m_j located on a vertex $x \neq s_j$ is preceded by a drop-off of the same message on x;
- An agent a_i can only pick-up (resp. drop-off) a message m_j if it is not carrying any message (resp. if it is carrying m_j).

Given a schedule S it is possible to compute its cost. Let d_i be the total distance traveled by agent a_i in S, then $\text{cost}(S) = \sum_{i=1}^{k} d_i \cdot c_i$. The goal is to compute a schedule S that minimizes its total cost $\text{cost}(S)$.

An agent a_i is *active* in a schedule S if a_i carries at least one message in S. A *restricted* schedule is a schedule such that (i) every message m_j is carried by a single agent with exactly one pick-up and one drop-off involving m_j (ii) each agent a_i returns to its starting location p_i as its last move. The following theorem from [2] shows that we can restrict our attention to restricted schedules if we are interested in computing approximate solutions.

Theorem 1 ([2]). *Let S^* be an optimal schedule for a given instance. There exists a restricted schedule S such that $\text{cost}(S) \leq 2 \cdot \text{cost}(S^*)$.*

From now on we will only consider restricted schedules (unless otherwise stated). For the sake of simplicity a restricted schedule S can be thought as consisting of a collection of k ordered sets $S_1, \ldots, S_k$, where S_i is the sequence of messages delivered by agent a_i. Indeed, once S_i is known, a minimum-cost strategy for agent a_i is to deliver all the messages contained in S_i one-by-one and by always moving along shortest paths.[3] Another nice property of restricted schedules is

---

[3] If the agent a_i is at vertex v, carries no message, and, according to its schedule S_i shall deliver message m_j, then a_i moves from v to s_j via a shortest path first, then picks-up message m_j from s_j, next moves from s_j to t_j via a shortest path, and finally drops-off message m_j on t_j.

that two restricted schedules can be joined together in order to obtain a new restricted schedule whose cost is upper bounded by the sum of the costs of the original schedules. More precisely, given two restricted schedules S^1 and S^2, we denote by $S^1 \circ S^2$ the restricted schedule in which each agent a_i first delivers all the messages so as in S_1 and then delivers all the messages so as in S_2. Observe that $\text{cost}(S^1 \circ S^2) \leq \text{cost}(S^1) + \text{cost}(S^2)$.

Due to space limitations, the proofs of Sect. 4 are omitted and will appear in the full version of the paper.

3 The Constant Approximation Algorithm for Few Agents

In this section we design a 8-approximation algorithm whose time complexity is exponential in k. We also show how to adapt such algorithm in order to obtain a polynomial time algorithm achieving an approximation ratio of $O(k^*)$, where $k^* \leq k$ is the number of active agents in an optimal solution.

3.1 Auxiliary Graph

We start by introducing an auxiliary graph that will be useful in the description of our approximation algorithms. Since we are working with restricted schedules, we can simplify the graph G by defining an auxiliary graph H as follows: For each message m_j, $V(H)$ contains a copy of the vertices s_j, t_j and, for each choice of $1 \leq j, j' \leq m$, the set $E(H)$ contains an edge $(s_j, t_{j'})$ of length $d_G(s_j, t_{j'})$ (see Fig. 1(a) for an example). Given a subgraph H' of H, we let $l(H') = \sum_{e \in E(H')} l_e$ denote the total length of H'.

Now, given a restricted schedule S, we can highlight the edges on the graph H that correspond to the paths followed by the agents in S. Formally, let $M = \{(s_j, t_j) \in E(H) \mid 1 \leq j \leq m\}$ be the set of edges that correspond to the paths from each source to its respective target. The set of *highlighted* edges for a schedule S is $E_S = M \cup \{(t_j, s_{j'}) \in E(H) \mid$ an agent in S delivers $m_{j'}$ immediately after delivering $m_j\}$.

In the rest of the paper, we denote by $l(S)$ the overall sum of lengths of highlighted edges for S, i.e., $l(S) = \sum_{e \in E_S} l_e$. Finally, given $M' \subseteq M$, we say that a restricted schedule S is a *restricted schedule w.r.t. M'* if S delivers all and only the messages m_j corresponding to the edges (s_j, t_j) in M'.

3.2 The Case of 1 Active Agent

To describe the algorithm, we first provide a simple procedure that computes a $O(1)$-approximate solution for the case in which an optimal restricted schedule S^* contains only 1 active agent. Such a simple procedure, that we call $\text{Tour}(T)$, takes as input a subgraph T of H, where T is a tree that spans the edges in M (i.e., $M \subseteq E(T)$), and computes a restricted schedule S with only 1 active agent (see Fig. 1(b)). More precisely, consider any Eulerian tour that visits each

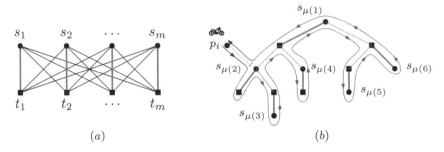

Fig. 1. (*a*): the auxiliary graph H. (*b*): Example of the tour $\texttt{Tour}(T)$ of the tree T. Green edges correspond to messages whose source and target vertices are depicted as circles and squares, respectively. Agent a_i starts from its position p_i, joints the tour at the closest source $s_{\mu(2)}$, and goes back to p_i. The sequence of messages it delivers in the corresponding restricted schedule is $\mu(2), \mu(3), \mu(4), \mu(5), \mu(6), \mu(1)$.

edge of T twice. Let $\mu(h)$ be the message that corresponds to the h-th edge of M, say (s_j, t_j), that is traversed from s_j to t_j in the Eulerian tour. Clearly, the overall length of such a tour is $2l(T)$. The procedure computes a restricted schedule S^i for every agent $i = 1, \ldots, k$ and outputs the cheapest one. In the schedule S^i all messages are delivered by a_i. More precisely, if j is the index such that $\mu(j)$ corresponds to the message whose start position $s_{\mu(j)}$ is closest to the initial position p_i of a_i, then $\langle \mu(j), \mu(j+1), \ldots, \mu(j+m-1) \rangle$, where indices are computed modulo m, is the ordered sequence of messages delivered by a_i in S^i.

Lemma 1. *Let $\widetilde{S}$ be a restricted schedule w.r.t. M and let T be a tree such that $M \subseteq E(T)$ and $l(T) \leq \alpha l(\widetilde{S})$, for some $\alpha \geq 1$. Then, the schedule S returned by procedure $\texttt{Tour}(T)$ satisfies $cost(S) \leq 2\alpha cost(\widetilde{S})$.*

Proof. Let a_i be a minimum-weight active agent in $\widetilde{S}$. Let s_j be the message source that is closest to p_i. Let j' be the index of the first message that is picked-up by a_i in $\widetilde{S}$. Using the facts that $\alpha \geq 1$ and $c_i d_G(p_i, s_{j'}) + c_i l(\widetilde{S}) \leq cost(\widetilde{S})$, we have that the cost of S is at most

$$cost(S) \leq cost(S^i) = 2c_i d_G(p_i, s_j) + 2c_i l(T)$$
$$\leq 2c_i d_G(p_i, s_{j'}) + 2\alpha c_i l(\widetilde{S}) \leq 2\alpha cost(\widetilde{S}). \qquad \square$$

Corollary 1. *Let S^* be an optimal restricted schedule and T a minimum-cost tree containing M. If there is only one active agent in S^*, then the call of $\texttt{Tour}(T)$ outputs a schedule S such that $cost(S) \leq 2cost(S^*)$.*

Proof. Since E_{S^*} induces a tree that contains M, we have that $l(T) \leq l(S^*)$. Using Lemma 1 with $\alpha = 1$, the cost of the restricted schedule S that is output by the call of $\texttt{Tour}(T)$ satisfies $cost(S) \leq 2cost(S^*)$. $\qquad \square$

3.3   How to Deal with More Active Agents

To deal with more than one active agent in an optimal restricted schedule S^*, we need to consider other schedules that provide good approximate solutions whenever the schedule computed by the call to $\texttt{Tour}(T)$ on a minimum-cost tree T that contains M does not guarantee a constant approximation. To do this, we need to introduce the concept of well-separated partitioning of M.

For a given restricted schedule S w.r.t. M and a set $M' \subseteq M$ we denote by $S_{M'}$ the subschedule of S induced by M'. More precisely, $S_{M'}$ is obtained from a copy of S in which we delete all the messages in $M \setminus M'$. We say that a partition of M into two sets M' and $M \setminus M'$, denoted by $\langle M', M \setminus M' \rangle$, is *well-separated* w.r.t. S if every active agent in S carries only messages that are either in M' or in $M \setminus M'$. By definition, given a restricted schedule S and a 2-partition $\langle M', M \setminus M' \rangle$ of M that is well-separated w.r.t. S, we have that $S = S_{M'} \circ S_{M \setminus M'} = S_{M \setminus M'} \circ S_{M'}$ and thus $\text{cost}(S) = \text{cost}(S_{M'}) + \text{cost}(S_{M \setminus M'})$. As the following lemma suggests, we can use a recursive algorithm to compute good approximate schedules.

Lemma 2. *Let $\widetilde{S}$ be a restricted schedule w.r.t. M, $\langle M', M \setminus M' \rangle$ a 2-partition of M that is well-separated w.r.t. $\widetilde{S}$, and let $\alpha \geq 1$ be a fixed value. Let S' be a restricted schedule w.r.t. M' such that $\text{cost}(S') \leq \alpha\text{cost}(\widetilde{S}_{M'})$. Similarly, let S'' be a restricted schedule w.r.t. $M'' = M \setminus M'$ such that $\text{cost}(S'') \leq \alpha\text{cost}(\widetilde{S}_{M''})$. Finally, let $S = S' \circ S''$. Then, $\text{cost}(S) \leq \alpha\text{cost}(\widetilde{S})$.*

Proof. We have $\text{cost}(S) \leq \text{cost}(S') + \text{cost}(S'') \leq \alpha\text{cost}(\widetilde{S}_{M'}) + \alpha\text{cost}(\widetilde{S}_{M''}) = \alpha\text{cost}(\widetilde{S})$.   □

Let $\widetilde{H}$ be a subgraph of H such that $M \subseteq E(\widetilde{H})$ and let S be a schedule w.r.t. M. We say that $\widetilde{H}$ is *separable* w.r.t. S if there exists a subgraph H' of $\widetilde{H}$ that contains only entire connected components of $\widetilde{H}$ and such that $\langle M', M \setminus M' \rangle$, with $M' = M \cap E(H')$, is well-separated w.r.t. S. See Fig. 2 for an example where the graph $\widetilde{H}$ consists of a forest of 6 trees.

Our algorithm, whose pseudocode is provided in Algorithm 1, takes a set M of messages and an integer k as inputs and returns a 8-approximate restricted schedule S of M with at most k active agents. To do so, the algorithm computes (i) a minimal (w.r.t. vertex deletions) minimum-cost forest F of k trees such that $M \subseteq E(F)$, and (ii) a tree T with $E(F) \subseteq E(T)$ that is obtained by augmenting F with a minimum-cost set of $k - 1$ edges. Clearly, T is a minimum-cost tree that contains all the edges of M.

Next, the algorithm computes a set of *candidate* schedules and outputs the cheapest of them. One candidate schedule considered by the algorithm is the one returned by the call of $\texttt{Tour}(T)$. As we will show, the cost of such a schedule is at most 4 times the cost of an optimal (fixed) restricted schedule S^*, under the assumption that F is not separable w.r.t. S^*.

To deal with the case in which F is separable w.r.t. S^*, the algorithm first guesses a subforest F' of F such that $\langle M', M \setminus M' \rangle$, with $M' = M \cap E(F')$,

---

Algorithm 1: Schedule(M,k) outputs a restricted schedule w.r.t. M with at most k active agents.

---

1 Let F be a minimum-cost forest of k trees such that $M \subseteq E(F)$
2 Let T be a minimum-cost tree such that $E(F) \subseteq E(T)$
3 **if** $k > 1$ **then**
4   **foreach** *forest* F' *containing from 1 up to* $k - 1$ *connected components of* F **do**
5          $M' \leftarrow M \cap E(F')$
6          $S_{F'} \leftarrow$ Schedule(M',1) $\circ$ Schedule($M \setminus M'$,$k - 1$)
7 **return** the cheapest schedule among all the $S_{F'}$ and Tour(T)

---

is a well-separated 2-partition of M w.r.t. S^*, and then recursively solves two corresponding subinstances. More precisely, the algorithm computes a schedule S' w.r.t. $M' = M \cap E(F')$ with 1 active agent only and a schedule S'' w.r.t. $M'' = M \setminus M'$ with at most $k - 1$ active agents, and adds the solution $S_{F'} = S' \circ S''$ to the candidate set. As we will prove, $\text{cost}(S') \leq 4\text{cost}(S^*_{M'})$ as well as $\text{cost}(S'') \leq 4\text{cost}(S^*_{M''})$. Hence, $\text{cost}(S_{F'}) \leq 4\text{cost}(S^*)$.

To optimize the overall time complexity so as it is bounded by $O^*(2^{k(k+1)/2})$, the forest F' guessed by the algorithm is not separable w.r.t. $S^*_{M'}$; furthermore, the number of active agents in $S^*_{M'}$ is upper bounded by the number of connected components of F'. As proved in the next lemma, this is enough to guarantee that the restricted schedule S' with only 1 active agent so as computed by the algorithm satisfies $\text{cost}(S') \leq 4\text{cost}(S^*_{M'})$.

Lemma 3. *Let* $\widetilde{S}$ *be a restricted schedule w.r.t.* M *with* k' *active agents,* F *be a minimal (w.r.t. vertex removal) minimum-cost spanning forest of at least* k' *trees such that* $M \subseteq E(F)$, *and* T *be a minimum-cost tree such that* $E(F) \subseteq E(T)$. *If* F *is not separable w.r.t.* $\widetilde{S}$, *then the schedule* S *w.r.t.* M *returned by the call of* Tour(T) *satisfies* $\text{cost}(S) \leq 4\text{cost}(\widetilde{S})$.

Proof. The set of highlighted edges $E_{\widetilde{S}}$ induces a forest $\widetilde{F}$ of k' paths that contains all edges of M. As a consequence

$$l(F) \leq l(\widetilde{F}) = l(\widetilde{S}). \tag{1}$$

Let $k'' \geq k'$ be the number of connected components of F and let $e_1, \ldots, e_{k''-1}$ be the $k'' - 1$ edges of $E(T) \setminus E(F)$. Since F is not separable w.r.t. S', there are $k'' - 1$ distinct highlighted edges $f_1, \ldots, f_{k''-1} \in E_{\widetilde{S}} \setminus M$ such that $l(e_h) \leq l(f_h)$ for every $h = 1, \ldots, k'' - 1$. As a consequence,

$$\sum_{h=1}^{k''-1} l(e_h) \leq \sum_{h=1}^{k''-1} l(f_h) \leq l(\widetilde{S}). \tag{2}$$

If we combine (1) with (2) we obtain $l(T) = l(F) + \sum_{h=1}^{k''-1} l(e_h) \leq 2l(\widetilde{S})$. Therefore, using Lemma 1, we have that $\text{cost}(S) \leq 4\text{cost}(\widetilde{S})$. The claim follows. $\square$

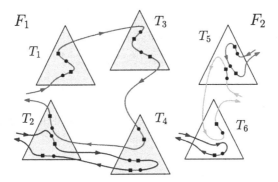

Fig. 2. Illustration of Lemma 4. The forest F consists of $k = 6$ trees $T_1, \ldots, T_6$. The schedule $\widetilde{S}$ is depicted as $\widetilde{k} = 5$ walks of its active agents. Let $\Lambda_i = M \cap E(T_i)$. Forest F is separable w.r.t. $\widetilde{S}$ and $\langle \Lambda_1 \cup \Lambda_2 \cup \Lambda_3 \cup \Lambda_4, \Lambda_5 \cup \Lambda_6 \rangle$ is well-separated w.r.t. $\widetilde{S}$. The subforest F' computed by the algorithm is $F_1 = \{T_1, T_2, T_3, T_4\}$.

We are now ready to prove the correctness of the algorithm.

Lemma 4. *Let $\widetilde{S}$ be a restricted schedule w.r.t. M with $\widetilde{k}$ active agents. Algorithm 1 called on inputs M and $k \geq \widetilde{k}$ returns a restricted schedule S w.r.t. M such that $cost(S) \leq 4cost(\widetilde{S})$.*

Proof. Let F be the forest of k trees as computed by the algorithm. Let T be the tree as computed by the algorithm. Clearly, the cost of the schedule S returned by the algorithm is at most the cost of the schedule S' that is computed by the call of $\texttt{Tour}(T)$. The proof is by induction on $\widetilde{k}$.

For the base case $\widetilde{k} = 1$, we have that F is not separable w.r.t. $\widetilde{S}$. Therefore, by Lemma 3, $cost(S') \leq 4cost(\widetilde{S})$. Hence, $cost(S) \leq 4cost(\widetilde{S})$.

For the inductive case $\widetilde{k} \geq 2$ we divide the proof into two cases according to whether F is separable w.r.t. $\widetilde{S}$ or not. If F is not separable w.r.t. $\widetilde{S}$, then, by Lemma 3, $cost(S') \leq 4cost(\widetilde{S})$; hence, $cost(S) \leq 4cost(\widetilde{S})$.

Now, we consider the case in which F is separable w.r.t. $\widetilde{S}$. We claim that there exists a subforest F' of F such that (see Fig. 2):

(i) $\langle M', M \setminus M' \rangle$, with $M' = M \cap E(F')$, is a well-separated 2-partition of M w.r.t. $\widetilde{S}$;

(ii) F' is not separable w.r.t. $\widetilde{S}_{M'}$;

(iii) the number of active agents in $\widetilde{S}_{M'}$ is at most the number of trees in F'.

Let $\langle F_1, \ldots, F_{k'} \rangle$, with $2 \leq k' \leq \widetilde{k}$, be the (unique) partition of the trees in F such that each F_i is not separable w.r.t. $\widetilde{S}_{M_i}$, where $M_i = M \cap E(F_i)$, and every active agent in $\widetilde{S}$ carries only messages that are all contained in a same set M_i. By definition, any forest F_i satisfies both (i) and (ii). To see that at least one of the forests F_i's also satisfies (iii), let k_i be the number of trees contained in F_i and let A_i be the set of active agents in $\widetilde{S}_{M_i}$. By definition, we have that the sets A_i's are pairwise disjoint. Therefore, $\sum_{i=1}^{k'} |A_i| = \widetilde{k}$. Since there are at least as many trees in F as active agents in $\widetilde{S}$, it must be the case that $k_i \geq |A_i|$ for at least one i, as otherwise $k = \sum_{i=1}^{k'} k_i < \sum_{i=1}^{k'} |A_i| = \widetilde{k} \leq k$ thus obtaining a contradiction.

Let $M' = M \cap E(F')$ and $M'' = M \setminus M'$. By Lemma 3, the recursive call of the algorithm on inputs M' and 1 returns a schedule S' whose cost is upper bounded by $4\mathrm{cost}(\widetilde{S}_{M'})$. Furthermore, using induction, the schedule S'' computed by the algorithm on inputs M'' and $k-1$ satisfies $\mathrm{cost}(S'') \leq 4\mathrm{cost}(\widetilde{S}_{M''})$ as $\widetilde{S}_{M''}$ contains at most $\widetilde{k}-1$ active agents.   □

We can finally state the main result of this section.

Theorem 2. *Algorithm 1 computes a 8-approximate solution in $O^*(2^{k(k+1)/2})$ time.*

Proof. By Lemma 4, the cost of the schedule returned by the algorithm is at most 4 times the cost of an optimal restricted schedule. Hence, using Theorem 1, the algorithm computes a 8-approximate solution.

Regarding the time complexity, the algorithm called with parameter k computes at most 2^k candidate solutions, i.e., one for each possible subset of trees contained in F, regardless of the set M provided in input. Moreover, to compute each candidate solution, the algorithm makes two recursive calls: the first one with parameter 1, that takes polynomial time w.r.t the input size, and the second one with parameter $k-1$. Since each candidate solution is computed in polynomial time, the time complexity of the algorithm is $O^*\left(\prod_{h=1}^{k} 2^h\right) = O^*\left(2^{\sum_{h=1}^{k} h}\right) = O^*\left(2^{k(k+1)/2}\right)$. The claim follows.   □

3.4 $O(k^*)$-Aproximation

We show how to modify Algorithm 1 to obtain a polynomial time algorithm that returns a $4k^*$-approximate schedule, where k^* is the number of active agents in a (fixed) optimal schedule (not necessarily restricted). The algorithm, whose pseudocode is given in Algorithm 2, computes the minimum-cost forest F of two trees T_1, T_2 such that $M \subseteq E(F)$ and augments it with the minimum-cost edge to get a minimum-cost tree T that contains M. The algorithm returns the cheapest of the following two schedules:

- the schedule returned by the call of $\mathrm{Tour}(T)$, which, as we will see, provides a $4k^*$-approximate solution when some agent of the optimal solution crosses the cut induced by T_1 and T_2;
- the schedule obtained by merging the two restricted schedules returned by the recursive calls on $M \cap E(T_i)$, with $i = 1, 2$.

Lemma 5. *Let $\widetilde{S}$ be a restricted schedule w.r.t. M with at most $\widetilde{k}$ active agents. Algorithm 2 computes a restricted schedule S w.r.t. M with at most $\widetilde{k}$ active agents and such that $\mathrm{cost}(S) \leq 2\widetilde{k}\,\mathrm{cost}(\widetilde{S})$.*

Proof. The proof is by induction on the size of M. For the base case in which $|M| = 1$ we have that $E(T) = M$. Therefore, $l(T) \leq l(\widetilde{S})$. Hence, from Lemma 1, the cost of the schedule returned by the call of $\texttt{Tour}(T)$ is at most $2\text{cost}(\widetilde{S})$.

To show the inductive case, we divide the proof into two cases, according to whether $\langle M', M \setminus M' \rangle$ is well-separated w.r.t. $\widetilde{S}$ or not. When $\langle M', M \setminus M' \rangle$ is well-separated w.r.t. $\widetilde{S}$, then, by inductive hypothesis, $\texttt{Schedule2}(M')$ returns a restricted schedule S_1 w.r.t. M' such that $\text{cost}(S_1) \leq 2\widetilde{k}_1\text{cost}(\widetilde{S}_{M'})$, where $\widetilde{k}_1$ is the number of active agents in $\widetilde{S}_{M'}$. Similarly, $\texttt{Schedule2}(M \setminus M')$ returns a restricted schedule S_2 w.r.t. $M \setminus M'$ such that $\text{cost}(S_2) \leq 2(\widetilde{k} - \widetilde{k}_1)\text{cost}(\widetilde{S}_{M \setminus M'})$, as $\widetilde{k} - \widetilde{k}_1$ is the number of active agents in $\widetilde{S}_{M \setminus M'}$. Therefore, the cost of the restricted schedule returned by Algorithm 2 is upper bounded by

$$\text{cost}(S_1 \circ S_2) \leq \text{cost}(S_1) + \text{cost}(S_2) \leq 2\widetilde{k}_1\text{cost}(\widetilde{S}_{M'}) + 2(\widetilde{k} - \widetilde{k}_1)\text{cost}(\widetilde{S}_{M \setminus M'})$$
$$< 2\widetilde{k}\text{cost}(\widetilde{S}).$$

Now consider the case in which $\langle M', M \setminus M' \rangle$ is not well-separated w.r.t. $\widetilde{S}$. We prove that $l(T) \leq \widetilde{k}l(\widetilde{S})$ and use Lemma 1 to derive that the cost of the tour returned by the algorithm – whose cost is upper bounded by the cost of the tour returned by the call of $\texttt{Tour}(T)$ – is at most $2\widetilde{k}\text{cost}(\widetilde{S})$. Let e' be the (unique) edge of T that is not in F. Since $\langle M', M \setminus M' \rangle$ is not well-separated w.r.t. $\widetilde{S}$, there is an active agent of $\widetilde{S}$ that delivers at least one message of M' and at least one message of $M \setminus M'$. This implies that such agent must traverse an edge in $E_{\widetilde{S}}$ whose length is lower bounded by $l_{e'}$. Now, let F' be a minimal (w.r.t. vertex deletion) minimum-cost subforest of F with $\widetilde{k}$ trees such that $M \subseteq E(F')$. Since $E_{\widetilde{S}}$ induces a forest $\widetilde{F}$ of $\widetilde{k}$ pairwise vertex-disjoint paths such that $M \subseteq E(\widetilde{F})$, we have that $l(F') \leq l(\widetilde{F})$. Furthermore, since e' is the longest edge of T, we also have that each of the $\widetilde{k} - 1$ edges of $E(T) \setminus E(F')$ has a length of at most $l_{e'} \leq l(\widetilde{F})$. Therefore,

$$l(T) = l(F') + \sum_{e \in E(T) \setminus E(F')} l_e \leq l(\widetilde{F}) + (\widetilde{k} - 1)l_{e'} \leq \widetilde{k}l(\widetilde{F}) \leq \widetilde{k}l(\widetilde{S}). \qquad \square$$

Since it is easy to see that there exists a restricted schedule with at most k^* active agents whose cost is at most twice the cost of an optimal (not restricted) schedule (e.g., by discarding all non-active agents in an optimal solution from the input instance and invoking Theorem 1), we have the following theorem:

Theorem 3. *Algorithm 2 computes a $4k^*$-approximate schedule in polynomial time, where k^* is the number of active agents in an optimal schedule.*

Proof. The time complexity of Algorithm 2 is polynomial since there are $O(m)$ recursive calls in total. Let S^* be an optimal (not necessarily restricted) schedule with k^* active agents and let $\widetilde{S}$ be a restricted schedule, with at most k^* active agents, and such that $\text{cost}(\widetilde{S}) \leq 2\text{cost}(S^*)$ (see Theorem 1). From Lemma 5, the cost of the schedule returned by Algorithm 2 is at most $2k^*\text{cost}(\widetilde{S})$ and hence upper bounded by $4k^*\text{cost}(S^*)$, $\qquad \square$

Algorithm 2: Schedule2(M) outputs a $4k^*$-approximate restricted schedule w.r.t. M.

1 compute a minimum-cost forest F of H with 2 trees T_1, T_2 such that $M \subseteq E(F)$
2 let T be a minimum-cost tree such that $E(F) \subseteq E(T)$
3 **if** $|M| > 1$ **then** $S' \leftarrow$ Schedule2(M') ∘ Schedule2($M \setminus M'$), where
   $M' = M \cap E(T_1)$
4 **return** the cheapest schedule between S' and Tour(T)

---

4   Agents of Two Types

In this section, we design a constant-factor approximation algorithm for the case in which each agent has one of two possible unitary movement costs, which we can assume (w.l.o.g.) to be 1 and $\gamma \geq 1$. The idea is to reduce our problem to the 2-Depot Heterogeneous Traveling Salesman (2-HTSP) problem for which a 3-approximation exists [17]. For technical convenience, we describe such reduction via a chain of reductions from/to intermediate problems. For each intermediate reduction, we prove that feasible solutions for a problem can be converted into a feasible solution for the other problem (and vice versa) by losing only a constant factor in the cost of the solution. We describe the chain of the reductions in the reverse order, starting from the 2-HTSP problem and arriving to our problem.

In the 2-HTSP problem we are given a set P of destinations that need to be visited by two heterogeneous vehicles that start from distinct depots $\{\delta_1, \delta_2\}$. The set P is partitioned in three subsets P_1, P_2, and $P_{1,2}$. The destinations in P_1 and P_2 must be visited by the first and the second vehicle, respectively, while each destination in $P_{1,2}$ can be visited by either of the vehicles. The traveling cost between two destinations depends on the vehicle: for $i \in \{1, 2\}$, let G_i be a complete undirected graph with vertex set $V(G_i) = \{\delta_i\} \cup P_i \cup P_{1,2}$. Each edge $e \in E(G_i)$ has a non-negative weight $w_i(e)$, and the edge weights satisfy the triangle inequality. A feasible solution of 2-HTSP consists of two tours T_1, T_2 where T_i is a closed walk in G_i that contains all the vertices in $P_i \cup \{\delta_i\}$, and each destination in $P_{1,2}$ is in one of T_1 and T_2. The goal is to find a solution that minimizes $\text{cost}(T_1, T_2) = \sum_{e \in E(T_1)} w_1(e) + \sum_{e \in E(T_2)} w_2(e)$. We will use the following result from [17]:

Theorem 4 ([17]). *There is a polynomial-time 3-approximation algorithm for 2-HTSP.*

4.1 Reducing 2-VWHTSP to 2-HTSP

We generalize the 2-HTSP problem by adding a non-negative weight $w_i(v)$ to each vertex in $V(G_i) \setminus \{\delta_i\}$ and by redefining the cost function as $\text{cost}(T_1, T_2) = \sum_{e \in E(T_1)} w_1(e) + \sum_{v \in V(T_1)} w_1(v) + \sum_{e \in E(T_2)} w_2(e) + \sum_{v \in V(T_2)} w_2(v)$, where we assume that $w(\delta_i) = 0$ for technical convenience. We name this generalized problem *2-depot Vertex-weighted Heterogenous Traveling Salesman Problem* (2-VWHTSP). Intuitively, we want to minimize the sum of the weights of the vertices visited by the two agents in addition to the cost of the respective tours.[4]

We now show how to reduce an instance I of 2-VWHTSP to an instance I' of 2-HTSP. We will refer to the objects (graphs, edge weights, costs, ...) in the definition of I' using the prime superscript. The instance I' is identical to I except for the absence of vertex weights, and for the fact that edge weights are redefined as $w_i'(u, v) = w_i(u, v) + \frac{w_i(u) + w_i(v)}{2}$. Next lemma shows that I' is indeed a valid instance of 2-HTSP.

Lemma 6. *The edge-weights of the graphs G_1' and G_2' in I' satisfy the triangle inequality.*

Notice that a feasible solution (T_1, T_2) for 2-VWHTSP is also a feasible solution for 2-HTSP and vice versa. The following lemma relates the cost of a solution in the two problems.

Lemma 7. $\text{cost}(T_1, T_2) = \text{cost}'(T_1, T_2)$.

Combining Lemma 6, Lemma 7, and Theorem 4 we immediately obtain the following upper-bound on the approximability of 2-VWHTSP.

Corollary 2. *2-VWHTSP admits a polynomial-time 3-approximation algorithm.*

4.2 Reducing VWHTSP to 2-VWHTSP

We now further generalize the 2-VWHTSP problem. The VWHTSP is defined similarly to 2-VWHTSP except that we allow multiple vehicles to tour each graph G_i. Formally, we are given a set P of destinations partitioned into three sets P_1, P_2, and $P_{1,2}$, and two non-empty sets D_1 and D_2 of depots. Each depot in D_i hosts a vehicle of *type i*. The traveling costs for vehicles of type i are encoded using a complete undirected graph G_i with vertex set $V(G_i) = D_i \cup P_i \cup P_{1,2}$. Each edge $e \in E(G_i)$ has a non-negative weight $w_i(e)$ and edge weights satisfy the triangle inequality. Similarly, each vertex $v \in V(G_i) \setminus D_i$ has a non-negative weight $w_i(v)$, and we let $w_i(\delta) = 0$ if $\delta \in D_i$. A solution is a collection $\mathcal{T}$ of tours, one from each depot $\delta \in D_1 \cup D_2$. The tour T_δ corresponding to a depot $\delta \in D_i$ is either empty or it is a closed walk in G_i that includes vertex δ. The solution $\mathcal{T}$ is feasible if each destination in P is contained in at least one tour in $\mathcal{T}$.

---

[4] Since the edge weights in G_1 (resp. G_2) satisfy the triangle inequality, we can assume that no vertex appears more than once in T_1 (resp. T_2).

The cost of $\mathcal{T}$ (to be minimized) is the sum of the costs of each individual tour, where the cost of a tour $T_\delta \in \mathcal{T}$ with $\delta \in D_i$ is $\sum_{e \in E(T_\delta)} w_i(e) + \sum_{v \in V(T_\delta)} w_i(v)$.

We reduce this problem to 2-VWHTSP by identifying all the depots of vehicles of the same type into a single depot and considering the metric closure of the resulting graphs. More precisely, given an instance I of VWHTSP, we define an instance I' of 2-VWHTSP in this way (we use the prime superscript to refer to the objects in the definition of I'): The set of destinations P' in I', and its partition into P_1', P_2', and $P_{1,2}'$, coincide with the respective sets in I. There are two depots δ_1' and δ_2'. In order to define the edge weights of G_i', consider the edge-weighted (multi-)graph H_i obtained from G_i by identifying all vertices in D_i into a single vertex δ_i'. The weight $w_i'(u, v)$ of an edge $(u, v) \in E(G_i')$ is the distance between u and v in H_i. Finally, each vertex $v \in V(G_i) \setminus \{\delta_i\}$ has weight $w_i'(v) = w_i(v)$.

Lemma 8. *Let $\mathcal{T}$ be a feasible solution for I. There exists a feasible solution (T_1', T_2') for I' such that $cost'(T_1', T_2') \leq cost(\mathcal{T})$.*

Lemma 9. *Let (T_1', T_2') be a feasible solution for I'. There exists a feasible solution $\mathcal{T}$ for I such that $cost(\mathcal{T}) \leq 2cost'(T_1', T_2')$.*

From Corollary 2, Lemma 8, and Lemma 9 it follows that:

Corollary 3. *VWHTSP admits a polynomial-time 6-approximation algorithm.*

4.3   Reducing the HWD Problem to VWHTSP

As final step, we reduce the instance of our problem where all the agents have a unitary movement cost of either 1 or γ to an instance of VWHTSP.

Definition 1. *A restricted schedule with delivery receipt (RSDR) is a restricted schedule in which, whenever an agent delivers a message m_j on t_j, it immediately travels back to s_j without picking up any other message along the way.*

As a consequence of the constrained structure of a RSDR, one can easily observe the following:

Remark 1. For any RSDR S, there is always a RSDR S' with $\text{cost}(S') \leq \text{cost}(S)$ and S' is such that: (i) for each vertex $v \in G$, all agents initially placed on v except (possibly) for the agent with minimum unit cost, are not active in S', and (ii) for each vertex v, all the messages with source vertex v are delivered by the same agent a, and no other message is delivered in-between by a.

Thanks to the above properties, we will henceforth assume (w.l.o.g.) that in our input instance at most one agent is initially positioned on each vertex, and that all source vertices of the messages to be delivered are distinct.[5]

We now show that RSDRs provide good approximations of restricted schedules.

---

[5] Indeed, we can discard all agents starting from the same vertex, except for one with minimum unit cost (selected arbitrarily in case of ties). We can further consolidate all messages with the same source u into a single "batch" message to be delivered to a new dummy vertex v. The distance from u to v is exactly the sum of the distances from u to the respective destinations of the replaced messages.

Lemma 10. *There exists a RSDR S such that $cost(S) \leq 3cost(OPT_R)$, where OPT_R is an optimal restricted schedule.*

At this point we are ready to define the instance I of VWHTSP. The depots D_1 (resp. D_2) in I are the initial positions of the agents a_i such that $c_i = 1$ (resp. $c_i = \gamma$). The sets P_1 and P_2 are empty, while $P_{1,2} = \{s_1, \ldots s_m\}$ is the set of all the source vertices. Every $(u, v) \in E(G_1)$ has weight $w_1(u, v) = d_G(u, v)$, while every $(u, v) \in E(G_2)$ has weight $w_2(u, v) = \gamma \cdot d_G(u, v)$. For each vertex $s_i \in P_{1,2}$, we set $w_1(s_i) = 2d_G(s_i, t_i)$ and $w_2(s_i) = 2\gamma \cdot d_G(s_i, t_i)$.

Lemma 11. *Let S be a feasible RSDR. There exists a feasible solution T of I such that $cost(T) \leq cost(S)$.*

Lemma 12. *Let T be a feasible solution for I. There exists a feasible RSDR S such that $cost(S) \leq cost(T)$.*

By using Lemma 11, Lemma 12, Lemma 10, Corollary 3, and Theorem 1, we immediately have:

Theorem 5. *There is a polynomial-time 36-approximation algorithm for the HWD problem when all agents have a unitary movement cost of either 1 or γ.*

5   A Polylogarithmic Approximation for the General Case

In this section we describe an approximation algorithm for the general case achieving an approximation ratio of $O(\log^2 n \cdot \log \min\{n, m\} \cdot \log \log n) = \widetilde{O}(\log^3 n)$. The idea is to reduce our problem to the group Steiner tree problem.

The group Steiner tree problem is the following. Let H be an undirected graph in which each edge $e \in E(H)$ has a non-negative weight $w(e)$. Let B be a collection of non-empty subsets of V. The objective is to find a *group Steiner tree*, i.e., a minimum weight subgraph of H that is a tree and contains at least one vertex from each of the groups.

Theorem 6 ([12]). *The group Steiner tree problem admits a polynomial-time $O(\log^2 |V(H)| \cdot \log |B| \cdot \log \log |V(H)|)$-approximation algorithm.*

Given an instance of HWD, we construct an instance I of group Steiner tree as follows: for each agent a_i we create a copy G_i of G in which each edge (u, v) has a weight $w_i(u, v) = c_i \cdot l_{uv}$. For each message m_j, we add a vertex μ_j to G_i and an edge (s_j, μ_j) of weight $c_i \cdot d_G(s, t_j)$. The graph H is obtained by starting from the disjoint union of all k graphs G_i, adding an additional vertex r, and adding an edge of weight 0 from r to vertex p_i in the copy of G_i, for each $i = 1, \ldots, k$. There is one group $b_j \in B$ for each message m_j, and it consists of all the vertices μ_j in the copies of $G_1, \ldots, G_k$. See Figs. 3(a) and (b) for an example.

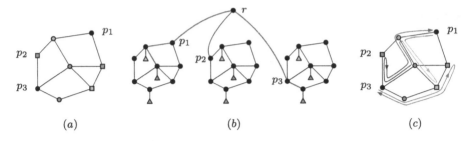

Fig. 3. (a) The graph G of our instance of HWD. The source and destination vertices s_j and t_j of each message m_j are depicted as a colored square and a colored circle, respectively (different colors correspond to different messages). Edge weights are not shown. (b) The graph H of the instance I of group Steiner tree. Vertices μ_j are depicted using triangles colored with the same colors of the vertices s_j and t_j of the corresponding message. The edges of a feasible group Steiner tree T are shown in red. (c) A set of walks on G obtained from an Eulerian tour of T, which collectively induce a feasible RSDR S. The portions of a walk in which an agent transports a message m_j from s_t to t_j and then travels back to s_j are drawn with the same color of s_j and t_j. The remaining portions of the walk are shown in red. Notice that agent a_2 is not active in S. (Color figure online)

Lemma 13. *Let S be a feasible RSDR. There is a group Steiner tree for I of total weight at most $\text{cost}(S)$.*

Proof. Given S, we denote by W_i the walk in G performed by agent a_i according to S. To prove the claim we show how to find, for each $i = 1, \ldots, k$, a subgraph G_i' of G_i of total weight at most $c_i \cdot \sum_{e \in E(W_i)} l_e$ and such that if a_i delivers message m_j then G' contains vertex μ_j.

The group Steiner tree from H can then be obtained by selecting any spanning tree of the graph resulting from the union of all G_is together with all the edges incident to r.

We now decompose the walk W_i into an alternating sequence of sub-walks $\langle \alpha_1, \beta_1, \alpha_2, \beta_2, \ldots, \alpha_h, \beta_h, \alpha_{h+1} \rangle$ where β_j corresponds to the portion of the walk in which a_i carries its j-th delivered message m_j from s_j to t_j and then travels back to s_j (as required by the definition of RSDR), while α_js represents the portions of W_i in which a_i travels from the initial position of a message to the next (or from/to p_i in case of α_1 and α_{h+1}).

The subgraph G_i is obtained as the union of the edges in $\bigcup_{j=1}^h E(\alpha_j)$ with the edges (s_j, μ_j) corresponding to message m_j delivered in some β_j. $\square$

Lemma 14. *Let T be a group Steiner tree for I of total weight w_T. There is a feasible RSDR S such that $\text{cost}(S) \leq 2w_T$.*

Proof. For each agent a_i, we call T_i the subgraph of T induced by the vertices in G_i. Notice that T_i is a (possibly empty) tree. We will use T_i to build a schedule S_i for agent a_i. The schedule S will be the union of all schedules $S_1, \ldots, S_k$.

If T_i is empty then S_i is also empty. Otherwise we must have $p_i \in V(T_i)$ and set M_i of messages delivered by a_i contains exactly the messages m_j for which the edge (s_j, μ_j) of G_i is also in T_i. The act of delivering these messages by travelling from their sources s_j to their target t_j and then back to s_j, as required by the definition of RSDR, costs exactly $2\sum_{m_j \in M_i} w(s_j, \mu_j)$.

Notice that all vertices μ_j for $m_j \in M_i$ must be leaves in T_i. Therefore the graph T_i' obtained from T_i by deleting all such μ_j is still a tree. The order in which the messages $m_j \in M_i$ are delivered by a_i according to S_i is the order in which the corresponding vertices s_j are first visited by an Eulerian tour of T_i' (that visits each edge twice) starting from p_i (see Figs. 3(b) and(c)). The energy consumed by a_i to travel from the source of a message to the next (and from/to p_i and the beginning/end of the schedule) is at most the total weight of the Eulerian tour, i.e., twice the weight of the edges in $E(T_i')$. We can hence conclude that the contribution of S_i to cost(S) is at most $2\sum_{e \in E(T_i)} w(e)$, implying that cost($S$) is at most twice the weight of T. □

We are now ready to state the main result of this section.

Theorem 7. *There is a polynomial time $O(\log^2 n \cdot \log\min\{m,n\} \cdot \log\log n)$-approximation algorithm for the HWD problem.*

Proof. The graph H in the instance I of group Steiner tree consists of the k graphs G_i plus the additional vertex r. By Remark 1 we can assume that $k \leq n$ and, since $|V(G_i)| = O(n)$ we have $|V(H)| = O(kn) = O(n^2)$. The number $|B|$ of groups in I coincides with the number of messages m, which can be assumed to be at most n (see again Remark 1). The claim follows by combining Lemma 14, Lemma 13, and Theorem 6. □

References

1. Bärtschi, A., et al.: Collaborative delivery with energy-constrained mobile robots. Theor. Comput. Sci. **810**, 2–14 (2020). https://doi.org/10.1016/j.tcs.2017.04.018
2. Bärtschi, A., Chalopin, J., Das, S., Disser, Y., Graf, D., Hackfeld, J., Penna, P.: Energy-efficient delivery by heterogeneous mobile agents. In: Vollmer, H., Vallée, B. (eds.) 34th Symposium on Theoretical Aspects of Computer Science, STACS 2017, Hannover, Germany, 8–11 March 2017. LIPIcs, vol. 66, pp. 10:1–10:14. Schloss Dagstuhl - Leibniz-Zentrum für Informatik (2017). https://doi.org/10.4230/LIPIcs.STACS.2017.10
3. Bärtschi, A., Graf, D., Mihalák, M.: Collective fast delivery by energy-efficient agents. In: Potapov, I., Spirakis, P.G., Worrell, J. (eds.) 43rd International Symposium on Mathematical Foundations of Computer Science, MFCS 2018, Liverpool, UK, 27–31 August 2018. LIPIcs, vol. 117, pp. 56:1–56:16. Schloss Dagstuhl - Leibniz-Zentrum für Informatik (2018). https://doi.org/10.4230/LIPIcs.MFCS.2018.56
4. Bärtschi, A., Graf, D., Penna, P.: Truthful mechanisms for delivery with agents. In: D'Angelo, G., Dollevoet, T. (eds.) 17th Workshop on Algorithmic Approaches for Transportation Modelling, Optimization, and Systems, ATMOS 2017, Vienna, Austria, 7–8 September 2017. OASICS, vol. 59, pp. 2:1–2:17. Schloss Dagstuhl - Leibniz-Zentrum für Informatik (2017). https://doi.org/10.4230/OASIcs.ATMOS.2017.2

5. Bärtschi, A., Tschager, T.: Energy-efficient fast delivery by mobile agents. In: Klasing, R., Zeitoun, M. (eds.) FCT 2017. LNCS, vol. 10472, pp. 82–95. Springer, Heidelberg (2017). https://doi.org/10.1007/978-3-662-55751-8_8

6. Berman, P., Demaine, E.D., Zadimoghaddam, M.: $O(1)$-Approximations for maximum movement problems. In: Goldberg, L.A., Jansen, K., Ravi, R., Rolim, J.D.P. (eds.) APPROX/RANDOM 2011. LNCS, vol. 6845, pp. 62–74. Springer, Heidelberg (2011). https://doi.org/10.1007/978-3-642-22935-0_6

7. Bilò, D., Disser, Y., Gualà, L., Mihal'ák, M., Proietti, G., Widmayer, P.: Polygon-constrained motion planning problems. In: Flocchini, P., Gao, J., Kranakis, E., Meyer auf der Heide, F. (eds.) ALGOSENSORS 2013. LNCS, vol. 8243, pp. 67–82. Springer, Heidelberg (2014). https://doi.org/10.1007/978-3-642-45346-5_6

8. Bilò, D., Gualà, L., Leucci, S., Proietti, G.: Exact and approximate algorithms for movement problems on (special classes of) graphs. Theor. Comput. Sci. **652**, 86–101 (2016). https://doi.org/10.1016/j.tcs.2016.09.007

9. Carvalho, I.A., Erlebach, T., Papadopoulos, K.: An efficient algorithm for the fast delivery problem. In: Gąsieniec, L.A., Jansson, J., Levcopoulos, C. (eds.) FCT 2019. LNCS, vol. 11651, pp. 171–184. Springer, Cham (2019). https://doi.org/10.1007/978-3-030-25027-0_12

10. Chalopin, J., Das, S., Mihal'ák, M., Penna, P., Widmayer, P.: Data delivery by energy-constrained mobile agents. In: Flocchini, P., Gao, J., Kranakis, E., Meyer auf der Heide, F. (eds.) ALGOSENSORS 2013. LNCS, vol. 8243, pp. 111–122. Springer, Heidelberg (2014). https://doi.org/10.1007/978-3-642-45346-5_9

11. Chalopin, J., Jacob, R., Mihalák, M., Widmayer, P.: Data delivery by energy-constrained mobile agents on a line. In: Esparza, J., Fraigniaud, P., Husfeldt, T., Koutsoupias, E. (eds.) ICALP 2014, Part II. LNCS, vol. 8573, pp. 423–434. Springer, Heidelberg (2014). https://doi.org/10.1007/978-3-662-43951-7_36

12. Charikar, M., Chekuri, C., Goel, A., Guha, S.: Rounding via trees: deterministic approximation algorithms for group Steiner trees and k-median. In: Proceedings of the Thirtieth Annual ACM Symposium on Theory of Computing, STOC 1998, pp. 114–123. Association for Computing Machinery, New York (1998). https://doi.org/10.1145/276698.276719

13. Demaine, E.D., et al.: Minimizing movement. ACM Trans. Algorithms **5**(3), 30:1–30:30 (2009). https://doi.org/10.1145/1541885.1541891

14. Gørtz, I.L., Molinaro, M., Nagarajan, V., Ravi, R.: Capacitated Vehicle Routing with Non-uniform Speeds. In: Günlük, O., Woeginger, G.J. (eds.) IPCO 2011. LNCS, vol. 6655, pp. 235–247. Springer, Heidelberg (2011). https://doi.org/10.1007/978-3-642-20807-2_19

15. Malik, W.A., Rathinam, S., Darbha, S.: An approximation algorithm for a symmetric generalized multiple depot, multiple travelling salesman problem. Oper. Res. Lett. **35**(6), 747–753 (2007). https://doi.org/10.1016/j.orl.2007.02.001

16. Xu, Z., Rodrigues, B.: A 3/2-approximation algorithm for the multiple TSP with a fixed number of depots. Informs J. Comput. **27**(4), 636–645 (2015). https://doi.org/10.1287/ijoc.2015.0650

17. Yadlapalli, S., Rathinam, S., Darbha, S.: 3-approximation algorithm for a two depot, heterogeneous traveling salesman problem. Optim. Lett. **6**(1), 141–152 (2012). https://doi.org/10.1007/s11590-010-0256-0

Graph Exploration by Energy-Sharing Mobile Agents

Jurek Czyzowicz[1], Stefan Dobrev[2], Ryan Killick[3], Evangelos Kranakis[3(✉)],
Danny Krizanc[4], Lata Narayanan[5], Jaroslav Opatrny[5], Denis Pankratov[5],
and Sunil Shende[6]

[1] Département d'Informatique, Université du Québec en Outaouais,
Gatineau, Canada
[2] Slovak Academy of Sciences, Bratislava, Slovakia
[3] School of Computer Science, Carleton University, Ottawa, Canada
kranakis@scs.carleton.ca
[4] Department of Mathematics and Computer Science, Wesleyan University,
Middletown, CT, USA
[5] Department of Computer Science and Software Engineering, Concordia University,
Montreal, Canada
[6] Department of Computer Science, Rutgers University, New Brunswick, USA

Abstract. We consider the problem of collective exploration of a known
n-node edge-weighted graph by k mobile agents that have limited energy
but are capable of energy transfers. The agents are initially placed at
an arbitrary subset of nodes in the graph, and each agent has an initial,
possibly different, amount of energy. The goal of the exploration problem
is for every edge in the graph to be traversed by at least one agent. The
amount of energy used by an agent to travel distance x is proportional
to x. In our model, the agents can *share* energy when co-located: when
two agents meet, one can transfer part of its energy to the other.

For an n-node path, we give an $O(n + k)$ time algorithm that either
finds an exploration strategy, or reports that one does not exist. For an
n-node tree with ℓ leaves, we give an $O(n + \ell k^2)$ algorithm that finds an
exploration strategy if one exists. Finally, for the general graph case, we
show that the problem of deciding if exploration is possible by energy-
sharing agents is NP-hard, even for 3-regular graphs. In addition, we
show that it is always possible to find an exploration strategy if the
total energy of the agents is at least twice the total weight of the edges;
moreover, this is asymptotically optimal.

Keywords: Energy · Exploration · Graph · Mobile agent · Path ·
Sharing · Tree

Research supported in part by NSERC grants.

© Springer Nature Switzerland AG 2021
T. Jurdziński and S. Schmid (Eds.): SIROCCO 2021, LNCS 12810, pp. 185–203, 2021.
https://doi.org/10.1007/978-3-030-79527-6_11

1   Introduction

The emergence of swarm robotics has inspired a number of investigations into the capabilities of a collection of autonomous mobile robots (or agents), each with limited capabilities. Such agents cooperate and work collaboratively to achieve complex tasks such as pattern formation, object clustering and assembly, search, and exploration. Collaboration on such tasks is achieved by, for example, decomposing the task at hand into smaller tasks which can be performed by individual agents. The benefits of the collaborative paradigm are manifold: smaller task completion time, fault tolerance, and the lower build cost and energy-efficiency of a collection of smaller agents as compared to larger more complex agents. Somewhat surprisingly, for example, a recent paper [16] shows that two agents can search for a target at an unknown location on the line with lower total energy costs than a single agent.

In this paper, we study the problem of collective exploration of a known edge-weighted graph by n mobile agents initially placed at arbitrary nodes of the graph. Many variants of the graph exploration problem have been studied previously; see Sect. 1.2 for a description of some of the related work. For our work, the goal of exploration is that *every edge* of the graph must be traversed by at least one agent. The weight of an edge is called its *length*. Every agent is equipped with a *battery/energy container* that has an initial amount of energy; the initial energies of different agents can be different. We assume that moving length x depletes the battery of an agent by exactly x.

Clearly then, for exploration to be possible, the sum of the initial energies of all agents has to be at least $\mathcal{E}$, the sum of all edge weights. However total energy $\mathcal{E}$ may not be sufficient; the *initial placement* of the agents plays a role in deciding if exploration is possible with the given energies. To see this, consider exploration by 2 agents of a path with 4 nodes, where each of the 3 edges has length 1. If the agents are initially placed at the two endpoints of the path, then total energy 3 suffices to explore the path. However if the two agents are initially placed at the middle two nodes of the path, it is not difficult to see that total energy 4 is necessary to complete the exploration.

In addition to initial placement of agents, and the total amount of energy, the initial *energy distribution* also affects the existence of an exploration strategy. To see this, suppose the 2 agents are placed at the middle nodes of the 4-node path. Consider first an energy distribution in which both agents have initial energy 2. Then one exploration strategy would be for both agents to explore half of the center edge, and turn around to travel to the endpoint. Next consider an energy distribution in which agent 1 has energy $3 + \epsilon$ for some $0 < \epsilon \leq 1$ and the agent 2 has energy $1 - \epsilon$. It is easy to see that exploration is impossible, even though the total energy of both agents is the same as in the first distribution.

Recently, several researchers have proposed a new mechanism to aid collaboration: *the capability to share energy*. In other words, when two agents meet, one can transfer a portion of its energy to the other. It is interesting to investigate what tasks might be made possible with this new capability, given the same initial amounts of energies. In [6,12–14,26], researchers have studied the problems of data delivery, broadcast, and convergecast by energy-sharing mobile agents.

In the example described above, where agent 1 has energy $3 + \epsilon$ for some $0 < \epsilon \leq 1$ and the agent 2 has energy $1 - \epsilon$, if energy transfer is allowed, agent 1 (with the higher energy) can first go to the endpoint closer to its initial position, then turn around, reach agent 2, and transfer its remaining energy ϵ to agent 2. This enables agent 2 to reach the other endpoint, thereby completing the exploration.

This simple example shows that energy-sharing capabilities make graph exploration possible in situations where it would have been impossible otherwise. Note that an algorithm for exploration with energy sharing requires not only an assignment of trajectories to agents that collectively explore the entire graph, but also an achievable schedule of energy transfers. In this paper, we are interested in exploration strategies for edge-weighted graphs by energy-sharing mobile agents. We give a precise definition of our model and the collaborative exploration problem below.

1.1 Model

We are given a *weighted graph* $G = (V, E)$ where V is a set of n vertices (or nodes), E a set of m edges, and each edge $a_i \in E$ is assigned a real number w_i, denoting its *length*. We have k *mobile agents* (or robots) $r_1, r_2, \ldots, r_k$ placed at some of the vertices of the graph. We allow more than one agent to be located in the same place. Each mobile agent (or agent for short) r_i can move with speed 1, and initially possesses a specific amount of *energy* equal to e_i for its moves. An agent can move in any direction along the edges of the graph G, it can stop if needed, and it can reverse its direction of moving either at a vertex, or after traversing a part of an edge. The energy consumed by a moving agent is linearly proportional to the distance x traveled; to simplify notation it is assumed to be equal to x. An agent can move only if its energy is greater than zero.

An important feature of our model is the possibility of *energy sharing* between agents: when two agents, say r_i and r_j, $i \neq j$, meet at some time at some location in the graph, agent r_i can transfer a portion of its energy to r_j. More specifically, if e_i' and e_j' are the energy levels of r_i and r_j at the time they meet then r_i can transfer to r_j energy $0 < e \leq e_i'$ and thus their energies will become $e_i' - e$ and $e_j' + e$, respectively.

In our model, each agent is assigned a *trajectory* to follow. We define a trajectory of an agent to be a sequence of edges or parts of edges that starts at the agent's initial position and forms a continuous walk in the graph. In addition, a trajectory specifies a *schedule* of energy transfers, i.e., all points on this walk (could be points different from vertices) where the agent is to receive/transfer energy from/to other agents, and for each such point the amounts of energy involved. We call a set of trajectories *valid* if the schedules of energy transfers among trajectories match, and energy levels are sufficient for the movement of agents. More specifically, for every transfer point on a trajectory of agent r_i where energy is to be received/transferred, there is exactly one agent r_j, $j \neq i$, whose trajectory contains the same transfer point transferring/receiving that amount of energy to/from r_i, and the transfers can scheduled on a time line. Furthermore, the energy of an agent, initially and after any energy transfer, must be always sufficient to continue to move along its assigned trajectory. We are interested in solving the following general problem of collaborative exploration:

Graph Exploration Problem: Given a *weighted graph* $G = (V, E)$ and k mobile agents $r_1, r_2, \ldots, r_k$ together with their respective initial energies $e_1, e_2, \ldots, e_k$ and positions $s_1, s_2, \ldots, s_k$ in the graph, find a valid set of trajectories that *explore* (or cover) all edges of the graph.

1.2 Related Work

The problems of exploration and searching have been investigated for over fifty years. The studied environments were usually graphs (e.g. [1,18,23,27]) and geometric two-dimensional terrains (e.g. [2,4,17]). The goal of such research was most often the minimization of the time of the search/exploration that was proportional to the distance travelled by the searcher. The task of searching consists of finding the target placed at an unknown position of the environment. The environment itself was sometimes known in advance (cf. [4,8,14,23]) but most research assumed only its partial knowledge, e.g. the type of graph, the upper bound on its size or its node degree, etc. Remarkably, there exist hundreds of papers for search in an environment as simple as a line (cf. [3]). The task of exploration consisted of constructing a traversal of the entire environment, e.g. in order to construct its map (see [22,27]). It is worth noting that performing a complete graph traversal does not result in acquiring the knowledge of the map (see [10]).

Most of the early research on search and exploration has been done for the case of a single searcher. When a team of collaborating searchers (also called agents or robots) is available, the main challenge is usually to partition the task among the team members and synchronize their efforts using available means of communication, cf. [5,9,19,21]. Unfortunately, for the centralized setting, already in the case of two robots in the tree environment known in advance, minimizing its exploration time is NP-hard, e.g., see [21].

The case of robots that can share energy has been recently studied for the tasks of data communication, [6,12–14,26]. In this research the robots are distributed in different places of the network, each robot initially possessing some amount of energy, possibly distinct for different robots. The energy is used proportionally to the distance travelled by the robot. The simplest communication task is *data delivery* (see [6,7,11,12]), where the data packet originally placed in some initial position in the environment has to be carried by the collaborating robots into the target place. Remarkably, when the robots cannot share energy, data delivery is an NP-hard problem even for the line network, (see [11]). When the robots are allowed to exchange a portion of energy while they meet in the tree of n nodes, [12] gives the $O(n)$-time solution for the data delivery. For energy sharing robots, the authors of [13] study the *broadcast problem*, where a single packet of data has to be carried to all nodes of the tree network, while [12] investigates also the *convergecast problem*, where the data from all tree nodes need to be accumulated in the memory of the same robot. In both cases efficient communication algorithms are proposed. A byproduct of [14] is an optimal exploration algorithm in the special case when all robots are initially positioned at the same node of the tree. When the energy sharing robots have small limited memory, able to carry only one or two data packets at a time, the simplest case of the data delivery problem is shown to be NP-hard in [6]. Further, in [20] bounds are proved in an energy model where robots can communicate when they are in the same node and the goal of robot team is to jointly explore an unknown tree.

1.3 Results of the Paper

We start in Sect. 2 with exploration of a path. Given an initial placement and energy distribution for k energy-sharing agents on an n-node path, we give an $O(n+k)$ algorithm to generate a set of valid trajectories whenever the exploration of the path is possible. We also show that a path can always be explored if the total energy of energy-sharing agents is $\frac{3}{2}$ times the total weight of edges in the path. In contrast, we show that there are energy configurations for which any total amount of energy is insufficient for path exploration *without* energy sharing.

In Sect. 3 we study exploration of trees. We first observe that without energy sharing the exploration of trees is NP-complete. Then, for an n-node tree, we give an $O(n + \ell k^2)$ algorithm that finds an exploration strategy if one exists, where ℓ is the number of leaves in the tree.

In Sect. 4, we consider exploration of general graphs. We show that the problem is NP-hard even for 3-regular graphs. In addition, we show that it is always possible to find an exploration strategy if the total energy of the agents is at least twice the total weight of the edges; moreover, this is asymptotically optimal, even for trees.

Therefore our results show that allowing energy to be shared between agents makes exploration possible in many situations when it would not be possible without sharing energy. Furthermore, the total energy needed for exploration is at most twice (at most 3/2) the total weight of the edges in the graph (path respectively), while there is no upper bound on the total energy needed for exploration if agents cannot share energy, even when the graph to be explored is a path. Due to space limitations, all missing proofs can be found in [15].

2 Exploring a Path

In this section we consider the case when the graph is a simple path on n nodes; without loss of generality, we assume that the path is embedded in the horizontal line segment $[0, 1]$, and we will refer to the movements of agents in their trajectories as being left/right movements on the segment. Clearly, in case the graph is given in the usual graph representation, this embedding can be obtained in $O(n+k)$ time. The path exploration problem can therefore be restated as follows:

Problem 1 (Segment Exploration). Given mobile agents $r_1, r_2, \ldots, r_k$ with energies $e_1, e_2, \ldots, e_k$, located initially in positions $0 \leq s_1 \leq s_2 \leq \cdots \leq s_k \leq 1$ of a line segment $[0, 1]$, respectively, find a set of valid trajectories of these agents that explore the segment, if possible.

A trajectory t_i of agent r_i explores a closed sub-segment a_i of $[0, 1]$ containing s_i. Let b_i^ℓ, b_i^r be the left, right end point of this sub-segment. We want to find a valid set of trajectories, i.e., a set that explores the line segment $[0, 1]$, and there exists a schedule for energy transfers such that every agent has enough energy to follow its trajectory.

We first observe that in the case of exploring a line segment with the possibility of energy sharing some assumptions on the shape of valid trajectories can be made without loss of generality.

1. The segments $a_1, a_2, \ldots, a_k$ explore (or cover) $[0, 1]$ and they don't overlap, i.e., $b_1^\ell = 0$, $b_n^r = 1$, and $b_i^r = b_{i+1}^\ell$ for $1 \leq i \leq k - 1$.
2. Trajectory t_i starts at s_i, goes straight to one of the endpoints of a_i. When both endpoints are different from s_i, it turns around and goes straight the other endpoint of a_i. Thus, in this case the trajectory *covers doubly* a sub-segment between s_i and the endpoint where it turns around, and the trajectory has a *doubly covered part* and a *singly covered part*.
3. A transfer of energy between two agents r_i and r_{i+1} may occur only at their *meeting point* b_i^r. Thus at b_i^r exactly one of the following occurs:
   (a) There is no energy transfer.
   (b) There is energy transfer from r_i to r_{i+1}. In that case t_{i+1} does not end at that point, it ends at b_{i+1}^r, and either $b_{i+1}^\ell = s_{i+1}$ or b_{i+1}^ℓ is a point where the trajectory t_{i+1} turns around to the right.
   (c) There is energy transfer from r_{i+1} to r_i. In that case t_i does not end at that point, it ends at b_i^ℓ and either $b_i^r = s_i$ or b_i^r is a point where the trajectory t_i turns around to the left.

The next lemma, stated without proof, specifies two additional restrictions that can be imposed on the nature of valid trajectories that will be applied by our algorithm.

Lemma 1. *Assume that the segment $[0, 1]$ can be explored by a set of valid trajectories $T = \{t_1, t_2, \ldots, t_k\}$ of the agents. Then there is a canonical set of valid trajectories $T' = \{t_1', t_2', \ldots, t_k'\}$ that explore the segment such that*

(i) If agent r_i receives energy from a right (left) neighbour then it receives it at its initial position s_i, and its trajectory may only go in straight line segment from s_i to the left (right).

(ii) For each trajectory, its singly covered part is at least as long as its doubly covered part.

We now describe a recursive, linear time algorithm for Problem 1 to find canonical trajectories as described in Lemma 1 above. The trajectories are assigned to agents from left to right, determining whether more energy needs to be transferred to complete the coverage on the left, or some surplus energy is to be transfused to agents on the right. If i is the index of the leftmost agent not used in the exploration of initial sub-segment $[0, \ell_i]$ and if tr_i is the energy deficit (negative) or surplus (positive) left after exploring this sub-segment using only agents 1 through $(i-1)$, then the procedure call $\text{PATH}(i, \ell_i, tr_i)$ decides whether a solution to the exploration problem for the remaining sub-segment $[\ell_i, 1]$ is possible via canonical trajectories. It does so by greedily deploying agent i to use the least amount of energy to cover at least the segment $[\ell_i, s_i]$: if this does not lead to energy deficit, then the trajectory of agent r_i is allowed to cover as much of the segment $[s_i, s_{i+1}]$ as it can, which determines the position ℓ_{i+1}.

Procedure. $\text{PATH}(i, \ell_i, tr_i)$

1: **if** $tr_i \leq 0$ **then**
2:    **if** $e_i < s_i - \ell_i + tr_i$ **then**   ▷ **Case 1.1** (deficit increases)
3:        # r_i waits to receive energy $|tr_{i+1}|$ from r_{i+1}. Trajectory t_i is from s_i to ℓ_i. Transfer $|tr_i|$ of energy to r_{i-1}
4:        $\ell_{i+1} \leftarrow s_i$
5:        $tr_{i+1} \leftarrow e_i + tr_i - (s_i - \ell_i)$
6:    **else if** $e_i \geq s_i - \ell_i + tr_i$ **then**   ▷ **Case 1.2** (deficit eliminated)
7:        # Using the values of ℓ_i, s_i and $e_i - |tr_i|$, select a canonical trajectory t_i originating in s_i, located between ℓ_i and s_{i+1} as in **Cases 1.2.1** to **1.2.3**. Transfer $|tr_i|$ of energy to r_{i-1}
8:        $tr_{i+1} \leftarrow e_i + tr_i - length(t_i)$
9:        $\ell_{i+1} \leftarrow right\_endpoint(t_i)$
10: **else**   ▷ **Case 2:** (Energy surplus)
11:    # A surplus of energy at ℓ_i implies that $\ell_i = s_i$. The trajectory t_i of r_i is "from s_i to the right, but at most to s_{i-1}".
12:    $\ell_{i+1} \leftarrow s_i + \min\{s_{i+1} - s_i, s_i + e_i + tr_i\}$
13:    $tr_{i+1} \leftarrow tr_i + e_i - (\min\{s_{i+1} - s_i, s_i + e_i + tr_i\} - s_i))$
14: **if** $(i < k)$ **then** return $\text{PATH}(i+1, \ell_{i+1}, tr_{i+1})$
15: **else if** $(\ell_{k+1} < 1)$ **or** $(tr_{k+1} < 0)$ **then**   ▷ Insufficient energy
16:    return with **solvable** $\leftarrow$ false
17: **else**
18:    return with **solvable** $\leftarrow$ true

Then, a recursive call to PATH is made with arguments $i+1$, ℓ_{i+1} and the resulting energy deficit or surplus tr_{i+1}. For an easier understanding of the algorithm, the description below is annotated in detail and Fig. 1 provides an example for each case encountered in the algorithm.

We use the following lemma to simplify the proof of the main theorem of this section.

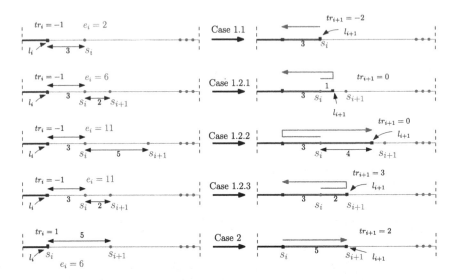

Fig. 1. Assignment of a trajectory to agent r_i by Procedure PATH. The trajectory established in each case is in red on the right part of the figure. Cases 1.1 to 1.2.3 deal with an energy deficit prior to an assignment of a trajectory to r_i, and Case 2 deals with a surplus of energy. In Cases 1.2.1 to 1.2.3 the deficit is eliminated. (Color figure online)

Lemma 2. *Let $t_1, t_2, \ldots, t_{i-1}$ be the trajectories and ℓ_i, tr_i be the values estab-lished by Procedure PATH after $i - 1$ recursive calls, $0 \leq i \leq k + 1$. These trajectories explore the segment $[0, \ell_i]$ using in total energy $(\sum_{j=1}^{i-1} e_j) - tr_i$ and this is the minimum energy required by the agents to explore the segment $[0, \ell_i]$. Furthermore, if $tr_i < 0$ (deficit) then $\ell_i = s_{i-1}$, if $tr_i > 0$ (surplus) then $\ell_i = s_i$, and if $tr_i = 0$ then $s_{i-1} \leq \ell_i \leq s_i$.*

Proof. The proof is done by induction on i and omitted for lack of space. □

Theorem 1. *Assume we are given mobile agents $r_1, r_2, \ldots, r_k$ with energies $e_1, e_2, \ldots, e_k$, located initially in positions $s_1 \leq s_2 \leq \cdots \leq s_k$ of a line segment $[0, 1]$ respectively. Let r_{k+1} be an additional "dummy agent" at position 1 with zero energy. Then the procedure call PATH$(1, 0, 0)$ on this instance runs in $O(k)$ time and terminates with **solvable** being true if and only if there are trajectories of agents that explore the line segment $[0, 1]$.*

Proof. It is clear from the description of the algorithm that it is linear in k. When the algorithm terminates with **solvable** being true, it is straightforward to see that a schedule can be determined for the agents, that creates a *valid* trajectory for each agent. To wit, in Round 1 all agents that receive no energy follow their trajectory and do the energy transfers as calculated. Notice that energy is received by agents when in their initial positions.

In Round i all agents that receive energy in Round $i-1$ follow their trajectory and do the energy transfers as calculated. Therefore, if the algorithm terminates with **solvable** being true, the exploration of segment $[0,1]$ is possible, and our algorithm returns valid trajectories for the agents to achieve this coverage. Thus we only need to show that the exploration of the segment $[0,1]$ is not possible when the algorithm terminates with **solvable** being false. In fact, **solvable** is set to false in the algorithm only if either $tr_{k+1} < 0$ or $\ell_{k+1} < 1$. By Lemma 2, if $tr_{k+1} < 0$ then we can cover the segment up to $l_{k+1} = s_k \leq 1$ but we need more than the given $(\sum_{j=1}^{k} e_j)$ in energy. If $tr_{k+1} = 0$ and $\ell_{k+1} < 1$ then $[0, \ell_{k+1}]$ is the maximum segment that can be explored by the agents using $(\sum_{j=1}^{k} e_j)$ energy. In both cases, the exploration of the entire segment $[0,1]$ is impossible with the given initial positions and energies. □

Consider the case when we apply our algorithm to an input instance with the sum of energies $\sum_{1}^{k} e_i \geq \frac{3}{2}$. Since in each trajectory the part covered doubly is less or equal the part covered singly, the energy deficit/surplus tr_{k+1} obtained after assigning a trajectory to agent r_k is at most $\sum_{1}^{k} e_i - \frac{3}{2}$, and it cannot be negative. Also ℓ_{k+1} cannot be less than 1 since there would be an unused surplus of energy of at least $\sum_{1}^{k} e_i - \frac{3\ell_{k+1}}{2} > 0$. Thus with $\sum_{1}^{k} e_i \geq \frac{3}{2}$ the algorithm terminates with valid exploration trajectories for the segment.

On the other hand when the input instance consists of a single agent r_1 located at point 0.5, the energy needed by r_1 to cover the segment $[0,1]$ is equal to $\frac{3}{2}$.

Corollary 1. *The segment* $[0,1]$ *can always be explored by k agents with canonical trajectories if the sum of their initial energies is at least $\frac{3}{2}$, but exploration may be impossible in some instances if the sum is less than $\frac{3}{2}$.*

Remark 1. If agents *cannot share energy*, regardless of k, exploration is impossible in an input instance where all k agents are co-located at 0, each with energy equal to $1 - \epsilon$, which gives total energy greater than $k - 1$. Thus, without energy-sharing, there is no upper bound on the total energy of agents that guarantees exploration of a path. We have also constructed a linear algorithm for the exploration of a path by agents that cannot share energy, however we cannot include it in this paper due to the limit on the number of pages.

3   Exploring a Tree

In this section we consider a restricted case of the graph exploration problem, specifically when the graph is a tree. First we observe that, *without energy exchange*, there is a straightforward reduction from the partition problem showing that the exploration is NP-hard even on a star graphs: Given an instance of the partition problem $S = \{a_1, a_2, \ldots, a_n\}$, let $T = \sum_{i=1}^{n} a_i/2$. We construct a star graph, with $n + 2$ edges incident on the central node. Of these, n edges have weight $a_1/2, a_2/2, \ldots, a_n/2$ respectively, and two additional edges each have cost T. Assume two agents are at the central node of the star graph with energy $3T/2$ each. Then there is a partition of the set S if and only if the there is an exploration strategy (without energy sharing) for the two agents on the star graph. However, for energy-sharing agents located on a tree we derive below a polynomial exploration algorithm (see also [21]).

Let T be an edge-weighted tree with k agents distributed across the n nodes of T with possibly several agents per node each of them with some non-negative energy. To simplify the design of our algorithm, we first preprocess the tree to transform it to a rooted binary tree where all the agents are located only at the leaves of the tree. We obtain such a tree from the initial tree T in four stages: (a) by taking all the agents at every non-leaf vertex v and shifting them to a new leaf node l_v that is added to the tree and connected to v via a zero-weight edge, (b) by repeatedly splitting vertices of degree more than 3 into trees of maximum degree 3 using zero-weight edges, (c) by collapsing any path with internal vertices of degree 2 into an edge whose weight equals the cumulative weight of the path, and (d) by converting the resulting 3-regular unrooted tree into a rooted one by splitting one of its edges and making its midpoint be the root of the tree. Without loss of generality, we will denote this new, rooted tree as T. We note these preprocessing steps have complexity $O(n+k)$. Our problem can be stated as follows:

Problem 2 (Tree Exploration). Let T be a rooted, edge-weighted binary tree obtained by preprocessing an unrooted edge-weighted tree with k agents at its nodes, so that all the agents are now located at leaves in T and have their given initial energies. For every node v, let a_v be the initial number of agents inside subtree T_v and let e_v be the sum of their initial energies. Let $w_e \geq 0$ be the weight of edge e. If possible, find a set of valid trajectories for the agents that explore every edge of T using only the given initial energies.

Now, consider any *feasible* exploration for the tree witnessed by a set of trajectories for the agents. The successful exploration of a subtree T_v may either have necessitated additional energy brought into the subtree from outside, or there may be a surplus of energy that could have gone out of the subtree to explore other parts of the tree. Also, exploration may have needed a transfer of agents into the subtree (over and above its a_v agents) or may have been accomplished with some agents made available to leave the subtree and contribute to the exploration of the rest of the tree.

We formalize this idea as follows. Let $B[v,i]$ denote the *maximum* possible total *surplus energy* that can *leave* the subtree T_v after it is fully explored so that i agents can *leave* the subtree with this total energy. Note that i counts only the *balance* of agents that depart from the tree, not individual arrivals and departures. Thus, we allow for i being negative (i.e., i agents enter the tree on balance), or $B[v,i]$ being negative (i.e., $-B[v,i]$ amount of energy is needed to be brought in from *outside* T_v to explore it fully). We remark that:

(i) when $i \leq 0$ and $B[v,i] \geq 0$, it means that an agent carrying excess energy *must* leave T_v but nevertheless, the overall balance of agents entering/leaving T_v is non-positive.
(ii) the $B[v,i]$ values do not take into consideration the energy expenditure that would be required to explore the edge from v to its parent node in the tree.

(iii) for node v, the value of i can only be in the interval $[-k + a_v,\ a_v]$, because, on balance, at most a_v agents can leave T_v and at most $k - a_v$ can enter it.

In order to simplify the calculation of $B[]$, we extend the definition of $B[]$ to edges as well: Let $e = (u, v)$ where u is the parent of v. As described above, $B[v, *]$ denotes the surplus energy leaving subtree T_v. $B[e, i]$ will denote the surplus energy available at u *along edge* e with a balance of i agents that could transit through u from the direction of v. We observe that agents *do* spend energy traversing e itself and can also stop in the middle of e, and hence the values $B[e, *]$ and $B[v, *]$ are different. Since node u has exactly two child edges below it, we can compute the $B[u, *]$ values by suitably combining the $B[]$ values of these edges.

It remains to show how to calculate $B[v, *]$ and $B[e, *]$ for each v and e. In principle, we can consider all the possibilities of what the agents can do, but in reality it is enough to consider only the best possible activity with the desired balance of agents. The calculation is performed by calling procedures HANDLEV-ERTEX and HANDLEEDGE (described below in pseudocode) respectively for each vertex and for each edge of T. The computation proceeds in a bottom-up manner starting from leaves, with the boolean arrays **done**$[v]$ and **done**$[e]$ being used to ensure this flow. In order to simplify the presentation in HANDLEEDGE, we assume that the assignment $B[e, i] \leftarrow y$ is shorthand for $B[e, i] \leftarrow \max(B[e, i],\ y)$ (with the initial values $B[e, *]$ being initialized to $-\infty$).

Our main result in this section is the following:

Theorem 2. *After transforming an unrooted tree with a specified distribution of initial agent locations and energies, procedure* HANDLEVERTEX, *when applied to the root of the resulting rooted binary tree, correctly solves the tree exploration problem for the original tree in $O(n + \ell k^2)$ time. It does so by correctly computing the optimal $B[v, i]$ values for every vertex v and all relevant i values for that*

Procedure. HANDLEVERTEX(v)

1: **if** v is a leaf **then**

2:      **for** $i = -k + a_v$ to a_v **do**

3:          $B[v, i] \leftarrow e_v$

4: **else**   ▷ v has two child edges e' and e''

5:      wait until done$[e']$ and done$[e'']$

6:      **for** $i = -k + a_v$ to a_v **do**

7:          $B[v, i] \leftarrow \max_{i' + i'' = i}(B[e', i'] + B[e'', i''])$

8: done$[v] \leftarrow$**true**

9: **if** v is the root **then**

10:     **if** there is $B[v, i] \geq 0$ with $i \geq 0$ **then**

11:         return **solvable**

12:     **else**

13:         return **not solvable**

---

vertex, in conjunction with procedure HANDLEEDGE *that correctly computes the optimal* $B[e, i]$ *for every edge* e *and all relevant* i *values for that edge.*

Procedure. HANDLEEDGE(e)

Require: $e = (u, v)$ where v is a child of u
1: wait until done$[v]$
2: **for** $i = -k + a_v$ to a_v **do**
3:     **if** $B[v, i] \leq 0$ **then**
4:         **if** $i < 0$ **then**
5:             $B[e, i] \leftarrow B[v, i] - |i| w_e$ ▷ Case 1a
6:         **else**
7:             $B[e, i] \leftarrow B[v, i] - (i + 2) w_e$ ▷ Cases 2a, 3a and 4a
8:     **else if** $i \leq 0$ **then**   ▷ $B[v, i] > 0$
9:         **if** $B[v, i] > (2 + |i|) w_e$ **then**
10:            $B[e, i] \leftarrow B[v, i] - (2 + |i|) w_e$ ▷ Cases 1c and 2c
11:         **else if** $i < 0$ **then**
12:            $B[e, i] \leftarrow i(w_e - B[v, i]/(2 + |i|))$ ▷
    Case 1b
13:         **else**   ▷ $i = 0$
14:            $B[e, -1] \leftarrow (B[v, 0] - 2 w_e)/2$ ▷ Case 2b
15:            $B[e, 0] \leftarrow B[v, 0] - 2 w_e$ ▷ Case 2b'
16:     **else**   ▷ $i > 0$ and $B[v, i] > 0$
17:         **if** $B[v, i] \geq i w_e$ **then**
18:            $B[e, i] \leftarrow B[v, i] - i w_e$ ▷ Cases 3c and 4c
19:         **else**   ▷ $i > 0$ and $B[v, i] < i w_e$
20:            $B[e, i] \leftarrow -(i + 2)(w_e - B[v, i]/i)$ ▷
    Cases 3b" and 4b
21:         **if** $i = 1$ **then**
22:            $B[e, -1] \leftarrow B[v, 1] - w_e$ ▷ Case 3b
23:            $B[e, 0] \leftarrow 2(B[v, 1] - w_e)$ ▷ Case 3b'
24: done$[e] \leftarrow$ **true**

The proof of Theorem 2 hinges on an inductive argument that shows that the $B[]$ values are correctly computed in a bottom-up manner starting at the leaves and working our way up the tree. The base case for the induction is for the leaf nodes, and follows directly from the construction (line 3 of HANDLEVERTEX: all the energy in a leaf node is surplus and can be utilized to explore the rest of the tree).

Our induction hypothesis is established by proving two concomitant lemmas.

Lemma 3. *Let* $e = (u, v)$ *be an edge in* T *with* u *being the parent of* v. *If the values* $B[v, *]$ *have been correctly computed, then procedure* HANDLEEDGE *correctly computes* $B[e, *]$, *where* $*$ *stands for all relevant values of* i.

Lemma 4. *Let v be an internal vertex with two child edges e' and e''. If $B[e', *]$ and $B[e'', *]$ have been correctly computed, then procedure* HANDLEVERTEX *correctly computes $B[v, *]$ where $*$ stands for all relevant values of i.*

It is easy to see after the $O(n + k)$ time preprocessing step to convert the original tree into a full binary tree, each leaf of the tree and subsequently, each edge of the tree can be processed in $O(k)$ time. To obtain the $B[]$ values for any internal node, we need to combine the k-vectors associated with the child edges (in step 7 of HANDLEVERTEX). Observe that there are two classes of internal nodes in the converted tree. The first class correspond to $O(k)$ nodes that contained a subset of agents in the original tree. Each such node, generated in stage (a) of the conversion phase, has a child that is a leaf in the converted tree (containing the same subset of agents). The second class contains the internal nodes generated in stage (b) of the conversion phase, as well as the nodes that were of degree at least 3 in the original tree, and the root obtained in stage (d). Observe that there are at most ℓ nodes in the second class. Let v be an internal node of the first class and let v' be its child that was added in preprocessing that has taken the v's agents. By construction, all the $B[v', *]$ values are equal to $e_{v'}$, and since the weight of e' is 0, $B[e', *] = e_{v'}$ as well. Hence, for such a node v we have $B[v, a_{e'} + a_{e''} - i] = e_{v'} + \max_{j=0}^{i} B[e'', a_{e''} - i]$ which can be for $i = 0$ to k computed in time $O(k)$. Consequently, the overall complexity of HANDLEVERTEX called for all $O(k)$ internal nodes of class one is $O(k^2)$. On the other hand, for each of $O(\ell)$ internal nodes from class two, the max function from step 7 of HANDLEVERTEX may be computed in $O(k)$ time, which leads to $O(\ell k^2)$ overall complexity of all the calls of the HANDLEVERTEX procedure for nodes of the second class. Applying Lemma 4 to the root of the tree, it is clear that the algorithm correctly decides whether or not the binary tree can be explored fully, and the computation takes $O(\ell k^2)$ time after the preprocessing step.

We further remark that if exploration is indeed feasible then in the same time complexity, standard post-processing, top-down techniques can be used to recover the trajectories (and the schedules) for the agents from the computed $B[]$ values by combining the schedules locally computed at each vertex and edge. The choice of the root vertex is arbitrary (after preprocessing) and does not influence the decision outcome – however, it does influence the computed schedule and the amount of energy left in the root, and there may be multiple feasible solutions (one for each $i \geq 0$ in the root's $B[]$ values). This completes the proof of Theorem 2.

4   General Graphs

Unfortunately, while the exploration problem for segments and trees admits very efficient solutions, for general graphs, exploration becomes intractable (unless P = NP). Indeed, we show that the graph exploration problem is NP-hard even in the case of 3-regular graphs by using a reduction from the Hamiltonian cycle problem. We also give an approximation algorithm.

4.1   NP Hardness for 3-Regular Graphs

Let G be a 3-regular graph on n nodes. We construct a graph M by replacing each edge $e = (u, v)$ of G by a meta-edge gadget $m(u, v)$ from Fig. 2 case a), where a and b are chosen so that $a > 5nb$ where n is the number of vertices of G. In addition, each meta-vertex (i.e., an image $m(v)$ of a vertex v of G) starts with one agent and $3a + 5b$ energy.

Note that the overall energy is $(3a + 5b)n$, while the overall weight of the edges ($3n/2$ of them in a 3-regular graphs) is $3n(a + b)$. Hence, a length at most $2bn$ can be crossed twice. As $a > 5bn$, this means no a-edge is crossed twice and at most $2n$ of b-edges are crossed twice.

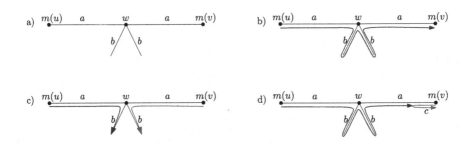

Fig. 2. a) the meta-edge gadget, b) covering gadget using one agent c) efficient covering of the gadget using two agents d) covering gadget using two agents so that at least one agent exits the gadget (Color figure online)

Lemma 5. *If only one agent x enters (w.l.o.g. from $m(u)$) a meta-edge $e = m(u, v)$, a total of $2a + 4b$ energy is spent ensuring e is fully explored. In such case x ends up in $m(v)$.*

Lemma 6. *Assume two agents x and y enter a meta-edge $e = m(u, v)$ from $m(u)$ and $m(v)$, respectively, and ensure e is fully explored. If no agent leaves e then the total energy spent in e is at least $2a + 2b$. If one or both agents leave e then all the leaving agents leave to the same meta-vertex, and the total energy spent in e is more than $2a + 4b$.*

Note that the second case of Lemma 6 is worse than Lemma 5 in terms of total energy expenditure, due to the extra cost of c (or $2c$). Still, it might be justified if the blue agent does not have enough energy for case b), or if the red agent does not have enough energy for case c).

Lets call a meta-edge *light* if it is covered by the first part of Lemma 6 (Fig. 2, case c)), otherwise it is *heavy*. Observe that each light meta-edge consumes 2 agents, while each heavy meta-edge consumes an excess of $2b$ energy compared to the weight of its edges. This yields:

Lemma 7. *If there is an exploration strategy for the input graph, the number of heavy edges is exactly n.*

By Lemma 5 and the second part of Lemma 6, a heavy meta-edge is traversed in one direction – lets call the halves *outgoing* and *incoming*.

Consider the directed graph $H = (V, E')$ formed by the heavy meta-edges, i.e., $e = (u, v) \in E'$ iff e is a heavy meta-edge from $m(u)$ to $m(v)$.

Lemma 8. *Each vertex of H has at least one incoming edge.*

Proof. As both light and outgoing edges consume agents, if v had no incoming edge, it would need 3 agents. Since each vertex starts with 1 agent, it is not possible for v to have 3 agents without an agent coming via an incoming edge. □

Because the number of heavy edges is exactly n, the heavy edges form a vertex-disjoint (vertex) cycle cover of H, i.e., each meta-vertex has one incoming, one outgoing and one light edge.

The problem is that the disjoint cycle cover is solvable in polynomial time. Hence, we need to modify the input so that there is a solution to the exploration problem if and only if the heavy edges form a single cycle of length n.

This is done by modifying the input into I as follows:

- the three edges incident to the initial vertex have weights adjusted to $a + \epsilon n$ for some small $\epsilon < b/3n$,
- the energy at the initial vertex is $3a + 5b + (2n)\epsilon$
- the energy at all other meta-vertices is $3a + 5b + \epsilon$

Lemma 9. *If the graph G is Hamiltonian then there is an exploration solution to the modified input I.*

Proof. Select the direction of the Hamiltonian cycle, its edges will be the heavy meta-edges. The *explorer* agent starting in the initial vertex takes all the energy available there and follows the Hamiltonian cycle. It collects $2a + 4b + \epsilon$ energy in each of the meta-vertices it crosses, while spending $2a + 4b$ on each heavy meta-edge. The agents located at other meta-vertices wake-up when the explorer arrives, take $a + b$ energy and explore half of the incident light meta-edge.

Note that when the explorer reaches i-th meta-vertex (not counting the initiator), it has $a + b + \epsilon n + i - 1$) energy remaining, except when it returns to the initiator, when it has only $a + b + \epsilon n$ energy as the last meta-edge it crossed has an extra ϵn cost. This is just sufficient to cover half of the incident light meta-edge, which is the last part not yet covered. □

Theorem 3. *The exploration problem is NP-hard for 3-regular graphs.*

Proof. Suppose there is an exploration solution for I. We claim that then the graph G is Hamiltonian. Note that since the sum of all ϵ is less than b, Lemma 7 and Lemma 8 still hold. Hence, the only way meta-edges incident to the starting vertex can be covered is if the agent returning to the starting vertex carries $a + b + \epsilon n$ energy. As the agent can gain only ϵ energy in each vertex it crosses (the remainder is used-up on crossing the heavy meta-edge and covering half of the incident light meta-edge), it needs to visit all n meta-vertices in order to collect sufficient energy, i.e., it has performed Hamiltonian cycle. The theorem then follows since the Hamiltonian cycle problem for 3-regular graphs is known to be NP-complete.   □

4.2   An Approximation Algorithm for General Graphs

Even though the graph exploration problem is NP-hard, it is still possible to obtain an efficient approximation algorithm for exploring arbitrary graphs that has an energy-competitive ratio at most 2. Specifically, the algorithm uses at most twice as much energy as the cumulative sum of the edge weights of the graph. First we state without proof a well-known result for agents on a cycle for which the reader is referred to [25] [Paragraph 3, Problem 21].

Lemma 10. *For any cycle and any initial positions of the agents there is an algorithm which explores the cycle if and only if the given sum of the energies of the agents is not less than the length of the cycle.*

Lemma 10 has some important consequences. Recall that a graph G is Eulerian if it is connected and all its vertices have even degrees.

Theorem 4. *For any Eulerian graph and any initial positions of the agents there is an algorithm which explores the graph provided that the sum of the energies of the agents at the start is not less than the sum of the edges of the given graph. Moreover, the algorithm has optimal energy consumption.*

Proof. Assume we have agents in such a graph so that the sum of the energies of the agents is at least equal to the sum of the length of the edges of the graph. Since the graph is Eulerian we can construct a cycle which traverses all the edges of the graph exactly once. By Lemma 10 there is an algorithm which assigns trajectories to the given sequence of agents and covers the entire graph. This proves Theorem 4.   □

Theorem 5. *Any graph can be explored by energy-sharing agents if the sum of their initial energies is at least twice the sum of edge weights. Moreover, this constant 2 cannot be improved even for trees.*

Proof. The original graph, say $G = (V, E)$, is not necessarily Eulerian. However, by doubling the edges of the graph we generate an Eulerian graph $G' = (V, E')$. The sum of the weights of the edges of G' is equal to twice the sum of the weights of the edges of G. Theorem 4 now proves that the graph G can be explored if the sum of their initial energies is at least twice the sum of edge weights in the graph.

Consider a star graph with $2k$ leaves, all edges are of weight 1, for a total weight of $2k$. Assume that we have k agents in the leaves of the star, and one agent in the center of the star. Agents in the leaves have energy 0, and the agent in the center $4k - 1$. To explore the graph the center agent can traverse

$2k - 1$ edges of the star twice and one edge once. It is easy to see that no other strategy can do it with less energy. Thus the energy of the middle agent cannot be any lower, and asymptotically, total energy in this instance equal to $4k - 1$ approaches the double of the cost of the edges. □

Remark 2. An improvement of the competitive ratio 2 of Theorem 5 is possible in specific cases by using a Chinese Postman Tour [24] (also known as Route Inspection Problem). Namely, in polynomial time we can compute the minimum sum of edges that have to be duplicated so as to make the graph Eulerian, and this additional sum of energies is sufficient for the exploration.

Assume we have a fixed configuration C of k agents $r_1, r_2, \ldots, r_k$ in a given graph G. We say that energy assignment $E = e_1, e_2, \ldots, e_k$ to agents in configuration C is *minimal* if exploration is possible with energies in E, but impossible when the energy level of any one agent is decreased. Let $|E| = \sum_{i=1}^{k} e_i$. We now investigate how large the ratio $|E_1|/|E_2|$ can be for two minimal assignments E_1 and E_2 of a given configuration C,

Claim. For any configuration of agent C and any two minimal energy assignments E_1 and E_2 the ratio $|E_1|/|E_2| \leq 2$, and this is asymptotically optimal.

5   Conclusion

We studied graph exploration by a group of mobile agents which can share energy resources when they are co-located. We focused on the problem of deciding whether or not it is possible to find trajectories for a group of agents initially placed in arbitrary positions with initial energies so as to explore the given weighted graph. The problem was shown to be NP-hard for 3-regular graphs while for general graphs it is possible to obtain an efficient approximation algorithm that has an energy-competitive ratio at most 2 (and this is shown to be asymptotically optimal). We also gave efficient algorithms for the decision problem for paths, trees, and Eulerian graphs. The problem considered is versatile and our study holds promising directions for additional research and interesting open problems remain by considering exploration with 1) optimal total energy consumption, 2) agents with limited battery capacity, 3) energy optimal placement of mobile agents, 4) time vs energy consumption tradeoffs for mobile agents with given speeds, 5) additional topologies, as well as 6) combinations of these.

References

1. Albers, S., Henzinger, M.R.: Exploring unknown environments. SIAM J. Comput. **29**(4), 1164–1188 (2000)
2. Albers, S., Kursawe, K., Schuierer, S.: Exploring unknown environments with obstacles. Algorithmica **32**(1), 123–143 (2002). https://doi.org/10.1007/s00453-001-0067-x

3. Alpern, S., Gal, S.: The Theory of Search Games and Rendezvous. Springer, Boston (2003). https://doi.org/10.1007/b100809
4. Baeza Yates, R., Culberson, J., Rawlins, G.: Searching in the plane. Inf. Comput. **106**(2), 234–252 (1993)
5. Baeza-Yates, R., Schott, R.: Parallel searching in the plane. Comput. Geom. **5**(3), 143–154 (1995)
6. Bampas, E., Das, S., Dereniowski, D., Karousatou, C.: Collaborative delivery by energy-sharing low-power mobile robots. In: Fernández Anta, A., Jurdzinski, T., Mosteiro, M.A., Zhang, Y. (eds.) ALGOSENSORS 2017. LNCS, vol. 10718, pp. 1–12. Springer, Cham (2017). https://doi.org/10.1007/978-3-319-72751-6_1
7. Bärtschi, A.: Efficient delivery with mobile agents. Ph.D. thesis, ETH Zurich (2017)
8. Beck, A.: On the linear search problem. Israel J. Math. **2**(4), 221–228 (1964). https://doi.org/10.1007/BF02759737
9. Burgard, W., Moors, M., Stachniss, C., Schneider, F.E.: Coordinated multi-robot exploration. IEEE Trans. Robot. **21**(3), 376–386 (2005)
10. Chalopin, J., Das, S., Kosowski, A.: Constructing a map of an anonymous graph: applications of universal sequences. In: Lu, C., Masuzawa, T., Mosbah, M. (eds.) OPODIS 2010. LNCS, vol. 6490, pp. 119–134. Springer, Heidelberg (2010). https://doi.org/10.1007/978-3-642-17653-1_10
11. Chalopin, J., Jacob, R., Mihalák, M., Widmayer, P.: Data delivery by energy-constrained mobile agents on a line. In: Esparza, J., Fraigniaud, P., Husfeldt, T., Koutsoupias, E. (eds.) ICALP 2014. LNCS, vol. 8573, pp. 423–434. Springer, Heidelberg (2014). https://doi.org/10.1007/978-3-662-43951-7_36
12. Czyzowicz, J., Diks, K., Moussi, J., Rytter, W.: Communication problems for mobile agents exchanging energy. In: Suomela, J. (ed.) SIROCCO 2016. LNCS, vol. 9988, pp. 275–288. Springer, Cham (2016). https://doi.org/10.1007/978-3-319-48314-6_18
13. Czyzowicz, J., Diks, K., Moussi, J., Rytter, W.: Broadcast with energy-exchanging mobile agents distributed on a tree. In: Lotker, Z., Patt-Shamir, B. (eds.) SIROCCO 2018. LNCS, vol. 11085, pp. 209–225. Springer, Cham (2018). https://doi.org/10.1007/978-3-030-01325-7_20
14. Czyzowicz, J., Diks, K., Moussi, J., Rytter, W.: Energy-optimal broadcast and exploration in a tree using mobile agents. Theor. Comput. Sci. **795**, 362–374 (2019)
15. Czyzowicz, J., et al.: Graph exploration by energy-sharing mobile agents. arxiv.org/pdf/2102.13062 (2021)
16. Czyzowicz, J., et al.: Energy consumption of group search on a line. In: Proceedings of ICALP, pp. 137:1–137:15 (2019)
17. Deng, X., Kameda, T., Papadimitriou, C.: How to learn an unknown environment. In: Proceedings of FOCS, pp. 298–303. IEEE Computer Society (1991)
18. Deng, X., Papadimitriou, C.H.: Exploring an unknown graph. J. Graph Theory **32**(3), 265–297 (1999)
19. Dereniowski, D., Disser, Y., Kosowski, A., Pajak, D., Uznański, P.: Fast collaborative graph exploration. Inf. Comput. **243**, 37–49 (2015)
20. Dynia, M., Łopuszański, J., Schindelhauer, C.: Why robots need maps. In: Prencipe, G., Zaks, S. (eds.) SIROCCO 2007. LNCS, vol. 4474, pp. 41–50. Springer, Heidelberg (2007). https://doi.org/10.1007/978-3-540-72951-8_5
21. Fraigniaud, P., Gasieniec, L., Kowalski, D.R., Pelc, A.: Collective tree exploration. Netw. Int. J. **48**(3), 166–177 (2006)
22. Kleinberg, J.M.: On-line search in a simple polygon. In: Proceedings of SODA, pp. 8–15 (1994)

23. Koutsoupias, E., Papadimitriou, C., Yannakakis, M.: Searching a fixed graph. In: Meyer, F., Monien, B. (eds.) ICALP 1996. LNCS, vol. 1099, pp. 280–289. Springer, Heidelberg (1996). https://doi.org/10.1007/3-540-61440-0_135
24. Kwan, M.-K.: Graphic programming using odd or even points. Acta Math. Sin. **10**, 263–266 (1960). MR 0162630. Translated in Chinese Mathematics **1**, 273–277 (1962)
25. Lovász, L.: Combinatorial Problems and Exercises. Elsevier, Amsterdam (1979)
26. Moussi, J.: Data communication problems using mobile agents exchanging energy. Ph.D. thesis, Université du Québec en Outaouais (2018)
27. Panaite, P., Pelc, A.: Exploring unknown undirected graphs. J. Algorithms **33**(2), 281–295 (1999)

Two-Agent Tree Evacuation

Henri Devillez, Béni Egressy[(⊠)], Robin Fritsch, and Roger Wattenhofer

ETH Zürich, Zürich, Switzerland
{hdevillez,begressy,rfritsch,wattenhofer}@ethz.ch

Abstract. We study the problem of evacuating two agents from a tree graph, through an unknown exit located at one of the nodes. Initially, the agents are located at the same starting node; they explore the graph until one of them finds the exit through which they can evacuate. The task is to minimize the time it takes until *both* agents evacuate, for a *worst case* placement of the exit. We consider two communication models, *global communication* where the agents can communicate at any time, and *local communication* where the agents can only communicate if they are at the same node at the same time. We show that the problem is NP-hard in both cases. We then present a 4/3-approximation algorithm for global and a 3/2-approximation algorithm for local communication.

1 Introduction

Imagine that two robots are trapped in a building. They have a map of the building, but most exits marked on the map are in fact blocked. Their goal is to find an exit that is still available, and evacuate. Armed with the map they devise a strategy to find an exit and evacuate as quickly as possible. How should they divide the work of checking all the locations for an available exit? In what order should they explore the locations? Should they meet up at some predefined location to exchange information?

More formally, we consider a group of k agents whose task is to find an exit node in a weighted graph $G = (V, E)$ and evacuate all agents through this exit. The agents all start at common node r, which we call the root. In the beginning, they know the graph and the edge weights and that at least one exit exists at one of the nodes, but not the location of the exit(s). In this paper, we study the case of $k = 2$ agents, one single exit, the graphs we consider will be trees. We are interested in worst case analysis so we can assume a single exit without loss of generality. Moreover two agents on a tree is the most fundamental case, encompassing already the challenges, trade-offs and insights of the more general setting. We will distinguish between two communication models. In the *local* model agents can only explicitly exchange information when they are at the same node at the same time. In the *global* model agents can exchange information at any time independent of their locations. Global communication is equivalent to a single central algorithm controlling all the agents.

T. Jurdziński and S. Schmid (Eds.): SIROCCO 2021, LNCS 12810, pp. 204–221, 2021.
https://doi.org/10.1007/978-3-030-79527-6_12

The objective will be to minimize the time for *all* agents to evacuate the graph. In other words we minimize the last exit time, or *evacuation time*. We can view this problem as a two player game, where one player defines the exploration-evacuation strategy for all the agents and the second player, the adversary, then chooses the worst possible exit location for this strategy.

An optimum algorithm is one that achieves the minimum worst case evacuation time. We first show that minimizing the worst case evacuation time for two agents in a tree is NP-hard. This motivates the search for approximation algorithms. Their performance is measured by the approximation ratio: The ratio of the worst case evacuation time of the given algorithm and the worst case evacuation time of an optimum algorithm.

We start our search in the global communication setting and show that a simple bi-directional depth-first search (DFS) strategy has an approximation ratio of 7/5. As our first major result, we then present the *Longest Path Global Algorithm* and show that it has a tight approximation ratio of 4/3. We then focus on the local communication setting and start again by showing that the simple bi-directional approach gives an approximation ratio of 2. As our second major result, we strengthen this result with a centroid-based algorithm, proving a tight approximation ratio of 3/2. Finally we ask how much worse local communication can be compared to global communication on the same graph and bound the worst case ratio of the two models between 4/3 and 3/2. We finish with concluding remarks, pointing the reader to a whole range of open questions for future work.

2 Related Work

One of the most fundamental classes of problems in the context of mobile agents are search problems. These include a whole range of related problems, such as ants searching for food [15,16,21], graph exploration [9,17,18], rendezvous problems [6,11–13,19], patrolling robots [25,26], and pursuit-evasion games [4, 5,22]. Another example are graph evacuation problems, where one or more agents search for an exit, through which they can evacuate. Evacuation problems are of two main types; geometrical problems, where agents need to evacuate some shape, such as a triangle, a square or a disk [20,24,28], and evacuation problems on graphs. The latter type has not been explored to a great extent; the problem has been considered on lines [1,3] and so-called m-rays [7,8,29], but not on general graphs. Borowiecki et al. [23] consider the problem of evacuating multiple agents from distinct nodes using multiple exits, but this problem is very different from ours with a focus on avoiding congestion and bottlenecks.

Another related problem is swarm exploration [14]. A swarm of mobile agents starting at the root of a tree has to visit every node, whilst staying within a distance of d, where d is called the range of the swarm. Unlike swarm exploration, graph evacuation does not put a hard constraint on the distance between agents, the agents stay close only when it is optimal.

To the best of our knowledge, our work is the first to consider evacuating two agents from a tree or graph through a single unknown exit. Although the geometric setting already leads to elaborate strategies and interesting insights [24, 28], graphs are a much more general and more widely applicable setting for multi-agent evacuation.

A related graph exploration problem is the multiple Traveling Salesmen Problem (mTSP) [10]. The mTSP is a generalization of the well-known traveling salesman problem (TSP), where more than one salesman is allowed to be used in the solution. Unlike mTSP, in graph evacuation one also has to consider how far apart the agents get during the exploration, as they eventually all have to converge to the exit.

3   Preliminaries

We start with an example to illustrate some important aspects of the problem.

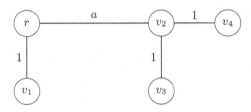

Fig. 1. An instance of tree evacuation. The agents start at r and $d(r, v_2) = a > 0$.

Take a look at Fig. 1. Let's first consider local communication. We observe that there are two competing strategies that could be optimal, depending on the value of a. The first is for the agents to stay together and explore everything together starting with v_1, then v_2, v_3, and finally v_4. By staying together, they can both evacuate immediately as soon as they find an exit. On the other hand the exploration is not parallelized and as such is not very efficient. The worst case is when the exit is located at v_4 giving an evacuation time of $a + 5$.

The second strategy is for the agents to split up at the beginning. The agents explore v_1 and v_3 in parallel, meeting up at v_2 to share information at time $t = a + 2$. The agents now know exactly where the exit is and can head straight there. The worst case is when the exit is at v_1 giving a total time of $2a + 3$. This strategy demonstrates the importance of the agents meeting to share information in the local communication setting.

Which strategy is better depends on the value of a. This example illuminates the two key aspects of the problem: to explore the graph efficiently in parallel, and to stay close enough in case the exit is found. A good algorithm has to balance these two (orthogonal) goals.

Let us now consider the same example with global communication to make another interesting observation. Let $a = 4$. We notice that the optimum strategy depends on whether the agents can abort traversing an edge when they are part way across. If they cannot, then splitting up would give a worst case evacuation time of $2a + 1 = 9$ with the exit at v_1, and staying together would also give a worst case evacuation time of $a + 5 = 9$. However if they can abort traversing the long edge, then the strategy of splitting up gives the optimum evacuation time 7. We will assume throughout the rest of the paper that agents can traverse an edge part way.

We start by showing that it is NP-hard to find the optimal strategy on trees.

Lemma 1. *Consider weighted tree evacuation with $k = 2$ agents. Finding a strategy to minimize the worst case evacuation time is NP-hard.*

Proof. We show this by reduction from PARTITION [2]. Let $S = (a_1, a_2, \ldots, a_n)$ be a multiset of positive integers, i.e., an instance of partition with $\sum_i a_i = 2M$. We construct the following star graph:

- Add root node r
- For each $a_i \in S$, we add node v_i and edge $e_i = (r, v_i)$ with weight $w(e_i) = a_i$
- In addition we add node v_{n+1} and edge $e_{n+1} = (r, v_{n+1})$ with weight $w(e_{n+1}) = 2M$

Let r be the starting node for the agents. Then this gives an instance of graph evacuation. We claim that there is a strategy with worst case evacuation time $4M$ if and only if there is a solution to the partition problem.

For the simple direction, if there is a solution to the partition problem, then the agents can explore nodes $\{r, v_1, \ldots, v_n\}$ and return to r in time $2M$. If either agent finds the exit, say at v_i, then the agents can evacuate in additional time $a_i \leq 2M$, giving at most $2M + a_i \leq 4M$ in total. On the other hand if the exit is at v_{n+1}, since the agents have already checked all the other vertices at time $2M$, they can go straight to v_{n+1} together and exit in total time $2M + 2M$.

Now suppose there is no solution to the partition problem. The agents can still choose to explore all nodes $\{r, v_1, \ldots, v_n\}$ first, leaving v_{n+1} till last. So first suppose node v_{n+1} is explored last. Then the adversary places the exit at v_{n+1}. Since there is no solution to the partition problem, exploring the other nodes and returning to r requires time strictly greater than $2M$ in total. So one of the agents will require strictly more than $2M + 2M = 4M$ to reach the exit. On the other hand, suppose the agents visit node v_{n+1} before exploring one of the nodes, say v_j. Then the adversary places the exit at v_j and the agent visiting v_{n+1} has to return, requiring at least $4M + a_j \geq 4M + 1$ to reach the exit at v_j.

Thus, deciding whether the optimum worst case evacuation time is greater than $4M$ is as hard as partition, so tree evacuation with 2 agents is NP-hard. □

Note that we do not use anywhere in the proof that the communication model is local or global. Note also that the proof can easily be extended to $k > 2$ agents, for example by simply adding $k - 2$ edges of length M.

Since finding the optimal strategy is NP-hard we will be looking for approximation algorithms. We use the following general lower bound on the cost OPT of the optimal algorithm to prove these approximation ratios.

Lemma 2. *Let TSP be the length of the shortest traversal of all vertices of a graph $G = (V, E)$, i.e. the solution to the traveling salesperson problem. Then $OPT \geq TSP/2$.*

Proof. For any order in which the agents explore the vertices, the adversary can choose the last node they explore to be the exit. That means, the two agents must together visit all vertices. Moreover, since they start and finish at common vertices (the root and the exit), they together perform a complete traversal of the graph. The length of the shortest traversal is TSP, so at least one of the agents must travel a distance of at least $TSP/2$, implying $OPT \geq TSP/2$.   □

This lemma applies to general graphs and any communication model. Since the shortest traversal of a tree graph uses every edge exactly twice, we get the following corollary for trees.

Corollary 3. *For a tree, $OPT \geq W$ where W is the total weight of the tree.*

Now we can prove an algorithm has an approximation ratio of at most c by showing that it always requires at most cW time to evacuate the agents.

Example 4. The best approximation ratio we can hope for using only this lower bound, $OPT \geq W$, is $3/2$ for either communication model.

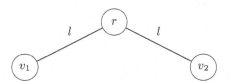

Fig. 2. Example of a tree graph with optimum worst case evacuation time $OPT = \frac{3}{2}W$. If the agents split up and reach v_1 and v_2 at the same time, then one of the agents will exit at time $3l$. If the agents do not split, then whichever leaf they explore first, the adversary can place the exit at the other, so that the agents again need $3l$ time to evacuate. Note also that $W = 2l$.

See Fig. 2 for an example of a tree with $OPT = \frac{3}{2}W$. Clearly no algorithm can do better than this, so we cannot get a better approximation ratio than $3/2$ if we rely solely on the lower bound $OPT \geq W$. To prove a better approximation ratio, we would need a tighter analysis between the approximation algorithm and an optimum algorithm. Therefore, motivated by Example 4, we give another lower bound for OPT.

Lemma 5. *Let v_1, v_2 be any two nodes of a tree rooted at r, with $d(r, v_1) \geq d(r, v_2)$. And let P_i denote the path from r to node v_i. Then $OPT \geq d(r, v_1) + 2d(v_2, P_1)$, where $d(v_2, P_1) = \min_{u \in P_1} d(v_2, u)$ is the shortest distance between v_2 and any node on the path P_1.*

Proof. Note that the adversary can force the two agents to explore all of the vertices in the graph, in particular both v_1 and v_2. Of course the agents can split up, whereby they visit v_1 and v_2 in parallel, but the adversary can place the exit at the node explored later by the agents. Therefore at least one of the agents visits both nodes. This gives a lower bound for OPT of

$$\begin{aligned} OPT &\geq \min\{d(r,v_1) + d(v_1,v_2), d(r,v_2) + d(v_2,v_1)\} \\ &= d(r,v_2) + d(v_2,v_1) \\ &= d(r,v_1) + 2\min_{u \in P_1} d(v_2,u) \\ &= d(r,v_1) + 2d(v_2,P_1) \end{aligned}$$

$\square$

In particular, applying Lemma 5 to v_1 and v_2 in Fig. 2 gives us a tight lower bound for OPT. The lemma gives $OPT \geq 3l$, and $3l$ is indeed the optimum.

4   Global Communication

In the global setting, a simple way to evacuate a general graph is for the two agents to follow a traversal of the graph in opposite directions.

Algorithm 1: Bi-directional traversal (BiT)

---

   input : A graph G with 2 agents at node r

   output: The agents explore and evacuate the graph

1 Find a shortest traversal R of G

2 **while** *the exit is not found* **do**

3 | The two agents traverse R in opposite directions starting from r

4 Both agents go directly to the exit

Lemma 6. *Algorithm 1 (BiT) has an approximation ratio of exactly 7/5 for 2-agent global evacuation on trees.*

We omit the proof due to space restrictions.[1] To achieve a better approximation ratio, we will use what we call a *longest path approach*. Given a tree, let the path P_L from root r to v_L be a longest path starting at r and let L denote its length. In a longest path approach, both agents explore the tree sequentially along P_L. In other words, an agent passes through each edge of P_L at most once during exploration, making excursions to explore subtrees along the way. Note that this is an optimal strategy for a single agent to explore a tree.

Let E' be the set of all edges not in P_L, with weight $w(E') = W - L$. The edges in E' form subtrees rooted along the path P_L. We would like each agent to explore half of E'. Let w be the walk from r to v_L of length $2W - L$ that traverses every edge on P_L once and all other edges twice (via a DFS along each subtree). Furthermore, let w' be the (non-connected) walk $w \backslash P_L$ of length $2(W - L)$. Let p be the midpoint of w'.

---

[1] The full version is available on our website: https://disco.ethz.ch/publications.

Algorithm 2: Longest Path Algorithm (LPA)

---

    input : A tree G with 2 agents at its root r, the longest path P_L, the walk w
             and the point p as defined previously
    output: The agents explore and evacuate the graph
1 **while** *the exit is not found* **do**
2   The two agents explore the graph in parallel
3   Agent 1 traverses w up to point p, then takes the shortest path from p to v_L
4   Agent 2 takes the shortest path from r to p and then traverses the
             remaining part of w to v_L
5 Both agents go directly to the exit

Following this algorithm, the agents arrive at v_L at the same time (if the exit is not found earlier), since they both traverse P_L, half of w' and the shortest path from p to P_L. In particular, the only part of E' they both explore is the shortest path from p to P_L.

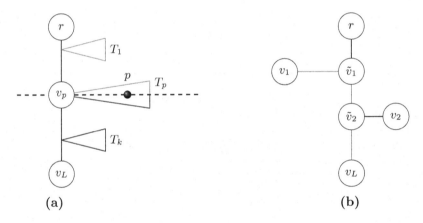

Fig. 3. (a) The longest path algorithm (LPA). The longest path P_L is the path from r to v_L. T_p is the subtree containing point p as described in the algorithm, and v_p is the root of T_p on P_L. Agent 1 explores the red edges and agent 2 the blue edges. (b) An upper bound (red) on $d(v_1, v_2)$ for a longest path algorithm. The node v_L is the furthest node from r, and v_1 and v_2 are the locations of the agents. (Color figure online)

Lemma 7. *If the two agents follow a longest path approach, then*

$$max\{d(v_1, v_L), d(v_2, v_L)\} \geq d(v_1, v_2)$$

at all times, where v_1 and v_2 are the positions of the agents at some time during exploration.

Proof. Let $\tilde{v}_i$ be the furthest node along P_L that agent i has reached. Without loss of generality, we assume that $\tilde{v}_1$ is closer to the root than $\tilde{v}_2$. See Fig. 3a. Thus, the distance between the agents is $d(v_1, \tilde{v}_1) + d(\tilde{v}_1, \tilde{v}_2) + d(\tilde{v}_2, v_2)$ while the distance between agent 1 and v_L is $d(v_1, v_L) = d(v_1, \tilde{v}_1) + d(\tilde{v}_1, \tilde{v}_2) + d(\tilde{v}_2, v_L)$. We observe that $d(\tilde{v}_2, v_2)$ cannot be greater than $d(\tilde{v}_2, v_L)$, as otherwise v_2 would be further away from the root than v_L. We conclude that $max(d(v_1, v_L), d(v_2, v_L)) \geq d(v_1, v_2)$. □

Theorem 8. *Algorithm 2 (LPA) has an approximation ratio of exactly 4/3 for 2-agent global evacuation on trees.*

Proof. We defer the lower bound for the approximation ratio to Example 9. In the following we prove the upper bound.

Let LPA be the worst case evacuation time of the LPA algorithm. Without loss of generality assume the exit is found by agent 1 at a node v_1 at time t_1 and that the second agent is at position v_2 at this moment. The evacuation time is then $t_1 + d(v_1, v_2)$. But if the adversary had placed the exit at v_L, then by Lemma 7 the evacuation time would have been at least $t_1 + max\{d(v_1, v_L), d(v_2, v_L)\} \geq t_1 + d(v_1, v_2)$. Therefore the worst case evacuation time occurs when the exit is at v_L. The agents reach v_L at the same time at

$$LPA = d(r, v_L) + \frac{2(W - L)}{2} + d(p, v_p) = W + d(p, v_p)$$

where p is as described in the algorithm and v_p is the closest node on P_L to p, in other words the root of the subtree containing p.

Let $L_2 = d(p, v_p) \leq L$. Applying Lemma 5 to p and v_L gives a lower bound of $OPT \geq L + 2L_2$. Combining this with the lower bound from Corollary 3 gives us the approximation ratio:

$$\frac{LPA}{OPT} \leq \frac{W + L_2}{\max\{W, L + 2L_2\}}$$

If $L_2 \leq W/3$, then we get the result with the lower bound of W. On the other hand if $L_2 > W/3$, then $W + L_2 < 4L_2$ and since $L \geq L_2$, also $L + 2L_2 \geq 3L_2$; thus we have $\frac{LPA}{OPT} < \frac{4L_2}{3L_2} = 4/3$. □

Example 9. 4/3 is a lower bound for the approximation ratio of any algorithm based on the longest path approach.

See Fig. 4 for an example of a tree where any algorithm visiting the furthest leaf last can only achieve an approximation ratio of at least 4/3. Therefore LPA is a best possible algorithm based on the longest path approach and the analysis in Theorem 8 is tight.

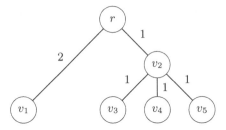

Fig. 4. Example of a tree where any algorithm visiting the furthest leaf last can achieve an approximation ratio of at best $4/3$. If the agents explore v_1 last, then they first explore in the direction of v_2; they can visit v_3 and v_4 respectively, returning to v_2 at time 3. The exit can still be at v_1 or v_5 so the best the agents can do is split up (or explore v_5 and then v_1 together), but with the exit at v_1, the agent(s) exploring v_5 will only reach the exit at time 8. On the other hand, an optimum strategy would be for agents 1 and 2 to explore v_1 and v_3 respectively; if the exit is found, they can evacuate in time 6, and otherwise agent 2 continues by exploring v_4, before the agents meet at v_2 at $t = 5$; and now the exit can be reached in 1 step. This gives an approximation ratio of $8/6 = 4/3$.

5 Local Communication

We turn our attention to the local communication model. Local communication is of course weaker than global communication and indeed there are graphs, where agents with local communication need significantly more time to evacuate in the worst case. We will show such examples at the end of the section, but first we present approximation algorithms for this communication model.

Example 10. Depth-first search (DFS) has an approximation ratio of 2 for 2-agent local evacuation on trees.

This observation is immediate. The length of a DFS traversal is $2W$, so if the agents walk together along the DFS route, they will evacuate in time at most $2W$. This can be improved slightly by ending the traversal at v_L, giving $2W - L$.

Next we propose an algorithm to improve this approximation ratio to $3/2$. We start with some definitions, before giving an outline of the algorithm.

Definition 11 (child subtree, centroid). *Given a tree G and a node v, a child subtree of v is defined as the connected subtree of G containing v and a connected component of $G \backslash \{v\}$. A node with k neighbours has k child subtrees.*

Given a tree G and a point p on edge (u, v), a child subtree of p is defined as above by treating p as a node of the graph. In other words, a child subtree of p is defined as the connected subtree of G containing p and a connected component of G without the edge (u, v). A point p on an edge has 2 child subtrees. Note that both child subtrees only contain part of the edge (u, v).

Given a weighted tree G with total weight W, the centroid of G is defined as the vertex or point c, such that all child subtrees of c have weight at most $W/2$.

We include a DFS-like algorithm for finding the centroid of a tree in the full version of the paper. Note that the centroid is unique for trees with positive edge weights, but this uniqueness is not needed in the algorithm. We can now give an outline of our algorithm for 2-agent local tree evacuation.

A key ingredient of the algorithm is that we use the centroid of the tree (c) as a meeting point in each iteration. The advantage of meeting at c is that every node of the graph is at distance at most $W/2$. So in particular if either agent finds the exit, then after meeting at c they can evacuate together in additional time at most $W/2$. This means we can safely assign a budget of W to each agent for exploring the child subtrees of c, see Fig. 6. Taking these budgets into account, the algorithm assigns child subtrees to the agents. We call the union of the unassigned child subtrees T. Note that T is a (connected) tree rooted at c.

Another key ingredient of the algorithm is that the agent with more leftover budget, can use its extra budget to start exploring T with a careful subroutine, which ensures that the unexplored edges form a *connected* subtree whilst guaranteeing a certain amount of further exploration. We start by presenting this subroutine and then we present the full algorithm.

Algorithm 3: Single Agent Lightest Subtree Algorithm (SALSA)

---

input : A tree G rooted at r with total weight $W = w(G)$
           An agent with an exploration budget $B = W + \Delta$, $\Delta \leq W$

output: Agent traverses a subtree of G in time at most B, starting and finishing at r. It leaves an unexplored connected subtree rooted at r_1 (possibly on an edge) with weight at most $W - \Delta$ and $d(r, r_1) \leq \Delta$.

1 **if** $B > w(G)$ **then**
2   **if** r *has a single child* **then**
3   **if** $d(r, r.child) \geq \Delta$ **then**
4   Move Δ units along the edge $e(r, r.child)$ and place r' here
5             $B' = B - 2\Delta$
6             $G' = G \setminus \{r\} \cup \{r'\}$
7   **else**
8             $r' = r.child$
9   Go to r'
10            $B' = B - 2d(r, r')$
11            $G' = G \setminus \{r\}$
12   **else**
13   Traverse lightest (lowest total weight) unexplored child subtree T_1 of r with DFS
14         $r' = r$
15         $B' = B - 2w(T_1)$
16         $G' = G \setminus T_1 \cup \{r\}$
17   Call SALSA(G', r', B')
18   Go back to r
19 **else**
20     $r_1 = r$

Lemma 12. *Algorithm 3 is correct. That is, it always terminates, the agent traverses a subtree of G rooted at r in total time at most B, and the agent leaves an unexplored connected subtree rooted at r_1 with total weight at most $W - \Delta$ and $d(r, r_1) \leq \Delta$.*

See Fig. 5(a) for an illustration of Algorithm 3 and see Fig. 5(b) for an example showing that the analysis in Lemma 12 is tight.

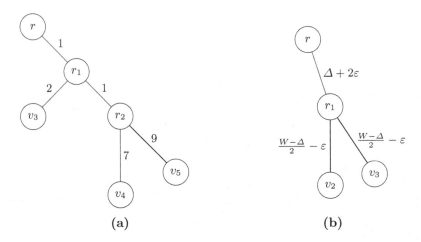

$$(a) \qquad\qquad (b)$$

Fig. 5. (a) Illustration of SALSA. Let $W = 20$ and $\Delta = 5$. Budget $B = 20 + 5$. First, the agent goes to r_1, then v_3, then r_2 and has budget $B' = 25 - 8 = 17$ left. The unexplored graph has weight $w(G') = 16 < B'$, so the agent continues by exploring the lightest child subtree, v_4. Since $B' = 17 \geq 2(7)$, this is fine. After this, the agent does not have enough budget to explore further. Total budget used is $2(11) = 22 \leq 25$ and the agent leaves an unexplored subtree of weight 9. This is less than $W - \Delta = 20 - 5$, as claimed in Lemma 12. (b) Worst case scenario showing that $W - \Delta$ is tight for the weight of the unexplored subtree. Budget is $B = W + \Delta$. After moving to r_1, the agent has budget $B' = W + \Delta - 2(\Delta + 2\varepsilon) < 2\left(\frac{W - \Delta}{2} - \varepsilon\right)$ left, so it can explore neither v_2 nor v_3. Instead the agent returns to r and r_1 becomes the new root.

Proof. We prove that before each recursive call of the algorithm, G' is an unexplored connected tree and its weight has decreased by at least the same amount as the decrease in $\Delta' = B' - W'$, where $W' = w(G')$. In addition, we have to show the agent's movements never exceed the budget B'. By recursively calling the algorithm until termination, this proves the lemma.

If r has a single child further away than Δ, then we are done since the agent can simply explore up to distance Δ along the edge and then return to r. This leaves an unexplored connected subtree rooted at r' as required. Clearly the budget is enough to do this and go back to r, since $B = W + \Delta \geq 2\Delta$.

If r has a single child closer than Δ, then the agent can move to the child at a cost of $d := d(r, r.child)$. The agent will incur the same cost again when returning to r at the end so we decrease the budget by $2d$. Note that G' is still an unexplored connected subtree. Moreover the weight of G' is d smaller than the weight of G at the start of the call. So we have

$$W' = w(G') = W - d$$
$$B' = B - 2d = W + \Delta - 2d = W' + (\Delta - d)$$

which implies $\Delta' = \Delta - d$.

For the remaining cases, we use the fact that a node r can have at most 1 child subtree of total weight greater than $\frac{1}{2}(W + \Delta)$. This is clear, else G would have weight greater than $W + \Delta \geq W$, which is not possible. Therefore we always have enough budget in line 13 of the algorithm to explore the lightest unexplored child subtree T_1. Since we explore a whole child subtree T_1 and leave all other child subtrees unexplored, G' is still an unexplored connected subtree. The weight of G' has decreased by $w(T_1)$ at a cost of $2w(T_1)$ budget, and the agent does not have to traverse any of T_1 on the way back to r at the end. So with $d = w(T_1)$ we have the same equations as above.

Finally note that when we explore a whole child subtree, then we do not increase $d(r, r')$, but we do decrease Δ'; and when we explore an edge, then we increase $d(r, r')$ by the same amount as we decrease Δ'. Therefore we ensure that we always have $d(r, r') \leq \Delta$. $\qquad\square$

Theorem 13. *Algorithm 4 (CMA) has an approximation ratio of exactly 3/2 for 2-agent local evacuation on trees.*

Proof. We include a lower bound example for the approximation ratio in the full version of the paper. Similarly, an algorithm for finding the centroid of a tree can be found in the full version.

For the upper bound we show that in each iteration of Algorithm 4 the agents explore the graph with a time to weight ratio of at most $\frac{3}{2}$. Moreover after every iteration the agents are left with an unexplored connected tree G', rooted at r', with both agents located at r'. And in the final iteration, when the agents evacuate, they find the exit and evacuate in time at most $\frac{3}{2}w(G')$. Combining these claims, we can conclude that the agents find the exit and evacuate in time at most $\frac{3}{2}W$. Together with Corollary 3 this proves the theorem.

We denote the child subtrees of the centroid by $\{T_{r'}, T_1, T_2, \ldots, T_k\}$, where the degree of the centroid is $k + 1$ and $T_{r'}$ is the subtree containing the starting node r'. If $r' = c$, $T_{r'}$ is the empty set and c has degree k. The child subtrees T_1 to T_k are ordered by increasing weight, i.e., $w(T_i) \geq w(T_{i-1})$ for all $i \geq 2$. Note that by definition of the centroid $w(T_i) \leq W/2$ for all $i = r', 1, \ldots, k$. The algorithm assigns $T_{r'}$ to agent 1. The algorithm then assigns each subtree in decreasing order of weight to the two agents, preferring always agent 1. Let W_1 and W_2 denote the total weights of subtrees assigned to agents 1 and 2 respectively.

Algorithm 4: Centroid Meeting Algorithm (CMA)

---

input : A tree G with 2 agents at its root r with total weight W

output: The agents explore and evacuate the graph

1 $G' = G$, $r' = r$

2 **while** *the exit is not found* **do**

3   Find the centroid of G' and call it c. Let $d = d(r', c)$

4   Agent 1 gets a budget of $B_1 = w(G')$

5   Agent 2 gets a budget of $B_2 = w(G')$

6   We assign the child subtrees of c to the agents as follows

7   **begin**

8   We assign the child subtree $T_{r'}$ containing r' to agent 1 and decrease the agent's budget by $2w(T_{r'}) - d$ (if $r' = c$, we choose $T_{r'}$ to be an empty set)

9   While agent 1's budget allows, we assign the unassigned child subtrees of c to agent 1 in decreasing order of weight, always at cost 2 times the weight

10   We decrease agent 2's budget by d (cost to get to c)

11   While agent 2's budget allows, we assign the unassigned child subtrees of c to agent 2 in decreasing order of weight, always at cost 2 times the weight

12   Let T be the union of the remaining unassigned subtrees

13   Agents 1 and 2 explore their assigned subtrees in parallel, finishing at c

14   Let b be the first agent to arrive at c at time t_b, let a be the second agent to arrive at t_a and let $B = t_a - t_b$

15   **if** $B > w(T)$ **then**

16   Agent b starts to explore T using SALSA with budget B (while agent a finishes)

17   G', r' = unexplored connected subtree and its root returned by SALSA

18   The agents meet at c and go to r'

19   **else**

20   Agent b waits for agent a at c

21         $G' = T$, $r' = c$

22 The agents meet at c and go directly to the exit

Agent 1 can fully explore its subtrees and reach c at time $2W_1 - d$, where $d := d(r', c)$ is the distance from the starting node to the centroid. Agent 2 can fully explore its subtrees and reach c at $2W_2 + d$.

Claim: $W_1 + W_2 \geq W/2$

Assume the claim is not true for a contradiction, and $W_1 + W_2 < W/2$. Since $w(T_i) \leq W/2$ for all child subtrees, we must have at least two child subtrees T_1 and T_2, which cannot be explored by either agent. We can assume $w(T_1) \leq w(T_2)$. Then since $W_1 + W_2 + w(T_1) + w(T_2) \leq W$, we must have $2w(T_1) \leq W - (W_1 + W_2)$. And since T_1 does not fit into either agent's budget, we have the inequalities

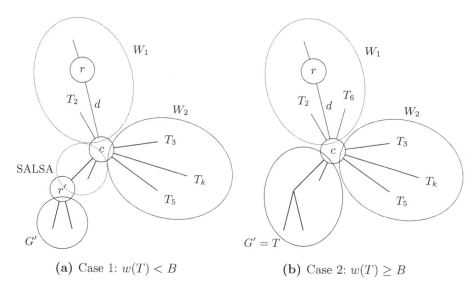

(a) Case 1: $w(T) < B$ **(b)** Case 2: $w(T) \geq B$

Fig. 6. Illustration of the two cases in Algorithm 4. In case 1, the agent with more budget left explores T with SALSA. In case 2, the agents do not explore T in this iteration.

$$2W_1 - d + (W - (W_1 + W_2)) \geq 2W_1 - d + 2w(T_1) > W$$
$$2W_2 + d + (W - (W_1 + W_2)) \geq 2W_2 + d + 2w(T_1) > W$$

which by adding up imply $2W > 2W$. Since this is a contradiction, we conclude that the claim is true.

Among the two agents, let agent a have a larger exploration time than agent b. Then we know the following about their respective exploration times t_a and t_b.

$$t_a = \max\{2W_1 - d, 2W_2 + d\}$$
$$t_b = \min\{2W_1 - d, 2W_2 + d\}$$
$$t_a + t_b = 2(W_1 + W_2) \geq W \tag{1}$$
$$t_a + t_b + 2w(T) = 2W \tag{2}$$

We now consider the two cases from the algorithm (see Fig. 6):

Case 1: $B > w(T)$

In this case agent b explores T using SALSA with budget $B = t_a - t_b$. We can apply Lemma 12 and we know that agent b can explore an additional weight of at least $\Delta = B - w(T) = t_a - t_b - w(T)$, leaving an unexplored subtree rooted at the new root r' (reassigned in line 17) at distance $d(c, r') \leq \Delta$.

Before the end of the iteration, the agents meet at the centroid c and then move to the new root r'. Using the above equations, we show that the iteration has efficient exploration with a time to weight ratio of at most $\frac{3}{2}$:

$$\text{total explored} = \frac{t_a + t_b}{2} + (t_a - t_b - w(T))$$

$$\text{time} = t_a + (t_a - t_b - w(T))$$

$$\frac{\text{time}}{\text{total explored}} = \frac{4t_a - 2t_b - 2w(T)}{3t_a - t_b - 2w(T)} \overset{(2)}{=} \frac{5t_a - t_b - 2W}{4t_a - 2W} \overset{(1)}{\leq} \frac{6t_a - 3W}{4t_a - 2W} = \frac{3}{2}$$

Case 2: $B \leq w(T)$

In this case we argue that even without any extra exploration by SALSA, the agents must have already explored efficiently with a time to weight ratio of at most $\frac{3}{2}$. By our claim, we have

$$t_a - t_b \leq w(T) \leq \frac{W}{2} \overset{(1)}{\leq} \frac{1}{2}(t_a + t_b).$$

Adding $t_a + t_b$ to the left and right sides we get $2t_a \leq 3(t_a + t_b)/2$. The agents have explored $(t_a + t_b)/2$ in time t_a giving

$$\frac{\text{time}}{\text{total explored}} = \frac{2t_a}{t_a + t_b} \leq \frac{3}{2}.$$

Thus we have shown that exploration is done with the required efficiency in each iteration. What remains to be shown is that in the final iteration, the agents find the exit and evacuate in time at most $\frac{3}{2}w(G')$. However this is clear from the choice of the meeting location c and the budgets $w(G')$. Since the agents meet at the centroid, any exit they find in the current iteration can be at a distance of at most $\frac{1}{2}w(G')$. And since they both arrive by $t = w(G')$, the evacuation time can be at most $\frac{3}{2}w(G')$ as required.   □

We finish with a lower bound on the worst case ratio between two agents with global communication versus two agents with local communication. Clearly, agents with global communication can always do at least as well as agents with local communication. However, what about in the worst case? How much worse can local communication be? We return to Fig. 4 to give an example where OPT_L is strictly larger than OPT_W. Recall that $OPT_W = 6$ and that any strategy visiting v_1 last would give an evacuation time of at least 8. Therefore with local communication we also explore v_1 and v_3 first. But now the agents have to meet at r to share the information; if they meet at v_2 it will be too late. But meeting at r leaves v_4 and v_5 unexplored, and the agents will have worst case evacuation time of 8, giving $OPT_L = 8$.

Together with Theorem 13 and Lemma 3, we bound the worst case ratio of local communication over global communication between 4/3 and 3/2.

6   Conclusion

To the best of our knowledge, our work is the first that considers evacuating two agents from a tree through a single unknown exit. We first show that the problem is NP-hard, motivating the search for approximation algorithms. Our main results are a 4/3-approximation algorithm for the global communication setting and a 3/2-approximation algorithm for the local communication setting.

The paper leaves a multitude of open questions for further research. One could search for better approximation algorithms to improve the approximation ratios. One could consider other communication models, such as blackboard communication [27] or communication with a limited radius. This paper focused on trees, but one could look at other graph classes. One could look at the case with more agents ($k > 2$) or different objectives, e.g., minimizing the average exit time of the agents. One could also consider the stochastic setting, where the exit is at a given node with some predetermined probability and the agents minimize the expected evacuation time. One could even look at a game theoretic scenario, where agents behave selfishly and do not go out of their way to inform the other agents about the exit location. How would this change the exploration strategy?

Acknowledgements. We would like to thank Nicolas Marxer and Tobias Zwahlen for fruitful discussions and the anonymous reviewers for their helpful comments.

References

1. Beck, A.: On the linear search problem. Israel J. Math. **2**(4), 221–228 (1964). https://doi.org/10.1007/BF02759737
2. Karp, R.M.: Reducibility among combinatorial problems. In: Miller, R.E., Thatcher, J.W., Bohlinger, J.D. (eds.) Complexity of Computer Computations. IRSS, pp. 85–103. Springer, Boston (1972). https://doi.org/10.1007/978-1-4684-2001-2_9
3. Gal, S.: Minimax solutions for linear search problems. SIAM J. Appl. Math. **27**(1), 17–30 (1974)
4. Parsons, T.D.: Pursuit-evasion in a graph. In: Alavi, Y., Lick, D.R. (eds.) Theory and Applications of Graphs. LNM, vol. 642, pp. 426–441. Springer, Heidelberg (1978). https://doi.org/10.1007/BFb0070400
5. Nowakowski, R., Winkler, P.: Vertex-to-vertex pursuit in a graph. Discrete Math. **43**(2–3), 235–239 (1983)
6. Alpern, S.: The rendezvous search problem. SIAM J. Control. Optim. **33**(3), 673–683 (1995)
7. Hejazi, R.F., Husain, T., Khan, F.I.: Landfarming operation of oily sludge in arid region–human health risk assessment. J. Hazard. Mater. **99**(3), 287–302 (2003)
8. López-Ortiz, A., Schuierer, S.: On-line parallel heuristics, processor scheduling and robot searching under the competitive framework. Theor. Comput. Sci. **310**(1–3), 527–537 (2004)
9. Fraigniaud, P., Ilcinkas, D., Peer, G., Pelc, A., Peleg, D.: Graph exploration by a finite automaton. Theor. Comput. Sci. **345**(2–3), 331–344 (2005)

10. Bektas, T.: The multiple traveling salesman problem: an overview of formulations and solution procedures. Omega **34**(3), 209–219 (2006)
11. Dessmark, A., Fraigniaud, P., Kowalski, D.R., Pelc, A.: Deterministic rendezvous in graphs. Algorithmica **46**(1), 69–96 (2006). https://doi.org/10.1007/s00453-006-0074-2
12. Kranakis, E., Krizanc, D., Rajsbaum, S.: Mobile agent rendezvous: a survey. In: Flocchini, P., Gąsieniec, L. (eds.) SIROCCO 2006. LNCS, vol. 4056, pp. 1–9. Springer, Heidelberg (2006). https://doi.org/10.1007/11780823_1
13. Czyzowicz, J., Gasieniec, L., Pelc, A.: Gathering few fat mobile robots in the plane. Theor. Comput. Sci. **410**(6–7), 481–499 (2009)
14. Czyzowicz, J., Pelc, A., Roy, M.: Tree exploration by a swarm of mobile agents. In: Baldoni, R., Flocchini, P., Binoy, R. (eds.) OPODIS 2012. LNCS, vol. 7702, pp. 121–134. Springer, Heidelberg (2012). https://doi.org/10.1007/978-3-642-35476-2_9
15. Feinerman, O., Korman, A.: Memory lower bounds for randomized collaborative search and implications for biology. In: Aguilera, M.K. (ed.) DISC 2012. LNCS, vol. 7611, pp. 61–75. Springer, Heidelberg (2012). https://doi.org/10.1007/978-3-642-33651-5_5
16. Feinerman, O., Korman, A., Lotker, Z., Sereni, J.-S.: Collaborative search on the plane without communication. In: Proceedings of the 2012 ACM Symposium on Principles of Distributed Computing, pp. 77–86 (2012)
17. Förster, K.-T., Wattenhofer, R.: Directed graph exploration. In: Baldoni, R., Flocchini, P., Binoy, R. (eds.) OPODIS 2012. LNCS, vol. 7702, pp. 151–165. Springer, Heidelberg (2012). https://doi.org/10.1007/978-3-642-35476-2_11
18. Megow, N., Mehlhorn, K., Schweitzer, P.: Online graph exploration: new results on old and new algorithms. Theor. Comput. Sci. **463**, 62–72 (2012)
19. Das, S., Dereniowski, D., Kosowski, A., Uznański, P.: Rendezvous of distance-aware mobile agents in unknown graphs. In: Halldórsson, M.M. (ed.) SIROCCO 2014. LNCS, vol. 8576, pp. 295–310. Springer, Cham (2014). https://doi.org/10.1007/978-3-319-09620-9_23
20. Czyzowicz, J., Kranakis, E., Krizanc, D., Narayanan, L., Opatrny, J., Shende, S.: Wireless autonomous robot evacuation from equilateral triangles and squares. In: Papavassiliou, S., Ruehrup, S. (eds.) ADHOC-NOW 2015. LNCS, vol. 9143, pp. 181–194. Springer, Cham (2015). https://doi.org/10.1007/978-3-319-19662-6_13
21. Emek, Y., Langner, T., Stolz, D., Uitto, J., Wattenhofer, R.: How many ants does it take to find the food? Theor. Comput. Sci. **608**, 255–267 (2015)
22. Förster, K.-T., Nuridini, R., Uitto, J., Wattenhofer, R.: Lower bounds for the capture time: linear, quadratic, and beyond. In: Scheideler, C. (ed.) SIROCCO 2014. LNCS, vol. 9439, pp. 342–356. Springer, Cham (2015). https://doi.org/10.1007/978-3-319-25258-2_24
23. Borowiecki, P., Das, S., Dereniowski, D., Kuszner, Ł.: Distributed evacuation in graphs with multiple exits. In: Suomela, J. (ed.) SIROCCO 2016. LNCS, vol. 9988, pp. 228–241. Springer, Cham (2016). https://doi.org/10.1007/978-3-319-48314-6_15
24. Brandt, S., Laufenberg, F., Lv, Y., Stolz, D., Wattenhofer, R.: Collaboration without communication: evacuating two robots from a disk. In: Fotakis, D., Pagourtzis, A., Paschos, V.T. (eds.) CIAC 2017. LNCS, vol. 10236, pp. 104–115. Springer, Cham (2017). https://doi.org/10.1007/978-3-319-57586-5_10

25. Gąsieniec, L., Klasing, R., Levcopoulos, C., Lingas, A., Min, J., Radzik, T.: Bamboo garden trimming problem (perpetual maintenance of machines with different attendance urgency factors). In: Steffen, B., Baier, C., van den Brand, M., Eder, J., Hinchey, M., Margaria, T. (eds.) SOFSEM 2017. LNCS, vol. 10139, pp. 229–240. Springer, Cham (2017). https://doi.org/10.1007/978-3-319-51963-0_18
26. Chuangpishit, H., Czyzowicz, J., Gąsieniec, L., Georgiou, K., Jurdziński, T., Kranakis, E.: Patrolling a path connecting a set of points with unbalanced frequencies of visits. In: Tjoa, A.M., Bellatreche, L., Biffl, S., van Leeuwen, J., Wiedermann, J. (eds.) SOFSEM 2018. LNCS, vol. 10706, pp. 367–380. Springer, Cham (2018). https://doi.org/10.1007/978-3-319-73117-9_26
27. Dorri, A., Kanhere, S.S., Jurdak, R.: Multi-agent systems: a survey. IEEE Access 6, 28573–28593 (2018)
28. Disser, Y., Schmitt, S.: Evacuating two robots from a disk: a second cut. In: Censor-Hillel, K., Flammini, M. (eds.) SIROCCO 2019. LNCS, vol. 11639, pp. 200–214. Springer, Cham (2019). https://doi.org/10.1007/978-3-030-24922-9_14
29. Brandt, S., Foerster, K.-T., Richner, B., Wattenhofer, R.: Wireless evacuation on m rays with k searchers. Theor. Comput. Sci. 811, 56–69 (2020)

Pebble Guided Near Optimal Treasure Hunt in Anonymous Graphs

Barun Gorain[1(✉)], Kaushik Mondal[2], Himadri Nayak[3], and Supantha Pandit[4]

[1] Indian Institute of Technology Bhilai, Raipur, Chhattisgarh, India
barun@iitbhilai.ac.in
[2] Indian Institute of Technology Ropar, Rupnagar, Punjab, India
kaushik.mondal@iitrpr.ac.in
[3] Indian Institute of Information Technology, Bhagalpur, Bhagalpur, India
himadri@iiitbhagalpur.ac.in
[4] Dhirubhai Ambani Institute of Information and Communication Technology,
Gandhinagar, Gujarat, India

Abstract. We study the problem of treasure hunt in a graph by a mobile
agent. The nodes in the graph are anonymous and the edges at any node
v of degree $deg(v)$ are labeled arbitrarily as $0, 1, \ldots, deg(v) - 1$. A mobile
agent, starting from a node, must find a stationary object, called *treasure*
that is located on an unknown node at a distance D from its initial position. The agent finds the treasure when it reaches the node where the
treasure is present. The *time* of treasure hunt is defined as the number
of edges the agent visits before it finds the treasure. The agent does not
have any prior knowledge about the graph or the position of the treasure.
An Oracle, that knows the graph, the initial position of the agent, and
the position of the treasure, places some pebbles on the nodes, at most
one per node, of the graph to guide the agent towards the treasure.

We target to answer the question: what is the fastest possible treasure
hunt algorithm regardless of the number of pebbles are placed?

We show an algorithm that uses $O(D \log \Delta)$ pebbles to find the treasure in a graph G in time $O(D \log \Delta + \log^3 \Delta)$, where Δ is the maximum
degree of a node in G and D is the distance from the initial position of
the agent to the treasure. We show an almost matching lower bound of
$\Omega(D \log \Delta)$ on time of the treasure hunt using any number of pebbles.

Keywords: Treasure hunt · Mobile agent · Anonymous graph ·
Pebbles

1 Introduction

1.1 Model and Problem Definition

Treasure hunt by a mobile agent is a well-studied problem in networks and related
areas. A mobile agent, starting from an initial position, has to find a stationary
object, called treasure. In practice, a treasure can be a missing person in a

© Springer Nature Switzerland AG 2021
T. Jurdziński and S. Schmid (Eds.): SIROCCO 2021, LNCS 12810, pp. 222–239, 2021.
https://doi.org/10.1007/978-3-030-79527-6_13

dark cave and a mobile robot must find the person. In networks applications, a software agent must find a computer virus or valuable data resource in a computer connected in a network.

The network is modeled as a graph where the nodes are unlabeled. The edges at a node v of degree $deg(v)$ are labeled as $0, 1, \ldots, deg(v) - 1$ arbitrarily. Thus, each edge has two port numbers associated with it at each of its incident vertices. A mobile agent, starting from a node, must find the treasure which is situated in an unknown node at distance D. The agent have no prior knowledge about the network or the value of D. The agent finds the existence of the treasure only when it reaches the node where the treasure is situated. The agent moves according to a deterministic algorithm where at each node, it chooses a port and move to the next node using the chosen port. At the start, the agent only knows the degree of the initial node. From a node u, when the agent reaches node v by using the port p at u, it learns the degree of the node v, and the port q at v through which it reaches v. For a network with maximum degree Δ, using a simple depth first search based algorithm, the agent can find the treasure in time $O(\Delta^D)$. But many practical applications required a faster treasure hunt algorithm. For example, consider the application of finding a person inside a mine by a mobile robot. The person may be lost and injured due to a sudden accident and therefore he or she must be found as fast as possible. In such scenarios, some external help is provided to the robot/agent in order to guide it towards the desired location faster. Two kind of external helps are mentioned in literature while solving network related problems using single of multiple agents. The first kind, such external help is provided to the agent by an oracle which gives some additional information in the form of a binary string, called *advice* [15,20]. One other way of providing this external help is to assign small labels to the nodes of the graph [9] such as road signs that may help to guide the agent(s) to follow a desired path. In this paper, we consider the second type of scenario where pebbles can be placed at the nodes as external information. An agent, looking at the placement of the pebbles, learns in which way it must traverse to find the treasure. To be specific, we consider the problem where some pebbles are placed in some nodes of the network by an oracle who knows the initial position of the agent and the position of the treasure. The position of the pebbles guides the agent towards the treasure. At any node, at most one pebble can be placed. The agent can see a pebble only after reaching that node. In this paper, we study what is the fastest possible algorithm for treasure hunt in anonymous graphs with pebbles. To be specific, we aim design the fastest algorithm for treasure hunt when any number of pebbles can be placed in the network.

1.2   Our Results

➤ We present an algorithm that finds the treasure in an anonymous graph in $O(D \log \Delta + \log^3 \Delta)$-time using $O(D \log \Delta)$ pebbles, where Δ is the maximum degree of a node in the graph and D is the distance from the initial position of the agent to the treasure.

➤ We prove that even if we supply any number of pebbles, any algorithm must require $\Omega(D \log \Delta)$-time to find the treasure in an anonymous graph.

Due to lack of space, all the proofs of the theorems and lemmas, and all the figures are omitted. The details can be found in [14].

1.3 Related Work

Treasure hunt by a mobile agent is well-studied [3,6,7,10,12,17,20,24] during the last few decades. In [3], Beck et al. introduced the problem of deterministic treasure hunt on a line. The authors proposed a deterministic algorithm with competitive ratio 9 and proved that this ratio is the best that can be achieved in case of line. A generalized version of [3] was studied by Demaine et al. [10] by considering cost of turns that agent makes along with the cost of the trajectory. Bouchard et al. [7] considered the treasure hunt problem in plane and showed a much improved bound with the assumption of angle information.

In the book [1], several problems related to treasure hunt are discussed. Most of the algorithms surveyed in this book are randomized. One such is the randomized treasure hunt in a star, where the treasure is present in one of the m rays passing through a common point [17]. In [20,24], it is shown that the problem of treasure hunt and the problem of rendezvous in graphs are closely related. Ricardo et al. studied the problem of finding an unknown fixed point on a line and in a grid [2]. More generalized studies are done in [16,18], where the objective is to search an unknown line in a plane. The author studied the problem of finding a target in a ring in [23] by multiple selfish agents participates and a game theoretic solution is proposed. Also, treasure hunt in a plane and in a grid by multiple agents are studied in [12,13,19]. In [12,19], the agents are considered to have bounded memory. Treasure hunt in plane is studied in [22] in the advice model. Treasure hunt in a tree network is studied in [4], where random faulty hints are provided to the agents. Treasure hunt in arbitrary graph is also studied in [6] considering the agent has unlimited memory. The game of pursuit-evasion, a closely related problem to treasure hunt, is considered in [5,8], where set of pursuers try to catch a fugitive trying to escape. Also treasure hunt in terrain in presence of obstacles was introduced in [21]. Another related problem is graph exploration and Disser et al. [11] recently proved a tight bound on number of pebbles required for a single mobile agent with constant memory to explore an undirected port labelled graph.

2 The Treasure Hunt Algorithm

In this section, we provide an $O(D \log \Delta + \log^3 \Delta)$-time algorithm for the treasure hunt problem using $O(D \log \Delta)$ pebbles.

Let G be a graph with maximum degree $\Delta \geq 2^{10}$. If $\Delta < 2^{10}$, then the algorithm described for the case when all nodes on the path from s to t are of 'small' degree (these small degree nodes are defined as light nodes later) can be applied.

Let $s, t \in G$ be the starting point of the agent, and position of the treasure in G, respectively. Let P be the shortest path between s and t of length D. Without loss of generality, we assume that the degree of the node s is at least 2. Otherwise, the first degree-3 node along P starting from s can be considered as the starting position of the agent. For any node $v \in G$, by $deg(v)$, we denote the degree of the node v. Let $\alpha_v = 1 + \lfloor \log deg(v) \rfloor$. For any node $w \in G$, by $w(0), w(1), \ldots, w(deg(w) - 1)$, we denote the neighbors of w that are connected through port numbered $0, 1, \ldots, deg(w) - 1$, at w respectively. For any two strings Γ_1 and Γ_2, by '$\Gamma_1 \cdot \Gamma_2$', we mean concatenation of Γ_1 and Γ_2. For any binary string Γ, by $\Gamma(i, j)$, we denote the substring of Γ starting from the i-th bit of Γ to the j-th bit of Γ. For two nodes $u, v \in G$, we denote the shortest distance between u and v in G by $dist(u, v)$.

Before providing the formal description of the algorithm, we give a high level idea of the pebble placement and discuss how these pebbles guide the agent towards the treasure. To help the reader understand the algorithm better, we describe the idea for trees first and then generalize this idea for general graphs.

High Level Idea of the Algorithm in a Tree Network: Here we assume that G is a rooted tree with root s. Let L_i be the set of nodes that are at distance i from s. Let $P = (s =) v_0, v_1, \ldots, v_{D-1}, v_D (= t)$ be the path from s to t, and let $p_0, p_1, \ldots, p_{D-1}$ be the sequence of port numbers corresponding to the path P such that from the node v_ℓ, the node $v_{\ell+1}$ can be reached by taking the edge with port number p_ℓ. For any node $v \in L_j$, let its i-th neighbor be the adjacent node in L_{j+1} to which v is connected via i-th largest port going to L_{j+1}. The pebbles are placed at the children of the nodes in P such that the placement of the pebbles corresponds the binary representation of the port numbers along the shortest path from the current node. To be more specific, let $b_0 b_1 \ldots b_{m-1}$ be the binary representation of the integer p_j, where $m = 1 + \lfloor \log deg(v_j) \rfloor$. For $0 \le i \le m - 1$, place a pebble at i-th neighbor of v_j, if $b_i = 1$. Hence, from the point of view of a node $v_j \in L_i$, each of its neighbors in L_{i+1} either contains a pebble or does not contain a pebble. Visiting each of the neighbor in increasing order of the port numbers and ignoring the port that connects to the parent of the current node, the agent, from the current node, can learn the binary representation of the integer p_j, by realizing a node with pebble as '1' and a node without pebble as '0'. Hence, the placement of pebbles in the above manner helps us to "encode" the port labeled path from s to t and the agent, with the help of this encoding, learn the port numbers from each node in P that leads to the next node towards the treasure.

Extending the Idea for General Graphs: The above method of pebble placement for trees can not be directly extended to general graphs. This is because in a rooted tree, no two nodes have common children. Hence, once the encoding is done after placing the pebbles, the agent can unambiguously decode this encoding. However, in the case of graphs, two consecutive nodes on P may have neighbors in common. Hence, if a pebble is placed on such a common neighbor, the agent can not distinguish for which node the pebble is placed. Also, since the nodes are anonymous, there is no way the agent can identify whether it is visiting a node that is a common neighbor to the previous or next node. We resolve this difficulty by encoding in the neighbors of a set of "*high*" degree nodes that do not share neighbors. These nodes are called *milestones* (we define this formally later). The details are explained below.

We say that a node is *heavy* if its degree is at least $80\lfloor \log \Delta \rfloor + 106$ (the reason for choosing this magical number is discussed in Remark 1). Otherwise, we say that the node is *light*. Let T be the *breadth first search (BFS)* tree, rooted at s, and for $0 \leq i \leq D$, let L_i denotes the set of nodes that are at a distance i from s. Clearly, $s \in L_0$, and $t \in L_D$. Let $P = (s =) v_0, v_1, \ldots, v_{D-1}, v_D (= t)$, be the shortest path from s to t, and let $p_0, p_1, \ldots, p_{D-1}$ be the sequence of port numbers corresponding to the path P such that from the node v_ℓ, the node $v_{\ell+1}$ can be reached by taking the edge with port number p_ℓ, for $0 \leq \ell < D$. For $0 \leq i \leq D - 1$, let B_i be the binary representation of the integer p_i of length x_i, where $x_i = 1 + \lfloor \log deg(v_i) \rfloor$.

First, consider a special case where each v_i, $0 \leq i \leq D - 1$, is light. A simple algorithm will work in this case: place a pebble at each of the nodes v_i, for $1 \leq i \leq D - 1$. The agent, at the starting node s, set $CurrentNode = s$. At each step, the agent visits all the neighbors of the $CurrentNode$ and move to the neighbor v, (except the node from where it reaches to $CurrentNode$) that contains a pebble. It then sets $CurrentNode = v$. The agent continues to explore in this way until the treasure is found. Since all the nodes on P are light, the time for treasure hunt is $O(D \log \Delta)$. If not all nodes are light on P, then a set of nodes called *milestones* are used to code the sequence of port numbers corresponding to the path P. We define a set of nodes as milestones in a recursive manner. To define the first milestone, we consider the following four cases based on the position of the heavy nodes in the BFS tree T: i) the node s is heavy, ii) the node s is light and a node in L_1 is heavy, iii) all the nodes in $L_0 \cup L_1$ are light and a node in L_2 is heavy, and iv) all the nodes in $L_0 \cup L_1 \cup L_2$ are light and $j \geq 3$ is the smallest integer for which L_j contains a heavy node that is at a distance 3 from v_{j-3}. From now onward, we distinguish these four cases as Case H, Case L-H, Case L-L-H, and Case L-L-L, respectively.

The first milestone is defined based on the above four cases as follows.

- **Case H:** $milestone_1 = s$.
- **Case L-H:** Let w be the node with maximum degree in L_1. If multiple nodes with maximum degree exists, then w is chosen as the node to which s is connected by the edge with minimum port number. Set $milestone_1 = w$.
- **Case L-L-H:** Let w be the node with maximum degree in L_2. If multiple nodes with maximum degree exists, then w is chosen as the node to which s is connected by a path of length 2 which is lexicographically shortest among all other paths to nodes with same degree. Set $milestone_1 = w$.
- **Case L-L-L:** If $j = 4$, and $v_1 \in \{s(0), s(1)\}$, then consider the set $W = \{w \in L_j | dist(s(0), w) = 3 \text{ or } dist(s(1), w) = 3\}$. Let w be the node in W whose degree is maximum among all nodes in W. If multiple nodes with maximum degree exists, then the node with maximum degree to which s is connected via lexicographically shortest path of length 4 is chosen as w.

Set $milestone_1 = w$. On the other hand, If $j > 4$ or $v_1 \notin \{s(0), s(1)\}$, let $W = \{w \in L_j | dist(v_{j-3}, w) = 3\}$. Let w be the node with maximum degree in W. If multiple nodes with maximum degree exists then w is chosen as the node to which v_{j-3} is connected by a path of length 3 that is lexicographically shortest among all other nodes with same degree. Set $milestone_1 = w$.

The subsequent milestones are defined recursively as follows. For $i \geq 1$, let $milestone_i \in L_j$. The first heavy node on P that is at a distance at least 3 from v_j is defined as $milestone_{i+1}$.

Intuitively, we encode in the neighbors of the milestones in a similar fashion as described above for the case of tree network. As the milestones are at least 3 distance apart, no two of them have common neighbors and hence decoding can be done unambiguously. However, there is another difficulty, that is the agent does not have any knowledge about the graph and hence does not know the value of Δ, the maximum degree of the graph. This restrict the agent to learn whether a node is heavy or light just by looking at its degree. We overcome this difficulty by placing some '*markers*'. By looking at these markers the agent can identify the possible position of the first milestone. Once the agent identify the first milestone, finding the other milestones are easy as the path towards the next milestone is carefully coded at the neighbors of the current milestone. If s itself is a heavy node, then it is defined as the first milestone. In order to help the agent to learn that this is the case, two pebbles are placed at $s(0)$, and $s(1)$, one at each. If s is light and a node in L_1 is heavy, then a pebble is placed at $s(0)$ and no pebble at $s(1)$. For Case L-L-H, a pebble is placed at $s(1)$ and no pebble is placed at $s(0)$. For the Case L-L-L, no pebbles are placed in either of the first two neighbors of s.

Another set of 'markers' are used to indicate the distance between two consecutive milestones. How these markers are placed will be explained later where formal descriptions of the pebble placements is provided.

We give the details of the pebble placement algorithm and the corresponding treasure hunt algorithm by the mobile agent below.

Pebble Placement: The placement of pebbles are done in three phases.

Phase 1: Placing pebbles at $s(0)$ and $s(1)$

- **Case H:** Place one pebble each at $s(0)$ and $s(1)$.
- **Case L-H:** Place a pebble at $s(0)$.
- **Case L-L-H:** Place a pebble at $s(1)$.
- **Case L-L-L:** No pebble is placed either at $s(0)$ or at $s(1)$.

Phase 2: Placing pebbles to encode the path between $milestone_1$ to $milestone_2$

- **Case H:** Here $milestone_1$ is the node s itself. Notice that, two pebbles are already placed at $s(0)$ and $s(1)$ during phase 1 to represent the marker corresponding to Case H. The other neighbors of s are used to encode the path P'

from s to $milestone_2$. To be specific, if the distance from s to $milestone_2$ is at most 5, then the entire path P' is coded in the neighbors of s. Otherwise, if the distance from s to $milestone_2$ is more than 5, then the first three port numbers and the last three port numbers are encoded at the neighbors of s. The difficulty here is to make the agent learn that how far $milestone_2$ is from s. To overcome this situation, another set of markers are encoded using the nodes $s(2)$ and $s(3)$. The case that $milestone_2$ is at distance 3, at distance 4, at distance 5 and at distance at least 6 are represented by markers '11', '10', '01', and '00', respectively and pebbles are placed similarly as explained in Phase 1. If $milestone_2$ is at distance at least 6 from $milestone_1$, the entire path from $milestone_1$ to $milestone_2$ is not coded. Instead, the first three and the last three sequence of port numbers are coded in the neighbors of $milestone_1$. Once the agent learns this coding, can compute the first three ports and the light nodes in between are used to guide the agent towards $milestone_2$. Here the difficulty is how to make the agent learn where the encoding ends as the neighbors which are not used for encoding may be mistaken as '0's. To overcome this difficulty, instead of simple binary encoding of the sequence of port numbers as explained in Case H, we use a *transformed binary encoding*: replace every '1' by '11' and every '0' by '10' of Γ. The advantage of this transformed encoding is that it does not contains the substring 00. The formal pebbles placement is described based on the distance of the second milestone as follows. Let ℓ be an integer such that $milestone_2 = v_\ell$.

1. $[\ell = 3]$: Here the path from $milestone_1$ to $milestone_2$ is v_0, v_1, v_2, v_3 and the corresponding sequence of port numbers is p_0, p_1, p_2. Let $\Gamma' = B_0 \cdot B_1 \cdot B_2$ and $\Gamma = 11 \cdot \Gamma'$.
2. $[\ell = 4]$: Here the path from $milestone_1$ to $milestone_2$ is v_0, v_1, v_2, v_3, v_4 and the corresponding sequence of port numbers is p_0, p_1, p_2, p_3. Let $\Gamma' = B_0 \cdot B_1 \cdot B_2 \cdot B_3$ and $\Gamma = 10 \cdot \Gamma'$.
3. $[\ell = 5]$: Here the path from $milestone_1$ to $milestone_2$ is $v_0, v_1, v_2, v_3, v_4, v_5$ and the corresponding sequence of port numbers is p_0, p_1, p_2, p_3, p_4. Let $\Gamma' = B_0 \cdot B_1 \cdot B_2 \cdot B_3 \cdot B_4$ and $\Gamma = 01 \cdot \Gamma'$.
4. $[\ell \geq 6]$: Here the path from $milestone_1$ to $milestone_2$ is $v_0, v_1, \ldots v_\ell$ and the corresponding sequence of port numbers is $p_0, p_1, \ldots p_\ell$. As mentioned earlier, the sequence of port numbers $p_0, p_1, p_2, p_{\ell-3}, p_{\ell-2}, p_{\ell-1}$ is coded in this case. Let $\Gamma' = B_0 \cdot B_1 \cdot B_2 \cdot B_{\ell-3} \cdot B_{\ell-2} \cdot B_{\ell-1}$ and $\Gamma = 00 \cdot \Gamma'$.

Let $\hat{\Gamma}$ be the transformed binary encoding of Γ and z be the length of the string $\hat{\Gamma}$. For $1 \leq i \leq z$, place a pebble on $s(1 + i)$, if the i-th bit of $\hat{\Gamma}$ is 1. If $\ell \geq 7$, then place a pebble on each of the nodes $v_4, \ldots, v_{\ell-3}$.

• **Case L-H:** In this case, the first milestone is selected as one of the neighbor w of s. Note that w may not be on the shortest path from s to t. For this reason we encode the path (or a subpath of the path) from s to $milestone_2$ in the neighbors of w. The agent, while executing the treasure hunt algorithm, first arrives at w, decode the path which is encoded in the neighbors of w, returns back to s and then moves according to this learned path.

In order to encode the path from s to $milestone_2$, a similar approach as in Case H can be applied. The sequence of port numbers from s to $milestone_2$ is encoded in the neighbors of w. As before, this is done based on the distance from s to $milestone_2$. However, a difficulty arises as $s(0)$ and/or $s(1)$ may also be neighbors of w and there is no way for the agent to learn through which port w is connected to $s(0)$ or $s(1)$. We overcome this difficulty in the following way.

Let Γ be the binary string of length z that we want to encode in the neighbors of w. Let $N_1(w), N_2(w), \ldots, N_5(w)$ be 5 sets of disjoint neighbors of w and the cardinality of each set is z. Since $s(0)$ and/or $s(1)$ may be neighbors of w, at least 3 of these 5 neighbor sets of w does not contain both $s(0)$ and $s(1)$. This implies that, if Γ is coded in each of these five sets, it is possible to code Γ correctly in the nodes of three sets. To be specific, the nodes of each of the $N_i(w)$ to encode Γ, and if $s(0)$ or $s(1)$ appears in this set then skip the corresponding bits of Γ while placing pebbles at the time of coding. The separation between the sets $N_i(w)$ can be learned by two consecutive zeros as the encoding is done using transformed binary encoding.

The formal description of the placement of pebbles in this case is given below. Let $milestone_2 = v_\ell$. Note that as per the definition of milestones, $l \geq 4$.

1. $[\ell = 4]$: Here the path from s to $milestone_2$ is v_0, v_1, v_2, v_3, v_4 and the corresponding sequence of port numbers is p_0, p_1, p_2, p_3. Let $\Gamma' = B_0 \cdot B_1 \cdot B_2 \cdot B_3$ and $\Gamma = 11 \cdot \Gamma'$.
2. $[\ell = 5]$: Here the path from s to $milestone_2$ is $v_0, v_1, v_2, v_3, v_4, v_5$ and the corresponding sequence of port numbers is p_0, p_1, p_2, p_3, p_4. Let $\Gamma' = B_0 \cdot B_1 \cdot B_2 \cdot B_3 \cdot B_4$ and $\Gamma = 10 \cdot \Gamma'$.
3. $[\ell = 6]$: Here the path from s to $milestone_2$ is $v_0, v_1, v_2, v_3, v_4, v_5, v_6$ and the corresponding sequence of port numbers is $p_0, p_1, p_2, p_3, p_4, p_5$. Let $\Gamma' = B_0 \cdot B_1 \cdot B_2 \cdot B_3 \cdot B_4 \cdot B_5$ and $\Gamma = 01 \cdot \Gamma'$.
4. $[\ell \geq 7]$: Here the path from s to $milestone_2$ is $v_0, v_1, \ldots v_\ell$ and the corresponding sequence of port numbers is $p_0, p_1, \ldots, p_\ell$. In this case, the sequence of port numbers $p_0, p_1, p_2, p_3, p_{\ell-3}, p_{\ell-2}, p_{\ell-1}$ is coded. Let $\Gamma' = B_0 \cdot B_1 \cdot B_2 \cdot B_3 \cdot B_{\ell-3} \cdot B_{\ell-2} \cdot B_{\ell-1}$ and $\Gamma = 00 \cdot \Gamma'$.

Let $\hat{\Gamma}$ be the transformed binary encoding of Γ and z is the length of $\hat{\Gamma}$. Let $N_i(w)$, for $1 \leq i \leq 5$, be the set z consecutive neighbors of w starting from the node $w((i-1)(z+2))$. To be specific, $N_i(w) = \{w((i-1)(z+2)), w((i-1)(z+2)+1), \ldots, w(((i-1)(z+2)+z-1))\}$. For each i, $1 \leq i \leq 5$, pebbles are placed at the nodes of $N_i(w)$ as follows. For $1 \leq a \leq z$, if the a-th bit of $\hat{\Gamma}$ is 1, then place a pebble at the node $w((i-1)(z+2)+a-1)$ only if $w((i-1)(z+2)+a-1) \notin \{s(0), s(1)\}$. If $\ell \geq 8$, then place a pebble at each of the nodes $v_5, \ldots, v_{\ell-3}$.

- **Case L-L-H:** The placement of pebbles in this case is similar to the placement in Case L-H. The path coded in the neighbors of w is a subpath of the path P starting from s. As before, depending on the position of the $milestone_2$, different sequences of port numbers are coded in the neighbors of $milestone_1$. Since $milestone_1 \in L_2$ in this case, $s(0)$, $s(1)$ may be connected to $milestone_1$.

For this reason, as before, the subpath is coded in five disjoint sets of neighbors of $milestone_1$.

Formal description of placements of pebbles in this case in described below. Let $milestone_2 = v_\ell$. As per the definition of milestones, $\ell \geq 5$.

1. $[\ell = 5]$: Here the path from s to $milestone_2$ is $v_0, v_1, v_2, v_3, v_4, v_5$ and the corresponding sequence of port numbers is p_0, p_1, p_2, p_3, p_4. Let $\Gamma' = B_0 \cdot B_1 \cdot B_2 \cdot B_3 \cdot B_4$ and $\Gamma = 11 \cdot \Gamma'$.
2. $[\ell = 6]$: Here the path from s to $milestone_2$ is $v_0, v_1, v_2, v_3, v_4, v_5, v_6$ and the corresponding sequence of port numbers is $p_0, p_1, p_2, p_3, p_4, p_5$. Let $\Gamma' = B_0 \cdot B_1 \cdot B_2 \cdot B_3 \cdot B_4 \cdot B_5$ and $\Gamma = 10 \cdot \Gamma'$.
3. $[\ell = 7]$: Here the path from s to $milestone_2$ is $v_0, v_1, v_2, v_3, v_4, v_5, v_6, v_7$ and the corresponding sequence of port numbers is $p_0, p_1, \ldots, p_\ell$. In this case, the sequence of port numbers $p_0, p_1, p_2, p_3, p_4, p_5, p_6$ is coded. Let $\Gamma' = B_0 \cdot B_1 \cdot B_2 \cdot B_3 \cdot B_4 \cdot B_5 \cdot B_6$ and $\Gamma = 01 \cdot \Gamma'$.
4. $[\ell \geq 8]$: Here the path from s to $milestone_2$ is $v_0, v_1, \ldots v_\ell$ and the corresponding sequence of port numbers is $p_0, p_1, \ldots, p_\ell$. In this case, the sequence of port numbers $p_0, p_1, p_2, p_3, p_4, p_{\ell-3}, p_{\ell-2}, p_{\ell-1}$ is coded. Let $\Gamma' = B_0 \cdot B_1 \cdot B_2 \cdot B_3 \cdot B_4 \cdot B_{\ell-3} \cdot B_{\ell-2} \cdot B_{\ell-1}$ and $\Gamma = 00 \cdot \Gamma'$.

Let $\hat{\Gamma}$ be the transformed binary encoding of Γ and z is the length of $\hat{\Gamma}$. Let $N_i(w)$, for $1 \leq i \leq 5$, be the set z consecutive neighbors of w starting from the node $w((i-1)(z+2))$. To be specific, $N_i(w) = \{w((i-1)(z+2)), w((i-1)(z+2)+1), \ldots, w(((i-1)(z+2)+z-1))\}$. For each i, $1 \leq i \leq 5$, pebbles are placed at the nodes of $N_i(w)$ as follows. For $1 \leq a \leq z$, if the a-th bit of $\hat{\Gamma}$ is 1, then place a pebble at the node $w((i-1)(z+2)+a-1)$ only if $w((i-1)(z+2)+a-1) \notin \{s(0), s(1)\}$. If $\ell \geq 8$, then place a pebble at each of the nodes $v_5, \ldots, v_{\ell-3}$.

Remark 1. It can be noted that maximum of 8 port numbers must be coded in this case in each of the five disjoint sets of neighbors of $milestone_1$. The transformed binary representation of each port can be of at most $2(1 + \lfloor \log \Delta \rfloor)$ length. Also, two bits are used as marker to represent the distance between first and second milestones. Hence in each set, a string of length $16(1 + \lfloor \log \Delta \rfloor) + 2$ is coded. Therefore, over all, among 5 sets, the nodes that are used to code the sequences of port numbers is $80\lfloor \log \Delta \rfloor + 90$. Also there are two zeros must be coded in between two consecutive sets to show separations between them and at the end at least 8 nodes kept blank (this is because if $s(1)$ appears in one of the first 4 blank nodes after these 5 sets). Hence the degree of $milestone_1$ must be at least $80\lfloor \log \Delta \rfloor + 106$. Since every milestone is heavy, and $\Delta \geq 2^{10}$ (for $\Delta \geq 2^{10}$, $\Delta \geq 80\lfloor \log \Delta \rfloor + 106$), therefore, such a coding can be done in the neighbors of $milestone_1$.

• **Case L-L-L:** This is the case where the two nodes $s(0)$ and $s(1)$ that are used for markers are not connected to $milestone_1$ as $milestone_1 \in L_j$, for some $j \geq 3$. Hence, it is easy to code the paths in the neighbors of $milestone_1$ like

Case H. The only difference here is, the subpath coded is a path starting from v_{j-3}. Depending on the position of $milestone_2$, either the sequence of port number corresponding to the entire path from v_{j-3} to $milestone_2$ or the sequence $p_{j-3}, p_{j-2}, p_{j-1}, p_j, p_{j+1}, p_{j+2}$, and the last three ports before $milestone_2$ are coded. For every light nodes starting from v_1 to v_{j-3}, a pebble is placed on these nodes that guides the agent towards $milestone_1$. One more difficulty here is the case when $v_1 \in \{s(0), s(1)\}$, as we can not place a pebble in any of the nodes $s(0), s(1)$, otherwise it is not possible to recognize the Case L-L-L. To overcome this difficulty, we place a pebble at s, if $milestone_1 \in L_3$. Now, the agent, starting from s, first identify the Case L-L-L by not seeing any pebbles in $s(0)$, and $s(1)$. If s contains a pebble, the agent learns that $milestone_1 \in L_3$. The coding in the neighbors of $milestone_1$ is done in the same way as described for Case H.

The formal description of the pebble placement is as follows. Let j be the integer such that $w = milestone_1 \in L_j$ and let ℓ be the integer such that $milestone_2 = v_\ell$.

1. **$[\ell - j = 3]$:** Here the path from v_{j-3} to $milestone_2$ is $v_{j-3}, v_{j-2}, v_{j-1}, v_j,$ $v_{j+1}, v_{j+2}, v_{j+3}$ and the corresponding sequence of port numbers is $p_{j-3},$ $p_{j-2}, p_{j-1}, p_j, p_{j+1}, p_{j+2}$. Let $\Gamma' = B_{j-3} \cdot B_{j-2} \cdot B_{j-1} \cdot B_j \cdot B_{j+1} \cdot B_{j+2}$ and $\Gamma = 11 \cdot \Gamma'$.

2. **$[\ell - j = 4]$:** Here the path from v_{j-3} to $milestone_2$ is $v_{j-3}, v_{j-2}, v_{j-1}, v_j,$ $v_{j+1},\ v_{j+2}, v_{j+3}, v_{j+4}$ and the corresponding sequence of port numbers is $p_{j-3}, p_{j-2}, p_{j-1}, p_j, p_{j+1}, p_{j+2}, p_{j+3}$. Let $\Gamma' = B_{j-3} \cdot B_{j-2} \cdot B_{j-1} \cdot B_j \cdot B_{j+1} \cdot B_{j+2} \cdot B_{j+3}$ and $\Gamma = 10 \cdot \Gamma'$.

3. **$[\ell - j = 5]$:** Here the path from v_{j-3} to $milestone_2$ is $v_{j-3}, v_{j-2}, v_{j-1}, v_j,$ $v_{j+1}, v_{j+2}, v_{j+3}, v_{j+4}, v_{j+5}$ and the corresponding sequence of port numbers is $p_{j-3}, p_{j-2}, p_{j-1}, p_j, p_{j+1}, p_{j+2}, p_{j+3}, p_{j+4}$. Let $\Gamma' = B_{j-3} \cdot B_{j-2} \cdot B_{j-1} \cdot B_j \cdot B_{j+1} \cdot B_{j+2} \cdot B_{j+3} \cdot B_{j+4}$ and $\Gamma = 01 \cdot \Gamma'$.

4. **$[\ell - j \geq 6]$:** Here the path from v_{j-3} to $milestone_2$ is $v_{j-3}, v_{j-2} \ldots v_\ell$ and the corresponding sequence of port numbers is $p_{j-3}, p_{j-2}, \ldots p_{\ell-1}$. Here, the sequence of port numbers $p_{j-3}, p_{j-2}, p_{j-1}, p_j, p_{j+1}, p_{j+2}, p_{j+3},$ $p_{\ell-3}, p_{\ell-2}, p_{\ell-1}$ is coded. Let $\Gamma' = B_{j-3} \cdot B_{j-2} \cdot B_{j-1} \cdot B_j \cdot B_{j+1} \cdot B_{j+2} \cdot B_{j+3} \cdot B_{\ell-3} \cdot B_{\ell-2} \cdot B_{\ell-1}$ and $\Gamma = 00 \cdot \Gamma'$.

Let $\hat{\Gamma}$ be the transformed binary encoding of Γ and z be the length of the string $\hat{\Gamma}$. For $1 \leq a \leq z$, place a pebble at $w(a - 1)$ if the a-th bit of $\hat{\Gamma}$ is 1. If $\ell - j \geq 7$, then place a pebble at each of the nodes $v_{j+4}, \ldots v_{\ell-3}$. Also, for $2 \leq i \leq j - 3$, place a pebble at each of the node v_i. If $j = 4$, place a pebble at s. If $v_1 \notin \{s(0), s(1)\}$, then place a pebble at v_1.

Phase 3: Placing pebbles to encode paths between other milestones
The coding of the paths between $milestone_j$ to $milestone_{j+1}$, for $j \geq 2$ are done in the similar fashion as described in Case H. The only difference here is the encoding is done in the neighbors of $milestone_j$ starting from $milestone_j(0)$. For the last milestone, the path from the last milestone to the treasure is coded in the same way as described for the other cases.

Let the total number of milestones be y. For $m = 2, 3, \ldots, y - 1$, let v_j be the node on P such that $milestone_m = v_j$ and $milestone_{m+1} = v_\ell$. For $m = y$, set $\ell = t$.

1. $\ell - j \leq 3$ then $\ell \leq j + 3$. The path from v_j to v_ℓ is $v_j, v_{j+1} \ldots v_\ell$ and the corresponding sequence of port numbers is $p_j, p_{j+1}, \ldots, p_{\ell-1}$. Let $\Gamma' = B_j \cdot B_{j+1} \cdots B_{\ell-1}$ and $\Gamma = 11 \cdot \Gamma'$.
2. $\ell - j = 4$ then $\ell = j + 4$. The path from v_j to v_ℓ is $v_j, v_{j+1}, v_{j+2}, v_{j+3}, v_{j+4}$ and the corresponding sequence of port numbers is $p_j, p_{j+1}, p_{j+2}, p_{j+2}, p_{j+3}$. Let $\Gamma' = B_j \cdot B_{j+1} \cdot B_{j+2} \cdot B_{j+3}$ and $\Gamma = 10 \cdot \Gamma'$.
3. $\ell - j = 5$ then $\ell = j + 5$. The path from v_j to v_ℓ is v_j, v_{j+1}, v_{j+2}, $v_{j+3}, v_{j+4}, v_{j+5}$ and the corresponding sequence of port numbers is p_j, p_{j+1}, $p_{j+2}, p_{j+2}, p_{j+3}, p_{j+4}$. Let $\Gamma' = B_j \cdot B_{j+1} \cdot B_{j+2} \cdot B_{j+3} \cdot B_{j+4}$ and $\Gamma = 10 \cdot \Gamma'$.
4. If $\ell - j \geq 6$, and $\ell \neq t$ then let Γ' be the binary representation of the sequence of port numbers $p_j, p_{j+1}, p_{j+2}, p_{\ell-3}, p_{\ell-2}, p_{\ell-1}$. If $\ell = t$ then Γ is the binary representation of the sequence of port numbers p_j, p_{j+1}, p_{j+2}. $\Gamma = 00 \cdot \Gamma'$.

Let $\hat{\Gamma}$ be the transformed binary encoding of Γ and z be the length of $\hat{\Gamma}$. For $1 \leq a \leq z$, place a pebble at $w(a - 1)$ if the a-th bit of Γ is 1. If $\ell - j \geq 7$, then place a pebble at each of the nodes $v_{j+4}, \ldots v_{t-3}$. If $\ell = t$, then place a pebble at each of the nodes v_{t-2} and v_{t-1}.

Treasure Hunt by the Mobile Agent. The agent follows the algorithm TREASUREHUNT (Algorithm 1) to find the treasure. Starting from the node s, it first visits the two nodes $s(0)$ and $s(1)$. If pebbles are found at both the nodes, then the agent follows SUBROUTINE_H; If a pebble is found at $s(0)$ but no pebble is found at $s(1)$, then the agent follows SUBROUTINE_L-H; If a pebble is found at $s(1)$ but no pebble is found at $s(0)$, then the agent follows SUBROUTINE_L-L-H, otherwise the agent follows SUBROUTINE_L-L-L if no pebbles are found in either of these two nodes.

Algorithm 1: TREASUREHUNT

---

1 Starting from s, the agent visits two nodes $s(0)$, and $s(1)$ one by one and comes back to s.
2 **if** *Both the nodes $s(0)$, and $s(1)$ contains a pebble each* **then**
3 | SUBROUTINE_H (Algorithm 2)
4 **else if** *$s(0)$ contains a pebble and $s(1)$ does not contain any pebble* **then**
5 | SUBROUTINE_L-H (Algorithm 3)
6 **else if** *$s(0)$ does not contain any pebble and $s(1)$ contains a pebble* **then**
7 | SUBROUTINE_L-L-H (Algorithm 4)
8 **else if** *Neither $s(0)$ nor $s(1)$ contains a pebble* **then**
9 | SUBROUTINE_L-L-L (Algorithm 5)

Algorithm 2: SUBROUTINE_H

---

1 $CurrentNode = s$.
2 The agent visits the neighbors of s starting from $s(2)$, in the increasing order of the port number through which s is connected to them until it finds two consecutive neighbors where no pebbles are placed.
3 Let $\hat{\Gamma} = b_2 b_3 \ldots b_z$ be the binary string where b_i is 1 if a pebble is found at $s(i)$ and the last two nodes visited in the previous step by the agent are $s(z+1)$ and $s(z+2)$. Let Γ be the string such that Γ' is the transformed binary encoding of Γ.
4 $CurrentIndex = 3$. $MinDistance = 3$
5 FINDNEXTMILESTONE($b_2, b_3, \Gamma, MinDistance$) (Algorithm 7)
6 PROGRESS($CurrentNode$) (Algorithm 8)

If two pebbles are found at each of the nodes $s(0)$ and $s(1)$, the agent learns that s is heavy. According to SUBROUTINE_H, the agent visits the nodes $s(2), s(3), \ldots$ until it found two nodes $s(z+1)$ and $s(z+2)$ such that no pebbles are found in both of these nodes. Let $\hat{\Gamma} = b_2 b_3 \ldots b_z$ be the binary string such that $b_i = 1$ if a pebble is found at $s(i)$, else $b_i = 0$. Let Γ be the string obtained from $\hat{\Gamma}$ by replacing each '11' by '1' and each '10' by 0 of $\hat{\Gamma}$ from left to right, taking two bits at a time. The first two bits of Γ represents the distance of $milestone_2$ from s. The agent, knowing the degree of s, compute $\alpha_s = 1 + \lfloor \log deg(s) \rfloor$. Let q_0 be the integer that is represented by the substring $\Gamma(3, 4 + \alpha_s)$. The agent moves along the port p to reach the node v_1. Once it moves to v_1, it learns its degree and computes α_{v_1}. It then compute the integer q_1 that is coded in the substring $\Gamma(5 + \alpha_s, 6 + \alpha_s + \alpha_{v_1})$. The agent moves along the port q_1 to reach the node v_2. The agent continues to move this way distances 3,4,5, if the first two bits represent the markers '11','10','01', respectively to reach $milestone_2$. For the marker '00' represented by $s(2)$ and $s(3)$, the agent moves distance 3 as per the above strategy, to reach a node v_3. It then visits all the neighbors of v_3 and move to the neighbor that contains a pebble. This process continues until for a node, none of its neighbors contains any pebble. In this case, the agent retrieve the next three ports encoded in the rest of the substring of Γ, one by one and moving to the respective node and move along three edges to reach to $milestone_2$.

If a pebble is found in $s(0)$ but no pebble is found in $s(1)$, the agent learns that $milestone_1 \in L_1$. In this case, it executes SUBROUTINE_L-H. The agent visits all the neighbor of s and finds the neighbor w with maximum degree. In case of tie, the agent moves to the node with maximum degree to which s is connected via smallest port number. This node w is $milestone_1$. The agent, after moving to w from s, starts visiting all the neighbors of w one by one until it finds four consecutive neighbors $w(z), w(z+1), w(z+2)$, and $w(z+3)$ none of which contain any pebble. The agent construct the binary string $\Gamma' = b_0 b_1 \ldots b_{z-1}$, where $b_i = 1$ if a pebble was found at $w(i)$, else $b_i = 0$. This string is split into substrings that are separated by the substring '00' and the agent computes the substring $\hat{\Gamma}$ whose occurrence among these substrings is maximum. Let Γ be the string obtained from $\hat{\Gamma}$ by replacing each '11' by '1' and each '10' by '0' of $\hat{\Gamma}$ from left to right, taking two bits at a time. The agent computes the ports one by one as described for SUBROUTINE_H and move towards the second milestone. The only difference here is after computing Γ, the agent comes back to s from $milestone_1$ and the path coded at Γ starts from s.

Algorithm 3: SUBROUTINE_L-H

1 The agent visits all the neighbors of s and let w be the node that have the maximum degree among all the neighbors of s. In case where multiple nodes with maximum degree exists, let w be the node to which s is connected via the smallest port number.

2 The agent moves to w. Let q be the incoming port at w of the edge (s, w).

3 The agent visits the neighbors of w in the increasing order of the port number through which w is connected to them until it finds four consecutive neighbors where no pebbles are placed.

4 Go back to s from w using port number q. $CurrentNode = s$.

5 Let $\Gamma' = b_0 b_1 \ldots b_{z'}$ be the binary string where b_i is 1 if a pebble is found at $w(i)$ and the last four nodes visited in the previous step by the agent are $w(z'), w(z'+1), w(z'+2), w(z'+3)$.

6 Partition Γ' into substrings that are separated by two consecutive zeros. Let $\hat{\Gamma}$ be the string that matches with most of these substrings. Let Γ be the string such that $\hat{\Gamma}$ is the transformed binary encoding of Γ.

7 $CurrentIndex = 3$. $MinDistance = 4$

8 FINDNEXTMILESTONE($b, b', \Gamma, MinDistance$) (Algorithm 7)

9 PROGRESS($CurrentNode$) (Algorithm 8)

Algorithm 4: SUBROUTINE_L-L-H

1 The agent visits all the neighbors of s and let w be the node the maximum degree node in L_2 to which s is connected through the lexicographically shortest path.

2 The agent moves to w.

3 The agent visits the neighbors of w in the increasing order of the port number through which w is connected to them until it finds four consecutive neighbors where no pebbles are placed.

4 Go back to s.

5 $CurrentNode = s$.

6 Let $\Gamma' = b_0 b_1 \ldots b_{z'-1}$ be the binary string where b_i is 1 if a pebble is found at $w(i)$ and the last four nodes visited in the previous step by the agent are $w(z'), w(z'+1), w(z'+2), w(z'+3)$.

7 Partition Γ' into substrings that are separated by consecutive zeros. Let $\hat{\Gamma}$ be the string that matches with most of these substrings. Let Γ be the string such that $\hat{\Gamma}$ is the transformed binary encoding of Γ.

8 $MinDistance = 5$. $CurrentIndex = 3$

9 FINDNEXTMILESTONE($b, b', \Gamma, MinDistance$) (Algorithm 7)

10 PROGRESS($CurrentNode$) (Algorithm 8)

Algorithm 5: SUBROUTINE_L-L-L

---

1 $CurrentNode = s$.

2 Visit all the neighbors of $CurrentNode$.

3 **if** *Treasure is found* **then**

4 | Stop and terminate.

5 **if** *a pebble found at a node v* **then**

6 | Move to v. Set $CurrentNode = v$. Go to Step 1.

7 **else**

8 | **if** $CurrentNode \neq s$ **then**

9 | | Visit all the paths from $CurrentNode$ of length 3. Let w be the node of maximum degree connected to $CurrentNode$ by the lexicographically shortest path of length 3.

10 | | Move to w. Store the incoming ports of the path from v to w in a stack.

11 | **else**

12 | | **if** *s contains a pebble* **then**

13 | | | Go to Step 8.

14 | | **else**

15 | | | Move to $s(0)$. Let q be the port number of the edge $(s, s(0))$ at $s(0)$. Visit all the neighbors of $s(0)$.

16 | | | **if** *a pebble is found at a neighbor v of $s(0)$* **then**

17 | | | | Move to v. Set $CurretNode = v$. Go to Step 1.

18 | | | **else**

19 | | | | Return to s using port q from $s(0)$. Move to $s(1)$. Let q' be the port number of the edge $(s, s(1))$ at $s(1)$. Visit all the neighbors of $s(1)$.

20 | | | | **if** *a pebble is found at a neighbor v of $s(1)$* **then**

21 | | | | | Move to v. Set $CurretNode = v$. Go to Step 1.

22 | | | | **else**

23 | | | | | Move back to s. Go to Step 8.

24 The agent visits the neighbors of w in the increasing order of the port number through which w is connected to them until it finds two consecutive neighbors where no pebbles are placed.

25 Let $\Gamma = b_0 b_1 \ldots b_{z-1}$ be the binary string where b_i is 1 if a pebble is found at the node $w(i)$ and the last two nodes visited in the previous step by the agent are $w(z)$ and $w(z+1)$. Let Γ be the string such that $\hat{\Gamma}$ is the transformed binary encoding of Γ.

26 Move back to $CurrentNode$ using the path stored in the stack. Set $CurrentIndex = 3$, $MinDistnace = 6$.

27 Algo FINDNEXTMILESTONE($b, b', \Gamma, MinDistance$)(Algorithm 7)

28 PROGRESS($CurrentNode$) (Algorithm 8)

If a pebble is found at $s(0)$ but no pebble at $s(1)$, the agent learns that $milestone_1 \in L_2$. In this case, the agent executes SUBROUTINE_L-L-H. From s, it explores all possible paths of length 2 and moves to the maximum degree node in L_2 to which s is connected through the lexicographically shortest path. After moving to w, the agent computes the binary string Γ in the same way as described in case of Algorithm 3 and proceed towards the second milestone.

Here, the string Γ that is computed by the agent, codes the path starting from s and the agent, after learning Γ, moves back to s and moves forward according to subpath coded in Γ towards the second milestone.

If no pebbles are found at both $s(0)$ and $s(1)$, the agent learns that $milestone_1$ is in L_j, for some $j \geq 3$ and executes SUBROUTINE_L-L-L. It then visits all the neighbors of s and identify the node v_1 by finding a neighbor with a pebble. Here, as mentioned in the pebble placement algorithm, the problem occurs when $v_1 \in \{s(0), s(1)\}$, as these two nodes are already used as marker and therefore no pebble can be placed here. In this case, the agent considers both $s(0)$ and $s(1)$ as possible candidates for v_1.

Once $milestone_2$ is reached, the agent moves according to Algorithm 8. Until the treasure is found, the agent, learn the sequence of port numbers that leads towards the next milestone by visiting the neighbors of the current milestone. Then following this sequence of port numbers and using the pebbles placed on the light nodes, the agent moves to the next milestone. This process continues until the treasure is found.

During the execution of the treasure hunt algorithm, the agent uses a set of global variables, $CurrentNode$, $MinDistance$, and $CurrentIndex$. The variable $CurrentNode$ denotes the node from which the current call of the algorithms are executed. The $MinDistance$ variable stores the integers which is the minimum number of ports that are coded in the neighbor of the current milestone. The $CurrentIndex$ indicates the position of the binary string (represents the sequence of port numbers towards the next milestone) from which the coding of the port number along the shortest path from $CurrentNode$ starts.

Algorithm 6: MOVEMENT(i,x,Γ)

1 Let p be the integer that is represented by the substring constructed from $\Gamma(i, x)$.
2 The agent move from the current node to the node u to which the current node is connected via port p.
3 **if** *Treasure found* **then**
4 | Stop and terminate.
5 **else**
6 | $CurrentNode = u$. $CurrentIndex = x + 1$

The following lemmas and the theorem ensure the correctness of the proposed algorithm.

Lemma 1. *Starting from the node s, the agent successfully reaches to $milestone_1$ in $O((dist(s, milestone_1) \log \Delta + \log^3 \Delta))$-time.*

In the next two lemmas, we prove that from $milestone_1$ the agent reaches to $milestone_2$ for each of the different cases. The first lemma proves this for the Case H and Case L-L-L and the second lemma proves this for the Case L-H and Case L-L-H.

Algorithm 7: FINDNEXTMILESTONE(a, b, Γ, i)

---

1 **if** $a = 1$ *and* $b = 1$ **then**
2 | **for** $j \leftarrow 1$ **to** i **do**
3 | | MOVEMENT($CurrentIndex$,$\alpha_{CurrentNode}$,Γ) (Algorithm 6)
4 **else**
5 | **if** $a = 1$ *and* $b = 0$ **then**
6 | | **for** $j = 1$ *to* $i + 1$ **do**
7 | | | MOVEMENT($CurrentIndex$,$\alpha_{CurrentNode}$,Γ)
8 | **else**
9 | | **if** $a = 0$ *and* $b = 1$ **then**
10 | | | **for** $j = 1$ *to* $i + 2$ **do**
11 | | | | MOVEMENT($CurrentIndex$,$\alpha_{CurrentNode}$,Γ)
12 | | **else**
13 | | | **for** $j = 1$ *to* i **do**
14 | | | | MOVEMENT($CurrentIndex$,$\alpha_{CurrentNode}$,Γ)
15 | | | **while** *a pebble is found in some neighbor of* $CurrentNode$ **do**
16 | | | | Move to the neighbor u of $CurrentNode$ that contains a pebble.
                      $CurrentNode = u$
17 | | | **for** $i = 1$ *to 3* **do**
18 | | | | MOVEMENT($CurrentIndex$,$\alpha_{CurrentNode}$,Γ)
19 PROGRESS($CurrentNode$) (Algorithm 8)

Algorithm 8: PROGRESS($CurrentNode$)

---

1 The agent visits the neighbors of $CurrentNode$ starting from $CurrentNode(0)$, in the increasing order of the port number through which $CurrentNode$ is connected to them until it finds two consecutive neighbors where no pebbles are placed.
2 Let $\hat{\Gamma} = b_0 b_1 \ldots b_z$ be the binary string where b_i is 1 if a pebble is found at the node connected to s through port i and the last two nodes visited in the previous step by the agent are $s(z + 1)$ and $s(z + 2)$. Let Γ be the string such that $\hat{\Gamma}$ is the transformed binary encoding of Γ.
3 Let b, b' be the first two bits of Γ.
4 $CurrentIndex = 3$. $MinDistance = 3$.
5 FINDNEXTMILESTONE($b, b', \Gamma, MinDistance$) (Algorithm 7)
6 PROGRESS($CurrentNode$) (Algorithm 8)

Lemma 2. *The agent successfully reaches to* $milestone_2$ *form* $milestone_1$ *for Case H and Case L-L-L.*

Lemma 3. *The agent successfully reaches to* $milestone_2$ *from* $milestone_1$ *for Case L-H and Case L-L-H.*

Lemma 4. *After reaching* $milestone_j$, *for some* $j \geq 2$, *the agent successfully either reaches to* $milestone_{j+1}$, *if exists, or finds the treasure.*

We now present our final result in the following theorem.

Theorem 1. *The agent finds the treasure in $O(D \log \Delta + \log^3 \Delta)$-time.*

3 Lower Bound

In this section, we show a lower bound $\Omega(D \log \Delta)$ for time of treasure hunt. To be specific, we construct a class of instances of treasure hunt such that if the time for treasure hunt is 'short', then any algorithm using any number of pebbles can not find the treasure within this short time for some instances.

Let T be a complete tree of height D where the degree of the root r and each internal node is Δ. There are $\Delta \cdot (\Delta - 1)^{D-1}$ leaves in T. Let $p = \Delta \cdot (\Delta - 1)^{D-1}$ and $u_1, \ldots, u_p$ be the leaves of T in lexicographical ordering of the shortest path from the root r. For $1 \le i \le p$, we construct an input B_i as follows. The tree T is taken as the input graph, r as the starting point of the agent, and u_i as the position of the treasure. Let $\mathcal{B}$ be the set of all inputs B_i, $1 \le i \le p$.

The following lemma is useful to prove the final lower bound result.

Lemma 5. *For any treasure hunt algorithm $\mathcal{A}$ taking t-time, then for all possible placements of pebbles, there are at most 2^t possible sequences of port numbers the agent may follow for the treasure hunt.*

The following theorem proves the lower bound result.

Theorem 2. *There exists a tree with maximum degree Δ (≥ 2) and diameter D (≥ 3) such that any deterministic algorithm must require $\Omega(D \log \Delta)$-time for the treasure hunt irrespective of the number of pebbles placed on the nodes of G.*

4 Conclusion

We propose an algorithm for the treasure hunt problem that finds the treasure in an anonymous graph in $O(D \log \Delta + \log^3 \Delta)$-time. We also prove a lower bound of $\Omega(D \log \Delta)$. Clearly, there is a small gap between the upper and lower bounds, however, the gap is smaller than any polynomial of Δ. A natural open question is to find tight upper and lower bounds for the problem. Another interesting problem is to study trade-off between number of pebble and time for treasure hunt in anonymous networks.

References

1. Alpern, S., Gal, S.: The Theory of Search Games and Rendezvous. International Series in Operations Research and Management Science, vol. 55. Springer, Boston (2003). https://doi.org/10.1007/b100809
2. Baeza-Yates, R.A., Culberson, J.C., Rawlins, G.J.E.: Searching in the plane. Inf. Comput. **106**(2), 234–252 (1993)
3. Beck, A., Newman, D.: Yet more on the linear search problem. Israel J. Math. **8**, 419–429 (1970). https://doi.org/10.1007/BF02798690

4. Boczkowski, L., Korman, A., Rodeh, Y.: Searching a tree with permanently noisy advice. In: ESA, pp. 54:1–54:13 (2018)
5. Bonato, A., Nowakowski, R.: The Game of Cops and Robbers on Graphs. American Mathematical Society, Providence (2011)
6. Bouchard, S., Dieudonné, Y., Labourel, A., Pelc, A.: Almost-optimal deterministic treasure hunt in arbitrary graphs. CoRR abs/2010.14916 (2020)
7. Bouchard, S., Dieudonné, Y., Pelc, A., Petit, F.: Deterministic treasure hunt in the plane with angular hints. Algorithmica **82**(11), 3250–3281 (2020). https://doi.org/10.1007/s00453-020-00724-4
8. Chung, T.H., Hollinger, G.A., Isler, V.: Search and pursuit-evasion in mobile robotics - a survey. Auton. Robots **31**(4), 299–316 (2011). https://doi.org/10.1007/s10514-011-9241-4
9. Cohen, R., Fraigniaud, P., Ilcinkas, D., Korman, A., Peleg, D.: Label-guided graph exploration by a finite automaton. ACM Trans. Algorithms **4**(4), 42:1–42:18 (2008)
10. Demaine, E.D., Fekete, S.P., Gal, S.: Online searching with turn cost. Theor. Comput. Sci. **361**(2), 342–355 (2006)
11. Disser, Y., Hackfeld, J., Klimm, M.: Tight bounds for undirected graph exploration with pebbles and multiple agents. J. ACM **66**(6), 40:1–40:41 (2019)
12. Emek, Y., Langner, T., Stolz, D., Uitto, J., Wattenhofer, R.: How many ants does it take to find the food? Theor. Comput. Sci. **608**, 255–267 (2015)
13. Fricke, G.M., Hecker, J.P., Griego, A.D., Tran, L.T., Moses, M.E.: A distributed deterministic spiral search algorithm for swarms. In: 2016 IEEE/RSJ (IROS), pp. 4430–4436 (2016)
14. Gorain, B., Mondal, K., Nayak, H., Pandit, S.: Pebble guided near optimal treasure hunt in anonymous graphs. CoRR abs/2103.05933 (2021)
15. Gorain, B., Pelc, A.: Deterministic graph exploration with advice. ACM Trans. Algorithms **15**(1), 8:1–8:17 (2019)
16. Jez, A., Lopuszanski, J.: On the two-dimensional cow search problem. Inf. Process. Lett. **109**(11), 543–547 (2009)
17. Kao, M., Reif, J.H., Tate, S.R.: Searching in an unknown environment: an optimal randomized algorithm for the cow-path problem. Inf. Comput. **131**(1), 63–79 (1996)
18. Langetepe, E.: Searching for an axis-parallel shoreline. Theor. Comput. Sci. **447**, 85–99 (2012)
19. Langner, T., Keller, B., Uitto, J., Wattenhofer, R.: Overcoming obstacles with ants. In: OPODIS, pp. 9:1–9:17 (2015)
20. Miller, A., Pelc, A.: Tradeoffs between cost and information for rendezvous and treasure hunt. In: OPODIS, pp. 263–276 (2014)
21. Pelc, A., Yadav, R.N.: Information complexity of treasure hunt in geometric terrains. CoRR abs/1811.06823 (2018)
22. Pelc, A., Yadav, R.N.: Cost vs. information tradeoffs for treasure hunt in the plane. CoRR abs/1902.06090 (2019)
23. Spieser, K., Frazzoli, E.: The cow-path game: a competitive vehicle routing problem. In: 2012 IEEE (CDC), pp. 6513–6520 (2012)
24. Ta-Shma, A., Zwick, U.: Deterministic rendezvous, treasure hunts, and strongly universal exploration sequences. ACM Trans. Algorithms **10**(3), 12:1–12:15 (2014)

Security and Efficiency of Network Communication

GMA: A Pareto Optimal Distributed Resource-Allocation Algorithm

Giacomo Giuliari$^{(\boxtimes)}$, Marc Wyss, Markus Legner, and Adrian Perrig

ETH Zürich, Universitätstrasse 6, 8092 Zürich, Switzerland
{giacomog,marc.wyss,markus.legner,adrian.perrig}@inf.ethz.ch

Abstract. To address the raising demand for strong packet delivery guarantees in networking, we study a novel way to perform graph resource allocation. We first introduce *allocation graphs*, in which nodes can independently set local resource limits based on physical constraints or policy decisions. In this scenario we formalize the *distributed path-allocation* (PA^{dist}) problem, which consists in allocating resources to paths considering only *local* on-path information—importantly, not knowing which other paths could have an allocation—while at the same time achieving the *global* property of never exceeding available resources.

Our core contribution, the global myopic allocation (GMA) algorithm, is a solution to this problem. We prove that GMA can compute *unconditional* allocations for all paths on a graph, while never over-allocating resources. Further, we prove that GMA is Pareto optimal with respect to the allocation size, and it has linear complexity in the input size. Finally, we show with simulations that this theoretical result could be indeed applied to practical scenarios, as the resulting path allocations are large enough to fit the requirements of practically relevant applications.

1 Introduction

Allocating resources such as bandwidth in a network has proven to be a difficult problem from both a theoretical and practical perspective: in many cases, networks consist of independent nodes without central controller and without a global view of the topology and available resources. Furthermore, these nodes often have their own policies on how to allocate resources. To the best of our knowledge, the theoretical networking literature is lacking solutions that address this distributed setting. In this paper, we consider *allocation graphs*, directed graphs consisting of independent nodes augmented with local policies, i.e., the amount of resources each node allocates for transit between any pair of neighbors. While we interpret the resources as bandwidth, other interpretations—like computations on behalf of the neighbors—are possible as well.

For any path in the allocation graph, we want to *myopically* compute a static allocation, i.e., based only on the local policies of on-path nodes. This allocation should guarantee that no local allocation is ever exceeded, even when all path allocations in the network are fully used simultaneously. This is resource allocation is therefore *unconditional*, since the size of one allocation is completely

© Springer Nature Switzerland AG 2021
T. Jurdziński and S. Schmid (Eds.): SIROCCO 2021, LNCS 12810, pp. 243–261, 2021.
https://doi.org/10.1007/978-3-030-79527-6_14

independent of any other allocation, and not determined by an admission process, and thus cannot be influenced by single off-path nodes. In particular, nodes do not need to keep track of allocations as each individual allocation is valid independently of whether or not any other allocations are used. We formalize the problem of finding the size of such allocations as the *distributed path allocation* (PA^{dist}) problem. Two major questions then arise: (i) Can unconditional resource allocation indeed be performed in a distributed setting, where nodes have only partial information on the network, without creating over-allocation? And (ii), since an allocation is implicitly created for every path in the network, can allocations be large enough to be useful in practice?

Our work addresses these problems, finding that it is possible to both avoid over-allocation and create allocations that meet the demands of a number of modern critical applications at the same time. We show this constructively, by proposing the first unconditional resource allocation algorithm: the *global myopic allocation* (GMA) algorithm. GMA interprets each node's local allocations both as capacity limits that must not be exceeded and as policy decisions about the relative importance of links to neighbors. It efficiently computes allocations that scale with these local policies, and ensures that capacities are not over-allocated. We prove that GMA fulfills all desired properties and that it is *Pareto optimal* with respect to all other algorithms that solve the PA^{dist} problem. Finally, we simulate GMA on random graphs, chosen to model real-world use cases; we evaluate the size of the resulting path allocations and show that they are viable for practical applications.

Practical Relevance of the PA^{dist} Problem. Over the past decades, computer networks have predominantly relied on the *best-effort* paradigm. Endpoints run congestion-control algorithms to prevent a congestion-induced collapse of the network [11,13], but no further guarantees for packet delivery or quality of service can be given. This has been shown to work reasonably well for many applications like web browsing, but it is becoming increasingly clear that it is far from optimal in terms of performance and fairness [7,19].

Although the networking community has developed several protocols to reserve resources for individual connections [3,4,16], none of them has seen widespread adoption because of their high complexity and poor scalability. These drawbacks arise in all these systems as they offer *conditional* allocations: endpoints can select the amount of resource to allocate, the rationale being that supply and demand will eventually lead to optimal resource utilization. However, this also means that all nodes have to store information about all individual requests, and check that new requests do not exceed resource capacity.

An unconditional resource allocation system based on the GMA algorithm avoids this problem. In a network of compliant sources using such a system, nodes do not need to keep track of allocations as each allocation is valid independently of whether or not any other allocations are used. Further, GMA guarantees that no over-allocation of bandwidth—and therefore congestion—occurs. Thus, strong delivery guarantees can be provided to the communications in this network, without the overhead required by conditional systems. Appendix A of the full paper [10] presents overview of the *critical* applications that would benefit the most from an unconditional resource allocation system.

2 Preliminaries: Formalizing Resource Allocation

We now introduce the formalism we use throughout the paper, and characterize the path-allocation (PA) problem. Although the PA problem arises from an applied networking context (as some of the terminology also suggests), we seek to provide a formulation that is not tied to networking, such that our solution can also be applied to other areas. Therefore, we define the problem with the abstraction of *allocation* graphs.

Allocation Graphs. We augment the standard directed graph definition, comprising nodes and edges, with a set of *interfaces* at every node.[1] An interface denotes the end of one of the edges attached to a node, while a *local interface*, which is not associated with any edge, represents internal sources or sinks (these concepts are shown in Figs. 1a and 1b on page 6). In an allocation graph, a *resource*—a generic quantity of interest—is associated with edges, and is a measure of supply. The *capacity* of an edge is a fixed, positive real number that represents the maximum amount of resource it can provide;[2] it is denoted by $cap_{i,\text{IN}}^{(k)}$, for the capacity of the edge incoming to interface i of node k, and $cap_{i,\text{OUT}}^{(k)}$ for the outgoing edge. Further, we assume that an *allocation matri $M^{(k)}$* is given for each node k. Allocation matrices are illustrated in Figs. 1b and 1c. An entry $M_{i,j}^{(k)}$ in the allocation matri, called *pair allocation*, denotes the maximum amount of resource that can be allocated in total to all the paths incoming at interface i and outgoing at interface j. Allocation matrices are non-negative and not necessarily symmetric. We call the maximum amount of resource that can be allocated from an interface i to every other interface the *divergent*, and the maximum amount of resource that can be allocated from every other interface towards an interface j the *convergent*. They are calculated as the sum of rows or columns of $M^{(k)}$, respectively:

$$DIV_i^{(k)} = \sum_j M_{i,j}^{(k)}, \qquad CON_j^{(k)} = \sum_i M_{i,j}^{(k)}. \tag{1}$$

The matrix $M^{(k)}$ must be defined to fulfill $\forall i.\ DIV_i^{(k)} \leq cap_{i,\text{IN}}^{(k)}, CON_i^{(k)} \leq cap_{i,\text{OUT}}^{(k)}$, that is, neither $DIV_i^{(k)}$ nor $CON_i^{(k)}$ respectively exceed the capacity of the incoming and outgoing edges, connected to interface i of node k.

Intuitively, an *interface pair* (i, j) is the logical connection between two interfaces of a node, and thus a pair allocation expresses the maximum amount of resource the node is willing to provide from one neighbor to the next. Allocation

---

[1] A node can be thought of as, e.g., an autonomous system in the Internet, or any other entity part of a distributed system that acts independently from other entities.

[2] We use dimensionless values for the resource; in practice, these could correspond to, e.g., bandwidth (in Gbps)) or computations per second.

matrices can therefore be seen as a way for nodes to encode policies on the level of service they want to grant to each pair of neighbors.

In this model, we represent a path of ℓ nodes $N^1, \ldots, N^\ell$ as a list of nodes and interface pairs $\pi = [(N^1, i^1, j^1), (N^2, i^2, j^2), \ldots, (N^\ell, i^\ell, j^\ell)]$.[3] To simplify the presentation, we will omit the nodes from the list when they are implicitly clear; we will also use the abbreviation $M_{i,j}^{(k)} \equiv M_{i^k,j^k}^{(N^k)}$. We say that a path is *terminated*, if the first interface of the first pair and the second interface of the last pair are local interfaces. Otherwise the path is called *preliminary*. A path is considered *simple* or *loop-free*, if it contains each node at most once. Furthermore, we use π^k to denote the *preliminary prefix-path of length k* of some terminated path π of length ℓ ($\pi^k = [(i^1, j^1), (i^2, j^2), \ldots, (i^k, j^k)]$ for $1 \leq k < \ell$). Finally, we call a path *valid*, if $M_{i,j}^{(1)}, \ldots, M_{i,j}^{(\ell)} > 0$, otherwise it is *invalid*.

The PA Problem. We are interested in the problem of allocating the resource on an allocation graph to paths. A *path allocation* is created when a certain amount of resource is allocated for that path, exclusively reserving this amount on every edge and interface pair of the path and thus making it unavailable for any other path. If the sum of the path allocations traversing an edge exceeds the capacity of the edge, we say that the edge is *over-allocated*. Similarly, an interface pair (i^k, j^k) is over-allocated if this sum is larger than its corresponding pair allocation $M_{i,j}^{(k)}$.

> Given an allocation graph and information on the allocation matrices, the PA problem is to calculate a path allocation for any path π in this graph with the following constraint:
>
> **C1 No-over-allocation:** For all allocation graphs, even if there is an allocation on every possible valid path in the graph, no edge and no interface pair is ever over-allocated.[4]

Solving the PA problem then requires finding an algorithm $\mathcal{A}$ that can compute such path allocation. We intentionally left underspecified the precise input that such an algorithm receives, as it depends on whether the algorithm is centralized or distributed. If centralized, $\mathcal{A}$'s input is the whole network topology, as well as the allocation matrices of all the nodes. Thus, the centralized PA problem can be viewed as a variant of the multicommodity flow problem [9], with the additional constraint that pair allocations have to be respected.

In the distributed version of the PA problem (PA^{dist}), the algorithm has to run consistently on each node, with partial information about the allocation graph. Since nodes on a path are assumed to be able to exchange information, we restrict this information by requiring $\mathcal{A}$'s input to contain only information about the path for which the path allocation is computed. This is captured by the following definition:

---

[3] This definition implicitly includes edges. Also, we assume that the interfaces match, i.e., $j^{(k-1)}$ and $i^{(k)}$ are interfaces at opposite ends of the same directed edge.

[4] Paths with loops, and of arbitrary length, are also included in this definition.

The PA^{dist} problem is to solve the PA problem with this additional restriction:

C2 Locality: The path allocation is a function of the on-path allocation matrices $M^{(1)}, \ldots, M^{(\ell)}$ only.

Among the set of algorithms that fit this definition, we are naturally interested in the ones that lead to higher path allocations. Since a precise optimality condition on the algorithm depends on the practical application for which it is used, we generally postulate that meaningful algorithms provide path allocations that cannot be strictly increased. This is captured by Pareto optimality:

Opt Optimality: Consider the class of all algorithms fulfilling the requirement of either PA or PA^{dist}. Algorithm $\mathcal{A}$ from this class is (Pareto) optimal if there is no other algorithm $\mathcal{B}$ from the same class that can provide at least the same path allocation for every path of every allocation graph, and a strictly better allocation for at least one path. Formally, if there exists a graph with a path π for which $\mathcal{B}(\pi) = \mathcal{A}(\pi) + \delta$ with $\delta > 0$, then there exists at least one other path π', possibly in a different graph, where $\mathcal{B}(\pi') = \mathcal{A}(\pi') - \delta'$ with $\delta' > 0$.[5]

In addition, we specify three supplementary properties that make an algorithm more amenable to practical settings. First, the algorithm should provide non-zero allocations for all valid paths, second, we require the algorithm to be efficient in the length of the path and the size of the on-path allocation matrices, and lastly, we enforce stricter requirements on the policy of individual nodes with the *monotonicity* property: if a node increases one of its pair allocations, we expect all path allocation crossing the interface pair to at least not decrease. Increasing one pair allocation also increases the corresponding divergent and convergent, while all other pair allocations that contribute to this convergent or divergent remain the same. Therefore the relative contribution of the increased pair allocation becomes higher, while the relative contribution of the other pair allocations decreases. This way, a node's allocation matrix can also be understood as a policy that defines the relative importance of its neighbors. Since a path containing loops might traverse the same node both through a pair allocation with increased importance and through one with decreased importance, monotonicity is only meaningful in the context of simple paths.[6]

S1 Usability: For every valid path π, the resulting allocation is positive ($\mathcal{A}\pi > 0$).

S2 Efficiency: Algorithm $\mathcal{A}$ should have at most polynomial complexity as a function of input size. Specifically, for PA^{dist} this means polynomial in the

---

[5] The loose constraint that π' is possibly in a different graph comes from the fact that because of the locality property in the PA^{dist} problem, the algorithm has no way to differentiate two graphs having a path with the same nodes and allocation matrices.

[6] For $i_1^k \neq i_2^k$, increasing $M_{i_1,j}^{(k)}$ decreases the relative contribution of $M_{i_2,j}^{(k)}$ (Eq. (1)).

total size of the allocation matrices of on-path nodes. This is a relatively loose requirement, we will show a linear algorithm in the following.

S3 Monotonicity: If the pair allocation of some node k on a simple path π is increased and all other allocations remain unchanged, the resulting allocation must not decrease: $M_{i,j}^{(k)} \leq \widetilde{M}_{i,j}^{(k)} \implies \mathcal{A}\pi \leq \widetilde{\mathcal{A}}(\pi)$.

The challenge of devising an optimal PA^{dist} algorithm is clear: $\mathcal{A}$ can only rely on a *myopic* view of the path, without any further knowledge about the larger graph. However, it has to achieve the *global* constraints of Pareto-optimality and no-over-allocation, which consider the result of performing allocations on all valid paths. In the remainder of the paper, we present the global myopic allocation (GMA) algorithm as a solution to the PA^{dist} problem. GMA fulfills requirements C1 and C2, and is optimal according to Opt, which we formally prove in Sect. 4. Furthermore, we prove in Appendix E of the full paper [10] that GMA also satisfies all the supplementary requirements (S1–S3). An additional property, *extensibility*, is presented and proven in Appendix F of the full paper [10].

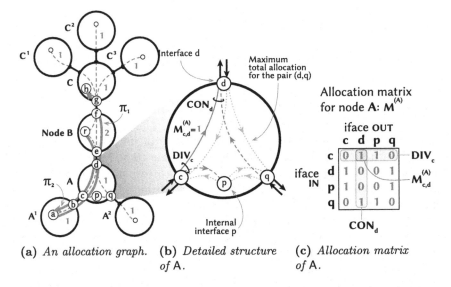

(a) *An allocation graph.*   (b) *Detailed structure of* A.   (c) *Allocation matrix of* A.

Fig. 1. Example of an allocation graph. Pair allocations are represented in Fig. 1a by dashed lines—their size shown by the number in the respective node. If two interfaces are not connected by dashed lines, their pair allocation is zero. All pair allocations are bidirectional, as shown in Fig. 1b. For clarity, we use globally unique interface identifiers. Fig. 1a also shows paths π_1 and π_2, used in the examples (π_3 is the reverse of π_2).

3   Introducing the GMA Algorithm

We present the GMA algorithm in three steps: starting from a simple first-cut approach, at each step we present a refinement of the previous algorithm. This section is meant to provide a profound yet intuitive understanding of the GMA algorithm and its properties—accompanied by the example in Fig. 1—leading to the final formulation of GMA in Eq. (10).

3.1   Step 1: Towards No-Over-Allocation

As a first attempt to achieve no-over-allocation, we take the pair allocation of the first node on a path, and multiply it by the ratio of the pair allocation and the divergent for each of the traversed interface pairs. With this approach, each node receives a *preliminary allocation* from the previous node, fairly splits it among all interfaces according to the pair allocations, and passes it on to the next node. This leads to the following formula:

$$\mathcal{A}_1\pi = M_{i,j}^{(1)} \cdot \prod_{k=2}^{\ell} \frac{M_{i,j}^{(k)}}{DIV_i^{(k)}}. \tag{2}$$

Example   *Consider the path* $\pi_1 = [(\mathsf{A^1}, \mathsf{a}, \mathsf{b}), (\mathsf{A}, \mathsf{c}, \mathsf{d}), (\mathsf{B}, \mathsf{e}, \mathsf{f}), (\mathsf{C}, \mathsf{g}, \mathsf{h})]$ *in Fig. 1. Then, Eq. (2) results in an allocation* $\mathcal{A}_1(\pi_1) = 1 \cdot \frac{1}{2} \cdot \frac{2}{4} \cdot \frac{1}{4} = \frac{1}{16}$.

To understand the idea behind this formula we consider some node k with interface i, connected through this interface to a neighboring node n. If node n can guarantee that the sum the preliminary allocations of all preliminary paths going towards node k is at most $DIV_i^{(k)}$, then $\mathcal{A}_1$ ensures that for each of node k's interfaces j, the sum of all preliminary allocations of all preliminary paths going through (i, j) is at most $M_{i,j}^{(k)}$. If all neighbors can provide this guarantee, no pair allocation of node k will be over-allocated, which implies that also none of its convergents will be over-allocated. If node k's convergents are smaller or equal to the corresponding divergents of its neighbors, also node k can give this guarantee to all of its neighbors. Therefore $\mathcal{A}_1$ will never cause over-allocation, if *every node's convergents are smaller or equal to the corresponding divergents of its neighbors*—which is an assumption we want to get rid of.

Example   *The graph in Fig. 1a ensures that the divergent of a node is always larger than the convergent of the previous node when going* upwards. *Going* downwards, *this is not the case. Indeed, already two paths* $\pi_2 = [(\mathsf{B}, \mathsf{r}, \mathsf{e}), (\mathsf{A}, \mathsf{d}, \mathsf{c}), (\mathsf{A^1}, \mathsf{b}, \mathsf{a})]$ *with* $\mathcal{A}_1(\pi_2) = 2 \cdot \frac{1}{2} \cdot \frac{1}{1} = 1$ *and* $\pi_3 = [(\mathsf{C}, \mathsf{h}, \mathsf{g}), (\mathsf{B}, \mathsf{f}, \mathsf{e}), (\mathsf{A}, \mathsf{d}, \mathsf{c}), (\mathsf{A^1}, \mathsf{b}, \mathsf{a})]$ *(reverse of π_1) with* $\mathcal{A}_1(\pi_3) = 1 \cdot \frac{2}{4} \cdot \frac{1}{2} \cdot \frac{1}{1} = \frac{1}{4}$ *together cause an over-allocation of interface pairs* (d, c) *and* (b, a).

3.2   Step 2: A General Solution for No-Over-Allocation

As over-allocation with $\mathcal{A}_1$ can only occur when some node's convergent is larger than the corresponding divergent of its neighbor, we can normalize each preliminary allocation to compensate this disparity. More concretely, if $CON_i^{(k-1)} > DIV_j^{(k)}$ for an on-path node k, the preliminary allocation from node $k - 1$ is multiplied with:

$$\frac{DIV_j^{(k)}}{CON_i^{(k-1)}} \cdot \frac{M_{i,j}^{(k)}}{DIV_j^{(k)}} = \frac{M_{i,j}^{(k)}}{CON_i^{(k-1)}}. \tag{3}$$

Adapting Eq. (2) to this modification gives rise to the following formula:

$$\mathcal{A}_2\pi = M_{i,j}^{(1)} \cdot \prod_{k=2}^{\ell} \frac{M_{i,j}^{(k)}}{\max\{CON_j^{(k-1)}, DIV_i^{(k)}\}}. \tag{4}$$

Example   We find $\mathcal{A}_2(\pi_3) = 1 \cdot \frac{2}{4} \cdot \frac{1}{4} \cdot \frac{1}{2} = \frac{1}{16} = \mathcal{A}_2(\pi_1); \mathcal{A}_2(\pi_2) = 2 \cdot \frac{1}{4} \cdot \frac{1}{2} = \frac{1}{4}$.

This algorithm will never cause over-allocation, which follows directly from our proof in Sect. 4.1. Unfortunately, $\mathcal{A}_2$ is neither monotonic nor Pareto optimal. We can see why this is the case by taking a closer look at the contribution of some node k to the calculated allocations, which consists of the values $(DIV_i^{(k)}, M_{i,j}^{(k)}, CON_j^{(k)})$. In Eq. (4), the only subterm depending on those values is

$$\frac{M_{i,j}^{(k)}}{\max\{CON_j^{(k-1)}, DIV_i^{(k)}\} \cdot \max\{CON_j^{(k)}, DIV_i^{(k+1)}\}}. \tag{5}$$

Increasing $M_{i,j}^{(k)}$ by $\delta > 0$, and thus, implicitly, also $DIV_i^{(k)}$ and $CON_j^{(k)}$ by δ, can potentially contribute twice to the denominator and only once to the nominator of Eq. (5), thereby reducing all the allocations going through the interface (i, j).

Example   Consider increasing the pair allocation (c, d) to $\widetilde{M}_{\mathsf{c},\mathsf{d}}^{(A)} = 9$, leaving everything else unchanged. Then, $\tilde{\mathcal{A}}_2(\pi_2) = 2 \cdot \frac{9}{10} \cdot \frac{1}{10} = \frac{18}{100} < \frac{1}{4} = \mathcal{A}_2(\pi_2)$.

In general, $\mathcal{A}_2$ provides suboptimal allocations when there is a node k with "*superfluous* allocations", i.e., where $DIV_i^{(k)} > CON_j^{(k-1)}$ and $CON_j^{(k)} > DIV_i^{(k+1)}$. We explain how to strictly improve this and present GMA in the next section.

3.3   Step 3: Monotonic and Pareto-Optimal Allocations

The main idea to resolve the violation of monotonicity and optimality is to implicitly *scale down* the three-tuple of a node k with superfluous allocations to $(s \cdot DIV_i^{(k)}, s \cdot M_{i,j}^{(k)}, s \cdot CON_j^{(k)})$ for $0 < s < 1$, such that either $s \cdot DIV_i^{(k)} \leq CON_j^{(k-1)}$ or $s \cdot CON_j^{(k)} \leq DIV_i^{(k+1)}$. The intuition is that a third algorithm, based on $\mathcal{A}_2$ but with scaled-down three-tuples, does not cause over-allocation while observing monotonicity. We will prove later in Sect. 4 that this statement holds.

For some arbitrary path, we now want to find a way to optimally scale down the three-tuple $(DIV_i^{(k)}, M_{i,j}^{(k)}, CON_j^{(k)})$ of each node k. The result is a new algorithm that takes the original inputs, scales them down implicitly, and finally uses $\mathcal{A}_2$ to compute the allocation.

As we prove in Appendix B of the full paper [10], down-scaling improves the resulting path allocation only for the case—as considered above—in which superfluous allocations are present ($DIV_i^{(k)} > CON_j^{(k-1)}$ and $CON_j^{(k)} > DIV_i^{(k+1)}$).[7] It is therefore sufficient to scale down the divergent of node k to the convergent of node $k-1$, any further scaling will not improve the allocation. This observation results in the following iterative algorithm.

On a path π with ℓ nodes, we start from node 1. As there is no previous node, scaling is not possible, and the scaling factor is $f^{(1)} = 1$. At the second node, the convergent of the first node can either be smaller than the divergent of the second node, or larger. In the first case, we scale down the three-tuple of the second node by $CON_j^{(1)}/DIV_i^{(2)}$. In the second, no scaling down is possible. In both cases we thus scale down the three-tuples of node 2 by $f^{(2)} = \min\{1, CON_j^{(1)}/DIV_i^{(2)}\}$, and so the first factor of the product in Eq. (4) becomes

$$\frac{M_{i,j}^{(2)} \cdot f^{(2)}}{\max\{CON_j^{(1)}, DIV_i^{(2)} \cdot f^{(2)}\}} = \frac{M_{i,j}^{(2)} \cdot f^{(2)}}{CON_j^{(1)}}. \tag{6}$$

At the third node this case distinction is repeated. However, recall that the convergent of the second node might have been scaled down, so we have to use the value $(f^{(2)} \cdot CON_j^{(2)})$ instead of $CON_j^{(2)}$ in the computation. Therefore, taking $f^{(3)} = \min\{1, (CON_j^{(2)} \cdot f^{(2)})/DIV_i^{(3)}\}$, we obtain the third factor of the product in Eq. (4):

$$\frac{M_{i,j}^{(3)} \cdot f^{(3)}}{\max\{CON_j^{(2)} \cdot f^{(2)}, DIV_i^{(3)} \cdot f^{(3)}\}} = \frac{M_{i,j}^{(3)} \cdot f^{(3)}}{CON_j^{(2)} \cdot f^{(2)}}. \tag{7}$$

Continuing this expansion, we can define the scaling factors f recursively for each node as

$$f^{(1)} = 1; \qquad f^{(k)} = \min\left\{1, \frac{CON_j^{(k-1)} \cdot f^{(k-1)}}{DIV_i^{(k)}}\right\}. \tag{8}$$

Overall, we modify Eq. (4) in the following way:

$$\mathcal{G}(\pi) = M_{i,j}^{(1)} \cdot \prod_{k=2}^{\ell} \frac{M_{i,j}^{(k)} \cdot f^{(k)}}{CON_j^{(k-1)} \cdot f^{(k-1)}} = f(\ell) \cdot \frac{\prod_{k=1}^{\ell} M_{i,j}^{(k)}}{\prod_{k=2}^{\ell} CON_j^{(k-1)}}, \tag{9}$$

---

[7] $CON_i^{(k-1)}$ and $DIV_i^{(k+1)}$ might have already been scaled down.

which is equivalent to computing $\mathcal{A}_2$ on the scaled-down input three-tuples. The last step follows from rearranging indices and realizing that $f^{(k)}$ can be factored out recursively, apart from the first ($f^{(1)} = 1$) and the last one. Instead of this recursive formulation, Eq. (9) can also be written as a direct formula (the proof can be found in Appendix C of the full paper [10]).

The *global myopic allocation (GMA) algorithm*:

$$\mathcal{G}(\pi) = \min_x \left(\prod_{k=1}^{x-1} \frac{M_{i,j}^{(k)}}{CON_j^{(k)}} \cdot M_{i,j}^{(x)} \cdot \prod_{k=x+1}^{\ell} \frac{M_{i,j}^{(k)}}{DIV_i^{(k)}} \right) \tag{10}$$

Example   *Consider again our example of Fig. 1a with* $\widetilde{M}_{c,d}^{(A)} = 9$. *In this case we have* $DIV_d^{(A)} = 10 > CON_e^{(B)} = 4$ *and* $CON_c^{(A)} = 10 > DIV_b^{(A^1)} = 1$. *The three-tuple of* A *can thus be scaled down by a factor of* $\frac{4}{10}$. *Using Eq.* *(10) for the path* π_2, *we find that the argument of the minimum is* A^1 *and* $\mathcal{G}(\pi_2) = \frac{2}{4} \cdot \frac{9}{10} \cdot 1 = \frac{9}{20} > \frac{18}{100} = \tilde{\mathcal{A}}_2(\pi_2)$.

4   Proofs of GMA's Properties

In this section, we prove that GMA's computation described in Eq. (10) satisfies the properties defined in Sect. 2. We prove the core property C1 in Sect. 4.1 and Opt in Sect. 4.2. Locality (C2) follows directly from Eq. (10), as the computation only involves allocation-matrix entries of the nodes on the path. The supplementary properties S1–S3 are proven in Appendix E of the full paper [10].

4.1   Proof of No-Over-Allocation (C1)

In this subsection we prove that there is no resource overuse of any of the pair allocation $M_{i,j}^{(k)}$, which, by the fact that convergent and divergent of an interface must be smaller than the capacity of the edge connected to it, implies that there is also no overuse on any edge of the graph. In the context of this proof, the + operator is not only used for addition, but also for list concatenation. We denote the set of non-local interfaces of some node k as $I_{ext}^{(k)}$. We will use the notation $M_{i,j}^{(k)}(\pi)$ to state more precisely which path the variable refers to. We want to prove that for every node k and all of its interface pairs, the corresponding pair allocation is greater than or equal to the sum of all resource allocations of all paths going through that interface pair. For this we distinguish the following cases an interface pair can be assigned to, and prove each case individually:

Case 1: The interface pair starts from a local interface: $(\perp, j)$
Case 2: The interface pair ends in a local interface: $(i, \perp)$
Case 3: The interface pair starts and ends in non-local interfaces: (i, j)

Case 1: We will prove a stronger statement, captured by the following lemma:

Lemma 1. *For an arbitrary node A and an arbitrary non-local interface j^A, let S_t^x be the set of* terminated *paths of length* at most x *that start in $(\perp, j^A)$, and S_p^x the set of* preliminary *paths of length* exactly x *that start in $(\perp, j^A)$. Then*

$$\forall x \geq 1: \sum_{\pi \in S_p^x} \mathcal{G}(\pi) + \sum_{\pi \in S_t^x} \mathcal{G}(\pi) \leq M_{\perp,j}^{(A)}. \tag{11}$$

We emphasize that, by the definition in Eq. (10), GMA not only allows to calculate allocations on terminated, but also on preliminary paths. The lemma implies our original statement, i.e., $\forall x \geq 1: \sum_{\pi \in S_t^x} \mathcal{G}(\pi) \leq M_{\perp,j}^{(A)}$.

Proof. We prove Lemma 1 by induction over x for arbitrary A and j^A.

Base Case ($x = 1$): We have $S_p^1 = \{\ [(\perp, j^A)]\ \}$ and $S_t^1 = \{\}$, which directly implies $\sum_{\pi \in S_p^1} \mathcal{G}(\pi) + \sum_{\pi \in S_t^1} \mathcal{G}(\pi) = M_{\perp,j}^{(A)} \leq M_{\perp,j}^{(A)}$.

Inductive Step

Induction Hypothesis: For a particular x: $\sum_{\pi \in S_p^x} \mathcal{G}(\pi) + \sum_{\pi \in S_t^x} \mathcal{G}(\pi) \leq M_{\perp,j}^{(A)}$.

To Show: $\sum_{\pi \in S_p^{x+1}} \mathcal{G}(\pi) + \sum_{\pi \in S_t^{x+1}} \mathcal{G}(\pi) \leq M_{\perp,j}^{(A)}$.

Definitions: For some preliminary path π of length ℓ, let node Z be the node that is connected to j^ℓ and let the corresponding interface of Z be i^Z. We define the *local extension* of a path π as $E_{\mathrm{loc}}(\pi) := \{\ \pi + [(i^Z, \perp)]\ \}$, the *non-local extension* of a path π as $E_{\mathrm{ext}}(\pi) := \cup_{j^Z \in I_{\mathrm{ext}}^{(Z)}} \{\ \pi + [(i^Z, j^Z)]\ \}$ and their union as $E(\pi) := E_{\mathrm{loc}}(\pi) \cup E_{\mathrm{ext}}(\pi)$.

Proof

$$\sum_{\pi \in S_p^{x+1}} \mathcal{G}(\pi) + \sum_{\pi \in S_t^{x+1}} \mathcal{G}(\pi) = \left(\sum_{\pi \in S_p^x} \sum_{\phi \in E_{\mathrm{ext}}(\pi)} \mathcal{G}(\phi) \right) + \left(\sum_{\pi \in S_t^x} \mathcal{G}(\pi) + \sum_{\pi \in S_p^x} \sum_{\phi \in E_{\mathrm{loc}}(\pi)} \mathcal{G}(\phi) \right) \tag{12a}$$

$$= \sum_{\pi \in S_p^x} \sum_{\phi \in E(\pi)} \mathcal{G}(\phi) + \sum_{\pi \in S_t^x} \mathcal{G}(\pi) \tag{12b}$$

$$= \sum_{\pi \in S_p^x} \sum_{\phi \in E(\pi)} \min\left(\mathcal{G}(\pi) \cdot \frac{M_{i,j}^{(Z)}}{DIV_i^{(Z)}}, \prod_{k=1}^{\ell} \frac{M_{i,j}^{(k)}}{CON_j^{(k)}} \cdot M_{i,j}^{(Z)} \right) + \sum_{\pi \in S_t^x} \mathcal{G}(\pi) \tag{12c}$$

$$\leq \sum_{\pi \in S_p^x} \sum_{\phi \in E(\pi)} \frac{M_{i,j}^{(Z)}}{DIV_i^{(Z)}} \cdot \mathcal{G}(\pi) + \sum_{\pi \in S_t^x} \mathcal{G}(\pi) = \sum_{\pi \in S_p^x} \mathcal{G}(\pi) + \sum_{\pi \in S_t^x} \mathcal{G}(\pi) \leq M_{\perp,j}^{(A)} \quad (12d)$$

In the step from Eq. (12b) to Eq. (12c), we used the fact that when extending the path, the argument of the minimum of Eq. (10) either stays the same, or the newly added node now minimizes the formula, which follows directly from Eq. (9). The transition in Eq. (12d) follows from $\sum_{\phi \in E(\pi)} M_{i,j}^{(Z)} = DIV_i^{(Z)}$.

Case 2: The proof is exactly the same as for case 1, except that we extend the path in the backward instead of the forward direction. The only change required is the adaptation of the definitions of local and non-local extensions of a path and we use $\sum_{\phi \in E(\pi)} M_{i,j}^{(Z)} = CON_j^{(Z)}$.

Case 3: Choose an arbitrary node A. Then choose arbitrary non-local interfaces $i^A, j^A \in I_{\text{ext}}^{(A)}$ of node A. Using exactly the same procedure as for the proof of case 2, but using (i^A, j^A) as the interface pair where the paths "end" (it does not terminate in a local interface), we can show that the sum of all resource allocations for all paths *ending* in (i^A, j^A) is always smaller or equal to $M_{i,j}^{(A)}$. We then choose an arbitrary path π that ends in (i^A, j^A). Using the same procedure as for the proof of case 1, but using (i^A, j^A) as the interface pair where the paths "begin" (it does not start in a local interface) and setting $\hat{M}_{i,j}^{(A)} := \mathcal{G}(\pi)$, we can show that the sum of the resource allocations of all the (terminated) paths that extend π never exceeds $\mathcal{G}(\pi)$. It follows that the sum of the resource allocations of all the paths going through (i^A, j^A) never exceeds $M_{i,j}^{(A)}$. $\qquad\square$

4.2 Proof of Optimality (Opt)

In this section we show that GMA is optimal according to Opt, which means that there is no better local (C2) algorithm that does not over-allocate any edge or interface pair (C1). As every invocation of a local algorithm is only based on the nodes of one path, and is oblivious of all the other nodes of the graph, in order to prevent overuse the algorithm has to consider all possible graphs containing this path. This insight is central for the proof of optimality and is formalized in the following lemma:

Lemma 2. *For every allocation graph and every one of its paths π, there exists another allocation graph that contains a path with the same sequence of allocation matrices, where the pair allocation $M_{i,j}^{(x)}$ of some on-path node x is fully utilized (there is no available resource left) if there is a GMA allocation on every path containing (x, i^x, j^x) in this new graph.*

Proof. Let π be an arbitrary path of an arbitrary allocation graph, and let x be the index for which Eq. (10) is minimized. We construct a new allocation graph around π as follows:

- Remove all the nodes that are not part of π.
- Keep the on-path nodes, their interfaces, and their allocation matrices as they are.
- For every node, create identical copies of the node for each of its occurrences on the path (multiple copies, in case the path contains loops) and only keep the edges to the previous and subsequent node on the path.
- For all these on-path nodes, attach new nodes to the non-local interfaces that are not already part of π. Those new nodes only have one local and one non-local interface (the interface through which they are attached to the on-path node).
- For every node $k \in \{1, \ldots, x-1\}$ and each of its interfaces $\tilde{i}$ to which a new node was attached, the pair allocation (from its local to its non-local interface) of the new node is set to $DIV_{\tilde{i}}^{(k)}$. This implies that also the divergent (at the local interface) and the convergent (at the non-local interface) of the new node are equal to $DIV_{\tilde{i}}^{(k)}$.
- For x, the newly attached nodes can have arbitrary allocation-matrix entries.
- For every node $k \in \{x+1, \ldots, \ell\}$ and each of its interfaces $\tilde{j}$ to which a new node was attached, the pair allocation (from its non-local to its local interface) of the new node is set to $CON_{\tilde{j}}^{(k)}$. This implies that also the divergent (at the non-local interface) and the convergent (at the local interface) of the new node are equal to $CON_{\tilde{j}}^{(k)}$.

Given that there is a GMA allocation on every possible path (in our new graph) going through (i^x, j^x), we want to show that $M_{i,j}^{(x)}$ is fully utilized. We characterize all possible paths for three cases: If $1 < x < \ell$ (case 1), a path starts at a local interface of some node $k \leq x-1$ or at the local interface of some of its attached nodes, and ends at a local interface of some node $m \geq x+1$ or at the local interface of some of its attached nodes. If $x = 1$ (case 2), every path starts at the local interface of x, and ends at a local interface of some node $k \geq 2$ or at the local interface of some of its attached nodes. If $x = \ell$ (case 3), every path starts at a local interface of some node $k \leq \ell-1$ or at the local interface of some of its attached nodes, and ends at the local interface of node ℓ.

Case 1: We use the following notation in order to simplify our proof:

$$au^{(u)} = \frac{M_{i,j}^{(u)}}{CON_j^{(u)}}, \quad b^{(u)} = \frac{M_{i,j}^{(u)}}{DIV_i^{(u)}} \tag{13}$$

Let R_u be the sum of all allocations of all the nodes $k \in \{1, \ldots, x-1\}$ starting either at a local interface or at the local interface of some of its attached nodes, and ending either at a local interface of node u or at the local interface of some of its attached nodes, divided by $M_{i,j}^{(x)}$. Thus, we need to prove

$$M_{i,j}^{(x)} \cdot \sum_{u=x+1}^{\ell} R_u = M_{i,j}^{(x)} \quad \Leftrightarrow \quad \sum_{u=x+1}^{\ell} R_u = 1. \tag{14}$$

We formulate two lemmas, which are proven in Appendix D of the full paper [10]:

Lemma 3. *For $a_1, \ldots, a_x > 0$: $\prod_{i=1}^{x} a_i + \sum_{k=1}^{x} \left((1 - a_k) \cdot \prod_{i=k+1}^{x} a_i \right) = 1$.*

Lemma 4. $R_\ell = \prod_{k=x+1}^{\ell-1} b^{(k)}$ *and* $R_u = \left(\prod_{k=x+1}^{u-1} b^{(k)} \right) \cdot (1 - b^{(u)})$ *(for $x + 1 \leq u \leq \ell - 1$).*

These lemmas immediately imply our proof goal:

$$\sum_{u=x+1}^{\ell} R_u = \sum_{u=x+1}^{\ell-1} R_u + R_\ell = \sum_{u=x+1}^{\ell-1} \prod_{k=x+1}^{u-1} b^{(k)} \cdot (1 - b^{(u)}) + \prod_{k=x+1}^{\ell-1} b^{(k)} = 1. \qquad (15)$$

Case 2+3: The proofs follow a simplified structure of the proof of case 1. □

Theorem 1. *GMA is Pareto optimal among all algorithms in the sense of Opt.*

Proof. This follows directly from Lemma 2: for a given path (nodes with their associated allocation matrices) there always exists a graph containing that path, where increasing the allocation calculated by GMA will cause overuse, which can only be prevented by decreasing allocations on other paths. □

5 GMA Provides Meaningful Allocations

A potential limitation of GMA is the size of the allocations it provides. We proved that GMA's path allocations are small enough that, even if all the paths have an allocation, no over-allocation occurs. In this section we show that GMA's path allocations are still large enough to satisfy the requirements of the critical applications that motivate this work (details in Appendix A of the full paper [10]). We do this by simulating GMA on random graphs, thereby exploring the trade-offs between graph topology and the resulting GMA allocation sizes.

5.1 Simulation Setup

Graph Topology. We use the well-known Barabási–Albert random graph model to generate allocation graphs [2]. This algorithm is designed to produce scale-free random graphs, which are found to well approximate real-life technological networks [6].

At the topological level, the size of a GMA allocation for some path depends on (i) the degree of the nodes on the path, as it determines the size of the allocation matrix, (ii) the length of the path, since Eq. (10) contains an iterative product on each node on the path, and (iii) the capacity of each on-path edge (discussed in the next paragraph). We aggregate the first two metrics at the graph level by considering the average node degree and the diameter of the graph, i.e., the length of the longest path.[8] Therefore, we generate 275 random graphs for our simulations, with 8 to 2048 nodes, varying average degree and diameter. Additional details on graph generation can be found in Appendix G of the full paper [10].

Resources and Allocation Matrices. In the simulations, we model the varying bandwidth of real-world network links by assigning different capacities to the edges of graphs. To assign capacity to edges based on a *degree–gravity* model: the capacity of a (directed) edge is selected proportionally to the product of the degrees of its adjacent nodes [15]. We discretize these values to 10 different levels from 40 to 400. This choice is motivated by real networks, where more connected nodes also tend to have higher forwarding capabilities.

Based on these edge capacities, we then create the allocation matrices. Although each node might have different policies, simulating those policies for the nodes introduces many additional degrees of complexity, beyond the scope of this evaluation. Therefore, we assume a simple *proportional sharing* policy to construct an allocation matrices, which we obtain by performing the following three steps for each node k and all its interfaces i and j: (i) $M_{i,j}^{(k)} \leftarrow cap_i^{(k)}$, while for the local interface $\perp$, $M_{\perp,j}^{(k)}, M_{i,\perp}^{(k)} \leftarrow \max_i\{cap_i^{(k)}\}$; (ii) $M_{i,j}^{(k)} \leftarrow M_{i,j}^{(k)} \cdot cap_j^{(k)}/CON_j^{(k)}$; (iii) if $DIV_i^{(k)} > cap_j^{(k)}$, then $M_{i,j}^{(k)} \leftarrow M_{i,j}^{(k)} \cdot cap_i^{(k)}/DIV_i^{(k)}$.

Path Selection. In this simulation, the goal is to create path allocations between every pair of nodes. Motivated again by networking practice, we consider allocations made on k-shortest paths, with $k \in \{1, 2, 3\}$. For $k = 1$, we create allocations on the single-shortest path for every pair of nodes. However, GMA can compute an allocation for *any* path in the graph. Therefore, if two nodes are able to use multiple paths simultaneously, the total allocation for the pair is the aggregate of the allocations on the individual paths. We then create allocations on the 2- and 3-shortest paths for every pair of nodes, and evaluate the advantage that multipath communication can provide.

Metrics: α-cover. Given a source node, the size of the GMA allocations to different destination nodes can vary greatly, and computing average statistics does not reflect the binary nature of critical application requirements: either the allocation exceeds the minimum usability threshold, or the allocation is not useful (see Appendix A of the full paper [10] for details).

Therefore, we introduce a new metric to aggregate this information and compare the effectiveness of GMA across different topologies, called α-cover. Given a source node in a graph and a path selection strategy, the node's α-cover is the fraction of destination nodes to which the sum of the path allocations computed over the available paths is more than α. Therefore, α-cover captures the size of the sub-graph with which the source node can communicate using an

---

[8] These two factors are closely related with each other and to the number of nodes in the graph: keeping the number of nodes fixed, a graph with higher average node degree will inevitably have smaller diameter.

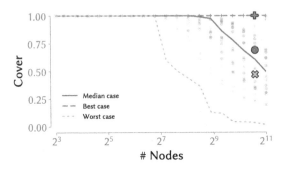

Fig. 2. *Minimum, maximum, and median single-path* 10^{-4}*-cover.* The high-lighted markers show the max ✚, median ●, and min ✖ cover for one specific graph (which is further analyzed in Figs. 5 and 6 in Appendix G).

adequately-sized GMA allocation. For example, a node with a 10^{-4}-cover of 0.7 can reach 70 % of the nodes in the graphs with an allocation of at least 10^{-4}. Naturally, higher values of α-cover are better. We define the median α-cover of a graph as the median of the α-covers of its nodes (and similarly for minimum and maximum). While different applications will require different values of α, we use a 10^{-4}-cover in all simulations. Again, this is motivated by practical considerations: if we set 1 unit of resource = 1 Gbps, 10^{-4} units correspond to 100 kbps. The applications that motivate this work, such as blockchains and inter-bank transaction clearing, can comfortably operate within this boundary.

5.2   Results

For each of the generated graphs, Fig. 2 relates its minimum, maximum, and median 10^{-4}-cover to the number of nodes, where we used the single shortest path selection scheme. We see that all graphs have a median cover in the upper 50 % range, while the minimum cover decreases to just a few percent for graphs with a high number of nodes. Graphs with lower median cover are the ones that have low or high diameter, as Fig. 5 in Appendix G shows. This confirms the observation that large allocation matrices (low diameter) or long paths (high diameter) decrease the size of allocations. Further, in all graphs, we find at least one node with cover greater than 89 %, and observe that the cover increases with the degree of the nodes: central nodes have therefore better cover, an important property in practical applications. An example is shown in Fig. 5 in Appendix G.

Figure 3 in Appendix G of the full paper [10] shows the improvement in the median cover of the graphs when using the 2- or 3-shortest path selection schemes in place of the single shortest path selection scheme. We see high returns for using additional paths, reaching over 120 % increase over single-path cover when using three paths instead of one. Graphs with lower number of nodes benefit less from the additional paths, as many already achieve perfect cover. A higher k could further increase the cover, but this exploration is left to future work.

6   Related Work

Flow Problems and Algorithms. A class of theoretical problems that are related to our path-allocation problem are *multi-commodity flow problems*, which have been studied extensively since the 1950s [9]. The variant which is most closely related to our setting is the *maximum concurrent flow problem* [17], where fairness between different commodities is taken into account, but the ratios are set by a central controller. All variants differ from our PA^{dist} problem in that they (i) do not consider independent nodes with their own properties and (ii) require a global knowledge of the topology. They have thus been applied mostly to centrally controlled networks [8].

Resource Allocation in Networks. Bandwidth guarantees were a central concept of virtual-circuit architectures like ATM [16]. For today's IP-based Internet, bandwidth reservations have been proposed in the Integrated Services (IntServ) architecture [4], in which they are negotiated through the Resource Reservation Protocol (RSVP) [5]. However, due to its high reliance on in-network state, IntServ has never been widely adopted. Further, these systems do not specify *how much* bandwidth should be allocated to flows. The Internet overwhelmingly relies on congestion control [11,13] as a distributed mechanism for bandwidth allocation between flows, which provides no guarantees to the communication partners and has no support to implement traffic policies. There exists a wide range of traffic-engineering systems suitable to intra-domain contexts, such as MPLS [14] with OSPF-TE [12] and RSVP-TE [1] or SDN-based solutions [18]. However, in contrast to GMA, which supports autonomous nodes, all these systems require a central controller.

7   Discussion and Conclusion

In this paper, we revisit an old networking and distributed-systems problem—how to allocate resources in a network of independent nodes when no central controller is available. After introducing the formalism of allocation graphs, in which each node is associated with *local* allocations based on available resources and policies, we ask a novel question: can an algorithm compute resource allocations for all paths in an allocation graph, without causing over-allocation, and relying only on local information? This is the foundation of the PA^{dist} problem. We answer with our *global myopic allocation* (GMA) algorithm, showing how these local decisions give rise to meaningful and sustainable *global* allocations. Further, we prove that these allocations are Pareto-optimal, and therefore cannot be trivially improved.

Relevance to Networking. The allocations calculated through GMA are static and depend only on the policies of on-path nodes; in particular, they are independent of other allocations and resource demands. They thus provide strong minimal resource guarantees that are valid under all networking conditions and are particularly relevant for applications where centralized solutions based on dedicated network infrastructure are too expensive or inherently impossible. By their very nature, these guaranteed allocations are smaller than what can be achieved through dynamic resource-allocation systems. However, our simulations show that, even under conservative assumptions, GMA provides sufficient communication bandwidth to virtually all pairs of nodes in small to medium-sized networks. Thus, GMA-based allocations with strong availability guarantees could *complement* other systems with higher network utilization but weaker guarantees, such as best-effort traffic.

Future Work. The novel results on graph resource allocation presented in this paper open many new and exciting avenues for future research, both theoretical and applied. First of all, this paper did not explore the *fairness* implications of GMA allocations. The properties of monotonicity and Pareto-optimality, along with the proportional use of pair allocations in the computation, point towards a strong *neighbor-based* fairness notion. We leave the analysis of such a notion to future work. Second, we see great potential for further research on PA^{dist} algorithms. For instance, Pareto optimality does not satisfy the question of whether GMA is optimal in a global sense, i.e., whether it maximizes a function over all path allocations—their sum, for example. The discovery of globally optimal PA^{dist} algorithms could lead to interesting theoretical advancements, with profound practical implications.

Finally, in this paper we have discussed how allocations can be *computed* in a distributed setting. This is orthogonal to the development of specific protocols necessary to communicate and authenticate necessary information and enforce the allocations. Future research could focus on the development of such a protocol and investigate its interplay with other networking paradigms like best-effort traffic and congestion control.

Acknowledgments. We would like to thank Mohsen Ghaffari for the illuminating discussions; Tobias Klenze, Simon Scherrer, Stefan Schmid, and Joel Wanner for their feedback on the manuscript; and the anonymous reviewers for their insightful comments. We gratefully acknowledge financial support from ETH Zurich and from the Zurich Information Security and Privacy Center (ZISC).

References

1. Awduche, D., Berger, L., Gan, D., Li, T., Srinivasan, V., Swallow, G.: RSVP-TE: Extensions to RSVP for LSP Tunnels. RFC 3209, IETF (2001)
2. Barabási, A.L., Albert, R.: Emergence of scaling in random networks. Science **286**(5439) (1999)
3. Basescu, C., et al.: SIBRA: scalable Internet bandwidth reservation architecture. In: NDSS (2016)
4. Braden, R., Clark, D., Shenker, S.: Integrated Services in the Internet Architecture: An Overview. RFC 1633, IETF (1994)
5. Braden, R., Zhang, L., Berson, S., Herzog, S., Jamin, S.: Resource ReSerVation Protocol (RSVP) - Version 1 Functional Specification. RFC 2205, IETF (1997)
6. Broido, A.D., Clauset, A.: Scale-free networks are rare. Nat. Commun. **10**(1), 1–10 (2019)

7. Brown, L., et al.: On the future of congestion control for the public internet. In: ACM HotNets (2020)

8. Chang, T., Tang, Y., Chen, Y., Hsu, W., Tsai, M.: Maximum concurrent flow problem in MPLS-based software defined networks. In: IEEE Global Communications Conference (GLOBECOM) (2018)

9. Ford Jr., L.R., Fulkerson, D.R.: A suggested computation for maximal multi-commodity network flows. Manage. Sci. **5**(1), 97–101 (1958)

10. Giuliari, G., Wyss, M., Legner, M., Perrig, A.: GMA: a pareto optimal distributed resource-allocation algorithm (2021). https://arxiv.org/abs/2102.10314

11. Jacobson, V.: Congestion avoidance and control. SIGCOMM CCR **18**(4), 314–329 (1988)

12. Katz, D., Kompella, K., Yeung, D.: Traffic Engineering (TE) Extensions to OSPF Version 2. RFC 3630, IETF (2003)

13. Kelly, F.P., Maulloo, A.K., Tan, D.K.: Rate control for communication networks: shadow prices, proportional fairness and stability. J. Oper. Res. Soc. **49**(3), 237–252 (1998)

14. Rosen, E., Viswanathan, A., Callon, R.: Multiprotocol Label Switching Architecture. RFC 3031, IETF (2001)

15. Saino, L., Cocora, C., Pavlou, G.: A toolchain for simplifying network simulation setup. In: International Conference on Simulation Tools and Techniques (2013)

16. Saitō, H.: Teletraffic Technologies in ATM Networks. Artech House (1994)

17. Shahrokhi, F., Matula, D.W.: The maximum concurrent flow problem. J. ACM **37**(2), 318–334 (1990)

18. Shu, Z., et al.: Traffic engineering in software-defined networking: measurement and management. IEEE Access **4**, 3246–3256 (2016)

19. Ware, R., Mukerjee, M.K., Seshan, S., Sherry, J.: Beyond Jain's fairness index: setting the bar for the deployment of congestion control algorithms. In: ACM HotNets (2019)

Testing Equality Under the Local Broadcast Model

Muhammad Samir Khan[1]($\boxtimes$) and Nitin H. Vaidya[2]

[1] Department of Computer Science, University of Illinois at Urbana-Champaign, Urbana, IL, USA
mskhan6@illinois.edu
[2] Department of Computer Science, Georgetown University, Washington DC, USA
nitin.vaidya@georgetown.edu

Abstract. In the *multiparty equality problem*, each of the n nodes starts with a k-bit input. If there is a mismatch between the inputs, then *at least one* node must be able to detect it. The cost of a multiparty equality protocol is the total number of bits sent in the protocol. We consider the problem of minimizing this communication cost under the *local broadcast* model for the case where the underlying communication graph is undirected. In the *local broadcast* model of communication, a message sent by a node is received identically by all of its neighbors. This is in contrast to the classical *point-to-point* communication model, where a message sent by a node to one of its neighbors is received only by its intended recipient.

Under point-to-point communication, there exists a simple protocol which is competitive within a factor 2 of the lower bound [1]. In this protocol, a rooted spanning tree is fixed and each node sends its entire input to its parent in the tree. On receiving a value from its child, a node compares it against its own input to check if the two values match. Ignoring lower order additive terms, a more complicated protocol comes within a factor 4/3 of the lower bound and is tight for certain classes of graphs [1]. Tight results, ignoring lower order terms, are also known for complete graphs [2,9].

We study the multiparty equality problem under the local broadcast model. Recently, our work has shown that the connectivity requirements for Byzantine consensus are lower in the local broadcast model as compared to the classical model [7,8]. In this work,

1. we identify a lower bound for the multiparty equality problem in this model.
2. we first identify simple protocols, wherein nodes are restricted to either transmit their entire input or not transmit anything at all, and find that these can cost $\Omega(\log n)$ times the lower bound using existing example for the set cover problem [12].

This research is supported in part by the National Science Foundation awards 1409416 and 1733872, and Toyota InfoTechnology Center. Any opinions, findings, and conclusions or recommendations expressed here are those of the authors and do not necessarily reflect the views of the funding agencies or the U.S. government.

T. Jurdziński and S. Schmid (Eds.): SIROCCO 2021, LNCS 12810, pp. 262–276, 2021.
https://doi.org/10.1007/978-3-030-79527-6_15

3. we then design a protocol to solve the problem within a constant factor of the lower bound.

Keywords: Communication complexity · Multiparty equality · Static protocols · Local broadcast

1 Introduction

In this paper, we study the *multiparty equality problem*, wherein n nodes are connected via an arbitrary undirected graph $G = (V, E)$. Each node $u \in V$ starts with a k-bit input $x(u)$. If $x(u) \neq x(v)$ for two distinct nodes $u, v \in V$, then *at least one* node in the graph must be able to detect the mismatch. The cost of a multiparty equality protocol is the total number of bits sent in the protocol. We want to minimize this communication cost.

This problem has been studied under the *point-to-point* communication model by Alon et al. [1] and Liang and Vaidya [9]. Under the point-to-point communication model, all links are private so that when a node transmits a message to a neighbor in the network, the other neighbors do not receive the message. Here, we consider the *local broadcast* communication model where a message sent by a node is received identically by all of its neighbors in the communication network. This communication model is inspired by wireless networks where a message sent by a wireless device is received by all devices in its immediate vicinity. Recently, it has been shown that the connectivity requirements for the Byzantine consensus problem are lower in the local broadcast model as compared to the point-to-point model [7,8].

To see the difference between the two communication models, consider the scenario where a node u intends to communicate its entire k-bit input with all of its neighbors. In the point-to-point communication model, node u will have to transmit its entire input on each of the incident edges separately. In contrast, in the local broadcast model, node u will have to transmit its input only once and all of its neighbors will receive the input identically.

When a node u transmits ℓ bits, under point-to-point channels, exactly ℓ bits are received by the recipient node. However, under local broadcast, *each* neighbor of u receives ℓ bits. So while the total number of bits transmitted in a protocol under the point-to-point model is exactly the same as the total number of bits received, this is not the case under the local broadcast model. The optimal protocols can be different depending on whether they minimize the number of bits transmitted or the number of bits received. We discuss these two different cost functions in Sect. 3. In this paper, we focus on the transmission cost.

We study *static* protocols [1,9], where the transmitting nodes (as well as the number of bits transmitted by the nodes) for each round of the protocol are pre-determined and independent of the inputs. We make the following contributions.

1. We give a lower bound on the transmission cost of multiparty equality under the local broadcast model.
2. We first introduce simple protocols, where each node can either transmit its entire input or not transmit at all. When a node receives a value from its neighbor, it compares it against its own input to check if the two values match. Under local broadcast, such simple protocols are related to special dominating sets. With point-to-point channels, the simple protocols consist of fixing a rooted spanning tree, with each node transmitting its input value to its parent. In the classical setting, these are competitive within a factor 2 of the corresponding lower bound [1]. Unfortunately, under the local broadcast model, we find that the simple protocols can be a factor $\Omega(\log n)$ worse than the identified lower bound.
3. We show that there exist static protocols that solve the multiparty equality problem within a constant factor of the lower bound. These are *linear* protocols in the sense that the value transmitted by any node is a linear function (over a finite field) of its input. This is in contrast with the point-to-point model where linear protocols do not perform any better than the simple protocols [1].

The best known protocol for arbitrary graphs under point-to-point communication is by Alon et al. [1]. It is a non-linear protocol that achieves a competitive factor of 4/3 against the lower bound, ignoring lower order additive terms. For certain classes of graphs, it is in fact optimal. Tight results, ignoring lower order terms, are also known for complete graphs [2,9] using non-linear protocols. Our results show that while there is no separation between linear and simple protocols in the point-to-point model, there is a clear separation between them in the local broadcast model.

The rest of the paper is organized as follows. We introduce the notation in Sect. 2. In Sect. 3, we formalize the problem and discuss the cost measure under the local broadcast model. A lower bound is given in Sect. 4. We present and analyze simple protocols in Sect. 5. In Sect. 6, we design a protocol that is competitive within factor 4 of the lower bound. Finally, we conclude in Sect. 7 and identify some open problems.

2 Notation

We consider an undirected communication graph $G = (V, E)$ of size $|V| = n$, which is fixed in advance. Throughout, we assume that the communication graph is connected, since the problem is not solvable in disconnected graphs. Each node u has a k-bit binary input $x(u)$.

Two nodes u and v are *neighbors* if $uv \in E$ is an edge in G. The *neighborhood* of a node u is the set of neighbors of u. It is denoted

$$N(u) := \{v \mid uv \in E\}.$$

The number of neighbors of u is the *degree* of node u, denoted by

$$d(u) := |N(u)|.$$

We use $N^+(u)$ to denote the set containing neighbors of u and u itself,

$$N^+(u) := N(u) + u.$$

Above, "+" denotes the union of a set with a singleton. We extend the definition of neighborhood to sets so that the neighborhood of a set S is the set of nodes not in S that have a neighbor in S,

$$N(S) := \{v \in V - S \mid uv \in E, u \in S\}.$$

For a set of nodes $S \subset V$,

- $\overline{S}$ is the set $V - S$.
- a *cut* is a partition $(S, \overline{S})$ of V.
- the set of edges that cross a cut $(S, \overline{S})$ is denoted by

$$E(S, \overline{S}) := \{uv \in E \mid u \in S, v \in \overline{S}\}.$$

- the *boundary* $B(S, \overline{S})$ of a cut $(S, \overline{S})$ is the set of nodes that have a neighbor on the other side of the cut, i.e.,

$$B(S, \overline{S}) := \{u \mid \exists uv \in E(S, \overline{S})\}.$$

- edges within the set S are denoted by

$$E[S] := \{uv \mid u, v \in S\}.$$

A subgraph of G is a graph whose node set and edge set are subsets of V and E respectively.

- For a subset of nodes $U \subset V$, $G[U]$ is a subgraph of G *node-induced by U*, with node set U and edge set $E[U]$.
- With a slight abuse of terminology, for a subset of edges $F \subset E$, $G[F]$ is a subgraph of G *edge-induced by F*, where all the endpoints of edges in F form the node set and F is the edge set. More specifically, the node set of $G[F]$ is given by $\{u \mid \exists uv \in F\}$.

3   Problem Statement and Cost Function

In the *Multiparty Equality Problem*, each node u starts with a k-bit binary input $x(u)$ and must output a single bit 0 or 1, meeting the following criteria. If all nodes have the same input, then all nodes must output 0. However, if there is a mismatch $x(u) \neq x(v)$, for any two distinct nodes u, v, then *at least one* node in the graph must output 1[1].

---

[1] Note that the node detecting a mismatch between inputs can propagate this to the rest of the graph with an overhead that is independent of k, but not of n.

Communication between nodes is via *local broadcast*. A message sent by a node u is received identically and reliably by each neighbor of u. Moreover, each neighbor can correctly identify u to be the transmitter of the message.

As in [1] and [9], we consider only the *static* protocols where the transmitters at each time step are pre-determined by the protocol and are independent of the inputs. We consider protocols where the total number of bits $c(u)$ transmitted by a node u is independent of the inputs. Note that under the local broadcast model, when a node u transmits $c(u)$ bits, a total of $d(u)c(u)$ bits are received by all the neighbors of u combined.

In the point-to-point model, a message transmitted by a node u is received by exactly one neighbor of u. So the total number of bits transmitted in a protocol is exactly the same as the total number of bits received. In contrast, in the local broadcast model, the number of bits transmitted is smaller than the number of bits received by factor equal to the degree of the transmitting node. Correspondingly, there are the following two cost functions. The *transmission cost* of a protocol is the total number of bits transmitted by all the nodes in the graph,

$$\sum_{u \in V} c(u).$$

The *reception cost* of a protocol is the total number of bits received by all the nodes in the graph,

$$\sum_{u \in V} d(u)c(u).$$

In this paper, we consider the transmission cost of protocols.

4   Lower Bound

The two party equality problem was introduced by Yao [13], who showed that both parties combined must transmit at least k bits to solve the problem. Note that, for two parties, the point-to-point model and the local broadcast model are equivalent. This argument can be extended for $n \geq 3$ parties by considering two-way partitions of the node set [1,3]. Let $(S, \overline{S})$ be an arbitrary cut of V. Consider the set of executions where all nodes in S always have the same input and all nodes in $\overline{S}$ always have the same input. Then this is equivalent to the two party equality problem. Thus, by the two party lower bound, there must be at least k bits shared across the cut.

Consider any multiparty equality protocol under the local broadcast model. Let $c(u)$ be the number of bits transmitted by a node u in the protocol. Then for any cut $(S, \overline{S})$, we have that there must be at least k bits transmitted across the cut. Under the local broadcast model, when a node transmits a message, it is sent identically on all its incident edges. Therefore, the total number of bits transmitted by the nodes at the boundary of the cut $(S, \overline{S})$ must be at least k, i.e.,

$$\sum_{u \in B(S, \overline{S})} c(u) \geq k.$$

Using $y(u) := c(u)/k$ to normalize the transmission by each node, we get the following linear program.

Linear Program $\mathcal{P}$:

minimize:
$$k \cdot \sum_{u \in V} y(u) \tag{1}$$

subject to:
$$\sum_{u \in B(S,\overline{S})} y(u) \geq 1 \qquad \forall (S, \overline{S}) : \emptyset \neq S \subsetneq V \tag{2}$$

$$y(u) \geq 0 \qquad \forall u \in V. \tag{3}$$

We use $\mathcal{P}$ to denote the above linear program given by Eqs. 1–3. The cost of $\mathcal{P}$ is the value of its optimal solution.

Theorem 1. *The cost of any static protocol that solves the multiparty equality problem under the local broadcast model is at least the cost of $\mathcal{P}$.*

The proof is an extension of the arguments for two parties. For any cut $(S, \overline{S})$, one can contract all nodes in S into one node and all nodes in $\overline{S}$ into another to get a two party problem.

Proof. Suppose, for the sake of contradiction, that a static protocol solves the multiparty equality problem but has a cost less than the optimal solution to $\mathcal{P}$. Then, there exists a cut $(S, \overline{S})$ such that $\sum_{u \in B(S,\overline{S})} c(u) < k$ for this protocol. By the pigeon hole principle, there exist two inputs α and β such that the nodes in $B(S, \overline{S})$ all transmit the same messages in the following three cases:

1. every node in the graph has input α.
2. every node in the graph has input β.
3. all nodes in S have input α and all nodes in $\overline{S}$ have input β.

Since all nodes in S (resp. $\overline{S}$) output 0 in case 1 (resp. case 2), therefore, all nodes output 0 in case 3, a contradiction.

5 Simple Protocols

In this section, we consider simple protocols where some subset of nodes is chosen to transmit their entire input. On receiving transmission from any of its neighbors, a node u compares the received value against its own input. If the values match for all the received messages, then u outputs 0. Otherwise, u outputs 1.

Definition 1. *A protocol is* simple *if every node either transmits its entire input, or does not transmit at all.*

This set of protocols is related to what is called the *weakly connected dominating set* of a graph. Consider a subset $S \subset V$ of nodes. Let $F := E[S] \cup E(S, \overline{S})$ be the set of edges that are incident on at least one node in S. Let $H := G[F]$ be the subgraph of G edge-induced by F. Then S is a *weakly connected dominating set* of G if H is a connected spanning subgraph of G.

Proposition 1. *A simple protocol solves the multiparty equality problem if and only if the set $S \subset V$ of nodes chosen to transmit their entire input is a weakly connected dominating set of G.*

Proof. We consider the two directions separately:

$\Rightarrow$ Consider a simple protocol that solves the multiparty equality problem by choosing a set $S \subset V$ of nodes to transmit their entire input. We show that S is a weakly connected dominating set of G. Let $F := E[S] \cup E(S, \overline{S})$ and $H := G[F]$.

1. H is a spanning subgraph of G: Suppose for the sake of contradiction that there is a node $u \notin H$. Then u neither sends nor receives any transmissions. Then no node in the graph G can distinguish between the case where all nodes in G have the same input and the case where u has a different input than the rest of the graph. This is a contradiction to the initial assumption that the protocol solves the multiparty equality problem.
2. H is a connected graph: Suppose for the sake of contradiction that H is not a connected graph so that there are at least two connected components A and B of H. Note that no messages are transmitted between A and B. Then no node in G can distinguish between the case where all nodes in G have the same input and the case where nodes in A have a different input than nodes in B. This is a contradiction to the initial assumption that the protocol solves the multiparty equality problem.

$\Leftarrow$ Suppose that $S \subset V$ is a weakly connected dominating set of G. As before, let $F := E[S] \cup E(S, \overline{S})$ and $H := G[F]$. Consider the corresponding simple protocol where nodes in S transmit their entire input, while all nodes compare the received values against their own input. Clearly no mismatch is detected when all nodes in G have the same input, and so all nodes output 0. So consider the case where two nodes u, v have mismatching inputs $x(u) \neq x(v)$. Since H is a connected spanning subgraph of G, so there exists at least one uv-path P in H. Furthermore, because $x(u) \neq x(v)$ so there exist two adjacent nodes w, z in P such that $x(w) \neq x(z)$. By construction of H, either $w \in S$ or $z \in S$ (or both). WLOG assume that $w \in S$ and it transmits its entire input in the protocol. Then z will receive a value different than its input and will output 1.

Note that the total cost of transmission is $k \cdot |S|$ where $|S|$ is the size of the weakly connected dominating set. The *minimum weakly connected dominating set problem* has been studied in the literature [4–6,11] and is known to be NP-complete.

As mentioned in Sect. 1, simple protocols in the point-to-point model are supported on a rooted spanning tree of G. These are within a factor 2 of the optimal and one can not do any better with linear protocols [1]. Even on complete graphs, non-linear protocols are needed to achieve the optimal cost [2,9]. Under local broadcast, it is easy to see that simple protocols are optimal for complete graphs (one node transmits its entire input). Unfortunately, the simple protocols suffer a gap of $\Omega(\log n)$ against the lower bound on arbitrary graphs.

Proposition 2. *There exist a family of graphs such that the cost of $\mathcal{P}$ is $O(k)$ while any dominating set has size $\Omega(k \cdot \log n)$.*

Proof (Proof Sketch). The family of graphs is based on Example 13.4 in [12] for establishing a lower bound on the integrality gap of a linear programming relaxation of the set cover problem. Using a common approximation preserving reduction from the set cover to the dominating set problem, one can get a graph G with the following properties. G has two parts A and B, both of size $n/2$. A is a complete graph and B is an independent set. Each node in A (resp. B) has exactly $(n+2)/4$ neighbors in B (resp. A). Furthermore, any dominating set has size at least $\log_2((n+2)/2)$.

We now give a solution y to $\mathcal{P}$. Pick an arbitrary node $s \in A$. Assign $y(s) := 1$. For each node $u \in A - s$, assign

$$y(u) := \frac{1}{|N(u) \cap B|}$$
$$= \frac{4}{n+2}.$$

For each node $u \in B$, assign $y(u) := 0$. To see that y is indeed a solution to $\mathcal{P}$, consider an arbitrary cut $(S, \overline{S})$. WLOG assume that $s \in S$. By construction of G (recall that A is a complete graph), if $A - S$ is non-empty, then $s \in B(S, \overline{S})$ and we have that

$$\sum_{u \in B(S,\overline{S})} y(u) \geq y(s)$$
$$= 1,$$

as required. So assume that $S \supseteq A$. Consider any node $t \in \overline{S} \subseteq B$. We have that

$$\sum_{u \in B(S,\overline{S})} y(u) \geq \sum_{u \in N(t)} y(u)$$
$$\geq \sum_{u \in N(t)} \frac{4}{n+2}$$
$$= 1.$$

The first inequality follows from the fact that all of t's neighbors are in $A \subseteq S$, and so $B(S, \overline{S}) \supseteq N(t)$. The second inequality follows from $y(u) \geq 4/(n+2)$ for each $u \in N(t)$, since $N(t) \subset A$. Finally, the equality follows from the fact that t has exactly $(n+2)/4$ neighbors by construction.

Recall that, by construction, any dominating set has size at least $\log_2((n+2)/2)$. This is a lower bound for any weakly connected dominating set as well. Therefore, any simple protocol has cost at least $k \cdot \log_2((n+2)/2)$. On the other hand, the solution y to $\mathcal{P}$ given above has value

$$k \cdot \sum_{u \in V} y(u) = k \left(y(s) + \sum_{u \in A - s} y(u) \right)$$

$$= k \left(1 + \left(\frac{n}{2} - 1 \right) \frac{4}{n+2} \right)$$

$$= k \left(1 + 2 \left(\frac{n-2}{n+2} \right) \right)$$

$$\leq 3k.$$

Therefore, the cost of $\mathcal{P}$ is at most $3k$.

6   Upper Bound

In this section, we constructively establish an upper bound on the multiparty equality problem, as stated in the following theorem.

Theorem 2. *For sufficiently large k, there exists a protocol that solves the multiparty equality problem with a cost of at most 4 times the cost of $\mathcal{P}$.*

We design a protocol that solves the multiparty equality problem under the local broadcast model. We start with an optimal solution y of the linear program $\mathcal{P}$ in Sect. 4. Note that y is an optimal solution to $\mathcal{P}$ for all values of $k > 0$. Since the linear program has integer entries, $y(u)$ is rational for each node u. Let q be an even integer such that $q \cdot y(u)$ is an integer for all u. Define two integers m and ℓ as follows.

$$m := q \cdot \sum_u y(u),$$

$$\ell := \frac{q}{2}.$$

For simplicity, we assume k is an integral multiple of both q and ℓ. To design our protocol, we will use an (m, ℓ)-Reed-Solomon code [10] over Galois field $GF(2^{k/\ell})$. Note that a code-word in this code consists of m symbols, with each symbol size being k/ℓ bits. Such a Reed-Solomon code exists so long as $2^{k/\ell} > m$. To satisfy this property, we assume that k is sufficiently large. In a Reed-Solomon (RS) code, k input bits are represented using ℓ symbols from $GF(2^{k/\ell})$, each symbol representing k/ℓ bits of the input. These ℓ symbols are then encoded into m symbols to obtain the corresponding code-word. Given any ℓ out of the m symbols of a code-word, the corresponding k-bit input can be correctly determined. We view the encoding of each of the m symbols as a function $\{0, 1\}^k \rightarrow \{0, 1\}^{k/\ell}$, since we will be applying the encodings to different inputs. Of the m total symbols in the code-word, each node u is assigned $q \cdot y(u)$ of them in the protocol. We describe how the nodes use these symbols later.

In the protocol, nodes are either red or blue. We describe how they are colored later. A red node broadcasts its entire input to its neighbors and always outputs 0. A blue node u computes its $q \cdot y(u)$ code symbols on its input $x(u)$ and broadcasts them to its neighbors. A blue node u performs checks (as discussed below) on all transmissions received from its neighbors. If all checks pass, then it outputs 0. Otherwise, it outputs 1. On receiving a transmission from a red neighbor r, u checks if the received value $x(r)$ is the same as $x(u)$. On receiving a transmission from a blue neighbor b, u computes the corresponding $q \cdot y(b)$ code symbols on its own input $x(u)$ and checks if they match with the received code symbols from b.

We now describe how to color the nodes for the protocol. We color the nodes in rounds. Initially, all nodes are colored white. In each round, at least one white node gets colored either red or blue. At the end, all nodes will be colored either red or blue. Let W_i, B_i, and R_i denote the set of white, blue, and red nodes at the end of round i, with $W_0 = V$ and $B_0 = R_0 = \emptyset$. In each round, we maintain that

1. the red and blue subgraph $G[R_i \cup B_i]$ is connected, and
2. no white node is a neighbor of a red node.

In round 1, we select an arbitrary node and color it red. All its neighbors are colored blue. In round i, we select an arbitrary white neighbor $u \in N(B_{i-1})$ of a blue node. Note that until all nodes are colored red or blue, such a white node always exists. There are two cases to consider.

1. If

$$\sum_{v \in N^+(u) \cap W_{i-1}} y(v) \geq \frac{1}{2},$$

   then we color u red and its white neighbors blue:

$$R_i := R_{i-1} + u,$$
$$B_i := B_{i-1} \cup \left(N(u) \cap W_{i-1} \right),$$
$$W_i := W_{i-1} \setminus \left(N^+(u) \cap W_{i-1} \right).$$

2. Otherwise we have that

$$\sum_{v \in N(u) \cap B_{i-1}} y(v) = \left(\sum_{v \in N^+(u)} y(v) \right) - \left(\sum_{v \in N^+(u) \cap W_{i-1}} y(v) \right)$$
$$\geq 1 - \frac{1}{2}$$
$$= \frac{1}{2}.$$

The first equality follows from the fact that 1) u itself is white, and 2) each neighbor of u is either white or blue, so that $N^+(u)$ can be partitioned into $N^+(u) \cap W_{i-1}$ and $N(u) \cap B_{i-1}$. The inequality follows because

$$\sum_{v \in N^+(u)} y(v) \geq 1 \qquad \text{from Eq. 2 in } \mathcal{P} \text{ with } S = \{u\},$$

and

$$\sum_{v \in N^+(u) \cap W_{i-1}} y(v) < \frac{1}{2}.$$

In this case, we color u blue:

$$R_i := R_{i-1},$$
$$B_i := B_{i-1} + u,$$
$$W_i := W_{i-1} - u.$$

Note that while the design of the protocol relies on knowing the solution to $\mathcal{P}$, the protocol itself is distributed where each red or blue node can run its part locally. In the following lemma, we use the coloring rounds $i \geq 1$ to inductively prove the correctness of the protocol.

Lemma 1. *For each $i \geq 1$, the protocol solves the multiparty equality problem in the subgraph $G[R_i \cup B_i]$.*

Proof. We proceed inductively. For the base case, $i = 1$. We have that $R_1 = r$ and $B_1 = N(r)$. If there is no mismatch between inputs, then clearly all nodes output 0. If there is a mismatch, then it must necessarily be between r and a blue node $b \in N(r)$. Since node r broadcasts its entire input, so node b is able to check that $x(r) \neq x(b)$ and so outputs 1, as required.

For the inductive step, assume that the protocol solves the multiparty equality problem in the subgraph $G[R_{i-1} \cup B_{i-1}]$. We show that it also solves the problem in the subgraph $G[R_i \cup B_i]$. If there is a mismatch between inputs of two nodes in $R_{i-1} \cup B_{i-1}$, then we are done by induction. So assume that all nodes in $R_{i-1} \cup B_{i-1}$ have the same input. Let $u \in N(B_{i-1})$ be the white node selected in round i. There are two corresponding cases to consider.

1. u got colored red in round i. Let $b \in B_{i-1} \cap N(u)$ be a neighbor of u which was blue at the end of round $i - 1$. Recall that all nodes in $R_{i-1} \cup B_{i-1}$ have identical input. If $x(u) \neq x(b)$, then b will output 1, as required. So suppose $x(u) = x(b)$. Therefore all nodes in $R_i \cup B_{i-1}$ have identical input. Consider an arbitrary node $b' \in B_i - B_{i-1}$ which got colored blue in round i. By construction, $b' \in N(u)$. So b' receives the entire input of u. If $x(b') \neq x(u)$, then b' will output 1. If $x(b') = x(u)$, then b' will output 0, as required.
2. u got colored blue in round i. Recall that u is the only node that got colored either red or blue in round i, i.e., $W_{i-1} - W_i = \{u\}$. Also, we have that

$$\sum_{v \in N(u) \cap B_{i-1}} y(v) \geq \frac{1}{2}.$$

So u must have received a total of at least $q/2 = \ell$ code symbols from nodes in B_{i-1}. u re-computes these code symbols on its own input $x(u)$ and checks against the received values. Since all nodes in B_{i-1} have the same input, by the property of RS codes, u outputs 0 if and only if $x(u)$ is the same as the inputs of nodes in B_{i-1}.

Therefore the protocol solves the multiparty equality problem in the subgraph $G[R_i \cup B_i]$, as required.

The following lemma bounds the transmission cost of the protocol.

Lemma 2. *The cost of transmission of the protocol is at most* $4k \cdot \sum_{u \in V} y(u)$.

Proof. The total number of bits transmitted by the red nodes is k times the number of red nodes, say t. Let $i_1 < i_2 < \cdots < i_t$ be the rounds where nodes $r_1, r_2, \ldots, r_t$ got colored red. We have that

$$t = \sum_{j=1}^{t} 1$$

$$\leq \sum_{j=1}^{t} \left(2 \cdot \sum_{v \in N^+(r_j) \cap W_{i_j - 1}} y(v) \right)$$

$$\leq 2 \cdot \sum_{u \in V} y(u).$$

For the first inequality, recall that $\sum_{v \in N^+(r_j) \cap W_{i_j - 1}} y(v) \geq 1/2$ for all $j \in [1, t]$ since r_j got colored red in round i_j. For the last inequality, note that $N^+(r_j) \cap W_{i_j - 1}$ and $N^+(r_{j'}) \cap W_{i_{j'} - 1}$ are disjoint for any distinct $j, j' \in [1, t]$. To see this, assume $j < j'$ so that $N^+(r_j) \cap W_{i_{j'} - 1}$ is empty because r_j got colored red and its neighborhood blue in round i_j. Thus, the total number of bits transmitted by red nodes is upper bounded by $2k \cdot \sum_{u \in V} y(u)$.

For the blue nodes, recall that each blue node u transmits $q \cdot y(u)$ code symbols, each of which consists of k/ℓ bits. So, the total number of bits transmitted by the blue nodes is at most

$$\frac{k}{\ell} \cdot \sum_{u \in V} q \cdot y(u) = \frac{2k}{q} \cdot q \cdot \left(\sum_{u \in V} y(u) \right)$$

$$= 2k \cdot \sum_{u \in V} y(u),$$

where the first equality follows from $\ell = q/2$.

It follows that the total number of bits transmitted by both the red and the blue nodes in the protocol is at most $4k \cdot \sum_{u \in V} y(u)$. □

Proof (Proof of Theorem 2). A protocol that solves the multiparty equality problem is given in this section. The proof of correctness follows from Lemma 1 while the transmission cost is bounded in Lemma 2. □

7   Conclusion and Open Problems

In this paper we have studied the multiparty equality problem under the local broadcast model on arbitrary graphs. We established a lower bound to the transmission cost using two-way partitions of nodes. We identified simple protocols and observed that they can cost $\Omega(\log n)$ times the lower bound in certain graphs. This is in contrast to the point-to-point model where simple protocols are within a factor 2 of the lower bound [1]. We also presented linear protocols, based on Reed-Solomon codes, that cost at most 4 times the lower bound.

We finish the paper with some open problems:

1. Can the lower bound be improved? Note that the lower bound for the point-to-point communication model [1] is also based on two-way partitions of nodes. If a better lower bound exists for the local broadcast model, can the same technique be used to improve the lower bound for the point-to-point model, or vice versa?
2. Can we improve on the given upper bound?
3. In this work, we considered the transmission costs of the protocols (Sect. 3). What do the protocols look like if they minimize reception cost instead?
   Let $\text{cost}_P(G)$ be the cost of an optimal protocol under point-to-point communication on a graph G. Let $\text{cost}_T(G)$ and $\text{cost}_R(G)$ be the transmission and reception costs of corresponding optimal protocols under local broadcast on a graph G. Then we have the following relationship between the three quantities.

   $$\text{cost}_T(G) \leq \text{cost}_P(G) \leq \text{cost}_R(G).$$

   The first inequality follows from the fact that any protocol P_p designed for the point-to-point model can be converted into a protocol P_b for the local broadcast model by having each node broadcast all the messages it transmits in P, without paying any additional transmission cost. The second inequality follows from the fact that any protocol P_b designed for the local broadcast model can be converted into a protocol P_p for the point-to-point model by having each node transmit all of its messages in P_b to all of its neighbors via point-to-point transmissions in P_p, without paying any additional reception cost.
4. A more generalized problem is where each node is assigned a weight. This weight is the per bit cost paid for communication by the node. This model generalizes both the transmission and reception cost variants.
5. In this work, we have considered static protocols (see Sect. 3) where the transmitters at each time step and the number of bits transmitted by each node are both independent of the input. Do "dynamic" protocols perform any better under local broadcast?

References

1. Alon, N., Efremenko, K., Sudakov, B.: Testing equality in communication graphs. IEEE Trans. Inf. Theory **63**(11), 7569–7574 (2017)
2. Alon, N., Moitra, A., Sudakov, B.: Nearly complete graphs decomposable into large induced matchings and their applications. In: Proceedings of the Forty-Fourth Annual ACM Symposium on Theory of Computing, STOC 2012, pp. 1079–1090. Association for Computing Machinery, New York (2012). https://doi.org/10.1145/2213977.2214074
3. Chattopadhyay, A., Rudra, A.: The range of topological effects on communication. In: Halldórsson, M.M., Iwama, K., Kobayashi, N., Speckmann, B. (eds.) ICALP 2015. LNCS, vol. 9135, pp. 540–551. Springer, Heidelberg (2015). https://doi.org/10.1007/978-3-662-47666-6_43
4. Chen, Y.P., Liestman, A.L.: Approximating minimum size weakly-connected dominating sets for clustering mobile ad hoc networks. In: Proceedings of the 3rd ACM International Symposium on Mobile Ad Hoc Networking & Computing, MobiHoc 2002, pp. 165–172. Association for Computing Machinery, New York (2002). https://doi.org/10.1145/513800.513821
5. Dubhashi, D., Mei, A., Panconesi, A., Radhakrishnan, J., Srinivasan, A.: Fast distributed algorithms for (weakly) connected dominating sets and linear-size skeletons. J. Comput. Syst. Sci. **71**(4), 467–479 (2005). https://doi.org/10.1016/j.jcss.2005.04.002. http://www.sciencedirect.com/science/article/pii/S002200000500053X
6. Dunbar, J.E., Grossman, J.W., Hattingh, J.H., Hedetniemi, S.T., McRae, A.A.: On weakly connected domination in graphs. Discrete Math. **167–168**, 261–269 (1997). Selected Papers 15th British Combinatorial Conference. https://doi.org/10.1016/S0012-365X(96)00233-6. http://www.sciencedirect.com/science/article/pii/S0012365X96002336
7. Khan, M.S., Naqvi, S.S., Vaidya, N.H.: Exact Byzantine consensus on undirected graphs under local broadcast model. In: Proceedings of the 2019 ACM Symposium on Principles of Distributed Computing, PODC 2019, pp. 327–336. Association for Computing Machinery, New York (2019). https://doi.org/10.1145/3293611.3331619
8. Khan, M.S., Tseng, L., Vaidya, N.H.: Exact Byzantine consensus on arbitrary directed graphs under local broadcast model. In: 23rd International Conference on Principles of Distributed Systems (OPODIS 2019). Leibniz International Proceedings in Informatics (LIPIcs), vol. 153, pp. 30:1–30:16. Schloss Dagstuhl-Leibniz-Zentrum fuer Informatik, Dagstuhl, Germany (2020). https://doi.org/10.4230/LIPIcs.OPODIS.2019.30. https://drops.dagstuhl.de/opus/volltexte/2020/11816
9. Liang, G., Vaidya, N.: Multiparty equality function computation in networks with point-to-point links. In: Kosowski, A., Yamashita, M. (eds.) SIROCCO 2011. LNCS, vol. 6796, pp. 258–269. Springer, Heidelberg (2011). https://doi.org/10.1007/978-3-642-22212-2_23
10. Reed, I.S., Solomon, G.: Polynomial codes over certain finite fields. J. Soc. Ind. Appl. Math. **8**(2), 300–304 (1960)
11. Swaminathan, V.: Weakly connected domination in graphs. Electron. Notes Discrete Math. **33**, 67–73 (2009). International Conference on Graph Theory and Its Applications. https://doi.org/10.1016/j.endm.2009.03.010. http://www.sciencedirect.com/science/article/pii/S1571065309000298

12. Vazirani, V.V.: Approximation Algorithms. Springer, Heidelberg (2003). https://doi.org/10.1007/978-3-662-04565-7
13. Yao, A.C.C.: Some complexity questions related to distributive computing (preliminary report). In: Proceedings of the Eleventh Annual ACM Symposium on Theory of Computing, STOC 1979, pp. 209–213. Association for Computing Machinery, New York (1979). https://doi.org/10.1145/800135.804414

A Distributed Computing Perspective of Unconditionally Secure Information Transmission in Russian Cards Problems

Sergio Rajsbaum$^{(\boxtimes)}$

Instituto de Matemáticas, Universidad Nacional Autónoma de México (UNAM), 04510 Mexico City, Mexico
rajsbaum@im.unam.mx

Abstract. The problem of A privately transmitting information to B by a public announcement overheard by an eavesdropper C is considered. To do so by a deterministic protocol, the inputs of the players must be correlated. Dependent inputs are traditionally represented using a deck of cards. There is a publicly known *signature* $(\mathbf{a}, \mathbf{b}, \mathbf{c})$, where $n = \mathbf{a} + \mathbf{b} + \mathbf{c} + \mathbf{r}$, and A gets $\mathbf{a}$ cards, B gets $\mathbf{b}$ cards, and C gets $\mathbf{c}$ cards, out of the deck of n cards. Using a deterministic protocol, A decides its announcement based on her hand.

Using techniques from coding theory, Johnson graphs, and additive number theory, a novel perspective inspired by distributed computing theory is provided, to analyze the amount of information that A needs to send, while preventing C from learning a single card of her hand. In one extreme, the generalized Russian cards problem, B wants to learn all of A's cards, and in the other, B wishes to learn *something* about A's hand.

Keywords: Johnson graphs · Russian cards problem · Information theoretic security · Combinatorial cryptography · Constant weight codes

1 Introduction

The idea that card games could be used to achieve security in the presence of computationally unbounded adversaries proposed by Peter Winkler [31] led to a long research line active up to now, see survey in [27]. It motivated Fischer and Wright [18] to consider *card games*, where A, B, C draw cards from a deck D of n cards, as specified by a *signature* $(\mathbf{a}, \mathbf{b}, \mathbf{c})$, with $n = \mathbf{a} + \mathbf{b} + \mathbf{c} + \mathbf{r}$. Nobody gets $\mathbf{r}$ cards, while A gets $\mathbf{a}$ cards, B gets $\mathbf{b}$ cards, and C gets $\mathbf{c}$ cards.

Fischer and Wright thought of the cards as representing correlated random initial local variables for the players, that have a simple structure. They were interested in knowing which distributions of private initial values allow A and B to obtain a key, that remains secret to C. Their protocols mostly use randomization, and they are information-theoretic secure. However, they do not keep the cards of A and B secret from C.

© Springer Nature Switzerland AG 2021
T. Jurdziński and S. Schmid (Eds.): SIROCCO 2021, LNCS 12810, pp. 277–295, 2021.
https://doi.org/10.1007/978-3-030-79527-6_16

Another research line started with an in depth, combinatorial and epistemic logic study of van Ditmarsch [12] of the *Russian cards* problem, presented at the Moscow Mathematics Olympiad in 2000, where the cards of A and B should be kept secret from C. Here A, B and C draw $(3, 3, 1)$ cards, respectively, from a deck of 7 cards. First A makes an announcement that allows B to identify her set of cards, while C cannot deduce a single card of A. After the announcement of A, B knows the cards of each player, and hence he may announce C's card, from which C learns nothing, but allows A to infer the cards of B. The problem has received a fair amount of attention since then[1] e.g. $[1, 2, 7–9, 13, 14, 24, 29, 30]$, in its *generalized* form of signature $(\mathbf{a}, \mathbf{b}, \mathbf{c})$, and other variants, including multi-round, multiplayer, and different security requirements. Solutions are based either on modular arithmetic or on combinatorial designs.

The original solution for $(3, 3, 1)$ uses modular arithmetic, where A announces the sum of her cards modulo 7, and then B announces C's card [25]. For the general case when $\mathbf{c} = 1$ (and $\mathbf{r} = 0$), solutions exist that announce the cards sum modulo an appropriate prime number greater or equal to n [7]. These solutions use only two announcements. A solution using three announcements for $(4, 4, 2)$ is reported in [13], and a four-step protocol where C holds approximately the square of the number of cards of A is presented in [9].

The relation to Steiner triple system and combinatorial designs goes back to 1847 Kirkman [23]. Using combinatorial designs Cordón-Franco et al. [9] prove that solutions exist when $\mathbf{a}$ is a power of a prime, and present the first solutions when $\mathbf{c} > \mathbf{a}$. The solution used 4 communication steps, as opposed to the usual 2-step protocols. Albert et al. [2] show that there is no 2-step solution if $c \geq a - 1$.

In addition to the papers mentioned above, through our new perspective, we have uncovered relations with other areas: intersecting families of sets, coding theory, additive number theory, and distributed computability.

The New Approach. Given a publicly known signature $(\mathbf{a}, \mathbf{b}, \mathbf{c})$, for a deck D of $n = \mathbf{a} + \mathbf{b} + \mathbf{c} + \mathbf{r}$ cards, the basic problem underlying the situations described above, is to design a safe protocol P_A, so that A makes a public announcement, $P_A(a)$, based on her hand, a. From the announcement $P_A(a)$, and using his own hand, b, B should learn something about A's hand. The announcement $P_A(a)$ is deterministically determined by the input of A, and the knowledge of the signature. No randomized solutions are considered in this paper.

In the language of e.g. [7,9,13], a protocol P_A should be *informative* for B and *safe* from C. A protocol is *safe* if C does not learn any of the cards of A. It is informative, if B learns the hand of A.

We introduce the notion of a protocol being *minimally informative,* where the goal is that B learns *something* about the hand of A. We prove that when $\mathbf{c} + \mathbf{r} = 1$, this is equivalent to B learning one card of A. If $\mathbf{c} + \mathbf{r} > 1$ then B learns even less; he learns that A has one of the cards of a set s, $|s| = \mathbf{c} + \mathbf{r}$.

We formalize this setting based on distributed computability [21], and more specifically when the least amount of communication is studied [11]. Using this

---

[1] The $\mathbf{r} = 0$ case is mostly considered here, as well as in the secret key research line.

formalization, we show that a protocol can be viewed as a coloring of the set of vertices $\mathscr{P}_\mathbf{a}(D)$, all subsets of size $\mathbf{a}$ of D, $P_A : \mathscr{P}_\mathbf{a}(D) \to \mathcal{M}$, for the set of messages $\mathcal{M}$ that A may send. Thus, $\mathscr{P}_\mathbf{a}(D)$ is the set of vertices of a Johnson graph $J(n, \mathbf{a})$, where $n = |D|$. We are interested in the question of how small can $\mathcal{M}$ be, i.e., the number of bits, $\log_2 |\mathcal{M}|$, that A needs to transmit to implement either and informative or a minimally informative safe protocol.

We show in Theorem 2 that P_A is informative if and only if P_A is a proper coloring of the d-*distance Johnson graph* $J^d(n, \mathbf{a})$, $d = \mathbf{c} + \mathbf{r}$. Vertices a, a' of $J^d(n, \mathbf{a})$ are adjacent whenever $\mathbf{a} - d \leq |a \cap a'|$. In particular, we have a Johnson graph when $d = 1$.

It is well-known that there is a family of maximal cliques of $J(n, \mathbf{a})$ of size $\mathbf{a} + 1$, e.g. [19]. It turns out, that the inputs of A that B with input b considers possible, form a maximal clique of $J^{\mathbf{c}+\mathbf{r}}(n, \mathbf{a})$, denoted $K_p(\bar{b})$. The clique $K_p(\bar{b})$ consists of all hands $a \subset \bar{b}$, $|a| = \mathbf{a}$, and hence $p = \binom{\mathbf{a}+\mathbf{c}+\mathbf{r}}{\mathbf{a}}$. Similarly, the hands that C considers possible with input c form a clique $K_p(\bar{c})$ of $J^{\mathbf{b}+\mathbf{r}}(n, \mathbf{a})$, and such cliques are of size $p = \binom{\mathbf{a}+\mathbf{b}+\mathbf{r}}{\mathbf{a}}$.

We show also in Theorem 2 that P_A is minimally informative if and only if P_A colors at least one edge of each clique $K_p(\bar{b})$ with two different colors. In contrast, informative requires that P_A colors every edge of $K_p(\bar{b})$ with two different colors.

Thus, the chromatic number of $J^d(n, \mathbf{a})$ determines the number of messages needed for a protocol P_A to be informative. There are many interesting open questions concerning the chromatic number of Johnson graphs [19, Chapter 16]. Upper bounds have been thoroughly studied for special cases, because they imply lower bounds on codes e.g. [5,15]. In addition to some special cases, only the trivial lower bound implied by the maximal cliques is known. Briefly, it is known that $n/2 \leq \chi(J(n, \mathbf{a})) \leq n$, often the chromatic number is a little bit smaller[2]. Indeed, using coding theory techniques we show the easy result that there is an informative protocol when $\mathbf{c} + \mathbf{r} = 1$ with $|\mathcal{M}| = n$ different messages (Lemma 5), and the more difficult new result for the general case, $\mathbf{c} + \mathbf{r} \geq 1$, that $(2n)^{\mathbf{c}+\mathbf{r}}$ different messages suffice, i.e., to properly color $J^{\mathbf{c}+\mathbf{r}}(n, \mathbf{a})$ (Lemma 6). It follows that $\Theta((\mathbf{c} + \mathbf{r}) \log n)$ bits are needed and sufficient for an informative protocol; the lower bound is implied by the size of the maximal cliques of $J^{\mathbf{c}+\mathbf{r}}(n, \mathbf{a})$, more details in Sect. 6.

Remarkably, only 1 bit suffices for minimal information transmission, when $\mathbf{b} < \lfloor n/2 \rfloor$. We study the minimal information problem in Sect. 4, where we present this and other results. We show that if additionally $\mathbf{c} \leq \lfloor n/2 \rfloor - 2$ the 1-bit protocol is also safe. Also, we present a reduction from an informative protocol, showing that when $\mathbf{c} + \mathbf{r} = 1$, as $\mathbf{a}$ grows from 3 up to roughly $n/2$, the number of different messages goes down from $n/3$ to 2, for a safe and minimally informative protocol. We find it surprising that there is a 1-bit protocol for $(3, 3, 1)$, with a 1-bit message, A can transfer one of her cards to B, privately.

---

[2] Apparently there is no $n, \mathbf{a}$ where it is known that $\chi(J(n, \mathbf{a})) < n-2$. In some special cases the exact number has been determined.

While the informative property requires that
all vertices of each maximal clique $K_p(\bar{b})$ are
colored differently by P_A, the safety property
requires the opposite, that not all vertices of
each maximal clique $K_p(\bar{c})$ are colored differently.
Thus, a protocol P_A can be informative and safe
only if $\mathbf{b} > \mathbf{c}$. In this case, while $K_p(\bar{c})$ induces a
clique in $J^{\mathbf{b+r}}(n, \mathbf{a})$, it does not induce a clique
in $J^{\mathbf{c+r}}(n, \mathbf{a})$.

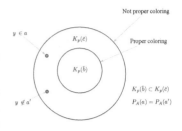

Safety requires that for each card y, there is a hand of A that includes y, and
another that does not include it, both equally colored, in the complement of the
hand of C.

We consider the protocol χ_{modn} in Sect. 5, that sends the sum of the cards
modulo n, for $\mathbf{c} + \mathbf{r} = 1$, and show that it is informative and safe, for $\mathbf{a}, \mathbf{b} \geq 3$,
$n \geq 7$. Indeed, while informative is a coding theory property, safety is an additive
number theory property. We prove safety using simple shifting techniques [19],
getting a generalization and simplification of results of [7].[3] Thus, only two additional messages are needed to make an informative protocol, also safe (w.r.t. the
best known solutions). We present an informative protocol for the general case
$\mathbf{c} + \mathbf{r} \geq 1$ based on more involved coding theory ideas and discuss safety, in
Sect. 6, but a detailed treatment is beyond the scope of this paper.

The Appendix includes additional details and some proofs, the other proofs
are in a companion technical report [27], together with an extensive discussion
of related work, and additional results.

2   Secure Information Transmission

The model and the problem are defined here, adapting the distributed computing
formalization of [21] to the case of an eavesdropper. In Sect. 2.1 we present the
representation of the inputs to A, B, C as a simplicial complex, which determines
the Johnson graphs that will play a central role in this paper. In Sect. 2.2 a
protocol is defined.

2.1   The Input Complex

Let $D = \{0, \ldots, n - 1\}$, $n > 1$, be the *deck* of n distinct cards. An element in
the deck is a *card*. A subset x of cards is a *hand*, $x \in \mathscr{P}(D)$. We may say for
short that x, $|x| = m$, is an *m-set* or *m-hand*, namely, if $x \in \mathscr{P}_m(D)$, the subsets
of D of size m. A *deal* $= (a, b, c)$ consists of three disjoint hands, meaning that
cards in a are dealt to A, cards in b to B, and cards in c to C. We say that
the hand is the *input* of the process. We call $\gamma = (\mathbf{a}, \mathbf{b}, \mathbf{c})$ the *signature* of the
deal $= (a, b, c)$ if $|a| = \mathbf{a}$, $|b| = \mathbf{b}$ and $|c| = \mathbf{c}$, following the notation introduced

---

[3] Cordón-Franco et al. [7] show that χ_{modn} is safe when n is prime using
[10, Theorem 4.1], analogous to the Cauchy-Davenport theorem, except for $(4, 3, 1)$,
$(3, 4, 1)$.

by Fischer and Wright [17]. We assume that A, B and C are aware of the deck and the signature.

It has been often assumed that $n = \mathbf{a} + \mathbf{b} + \mathbf{c}$, but as we shall see, it is natural to consider the case where nobody gets $\mathbf{r}$ cards, $n = \mathbf{a} + \mathbf{b} + \mathbf{c} + \mathbf{r}$. While A and B get at least one card, $\mathbf{a}, \mathbf{b} \geq 1$, C may get none $\mathbf{c} \geq 0$.

All possible deals for a given signature over D are represented by a simplicial complex. The vertices are of the form (Y, y), $Y \in \{A, B, C\}$, and y a hand. Such a vertex is called a Y-vertex. The *input complex* $\mathcal{I}(\mathbf{a}, \mathbf{b}, \mathbf{c})$, or $\mathcal{I}$ for short, for signature $\gamma = (\mathbf{a}, \mathbf{b}, \mathbf{c})$ is defined as follows. The facets of $\mathcal{I}$ are all the sets $\{(A, a), (B, b), (C, c)\}$, where a, b, c is a deal of signature γ. The input complex $\mathcal{I}$ consists of all such facets, together with all their subsets.

Notice that the A-vertices of $\mathcal{I}$ are in a one-to-one correspondence with all subsets of size $\mathbf{a}$ of D, $\mathscr{P}_\mathbf{a}(D)$, the B-vertices with $\mathscr{P}_\mathbf{b}(D)$, the C-vertices with $\mathscr{P}_\mathbf{c}(D)$. Indeed, when $\mathbf{c} = 0$, there is a single vertex for C in $\mathcal{I}$.

Example 1. In distributed computing the input complex with a signature $\gamma = (1, 1, 1)$ for three processes has been considered, representing that processes get distinct input names from a set of n names [3]. The figure from [22] shows that in the case of $n = 4$, the complex is a torus subdivided into triangles. The vertices of each triangle are colored black, gray, and white to represent the three processes. Inside the vertex is the card dealt to the corresponding process.

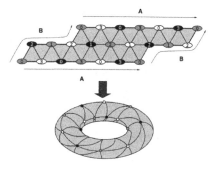

2.2 Informative and Safe Protocols

Fix an input complex $\mathcal{I}$ over D, $n = \mathbf{a} + \mathbf{b} + \mathbf{c} + \mathbf{r}$. The announcement of A is defined by a deterministic function $P_A(a) = M$, for each input vertex $(A, a) \in \mathcal{I}$, where M belongs to $\mathcal{M}$, the domain of possible messages that A may send. We say that P_A is the *protocol* of A. For B, there is a *decision function* $\delta_B(b, M)$ that produces a set of cards in $\mathscr{P}(D)$, based on the input b of B, and the message M received[4].

In the language of e.g. [7,9,13], a protocol should be informative for B and safe from C. If a protocol is informative, B should learn the hand of A. We define also the notion of minimally informative. The goal is that B learns *something* about the hand of A, after listening to an announcement M made by A.

More precisely, by P_A being minimally informative we mean that if b is the input of B, then it is not the case that A sends the same message, on all of her possible inputs. If this is the case, clearly B does not learn anything from her message, as

---

[4] Since we have fixed D and the input complex $\mathcal{I}$, implicitly $P_A(a)$ and $\delta_B(b, M)$ depend on these parameters, in addition to the specific input a, resp. (b, M). This is what we mean when we say that the players know the input complex.

by just looking at his input b, he knows in advance which message A will send. As we shall see in Theorem 2, this is equivalent to B learning that A has one of the cards of a set s, $|s| = n - \mathbf{a} - \mathbf{b}$. Thus, if $n = \mathbf{a} + \mathbf{b} + \mathbf{c} + \mathbf{r}$, with $\mathbf{c} + \mathbf{r} = 1$, then B should learn one of the cards in the hand of A. When $\mathbf{b} = 1$, B should learn that A has one of the cards in a set s, $|s| = n - \mathbf{a} - 1$, more than the trivial guess s, $s = D\backslash b$, where b is B's input card. When $\mathbf{c} + \mathbf{r} = 0$ without any communication B knows the hand of A, so it does not make sense to define a protocol where B learns less information. Notice that when $\mathbf{c} + \mathbf{r} \geq 1$, we have that $n - \mathbf{a} - \mathbf{b} \geq 1$, and the following minimally informative definition makes sense.

Definition 1 (Informative and minimally informative). *Let P_A be a protocol. If there exists δ_B, such that for any given input edge $\{(A, a), (B, b)\} \in \mathcal{I}$, with $M = P_A(a)$,*

- *$\delta_B(b, M) = a$, the protocol is* informative,
- *for $\mathbf{c} + \mathbf{r} \geq 1$, $\delta_B(b, M) = s \in \mathscr{P}_{\mathbf{c}+\mathbf{r}}(D)$, such that $a \cap s \neq \emptyset$, the protocol is* minimally informative.

The previous definition does not talk about C. Indeed, it is based only on the graph which is the subcomplex of $\mathcal{I}$ induced by the A-vertices and the B-vertices. A protocol is safe if C cannot tell who holds even a single card (that she does not hold). Consider a deal $I = \{(A, a), (B, b), (C, c)\} \in \mathcal{I}$. Let $P_A(a) = M$ be the announcement sent by A, and denote it also by $P_A(I)$. Two deals $I, I' \in \mathcal{I}$ are *initially indistinguishable* [4] to C with input c if $(C, c) \in I, I'$. And they are *indistinguishable after the protocol*, if additionally $P_A(I) = P_A(I')$. We require then that for C there are always two indistinguishable inputs of A, a, a', after the protocol, such that $x \in a$ and $x \notin a'$ or else $x \notin a$ and $x \in a'$. More precisely, for a vertex (C, c), let M be a *possible* message, namely, such that there exists $I = \{(A, a), (B, b), (C, c)\} \in \mathcal{I}$, and $P_A(I) = M$. For a hand c, let $\bar{c} = D\backslash c$, and $\triangle$ the symmetric difference operator.

Definition 2 (Safety). *A protocol P_A is* safe, *if for any (C, c), any $x \in \bar{c}$, and any possible message M for (C, c), there are edges $I = \{(A, a), (C, c)\} \in \mathcal{I}$, and $I' = \{(A, a'), (C, c)\} \in \mathcal{I}$, with $P_A(I) = P_A(I') = M$ such that $x \in a \triangle a'$.*

Notice that while $\mathbf{a}, \mathbf{b} \geq 1$, the previous definition applies even when $\mathbf{c} = 0$.

3 Protocol as Vertex Coloring

We represent subcomplexes of $\mathcal{I}$ as Johnson graphs in Sect. 3.1. We reformulate the information transmission problem as vertex colorings of Johnson graphs in Sect. 3.2. Implications of the reformulation are presented in Sect. 3.3.

3.1 Representing Indistinguishability by Johnson Graphs

The situation when B has input b is represented by a vertex $(B, b) \in \mathcal{I}$. The A-vertices that B considers possible with input b, are the A-neighbors of (B, b) in

$\mathcal{I}$. Thus, we define (following [11], but used since [32] in information theory) the graph $\mathcal{G}_B$ in terms of $\mathcal{I}$, as follows. The vertices of $\mathcal{G}_B$ consist of all the A-vertices of $\mathcal{I}$. There is an edge joining two vertices $(A, a), (A, a')$ if and only if there are edges in $\mathcal{I}$ connecting them with the same vertex (B, b). To analyze $\mathcal{G}_B$, we omit the id A from the vertices, and let $V(\mathcal{G}_B) = \mathscr{P}_{\mathbf{a}}(D)$. Thus, for two distinct $a, a' \in \mathscr{P}_{\mathbf{a}}(D)$, $\{a, a'\} \in E(\mathcal{G}_B)$ iff $\exists b \in \mathscr{P}_{\mathbf{b}}(D)$ such that $a, a' \subseteq \bar{b} = D - b$. If $\mathbf{r} = \mathbf{c} = 0$, and $n = \mathbf{a} + \mathbf{b}$, there are no two such distinct deals a, a', and the graph has no edges.

The graph $\mathcal{G}_C$ is defined analogously, on the same set of vertices, $V(\mathcal{G}_C) = \mathscr{P}_{\mathbf{a}}(D)$. When C has input c there is a vertex $(C, c) \in \mathcal{I}$. The A-vertices that C considers possible with input c, are the A-neighbors of (C, c) in $\mathcal{I}$. Thus, for two distinct $a, a' \in \mathscr{P}_{\mathbf{a}}(D)$, $\{a, a'\} \in E(\mathcal{G}_C)$ iff $\exists c \in \mathscr{P}_{\mathbf{c}}(D)$ such that $a, a' \subseteq \bar{c}$.

Lemma 1. *For $a, a' \in V(\mathcal{G}_B)$, $n = \mathbf{a} + \mathbf{b} + \mathbf{c} + \mathbf{r}$, $\mathbf{r} \geq 0$, we have that $\{a, a'\} \in E(\mathcal{G}_B)$ iff $\mathbf{a} - (\mathbf{c}+\mathbf{r}) \leq |a \cap a'|$. Similarly, $\{a, a'\} \in E(\mathcal{G}_C)$ iff $\mathbf{a} - (\mathbf{b}+\mathbf{r}) \leq |a \cap a'|$.*

Definition 3 (Distance d Johnson graph). *For a set of n elements, the graph $J^d(n, m)$, $0 \leq d \leq m$, has as vertices all m-subsets. Two vertices a, a' are adjacent whenever $m - d \leq |a \cap a'|$. When $d = 1$, we have a Johnson graph, denoted $J(n, m)$.*

We have our basic theorem for the rest of the paper.

Theorem 1. *The graph $\mathcal{G}_B$ for signature $(\mathbf{a}, \mathbf{b}, \mathbf{c})$ is equal to the graph $J^{\mathbf{c}+\mathbf{r}}(n, \mathbf{a})$. In particular, $\mathcal{G}_B$ is a Johnson graph, $J(n, \mathbf{a})$, exactly when $\mathbf{c}+\mathbf{r} = 1$. Similarly, $\mathcal{G}_C$ is equal to $J^{\mathbf{b}+\mathbf{r}}(n, \mathbf{a})$.*

The vertices of A that B considers possible with input b, are the A-neighbors of (B, b) in $\mathcal{I}$. They are denoted $K_p(\bar{b})$, where $\bar{b} = D - b$. They induce a clique in $\mathcal{G}_B$ (overloading notation the clique itself is also sometimes denoted by $K_p(\bar{b})$). The vertices in $K_p(\bar{b})$ are all $a \subseteq \bar{b}$ with $|a| = \mathbf{a}$. Thus, when B has input b, B considers possible that A has any input a, $a \in K_p(\bar{b})$. Notice that if $\mathbf{c} + \mathbf{r} = 0$ and $n = \mathbf{a} + \mathbf{b}$, then B with input b considers possible only one input for A, namely, $\bar{b}$. In this case, $E(\mathcal{G}_B) = \emptyset$.

Lemma 2. *For each hand b of B, the possible inputs of A induce a clique $K_p(\bar{b})$ in $\mathcal{G}_B$, $p = \binom{n-\mathbf{b}}{\mathbf{a}}$, consisting of all $a \in \mathscr{P}_{\mathbf{a}}(D)$, such that $a \subset \bar{b}$. Similarly, for $\mathcal{G}_C$, the vertices $K_p(\bar{c})$ consisting of all $a \in \mathscr{P}_{\mathbf{a}}(D)$ such that $a \subset \bar{c}$, induce a clique in $\mathcal{G}_C$.*

We have illustrated the following in the figure of the Introduction.

Remark 1 (Subgraphs). If $\mathbf{b} \leq \mathbf{c}$ then $J^{\mathbf{b}+\mathbf{r}}(n, \mathbf{a})$ is a subgraph of $J^{\mathbf{c}+\mathbf{r}}(n, \mathbf{a})$ on the same set of vertices. Hence, for each $b \in \mathscr{P}_{\mathbf{b}}(D)$, $c \in \mathscr{P}_{\mathbf{c}}(D)$, both $K_p(\bar{b})$ and $K_p(\bar{c})$ induce cliques in $J^{\mathbf{c}+\mathbf{r}}(n, \mathbf{a})$. Furthermore, if $b \subseteq c$, then $K_p(\bar{c}) \subseteq K_p(\bar{b})$.

3.2   Protocol as Vertex Coloring of a Johnson Graph

Consider a protocol P_A for signature $(\mathbf{a}, \mathbf{b}, \mathbf{c})$, with $n = \mathbf{a} + \mathbf{b} + \mathbf{c} + \mathbf{r}$. In light of Theorem 1, we take the view of P_A as a vertex coloring, $P_A : \mathscr{P}_{\mathbf{a}}(D) \to \mathcal{M}$. For vertex $(A, a) \in \mathcal{I}$, $P_A(a)$ is the message $M \in \mathcal{M}$, sent by A when she has input a. We assume that P_A is surjective. The set of A-vertices colored M is $P_A^{-1}(M)$.[5]

Recall that a vertex coloring of a graph is *proper* if each pair of adjacent vertices have different colors. The following theorems reformulate the informative and safety notions of Definitions 1 and 2.

Theorem 2 (Informative characterization). *Let $P_A : \mathscr{P}_{\mathbf{a}}(D) \to \mathcal{M}$ be a protocol.*

- *P_A is informative if and only if P_A is a proper vertex coloring of $J^{\mathbf{c}+\mathbf{r}}(n, \mathbf{a})$.*
- *When $\mathbf{c} + \mathbf{r} \geq 1$, P_A is minimally informative if and only if for each $b \in \mathscr{P}_{\mathbf{b}}(D)$ there is some edge $\{a, a'\}$ in the clique $K_p(\bar{b})$ of $J^{\mathbf{c}+\mathbf{r}}(n, \mathbf{a})$, such that $P_A(a) \neq P_A(a')$.*

By Lemma 10, for the case when $\mathbf{c} + \mathbf{r} = 1$ (recall Theorem 1), we have that B learns at least one card of A (Lemma 11).

Recall from Sect. 3.1 the graph $\mathcal{G}_C$. The vertices of $\mathcal{G}_C$ consist of all the A-vertices of $\mathcal{I}$. There is an edge joining two vertices $(A, a), (A, a')$ if and only if there are edges in $\mathcal{I}$ connecting them with the same vertex (C, c). Then, $V(\mathcal{G}_C) = V(\mathcal{G}_B) = \mathscr{P}_{\mathbf{a}}(D)$, and for two distinct hands a, a' of size $\mathbf{a}$, $\{a, a'\} \in E(\mathcal{G}_C)$ iff $\exists c \in \mathscr{P}_{\mathbf{c}}(D)$ such that $a, a' \subseteq \bar{c} = D - c$. Namely, we have the graph $J^{\mathbf{b}+\mathbf{r}}(n, \mathbf{a})$, where $K_p(\bar{c})$ induces a clique, for every $c \in \mathscr{P}_{\mathbf{c}}(D)$. In the following the set of colors of vertices of a clique is denoted, $P_A(K_p(\bar{c})) = \{M \mid P(a) = M, a \in K_p(\bar{c})\}$. The following equivalence is straightforward.

Theorem 3 (Safety characterization). *Let $P_A : \mathscr{P}_{\mathbf{a}}(D) \to \mathcal{M}$. The following conditions are equivalent.*

1. *P_A is safe.*
2. *Consider any $c \in \mathscr{P}_{\mathbf{c}}(D)$, and any $y \in \bar{c}$. For each $M \in P_A(K_p(\bar{c}))$, there exist $a, a' \in K_p(\bar{c})$ with $P_A(a) = P_A(a') = M$ such that $y \in a \triangle a'$.*

In a *two-step protocol* first A and then B makes an announcement, both heard by C. If a protocol P_A is informative and safe, and $\mathbf{r} = 0$, one may assume that P_B, the protocol of B, is simply to announce C's set of cards.

Corollary 1. *There is a 2-step solution for the Russian problem $(\mathbf{a}, \mathbf{b}, \mathbf{c})$, $n = \mathbf{a} + \mathbf{b} + \mathbf{c} + \mathbf{r}$ with A making the first announcement, if and only if there is a safe proper coloring of $J^{\mathbf{c}+\mathbf{r}}(n, \mathbf{a})$.*

---

[5] Thus, $P_A^{-1}(M)$ is equivalent to an "announcement" by A in the terminology of [2], or the "alternative hands" for A, in the notation of [12, Proposition 24].

3.3 General Bounds

For a protocol $P_A : \mathscr{P}_{\mathbf{a}}(D) \to \mathcal{M}$, the protocol $\bar{P}_A : \mathscr{P}_{n-\mathbf{a}}(D) \to \mathcal{M}$ is defined by

$$\bar{P}_A(a) = P_A(\bar{a}),$$

where as usual, $\bar{a} = D \backslash a$. The following main result of the section shows that there is a safe proper coloring of $J(n, \mathbf{a})$ iff there is a safe proper coloring of $J(n, n - \mathbf{a})$. Remarkably, this result does not hold for minimally informative protocols (see Corollary 3).

Theorem 4 (duality). *Assume* $\mathbf{c} + \mathbf{r} = 1$*, so* $n = \mathbf{a} + \mathbf{b} + 1$*. A protocol* P_A *is informative and safe for* $(\mathbf{a}, \mathbf{b}, \mathbf{c})$ *if and only if the protocol* $\bar{P}_A$ *is informative and safe for* $(\mathbf{b} + 1, \mathbf{a} - 1, \mathbf{c})$*.*

For instance, there is solution for the $(4, 2, 1)$ case, because it is equivalent to a solution to $(3, 3, 1)$, the classic Russian cards case[6]. However, there is no solution for the $(2, 4, 1)$ case, as we show in the next theorem (and was observed in [2]). The reason is that in this case we get the graph $J(7, 2)$, which has no safe proper coloring. Thus, while we assume that A makes the first announcement; to analyze the other case, one may exchange values of $\mathbf{a}$ and $\mathbf{b}$. It may be more convenient that A makes the first announcement, or that B makes it, in terms of both solvability and communication complexity. For the first case, a coloring has to be found for $J(n, \mathbf{a})$, and for the second case, one for $J(n, \mathbf{b})$.

Theorem 5. *If* $\mathbf{c} + \mathbf{r} \geq \min\{\mathbf{a}, n - \mathbf{a}\} - 1$*,* $\mathbf{c} \geq 1$*, then there is no safe proper coloring of* $J^{\mathbf{c}+\mathbf{r}}(n, \mathbf{a})$*.*

Recall that a protocol can be informative and safe only if $\mathbf{b} > \mathbf{c}$ (Remark 3). Thus, combining this fact with Theorem 5, we get the following, that includes several particular cases of interest, some previously observed[7].

Corollary 2. *There is no informative and safe protocol if* $\mathbf{c} \geq \mathbf{b}$ *or if* $\mathbf{c} + \mathbf{r} \geq \min\{\mathbf{a}, n - \mathbf{a}\} - 1$*,* $\mathbf{c} \geq 1$*.*

4 Minimal Information Transmission

We study first the protocol, χ_2, that sends the sum of the cards modulo 2. We show in Sect. 4.1 that χ_2 is minimally informative only if $\mathbf{b} < \lfloor n/2 \rfloor$. Thus, χ_2 is not minimally informative for the classic Russian cards case $(3, 3, 1)$.

In Sect. 4.2 we describe how to transform an informative protocol into a minimally informative protocol. Applying the reduction to $\chi_{mod\,n}$, when $\mathbf{c} + \mathbf{r} = 1$,

---

[6] This is the example of [2], "we get a 7-line good announcement for $(4, 2, 1)$. It may further be observed that this is the complement of a 7-line good announcement for $(3,3,1)$ as found above (for no apparent reason related to designs)".

[7] Using two different proof techniques, it was shown that if $\mathbf{a} \leq \mathbf{c} + 1$, there is no informative and safe solution ($\mathbf{r} = 0$), in [2, Corollary 2]) and [29, Theorem 6].

as $\mathbf{a}$ grows from 3 up to roughly $n/2$, the number of different messages goes down from $n/3$ to 2.

This reduction shows that there is a safe minimally informative protocol for the Russian cards case $(3, 3, 1)$ using 3 messages. Finally, we present a solution to the Russian cards case using only 2 messages, in Sect. 4.1. Given that there is no uniform safe informative protocol using 6 messages [27], indeed this 2-message protocol splits color classes of an informative protocol.

4.1 Minimal Information with 2 Messages

For signature $(\mathbf{a}, \mathbf{b}, \mathbf{c})$, with $n = \mathbf{a} + \mathbf{b} + \mathbf{c} + \mathbf{r}$, consider a protocol $\chi_2 : \mathscr{P}_\mathbf{a}(D) \to \{0, 1\}$, defined by

$$\chi_2(a) = \sum x \in a \pmod 2.$$

The Protocol χ_2 is Minimally Informative. Recall Lemma 2. For each input vertex (B, b) denoting that B gets hand b, there are $m = \binom{n-\mathbf{b}}{\mathbf{a}}$ possible hands a_i for A, corresponding to vertices (A, a_i). In $J^{\mathbf{c}+\mathbf{r}}(n, \mathbf{a})$ these vertices form a maximal clique $K_p(\bar{b})$ of $\mathcal{G}_B$, $p = \binom{n-\mathbf{b}}{\mathbf{a}}$, consisting of all hands $a \subset \bar{b}$, $|a| = \mathbf{a}$. If $\mathbf{b} \geq \lfloor n/2 \rfloor$ then for b of size $\mathbf{b}$, $\bar{b}$ may consist of cards of the same parity, and thus all $a \subset \bar{b}$, $|a| = \mathbf{a}$ have the same parity, and χ_2 is not minimally informative.

Lemma 3. *Assume that $\mathbf{c} + \mathbf{r} \geq 1$, $\mathbf{a} \geq 1$, $\mathbf{b} < \lfloor n/2 \rfloor$. Then χ_2 is a minimally informative protocol.*

The Protocol χ_2 is Safe. Lemma 3 implies that χ_2 is minimally informative when $n = 7, \mathbf{a} = 3, \mathbf{b} = 2, \mathbf{c} = 2, \mathbf{r} = 0$, namely, for $J^2(7, 3)$. But it is not safe, because if C has hand $\{1, 3\}$ and the announcement is 0 she knows that A does not have card 5. Or if the announcement is 1, she knows that A has card 5. More generally, the number of odd cards in D is $\lfloor n/2 \rfloor$. If $\mathbf{c} = \lfloor n/2 \rfloor - 1$ then when C holds $\mathbf{c}$ odd cards she can deduce from the announcement whether A holds the remaining odd card. Thus, assume that $\mathbf{c} \leq \lfloor n/2 \rfloor - 2$, and additionally, $\mathbf{a} \geq 2$ (Remark 4).

In Sect. 5.2 we discuss the modulo n case and the relation of proving safety with additive number theory. The proof for the modulo 2 case provides a simple illustration of the ideas.

Lemma 4. *Assume that $\mathbf{a}, \mathbf{b} \geq 2$ and $\mathbf{c} \leq \lfloor n/2 \rfloor - 2$. Then χ_2 is a safe protocol.*

Combining Lemma 3 and Lemma 4 we get the following theorem.

Theorem 6. *Let $n = \mathbf{a} + \mathbf{b} + \mathbf{c} + \mathbf{r}$. If $\mathbf{a}, \mathbf{b} \geq 2$, $\mathbf{c} \leq \lfloor n/2 \rfloor - 2$, $\mathbf{c} + \mathbf{r} \geq 1$, and $\mathbf{b} < \lfloor n/2 \rfloor$, then χ_2 is minimally informative and safe.*

Thus, for example, when $n = 7$, $\mathbf{a} = 3$, $\mathbf{b} = 2$, $\mathbf{c} = 1, \mathbf{r} = 1$, namely, $J^2(7, 3)$, then χ_2 is both minimally informative and safe. Similarly for $n = 7$, $\mathbf{a} = 4$, $\mathbf{b} = 2$, $\mathbf{c} = 1, \mathbf{r} = 0$, namely, $J(7, 4)$. Which is interesting, because it shows that the duality Theorem 4 does not hold for minimally informative protocols; notice that $J(7, 4) \cong J(7, 3)$, but $\bar{\chi}_2$ is not minimally informative for $J(7, 3)$ (neither is χ_2). More generally, we get the following.

Corollary 3. *Assume* $c + r = 1$. *Then,* χ_2 *is minimally informative and safe, whenever* $a > \lceil n/2 \rceil - 1$ *and* $b < \lfloor n/2 \rfloor$.

The Russian Cards Case with Two Messages. The following protocol χ is a minimally informative 2-coloring of $J(7,3)$.

$$\chi^{-1}(0) = \{012, 013, 014, 015, 016, 023, 024, 025, 036, 046, 056, 126, 134, 135,$$
$$234, 236, 245, 246, 345, 356, 456\}$$
$$\chi^{-1}(1) = \{026, 034, 035, 045, 123, 124, 125, 136, 145, 146, 156, 235, 256, 346\}$$

The solution was found by Zoe Leyva-Acosta and Eduardo Pascual-Aseff, using a computer program.

4.2 Reducing Informative to Minimally Informative Protocols

As observed in Sect. 4.1, the protocol χ_2 is not minimally informative when $a \leq \lceil n/2 \rceil - 1$ or $b \geq \lfloor n/2 \rfloor$, and thus, in particular, for the Russian cards problem $(3, 3, 1)$, $r = 0$. We present here a protocol for this case, based on the χ_{modn} protocol studied in Sect. 5. Notice that the protocol χ_{modn} is safe and informative when $c + r = 1$.

The protocol uses the idea that, merging two color classes of a protocol P_A, $P_A^{-1}[M] \cup P_A^{-1}[M']$, leads to a new protocol that preserves safety (but possibly not informative properties). Actually, the idea works for any safe and informative protocol $P_A : \mathscr{P}_a(D) \to \mathcal{M}$. If $|\mathcal{M}| = m$, let us denote $\mathcal{M} = \mathbb{Z}_m$.

If $P_A : \mathscr{P}_a(D) \to \mathbb{Z}_m$ is a safe proper coloring of $J^{c+r}(n, a)$, $c + r \geq 1$, define the protocol, $P_A^{[p]} : \mathscr{P}_a(D) \to \mathbb{Z}_{\lceil m/(p-1) \rceil}$, where

$$P_A^{[p]}(a) = P_A(a) \pmod{\lceil m/(p-1) \rceil},$$

$p = \binom{a+c+r}{a} = \binom{n-b}{a}$.

Theorem 7 (Information reduction). *If* P_A *is a safe and informative protocol then* $P_A^{[p]}$ *is a safe and minimally informative protocol. Thus, if* m *is the different number of messages used by* P_A, *then* $\lceil m/(p-1) \rceil$ *is the number of messages used by* $P_A^{[p]}$.

In the case of $c + r = 1$, the protocol χ_{modn} studied in Sect. 5 is a safe and informative protocol (Theorem 8), using n different messages. In this case, $p = a + 1$. Thus we have the following.

Corollary 4. *The protocol* $\chi_{modn}^{[a+1]}$ *is minimally informative and safe for* $a, b \geq 3$, $c + r = 1$, *using* $\lceil n/a \rceil$ *different messages.*

Notice that not every minimally informative safe protocol can be obtained by reduction from an informative protocol. Theorem 6 states that χ_2 is minimally informative and safe in some cases where

$$c \geq b \quad \text{or} \quad c + r \geq \min\{a, n - a\} - 1. \tag{1}$$

For instance, the case of signature $(6, 6, 8)$, $\mathbf{r} = 0$, satisfies the hypothesis of the theorem and hence χ_2 is minimally informative and safe. But recall that in such cases (1) there is no informative and safe protocol (Corollary 2).

5 The Modular Protocol χ_{modn} for $\mathbf{c} + \mathbf{r} = 1$

For signature $(\mathbf{a}, \mathbf{b}, \mathbf{c})$, with $n = \mathbf{a} + \mathbf{b} + \mathbf{c} + \mathbf{r}$, consider the protocol χ_{modn} : $\mathscr{P}_{\mathbf{a}}(D) \rightarrow \mathbb{Z}_n$, defined by

$$\chi_{modn}(a) = \sum x \in a \pmod{n}.$$

All operations in this section are modulo n, working in $\mathbb{Z}_n$, even when not explicitly stated. We show that χ_{modn} is informative and safe when $\mathbf{c} + \mathbf{r} = 1$. It is easy to see that χ_{modn} is not informative when $\mathbf{c} + \mathbf{r} > 1$, and more complicated techniques are needed, discussed in Sect. 6.

5.1 χ_{modn} Is Informative and Coding Theory

The result that χ_{modn} is informative when $\mathbf{c} + \mathbf{r} = 1$ is known and easy [7]. But our perspective that this is equivalent to being a proper vertex coloring of $J(n, \mathbf{a})$ exposes the connection with coding theory. It is actually the argument (generalized in Sect. 6 to $\mathbf{c} + \mathbf{r} > 1$) behind the proof that shows a lower bound on $A(n, 4, w)$, the maximum number of codewords in any binary code of length n, constant weight w, and Hamming distance 4 [20, Theorem 1].

Lemma 5. *For* $\mathbf{c} + \mathbf{r} = 1$, χ_{modn} *is a proper vertex coloring of* $J(n, \mathbf{a})$, *for* $1 \leq \mathbf{a} < n$.

5.2 If $\mathbf{c} + \mathbf{r} = 1$ Then χ_{modn} Is Safe

Now we show that when $\mathbf{c} + \mathbf{r} = 1$, the codes described in Sect. 5.1, defined by χ_{modn}^{-1}, are safe. We prove it using the additive number theory properties [27].

Theorem 8. *The protocol* χ_{modn} *is informative and safe when* $\mathbf{c} + \mathbf{r} = 1$, $\mathbf{a}, \mathbf{b} \geq 3$, $n \geq 7$.

This theorem generalizes and simplifies results of [7].[8]

---

[8] In [7, Corollary 9] it is shown that the protocol is safe when n prime, with a proof based on a non-trivial theorem by Dias da Silva and Hamidoune [10, Theorem 4.1]. Which is analogous to the Cauchy-Davenport theorem, the first theorem in additive group theory [26]. Then, this result was extended to [7, Theorem 13], proving that a protocol that announces the sum of the cards modulo p is safe, except for $(4, 3, 1)$, $(3, 4, 1)$, where p is the least prime greater than or equal to $\mathbf{a} + \mathbf{b} + 1$.

6 Informative Transmission: The General Case $\mathbf{c} + \mathbf{r} \geq 1$

In this section we discuss an informative solution when $\mathbf{c} + \mathbf{r} \geq 1$. As far as we know, this is the first general informative protocol, and there is no safe and informative general solution known. Swanson et al. [30] discuss informative protocols and their relation to combinatorial designs. They explain the combinatorial difficulty of the case $\mathbf{c} + \mathbf{r} \geq 1$.

We are now behind the classic coding theory proof that shows a lower bound on $A(n, 2\delta, w)$, the maximum number of codewords in any binary code of length n, constant weight w, and Hamming distance 2δ. Namely, the proof that shows that the vertices in $\chi_{mod\,n}^{-i}$ in this case define a binary code of length n, constant weight w, and Hamming distance 2δ. We reuse the coding theory argument from [20, Theorem 4]. Let q be a primer power (positive integer power of a single prime number), $q \geq n$. Let the elements of the Galois field $GF(q)$ be $w_0, w_1, \ldots, w_{q-1}$. For a vertex a of $J^d(n, \mathbf{a})$, let $a_i = 1$ if $i \in a$, and else $a_i = 0$. Namely, for the following lemma we view a as a vector $a = (a_0, \ldots, a_{n-1}) \in \mathbb{F}_\mathbf{a}^n$. Define $\bar{\chi}(a)$ to be the vector $(\chi_1(a), \chi_2(a), \ldots, \chi_d(a))$,

$$\chi_1(a) = \sum_{a_i=1} w_i,$$

$$\chi_2(a) = \sum_{\substack{i<j \\ a_i=a_j=1}} w_i w_j, \tag{2}$$

$$\chi_3(a) = \sum_{\substack{i<j<k \\ a_i=a_j=a_k=1}} w_i w_j w_k,$$

$$\ldots$$

Then, for $v \in GF(q)^d$, the set of vertices colored v is $\bar{\chi}^{-1}(v)$.

Lemma 6. $\bar{\chi}$ is a proper vertex coloring of $J^d(n, \mathbf{a})$, $d \geq 1$, $d < \min\{\mathbf{a}, n - \mathbf{a}\}$.

Thus, the set of colors needed is of size at most q^d. Which implies that there is always a set of size at most $(2n)^d$ to properly color $J^d(n, \mathbf{a})$, because Bertrand's postulate states that there is a prime p such that $n < p \leq 2n$.

On the other hand, there is a corresponding (asymptotically in terms of n, for $\mathbf{c} + \mathbf{r}$ constant) lower bound[9]. Namely, by Lemma 2, the cliques $K_p(\bar{b})$ in $\mathcal{G}_B$ have size $p = \binom{\mathbf{a+c+r}}{\mathbf{a}}$, and by Lemma 7, $J^d(n, m) \cong J^d(n, n - m)$. Thus,

Theorem 9. $\Theta((\mathbf{c} + \mathbf{r}) \log n)$ bits are needed and sufficient for an informative protocol.

---

[9] Recall that $\binom{z+k}{k} = \frac{k^z}{\Gamma(z+1)}(1 + \frac{z(z+1)}{2k} + O(k^{-2}))$, as $k \to \infty$. Thus, in more detail, the lower bound in the number of bits is $\Theta((\mathbf{c} + \mathbf{r}) \log n - (\mathbf{c} + \mathbf{r}) \log(\mathbf{c} + \mathbf{r}))$.

7   Conclusions

We have presented a new perspective inspired by distributed computing on the basic problem of safe information transmission from A to B in the face of an eavesdropper C. The formalization in terms of Johnson graphs, facilitated using known results about these graphs, closely related to coding theory, and motivated developing new additive number theory proofs. We were able thus to prove new results, as well as explaining and unifying previously known results. We considered the standard informative notion, requiring the B learns the hand of A, and defined the new notion, of minimal information transfer.

Many interesting avenues remain for future work. Some problems would imply solutions in coding theory, where much research has been done. A detailed study of the general case $d \geq 1$ is beyond the scope of this paper. The colorings for minimal information transmission do not seem to have been studied before, and many cases remain open.

Many other interesting problems remain open, about the relation with combinatorial designs (that has been thoroughly studied e.g. [30]), about stronger security requirements e.g. [24], about fault-tolerant solutions [21], and more than two parties e.g. [14], and randomized protocols [16]. It would be interesting to understand the role of Johnson graphs in multi-round protocols; there exists work from the secret sharing side e.g. [17], from the Russian cards side [9,13], and from the distributed computing side [6,11].

Acknowledgements. We would like to thank Jorge Armenta, Hans van Ditmarsch, Zoe Leyva-Acosta, and Eduardo Pascual-Aseff for their many comments. This work was supported by the UNAM-PAPIIT project IN106520.

A   Appendix

It is easy to see and well-known that $J(n, m)$ is isomorphic to $J(n, n - m)$. The same holds for the distance d version.

Lemma 7. *The following are isomorphic graphs* $J^d(n, m) \cong J^d(n, n - m)$.

Remark 2 (Maximal cliques).   There are two families of maximal cliques in $J(n, m)$. For the first, take all $n - m + 1$ of the m-subsets that contain a fixed $(m - 1)$-subset; for the second, take the m-subsets of a fixed set of size $m + 1$. When $n = 2m$ the cliques in these two families have the same size. Maximality of the cliques is implied by Erdös–Ko–Rado Theorem [19, Chapter 6]. In the case of $J^d(n, m)$, we have already encountered one family in Lemma 2. For each $(m+d)$-subset $\bar{b}$, there is a clique in $J^d(n, m)$, denoted $K_p(\bar{b})$. The vertices of $K_p(\bar{b})$ are all m-subsets of $\bar{b}$. We will encounter the other family as well, $K'_p(b)$. A clique $K'_p(b)$ is obtained by taking the m-subsets that contain a fixed $(m - d)$-subset b.

We recall a simple but useful *shifting* technique in Johnson graphs, and even more generally in intersecting set families [19], we use the following version. For a hand a, and cards i, j, with $i \notin a$, $j \in a$,

$$a_{ij} = (a \backslash j) \cup \{i\},$$

denoted by an arc $a \xrightarrow{ij} a_{ij}$. Notice that, $\{a, a_{ij}\} \in E(J(n, m))$, and if a' is reachable from a by d arcs, then $\{a, a'\} \in E(J^d(n, m))$.

For a hand s, we say that a' is *s-reachable* from a if there is a directed path from a to a' defined by a (possibly empty) sequence of arcs $\xrightarrow{ij}$, all of them with $i \in s$. (For the following cf. [28, Lemma 1]).

Lemma 8. *Let $a \in V(K_p(\bar{b}))$. Let $s = \bar{b} \backslash a$. Thus, $|s| = d$. Then, $V(K_p(\bar{b}))$ is the set of s-reachable vertices from a.*

Proof. First, notice that a is s-reachable from itself. Now, let a' be any other vertex of $K_p(\bar{b})$. If $2d' = |a \triangle a'|$, $d' \leq d$, order the cards in $a \backslash a'$ as $x_1, \ldots, x_{d'}$ and those in $a' \backslash a$ as $x'_1, \ldots, x'_{d'}$. Then, a' is reachable from a by the path

$$a = a_0 \xrightarrow{x'_1 x_1} a_1 \xrightarrow{x'_2 x_2} a_2 \cdots \xrightarrow{x'_{d'} x_{d'}} a_{d'} = a'.$$

Lemma 9. *Let $K_p(\bar{b})$ be a clique of $J^d(n, m)$. For any set of k vertices, $1 \leq k < p$, $\{a_1, \ldots, a_k\} \subset K_p(\bar{b})$, there exists a set $s \subset \bar{b}$, $|s| = d$, such that for any a_i, $a_i \cap s \neq \emptyset$.*

Proof. Pick $a \in K_p(\bar{b})$ not in $\{a_i\}$. Let $s = \bar{b} \backslash a$, $|s| = d$. Since $K_p(\bar{b})$ is the set of s-reachable vertices from a (Lemma 8), all other vertices in $K_p(\bar{b})$ are s-reachable from a, $s = \bar{b} \backslash a$. And hence, for the subset $\{a_i\}$ of those vertices, we have that for any a_i, $a_i \cap s \neq \emptyset$.

In particular, when $d = 1$, the following holds.

Lemma 10. *Consider $J(n, m)$ and any $K_{m+1}(\bar{b})$. For any set of k vertices, $1 \leq k \leq m + 1$, $\{a_1, \ldots, a_k\} \subseteq K_{m+1}(\bar{b})$, it holds that $|\cap a_i| = m + 1 - k$.*

Proof. Consider the a_i vertices in order $a_1, \ldots, a_k$, and the shiftings

$$a_1 \xrightarrow{x'_1 x_1} a_2 \xrightarrow{x'_2 x_2} a_3 \cdots a_{k-1} \xrightarrow{x'_{k-1} x_{k-1}} a_k,$$

where $a_{i+1} \backslash a_i = x'_i$ and $a_i \backslash a_{i+1} = x_i$. Thus, by induction on i, for each $i \geq 1$, $|a_1 \cap a_2 \cap \ldots \cap a_i| = m + 1 - i$.

Lemma 11. *Let $\mathbf{c} + \mathbf{r} = 1$. For a minimally informative protocol P_A, there exists a decision function for B, δ_B, such that when the hand of A is a and $P_A(a) = M$, then $\delta_B(b, M) = x$, for some $x \in a$.*

The following argument is similar to [12, Proposition 29].

Lemma 12. *Let* $a \geq 2$, $c \geq 1$, P_A *be a safe protocol. Consider any* M. *For any vertex* $a \in P_A^{-1}(M)$, *any* $z \in a$, *and any card* y, *there must be another vertex* $a' \in P_A^{-1}(M)$ *that also includes card* z, *and* $y \in a \triangle a'$.

Remark 3 (Safety).

- Informative requires P_A to be a proper vertex coloring of $J^{c+r}(n, \mathbf{a})$, while safety requires that P_A is not a proper vertex coloring of $J^{b+r}(n, \mathbf{a})$. Thus, by Remark 1, a protocol can be informative and safe only if $\mathbf{b} > \mathbf{c}$. In this case, while $K_p(\bar{c})$ induces a clique in $J^{b+r}(n, \mathbf{a})$, it does not induce a clique in $J^{c+r}(n, \mathbf{a})$, by Remark 2. (cf. [2, Lemma 2]).
- Joining color classes $P_A^{-1}[M] \cup P_A^{-1}[M']$ of a protocol preserves safety, but not necessarily informative properties (see Sect. 4.2).

Remark 4 (The assumption $\mathbf{a} \geq 2$*).* A simple consequence of Theorem 3 is that we should concentrate on the case that $\mathbf{a} \geq 2$. If $\mathbf{a} = 1$ then a safe protocol P_A must always send the same message M. Otherwise, if $P_A(y) \neq P_A(y')$ for $y, y' \in D$, then when C has a hand c, such that $y, y' \in \bar{c}$, then when C hears $P_A(y)$ she knows that A does not have card y'. Thus a safe protocol P_A cannot be minimally informative, and thus cannot be informative either.

Theorem 4. *Assume* $\mathbf{c} + \mathbf{r} = 1$, *so* $n = \mathbf{a} + \mathbf{b} + 1$. *A protocol* P_A *is informative and safe for* $(\mathbf{a}, \mathbf{b}, \mathbf{c})$ *if and only if the protocol* $\bar{P}_A$ *is informative and safe for* $(\mathbf{b} + 1, \mathbf{a} - 1, \mathbf{c})$.

Proof. There are two cases: $\mathbf{c} = 1, \mathbf{r} = 0$, and $\mathbf{c} = 0, \mathbf{r} = 1$. First we show the equivalence for the informative property, in both cases.

Notice that $n - \mathbf{a} = \mathbf{b} + 1$. By Lemma 7, we have that $J(n, \mathbf{a}) \cong J(n, n - \mathbf{a})$, under the isomorphism $f(a) = \bar{a}$. Thus, if P_A is an informative, i.e., proper vertex coloring of $J(n, \mathbf{a})$, then $\bar{P}_A(a) = P_A(f(a))$ is a proper vertex coloring of $J(n, n - \mathbf{a})$.

Now, consider the case $\mathbf{c} = 1, \mathbf{r} = 0$, and assume that P_A is safe for $(\mathbf{a}, \mathbf{b}, 1)$. That is, for every card $c \in \mathscr{P}_\mathbf{c}(D)$, $\mathbf{c} = 1$, $y \in \bar{c}$, and $M \in P_A(K_p(\bar{c}))$, there exists $a, a' \in K_p(\bar{c})$, $P_A(a) = P_A(a') = M$ such that $y \in a \triangle a'$.

To prove that $\bar{P}_A$ is safe, we need to consider a card $c \in \mathscr{P}_\mathbf{c}(D)$, and the vertices of $K'_p(\bar{c})$ in $J(n, n - \mathbf{a})$, which are $\bar{a} \in \mathscr{P}_{n-\mathbf{a}}(D)$, such that $\bar{a} \subseteq \bar{c}$.

Let $y \in \bar{c}$, $\bar{a} \in K'_p(\bar{c})$ with $\bar{P}_A(\bar{a}) = M$. Suppose $y \in a$ (the case when $y \notin a$ is similar). Thus, $P_A(a) = M$ and $c \in a$. By Lemma 12 there exists $a' \in \mathscr{P}_\mathbf{a}(D)$, $y \notin a'$, $P_A(a') = M$, such that $c \in a'$.

Now, let $a' \in \mathscr{P}_\mathbf{a}(D)$, $y \notin a'$, $P_A(a') = M$, with $c \in a'$. Then, c is in both a and a', and hence c is in neither $\bar{a}$ nor $\bar{a}'$. Namely, $\bar{a}, \bar{a}' \in K'_p(\bar{c})$. But $\bar{P}_A(\bar{a}) = P_A(\bar{a}') = M$. And we are done, because $y \in \bar{a} \triangle \bar{a}'$.

For the converse, assume P_A is safe for $(\mathbf{b} + 1, \mathbf{a} - 1, 1) = (n - \mathbf{a}, \mathbf{a} - 1, 1)$, and consider $c \in \mathscr{P}_\mathbf{c}(D)$, and the vertices of $K_p(\bar{c})$ in $J(n, \mathbf{a})$, which are $a \in \mathscr{P}_\mathbf{a}(D)$, such that $a \subseteq \bar{c}$.

Let $y \in \bar{c}$, $a \in K_p(\bar{c})$ with $P_A(a) = M$. Suppose $y \in a$ (the case when $y \notin a$ is similar). Consider $\bar{a}$, and hence $\bar{P}_A(\bar{a}) = P_A(a)$. Thus, $c \in \bar{a}$. By Lemma 12 there exists $\bar{a}' \in \mathscr{P}_{n-\mathbf{a}}(D)$, $y \notin \bar{a}'$, $\bar{P}_A(\bar{a}') = M$, such that $c \in \bar{a}'$. Then, c is in both $\bar{a}$ and $\bar{a}'$, and hence c is in neither a nor a'. Namely, $a, a' \in K_p(\bar{c})$. But $P_A(a) = P_A(a') = M$. And we are done, because $y \in a \triangle a'$.

Finally, we prove the safety equivalence, for the second case, where $\mathbf{c} = 0, \mathbf{r} = 1$. Solving the weak Russian cards problem for the case $(\mathbf{a}, \mathbf{b}, 0)$ is equivalent to solving it for the case $(\mathbf{b} + 1, \mathbf{a} - 1, 0)$. This case is easier, it does not need Lemma 12. If P_A is safe for $(\mathbf{a}, \mathbf{b}, 0)$, then we take c and $\bar{c}$ as the empty set. Then, for any $y \in D$, and M, there exists a, a' such that $P_A(a) = P_A(a')$, such that $y \in a \triangle a'$. Then, $y \in \bar{a} \triangle \bar{a}'$, which is what is needed for $\bar{P}_A$ to be safe, since $\bar{P}_A(\bar{a}) = \bar{P}_A(\bar{a}')$. The converse is similar.

References

1. Albert, M., Cordón-Franco, A., van Ditmarsch, H., Fernández-Duque, D., Joosten, J.J., Soler-Toscano, F.: Secure communication of local states in interpreted systems. In: Abraham, A., Corchado, J.M., González, S.R., De Paz, S.J.F. (eds.) International Symposium on Distributed Computing and Artificial Intelligence. AINSC, vol. 91, pp. 117–124. Springer, Heidelberg (2011). https://doi.org/10.1007/978-3-642-19934-9_15
2. Albert, M.H., Aldred, R.E.L., Atkinson, M.D., van Ditmarsch, H., Handley, C.C.: Safe communication for card players by combinatorial designs for two-step protocols. Australas. J Comb. **33**, 33–46 (2005)
3. Attiya, H., Bar-Noy, A., Dolev, D., Peleg, D., Reischuk, R.: Renaming in an asynchronous environment. J. ACM **37**(3), 524–548 (1990)
4. Attiya, H., Rajsbaum, S.: Indistinguishability. Commun. ACM **63**(5), 90–99 (2020)
5. Brouwer, A.E., Etzion, T.: Some new distance-4 constant weight codes. Adv. Math. Commun. **5**, 417–424 (2011)
6. Conde, R., Rajsbaum, S.: The complexity gap between consensus and safe-consensus. In: Halldórsson, M.M. (ed.) SIROCCO 2014. LNCS, vol. 8576, pp. 68–82. Springer, Cham (2014). https://doi.org/10.1007/978-3-319-09620-9_7
7. Cordón-Franco, A., van Ditmarsch, H., Fernández-Duque, D., Joosten, J.J., Soler-Toscano, F.: A secure additive protocol for card players. Australas. J Comb. **54**, 163–176 (2012)
8. Cordón-Franco, A., van Ditmarsch, H., Fernández-Duque, D., Soler-Toscano, F.: A geometric protocol for cryptography with cards. Des. Codes Crypt. **74**(1), 113–125 (2013). https://doi.org/10.1007/s10623-013-9855-y
9. Cordón-Franco, A., Van Ditmarsch, H., Fernández-Duque, D., Soler-Toscano, F.: A colouring protocol for the generalized Russian cards problem. Theor. Comput. Sci. **495**, 81–95 (2013)
10. Da Silva, J.A.D., Hamidoune, Y.O.: Cyclic spaces for Grassmann derivatives and additive theory. Bull. Lond. Math. Soc. **26**(2), 140–146 (1994)
11. Delporte-Gallet, C., Fauconnier, H., Rajsbaum, S.: Communication complexity of wait-free computability in dynamic networks. In: Richa, A.W., Scheideler, C. (eds.) SIROCCO 2020. LNCS, vol. 12156, pp. 291–309. Springer, Cham (2020). https://doi.org/10.1007/978-3-030-54921-3_17
12. van Ditmarsch, H.: The Russian cards problem. Stud. Logica. **75**, 31–62 (2003). https://doi.org/10.1023/A:1026168632319

13. van Ditmarsch, H., Soler-Toscano, F.: Three steps. In: Leite, J., Torroni, P., Ågotnes, T., Boella, G., van der Torre, L. (eds.) CLIMA 2011. LNCS (LNAI), vol. 6814, pp. 41–57. Springer, Heidelberg (2011). https://doi.org/10.1007/978-3-642-22359-4_4

14. Duan, Z., Yang, C.: Unconditional secure communication: a Russian cards protocol. J. Comb. Optim. **19**(4), 501–530 (2010). https://doi.org/10.1007/s10878-009-9252-7

15. Etzion, T., Bitan, S.: On the chromatic number, colorings, and codes of the Johnson graph. Discrete Appl. Math. **70**(2), 163–175 (1996)

16. Fischer, M.J., Paterson, M.S., Rackoff, C.: Secret bit transmission using a random deal of cards. In: Feigenbaum, J., Merritt, M. (eds.) Distributed Computing and Cryptography, Proceedings of a DIMACS Workshop. DIMACS Series in Discrete Mathematics and Theoretical Computer Science, Princeton, New Jersey, USA, 4–6 October 1989, vol. 2, pp. 173–182. DIMACS/AMS (1989)

17. Fischer, M.J., Wright, R.N.: Multiparty secret key exchange using a random deal of cards. In: Feigenbaum, J. (ed.) CRYPTO 1991. LNCS, vol. 576, pp. 141–155. Springer, Heidelberg (1992). https://doi.org/10.1007/3-540-46766-1_10

18. Fischer, M.J., Wright, R.N.: An efficient protocol for unconditionally secure secret key exchange. In: Proceedings of the Fourth Annual ACM-SIAM Symposium on Discrete Algorithms, SODA 1993, p. 475–483. Society for Industrial and Applied Mathematics (1993)

19. Godsil, C., Meagher, K.: Erdős-Ko-Rado Theorems: Algebraic Approaches. Cambridge Studies in Advanced Mathematics, Cambridge University Press, Cambridge (2015)

20. Graham, R., Sloane, N.: Lower bounds for constant weight codes. IEEE Trans. Inf. Theory **26**(1), 37–43 (1980)

21. Herlihy, M., Kozlov, D., Rajsbaum, S.: Distributed Computing Through Combinatorial Topology. Elsevier-Morgan Kaufmann, Amsterdam (2013)

22. Herlihy, M., Shavit, N.: The topological structure of asynchronous computability. J. ACM **46**(6), 858–923 (1999)

23. Kirkman, T.: On a problem in combinations. Camb. Dublin Math. J. **2**, 191–204 (1847)

24. Landerreche, E., Fernández-Duque, D.: A case study in almost-perfect security for unconditionally secure communication. Des. Codes Crypt. **83**(1), 145–168 (2016). https://doi.org/10.1007/s10623-016-0210-y

25. Makarychev, K.S., Makarychev, Y.S.: The importance of being formal. Math. Intell. **23**(1), 41–42 (2001). https://doi.org/10.1007/BF03024516

26. Mann, H.: Additive group theory-a progress report. Bull. Am. Math. Soc. **79**(6), 1069–1075 (1973)

27. Rajsbaum, S.: A distributed computing perspective of unconditionally secure information transmission in Russian cards problems, September 2020. https://arxiv.org/abs/2009.13644

28. Ramras, M., Donovan, E.: The automorphism group of a Johnson graph. SIAM J. Discrete Math. **25**(1), 267–270 (2011)

29. Swanson, C.M., Stinson, D.R.: Combinatorial solutions providing improved security for the generalized Russian cards problem. Des. Codes Crypt. **72**(2), 345–367 (2014). https://doi.org/10.1007/s10623-012-9770-7

30. Swanson, C.M., Stinson, D.R.: Additional constructions to solve the generalized Russian cards problem using combinatorial designs. Electron. J. Comb. **21**(3) (2014). https://doi.org/10.37236/4019

31. Winkler, P.: The advent of cryptology in the game of bridge. Cryptologia **7**(4), 327–332 (1983)
32. Witsenhausen, H.: The zero-error side information problem and chromatic numbers (corresp.). IEEE Trans. Inf. Theor. **22**(5), 592–593 (1976). https://doi.org/10.1109/TIT.1976.1055607

Synchronous Concurrent Broadcasts for Intermittent Channels with Bounded Capacities

Volker Turau[(✉)]

Institute of Telematics, Hamburg University of Technology, 21073 Hamburg, Germany
turau@tuhh.de

Abstract. In this work we extend the recently proposed synchronous broadcast algorithm *amnesiac flooding* to the case of intermittent communication channels. In amnesiac flooding a node forwards a received message in the subsequent round. There are several reasons that render an immediate forward of a message impossible: Higher priority traffic, overloaded channels, etc. We show that postponing the forwarding for one or more rounds prevents termination. Our extension overcomes this shortcoming while retaining the advantages of the algorithm: Nodes don't need to memorize the reception of a message to guarantee termination and messages are sent at most twice per edge. This extension allows to solve more general broadcast tasks such as multi-source broadcasts and concurrent broadcasts for systems with bounded channel capacities.

1 Introduction

Broadcasting is the task of delivering a message from one network node to all other nodes. Broadcast algorithms constitute a fundamental component of many distributed systems and are often used as subroutines in more complex algorithms. There are numberless applications of broadcast. Demers et al. discuss the maintenance of a database replicated at many sites in a large corporate network [3]. Each database update can be injected at various nodes, and these updates must be propagated to all nodes in the network. The replica become fully consistent only when all updating activity has stopped and the system has become quiescent. The efficiency of the broadcasting algorithm determines the rate of updates the system can handle.

A common broadcasting algorithm is flooding. The originator v_0 of a message m forwards m to all neighbors and when a node receives m for the first time, it sends it to all its neighbors in the communication graph $G(V, E)$. Flooding uses $2|E|$ messages and terminates after at most $\epsilon_G(v_0) + 1$ rounds, $\epsilon_G(v_0)$ denotes the maximal distance of v_0 to any other node. In this form flooding is a stateful algorithm, it requires each node to keep a record of already forwarded messages. This requires storage per node in the order of the number of broadcasted messages. Since nodes are unaware of the termination of the broadcast, these records have to be stored for an unknown time.

© Springer Nature Switzerland AG 2021
T. Jurdziński and S. Schmid (Eds.): SIROCCO 2021, LNCS 12810, pp. 296–312, 2021.
https://doi.org/10.1007/978-3-030-79527-6_17

For synchronous distributed systems stateless broadcasting algorithms are known. Hussak and Trehan proposed *amnesiac flooding* ($\mathcal{A}_{AF}$) [6]. Every time a node receives message m, it forwards it to those neighbors from which it didn't receive m in the current round. In contrast to classic flooding, a node may forward a message twice. Surprisingly amnesiac flooding terminates and each message is sent at most twice per edge. Crucial for the termination of $\mathcal{A}_{AF}$ is that the forwarding of messages is always performed in the round immediately following the reception. We show in Sect. 4 that algorithm $\mathcal{A}_{AF}$ no longer terminates when message forwarding is suspended for some rounds. There can be several reasons for suspending forwarding, when traffic with a priority higher than broadcast has to be handled, or when the capacity of a communication channel is exhausted due to several concurrent broadcasts. Surprisingly it requires only a simple extension to make $\mathcal{A}_{AF}$ to work correctly despite a limited number of suspensions. Our first contribution is the extended algorithm $\mathcal{A}_{AFI}$ described in Sect. 4.

Our first result enables us to prove that algorithm $\mathcal{A}_{AF}$ is also correct for multi-source broadcasting, i.e., several nodes broadcast the same message m in different rounds, provided a broadcast of m is invoked before m reaches the invoking node from another broadcast. In Sect. 5 we prove that in this case $\mathcal{A}_{AF}$ delivers m after at most $Diam(G)$ rounds and forwards m at most $2|E|$ times. If the communication channel is unavailable f times then $\mathcal{A}_{AFI}$ delivers m after at most $Diam(G) + 2f$ rounds, m is still forwarded at most $2|E|$ times.

While algorithm $\mathcal{A}_{AFI}$ is of interest on its own, it can also be used to solve the general task of multi-message broadcast in systems with bounded channel capacities. Multi-message broadcast means that multiple nodes initiate broadcasts of different messages, even when broadcasts from previous initiations have not yet terminated. If channel capacities are bounded, nodes can forward only a limited number of messages per round. Bounded channel capacities occur in communication systems utilizing TDMA, where communication is performed in fixed length slots and therefore only b messages can be sent in one round. If more than b messages are in the sending queue, then the forwarding of some messages has to be postponed for at least one round. In Sect. 6 we present two algorithms $\mathcal{A}_{AFIs}$ and $\mathcal{A}_{AFIF}$ for this task. The advantage of these algorithms is that compared to classic flooding besides the unavoidable message buffer no state information has to be maintained. Theorem 1 summarizes our third contribution.

Theorem 1. *Let S be a sequence of message broadcasts (identical or different messages) by the nodes of a graph $G(V, E)$ in arbitrary rounds under the restriction that a broadcast of message m is invoked before m reaches the invoking node from a broadcast of another node. If in each round each node can send at most b messages to each neighbor algorithm $\mathcal{A}_{AFIF}$ eventually terminates and delivers each message of S. Nodes don't need to memorize the reception of a message. If G is bipartite each message is forwarded $|E|$ times, otherwise $2|E|$ times.*

2   State of the Art

Broadcasting as a service in distributed systems can be realized in two ways: Either by using a pre-constructed structure such as a spanning tree or by performing the broadcast each time from scratch. In the first case a broadcast can be performed with $n - 1$ messages. In the second case a broadcast can be realized by $2(n - 1)$ messages by traversing the graph in a DFS style and carrying the identifiers of the visited nodes along with the messages. This requires messages that store up to n node identifiers. If the message size is restricted to $o(n)$ and only a fixed number of messages can be sent per round per link then each deterministic broadcast algorithm has message complexity $\Omega(|E|)$, Thm. 23.3.6 [9]. For a detailed analysis of broadcast algorithms we refer to Sec. 23 of [9].

In this work we focus on broadcast algorithms that do not rely on a pre-constructed structure and use limited communication channels. The most basic algorithm of this category is flooding as described above. Flooding uses $2|E|$ messages and terminates after at most $\epsilon_G(v_0) + 1$ rounds, these bounds hold in the synchronous and asynchronous model [9]. It requires each node to maintain for each message a record that the message has been forwarded. These records have to be kept for an unknown time. This requires storage per node proportional to the number of disseminated messages. Amnesiac flooding $\mathcal{A}_{\mathsf{AF}}$ overcomes this limitation in synchronous systems and is thus stateless [6]. $\mathcal{A}_{\mathsf{AF}}$ delivers a broadcasted message twice to each node. Thus, we have to distinguish between delivery and termination time. $\mathcal{A}_{\mathsf{AF}}$ delivers a message (resp. terminates) for an initiator v_0 on any finite graph in at most $\epsilon_G(v_0)$ (resp. $\epsilon_G(v_0) + Diam(G) + 1$) rounds, where $Diam(G)$ is the diameter of G. The termination time compared to standard flooding increases almost by a factor of 2. Amnesiac flooding was also analyzed for sets of initiators [13]. A stateless broadcasting algorithm with the same time complexity as classic flooding has recently been proposed in [11].

A problem related to broadcast is rumor spreading. It describes the dissemination of information in networks through pairwise interactions. A simple model for rumor spreading is that in each round, each node that knows the rumor, forwards it to a randomly chosen neighbor. For many topologies, this strategy is a very efficient way to spread a rumor. With high probability the rumor is received by all vertices in time $\Theta(\log n)$, if the graph is a complete graph or a hypercube [4,5]. New results about rumor spreading can be found in [8].

Intermittent channel availability is no issue for classic flooding and thus has not been considered. Broadcasting in distributed systems with bounded channel capacities has received little attention. Hussak et al. consider a model where a node can send only a single message per edge per round [7]. They propose a variant of amnesiac flooding to handle many nodes invoking broadcasts of different messages in different rounds. They show that their algorithm terminates, but delivery to all nodes is only guaranteed in the case that a single node broadcasts different messages. Our work is more general and uses a different approach.

Raynal et al. present a broadcast algorithm suited for dynamic systems where links can appear and disappear [10]. Some algorithms of [7] also maintain their properties in case edges or nodes disappear over time. Casteigts et al. analyze broadcasting with termination detection in time-varying graphs [2]. They prove that the solvability and complexity of this problem varies with the metric considered, as well as with the type of a priori knowledge available to nodes. Adamek et al. present a stateless planar geocasting algorithm relying on coordinates [1].

3   Notation and Model

In this work $G(V, E)$ denotes a finite, connected, undirected graph with $n = |V|$. Let $v, u \in V$, $d_G(v, u)$ denotes the distance between v and u in G, $N(v)$ the set of neighbors and $\epsilon_G(v)$ the *eccentricity* of v in G, i.e., the greatest distance between v and any other node in G. $Diam(G)$ denotes the maximum eccentricity of any node of G. An edge $(u, w) \in E$ is called a *cross edge* with respect to a node v_0 if $d_G(v_0, u) = d_G(v_0, w)$. Δ denotes the maximal node degree in G. Each node has a unique id and is aware of the ids of its neighbors but does not have any knowledge about graph parameters such as the number of nodes or diameter.

The goal of a broadcasting algorithm is to disseminate a message created by a node to all nodes of the network. Messages are assumed to be distinguishable, each having unique id. No message is lost in transit. A broadcast is said to *terminate* when all network events (message sends/receives) that were caused by that broadcast have ceased. A broadcast message is said to have been *delivered*, if it has been received by all the nodes in the network.

In this paper we consider synchronous distributed systems, i.e., algorithms are executed in rounds of fixed length and all messages sent by all nodes in a particular round are received and processed in the next round. In Sect. 6 we assume that in each round each node can only send a constant number b of messages to a subset of its neighbors. This can be realized by a network-level broadcast, where each message contains the identifiers of the receivers. This requires $O(b \log n)$ bits in each messages. Besides this, each message has just enough space to contain the information to be disseminated. In particular two messages cannot be aggregated into one.

4   Handling Intermittent Channels

In this section we extend $\mathcal{A}_{\mathsf{AF}}$ so that it operates correctly with intermittent channel availabilities. Algorithm 1 recaps the details of amnesiac flooding $\mathcal{A}_{\mathsf{AF}}$ as described in [6]. A node that wants to flood a message m sends m to all neighbors. Every time a node receives m, it forwards it to those neighbors from which it didn't receive m in the current round. The code in Algorithm 1 shows the handling of a single message m. If several messages are broadcasted concurrently, each requires its own set M.

An attempt to handle channel unavailabilities is to postpone the sending of some messages to the next round when the channel is again available. Messages received in the mean time are treated as before, the senders are inserted into M. Unfortunately, this modification of $\mathcal{A}_{\mathsf{AF}}$ may not terminate. Figure 1 presents an illustrative example. In the graph depicted in the top left node v_0 broadcasts a

---

Algorithm 1: Algorithm $\mathcal{A}_{AF}$ distributes a message m in the graph G

---

input : A graph $G = (V, E)$, a subset S of V, and a message m.

In round 1 each node $v \in S$ sends message m to each neighbor in G;
Each node v executes in every round $i > 1$

> $M := N(v)$;
> **foreach** receive(w, m) **do**
>> $M := M \setminus \{w\}$;
>
> **if** $M \neq N(v)$ **then**
>> **forall** $u \in M$ **do** send(u, m);

---

message m in round 0. Suppose that node v_2 (resp. v_3) cannot send messages in rounds $2, 3$ and 4 (resp. in round 2). We show that forwarding messages in the first available round may prevent termination. In the first round v_0 sends m to v_1, v_2 and v_3. In round 2 nodes v_2 and v_3 cannot forward m and postpone the sending. Node v_3 postpones this to round 3. In this round v_2 also receives a message from v_1. In rounds 3 and 4 node v_2 in addition receives a message from node v_5. These three events cannot be handled immediately and are also postponed. In round 5 the channel becomes available for node v_2, but in the meantime v_2 has received a message from all its neighbors and thus $\mathcal{A}_{AF}$ will not send m to any of v_2's neighbors. From this round on the channel is continuously available and thus $\mathcal{A}_{AF}$ can be executed in its original form. In round 9 the algorithm reaches the same configuration as in round 5. Thus, the algorithm does not terminate.

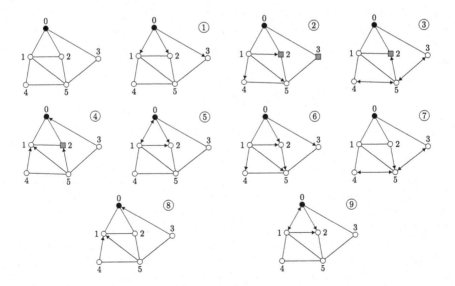

Fig. 1. A naive extension of algorithm $\mathcal{A}_{AF}$ does not terminate in case of intermittent channel availability. The configuration of round 5 repeats itself in round 9.

There is no striking reason for the failure of this naive attempt to fix $\mathcal{A}_{AF}$. To analyze the failure we reconsider the proof of termination of the original algorithm $\mathcal{A}_{AF}$ in [13]. This paper introduces for a given graph G and a broadcasting node v_0 the bipartite auxiliary graph $\mathcal{G}(v_0)$ and shows that executions of $\mathcal{A}_{AF}$ on G and $\mathcal{G}(v_0)$ are tightly coupled. $\mathcal{G}(v_0)$ is a double cover of G that consists of two copies of G, where the cross edges with respect to v_0 are removed. Each cross edges is replaced by two edges leading from one copy of G to the other. Figure 2 depicts $\mathcal{G}(v_0)$ for the graph shown in Fig. 1 (see Def. 3 in [13] for details).

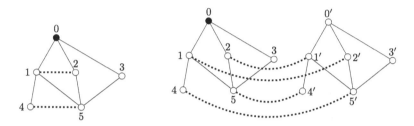

Fig. 2. The dashed lines on the left show the cross edges of G (v_0 is the broadcasting node). The graph $\mathcal{G}(v_0)$ is shown on the right, dashed edges are the replacement edges.

An important observation is that $\mathcal{G}(v_0)$ is bipartite and that in every round of $\mathcal{A}_{AF}$ the nodes that send messages have the same color in a 2-coloring of graph $\mathcal{G}(v_0)$. Figure 3 shows the separation of the nodes of $\mathcal{G}(v_0)$ into two color classes for the graph in Fig. 2. An analysis of the execution of Fig. 1 shows that in some rounds, nodes with different colors forward the message (e.g., in round 3).

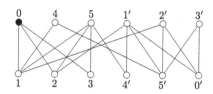

Fig. 3. Concurrently forwarding nodes in $\mathcal{A}_{AF}$ either all belong the top or bottom row.

4.1 Algorithm $\mathcal{A}_{AFI}$

The last observation leads to the following extension of $\mathcal{A}_{AF}$ for intermittent availabilities. If a message cannot be forwarded in the current round, it will be postponed until the next available round with the same parity, i.e., if the blocked round is odd (resp. even), the message will be forwarded in the next available odd (resp. even) round. This approach guarantees that as in $\mathcal{A}_{AF}$ all nodes that concurrently send messages belong to same of the two node sets.

Algorithm 2 shows a realization $\mathcal{A}_{AFI}$ of this idea. Compared to $\mathcal{A}_{AF}$ the new algorithm maintains two sets for the senders of the message in the variable M, one for messages that arrive in odd rounds and one for even rounds. The parity is maintained by the Boolean variable *parity*. The initialization of *parity* does not need be the same for all nodes. The symbol $\perp$ is used to indicate that no message has arrived in rounds with the specified parity. This is needed to distinguish this situation from the case that a node wants to broadcast a message, in this case $M[parity]$ is assigned the empty set. If we insert a node w into $M[parity]$ when $M[parity] = \perp$ then $M[parity] = \{w\}$ afterwards. Messages sent in round i are received in round $i + 1$. Hence, in round 1 no message is received.

Algorithm 2: Algorithm $\mathcal{A}_{AFI}$ distributes a message m in the graph G

Initialization
    parity:= true;
    $M[true] := M[false] := \perp$;

Upon receiving message m from w:
    $M[parity].add(w)$;

if channel is available and $M[parity] \neq \perp$ **then**
    | **forall** $u \in N(v) \setminus M[parity]$ **do** send(u, m);
    | $M[parity] := \perp$;

At the end of each round
    parity := $\neg parity$;

function broadcast(m)
    $M[parity] := \emptyset$;

Figure 4 shows an execution of algorithm $\mathcal{A}_{AFI}$ for the graph of Fig. 1, given that node v_2 (resp. v_3) cannot send in rounds 2 to 4 (resp. 2). The execution terminates after round 5, with no indeterminacy the algorithm would already terminate in 4 rounds (see [12] for details).

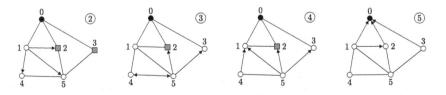

Fig. 4. Execution of $\mathcal{A}_{AFI}$ for the graph of Fig. 1. Round 1 is the same as in Fig. 1. In round 6 node v_2 does not need to forward the message because, it received messages from all neighbors in odd rounds (1, 3, 5). Whereas v_2 has to send a message to v_0 in round 5 because it only received the message from v_1 and v_5 in even rounds 2 and 4.

Clearly this extension of $\mathcal{A}_{\mathsf{AF}}$ is no longer stateless, but because of message buffering no stateless algorithm can handle channel unavailabilities.

4.2   Correctness and Complexity of Algorithm $\mathcal{A}_{\mathsf{AFI}}$

To formally describe a node's channel availability for message forwarding the concept of an availability scheme is introduced. Let $A : V \times \mathbb{N} \longrightarrow \{true, false\}$ be a predicate. Node v can send a message in round c_v only if $A(v, c_v) = true$. A is called an *availability scheme* for G and v_0 if the number of pairs $(v, i) \in V \times \mathbb{N}$ with $A(v, i) = false$ is bounded by a constant c. Note that this concept is only used in the formal proof. Nodes do not need to have a common round counter. The availability scheme for Fig. 1 is $A(v_2, 2) = A(v_2, 3) = A(v_2, 4) = A(v_3, 2) = false$ and *true* otherwise. WLOG we always assume that $A(v_0, 1) = true$.

For a given availability scheme A we construct a directed bipartite graph $\mathcal{B}_A(v_0)$ such that the execution of $\mathcal{A}_{\mathsf{AFI}}$ on G with respect to A is equivalent to the execution of amnesiac flooding $\mathcal{A}_{\mathsf{AF}}$ on $\mathcal{B}_A(v_0)$. The starting point for the construction of $\mathcal{B}_A(v_0)$ is the double cover $\mathcal{G}(v_0)$ of G as defined in Sect. 4. To keep the notation simple we will omit the reference to the originating node v_0 and refer to the two graphs as $\mathcal{B}_A$ and $\mathcal{G}$.

First we extend the definition of the availability scheme A to all nodes of $\mathcal{G}$, i.e., $A : V \cup V' \times \mathbb{N} \longrightarrow \{true, false\}$. For each node $v' \in V'$ let $A(v', i) = A(v, i)$ for all $i \in \mathbb{N}$. The nodes of $\mathcal{B}_A$ are of two different types: copies of nodes of $\mathcal{G}$ and so called *dummy nodes*. We define $\mathcal{B}_A$ inductively, layer by layer. There can be copies of the same node v of $\mathcal{G}$ on several layers of $\mathcal{B}_A$, but the nodes of a single layer of $\mathcal{B}_A$ are copies of different nodes of $\mathcal{G}$. Therefore, we do not cause ambiguity when we denote the copies of the nodes by their original names. The construction of $\mathcal{B}_A$ is based on a function *originator*, that assigns to each node v of $\mathcal{B}_A$ a set of neighbors of v in $\mathcal{G}$. This function is also defined recursively.

Layer 0 of $\mathcal{B}_A$ consists of copy of v_0 with $originator(v_0) = \emptyset$. Layer 1 consists of copies of the neighbors of v_0 in $\mathcal{G}$, these are also the neighbors of v_0 in G. All layer 1 nodes are successors of v_0 and the *originator* of these nodes is $\{v_0\}$. Next assume that layers 0 to i with $i \geq 0$ are already defined including the function *originator*. We first define the nodes of layer $i + 1$ and afterwards the function originator. For each node of layer i we also define the successors. We do this first for nodes which are copies of nodes of $\mathcal{G}$ and afterwards for dummy nodes.

Let v be a node of layer i that is a copy of a node of $\mathcal{G}$. If $originator(v) = N_{\mathcal{G}}(v)$ then v has no successor in layer $i + 1$. Assume $originator(v) \neq N_{\mathcal{G}}(v)$. First consider the case $A(v, i+1) = true$. Let $U = N_{\mathcal{G}}(v) \backslash originator(v)$. For each $u \in U$ we do the following: If layer $i + 1$ already contains a copy of u then we make it a successor of v. Otherwise, we insert a new copy of u into layer $i + 1$ and make it a successor of v. If $A(v, i + 1) = false$ then we create a new dummy node, insert it into layer $i + 1$, and make it the single successor of v. Finally, let v be a dummy node of layer i and w its single predecessor in layer $i - 1$. If layer $i + 1$ already contains a copy of w then we make it a successor of v. Otherwise, we create a new copy of w, insert it into layer $i + 1$, and make it v's successor.

To define *originator* for each node v of layer $i + 1$ let $pred(v)$ be the set of predecessors of a node v in $\mathcal{B}$. With $pred_d(v)$ we denote the dummy nodes in $pred(v)$. Since dummy nodes only have a single predecessor we denote the predecessor in this case also by $pred(v)$. If v is not a dummy node then we define

$$originator(v) = \bigcup_{w \in pred_d(v)} originator(w) \ \cup \ pred(v) \backslash pred_d(v)$$

otherwise $originator(v) = originator(pred(v))$. Note that $\mathcal{B}_A$ is bipartite, since nodes of the same layer are not connected. Figure 5 shows the graph $\mathcal{B}_A$ for the graph of Fig. 1 and availability scheme A. The dummy nodes are labeled a to d. We have $originator(a) = originator(b) = \{v_0\}$, $originator(c) = \{v_1\}$, and $originator(d) = \{v_0, v_5\}$. Also, $originator(v_2) = \{v_0, v_5, v_{1'}\}$ in layer 5.

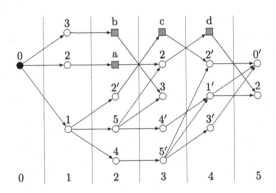

Fig. 5. The graph $\mathcal{B}_A$ for the availability scheme A has four dummy nodes.

We orient the edges of $\mathcal{G}$ by executing a breadth-first search starting in v_0. The union of the successors and predecessors of a node in $\mathcal{G}$ are precisely the neighbors of the node in G. The next lemma follows from Lemma 5 of [13].

Lemma 1. *Let v be a node of layer $i \geq 0$ of $\mathcal{G}$. The predecessors of v in $\mathcal{G}$ are copies of the nodes in G that send in round i of an execution of $\mathcal{A}_{\mathsf{AF}}$ a message to v and the successors of v in $\mathcal{G}$ receive a message from v in round $i + 1$.*

Proof. Suppose that a node w sends in round i a message to a node v. By Lemma 5 of [13] w is a node of layer $i - 1$ and either v or v' is a successor of w in $\mathcal{B}$ or w' is a node of layer $i - 1$ and v' is a successor of w. Note that in $\mathcal{B}$ a node of G and its copy cannot be in the same layer. The second statement also follows from this lemma. $\square$

Let A be any availability scheme for G and v_0. Lemma 2 is easy to prove.

Lemma 2. *Let v be a node of $\mathcal{G}$. For each copy u of v in $\mathcal{B}_A$ we have $N_{\mathcal{G}(v_0)}(v) = originator(u) \cup succ(u)$. If none of the predecessors of v in $\mathcal{B}$ is a dummy node then $N_{\mathcal{G}(v_0)}(v) = pred(u) \cup succ(u)$.*

To illustrate the last lemma we consider the execution from Fig. 4 and the corresponding graph $\mathcal{B}_A$ in Fig. 5. Let $i = 4$ and consider node v_2. The copy of v_2 on layer 4 is called $v_{2'}$. Figure 5 shows that $originator(v_2) = \{v_5, v_1\}$. From Fig. 4 we see that node v_2 receives a message from node v_1, i.e., $v_1 \in v_2.M[parity]$. Since $A(v_2, 3) = false$ node v_2 could not send a message in round 3. Hence the sender v_1 of the message received in round 3 is still in $v_2.M[parity]$. This yields $v_2.M[parity] = \{v_5, v_1\}$, since $A(v_2, 1) = true$.

For an availability scheme A and $k \geq 0$ we define a new availability scheme A_k as follows. We consider the nodes of $\mathcal{B}_A$ in any arbitrary but fixed order and define a total order on the set of pairs $(v, i) \in V \times \mathbb{N}$ with $A(v, i) = false$ as follows: $(v, i) < (w, j)$ if and only if $i < j$ or $i = j$ and $v < w$. Then we define $A_k(v, i) = false$ for all but the first k pairs (v, i), i.e., A_k has value $false$ for exactly k pairs (v, i). Note that there exists $c \geq 0$ such that $A = A_c$.

Lemma 3. *There is a one-to-one mapping between the edges of $\mathcal{G}$ and those edges of $\mathcal{B}_A$ that are not incident to a dummy node.*

Proof. It suffices to prove that the lemma holds for each A_k with $k \geq 0$. The proof is by induction on k. If $k = 0$ then the result is trivially true since $\mathcal{B}_{A_0} = \mathcal{G}$. Assume the theorem is true for $k \geq 1$. Consider the graph $\mathcal{B}_{A_{k-1}}$. Let (v, i) be the kth pair with $A(v, i) = false$. If layer $i - 1$ of $\mathcal{B}_{A_{k-1}}$ contains no copy of v then $\mathcal{B}_{A_{k-1}} = \mathcal{B}_{A_k}$ and we are done. Suppose there exists a copy of v on layer $i - 1$ of $\mathcal{B}_{A_{k-1}}$. We inductively define two sequences of sets X_j, $\overline{X}_j$ $(j \geq 1)$ of nodes of $\mathcal{B}_{A_{k-1}}$ (see Fig. 6). Nodes of X_j, $\overline{X}_j$ are in layer $i - 1 + j$ of $\mathcal{B}_{A_{k-1}}$. X_1 is the set of nodes of layer i that have v as the single predecessor in layer $i - 1$ and $\overline{X}_1 = succ(v) \setminus X_1$, where $succ(v)$ denotes the successors in $\mathcal{B}_{A_{k-1}}$. Thus, each node in $\overline{X}_1$ has besides v another predecessor in layer $i - 1$. Suppose we already defined $X_{j-1}, \overline{X}_{j-1}$. Then X_j is the set of nodes of layer $i - 1 + j$ that have only predecessors in X_{j-1}, i.e., $pred(X_j) \subseteq X_{j-1}$. $\overline{X}_j$ consists of those nodes of layer $i - 1 + j$ that have predecessors in X_{j-1} and in $\overline{X}_{j-1}$, i.e., for each $w \in \overline{X}_j$ we have $pred(w) \cap X_{j-1} \neq \emptyset$ and $pred(w) \cap \overline{X}_{j-1} \neq \emptyset$. Hence, $succ(X_{j-1}) = X_j \dot\cup \overline{X}_j$. Note that none of the nodes of X_j, $\overline{X}_j$ are dummy nodes, therefore $N_{\mathcal{G}}(u) = pred(u) \cup succ(u)$ for each $u \in X_j \cup \overline{X}_j$ by Lemma 2. Since the theorem is true for A_{k-1}, there exist t such that $X_t = \emptyset$. Note that $X_j \neq \emptyset$ for $j = 1, \ldots t - 1$ while $\overline{X}_j$ can be empty for any j.

Next, we show how $\mathcal{B}_{A_k}$ can be derived from $\mathcal{B}_{A_{k-1}}$. The two graphs coincide completely in the first $i - 1$ layers. In subsequent layers nodes that are not reachable from v in layer $i - 1$ also are identical. The single successor of v in layer i is the dummy node. This node itself has as successor a copy of v on layer $i+1$. Clearly this copy of v is also the successor of all nodes in $\overline{X}_1$ in layer i. The successors of the copy of v on layer $i+1$ are copies of the nodes of set X_1. Nodes in $\overline{X}_2$ on layer $i + 1$ are the predecessors of nodes in X_1. All these statements are an immediate consequence of Lemma 2. Similarly it follows that each layer $i - 1 + j$ for $j \geq 3$ contains copies of the nodes of set X_{j-2}. Their predecessors are copies of the nodes in X_{j-3} and $\overline{X}_{j-1}$.

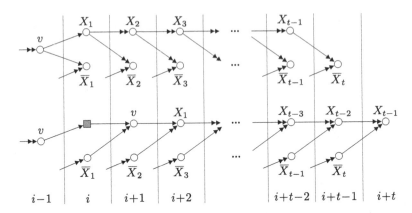

Fig. 6. The top row illustrates the definition of X_j and $\overline{X}_j$ for $\mathcal{B}_{A_{k-1}}$. The lower row displays the changes in $\mathcal{B}_{A_k}$ compared with $\mathcal{B}_{A_{k-1}}$. The last row indicates the number of the layer. The symbol $\twoheadrightarrow$ indicates that there can be several edges.

Thus, in $\mathcal{B}_{A_k}$ some edges from $\mathcal{B}_{A_{k-1}}$ are reversed: The orientation of edges from X_j to $\overline{X}_{j+1}$ and from v to $\overline{X}_1$ is reversed. This analysis also shows that $\mathcal{B}_{A_k}$ only has two additional edges, those adjacent to the new dummy node. In the worst case, $\mathcal{B}_{A_k}$ consists of two more layers compared to $\mathcal{B}_{A_{k-1}}$. □

To ease the formulation of the next lemma we introduce another definition. Let u be a node of G. For a copy of u in layer i of $\mathcal{B}_A$ we denote the originators in $\mathcal{B}_A$ of this copy of v by $originator^i(v)$. Furthermore, the set $M[parity]$ of node u immediately before checking channel availability in round i during an execution of $\mathcal{A}_{\mathsf{AFI}}$ on G is denoted by $v.M^i[parity]$.

Lemma 4. *Let u be a non-dummy node of layer i of $\mathcal{B}_A$. Then $u.M^i[parity] = originator^i(u)$.*

Proof. We use the notation introduced in the proof of Lemma 3. As before we prove by induction on k that the lemma holds for A_k. If $k = 0$ then the result holds by Lemma 1 since $\mathcal{B}_{A_0} = \mathcal{G}$. Assume the lemma is true for $k \geq 1$. We consider the graph $\mathcal{B}_{A_{k-1}}$. Let (v, i) be the kth pair with $A(v, i) = false$. If in layer $i - 1$ of $\mathcal{B}_{A_{k-1}}$ there exists no copy of v then $\mathcal{B}_{A_{k-1}} = \mathcal{B}_{A_k}$ and we are done. Suppose there exists a copy of v on layer $i - 1$ of $\mathcal{B}_{A_{k-1}}$. From Fig. 6 we see that we only have to consider the cases $u = v$, $u \in X_j$, and $u \in \overline{X}_j$. Remember that there are no dummy nodes in X_j, $\overline{X}_j$.

First consider the case that u is the copy of v in layer $i + 1$ in $\mathcal{B}_{A_k}$ (see Fig. 6). In round $i + 1$ in $\mathcal{B}_{A_k}$ the nodes in $\overline{X}_1$ do not receive the message from v because $A(v, i) = false$. Since each node in $\overline{X}_1$ still receives the message from another node, each of them must forward the message in round i to v. Hence, $v.M^{i+1}[parity] = v.M^{i-1}[parity] \cup \overline{X}_1$. On the other hand $originator^{i+1}(v) = originator^{i-1}(v) \cup \overline{X}_1$. By induction $originator^{i-1}(v) = v.M^{i-1}[parity]$.

Next consider the case $u \in X_1$. Then u is on layer $i + 2$ of $\mathcal{B}_k$. Since in $\mathcal{B}_{A_{k-1}}$ each node in X_1 receives in round i only the message from v, node v sends the message to each node in X_1 in round $i+1$. Furthermore, since for $\mathcal{B}_{A_{k-1}}$ each node in $\overline{X}_2$ received in round $i+1$ a message from a node in X_1, each node of $\overline{X}_2$ sends $\mathcal{B}_{A_k}$ the message to at least one node of X_1. In particular node u receives in round $i+2$ the message from its predecessors in $\overline{X}_2$ for $\mathcal{B}_{A_k}$. Clearly, u does not receive the message from any other node. Thus, $u.M^{i+2}[parity] = originator^{i+2}(u)$. The cases $u \in X_j$ with $j > 1$ and $u \in \overline{X}_j$ with $j \geq 1$ can be proved similarly.   □

Lemma 5. *During round i of an execution of $\mathcal{A}_{AFI}$ on G a node v sends the message to a neighbor w if and only if the copy of v in layer $i-1$ of $\mathcal{B}_A$ is the predecessor of a copy of w in layer i of $\mathcal{B}_A$.*

Proof. If during the execution of $\mathcal{A}_{AFI}$ node v sends messages in round i to w then $A(v,i) = true$ and $N(v) \neq v.M[parity]$. By the Lemma 4 we have $w \in N(v) \setminus originator(v)$. Thus, by construction w is a successor of v in $\mathcal{B}_A$. Conversely, if w is successor of v in $\mathcal{B}_A$ then $A(v,i) = true$ and $v \in N(v) \setminus originator(v)$. Again Lemma 4 gives the desired result.   □

The last lemma implies that executing $\mathcal{A}_{AFI}$ on G is *equivalent* to executing $\mathcal{A}_{AF}$ on $\mathcal{B}_A$. The reason is that $\mathcal{B}_A$ is bipartite and executing $\mathcal{A}_{AF}$ on a bipartite graph starting at the root is equivalent to synchronous flooding the bipartite graph. This is formulated in the following theorem.

Theorem 2. *Let G be a graph G and A an availability scheme for G. Let $f = |\{(v,i) \mid A(v,i) = false\}|$. Algorithm $\mathcal{A}_{AFI}$ delivers a broadcasted message (resp. terminates) after at most $Diam(G) + 2f$ (resp. $2Diam(G) + 2f + 1$) rounds. If G is bipartite each message is forwarded $|E|$ times, otherwise $2|E|$ times.*

Proof. Lemma 5 implies that $\mathcal{A}_{AFI}$ terminates after d rounds where d is the height of $\mathcal{B}_A$. The proof of Lemma 3 shows that each pair (v,i) with $A(v,i) = false$ increases the depth by at most 2. By Thm. 1 of [13] the depth of $\mathcal{G}$ is at most $2Diam(G) + 1$. By Lemma 3 and Lemma 4 $\mathcal{A}_{AFI}$ sends $2|E|$ messages.   □

5   Multi-source Broadcasts

A variant of broadcasting is multi-source broadcasting, where several nodes invoke a broadcast of the same message, i.e., with the same message id, possibly in different rounds. This problem is motivated by disaster monitoring: A distributed system monitors a geographical region. When multiple nodes detect an event, each of them broadcasts this information unless it has already received this information. Multi-source broadcasting for the case that all nodes invoke the broadcast in the same round was already analyzed in [13]. This variant can be reduced to the case of single node invoking the broadcast by introducing a virtual source v^* connected by edges to all broadcasting nodes.

In this section we consider the general case where nodes can invoke the broadcasts in arbitrary rounds. First we show that broadcasting one message with algorithm $\mathcal{A}_{AF}$ also terminates in this case and that overlapping broadcasts complement each other in the sense that the message is still forwarded only $2|E|$ resp. $|E|$ times. Later we extend this to the case of intermittent channels.

Theorem 3. *Let $v_1, \ldots, v_k$ be nodes of G that initiate a broadcast of the same message m in rounds $r_1, \ldots, r_k$. Each broadcast is invoked before m reaches the invoking node. Algorithm $\mathcal{A}_{\mathsf{AF}}$ delivers m after $Diam(G)$ rounds and terminates after at most $2Diam(G) + 1$ rounds and m is forwarded at most $2|E|$ times.*

Proof. WLOG we assume $r_1 = 0$. For each i with $r_i > 0$ we attach to node v_i a path $P_i = u_1^i, \ldots, u_{r_i}^i$ with r_i new nodes, i.e., $u_{r_i}^i$ is connected to v_i by an edge. The extended graph is called G°. Let $S = \{u_1^i \mid r_i > 0\} \cup \{v_i \mid r_i = 0\}$. If in G° all nodes in S broadcast in round 0 message m then in round $r_i + 1$ each node v_i sends m to all its neighbors in G. Thus, the forwarding of m along the edges of G is identical in G and G°. By Thm. 1 of [13] algorithm $\mathcal{A}_{\mathsf{AF}}$ delivers m after $d_{G^\circ}(S, V^\circ)$ rounds and terminates after at most $d_{G^\circ}(S, V^\circ) + 1 + Diam(G^\circ)$ rounds, V° is the set of nodes of G°. Also, in G° message m is forwarded at most twice via each edge. Thus, in G message m is forwarded at most $2|E|$ times.

To prove the upper bounds for the delivery and termination time we reconsider the proof of Thm. 1 of [13]. This proof constructs from G° a new graph G^* by introducing a new node v^* and connecting it to all nodes in S. It is then shown that the termination time of invoking the broadcast in G° by all nodes of S in round 0 is bounded by $d - 1$, where d is the depth of the bipartite graph $\mathcal{G}(v^*)$ corresponding to G^*. Note that we are only interested in the termination time of the nodes of G in G°. Thus, we only have to bound the depth of the copies of the nodes of G in $\mathcal{G}(v^*)$. Since broadcasts are invoked before m is received for the first time we have $r_i \leq ecc_G(v_1)$. Thus, the depth of the first copy of each node has depth at most $ecc_G(v_1) + 1 \leq Diam(G) + 1$ in $\mathcal{G}(v^*)$. Hence, delivery in G takes place after $Diam(G)$ rounds. The second copy of each node of G is at most in distance $1 + Diam(G)$ from one of the first copies of the nodes of G in $\mathcal{G}(v^*)$. Thus, termination in G is after at most $2Diam(G) + 1$ rounds. $\square$

The stated upper bounds are the worst case. Depending on the locations of the nodes v_i and the values of r_i the actual times can be much smaller. Next we extent Theorem 3 to tolerate intermittent channel availabilities.

Theorem 4. *Let A be an availability scheme for a graph G. Let $v_1, \ldots, v_k$ be nodes of G that broadcast the same message m in rounds $r_1, \ldots, r_k$. Each broadcast is invoked before m reaches the invoking node. Algorithm $\mathcal{A}_{\mathsf{AFI}}$ delivers m (resp. terminates) in at most $Diam(G) + 2f$ (resp. $2Diam(G) + 2f + 1$) rounds after the first broadcast with $f = |\{(v, i) \mid A(v, i) = false\}|$. Message m is forwarded at most $2|E|$ times.*

Proof. In the proof of Theorem 3 it is shown that broadcasting the same message m in different rounds by different nodes is equivalent to the single broadcast of m by a single node v^* in the graph G^*. Applying Theorem 2 to G^* and v^* shows that $\mathcal{A}_{\mathsf{AF}}$ delivers m to all nodes of G^* for any availability scheme. Hence, Theorem 3 also holds for any availability scheme. $\square$

6 Multi-message Broadcasts

While algorithm $\mathcal{A}_{\mathsf{AFI}}$ is of interest on its own, it can be used as a building block for more general broadcasting tasks. In this section we consider *multi-message broadcasts*, i.e., multiple nodes initiate broadcasts, each with its own message, even when broadcasts from previous initiations have not completed. We consider this task under the restriction that in each round each node can forward at most b messages to each of its neighbors. Without this restriction we can execute one instance of $\mathcal{A}_{\mathsf{AF}}$ for each broadcasted message. Then each messages is delivered (resp. the broadcast terminates) in $ecc(v_0)$ (resp. $ecc(v_0) + 1 + Diam(G)$) rounds [13]. The restriction enforces that only b instances of $\mathcal{A}_{\mathsf{AF}}$ can be active in each round, additional instances have to be suspended. First consider the case $b = 1$.

Multi-message broadcast can be solved with an extension of algorithm $\mathcal{A}_{\mathsf{AFI}}$. We use an associative array *messTbl* to store the senders of suspended messages according to their parity. Message identifiers are the keys, the values correspond to variable M of Algorithm 2. Any time a node v receives a message m with identifier id from a neighbor w it is checked whether $v.messTbl$ already contains an entry with key id for the current *parity*. If not, a new entry is created. Then w is inserted according to the actual value of *parity* into $v.messTbl[id]$. When all messages of a round are received all values in $v.messTbl$ with the current *parity* are checked, if a value equals $N(v)$ then it is set to $\bot$. In this case v received message id from all neighbors and no action is required. After this cleaning step, an entry of *messTbl* is selected for which the value with the current *parity* is not $\bot$. Selection is performed according to a given criterion. The message belonging to this entry is sent to all neighbors but those listed in the entry. Finally the entry is set to $\bot$. The details of this algorithm can be found in [12]. The delivery order of messages depends on the selection criterion. The variant of this algorithm which always selects the method with the smallest id is called $\mathcal{A}_{\mathsf{AFI^s}}$.

Theorem 5. *Algorithm $\mathcal{A}_{\mathsf{AFI^s}}$ eventually delivers each message of any sequence of broadcasts of messages with different identifiers. If G is bipartite, each message is forwarded $|E|$ times, otherwise $2|E|$ times.*

Proof. The message with the smallest identifier id_1 is always forwarded first by $\mathcal{A}_{\mathsf{AFI^s}}$. Thus, this message is forwarded as in amnesiac flooding. Hence, it is delivered after at most $2Diam(G) + 1$ rounds after it is broadcasted [13]. Next we define an availability scheme A_1: $A_1(v, i) = \textit{false}$ if during round i of algorithm $\mathcal{A}_{\mathsf{AFI^s}}$ node v forwards message id_1, otherwise let $A_1(v, i) = \textit{true}$. Then the message with the second smallest identifier id_2 is forwarded as with algorithm $\mathcal{A}_{\mathsf{AFI}}$ for availability scheme A_1. Thus, by Theorem 2 this message is eventually delivered. Next define availability scheme A_2 similarly to A_1 with respect to the messages with ids id_1 and id_2 and apply again Theorem 2, etc.   □

Forwarding the message with the smallest id is only one option. Other selection criteria are also possible, but without care starvation can occur. The variant, where the selection of the forwarded message is fair, is called $\mathcal{A}_{\mathsf{AFI^F}}$. Fairness in this context means, that each message is selected after at most a fixed number of selections. This fairness criteria limits the number of concurrent broadcasts. If message selection is unfair for one of the nodes, then continuously inserting new messages results in starvation of a message. We have the following result.

Theorem 6. *If in each round each node can forward only one message to each of its neighbors algorithm Algorithm $\mathcal{A}_{\mathsf{AFIF}}$ eventually terminates and delivers each message of any sequence of broadcasts of messages with different identifiers. If G is bipartite, each message is forwarded $|E|$ times, otherwise $2|E|$ times.*

Proof. Whenever the associative array *messTbl* of a node is non-empty, the node will forward a message in the next round with the adequate parity. The fairness assumption implies that whenever m is inserted into $w.messTbl$ for a node w then after a bounded number of rounds it will be forwarded and removed from $w.messTbl$. Thus, the forwarding of m makes progress.

Let m be a fixed message that is broadcasted in some round i_m. Denote by f_j the number of forwards of message m up to round j. For each j we define an availability scheme A_j as follows: $A_j(v, i) = true$ for all $i > j$ and all $v \in V$. Furthermore, $A_j(v, i) = true$ for $i \leq j$ and $v \in V$ if during round i node v forwards message m. For all other pairs let $A_j(v, i) = false$. Hence, there are only finitely many pairs (v, i) such that $A_j(v, i) = false$. Clearly for all j, message m is forwarded during the first j rounds as with algorithm $\mathcal{A}_{\mathsf{AFI}}$ with respect to A_j. Thus, by Theorem 2 $f_j \leq 2m$. Hence, there exist $j_m \geq i_m$ such that in round j_m each node has received the message and after this round the message is no longer in the system. Hence, the result follows from Theorem 2.   □

The case $b > 1$ is proved similarly. We only have to make a single change to $\mathcal{A}_{\mathsf{AFIF}}$. After the cleaning step we select up to b entries of *messTbl* and send the corresponding messages. The proof of Theorem 7 is similar to that of Theorem 6.

Theorem 7. *If in each round each node can forward at most $b \geq 1$ messages to each of its neighbors algorithm $\mathcal{A}_{\mathsf{AFIF}}$ eventually terminates and delivers each message of any sequence of broadcasts of messages with different identifiers. If G is bipartite, each message is forwarded $|E|$ times, otherwise $2|E|$ times.*

Finally, Theorem 1 follows directly from Theorem 4 and Theorem 7.

7   Discussion and Conclusion

In this paper we proposed extensions to the synchronous broadcast algorithm amnesiac flooding. The main extension allows to execute the algorithm for systems with intermittent channels. While this is of interest on its own, it is the basis to solve the general task of multi-message broadcast in systems with bounded channel capacities. The extended algorithm delivers messages broadcasted by multiple nodes in different rounds, even when broadcasts from previous invocations have not completed, while each of the messages is forwarded at most $2|E|$ times. The main advantage of amnesiac flooding remains, nodes don't need to memorize the reception of a message to guarantee termination.

We conclude by discussing two shortcomings of amnesiac flooding. $\mathcal{A}_{\mathsf{AF}}$ delivers a broadcasted message twice to each node. To avoid duplicate delivery, nodes have to use a buffer. Upon receiving a message m a node checks whether the id of m is contained in its buffer. If not then m is delivered to the application and m's id is inserted into the buffer. Otherwise, m's id is removed from the buffer and not delivered. This also holds for algorithm $\mathcal{A}_{\mathsf{AFIF}}$.

Amnesiac flooding satisfies the FIFO order, i.e., if v_0 broadcasts a message m before it broadcasts message m' then no node delivers m' unless it has previously delivered m. This is no longer guaranteed for $\mathcal{A}_{\mathsf{AFI}}$: Suppose that v_0 broadcasts m resp. m' in rounds i resp. $i+1$. Let $w \in N(v_0)$ with $A(w, i+2) = false$ and $A(v, j) = true$ for all other pairs. Then w forwards m' in round $i+3$ while it forwards m in round $i+4$. Thus, a neighbor u of w receives m' before m.

References

1. Adamek, J., Nesterenko, M., Robinson, S., Tixeuil, S.: Stateless reliable geocasting. In: 2017 IEEE 36th Symposium on Reliable Distributed Systems, pp. 44–53 (2017)
2. Casteigts, A., Flocchini, P., Mans, B., Santoro, N.: Deterministic computations in time-varying graphs: broadcasting under unstructured mobility. In: Calude, C.S., Sassone, V. (eds.) TCS 2010. IAICT, vol. 323, pp. 111–124. Springer, Heidelberg (2010). https://doi.org/10.1007/978-3-642-15240-5_9
3. Demers, A., et al.: Epidemic algorithms for replicated database maintenance. In: Proceedings 6th Annual Symposium on Principles of Distributed Computing, PODC, pp. 1–12. ACM (1987). https://doi.org/10.1145/41840.41841
4. Feige, U., Peleg, D., Raghavan, P., Upfal, E.: Randomized broadcast in networks. In: Asano, T., Ibaraki, T., Imai, H., Nishizeki, T. (eds.) SIGAL 1990. LNCS, vol. 450, pp. 128–137. Springer, Heidelberg (1990). https://doi.org/10.1007/3-540-52921-7_62
5. Frieze, A.M., Grimmett, G.R.: The shortest-path problem for graphs with random arc-lengths. Discrete Appl. Math. **10**(1), 57–77 (1985)
6. Hussak, W., Trehan, A.: On the termination of flooding. In: Paul, C., Bläser, M. (eds.) 37th Symposium on Theoretical Aspects of Computer Science (STACS). LIPIcs, vol. 154, pp. 17:1–17:13 (2020). https://doi.org/10.4230/LIPIcs.STACS.2020.17
7. Hussak, W., Trehan, A.: Terminating cases of flooding. CoRR abs/2009.05776 (2020). https://arxiv.org/abs/2009.05776
8. Mocquard, Y., Sericola, B., Anceaume, E.: Probabilistic analysis of rumor-spreading time. INFORMS J. Comput. **32**(1), 172–181 (2020)
9. Peleg, D.: Distributed Computing: A Locality-Sensitive Approach. SIAM Society for Industrial and Applied Mathematics, Philadelphia (2000)
10. Raynal, M., Stainer, J., Cao, J., Wu, W.: A simple broadcast algorithm for recurrent dynamic systems. In: IEEE 28th International Conference on Advanced Information Networking and Applications, pp. 933–939 (2014). https://doi.org/10.1109/AINA.2014.115
11. Turau, V.: Stateless information dissemination algorithms. In: Richa, A.W., Scheideler, C. (eds.) SIROCCO 2020. LNCS, vol. 12156, pp. 183–199. Springer, Cham (2020). https://doi.org/10.1007/978-3-030-54921-3_11

12. Turau, V.: Synchronous concurrent broadcasts for intermittent channels with bounded capacities. CoRR abs/2011.05772 (2020). https://arxiv.org/abs/2011.05772

13. Turau, V.: Amnesiac flooding: synchronous stateless information dissemination. In: Bureš, T., et al. (eds.) SOFSEM 2021. LNCS, vol. 12607, pp. 59–73. Springer, Cham (2021). https://doi.org/10.1007/978-3-030-67731-2_5

Network and Graph Structures

Fault-Tolerant Distance Labeling
for Planar Graphs

Aviv Bar-Natan[1], Panagiotis Charalampopoulos[2] (ID), Paweł Gawrychowski[3] (ID),
Shay Mozes[2] (ID), and Oren Weimann[1]([✉]) (ID)

[1] University of Haifa, Haifa, Israel
`oren@cs.haifa.ac.il`
[2] The Interdisciplinary Center Herzliya, Herzliya, Israel
`panagiotis.charalampopoulos@post.idc.ac.il`
[3] University of Wrocław, Wrocław, Poland
`gawry@cs.uni.wroc.pl`

Abstract. In fault-tolerant distance labeling we wish to assign short labels to the vertices of a graph G such that from the labels of any three vertices u, v, f we can infer the u-to-v distance in the graph $G \setminus \{f\}$. We show that any directed weighted planar graph (and in fact any graph in a graph family with $O(\sqrt{n})$-size separators, such as minor-free graphs) admits fault-tolerant distance labels of size $O(n^{2/3})$. We extend these labels in a way that allows us to also count the number of shortest paths, and provide additional upper and lower bounds for labels and oracles for counting shortest paths.

Keywords: Forbidden-set distance labels · Planar graphs · Fault-tolerant distance labels · Counting shortest paths

1 Introduction

Computing distances in graphs is one of the most basic and important problems in graphs theory, both from theoretical and practical points of view. In this work we consider distance labeling schemes, in which one preprocesses a network to assign labels to the vertices, so that the distance between any two vertices u and v can be recovered from just the labels of u and v (and no other information). The main criteria of interest are foremost the size of the label, and to a lesser extent the time it takes to recover the distance from a given pair of labels (query time). Distance labeling schemes are useful in the distributed setting, where it is advantageous to be able to infer distances based only on local information such as the labels of the source and destination. This is the case in communication networks or in disaster stricken areas, where communication with a centralized entity is infeasible or downright impossible.

   Considering the latter scenario of disaster management, it is not only likely that a disastrous event makes communication with a centralized entity impossible, but also that parts of the network are affected by the disaster, and that

© Springer Nature Switzerland AG 2021
T. Jurdziński and S. Schmid (Eds.): SIROCCO 2021, LNCS 12810, pp. 315–333, 2021.
https://doi.org/10.1007/978-3-030-79527-6_18

only shortest paths that avoid affected parts of the network should be considered when computing distances. Forbidden-set distance labeling schemes assign labels to vertices, so that, for any pair of vertices u and v, and any set F of failed vertices, the length of a shortest u-to-v path that avoids all vertices in F can be recovered just from the labels of u, v, and of the vertices in F. In this work we study forbidden-set distance labeling schemes in directed planar networks. We also study the extension of such schemes to capture not only the distance from u to v, but also the number of distinct u-to-v shortest paths.

For unweighted graphs, we measure the label size in bits. For weighted graphs and queries concerning lengths of the shortest paths, we assume that the distance between any two nodes fits in a single machine word, and measure the label size in words. For queries concerning the number of shortest paths, unless mentioned otherwise, we assume that the number of shortest paths between any two nodes fits in a single machine word, and measure the label size in words.

1.1 Related Work

Labeling schemes provide a clean and natural model for studying how to distribute information about a graph. Problems considered in this model include adjacency [4–6,10,30,42], flows and connectivity [27,32,36], and Steiner tree [41]. See [43] for a recent survey. We specifically focus on distance labeling schemes.

Distance Labeling Schemes. Embedding distance information into labels was studied by Graham and Pollak [25] in the 1970's in the so-called squashed cube model. In 2000, Peleg [40] formalized the notion of distance labeling schemes, and provided schemes with polylogarithmic label size (in bits) and query time for trees, interval graphs and permutation graphs. Gavoille et al. [22] showed that for general graphs, the label size is $\Theta(n)$, and for trees, $\Theta(\log^2 n)$. For (unit-weight) planar graphs they showed a lower bound of $\Omega(n^{1/3})$, and an upper bound of $O(\sqrt{n} \log n)$ bits. The upper bound was recently improved to $O(\sqrt{n})$ [24], but the rare *polynomial* gap between the lower and upper bound remains an interesting and important open problem. For weighted planar graphs Gavoille et al. gave tight (up to polylogarithmic factors) $\tilde{\Theta}(n^{1/2})$ upper and lower bounds.

Approximate Distance Labeling Schemes. Since exact distance labels typically require polynomial size labels [22], researchers have sought smaller labels that yield approximate distances. Gavoille et al. [21] studied such labels for general graphs and various graph families. Specifically, for planar graphs, they presented $O(n^{1/3} \log n)$-bit labels that provide a 3-approximation of the distance. In the same year, Gupta et al. [26] presented smaller 3-approximate labels, requiring only $O(\log^2 n)$ bits, and Thorup gave $(1 + \epsilon)$-approximate labels of size $O(\log n/\epsilon)$, for any fixed $\epsilon > 0$ [44]. The latter result was generalized to H-minor free graphs by Abraham and Gavoille in [3].

Forbidden-Set Distance Labeling Schemes. Forbidden-set labels were introduced in the context of routing labels by Feigenbaum et al. [18,19], and studied by several others [1,2,14,15,45]. Exact forbidden-set labeling schemes of polylogarithmic size are given in [15,45] for graphs of bounded treewidth or cliquewidth.

For unweighted graphs of bounded doubling dimension, forbidden-set labels with polylogarithmic size and $(1+\epsilon)$-stretch are also known [2]. For undirected planar graphs, and for any fixed $\epsilon > 0$, Abraham et al. [1] presented a forbidden-set labeling scheme of polylogarithmic size such that a $(1 + \epsilon)$-approximation of the shortest path between vertices u and v that avoids a set F of failed vertices can be recovered from the labels of u, v, and the labels of the failed vertices in $\tilde{O}(|F|^2)$ time[1].

Other Related Work. There are many other concepts related to distances in the presence of failures. In the replacement paths problem we are given a graph along with a source and sink vertices, and the goal is to efficiently compute all shortest paths between the source and the destinations for every possible single-edge failure in the graph. In planar graphs this problem can be solved in nearly linear time [16,35,46]. For the single source, single failure version of the problem (i.e. when only the source vertex is fixed at construction time, and the query specifies just the target and a single failed vertex), Baswana et al. [8] presented an oracle with size and construction time $O(n\log^4 n)$ that answers queries in $O(\log^3 n)$ time. Building upon this oracle, they then present an oracle of size $\tilde{O}(n^2/q)$ supporting arbitrary distance queries subject to a single failure in time $\tilde{O}(q)$ for any $q \in [1, n^{1/2}]$. The authors of [13] show how to construct in $\tilde{O}(n)$ time an oracle of size $\tilde{O}(n)$ that, given a source vertex u, a target vertex v, and a set F of k faulty vertices, reports the length of a shortest u-to-v path in $G \setminus F$ in $\tilde{O}(\sqrt{kn})$ time. They further show that for any $r \in [1, n]$ there exists an $\tilde{O}(\frac{n^{k+1}}{r^{k+1}}\sqrt{nr})$-size oracle that answers queries in time $\tilde{O}(k\sqrt{r})$. Recently, Italiano et al. [28] gave an oracle of size $O(n\log n)$ and construction time $O(n\log^2 n/\log\log n)$ that supports reachability queries subject to a single failure in time $O(\log n)$.

Another related concept is that of dynamic distance oracles. Here a graph is preprocessed so as to efficiently support distance queries between arbitrary pairs of vertices as well as updates to the graph. Updates may include deletion of edges or vertices (decremental updates), or also addition of new edges and vertices (fully dynamic). Fakcharoenphol and Rao [17] presented distance oracles that require $\tilde{O}(n^{2/3})$ and $\tilde{O}(n^{4/5})$ amortized time per update and query for non-negative and arbitrary edge-weight updates respectively[2]. The space required by these oracles is $O(n\log n)$. The extensions of this result in [13,29,31,33] yield a dynamic oracle that can handle arbitrary edge weight updates, edge deletions and insertions (not violating the planarity of the embedding) and vertex deletions, as well as answer distance queries, in $\tilde{O}(n^{2/3})$ time each.

Counting Shortest Paths. In the (non-faulty) counting version of shortest paths labeling, given the labels of vertices s and t we wish to return the *number* of shortest s-to-t paths in G (i.e. paths whose length is equal to $d(s,t)$).

---

[1] The $\tilde{O}(\cdot)$ notation suppresses $\log^{O(1)} n$ factors.

[2] Though this is not mentioned in [17], the query time can be made worst case rather than amortized by standard techniques.

This problem (without faults) was recently studied in [9] where labels[3] of size $\Theta(\sqrt{n})$ were constructed under the assumption that the number of shortest paths between any two nodes fits in a constant number of machine words. In the general case where the numbers consist of L bits, the obtained labels consist of $O(\sqrt{n} \cdot L)$ bits. As already observed in [9], it is easy to construct an unweighted graph where $L = n - 1$ making the labels consist of $\Theta(n^{1.5})$ bits, that is, more than in a naive encoding storing the whole graph in every label. However, the following simple construction shows that we cannot hope to construct labels consisting of $o(n)$ bits without bounding L: given n bits $b_0, \ldots, b_{n-1}$ we construct a graph consisting of a path $s = u_0 - u_1 - \cdots - u_{n-1}$ and another path $v_1 - v_2 - \cdots - v_n = t$ in which every edge is duplicated (i.e., there are two parallel edges between each pair v_i, v_{i+1}). Finally, for every $i = 0, \ldots, n-1$ such that $b_i = 1$, we add an edge $u_i - v_{i+1}$. Then the number of shortest s-to-t paths is exactly $\sum_{i=0}^{n-1} b_i \cdot 2^{n-1-i}$, and so by an encoding argument the total number of bits in the labels of s and t must be at least n. Therefore, when counting shortest paths we will measure the size of a label in the number of machine words, each long enough to store the number of shortest paths between any two nodes in the graph.

We highlight one interesting application where our scheme for counting shortest s-to-t paths that avoid nodes $v_1, v_2, \ldots, v_k$ can be modified to obtain a better bound on the sizes of the labels in bits. Say that instead of counting such shortest paths we would like to check if avoiding nodes $v_1, v_2, \ldots, v_k$ increases the length of the shortest path. In such case, we only need to check if the number of shortest s-to-t paths that avoid nodes $v_1, v_2, \ldots, v_k$ is nonzero. Because the number of shortest paths is always at most 2^n, by well known properties of prime numbers, choosing a random prime p consisting of $\Theta(k \cdot \log n)$ bits guarantees that with high probability, for every $s, t, v_1, v_2, \ldots, v_k$, the number of shortest paths counted modulo p is nonzero if and only if the number of shortest paths is nonzero. Our scheme (as well as the scheme of [9]) can be used for counting modulo p, so we obtain labels consisting of $\tilde{O}(\sqrt{n} \cdot k)$ bits for such queries.

1.2   Our Results

- In Sect. 3 we present a single-fault distance labeling scheme (forbidden-set labeling scheme for a set of cardinality 1). The label size is $O(n^{2/3})$, the query time is $\tilde{O}(\sqrt{n})$, and time to construct all labels is $\tilde{O}(n^{5/3})$. Our labeling scheme extends (with no overhead in the label size) to a labeling scheme for counting shortest paths (with a single fault).
- In Sect. 4 we extend the counting labels of [9] to the following fault-tolerant variant. Given the labels of vertices $s, t, v_1, v_2, \ldots, v_k$, we wish to return the number of s-to-t paths that avoid vertices $v_1, \ldots, v_k$ and whose length is equal to $d(s, t)$ (the original s-to-t distance in G). We show that the labeling of [9] (with labels of size $\tilde{O}(\sqrt{n})$) actually works in this more general setting.

---

[3] In [9], the authors actually considered the oracle version of the problem, but their solution can be easily applied for labeling as well.

A naive query to such labeling takes $\tilde{O}(\sqrt{n} \cdot k^2)$ time, we show how to improve this to $\tilde{O}(\sqrt{n} \cdot k)$.

- In Sect. 5 we show a lower bound of $\Omega(\sqrt{nL})$ on the label-size (in bits) for counting shortest paths (without faults), in graphs in which the number of distinct shortest paths between any two nodes consists of at most L bits.
- In the full version of this paper [7] we show a lower bound (conditioned on the hardness of online boolean matrix-vector multiplication) on dynamic oracles for counting shortest paths. We prove that for such oracles, either the query time or the update time must be $\Omega(\sqrt{n})$ (up to subpolynomial factors).

We focus on planar graphs but in fact all our results (except for the efficient preprocessing time and query time in Sect. 3) hold for any graph family with $O(\sqrt{n})$-size separators (such as H-minor free graphs and bounded genus graphs). This is also the case for the standard (i.e. without failures) labeling scheme of Gavoille et al. [22]. However, while their $\tilde{O}(n^{1/2})$-size labels are obtained with a straightforward application of separators, our $O(n^{2/3})$-size (fault-tolerant) labels are obtained with a non-standard and intricate use of separators.

A main open question that is left unanswered by our work is the existence of non-trivial forbidden-set distance labels tolerating more than a single fault. Labels for approximate distances [1] also rely on separators, and do handle multiple failures. In the failure-free case, the labels of [1] consist of distances to a small (logarithmic) sample of vertices on some separators, called connections. To handle failures, the label of each vertex u also stores the failure-free labels of the connections of u. This only increases the label-size by a polylogarithmic factor. In case of exact distances, the size of the failure-free labels is $\Omega(\sqrt{n})$, so this approach seems unsuitable.

Another natural open question is whether the gap between our $O(n^{2/3})$-size fault-tolerant labels and the $\tilde{O}(n^{1/2})$-size labels without failures is actually required and tight. We observe that the existing lower bound technique of Gavoille et al. cannot be extended to show a lower bound above $\Omega(\sqrt{n})$ for fault-tolerant labels. The reason is that their technique uses a global argument showing that if we wish to encode the distances between a subset S of $k \leq \sqrt{n}$ vertices then all their labels together require size $\Omega(k^2)$. However, even in the presence of (any number of) failures, encoding distances can be done with total size $\tilde{O}(k^2)$ (simply store for every $u, v \in S$ the length of the shortest u-to-v path that is internally disjoint from S).

2 Preliminaries

Throughout the paper we consider as input a weighted directed planar graph G, embedded in the plane. We assume that the input graph has no negative length cycles. We can transform the graph in a standard way, in $O(n \frac{\log^2 n}{\log \log n})$ time, so that all edge weights are non-negative and distances are preserved [39].

Separators and Recursive Decompositions. Miller [37] showed how to compute a Jordan curve that intersects the graph at a set of nodes $Sep(G)$ of size $O(\sqrt{n})$ and separates G into two pieces with at most $2n/3$ vertices each. Jordan curve separators can be used to recursively separate a planar graph until pieces have constant size. The authors of [34] show how to obtain a complete recursive decomposition tree $\mathcal{T}$ of G in $O(n)$ time. $\mathcal{T}$ is a binary tree whose nodes correspond to subgraphs of G (called *pieces*), with the root being all of G and the leaves being pieces of constant size. We identify each piece P with the node representing it in $\mathcal{T}$ (we can thus abuse notation and write $P \in \mathcal{T}$), with its boundary ∂P (i.e. vertices that belong to some separator along the recursive decomposition used to obtain P), and with its separator $Sep(P)$. We denote by $\mathcal{T}[P,Q]$ the P-to-Q path in $\mathcal{T}$ (and also use $\mathcal{T}(P,Q]$, $\mathcal{T}[P,Q)$, and $\mathcal{T}(P,Q)$).

An *r-division* [20] of a planar graph, for $r \in [1, n]$, is a decomposition of the graph into $O(n/r)$ pieces, each of size $O(r)$, such that each piece P has $O(\sqrt{r})$ boundary vertices (denoted ∂P). Another desired property of an r-division is that the boundary vertices lie on a constant number of faces (called holes) of the piece. For every r larger than some constant, an r-division with few holes is represented in the decomposition tree $\mathcal{T}$ of [34]. It is convenient to describe the r-division by truncating $\mathcal{T}$ at pieces of size $O(r)$, that also satisfy the other required properties. We refer to those pieces (the leaves of $\mathcal{T}$ after truncation) as *regions* and denote by R_u the region containing vertex u (if u belongs to multiple regions, we arbitrarily designate one of them as R_u).

Dense Distance Graphs and FR-Dijkstra. The *dense distance graph* of a set of vertices U that lie on a constant number of faces of a planar graph H, denoted $DDG_H(U)$ is a complete directed graph on the vertices of U. Each edge (u, v) has weight $d_H(u, v)$, equal to the length of the shortest u-to-v path in H. $DDG_H(U)$ can be computed in time $O((|U|^2 + |H|)\log|H|)$ using the multiple source shortest paths (MSSP) algorithm [11,33]. Thus, computing $DDG_P(\partial P)$ over all pieces of the recursive decomposition of G requires time $O(n\log^2 n)$ and space $O(n\log n)$. We next give a –convenient for our purposes– interface for FR-Dijkstra [17], which is an efficient implementation of Dijkstra's algorithm on any union of DDGs. The algorithm exploits the fact that, due to planarity, certain submatrices of the adjacency matrix of $DDG_H(U)$ satisfy the Monge property (A matrix M satisfies the Monge property if, for all $i < i'$ and $j < j'$, $M_{i,j} + M_{i',j'} \le M_{i',j} + M_{i,j'}$ [38]). The interface is specified in the following theorem, which was essentially proved in [17], with some additional components and details from [31,39].

Theorem 1 [17,31,39]. *Given a set Y of DDGs, Dijkstra's algorithm can be run on the union of any subset of Y with $O(N)$ vertices in total (with multiplicities) and an arbitrary set of $O(N)$ extra edges in time $O(N\log^2 N)$.*

3   Single-Fault Labeling for Reporting Shortest Paths

Warm-up. As a warm-up, we first sketch a simple labeling scheme that assigns a label of size $O(n^{4/5})$ to each vertex. Consider an r-division for $r = n^{4/5}$, and let $\mathcal{R}$ be the set of its regions. The label of each vertex u consists of the following:

(a) The r-division $\mathcal{R}$. Space: $O(n/r)$.
(b) For each region R in the r-division, the length of the shortest path in G, among paths that are internally disjoint from R, from u to $\bigcup_{P \in \mathcal{R}} \partial P$, and from $\bigcup_{P \in \mathcal{R}} \partial P$ to u. There are $O(n/r)$ regions and for each of them we store $O(n/r \cdot \sqrt{r})$ distances. Space: $O(n^2/r^{3/2})$.
(c) The region R_u and the ∂R_u-to-∂R_u distances in $G \setminus \{u\}$. Space: $O(r)$.

The space is thus $O(n/r + n^2/r^{3/2} + r) = O(n^{4/5})$.

Let us now consider a query (u, v, f), and assume, for simplicity, that no two of u, v and f are contained in a single region. We have two cases. If there is a shortest u-to-v path in $G \setminus \{f\}$ that is vertex-disjoint from R_f, then the u-to-∂R_v distances among paths internally-disjoint from R_f (item (b)), together with R_v, which is stored for v (item (c)), allow us to retrieve the length of this path. In the other case, we employ the u-to-∂R_f distances among paths internally-disjoint from R_f (item (b)), the information stored in item (c) for f, and the ∂R_f-to-v distances among paths internally-disjoint from R_f (item (b)).

It is not difficult to combine this approach with the distance-labeling scheme of Gavoille et al. [22] for the failure-free setting to obtain labels of size $O(n^{3/4})$. (Item (b) has to be modified to store distances to separators of ancestors of R_u instead of distances to $\bigcup_{P \in \mathcal{R}} \partial P$, requiring $O(n^{3/2}/r)$ space.) In the approach that we present below, we rely on separators in a more sophisticated and delicate manner to obtain labels of size $O(n^{2/3})$.

The Label. Recall that an r-division is represented by a decomposition tree $\mathcal{T}$, whose root corresponds to G. The internal nodes of $\mathcal{T}$ correspond to pieces of G. The two children of a piece $P \in \mathcal{T}$ are the subgraphs of P external and internal to $Sep(P)$. The leaves of $\mathcal{T}$ are the regions of the r-division.

The label of each vertex u in G consists of the following information:

(i) The entire recursive decomposition tree $\mathcal{T}$. Space: $O(n/r)$.
(ii) For each region R in the r-division, the shortest path distances in G from u to ∂R among paths that are internally disjoint from R. There $O(n/r)$ regions and each of them has $O(\sqrt{r})$ boundary nodes. Space: $O(n/\sqrt{r})$.
(iii) The region R_u and the ∂R_u-to-∂R_u distances in $G \setminus \{u\}$. Space: $O(r)$.
(iv) For each piece $P \in \mathcal{T}$ with sibling Q, for each $p \in \partial P \setminus Q$, the shortest path distance from u to p in $G \setminus (P \cup Q) \cup \{p\}$, and the shortest path distance from p to u in $G \setminus Q$. Space: $O(\sum_{P \in \mathcal{T}} \partial P) = O(n/\sqrt{r})$, c.f. [23].
(v) For each ancestor piece P of R_u in $\mathcal{T}$, for each vertex p of $Sep(P) \setminus \partial P$, the shortest path distance from u to p among paths in $P \setminus \partial P$ that are internally disjoint from $Sep(P)$, and the shortest path distance in $P \setminus \partial P$ from p to u. Space: $O(\sqrt{n})$, c.f. [23].

The overall space required by the above five items is $O(n/r + n/\sqrt{r} + r + n/\sqrt{r} + \sqrt{n})$, which is $O(n^{2/3})$ for $r = n^{2/3}$.

The Query. Upon query (u, v, f) we say that a path is a (u, v, f)-path if it is a u-to-v path in G that avoids f, and we seek the shortest (u, v, f)-path, which we denote by S. Let X denote the lowest node in T that is an ancestor of R_f and of at least one of $\{R_u, R_v\}$. Let us assume without loss of generality that X is an ancestor of R_u. We return the minimum of the following three:

1. S includes a vertex of ∂R_f.
   The length of this path is found with a SSSP computation on the (non-planar) graph G_1 whose vertices are u, v, and $\partial R_f \setminus \{f\}$ and whose edges are in one-to-one correspondence with the distances specified below, i.e. for each a-to-b distance, there is an edge from a to b with length equal to that distance:
   - the u-to-$\partial R_f \setminus \{f\}$ distances from item (ii) in u's label (or the u-to-$\partial R_f \setminus \{f\}$ distances in $R_f \setminus \{f\}$, which can be computed from item (iii), if $R_u = R_f$);
   - the $\partial R_f \setminus \{f\}$-to-$\partial R_f \setminus \{f\}$ distances from item (iii) in f's label;
   - the $\partial R_f \setminus \{f\}$-to-$v$ distances from item (ii) in v's label (or the $\partial R_f \setminus \{f\}$-to-$v$ distances in $R_f \setminus \{f\}$, which can be computed from item (iii), if $R_v = R_f$).

2. S avoids R_f but includes a boundary vertex of some piece on $T[X, R_f]$.
   The length of this path is found with a SSSP computation on the graph G_2 whose vertices are u, v, and ∂P of all nodes P that are siblings of some node Q on the X-to-R_f path in T. The edges are in one-to-one correspondence with the u-to-∂P distances from item (iv) in u's label and the ∂P-to-v distances from item (iv) in v's label.

3. S avoids all boundary vertices of all the pieces on $T[X, R_f]$.
   This is required only for the case where the lowest common ancestor of R_u and R_v is not an ancestor of R_f (otherwise, it is an ancestor of X and a u-to-v path cannot avoid the boundary vertices of X). The length of this path is found with a SSSP computation on the graph G_3 whose vertices are u, v, and $Sep(P) \setminus \partial P$ of all nodes P on $T(X, R_u)$. The edges are in one-to-one correspondence with the u-to-$Sep(P)$ distances from item (v) in u's label and the $Sep(P)$-to-v distances from item (v) in v's label. If $R_u = R_v$, the shortest path may not cross any of these separators; in that case the distance may be retrieved by a single SSSP computation in $R_u \setminus \{f\}$ (item (iii)).

Correctness. Let us consider the three options for the shortest (u, v, f)-path S (an illustration is provided in Fig. 1).

1. S includes a vertex of ∂R_f. Let a (resp. b) denote the first (resp. last) vertex of S that belongs to $\partial R_f \setminus \{f\}$. The path S can be partitioned into a u-to-a prefix, an a-to-b infix, and a b-to-v suffix. All three subpaths are represented in G_1, and all paths represented in G_1 do not include f.

2. S avoids R_f but includes a boundary vertex of some piece on $T[X, R_f]$. First observe that all u-to-v paths in G_2 avoid some (not necessarily proper) ancestor of R_f and therefore also avoid f. To see that S is represented in G_2, let Q denote the unique piece on $T(X, R_f]$ such that S avoids Q but visits its sibling P (such a piece Q must exist because S avoids R_f but visits some piece on $T[X, R_f]$). Since S visits P it must visit some vertex of ∂P. Let p be the first such vertex of S. Partition S into a shortest u-to-p path in $G \setminus (Q \cup P) \cup \{p\}$ and a shortest p-to-v path in $G \setminus Q$. These two subpaths are represented in G_2.

3. S avoids all boundary vertices of all the pieces on $T[X, R_f]$. If S does not visit ∂R_u (and thus $R_u = R_v$) then we find S with an SSSP computation in $R_u \setminus \{f\}$. Otherwise, S visits a separator vertex in of some piece that is a proper ancestor of R_u. Let P be the rootmost such piece. Since S avoids ∂X we have that S is restricted to X and hence P is a descendant of X. In fact, P must be a *proper* descendant of X (otherwise, S visits $Sep(X)$ and therefore visits the boundary of both child-pieces of X including the one on $T[X, R_f]$, a contradiction). We therefore have that $P \in T(X, R_u)$ and S is restricted to P. Also observe that S avoids ∂P because otherwise S must visit a separator vertex of some ancestor of P, contradicting P being rootmost. Let p be the first vertex of S that belongs to $Sep(P)$. S can be decomposed into a shortest path from u to p in $P \setminus \partial P$ that is internally disjoint from $Sep(P)$, and a suffix that is a shortest path from p to v in $P \setminus \partial P$; S is thus represented in G_3. To see that no path represented in G_3 contains f, observe that P may contain f, but since R_f is not a descendant of P, f must be a vertex of ∂P and so is not visited by any path represented in G_3.

We thus arrive at the following result.

Theorem 2. *Given a directed planar graph G of size n, with real edge-lengths, we can assign an $O(n^{2/3})$-size label to each vertex of G such that upon query (u, v, x), where $u, v, x \in V(G)$, the length of the shortest u-to-v path in $G \setminus \{x\}$ can be retrieved from the labels of u, v and x.*

Remark 1. Any graph G of size n from a family of graphs that hereditarily admits $O(\sqrt{n})$-size separators (such as H-minor free graphs and bounded genus graphs) can be recursively decomposed so that we get an r-division (perhaps not with the few-holes property). As our labeling scheme does not require the few-holes property, Theorem 2 actually applies to any such graph family.

Extension for Counting. We now show how to extend our single-fault labeling from reporting u-to-v shortest paths in $G \setminus \{f\}$ to counting the number of u-to-v shortest paths in $G \setminus \{f\}$. Our modification does not increase the label size (assuming that each number we store fits into a single word, see the discussion in the introduction). However, the efficient query algorithm cannot be applied, leading to $\tilde{O}(n^{2/3})$ query time.

In order to extend the labeling scheme for counting, for every u-to-v shortest path distance which is stored in our label, we also store the number of such

u-to-v shortest paths. The change in query time is that instead of the SSSP computations on G_1, G_2, G_3 we use an SSSP computation that counts shortest paths. That is, for each edge in G_i there is a value representing its multiplicity (the value we added to the label), and we want to compute the number of shortest paths with respect to the multiplicities. This extension can be achieved by a trivial extension to Dijkstra's algorithm, resulting in $\tilde{O}(n^{2/3})$ query time (In contrast, FR-Dijkstra has no known extension for counting shortest paths). The following lemma proves the correctness of our labeling scheme.

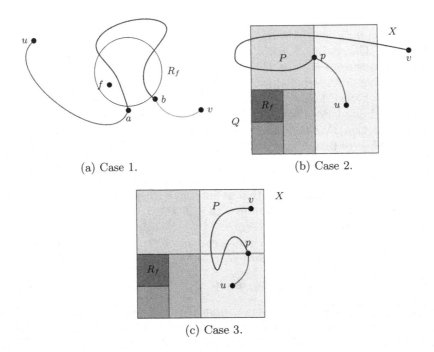

(a) Case 1.   (b) Case 2.

(c) Case 3.

Fig. 1. An illustration of the 3 different cases that arise for the query. In the figures we assume that $u, v \notin R_f$ and the different colors in each path represent its decomposition as defined in the proof of correctness. In the figure for Case 2, the blue piece denotes R_f, while the siblings of its ancestors in $T(X, R_f]$ are denoted by different scales of gray; the deeper the piece is in T, the darker its color. Piece Q is denoted be the red-dashed rectangle. For Case 3, the setting is the same and in our illustration P is the child of X that is not an ancestor of R_f. $Sep(P)$ is denoted by green. (Color figure online)

Lemma 1. *Every shortest path from u to v in $G \setminus \{f\}$ is represented exactly once in the query graphs G_1, G_2, G_3.*

Proof. The same argument as in the correctness subparagraph proves that every shortest path is represented at least once in the query graphs. It remains to show that every path is represented at most once. Let us consider the three cases for a shortest (u, v, f)-path:

1. S includes a vertex of ∂R_f. S is not represented in G_2, G_3 because every path that is represented there must avoid an ancestor of R_f. S is represented exactly once in G_1 because it has a unique decomposition into subpaths $S_1 S_2 S_3$ where S_1 is from u to the first vertex b_1 of S in ∂R_f, S_2 is from b_1 to the last vertex b_2 of S in ∂R_f, and S_3 is from b_2 to v.

2. S avoids R_f but includes a boundary vertex of some piece on $T[X, R_f]$. S is not represented in G_1 because all the paths that are represented there touch R_f, it is also not represented in G_3 since every path there avoids all boundary vertices of all pieces in $T[X, R_f]$. To prove that S is represented in G_2 exactly once we again show that S can be uniquely decomposed into three subpaths in G_2. Let P be the sibling of some piece $Q \in T[X, R_f]$ s.t. S visits P, and let $p \in \partial P \cap S$. If P is not the deepest such piece, then S also visits Q but the edge (p, v) in G_2 counts only paths in $G \setminus Q$, hence S is not represented as a $u - p - v$ path in G_2. If P is the deepest such piece but p is not the first vertex in ∂P that S visits, then the u-to-p subpath of S is not represented as an edge (u, p) in G_2 since only paths in $G \setminus (P \cup Q) \cup \{p\}$ are.

3. S avoids all boundary vertices of all the pieces on $T[X, R_f]$. S is not represented in G_1, G_2 because every path that is represented there touches some piece in $T[X, R_f]$. It is counted exactly once in G_3 by a similar argument to case 2 above: S is counted once in G_3 by the first separator vertex that S visits in the rootmost piece that it visits. Finally, in the case where $R_u = R_v = R_f$, we perform Dijkstra (with its extension for counting) on $R_u \setminus \partial R_u$.

Efficient Queries for Planar Graphs. We can easily achieve $\tilde{O}(n^{2/3})$ query-time, since this is the size of the graphs that we construct and can thus perform Dijkstra for SSSP computations. This query time applies to any graph family with $\sqrt{n}$-size separators, such as minor-free graphs. On planar graphs, in order to perform queries more efficiently we have to assume random access to the labels of vertices u, v and x; retrieving them would require $O(n^{2/3})$ time. We present an $\tilde{O}(\sqrt{n})$-time query algorithm for planar graphs at the expense of increasing the labels' size by polylogarithmic factors.

Let us now formally state the main result of [8].

Theorem 3 [8]. *Given a weighted directed planar graph G of size n and a source $s \in V(G)$, we can construct in $O(n \log^4 n)$ time an $O(n \log^4 n)$-size data structure, that upon query (v, x), for $v, x \in V(G)$, returns the s-to-v distance in $G \setminus \{x\}$ in time $O(\log n)$.*

Cases 2 & 3. G_2 and G_3 are of size $O(\sqrt{n})$ and they can be constructed in $O(\sqrt{n})$ time from the labels of u, v and f. We can compute SSSPs in these graphs in $O(\sqrt{n} \log n)$ time using Dijkstra's algorithm. We handle the subcase of Case 3 in which $R_u = R_v$ and the sought shortest path does not cross ∂R_u as follows. The label of u additionally stores the single-source single-failure distance oracle of Theorem 3 for graph $R_u \setminus (\partial R_u \setminus \{u\})$ and source u. It occupies $\tilde{O}(r) = \tilde{O}(n^{2/3})$ additional space. Upon query, we simply query this oracle with (v, x).

*C*ase 1. This is the only involved case, as G_1 can be of size $\Theta(r) = \Theta(n^{2/3})$ and we aim at performing SSSP computations in time $\tilde{O}(\sqrt{n})$. Let us note that the distances of u to $\partial R_f \setminus \{f\}$ in the case that $R_u = R_f$ can be computed in time $\tilde{O}(\sqrt{r}) = \tilde{O}(n^{1/3})$ if we have stored the oracle of Theorem 3 for graph R_u and source u in the label of u. The case $R_v = R_f$ can be treated analogously.

In order to perform efficient SSSP computations we resort to FR-Dijkstra (Theorem 1). We first make a minor modification to item (iii) of the label so that the Monge property required for FR-Dijkstra is satisfied: instead of storing ∂R_u-to-∂R_u distances in $G \setminus \{u\}$, we instead store ∂R_u-to-∂R_u distances in $R \setminus \{u\}$ and ∂R_u-to-∂R_u distances in $G \setminus ((R \setminus \partial R) \cup \{u\})$. This ensures that the set of vertices over which the *DDG*s are built lie on a constant number of faces of the reference graph. The size of the label is unaffected by this modification. We can then use Theorem 1 in a straightforward way to compute the sought shortest path in time $\tilde{O}(\sqrt{r}) = \tilde{O}(n^{1/3})$.

Efficient Preprocessing for Planar Graphs. The labels can be naively constructed in $O(n^2)$ time. This is true for any graph family with $\sqrt{n}$-size separators. For planar graphs, we show that the construction time can be improved to $\tilde{O}(n^{5/3})$.

The complete recursive decomposition of G, required for item (i), can be computed in $O(n)$ time [34]. For the rest of the items, we use MSSP data structure for an appropriate subgraph of G, or of the reverse graph of G, i.e. G with all its edges reversed.

The multiple-source shortest paths (MSSP) data structure [33] represents all shortest path trees rooted at the vertices of a single face g in a planar graph. It can be constructed in $O(n \log n)$ time, requires $O(n \log n)$ space, and can report any distance between a vertex of f and any other vertex in the graph in $O(\log n)$ time. Using a simple modification of the underlying graph, presented in [13], we can ensure that MSSP returns the length of the shortest path that is internally disjoint from a prespecified subset of the vertices of g.

To compute the information required for item (ii) of the labels, we build an MSSP data structure for the reverse graph of $G \setminus (R \setminus \partial R)$ for each piece R in the r-division and each of the $O(1)$ holes g on which the vertices of ∂R lie. We then query the sought distances. The time required to construct the MSSP data structures is $\tilde{O}(n^2/r) = \tilde{O}(n^{4/3})$ and the time required for computing the distances is $\tilde{O}(n^2/\sqrt{r}) = \tilde{O}(n^{5/3})$. The precomputations for items (iii), (iv) and the first part of item (v) can be done analogously –for item (iii) we store the distances described in the description of the efficient query implementation.

For the second part of item (v), we can not make use of MSSP, as the shortest path from u to $p \in Sep(P)$ is allowed to cross $Sep(P)$. We can instead build an $\tilde{O}(|P|)$-size exact distance oracle for $P \setminus \partial P$ in $\tilde{O}(|P|^{3/2})$ time that answers distance queries in $\tilde{O}(|P|^\epsilon)$ time, for any constant $\epsilon > 0$ [12]; we pick $\epsilon = 1/6$. We then query this oracle for the all distances we need to compute in $P \setminus \partial P$. Over all pieces, the preprocessing time is $\tilde{O}(n^{3/2})$ and the sought distances are retrieved in $\tilde{O}(n^{3/2} \cdot n^{1/6}) = \tilde{O}(n^{5/3})$

To wrap up, the global preprocessing time is $\tilde{O}(n^{5/3})$ and is upper bounded by the total size of the labels up to polylogarithmic factors.

4 Labeling for Counting Shortest Paths

In this section we design labels such that given the labels of any $k + 2$ vertices $s, t, v_1, v_2, \ldots, v_k$, we should return the number of s-to-t paths that avoid vertices $v_1, \ldots, v_k$ and whose length is equal to $d(s, t)$ (the original s-to-t distance in G). Note that this is the same as returning the number of shortest s-to-t paths in $G \setminus \{v_1, v_2, \ldots, v_k\}$ only if the length of the shortest s-to-t path does not change when $\{v_1, v_2, \ldots, v_k\}$ fail. We show that the labeling of [9] (with labels of size $O(\sqrt{n})$) actually works in this more general setting and show how to perform a query in $\tilde{O}(\sqrt{n} \cdot k)$ time. We assume in this section that edge weights are positive.

The Label. We first compute a complete recursive decomposition of G. The label of each vertex v in G then consists of the following information:

(i) For each ancestor piece P of v, for every $u \in Sep(P)$, the number $p_1(v, u)$ and length $d_1(v, u)$ of all v-to-u shortest paths in $P \setminus Sep(P) \cup \{u\}$.
(ii) For each ancestor piece P of v, for every $u \in Sep(P)$, the number $p_2(u, v)$ and length $d_2(u, v)$ of all u-to-v shortest paths in $P \setminus \partial P$.

In what follows, in the case that u is in many separators of ancestor pieces of v, when referring to $d_1(v, u)$, $p_1(v, u)$, $d_2(u, v)$ and $p_2(u, v)$ we mean the values computed for the rootmost such piece.

The Query - Without Faults. When there are no faulty vertices, every s-to-t shortest path Q in G is uniquely determined by a piece P in the recursive decomposition and a vertex $u \in Sep(P)$. The piece P is the rootmost ancestor piece of s in the recursive decomposition s.t. Q visits $Sep(P)$ and therefore does not visit ∂P. Such a piece P must be an ancestor of both s and t. The vertex $u \in Sep(P)$ is the first vertex of $Sep(P)$ visited by Q. Q can thus be decomposed into a prefix Q_1 in $P \setminus Sep(P) \cup \{u\}$ from s to u, and a suffix Q_2 in $P \setminus \partial P$ from u to t. For every possible u we have the number of such Q_1 in (i) of s and the number of such Q_2 in (ii) of t. We therefore add the term $p_1(s, u) \cdot p_2(u, t)$ to the answer. However, we only wish to add this term if $d(s, u) + d(u, t) = d(s, t)$ (otherwise, we are counting non-shortest paths). We have $d(s, u) + d(u, t)$ from the labels of s and t. We compute $d(s, t)$ as follows. Let $A[v]$ be the union of separator vertices of all ancestors of v. Then

$$d(s, t) = \min_{u \in A[s] \cap A[t]} (d_1(s, u) + d_2(u, t)), \tag{1}$$

and the overall query is computed as

$$paths(s, t) = \sum_{\substack{u \in A[s] \cap A[t] \text{ s.t} \\ d_1(s,u)+d_2(u,t)=d(s,t)}} p_1(s, u) \cdot p_2(u, t) \tag{2}$$

It takes $\tilde{O}(\sqrt{n})$ time to perform such query because there are $O(\sqrt{n})$ vertices in $A[s] \cap A[t]$ and for each of them we perform $\tilde{O}(1)$ calculations. We also compute $d(s, t)$ beforehand in $\tilde{O}(\sqrt{n})$ time.

The Query - with Faults. We begin with an $\tilde{O}(\sqrt{n} \cdot k^2)$ time query and then improve this to $\tilde{O}(\sqrt{n} \cdot k)$. We order the faulty vertices in the increasing order of their distances from s in G, and index them $v_1, \ldots, v_k$ accordingly. For convenience we refer to s as v_0 and to t as v_{k+1}. Denote by $R[j]$ the number of s-to-v_j shortest paths in G that avoid $v_1, \ldots, v_{j-1}$. Denoting by $paths(v_i, v_j)$ the number of v_i-to-v_j shortest paths in G we obtain the recurrence:

$$R[j] = paths(s, v_j) - \sum_{\substack{i<j \text{ s.t.} \\ d(s,v_i)+d(v_i,v_j)=d(s,v_j)}} R[i] \cdot paths(v_i, v_j) \qquad (3)$$

To see why this recurrence holds, it suffices to show that every shortest path Q in G from s to v_j that visits at least one of $v_1, \ldots, v_{j-1}$ is counted in the second term exactly once. It is clear that every such path Q is counted at least once, because it can be decomposed into a prefix composed of a shortest path from s to the first v_i that Q visits (i.e. is counted by $R[i]$) and a suffix composed of a v_i-to-v_j path (i.e. counted by $paths(v_i, v_j)$). To see why every path Q is counted at most once, notice that every such path Q visits the faulty vertices monotonically with respect to their ordering. In other words, if Q visits some v_i and then some v_j then $i < j$. This holds because if v_i is on a shortest path from s to v_j then $d(s, v_i) < d(s, v_j)$, and by our ordering of the faulty vertices $i < j$. Since $R[i]$ only counts paths that are internally disjoint from failed vertices, the only time Q is counted is when we count paths of the form $s \rightsquigarrow v_i \rightsquigarrow v_j$, where v_i is the first faulty vertex Q visits.

Given $R[1], \ldots, R[j-1]$ we can compute $R[j]$ in $\tilde{O}(\sqrt{n} \cdot j)$ using the recurrence. For each faulty vertex v_i with $i < j$ we perform a $paths(v_i, v_j)$ query as described above which takes $\tilde{O}(\sqrt{n})$ time, so the overall complexity is $\tilde{O}(\sqrt{n} \cdot k^2)$.

Improved Query Time. We now show how to improve the query time from $\tilde{O}(\sqrt{n} \cdot k^2)$ to $\tilde{O}(\sqrt{n} \cdot k)$. In order to achieve this, we cannot afford to compute $paths(v_i, v_j)$ for every pair i, j. Instead, we will express $R[j]$ as a summation over $O(\sqrt{n})$ terms that we can compute in $\tilde{O}(1)$ time.

By combining Eqs. (2) and (3), and since $paths(s, v_j)$ can be computed in $\tilde{O}(\sqrt{n})$ time, we get that computing $R[j]$ boils down to computing the following double summation:

$$\sum_{\substack{i<j \text{ s.t.} \\ d(s,v_i)+d(v_i,v_j)=d(s,v_j)}} R[i] \sum_{\substack{u \in A[v_i] \cap A[v_j] \text{ s.t} \\ d_1(v_i,u)+d_2(u,v_j)=d(v_i,v_j)}} p_1(v_i, u) \cdot p_2(u, v_j) \qquad (4)$$

The above sum counts all s-to-v_j shortest paths Q that can be decomposed into three parts:

Q_1 - a shortest s-to-v_i path in G (for some v_i) that avoids $v_1, \ldots, v_{i-1}$.

Q_2 - a shortest v_i-to-u path in $P \setminus Sep(P) \cup \{u\}$ for some $u \in Sep(P)$, where P is defined as the rootmost ancestor of v_i s.t. Q touches $Sep(p)$ (u is the first vertex of $Sep(P)$ in Q_2).

Q_3 - a shortest u-to-v_j path in $P \setminus \partial P$.

We use the same decomposition into Q_1, Q_2, Q_3 but sum the terms differently. Denoting $D(s, u) = \min_i (d(s, v_i) + d_1(v_i, u))$ we compute:

$$\sum_{\substack{u \in A[v_j] \text{ s.t.} \\ D(s,u)+d_2(u,v_j)=d(s,v_j)}} p_2(u, v_j) \qquad \sum_{\substack{i<j \text{ s.t. } u \in A[v_i] \text{ and} \\ d(s,v_i)+d_1(v_i,u)=D(s,u)}} R[i] \cdot p_1(v_i, u) \qquad (5)$$

Let us explain Eq. (5). Denote the inner summation term (in blue) as $F_j(u)$. $F_j(u)$ counts the number of combinations for $Q_1 Q_2$ by iterating over every faulty vertex v_i where $i < j$ and $u \in A[v_i]$. For a fixed v_i, the number of such combinations is $R[i] \cdot p_1(v_i, u)$. Among all $Q_1 Q_2$ combinations, we only want to sum combinations $Q_1 Q_2$ that have length $d(s, u)$. Ideally, this could be imposed by adding the condition $d(s, v_i) + d_1(v_i, u) = d(s, u)$ to the inner sum. However, we cannot compute $d(s, u)$ because we do not have the label of u. Instead, we add the condition $d(s, v_i) + d_1(v_i, u) = D(s, u)$ where $D(s, u) = \min_i (d(s, v_i) + d_1(v_i, u))$ (observe that $D(s, u) \geq d(s, u)$). This condition is easy to check using $d_1(v_i, u)$ stored in the label of v_i and the value $d(s, v_i)$ which can be computed beforehand using Eq. (1). The counting remains correct because in the outer sum we check that $D(s, u) + d_2(u, v_j) = d(s, v_j)$ which only holds if $D(s, u) = d(s, u)$ (because when $D(s, u) > d(s, u)$ then by the triangle inequality we have that $D(s, u) + d_2(u, v_j) > d(s, u) + d_2(u, v_j) \geq d(s, v_j)$). Note that even if $D(s, u) = d(s, u)$ it may be that $D(s, u) + d_2(u, v_j) > d(s, v_j)$. This happens in the case that there are no s-to-v_j shortest paths that visit u. In other words, we check that a path $Q_1 Q_2 Q_3$ is shortest by verifying that $d(s, v_i) + d_1(v_i, u) + d_2(u, v_j) = d(s, v_j)$. This is true iff $D(s, u) = d(s, u)$ and $d_2(u, v_j) = d(u, v_j)$ which means that $Q_1 Q_2 Q_3$ is indeed a shortest path.

Observe that in the inner sum we consider only $i < j$. This is because for $i \geq j$ none of the paths from s to v_j that visit v_i is shortest due to the ordering of the faulty vertices.

As for the outer sum, it counts the number of Q_3 paths for every $u \in A[v_j]$. Overall, we iterate over every $u \in A[v_j]$ and multiply $F_j(u)$ (the number of $Q_1 Q_2$ paths) by $p_2(u, v_j)$ (the number of Q_3 paths) and obtain the answer.

Overall, in the j'th iteration we compute $R[j]$ using the $F_j(u)$ values according to Eq. (5). Notice that $F_{j+1}(u)$ is either equal to $F_j(u)$ or to $F_j(u) + R[j] \cdot p_1(v_j, u)$. We can therefore compute $F_{j+1}(u)$ for every $u \in A[v_j]$ using the just computed $R[j]$ and $F_j(u)$. This takes total $\tilde{O}(\sqrt{n})$ time and $\tilde{O}(\sqrt{n} \cdot k)$ time over all the $k + 2$ iterations.

In order to check the distance restrictions in the summations we precompute $d(s, v_j)$ for every $0 \leq j \leq k + 1$ and $D(s, u)$ for every $u \in \bigcup_{0 \leq i \leq k+1} A[v_i]$. The former ($d(s, v_j)$) is computed using (1), and the latter ($D(s, u)$) is computed by iterating over every i and $u \in A[v_i]$ and maintaining the minimum value for each $D(s, u)$. Thus, the precomputation of $D(s, u)$ and $d(s, v_j)$ takes $\tilde{O}(\sqrt{n} \cdot k)$ time.

5   A Lower Bound on Labels for Counting Shortest Paths

In this section we prove the following lower bound on labeling schemes for counting shortest paths (without faults) in graphs such that the number of distinct shortest paths between any two nodes consists of at most L bits.

The proof is a modification of the approach of Gavoille et al. [22] for standard distance labeling. Their proof proceeds by assigning weights to the edges of a $\sqrt{n} \times \sqrt{n}$ grid graph so that the shortest path from the i-th node in the first column to the j-th node in the first row consists of $j-1$ horizontal edges, followed by $i-1$ vertical edges. Then, the proof hides a single bit in every intersection by creating or not a shortcut. The shortest paths defined above are still of the same form, up to using the shortcut in case it exists: horizontal edges, possibly a shortcut, and then vertical edges.

Theorem 4. *Any labeling scheme for counting shortest paths in planar graphs such that the number of distinct shortest paths between any two nodes consists of at most L bits requires labels consisting of $\Omega(\sqrt{nL})$ bits.*

Proof. Let us consider a $\sqrt{m} \times \sqrt{m}$ grid graph, weighted as in the proof of Gavoille et al. from [22]. In every intersection, instead of a single s-to-t shortcut, we introduce an $O(L)$-size gadget – essentially the one described in the introduction, in our proof that labels of $o(n)$ bits cannot exist if L is unbounded.

More specifically, suppose that we are given $L-1$ bits $b_0, \ldots, b_{L-2}$. Each edge of the gadget will have weight equal to $1/L$ times the weight of the shortcut in the proof of Gavoille et al. The gadget consists of a path $s = u_0 - u_1 - \cdots - u_{L-1}$ and another path $v_1 - v_2 - \cdots - v_L = t$ in which every edge is duplicated (i.e., there are two parallel edges between each pair v_i, v_{i+1}). Finally, for every $i = 0, \ldots, L-2$ such that $b_i = 1$, we add an edge $u_i - v_{i+1}$. The number of shortest s-to-t paths in the gadget is exactly $\sum_{i=0}^{L-2} b_i \cdot 2^{L-1-i}$. Note that this number is congruent to 0 modulo 2. The size of the graph is $n = \Theta(mL)$.

Now, the number of shortest paths from the i-th node in the first column to the j-th node in the first row is 1 if all b_i's are equal to 0 for the gadget at intersection (i, j); otherwise it is equal to $\sum_{i=0}^{L-2} b_i \cdot 2^{L-1-i}$. Hence, each pair (i, j) allows us to recover $\Theta(L)$ distinct bits. Thus, the labels must consist of $\Omega((\sqrt{m} - 1)^2 L / (2\sqrt{m} - 1)) = \Omega(\sqrt{m}L) = \Omega(\sqrt{nL})$ bits.

We leave the problem of closing the gap between this $\Omega(\sqrt{nL})$ lower bound and the $O(\sqrt{nL})$ upper bound open for further investigation.

References

1. Abraham, I., Chechik, S., Gavoille, C.: Fully dynamic approximate distance oracles for planar graphs via forbidden-set distance labels. In: 44th STOC, pp. 1199–1218 (2012). https://doi.org/10.1145/2213977.2214084
2. Abraham, I., Chechik, S., Gavoille, C., Peleg, D.: Forbidden-set distance labels for graphs of bounded doubling dimension. ACM Trans. Algorithms 12(2), 22:1–22:17 (2016). https://doi.org/10.1145/2818694

3. Abraham, I., Gavoille, C.: Object location using path separators. In: 25th PODC, pp. 188–197. ACM (2006). https://doi.org/10.1145/1146381.1146411
4. Alon, N., Nenadov, R.: Optimal induced universal graphs for bounded-degree graphs. In: 28th SODA, pp. 1149–1157 (2017). https://doi.org/10.1137/1.9781611974782.74
5. Alstrup, S., Dahlgaard, S., Knudsen, M.B.T.: Optimal induced universal graphs and adjacency labeling for trees. J. ACM **64**(4), 27:1–27:22 (2017). https://doi.org/10.1145/3088513
6. Alstrup, S., Kaplan, H., Thorup, M., Zwick, U.: Adjacency labeling schemes and induced-universal graphs. SIAM J. Discret. Math. **33**(1), 116–137 (2019). https://doi.org/10.1137/16M1105967
7. Bar-Natan, A., Charalampopoulos, P., Gawrychowski, P., Mozes, S., Weimann, O.: Fault-tolerant distance labeling for planar graphs. CoRR abs/2102.07154 (2021)
8. Baswana, S., Lath, U., Mehta, A.S.: Single source distance oracle for planar digraphs avoiding a failed node or link. In: 23rd SODA. pp. 223–232 (2012). https://doi.org/10.1137/1.9781611973099.20
9. Bezáková, I., Searns, A.: On counting oracles for path problems. In: 29th ISAAC, pp. 56:1–56:12 (2018). https://doi.org/10.4230/LIPIcs.ISAAC.2018.56
10. Bonichon, N., Gavoille, C., Labourel, A.: Short labels by traversal and jumping. Electron. Not. Discrete Math. **28**, 153–160 (2007). https://doi.org/10.1016/j.endm.2007.01.022
11. Cabello, S., Chambers, E.W., Erickson, J.: Multiple-source shortest paths in embedded graphs. SIAM J. Comput. **42**(4), 1542–1571 (2013). https://doi.org/10.1137/120864271
12. Charalampopoulos, P., Gawrychowski, P., Mozes, S., Weimann, O.: Almost optimal distance oracles for planar graphs. In: 51st STOC, pp. 138–151 (2019). https://doi.org/10.1145/3313276.3316316
13. Charalampopoulos, P., Mozes, S., Tebeka, B.: Exact distance oracles for planar graphs with failing vertices. In: 30th SODA, pp. 2110–2123 (2019). https://doi.org/10.1137/1.9781611975482.127
14. Courcelle, B., Gavoille, C., Kanté, M.M.: Compact labelings for efficient first-order model-checking. J. Comb. Optim. **21**(1), 19–46 (2009). https://doi.org/10.1007/s10878-009-9260-7
15. Courcelle, B., Twigg, A.: Constrained-path labellings on graphs of bounded clique-width. Theory of Comput. Syst. **47**(2), 531–567 (2010). https://doi.org/10.1007/s00224-009-9211-9
16. Emek, Y., Peleg, D., Roditty, L.: A near-linear-time algorithm for computing replacement paths in planar directed graphs. ACM Trans. Algorithms **6**(4), 64:1–64:13 (2010). https://doi.org/10.1145/1824777.1824784
17. Fakcharoenphol, J., Rao, S.: Planar graphs, negative weight edges, shortest paths, and near linear time. J. Comput. Syst. Sci. **72**(5), 868–889 (2006). https://doi.org/10.1016/j.jcss.2005.05.007
18. Feigenbaum, J., Karger, D.R., Mirrokni, V.S., Sami, R.: Subjective-cost policy routing. In: 1st WINE, pp. 174–183 (2005). https://doi.org/10.1007/11600930_18
19. Feigenbaum, J., Karger, D.R., Mirrokni, V.S., Sami, R.: Subjective-cost policy routing. Theor. Comput. Sci. **378**(2), 175–189 (2007). https://doi.org/10.1016/j.tcs.2007.02.020
20. Frederickson, G.N.: Fast algorithms for shortest paths in planar graphs, with applications. SIAM J. Comput. **16**(6), 1004–1022 (1987). https://doi.org/10.1137/0216064

21. Gavoille, C., Katz, M., Katz, N.A., Paul, C., Peleg, D.: Approximate distance labeling schemes. In: 9th ESA, pp. 476–487 (2001). https://doi.org/10.1007/3-540-44676-1_40

22. Gavoille, C., Peleg, D., Pérennes, S., Raz, R.: Distance labeling in graphs. J. Algorithms **53**(1), 85–112 (2004). https://doi.org/10.1016/j.jalgor.2004.05.002

23. Gawrychowski, P., Mozes, S., Weimann, O., Wulff-Nilsen, C.: Better tradeoffs for exact distance oracles in planar graphs. In: 29th SODA, pp. 515–529 (2018). https://doi.org/10.1137/1.9781611975031.34

24. Gawrychowski, P., Uznański, P.: A note on distance labeling in planar graphs. CoRR abs/1611.06529 (2016)

25. Graham, R.L., Pollak, H.O.: On embedding graphs in squashed cubes. In: Alavi, Y., Lick, D.R., White, A.T. (eds.) Graph Theory and Applications. LNM, vol. 303, pp. 99–110. Springer, Heidelberg (1972). https://doi.org/10.1007/BFb0067362

26. Gupta, A., Kumar, A., Rastogi, R.: Traveling with a pez dispenser (or, routing issues in MPLS). In: 42nd FOCS, pp. 148–157 (2001). https://doi.org/10.1109/SFCS.2001.959889

27. Hsu, T., Lu, H.: An optimal labeling for node connectivity. In: 20th ISAAC (2009). https://doi.org/10.1007/978-3-642-10631-6_32

28. Italiano, G.F., Karczmarz, A., Parotsidis, N.: Planar reachability under single vertex or edge failures. In: 32nd SODA, pp. 2739–2758 (2021). https://doi.org/10.1137/1.9781611976465.163

29. Italiano, G.F., Nussbaum, Y., Sankowski, P., Wulff-Nilsen, C.: Improved algorithms for min cut and max flow in undirected planar graphs. In: 43rd STOC, pp. 313–322 (2011). https://doi.org/10.1145/1993636.1993679

30. Kannan, S., Naor, M., Rudich, S.: Implicit representation of graphs. SIAM J. Discrete Math. **5**(4), 596–603 (1992). https://doi.org/10.1137/0405049

31. Kaplan, H., Mozes, S., Nussbaum, Y., Sharir, M.: Submatrix maximum queries in monge matrices and partial monge matrices, and their applications. ACM Trans. Algorithms **13**(2), 26:1–26:42 (2017). https://doi.org/10.1145/3039873

32. Katz, M., Katz, N.A., Korman, A., Peleg, D.: Labeling schemes for flow and connectivity. SIAM J. Comput. **34**(1), 23–40 (2004). https://doi.org/10.1137/S0097539703433912

33. Klein, P.N.: Multiple-source shortest paths in planar graphs. In: 16th SODA, pp. 146–155 (2005). http://dl.acm.org/citation.cfm?id=1070432.1070454

34. Klein, P.N., Mozes, S., Sommer, C.: Structured recursive separator decompositions for planar graphs in linear time. In: 45th STOC, pp. 505–514 (2013). https://doi.org/10.1145/2488608.2488672

35. Klein, P.N., Mozes, S., Weimann, O.: Shortest paths in directed planar graphs with negative lengths: A linear-space $O(n \log^2 n)$-time algorithm. ACM Trans. Algorithms **6**(2), 30:1–30:18 (2010). https://doi.org/10.1145/1721837.1721846

36. Korman, A.: Labeling schemes for vertex connectivity. ACM Trans. Algorithms **6**(2), 39:1–39:10 (2010). https://doi.org/10.1145/1721837.1721855

37. Miller, G.L.: Finding small simple cycle separators for 2-connected planar graphs. In: 16th STOC, pp. 376–382 (1984). https://doi.org/10.1145/800057.808703

38. Monge, G.: Mémoire sur la théorie des déblais et des remblais. De l'Imprimerie Royale (1781)

39. Mozes, S., Wulff-Nilsen, C.: Shortest paths in planar graphs with real lengths in $O(n \log^2 n / \log \log n)$ time. In: 18th ESA, pp. 206–217 (2010). https://doi.org/10.1007/978-3-642-15781-3_18

40. Peleg, D.: Proximity-preserving labeling schemes. J. Graph Theory **33**(3), 167–176 (2000)

41. Peleg, D.: Informative labeling schemes for graphs. Theor. Comput. Sci. **340**(3), 577–593 (2005). https://doi.org/10.1016/j.tcs.2005.03.015
42. Petersen, C., Rotbart, N., Simonsen, J.G., Wulff-Nilsen, C.: Near-optimal adjacency labeling scheme for power-law graphs. In: 43rd ICALP, pp. 133:1–133:15 (2016). https://doi.org/10.4230/LIPIcs.ICALP.2016.133
43. Rotbart, N.G.: New Ideas on Labeling Schemes. Ph.D. thesis, University of Copenhagen (2016)
44. Thorup, M.: Compact oracles for reachability and approximate distances in planar digraphs. J. ACM **51**(6), 993–1024 (2004). https://doi.org/10.1145/1039488.1039493
45. Twigg, A.D.: Compact forbidden-set routing. Tech. Rep. UCAM-CL-TR-678, University of Cambridge, Computer Laboratory (2006). https://www.cl.cam.ac.uk/techreports/UCAM-CL-TR-678.pdf
46. Wulff-Nilsen, C.: Solving the replacement paths problem for planar directed graphs in $O(n \log n)$ time. In: 21st SODA, pp. 756–765 (2010). https://doi.org/10.1137/1.9781611973075.62

Constant Round Distributed Domination on Graph Classes with Bounded Expansion

Simeon Kublenz, Sebastian Siebertz$^{(\boxtimes)}$ ⓘ, and Alexandre Vigny ⓘ

University of Bremen, Bremen, Germany
{kublenz,siebertz,vigny}@uni-bremen.de

Abstract. We show that the dominating set problem admits a constant factor approximation in a constant number of rounds in the LOCAL model of distributed computing on graph classes with bounded expansion. This generalizes a result of Czygrinow et al. for graphs with excluded topological minors.

Keywords: Dominating set · LOCAL algorithm · Bounded expansion graph classes

1 Introduction

A dominating set in an undirected and simple graph G is a set $D \subseteq V(G)$ such that every vertex $v \in V(G)$ either belongs to D or has a neighbor in D. The MINIMUM DOMINATING SET problem takes as input a graph G and the objective is to find a minimum size dominating set of G. The decision problem whether a graph admits a dominating set of size k is NP-hard [23] and this even holds in very restricted settings, e.g. on planar graphs of maximum degree 3 [17].

Consequently, attention shifted from computing exact solutions to approximating near optimal dominating sets. The simple greedy algorithm computes an $\ln n$ approximation (where n is number of vertices of the input graph) of a minimum dominating set [21,29], and for general graphs this algorithm is near optimal – it is NP-hard to approximate minimum dominating sets within factor $(1 - \epsilon) \ln n$ for every $\epsilon > 0$ [10].

Therefore, researchers tried to identify restricted graph classes where better (sequential) approximations are possible. The problem admits a PTAS on classes with subexponential expansion [19]. Here, expansion refers to the edge density of bounded depth minors, which we will define in detail below. Important examples of classes with subexponential expansion include the class of planar graphs and more generally classes that exclude some fixed graph as a minor. The dominating set problem admits a constant factor approximation on classes of bounded degeneracy (equivalently, of bounded arboricity) [5,28] and an $\mathcal{O}(\ln \gamma)$ approximation (where γ denotes the size of a minimum dominating set) on classes of bounded VC-dimension [7,14]. In fact, the greedy algorithm can be modified to

© Springer Nature Switzerland AG 2021
T. Jurdziński and S. Schmid (Eds.): SIROCCO 2021, LNCS 12810, pp. 334–351, 2021.
https://doi.org/10.1007/978-3-030-79527-6_19

yield a constant factor approximation on graphs with bounded degeneracy [22] and an $\mathcal{O}(\ln \gamma)$ approximation on biclique-free graphs (graphs that exclude some fixed complete bipartite graph $K_{t,t}$ as a subgraph) [33]. However, it is unlikely that polynomial-time constant factor approximations exist even on $K_{3,3}$-free graphs [33]. The general goal in this line of research is to identify the broadest graph classes on which the dominating set problem (or other important problems that are hard on general graphs) can be approximated efficiently with a certain guarantee on the approximation factor. These limits of tractability are often captured by abstract notions, such as expansion, degeneracy or VC-dimension of graph classes.

In this paper we study the distributed time complexity of finding dominating sets in the classic LOCAL model of distributed computing, which can be traced back at least to the seminal work of Gallager, Humblet and Spira [16]. In this model, a distributed system is modeled by an undirected (connected) graph G, in which every vertex represents a computational entity of the network and every edge represents a bidirectional communication channel. The vertices are equipped with unique identifiers. In a distributed algorithm, initially, the nodes have no knowledge about the network graph. They must then communicate and coordinate their actions by passing messages to one another in order to achieve a common goal, in our case, to compute a dominating set of the network graph. The LOCAL model focuses on the aspects of communication complexity and therefore the main measure for the efficiency of a distributed algorithm is the number of communication rounds it needs until it returns its answer.

Kuhn et al. [25] proved that in r rounds on an n-vertex graphs of maximum degree Δ one can approximate minimum dominating sets only within a factor $\Omega(n^{c/r^2}/r)$ and $\Omega(\Delta^{1/(r+1)}/r)$, respectively, where c is a constant. This implies that, in general, to achieve a constant approximation ratio, we need at least $\Omega(\sqrt{\log n/\log\log n})$ and $\Omega(\log\Delta/\log\log\Delta)$ communication rounds, respectively. Kuhn et al. [25] also presented a $(1+\epsilon)\ln\Delta$-approximation in that runs in $\mathcal{O}(\log(n)/\epsilon)$ rounds for any $\epsilon > 0$, Barenboim et al. [6] presented a deterministic $\mathcal{O}((\log n)^{k-1})$-time algorithm that provides an $\mathcal{O}(n^{1/k})$-approximation, for any integer parameter $k \geqslant 2$. More recently, the combined works of Rozhon, Ghaffari, Kuhn, and Maus [18,32] provide an algorithm computing a $(1+\epsilon)$-approximation of the dominating set in poly$(\log(n)/\epsilon)$ rounds [32, Corollary 3.11].

For graphs of degeneracy a (equivalent to arboricity up to factor 2), Lenzen and Wattenhofer [28] provided an algorithm that achieves a factor $\mathcal{O}(a^2)$ approximation in randomized time $\mathcal{O}(\log n)$, and a deterministic $\mathcal{O}(a\log\Delta)$ approximation algorithm with $\mathcal{O}(\log\Delta)$ rounds. Graphs of bounded degeneracy include all graphs that exclude a fixed graph as a (topological) minor and in particular, all planar graphs and any class of bounded genus.

Amiri et al. [1] provided a deterministic $\mathcal{O}(\log n)$ time constant factor approximation algorithm on classes of bounded expansion (which extends also to connected dominating sets). Czygrinow et al. [8] showed that for any given $\epsilon > 0$, $(1+\epsilon)$-approximations of a maximum independent set, a maximum matching, and a minimum dominating set, can be computed in $\mathcal{O}(\log^* n)$ rounds in planar graphs, which is asymptotically optimal [27].

Lenzen et al. [26] proposed a constant factor approximation on planar graphs that can be computed in a constant number of communication rounds (see also [35] for a finer analysis of the approximation factor). Wawrzyniak [34] showed that message sizes of $\mathcal{O}(\log n)$ suffice to give a constant factor approximation on planar graphs in a constant number of rounds. In terms of lower bounds, Hilke et al. [20] showed that there is no deterministic local algorithm (constant-time distributed graph algorithm) that finds a $(7 - \epsilon)$-approximation of a minimum dominating set on planar graphs, for any positive constant ϵ.

The results for planar graphs were gradually extended to classes with bounded genus [2,3], classes with sublogarithmic expansion [4] and eventually by Czygrinow et al. [9] to classes with excluded topological minors. Again, one of the main goals in this line of research is to find the most general graph classes on which the dominating set problem admits a constant factor approximation in a constant number of rounds (Fig. 1).

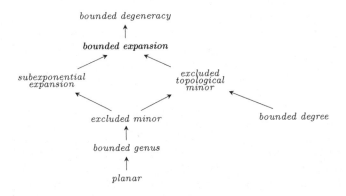

Fig. 1. Inclusion diagram of the mentioned graph classes.

We take a step towards this goal and generalize the result of Czygrinow et al. [9] to classes of bounded expansion. The notion of bounded expansion was introduced by Nešetřil and Ossona de Mendez [30] and offers an abstract definition of uniform sparseness in graphs. It is based on bounding the density of shallow minors. Intuitively, while a minor is obtained by contracting arbitrary connected subgraphs of a graph to new vertices, in an r-shallow minor we are only allowed to contract connected subgraphs of radius at most r.

A class of graphs has bounded expansion if for every radius r the set of all r-shallow minors has edge density bounded by a constant depending only on r. We write $\nabla_r(G)$ for the maximal edge density of an r-shallow minor of a graph G. Of course, every class $\mathscr{C}$ that excludes a fixed graph H as a minor has bounded expansion. For such classes there exists an absolute constant c such that for all $G \in \mathscr{C}$ and all r we have $\nabla_r(G) \leqslant c$. Special cases are the class of planar graphs, every class of graphs that can be drawn with a bounded number of crossings, and every class of graphs that embeds into a fixed surface. Every class of intersection graphs of low density objects in low dimensional Euclidean space has polynomial expansion, that is, the function ∇_r is bounded polynomially in r on $\mathscr{C}$. Also every class $\mathscr{C}$ that excludes a fixed graph H as a topological minor has bounded expansion. Important special cases are classes of bounded degree and classes of graphs that can be drawn with a linear number of crossings Further examples include classes with bounded queue-number, bounded stack-number or bounded non-repetitive chromatic number and the class of Erdös-Rényi random graphs with constant average degree d/n, $G(n, d/n)$, has asymptotically almost surely bounded expansion. See [19,31] for all these examples.

Hence, classes of bounded expansion are much more general than classes excluding a topological minor. On the other hand, maybe not surprisingly, when performing local computations, it is not properties of minors or topological minors, but rather of shallow minors that allow the necessary combinatorial arguments in the algorithms. This observation was already made in the study of the kernelization complexity of dominating set on classes of sparse graphs [11–13,15,24]. On the other hand, degenerate classes are those classes where only $\nabla_0(G)$ is bounded. These classes are hence more general than classes of bounded expansion.

The algorithm of Czygrinow et al. [9] is based on an quite complicated iterative process of choosing dominating vertices from so called *pseudo-covers*. Based on the fact that classes with excluded topological minors in particular exclude some complete bipartite graph $K_{t,t}$ as a subgraph it is proved that this iterative process terminates after at most t rounds and produces a good approximation of a minimum dominating set.

In this paper we make three contributions. First, we simplify the arguments used by Czygrinow et al. and give a much more accessible description of their algorithm. Second, we identify the property that $\nabla_1(G)$ is bounded by a constant as the key property that makes the algorithm work. Classes with only this restriction are even more general than bounded expansion classes, hence, we generalize the algorithm to the most general classes on which it (and similar approaches based on covers or pseudo-covers) can work. We demonstrate that the pseudo-covering method cannot be extended e.g. to classes of bounded degeneracy. Finally, Czygrinow et al. explicitly stated that they did not aim to optimize any constants, and as presented, the constants in their construction are enormous. We optimize the bounds that arise in the algorithm in terms of $\nabla_1(G)$. Even though the constants are still large, they are by magnitudes smaller than those in the original presentation.

Theorem 1. *There exists a LOCAL algorithm that for any given graph G and an upper bound on $\nabla_1(G)$ as input computes in a constant number of rounds a dominating set of size $\mathcal{O}(\nabla_1(G)^{4t\nabla_1(G)+t}) \cdot \gamma(G)$, where $t \leqslant 2\nabla_1(G) + 1$ is minimum such that $K_{t,t} \nsubseteq G$.*

Before we go into the technical details let us give an overview of the algorithm. The algorithm works in three steps, in each step ($i \in \{1, 2, 3\}$) computing a small set D_i that is added to the dominating set.

1. Compute the set D_1 of all v such that $N(v)$ cannot be dominated by a small number (the constant $2\nabla_1(G)$) of vertices different from v. Remove D_1 from G and mark all its neighbors as dominated. The fact that $|D_1|$ is linearly bounded in $\gamma(G)$ goes back to work of [26] and we prove our bounds in Lemma 1.
2. In parallel for every vertex $v = v_1$ we compute all so called *domination sequences* $v_1, \ldots, v_s$, defined formally in Definition 3. This step is based on the construction of pseudo-covers as in the work of Czygrinow et al. [9]. We add all vertices v_s to the set D_2. We prove that this set is small compared to $\gamma(G)$ in Lemma 10. Remove D_2 from G and mark its neighbors as dominated.
3. All remaining vertices have small degree, as proved in Corollary 2, and hence in a final step we can add all non-dominated vertices to a set D_3. We finally return the set $D_1 \cup D_2 \cup D_3$.

The main open question that remains in this line of research is whether we can compute constant factor approximations of minimum dominating sets in a constant number of rounds in classes of bounded degeneracy.

2   Preliminaries

In this section we fix our notation and prove some basic lemmas required for the algorithm. We use standard notation from graph theory and refer to the literature for extensive background. For an undirected and simple graph G we denote by $V(G)$ the vertex set and by $E(G)$ the edge set of G. We also refer to the literature, for the formal definition of the LOCAL model of distributed computing.

A graph H is a minor of a graph G, written $H \preceq G$, if there is a set $\{G_v : v \in V(H)\}$ of pairwise vertex disjoint and connected subgraphs $G_v \subseteq G$ such that if $\{u, v\} \in E(H)$, then there is an edge between a vertex of G_u and a vertex of G_v. We call $V(G_v)$ the *branch set* of v and say that it is *contracted* to the vertex v.

For a non-negative integer r, a graph H is an *r-shallow minor* of G, written $H \preceq_r G$, if there is a set $\{G_v : v \in V(H)\}$ of pairwise vertex disjoint connected subgraphs $G_v \subseteq G$ of radius at most r such that if $\{u, v\} \in E(H)$, then there is an edge between a vertex of G_u and a vertex of G_v. Observe that a 0-shallow minor of G is just a subgraph of G.

We write $\nabla_r(G)$ for $\max_{H \preceq_r G} |E(H)|/|V(H)|$. Observe that $\nabla_0(G)$ denotes the maximum average edge density of G and $2\nabla_0(G)$ bounds the degeneracy of G, which is defined as $\max_{H \subseteq G} \delta(H)$. Here, $\delta(H)$ denotes the minimum degree of H. A class $\mathscr{C}$ of graphs has *bounded expansion* if there is a function $f : \mathbb{N} \to \mathbb{N}$ such that $\nabla_r(G) \leq f(r)$ for all graphs $G \in \mathscr{C}$. This is equivalent to demanding that the degeneracy of each r-shallow minor of G is functionally bounded by r.

We write $K_{s,t}$ for the complete bipartite graph with partitions of size s and t, respectively. Observe that $K_{t,t}$ has $2t$ vertices and t^2 edges, hence, if $\nabla_0(G) < t/2$, then G excludes $K_{t,t}$ as a subgraph.

For a graph G and $v \in V(G)$ we write $N(v) = \{w : \{v, w\} \in E(G)\}$ for the *open neighborhood* of v and $N[v] = N(v) \cup \{v\}$ for the *closed neighborhood* of v. For a set $A \subseteq V(G)$ let $N[A] = \bigcup_{v \in A} N[v]$. We write $N_r[v]$ for the set of vertices at distance at most r from a vertex v. A dominating set in a graph G is a set $D \subseteq V(G)$ such that $N[D] = V(G)$. We write $\gamma(G)$ for the size of a minimum dominating set of G. For $W \subseteq V(G)$ we say that a set $Z \subseteq V(G)$ *dominates* or *covers* or is a *cover* of W if $W \subseteq N[Z]$. Observe that we do not require $Z \cap W = \varnothing$ as Czygrinow et al. do for covers.

The following lemma is one of the key lemmas used for the algorithm. It goes back to [26].

Lemma 1. *Let G be a graph. Then there are less than $2\gamma(G)$ vertices v with the property that $N(v)$ cannot be dominated by at most $2\nabla_1(G)$ vertices different from v.*

Proof. Let $\gamma = \gamma(G)$ and $\nabla_1 = \nabla_1(G)$ and assume that there are 2γ such vertices $a_1, \ldots, a_{2\gamma}$. We proceed towards a contradiction. Let $\{d_1, \ldots, d_\gamma\}$ be a minimum dominating set. At least γ of the a_i's are not in this dominating set. We can hence assume w.l.o.g. that $\{a_1, \ldots, a_\gamma\}$ and $\{d_1, \ldots, d_\gamma\}$ are two disjoint sets of vertices.

We build a 1-shallow minor H of the graph G with the following 2γ branch sets. For every $i \leqslant \gamma$, we have a branch set $A_i = \{a_i\}$ and a branch set $D_i = N[d_i] \backslash (\{a_1, \ldots, a_\gamma\} \cup \bigcup_{j<i} N[d_j] \cup \{d_{i+1}, \ldots, d_\gamma\})$. We call the associated vertices of H $a_1', \ldots, a_\gamma', d_1', \ldots, d_\gamma'$.

Since $\{d_1, \ldots, d_\gamma\}$ is a dominating set of G and by assumption on $N(a_i)$, we have that in H, every a_i' is connected to at least $2\nabla_1 + 1$ of the d_j'. We therefore have that $|V_H| = 2\gamma$ and $|E_H| \geqslant \gamma(2\nabla_1 + 1)$, hence $|E_H| > |V_H|\nabla_1$, a contradiction.

Note that we cannot locally determine the number $\nabla_1(G)$. We must hence assume that it is given with the input. Observe that similarly, the algorithm of Czygrinow et al. works with the assumption that the input excludes a complete graph with t vertices as a topological minor. This implies a bound on the edge density of topological minors in G, which can be seen as being given with the input.

The algorithm proceeds in three phases. The first phase is based on Lemma 1 as follows. In the LOCAL model we can learn the distance-2 neighborhood $N_2[v]$ of every vertex v in 2 rounds, and then locally check whether $N(v)$ can be dominated by at most $2\nabla_1(G)$ vertices.

We let D_1 be the set of all vertices that do not have this property. By Lemma 1 we have $|D_1| \leqslant 2\gamma(G)$. We remove D_1 from the graph and mark all its neighbors as dominated in one additional round.

In the following we fix a graph G and we assume that $N(v)$ can be dominating by at most $2\nabla_1(G)$ vertices different from v for all $v \in V(G)$. We write ∇_1 for $\nabla_1(G)$ and we let $t \leqslant 2\nabla_0(G) + 1$ be the smallest positive integer such that G excludes $K_{t,t}$ as a subgraph. Note that this number is not required as part of the input. We let $k := 2\nabla_1$.

Example 1. A planar n-vertex graph has at most $3n - 6$ edges. A minor of a planar graph is again planar, hence for planar graphs G we have $\nabla_r(G) \leqslant 3$ for all $r \geqslant 0$ and $k = 2\nabla_1(G) \leqslant 6$.

We also fix a minimum dominating set D of G of size γ. The following lemma is proved exactly as Lemma 1.

Lemma 2. *There are less than 2γ vertices v with the property that $N(v)$ cannot be dominated by at most $2\nabla_1$ vertices from D and different from v.*

Unfortunately, we cannot determine these vertices locally, as it requires knowledge of D, however, this structural property is very useful for our further argumentation.

Denote by $\hat{D}$ the set of all vertices v whose neighborhood cannot be dominated by $2\nabla_1$ vertices of D different from v. Let $D' = D \cup \hat{D}$.

According to Lemma 2, D' contains at most 3γ vertices. Let us stress that D' will never be computed by our LOCAL algorithm. We only use its existence in the correctness proofs.

We can apply these lemmas to obtain a constant factor approximation for a dominating set only if $\nabla_1(G)$ is bounded by a constant. For example in graphs of bounded degeneracy in general the number of vertices that dominate the neighborhood of a vertex can only be bounded by $\gamma(G)$. Hence, the approach based on covers and pseudo-covers that is employed in the following cannot be extended to degenerate graph classes.

Example 2. Let $G(\gamma, m)$ be the graph with vertices v_i for $1 \leqslant i \leqslant \gamma$, w^j for $1 \leqslant j \leqslant m$ and s_i^j for $1 \leqslant i \leqslant \gamma, 1 \leqslant j \leqslant m$. We have the edges $\{v_1, w^j\}$ for $1 \leqslant j \leqslant m$, hence v_1 dominates all w^j. We have the edges $\{w^j, s_i^j\}$ for all $1 \leqslant i \leqslant \gamma, 1 \leqslant j \leqslant m$, hence, the s_i^j are neighbors of w^j. Finally, we have the edges $\{v_i, s_i^j\}$, that is, v_i dominates the ith neighbor of w_j. Hence, for $m > \gamma$, $G(\gamma, m)$ has a dominating set of size γ and m vertices whose neighborhood can be dominated only by $\gamma(G)$ vertices. Lemma 1 implies that $\gamma < 2\nabla_1$, and as we can choose m arbitrary large, we cannot usefully apply Lemma 1. Furthermore, $G(\gamma, m)$ is 2-degenerate, showing that these methods cannot be applied on degenerate graph classes (Fig. 2).

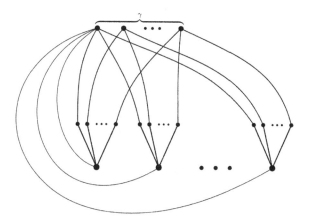

Fig. 2. A 2-degenerate graph where for many $v \in V(G)$ the set $N(v)$ can only be dominated by at least γ vertices different from v.

3   Covers and Pseudo-covers

Intuitively, the vertices from a cover of a set W can take different roles. A few vertices of a cover may cover almost the complete set W, while a few others are only there to cover what was left over. The key observation of Czygrinow et al. is that in classes that exclude some $K_{t,t}$ as a subgraph, there can only be few of such high degree covering vertices, while there can be arbitrarily many vertices that cover at most $t-1$ vertices of W (the same vertices can be covered over and over again). This observation can be applied recursively and is distilled into the following two definitions. Recall that by the processing carried out in the first phase of the algorithm we know that every neighborhood $N(v)$ can be covered by $k = 2\nabla_1$ vertices different from v. We recall all fixed parameters for easy to find reference.

- G : fixed graph.
- γ : $\gamma(G)$.
- ∇_1 : $\nabla_1(G)$.
- t : smallest integer such that G excludes $K_{t,t}$ as a subgraph
- D_1 : defined and computed in Lemma 1.
- D : fixed dominating set of G of size γ (not computed).
- $\hat{D}$: defined in Lemma 2 (not computed).
- D' : $D \cup \hat{D}$ (not computed).

Following the presentation of [9], we name and fix these constants for the rest of this article.

> - $k := 2\nabla_1$.
> - $\alpha := 1/k$.
> - $\ell := 8\nabla_1/\alpha^2 + 1 = 4k^3 + 1$.
> - $q := 4k^4$.

Definition 1. *A vertex $z \in V(G)$ is α-strong for a vertex set $W \subseteq V(G)$ if $|N[z] \cap W| \geq \alpha|W|$.*

The following is the key definition by Czygrinow et al. [9].

Definition 2. *A* pseudo-cover *(with parameters α, ℓ, q, k) of a set $W \subseteq V(G)$ is a sequence $(v_1, \ldots, v_m)$ of vertices such that for every i we have*

- $|W \setminus \bigcup_{j \leq m} N[v_j]| \leq q$,
- v_i *is α-strong for* $W \setminus \bigcup_{j < i} N[v_j]$,
- $|N[v_i] \cap (W \setminus \bigcup_{j < i} N[v_j])| \geq \ell$,
- $m \leq k$.

Intuitively, all but at most q elements of the set W are covered by the $(v_i)_{i \leq m}$. Additionally, each element of the pseudo-cover dominates both an α-fraction of what remains to be dominated, and at least ℓ elements. Note that with our choice of constants, if there are more than q vertices not covered yet, any vertex that covers an α-fraction of what remains also covers at least ℓ elements.

The next lemma shows how to derive the existence of pseudo-covers from the existence of covers.

Lemma 3. *Let $W \subseteq V(G)$ be of size at least q and let Z be a cover of W with k elements. There exists an ordering of the vertices of Z as $z_1, \ldots, z_k$ and $m \leq k$ such that $(z_1, \ldots, z_m)$ is a pseudo-cover of W.*

Proof. We build the order greedily by induction. We order the elements by neighborhood size, while removing the neighborhoods of the previously ordered vertices. More precisely, assume that $(z_1, \ldots, z_i)$ have been defined for some $i \geq 0$. We then define z_{i+1} as the element that maximizes $|N[z] \cap (W \setminus \bigcup_{j \leq i} N[z_j])|$.

Once we have ordered all vertices of Z, we define m as the maximal integer not larger than k such that for every $i \leq m$ we have:

- z_i is α-strong for $W \setminus \bigcup_{j < i} N[z_j]$, and
- $|N[z_i] \cap (W \setminus \bigcup_{j \leq i} N[z_j])| \geq \ell$.

This made sure that $(z_1, \ldots, z_m)$ satisfies the last 3 properties of a pseudo-cover of W. It only remains to check the first one. To do so, we define $W' := W \setminus \bigcup_{i \leq m} N[z_i]$. We want to prove that $|W'| \leq q$. Note that because Z covers W, if $m = k$ we have $W' = \emptyset$ and we are done. We can therefore assume that $m < k$ and $W' \neq \emptyset$. Since Z is a cover of W, we also know that $(z_{m+1}, \ldots z_k)$ is a cover of W', therefore there is an element in $(z_{m+1}, \ldots z_k)$ that dominates at least a $1/k$ fraction of W'. Thanks to the previously defined order, we know that z_{m+1}

is such element. Since $\alpha = 1/k$, it follows that z_{m+1} is α-strong for W'. This, together with the definition of m, we have that $|N[z_i] \cap (W \setminus \bigcup_{j<i} N[z_j])| < \ell$ meaning that $|N[z_{m+1}] \cap W'| < \ell$. This implies that $|W'|/k < \ell$. And since $\ell = q/k$, we have $|W'| < q$. Hence, $(z_1, \ldots, z_m)$ is a pseudo-cover of W.

While there can exist unboundedly many covers for a set $W \subseteq V(G)$, the nice observation of Czygrinow et al. was that the number of pseudo-covers is bounded whenever the input graph excludes some biclique $K_{s,t}$ as a subgraph. We do not state the result in this generality, as it leads to enormous constants. Instead, we focus on the case where small covers exist, that is, on the case where $\nabla_1(G)$ is bounded and optimize the constants for this case.

Lemma 4. *Let $W \subseteq V(G)$ of size at least $8\nabla_1/\alpha^2$. Then there are at most $4\nabla_1/\alpha$ vertices that are α-strong for W.*

Proof. Assume that there is such a set W with at least $c := 4\nabla_1/\alpha$ vertices that are α-strong for W. We build a 1-shallow minor H of the graph G with $|W|$ branch sets. Each branch set is either a single element of W, or a pair $\{w, a\}$, where w is in W and a is an α-strong vertex for W, connected to w, and that is not in W. This is obtained by iteratively contracting one edge of an α-strong vertex with a vertex of W. This is possible because $\alpha|W| > c$, so during the process and for any α-strong vertex we can find a connected vertex in W that is not part of any contraction.

Once this is done, we have that $|V_H| = |W|$. For the edges, each of the α-strong vertices can account for $\alpha|W|$ many edges. We need to subtract c^2 from the total as we do not count twice an edge between two strong vertices. Therefore $|E_H| \geq c\alpha|W| - c^2$. Note also that because $|W| \geq 8\nabla_1/\alpha^2$, we have that $2\nabla_1 \geq (4\nabla_1)^2/(\alpha^2|W|)$. All of this together leads to:

$$\frac{|E_H|}{|V_H|} \geq \frac{c\alpha|W| - c^2}{|W|} \geq 4\nabla_1 - \frac{(4\nabla_1)^2}{\alpha^2\,|W|} \geq 4\nabla_1 - 2\nabla_1 > \nabla_1$$

This contradicts the definition of ∇_1.

This leads quickly to a bound on the number of pseudo-covers.

Lemma 5. *For every $W \subseteq V(G)$ of size at least ℓ, the number of pseudo-covers is bounded by $2(4\nabla_1(G)/\alpha)^k$.*

The proof of the lemma is exactly as the proof of Lemma 7 in the presentation of Czygrinow et al. [9], we therefore refrain from repeating it here.

We write $\mathcal{T}(v)$ for the set of all pseudo-covers of $N(v)$ and $\mathcal{P}(v)$ for the set of all vertices that appear in a pseudo-cover of $N(v)$.

Corollary 1. *For every $v \in V(G)$ with $|N(v)| > \ell$, we have $|\mathcal{T}(v)| \leq 2(2k^2)^k$ and $|\mathcal{P}(v)| \leq 2k(2k^2)^k \leq (2k)^{2k+1}$.*

4   Finding Dominators

Recall that by Lemma 2 for every $v \in V(G)$ we can cover $N(v)$ with at most k vertices from D'. To first gain an intuitive understanding of the second phase of the algorithm, where we construct a set $D_2 \subseteq V(G)$, let us consider the following iterative procedure.

Fix some $v \in V(G)$. Let $v_1 = v$ and $B_1 := N(v)$ and assume $|B_1| \geq k^{t-1}(2t-1)$. We consider s vertices $v_1, v_2 \ldots, v_s$ as follows. Choose as v_2 an arbitrary vertex different from v_1 that dominates at least $k^{t-2}(2t-1)$ vertices of B_1, that is, a vertex that satisfies $|N[v_2] \cap B_1| \geq k^{t-2}(2t-1)$. Note that any vertex v_2 that dominate a $1/k$-fraction of B_1 can be such vertex, i.e. it is enough for v_2 to be α-strong for B_1.

Let $B_2 := N(v_2) \cap B_1$. Observe that we consider the open neighborhood of v_2 here, hence B_2 does not contain v_2. Hence, $|B_2| \geq k^{t-2}(2t-1)-1 \geq k^{t-2}(2t-2)$. We continue to choose vertices $v_3, \ldots$ inductively just as above. That is, if the vertices $v_1, \ldots, v_i$ and sets $B_1, \ldots, B_i \subseteq V(G)$ have been defined, we choose the next vertex v_{i+1} as an arbitrary vertex not in $\{v_1, \ldots, v_i\}$ that dominates at least $k^{t-i-1}(2t-i)$ vertices of B_i, that is, a vertex with $|N[v_{i+1}] \cap B_i| \geq k^{t-i-1}(2t-i)$ and let $B_{i+1} := N(v_{i+1}) \cap B_i$, of size at least $k^{t-i-1}(2t-i-1)$.

Lemma 6. *Assume $|N(v)| \geq k^{t-1} \cdot (2t-1)$. Let $v_1, \ldots, v_s$ be a maximal sequence obtained as above. Then $s < t$ and $D' \cap \{v_1, \ldots, v_s\} \neq \emptyset$.*

Proof. Assume that we can compute a sequence $v_1, v_2, \ldots, v_t$. By definition, every v_i is connected to every vertices of B_t. For every $1 \leq i \leq t$ we have $|B_i| \geq k^{t-i}(2t-i)$ and therefore $|B_t| \geq t$. This shows that the two sets $\{v_1, \ldots, v_t\}$ and B_t form a $K_{t,t}$ as a subgraph of G. Since this is not possible, the process must stop having performed at most $t-1$ rounds.

We now turn to the second claim of the lemma. Assume that $v_1, v_2, \ldots, v_s$ is a maximal sequence for some $s < t$. We assume $v_1 \notin \hat{D}$, otherwise, we are done, as $\hat{D} \subseteq D'$. Because $s < t$, we have that B_s is not empty. Because $B_s \subseteq B_1 = N(v_1)$, we have that B_s can be dominated with at most k elements of D (by definition of $\hat{D}$), and in particular by at most k elements of D'. Therefore, there must be an element v of D' that dominates a $1/k$ fraction of B_s. If v was not one of the $v_1, \ldots, v_s$, we could have continued the sequence by defining $v_{s+1} := v$. Since the sequence is maximal, v must be one of the $v_1, \ldots, v_s$, which leads to $D' \cap \{v_1, \ldots, v_s\} \neq \emptyset$.

We aim to carry out this iterative process in parallel for all vertices $v \in V(G)$ with a sufficiently large neighborhood. Of course, in the process we cannot tell when we have encountered the element of D'. Hence, from the constructed vertices $v_1, \ldots, v_s$ we will simply choose the element v_s into the dominating set. Unfortunately, this approach alone can give us arbitrarily large dominating sets, as we can have many choices for the vertices v_i, while already v_1 was possibly optimal. We address this issue by restricting the possible choices for the vertices v_i.

Definition 3. *For any vertex $v \in V(G)$, a k-dominating-sequence of v is a sequence $(v_1, \ldots, v_s)$ for which we can define sets $B_1, \ldots, B_s$ such that:*

- $v_1 = v$, $B_1 \subseteq N(v_1)$,
- *for every $i \leqslant s$ we have $B_i \subseteq N(v_i) \cap B_{i-1}$,*
- $|B_i| \geqslant k^{t-i}(2t - i + (t - i)q)$
- *and for every $i \leqslant s$ we have $v_i \in \mathcal{P}(v_{i-1})$.*

A k-dominating-sequence $(v_1, \ldots, v_s)$ is maximal *if there is no vertex u such that $(v_1, \ldots, v_s, u)$ is a k-dominating-sequence.*

Note that this definition requires $|N(v)| \geqslant k^{t-1}(2t - 1 + (t - 1)q)$. For a vertex v with a not sufficiently large neighborhood, there are no k-dominating-sequences of v. We show two main properties of these dominating-sequences. First, Lemma 7 shows that a maximal dominating sequence must encounter D' at some point. Second, with Lemma 8 to 10, we show that collecting all "end points" of all maximal dominating sequences results in a set D_2 of size linear in the size of D'. While D' cannot be computed, we can compute D_2.

Lemma 7. *Let v be a vertex and let $(v_1, \ldots, v_s)$ be a maximal k-dominating-sequence of v. Then $s < t$ and $D' \cap \{v_1, \ldots, v_s\} \neq \varnothing$.*

Proof. The statement $s < t$ is proved exactly as for Lemma 6.

To prove the second statement we assume, in order to reach a contradiction, that $D' \cap \{v_1, \ldots, v_s\} = \varnothing$. We have that $B_s \subseteq N(v_s)$, and remember that $N(v_s)$ can be dominated by at most k elements of D'. By Lemma 3, we can derive a pseudo-cover $S = (u_1, \ldots, u_m)$ of $N(v_s)$, where $m \leqslant k$ and every u_i is an element of D'. Let X denote the set (of size at most q) of vertices not covered by S. As S contains at most k vertices there must exist a vertex u in S that covers at least a $1/k$ fraction of $B_s \setminus X$. By construction, we have that $|B_s| \geqslant k^{t-s} \cdot (2t - s + (t - s)q) \geqslant k(t + q)$ because $s < t$. Therefore $|B_s \setminus X| \geqslant k$ and we have

$$|N[u] \cap B_s| \geqslant \frac{|B_s| - q}{k} \geqslant \frac{k^{t-s}(2t - s + (t - s)q) - q}{k},$$

hence

$$|N[u] \cap B_s| \geqslant \frac{k^{t-s}(2t - s + (t - s - 1)q)}{k} \geqslant k^{t-s-1}(2t - s + (t - s - 1)q),$$

and therefore

$$|N(u) \cap B_s| \geqslant |N[u] \cap B_s| - 1 \geqslant k^{t-s-1}(2t - s - 1 + (t - s - 1)q).$$

So we can continue the sequence $(v_1, \ldots, v_s)$ by defining $v_{s+1} := u$. In conclusion if $(v_1, \ldots, v_s)$ is a maximal sequence, it contains an element of D'.

The goal of this modified procedure is first to ensure that every maximal sequence contains an element of D' and second, to make sure that there are not to many possible v_s (which are the elements that we pick for the dominating set). This is illustrated in the following example and formalized right after that.

Example 3. Consider the case of planar graphs. Since these graph exclude $K_{3,3}$, i.e. $t = 3$, we have that every maximal sequence is of length 1 or 2. For every v of sufficiently large neighborhood we consider every maximal k-dominating-sequence (v_1, v_s) of v. We then add v_s to the set D_2. We want to show that $|D_2|$ is linearly bounded by $|D'|$ and hence by $\gamma(G)$.

If $s = 1$, then we have $v_s \in D'$ and we are good.

If $s = 2$, we have two possibilities. If v_2 is in D', we are good. If however, v_2 is not in D', then v_1 is in D'. Additionally, v_2 is in some pseudo-cover S of v_1, i.e. $v_2 \in \mathcal{P}(v_1)$.

By Corollary 1, we have $|\mathcal{P}(v_1)| \leqslant (2k)^{2k+1}$ (and in fact this number is much smaller in the case of planar graphs). Therefore we have $|D_2| \leqslant ((2k)^{2k+1}+1)|D'|$.

We generalize the ideas of Example 3, by explaining what a "few possible choices" in the discussion before Definition 3 means.

Lemma 8. *For any maximal k-dominating-sequence $(v_1, \ldots, v_s)$, and for any $i \leqslant s - 1$, we have that*

- $v_{i+1} \in \mathcal{P}(v_i)$,
- $|N(v_i)| \geqslant \ell$, *and*
- $|\mathcal{P}(v_i)| \leqslant (2k)^{2k+1}$.

Proof. By construction $v_{i+1} \in \mathcal{P}(v_i)$, furthermore, v_i dominates at least B_i, and $|B_i| \geqslant k^{t-i}(2t - i + (t - i)q) \geqslant q > \ell$. We conclude with Collorary 1.

We now for every $v \in V(G)$ compute all maximal k-dominating-sequences starting with v. Obviously, as every v_i in any k-dominating-sequences of v dominates some neighbors of G, we can locally compute these steps after having learned the 2-neighborhood $N_2[v]$ of every vertex in two rounds in the LOCAL model of computation.

For a set $W \subseteq V(G)$ we write $\mathcal{P}(W) = \bigcup_{v \in W} \mathcal{P}(v)$. Remember that the definition of $\mathcal{P}(v)$ requires that $|N(v)| > \ell$. We simply extend the notation with $\mathcal{P}(v) = \varnothing$ if $|N(v)| \leqslant \ell$. We now define

$$\mathcal{P}^{(1)}(W) := \mathcal{P}(W)$$

additionally, for $1 < i < t$

$$\mathcal{P}^{(i)}(W) := \mathcal{P}(\mathcal{P}^{(i-1)}(W))$$

and finally, for every $1 \leqslant i \leqslant t$

$$\mathcal{P}^{(\leqslant i)}(W) := \bigcup_{1 \leqslant j \leqslant i} \mathcal{P}^{(j)}(W).$$

Using Lemma 8, for every k-dominating-sequence $(v_1, \ldots, v_s)$ we have that $v_s \in \mathcal{P}^{(\leqslant k)}(v_1)$. More generally, for every $i \leqslant s$, we have that $v_s \in \mathcal{P}^{(\leqslant t)}(v_i)$.

> We define D_2 as the set of all $u \in V(G)$ such that there is some vertex $v \in V(G)$, and some maximal k-dominating-sequence $(v_1, \ldots, v_s)$ of v with $u = v_s$.

This leads to the following lemma.

Lemma 9. $D_2 \subseteq \mathcal{P}^{(\leq t)}(D')$.

Proof. This uses the observation made above the statement of this lemma, together with Lemma 7.

Note that while we don't know how to compute D', this section explained how to compute D_2 in 2 rounds with the LOCAL model of computation.

Lemma 10. $|D_2| \leq (2k)^{t(2k+1)} \cdot |D'|$

Proof. Corollary 1 gives us that $|\mathcal{P}(v)| \leq 2k(2k^2)^k$ for every $v \in V(G)$ with $|N(v)| > \ell$. As $\mathcal{P}(W) \leq \sum_{v \in W} |\mathcal{P}(v)|$, we have $P(W) \leq |W| \cdot (2k)^{2k+1}$. A naive induction yields that for every $i \leq t$,

$$|\mathcal{P}^{(\leq i)}(W)| \leq c^i |W|,$$

where $c = (2k)^{2k+1}$. Hence with this and Lemma 9 we have

$$|D_2| \leq (2k)^{t(2k+1)} \cdot |D'|$$

5   Cleaning up

We now show that after defining and computing D_2 as explained in the previous section, every neighborhood is almost entirely dominated by D_2. More precisely, for every vertex v of the graph $|\{v' \in N(v) : v' \notin N(D_2)\}| < k^{t-1}(2t-1+(t-1)q)$ holds.

Before explaining why this holds, note that it implies that, in particular, the vertices of D have at most $k^{t-1}(2t-1+(t-1)q)$ non-dominated neighbors. Since every vertex is either in D or a neighbor of some element in D, this implies that in the whole graph there are at most $k^{t-1}(2t-1+(t-1)q) \cdot \gamma$ non-dominated vertices left.

> We can therefore define $D_3 := \{v \in V(G) : v \notin N(D_2)\}$ and have that $|D_3| \leq k^{t-1}(2t-1+(t-1)q) \cdot \gamma$, and that $D_1 \cup D_2 \cup D_3$ is a dominating set of G.

We now turn to the proof of the above claim.

Lemma 11. *For every vertex v of the graph, the following holds:*

$$|\{v' \in N(v) : v' \notin N(D_2)\}| < k^{t-1}(2t-1+(t-1)q).$$

Proof. Assume, for the sake of reaching a contradiction, that there is a vertex v such that $|\{v' \in N(v) \; : \; v' \notin N(D_2)\}| \geqslant k^{t-1}(2t - 1 + (t-1)q)$.

We then define $B_1 := \{v' \in N(v) \; : \; v' \notin N(D_2)\}$.

Exactly as in the proof of Lemma 7, we have that B_1 can be dominated by at most k elements of D'. Hence by Lemma 3, we can derive a pseudo-cover $S = (u_1, \ldots, u_m)$ of B_1, where $m \leqslant k$ and every u_i is an element of D'. This leads to the existence of some vertex u in S that covers at least a $1/k$ fraction of $B_1 \setminus X$. This yields a vertex v_2, and a set B_2.

We can then continue and build a maximal k-dominating-sequence $(v_1, \ldots v_s)$ of v. By construction, this sequence has the property that every v_i dominates some elements of B_1. This is true in particular for v_s, but also we have that $v_s \in D_2$, hence a contradiction.

Corollary 2. *The graph contains at most $k^{t-1}(2t-1+(t-1)q)\cdot\gamma$ non-dominated vertices. In particular, the set D_3 has at most this size.*

6   The Algorithm

In this final section we summarize the algorithm.

1. Compute the set D_1 of all v such that $N(v)$ cannot be dominated by $2\nabla_1(G)$ vertices different from v. Remove D_1 from G and mark all its neighbors as dominated.
2. In parallel for every vertex $v = v_1$ compute all k-domination sequences $v_1, \ldots, v_s$. Add all vertices v_s to the set D_2. Remove D_2 from G and mark its neighbors as dominated. This is done as follows.
   We can learn the neighborhood $N_2[v]$ for every vertex v in 2 rounds. In the LOCAL model we can then compute the pseudo-covers without further communication. In two additional rounds can compute the domination sequences from the pseudo-covers (as we need to consider only elements from $N_2[v_1]$). We report in 2 additional rounds that v_s belongs to D_2 and one more round to mark the neighbors of D_2 as dominated.
3. In the final round we add all non-dominated vertices to a set D_3 and return the set $D_1 \cup D_2 \cup D_3$.

According to Lemma 1, Lemma 10 and Colloary 2 the algorithm computes a $2 + 3(2k)^{t(2k+1)} + k^{t-1}(2t - 1 + (t-1)q)$ approximation. This is an absolute constant in $\mathcal{O}(\nabla_1^{4t\nabla_1+t})$ depending only on $\nabla_1(G)$, as also $t < 2\nabla_1$.

7   Conclusion

We simplified the presentation and generalized the algorithm of Czygrinow et al. [9] from graph classes that exclude some topological minor to graph classes $\mathcal{C}$ where $\nabla_1(G)$ is bounded by an absolute constant for all $G \in \mathcal{C}$. This is a property in particular possessed by classes with bounded expansion, which include many commonly studied sparse graph classes.

It is an interesting and important question to identify the most general graph classes on which certain algorithmic techniques work. The key arguments of Lemma 1 and Lemma 2 work only for classes with $\nabla_1(G)$ bounded by an absolute constant. We need different methods to push towards classes with only $\nabla_0(G)$ bounded, which are the degenerate classes.

The obtained bounds are still large, but by magnitudes smaller than those obtained in the original work of Czygrinow et al. [9]. It will also be interesting to optimize the algorithm for planar graphs, where additional topological arguments can help to strongly optimize constants and potentially beat the currently best known bound of 52 [26, 35].

References

1. Akhoondian Amiri, S., Ossona de Mendez, P., Rabinovich, R., Siebertz, S.: Distributed domination on graph classes of bounded expansion. In: Proceedings of the 30th on Symposium on Parallelism in Algorithms and Architectures, pp. 143–151 (2018)
2. Akhoondian Amiri, S., Schmid, S., Siebertz, S.: A local constant factor MDS approximation for bounded genus graphs. In: Proceedings of the 2016 ACM Symposium on Principles of Distributed Computing, pp. 227–233 (2016)
3. Amiri, S.A., Schmid, S.: Brief announcement: a log*-time local MDS approximation scheme for bounded genus graphs. In: Proceedings of DISC (2016)
4. Amiri, S.A., Schmid, S., Siebertz, S.: Distributed dominating set approximations beyond planar graphs. ACM Trans. Algorithms (TALG) 15(3), 1–18 (2019)
5. Bansal, N., Umboh, S.W.: Tight approximation bounds for dominating set on graphs of bounded arboricity. Inf. Process. Lett 122, 21–24 (2017)
6. Barenboim, L., Elkin, M., Gavoille, C.: A fast network-decomposition algorithm and its applications to constant-time distributed computation. Theoret. Comput. Sci. 751, 2–23 (2018)
7. Brönnimann, H., Goodrich, M.T.: Almost optimal set covers in finite VC-dimension. Discrete Comput. Geom. 14(4), 463–479 (1995)
8. Czygrinow, A., Hańćkowiak, M., Wawrzyniak, W.: Fast distributed approximations in planar graphs. In: Taubenfeld, G. (ed.) DISC 2008. LNCS, vol. 5218, pp. 78–92. Springer, Heidelberg (2008). https://doi.org/10.1007/978-3-540-87779-0_6
9. Czygrinow, A., Hanckowiak, M., Wawrzyniak, W., Witkowski, M.: Distributed approximation algorithms for the minimum dominating set in k_h-minor-free graphs. In: 29th International Symposium on Algorithms and Computation (ISAAC 2018). Schloss Dagstuhl-Leibniz-Zentrum fuer Informatik (2018)
10. Dinur, I., Steurer, D.: Analytical approach to parallel repetition. In: Proceedings of the Forty-Sixth Annual ACM Symposium on Theory of Computing, pp. 624–633 (2014)
11. Drange, P.G., et al.: Kernelization and sparseness: the case of dominating set. In: 33rd Symposium on Theoretical Aspects of Computer Science, STACS 2016, pp. 31:1–31:14 (2016)
12. Eiben, E., Kumar, M., Mouawad, A.E., Panolan, F., Siebertz, S.: Lossy kernels for connected dominating set on sparse graphs. SIAM J. Discrete Math. 33(3), 1743–1771 (2019)

13. Eickmeyer, K., et al.: Neighborhood complexity and kernelization for nowhere dense classes of graphs. In: 44th International Colloquium on Automata, Languages, and Programming, ICALP 2017, 10–14 July 2017, Warsaw, Poland, pp. 63:1–63:14 (2017)
14. Even, G., Rawitz, D., Shahar, S.M.: Hitting sets when the VC-dimension is small. Inf. Process. Lett. **95**(2), 358–362 (2005)
15. Fabianski, G., Pilipczuk, M., Siebertz, S., Torunczyk, S.: Progressive algorithms for domination and independence. In: 36th International Symposium on Theoretical Aspects of Computer Science, STACS 2019, 13–16 March 2019, Berlin, Germany, pp. 27:1–27:16 (2019)
16. Gallager, R.G., Humblet, P.A., Spira, P.M.: A distributed algorithm for minimum-weight spanning trees. ACM Trans. Program. Langu. Syst. (TOPLAS) **5**(1), 66–77 (1983)
17. Garey, M.R., Johnson, D.S.: Computers and Intractability, vol. 174. Freeman San Francisco (1979)
18. Ghaffari, M., Kuhn, F., Maus, Y.: On the complexity of local distributed graph problems. In: STOC, pp. 784–797. ACM (2017)
19. Har-Peled, S., Quanrud, K.: Approximation algorithms for polynomial-expansion and low-density graphs. SIAM J. Comput. **46**(6), 1712–1744 (2017)
20. Hilke, M., Lenzen, C., Suomela, J.: Brief announcement: local approximability of minimum dominating set on planar graphs. In: Proceedings of the 2014 ACM Symposium on Principles of Distributed Computing, pp. 344–346 (2014)
21. Johnson, D.S.: Approximation algorithms for combinatorial problems. J. Comput. Syst. Sci. **9**(3), 256–278 (1974)
22. Jones, M., Lokshtanov, D., Ramanujan, M., Saurabh, S., Suchý, O.: Parameterized complexity of directed Steiner tree on sparse graphs. SIAM J. Discrete Math. **31**(2), 1294–1327 (2017)
23. Karp, R.M.: Reducibility among combinatorial problems. In: Miller, R.E., Thatcher, J.W., Bohlinger, J.D. (eds.) Complexity of Computer Computations, pp. 85–103. Springer, Boston (1972). https://doi.org/10.1007/978-1-4684-2001-2_9
24. Kreutzer, S., Rabinovich, R., Siebertz, S.: Polynomial kernels and wideness properties of nowhere dense graph classes. ACM Trans. Algorithms (TALG) **15**(2), 1–19 (2018)
25. Kuhn, F., Moscibroda, T., Wattenhofer, R.: Local computation: lower and upper bounds. J. ACM **63**(2), 17:1–17:44 (2016)
26. Lenzen, C., Pignolet, Y.A., Wattenhofer, R.: Distributed minimum dominating set approximations in restricted families of graphs. Distrib. Comput. **26**(2), 119–137 (2013)
27. Lenzen, C., Wattenhofer, R.: Leveraging Linial's locality limit. In: Taubenfeld, G. (ed.) DISC 2008. LNCS, vol. 5218, pp. 394–407. Springer, Heidelberg (2008). https://doi.org/10.1007/978-3-540-87779-0_27
28. Lenzen, C., Wattenhofer, R.: Minimum dominating set approximation in graphs of bounded arboricity. In: Lynch, N.A., Shvartsman, A.A. (eds.) DISC 2010. LNCS, vol. 6343, pp. 510–524. Springer, Heidelberg (2010). https://doi.org/10.1007/978-3-642-15763-9_48
29. Lovász, L.: On the ratio of optimal integral and fractional covers. Discrete Math. **13**(4), 383–390 (1975)
30. Nešetřil, J., de Mendez, P.O.: Grad and classes with bounded expansion I. decompositions. Eur. J. Comb. **29**(3), 760–776 (2008)
31. Nešetřil, J., de Mendez, P.O., Wood, D.R.: Characterisations and examples of graph classes with bounded expansion. Eur. J. Comb. **33**(3), 350–373 (2012)

32. Rozhon, V., Ghaffari, M.: Polylogarithmic-time deterministic network decomposition and distributed derandomization. In: STOC, pp. 350–363. ACM (2020)
33. Siebertz, S.: Greedy domination on biclique-free graphs. Inf. Process. Lett. **145**, 64–67 (2019)
34. Wawrzyniak, W.: Brief announcement: a local approximation algorithm for MDS problem in anonymous planar networks. In: Proceedings of the 2013 ACM Symposium on Principles of Distributed Computing, pp. 406–408 (2013)
35. Wawrzyniak, W.: A strengthened analysis of a local algorithm for the minimum dominating set problem in planar graphs. Inf. Process. Lett. **114**(3), 94–98 (2014)

Approximate Minimum Directed Spanning Trees Under Congestion

Christoph Lenzen[1] and Hossein Vahidi[1,2](✉)

[1] MPI for Informatics, Saarbrücken, Germany
{clenzen,hovahidi}@mpi-inf.mpg.de
[2] Saarbrücken Graduate School of Computer Science, Saarbrücken, Germany

Abstract. The *minimum directed spanning tree* (MDST) problem has until recently not been studied in distributed computing models. This fundamental task generalizes the well-studied minimum spanning tree problem, by asking for a minimum weight spanning tree rooted at some specified node of a directed network. In their DISC 2019 paper [9], Fischer and Oshman reduce the MDST problem to the single-source shortest path (SSSP) problem, with a polylogarithmic increase in running time. This holds both in the Congest and Congested Clique models.

Fischer and Oshman further suggest the possibility that an *approximate* SSSP algorithm could be leveraged in computing an *approximate* MDST. We extend their analysis to show that this is indeed the case: For $\varepsilon > 0$, using a $(1 + \varepsilon)$-approximation to SSSP running in R rounds we can compute a $(1 + \varepsilon)$-approximate MDST in $\tilde{O}(R)$ rounds ($\tilde{O}$-notation neglects polylogarithmic factors in the number n of nodes in the graph.). In particular, this implies the following improvements in the state of the art for $(1 + o(1))$-approximation of MDST.

- An $\tilde{O}(n^{1-2/\omega+o(1)}) \subset \tilde{O}(n^{0.158})$-round Congested Clique algorithm, where $\omega < 2.373$ is the fast matrix multiplication exponent [3].
- An $\tilde{O}(\lambda^2)$-round Congested Clique algorithm in graphs where each edge has an at most factor $\lambda \geq 1$ heavier reverse edge [1].
- An $\tilde{O}(\lambda^2(\sqrt{n} + D))$-round Congest algorithm in the same family of graphs [1]. For $\lambda \in \log^{O(1)} n$, the resulting running time of $\tilde{O}(\sqrt{n}+D)$ is unconditionally tight up to a polylogarithmic factor [21].

1 Introduction

Finding the minimum-weight spanning tree (MST) of a weighted undirected graph is a fundamental problem, which is well-studied in both sequential and distributed settings. In the more general minimum *directed* spanning tree (MDST) problem, we are given a weighted directed graph $G = (V, E, w)$ and a node $r \in V$. The goal is to determine a minimum-weight spanning tree rooted at r.

© Springer Nature Switzerland AG 2021
T. Jurdziński and S. Schmid (Eds.): SIROCCO 2021, LNCS 12810, pp. 352–369, 2021.
https://doi.org/10.1007/978-3-030-79527-6_20

In this work, we study the task of finding a directed spanning tree (DST) rooted at r whose weight is at most by a factor of $1+\varepsilon$ larger than the optimum, or solving $(1+\varepsilon)$-approximate MDST for short, in the Congest and Congested Clique models.

The Congest and Congested Clique Models. In the Congest model, the network is represented by a weighted n-node graph $G = (V, E, w)$, where each node $v \in V$ has a unique $O(\log n)$-bit identifier. Initially, each node knows only its identifier and the weights of its incident edges, and it must determine which of its incident edges belong to the DST the algorithm chooses. Computation proceeds in synchronous compute-send-receive rounds, and we seek to minimize the number of communication rounds until all nodes have determined their local output and terminated. Message size is restricted to $O(\log n)$ bits, where each node may send a different message to each of its neighbors in each round. To avoid the complication that distances cannot be encoded by a single message, we follow the common convention to assume that edge weights are integers from a range that is polynomially bounded in n. The Congested Clique model is identical, except that each node may send an $O(\log n)$-bit message to each other node, not just its neighbors.

State of the Art. While both the MST and the MDST problem have been extensively studied in the sequential setting, there is a surprising disparity in the distributed context. In all likelihood, the MST problem is *the* most well-studied task in the Congest model, and it received substantial attention in the Congested Clique as well. In contrast, despite its many applications, the community completely ignored the MDST problem until recently. Drawing inspiration from sequential [7,10] and PRAM algorithms [17], Fischer and Oshman [9] presented a reduction of MDST to single-source shortest path in directed graphs (SSSP), the task of computing a shortest path tree with given root s. Their reduction incurs a round overhead of $\log^{O(1)} n$. Plugging in the currently best known algorithms for SSSP, one obtains a randomized $\tilde{O}(\sqrt{n}D^{1/4} + D)$-round Congest [4] and a deterministic $\tilde{O}(n^{1/3})$-round Congested Clique [3] algorithm, respectively.

Moreover, Fischer and Oshman show that in both models, MDST is at least as hard as finding a shortest path between two designated nodes $s, t \in V$. Thus, the round complexity of MDST is wedged in between those of SSSP and s-t path in both models. In Congest, even approximating s-t path in undirected graphs or an MST require $\tilde{\Omega}(\sqrt{n} + D)$ rounds [8,20,21]. In the Congested Clique, no non-trivial lower bounds are known, and finding even slightly super-constant such bounds would imply long-sought statements on circuit complexity [6].

However, the complexity of (directed) SSSP and s-t path are incompletely understood in either model, with polynomial gaps between upper and lower bounds. In addition, it is an open question whether *approximation* is easier. Currently, faster $(1+\varepsilon)$-approximate SSSP algorithms for non-negative weights are known for the Congested Clique [3] and for special cases in Congest [1]. Thus, a reduction based on SSSP approximation is of interest. Indeed, Fischer and Oshman conjecture that a $(1+\varepsilon)$-approximation to SSSP can be leveraged in their reduction to obtain a $(1+\varepsilon)^{\lceil \log n \rceil}$-approximation to MDST [9].

Our Contribution. We prove the stronger result that using a $(1+\varepsilon)$-approximate SSSP algorithm in the Fischer-Oshman framework, without modification, results in a $(1+\varepsilon)$-approximation to MDST. This implies the following theorems.

Theorem 1. *For $\varepsilon > 0$, denote by $T_{\text{SSSP}}(n, D, \varepsilon)$ the round complexity of a $(1 + \varepsilon)$-approximate SSSP Congest algorithm on directed n-node graphs with non-negative weights and (undirected) diameter D. Then a $(1 + \varepsilon)$-approximate MDST can be computed in $\tilde{O}(T_{\text{SSSP}}(n, D, \varepsilon))$ rounds in the Congest model.*

Theorem 2. *For $\varepsilon > 0$, denote by $T_{\text{SSSP}}(n, D, \varepsilon)$ the round complexity of a $(1+\varepsilon)$-approximate SSSP Congested Clique algorithm on directed n-node graphs with non-negative weights and (undirected) diameter D. Then a $(1 + \varepsilon)$-approximate MDST can be computed in $\tilde{O}(T_{\text{SSSP}}(n, D, \varepsilon))$ rounds in the Congested Clique.*

We note that the restriction to non-negative edge weights is natural when using approximation algorithms, as negative edge weights could cancel out with positive weights to result in a very light MDST despite heavy edges. This would decouple the notions of SSSP and MDST approximation to the point of meaninglessness, where, e.g., only an exact MDST has a negative total weight. Thus, any multiplicative MDST approximation would have to be an exact solution.

The above results are derived by generalizing the analysis of Fischer and Oshman in a model-independent way. Thus, whenever their framework can be applied, the same holds for our generalization[1]. However, for the sake of conciseness we confine the presentation to these two prominent models. In these models, pluggin in the most recent SSSP approximations yields the following.

Corollary 1 ([3,15]). *For $\varepsilon > 0$, in the Congested Clique a $(1 + \varepsilon)$-approximate MDST with non-negative weights can be found in $n^{1-2/\omega+o(1)} \subset O(n^{0.158})$ rounds, where ω is the matrix multiplication exponent in the Congested Clique.*

Corollary 2 ([1]). *Suppose $G = (V, E, w)$ satisfies that for each $(u, v) \in E$, it holds that $(v, u) \in E$ and $0 \leq w(u, v) \leq \lambda w(v, u)$. Then, for $\varepsilon > 0$, in the Congested Clique a $(1+\varepsilon)$-approximate MDST can be found in $\tilde{O}(\lambda^2/\varepsilon^2)$ rounds.*

Corollary 3 ([1]). *Suppose $G = (V, E, w)$ satisfies that for each $(u, v) \in E$, it holds that $(v, u) \in E$ and $0 \leq w(u, v) \leq \lambda w(v, u)$. Then, for $\varepsilon > 0$, in the Congest model a $(1+\varepsilon)$-approximate MDST can be found in $\tilde{O}((\sqrt{n}+D)\lambda^2/\varepsilon^{3/2})$ rounds w.h.p[2]. Deterministic correctness (i.e., only the running time bound could be violated) can be achieved in $\tilde{O}((\sqrt{n} + D)\lambda^2/\varepsilon^3)$ rounds w.h.p.*

Note that for $\lambda \in \log^{O(1)} n$ this matches the lower bound of $\tilde{\Omega}(\sqrt{n} + D)$ for shortest *s-t* path approximation from [21] up to a polylogarithmic factor.

---

[1] For example, [9] also discusses a modification to the Congest model in which directed edges enable communication in one direction only. Similarly, we expect that the approach is efficient in the k-machine and semi-streaming models.

[2] W.h.p. stands for with high probability, which means with probability at least $1 - 1/n^c$ for a freely chosen, but fixed constant $c > 0$.

On the technical level, we obtain our results by generalizing the analysis of the Fischer-Oshman framework. Intuitively, one might expect that it is sufficient to plug in the approximate SSSP algorithm instead of an exact routine. This turns out to be correct, but proving it requires to overcome a technical hurdle.

The exact MDST algorithm by Edmonds [7] heavily exploits that the graph manipulations it performs do not change the "remaining" MDST. More precisely, it first computes an edge set that may contain cycles, contracting these cycles whenever they are formed. It then updates edge weights in such a way that the set of MDST edges that are still to be selected are not affected by such changes. Once the selected subgraph is spanning, i.e., all nodes can be reached from r, Edmonds iteratively uncontracts all selected cycles and determines for each of them which edge has to be removed to obtain an MDST.

Fischer and Oshman simulate Edmonds algorithm in a manner that parallelizes well, yet can be efficiently implemented in distributed models. As their algorithm computes the same MDST as the one by Edmonds, the main challenge they face is efficient implementation. In contrast, our main obstacle is to relate the computed DST to an optimal MDST. Since we do not solve SSSP exactly, we choose different edges as Edmonds' algorithm, which in turn means that future SSSP instances might differ wildly from those in the exact algorithm. Hence, while we can build on [9] for an efficient implementation, our challenge is to argue that the computed DST is actually a good approximation to an MDST.

Facing this challenge from scratch would be a difficult task. As the immediate connection to an MDST breaks down, it is unclear how the complex evolution of the intermediate subgraphs could be tied to an MDST by an ad hoc argument. Even if one could be found, it would likely result in a proof repeating many of the steps for the exact setting.

We follow a different route, by re-interpreting the run of the approximation algorithm as a run of the *exact* algorithm on an *approximation* of the input graph. The effect of the modifications of the graph on the weight of an MDST can be easily bounded. The modifications of the graph are limited to scaling all edge weights by factor $1 + \varepsilon$ and performing some simple changes to the graph forcing the exact algorithm to contract the exact same regions as the approximation algorithm. This also means that the exact algorithm incurs the same cost as the approximation algorithm on the original graph. Since the MDST of the modified graph is at most by factor $1 + \varepsilon$ more costly than the original graph (as the original edge set is still present, albeit with factor $1 + \varepsilon$ larger cost), the same follows for the approximate solution on the original graph. Overall, this results in a proof of the conjecture by Fischer and Oshman, without the need for any non-trivial modification to their algorithmic framework.

Further Related Work

Sequential MDST Computation. Gabow et al. [10] provided an efficient implementation of an approach proposed independently by Edmonds [7], Bock [2] and, Chu and Liu [5], with step complexity $O(m + n \log n)$. The algorithm goes through a series of steps, also called Edmonds steps, and at each step, every vertex (except the root r) selects the lightest incoming edge, remembers its weight, and subtracts it from the weight of all the incoming edges. The idea is that to reach a vertex, we need to pay at least as much as its lightest incoming edge. Then, all zero-weight cycles are contracted and we continue these steps recursively until there is only one component left. The sum of the weights subtracted by vertices through these steps is equal to the cost of an MDST of the graph. Finding an MDST requires a careful but simple unpacking of the contractions.

Lovasz' Algorithm. The framework by Fischer and Oshman can be seen as a less aggressive way of parallelizing Edmonds steps than in Lovasz' PRAM algorithm [17]. For $\lceil \log n \rceil$ iterations, Lovasz performs an all-pairs shortest paths computation to find shortest paths that, similar to Edmonds approach, could be selected sequentially into an MDST. As in each of the iterations, each of the components induced by the currently selected edges but the one containing r is guaranteed to connect to another component, in the end only a single component remains. Then a similar unpacking procedure yields an MDST. The key observation by Fischer and Oshman is that it is perfectly sufficient to find for each component the shortest path leaving it (when flipping the directions of all edges). This more conservative approach avoids that the computations of different components "overlap," which causes the need for an all-pairs shortest path algorithm for Lovasz, yet also ensures termination within $\lceil \log n \rceil$ iterations.

MST in Congest. While the MDST problem has been the neglected child in the family of global Congest problems, its little brother, finding an MST in an undirected graph, has been showered with attention; we make no attempt at covering these results here, see [19] for a recent survey. In part, this is likely due to habit, as MST is a canonical global problem that lends itself well to studying new models and complexity measures. On the other hand, the problem is closely related to testing whether a given subgraph is connected. Any MST algorithm can solve this task, and the lower bound of $\tilde{\Omega}(\sqrt{n} + D)$ due to Das Sarma et al. [21] applies to both tasks. Due to the $\tilde{O}(\sqrt{n} + D)$-round algorithm by Kutten and Peleg [14], this implies that there appears to be virtually no difference between the two problems. As many Congest algorithms for global problems need to test subgraphs for connectivity, this close connection means that insights on MST construction frequently transfer to tasks which appear unrelated at first sight. It also explains why so many problems turn out to have round complexity $\tilde{\Theta}(\sqrt{n} + D)$.

We remark that for MST, it is known that allowing approximate solutions or randomization does not make the job easier [8,21]. As discussed above, for the MDST problem this will depend on whether either makes SSSP (or possibly s-t path) easier in the considered models, with remains open to date.

MST in the Congested Clique. The Congested Clique was introduced by Lotker et al. in 2003 [16][3]. Naturally, the MST problem served as their guinea pig,

---

[3] In the MST problem, heavy edges can be added without changing the solution. Hence, decoupling problem and communication graph was formalized only later.

and they provided an $O(\log \log n)$-round algorithm. After more than a decade of silence, a flurry of results [11–13] culminated in a deterministic constant-round solution [18].

2   Preliminaries

Let $G = (V, E, w)$ be an n-node directed graph with edge weight function w. Let $S \subseteq V(G)$ be a vertex set. Then, the corresponding induced subgraph in G is denoted by $G[S] = (S, E')$, where $E' = \{(u, v) \mid u, v \in S$ and $(u, v) \in E(G)\}$. Moreover, the weight of subgraph $H \subseteq G$, denoted by $w_G(H)$, is the sum of the weight of its edges. For any graph H, $V(H)$ and $E(H)$ denote its vertex and edge set, respectively, and w_H its weight function. A subgraph is weakly connected, if its underlying undirected graph is connected. Weakly connected components are defined accordingly. For $u, v \in V$, let $\operatorname{dist}_G(u, v)$ be the weight of the shortest path from u to v in G. Denote by $B_G(v, r)$ the ball of radius r around node v, i.e., $\{u \mid \operatorname{dist}_G(u, v) \leq r\}$. An s-t path P can be represented as a tuple of its vertices in the order of appearance, e.g., $P = (s, v_1, \ldots, v_k, t)$.

Contraction of an edge $e = (u, v)$ is the following operation. We combine u and v into a supernode x that keeps all the incident edges of u and v. Then, self-loops are removed and in the case of parallel edges between two nodes we only keep the lightest edge. Contracting a ball $B_G(v, r)$ is similar, in that all nodes inside the ball are merged into a supernode x. However, an edge $(u, u') \in (G \setminus B_G(v, r)) \times B_G(v, r)$ gives rise to edge (u, x) of weight $w_G(u, u') + \operatorname{dist}_G(u', v) - r$. Analogously, outgoing edge $(u, u') \in B_G(v, r) \times (G \setminus B_G(v, r))$ results in edge (x, u') of weight $w_G(u, u') + \operatorname{dist}_G(v, u) - r$. Again, self-loops are removed and only the lightest edge is kept. Finally, we will need to contract "approximate" balls, where we consider $B_T(v, r)$ in a graph G, with T being a tree. In such a case, we replace the dist_G terms by dist_T, even for edges that are present in G, but not in T. Note that this can result in negative edge weights. In such a case, the resulting contracted edge will be assigned weight 0.

When referring to an *uncontraction*, this means to reverse the above process. If we uncontract a graph with a selected spanning tree T that resulted from contraction of G, each edge of T induces a marked edge in G, which caused it to be assigned its weight. For convenience, we refer to this as *uncontracting* T.

3   Exact MDST Computation

We will modify the Fischer-Oshman approach [9] to provably work with approximate SSSP computations. For an intuitive understanding as well as a formal proof, it is instructive to revisit their technique.

In the following and throughout this paper, w.l.o.g. let us make the following assumptions. First, the input graph $G = (V, E, w)$ has indeed a spanning tree rooted at r, i.e., an MDST rooted at r exists. Otherwise the algorithm will simply fail to compute such an MDST, and this can be verified fast enough in the considered models. Second, we assume that there is no edge with endpoint

r, as no DST with root r contains such an edge. Finally, we assume that all edge weights are different; any kind of consistent tie-breaking mechanism results in equivalent behavior.

A Variant of Edmonds' Algorithm. In MST construction, it is commonly exploited that the lightest edge of a cut, and in particular the lightest incident edge to each node, are part of the MST. Crucially, these statements assume a consistent tie-breaking mechanism in place, which ensures that no cycle can be closed when selecting all such edges concurrently: it does not matter which edge of a cycle in which all edges have the same weight is selected, but one edge must be excluded. In the directed setting, it is no longer arbitrary which edge of a directed cycle of "candidate edges" is excluded, as for reachability it now matters at which node the path from the root to the cycle in the MDST ends. Lemma 1 provides a highly useful structural property of MDSTs corresponding to these observations.

Lemma 1 (implicit in [7]). *Define $G' = (V, E, w')$ by setting $w'(u,v) := w(u,v) - \min_{(u',v) \in E}\{w(u',v)\}$ for all $(u,v) \in E$. Then an MDST T of G is also an MDST of G', where $w(T) = w'(T) + \sum_{v \in V \setminus \{r\}} \min_{(u',v) \in E}\{w(u',v)\}$. Moreover, let $E_0 := \{(u,v) \in E \mid w'(u,v) = 0\}$ denote the pseudo-forest[4] given by the 0-weight edges of G'. Then for each cycle C in E_0 there is a unique edge $(u,v) \in C \setminus T$.*

Proof. Each non-root node has exactly one incoming edge in any DST, so the weight of *each* DST rooted at r changes by $\sum_{v \in V \setminus \{r\}} \min_{(u',v) \in E}\{w(u',v)\}$ when replacing w by w'. For the second claim, observe that any cycle C in E_0 must have at least one of its edges not be part of T. So assume for contradiction that there is a cycle C such that $|T \cap (V \setminus C \times C)| > 1$. Let $(u,v) \in T \cap (V \setminus C \times C)$ and denote by $(u',v) \in E_0$ the unique edge in E_0 with endpoint v. Then $T' := T \setminus (u,v) \cup (u',v)$ is a DST: there is still some node in C reachable from r in $T \setminus (u,v)$, which then inductively applies to all its successors in C, including u'. However, $w'(u,v) > 0$ and $w'(u',v) = 0$ by choice of E_0, implying that $w'(T') < w'(T)$, a contradiction to the already established claim that T is an MDST of G'. □

Lemma 1 suggests the following procedure to compute an MDST. For each non-root node select the cheapest incoming edge and subtract its weight from all incoming edges of the node. Contract the resulting 0-weight cycles and repeat the process on all the newly created supernodes until no non-root node without a selected incoming edge remains. At this point, the 0-weight edges form an MDST of the current graph (this will be shown in the proof of Lemma 2). To get an MDST of the original graph, we go in the reverse order, uncontracting the 0-weight cycles of the previous step, and adjusting the MDST to the graph resulting from uncontraction. To achieve the latter, for each new node without an incoming edge in the old MDST, we pick a 0-weight incoming edge from the uncontracted cycle. Lemma 2 shows that this procedure, whose pseudocode is given in Algorithm 1, indeed yields an MDST of G.

---

[4] By the above assumptions, each non-root node has exactly one 0-weight incoming edge, while the root has none. However, E_0 might contain cycles.

Algorithm 1. Finding an MDST of a Graph

```
1: procedure EDMONDS(G = (V, E, w))
2:     i := 0, G^(0) := (V^(0), E^(0), w^(0)) := G
3:     while (V^(i), {e_v^(i) | v ∈ V^(i)}) is not a DST of G^(i) do
4:         i ← i + 1
5:         Each node v ∈ V^(i-1) \ {r} sets e_v^(i) := argmin_{(u,v)∈E^(i-1)} {w^(i-1)(u, v)}
6:         For each (u, v) ∈ E^(i-1), set w^(i)(u, v) := w^(i-1)(u, v) − w^(i-1)(e_v^(i))
7:         Contract all 0-weight cycles, resulting in G^(i) = (V^(i), E^(i), w^(i))
8:     Set T^(i) := {e_v^(i) | v ∈ V^(i)}                         ▷ uncontraction phase
9:     while i > 0 do
10:        Initialize T^(i-1) by the set of edges obtained by uncontracting G^(i) to G^(i-1)
11:        Let X be the set of nodes that have been in a zero-cycle before contraction
12:        for each v ∈ X without an incoming edge in T^(i) do
13:            T^(i-1) ← T^(i-1) ∪ {e_v^(i-1)}          ▷ add its incoming zero-weight edge
14:        i ← i − 1
15:    return T^(0)
```

Lemma 2 (implicit in [7]). *Algorithm 1 computes an MDST of G. Denoting by $i_{\max}$ the maximum value of i throughout the procedure, its weight equals $\sum_{i=1}^{i_{\max}} \sum_{v \in V^{(i-1)}\setminus\{r\}} w^{(i-1)}(e_v^{(i)})$.*

Proof. Observe that contracting a cycle of weight 0 in a graph without negative edge weights cannot change the cost of an MDST: Regardless of how an MDST of the graph after contraction looks like, we can connect all nodes in the cycle at cost 0 in the original graph, and we can delete a non-cycle edge (of cost at least 0) for each cycle this closes. Because Lines 5 and 6 ensure that the new weights satisfy this property, applying Lemma 1 inductively to the first while loop shows that $\sum_{i=1}^{i_{\max}} \sum_{v \in V^{(i-1)}\setminus\{r\}} w^{(i-1)}(e_v^{(i)})$ is precisely the cost of an MDST of G.

Hence, it remains to show that the computed edge set $T^{(0)}$ is indeed an MDST. To this end, we show by induction that $T^{(i)}$ is an MDST of $G^{(i)}$ for all $i \in \{0, \ldots, i_{\max}\}$. To anchor the induction at $i = i_{\max}$, note that by Lines 5 and 6, it holds that $w^{(i_{\max})}(e_v^{(i)}) = 0$ for all $v \in V^{(i_{\max})}$ and $w^{(i_{\max})}(u, v) \geq 0$ for all $(u, v) \in E^{(i_{\max})}$. Hence, by the halting criterion of the first loop, $T^{(i_{\max})}$ is indeed an MDST of $G^{(i_{\max})}$. Assuming that the claim holds for $i > 0$, Line 13 and the fact that $T^{(i)}$ is a tree ensure that each non-root node has indegree 1. Moreover, as $T^{(i)}$ is spanning, we can reach each node $v \in V^{(i)}$ from r by taking the edges in $E^{(i-1)}$ corresponding to the respective path in $T^{(i)}$ and, wherever a path node gets uncontracted into a cycle C, adding the path in C connecting the endpoint of the incoming edge to the node with the outgoing edge (or v if it is on the cycle). Thus, $T^{(i-1)}$ is a spanning pseudo-forest, implying that it must be a DST. The minimality of $w(T^{(i-1)})$ follows from the fact that $T^{(i)}$ is an MDST of $G^{(i)}$, the weight changes of Line 13, and Lemma 1.   □

The Fischer-Oshman Framework. The above observations are promising in that in each iteration, all (weakly) connected components can operate concurrently.

Despite the technical obstacle that cycle contraction is problematic in Congest, because the communication graph does not change, Fischer and Oshman show how to perform all operations with sufficient efficiency. However, a second, more important hurdle is that the above procedure might require a lot of iterations. In the worst case, each added edge closes another cycle rather than reducing the number of connected components. This means that $\Omega(n)$ contractions could be performed sequentially, resulting in a slow algorithm.

More concretely, note that after selecting the lightest incoming edges, the resulting subgraph has exactly one cycle in each weakly connected non-root component. After contraction, we get a forest whose roots are the nodes resulting from cycle contraction. These roots are exactly the "new" nodes selecting new edges, while all other nodes stick to their previously selected edges whose reduced weight is 0. Such a node selecting a new edge and immediately contracting the resulting cycle is referred to as an *Edmonds step*. If both endpoints of the edge selected by an Edmonds step are in the same weakly connected component, another cycle within this component is formed, whose contraction might eliminate no more than a few nodes.

Let H be a non-root component formed by the currently selected edges and let C_H be the unique cycle at the heart of H. The crucial insight Fischer and Oshman exploit is the following. The iterations of the above Algorithm 1 on H until an edge into the component is selected are equivalent to running Dijkstra's algorithm on the component, where the contracted cycle, C_H, is the source, and we reverse edges. Thus, the selected edges contain a shortest path P of weight β_H from outside the connected component to the (original) cycle. Equivalently, we can find β_H and contract $B_H(C_H, \beta_H)$, i.e., a ball of radius β_H centered at C_H, where edges that are only partially inside the ball lose a respective share of their weight. Note that this does not affect other components, until the resulting 0-weight edge connecting to another component is contracted. Hence, this operation can be performed on all weakly connected non-root components concurrently, and Fisher and Oshman formalize how to achieve this using a call to a single, globally operating SSSP instance. Doing so constitutes a *mega-step* in the Fischer-Oshman terminology. As each component gets merged with at least one other component in a mega-step, the process terminates after at most $\lceil \log n \rceil$ mega-steps.

Fischer and Oshman prove that the necessary bookkeeping and the later uncontractions can be efficiently implemented in both the Congest and Congested Clique models, rendering the SSSP algorithm the subroutine that dominates the round complexity. In Congest this implementation is rather involved. Fortunately, as we will show that we can replace the exact SSSP computation with an approximate one *in a blackbox fashion,* we can confine our presentation to the abstract viewpoint of explicitly performing contractions and uncontractions. We summarize the relevant structural results by Fischer and Oshman as follows.

Lemma 3 (Fischer and Oshman [9]). *Denote by $G^{(i)} = (V^{(i)}, E^{(i)}, w^{(i)})$ the graph after i mega-steps. Denote by $H \not\ni \{r\}$ a weakly connected component of* the selected edges and by C_H its unique node with indegree 0. Then contracting $B_{G^{(i)}}(C_H, \beta_H)$ simulates multiple Edmonds steps on H.

A mega-step is performed by executing these operations on each weakly connected non-root component and then contracting 0-weight cycles. We stress that, while the intuition as to why the algorithm is correct remains the same as for Algorithm 1 – both can be decomposed into a sequence of Edmonds steps – the iterations of the first loop of Algorithm 1 cannot be consistently mapped to mega-steps.

Nonetheless, constructing an MDST after contracting the graph into a root component is done in a similar fashion. One uncontracts in reverse order of the mega-steps, operating on all components in parallel. In this process, one maintains the invariant that the current tree $T^{(i)}$ is an MDST of the current graph $G^{(i)}$, starting with $G^{(i_{\max})}$. After uncontracting to $G^{(i-1)}$, we need to connect to the cycle of each component H, which is done by selecting the computed shortest path π_H from outside of H to its cycle. Finally, the remaining nodes without incoming edge add their previously selected edge of weight 0. This ensures reachability of all nodes in the component, as (i) all path nodes are reachable from the "parent" component, (ii) all nodes on the cycle are reachable from the endpoint of the path along the cycle edges, and (iii) the remaining nodes are attached to the path and cycle nodes by a forest of 0-weight edges. Because $T^{(i)}$ was a DST, so is $T^{(i-1)}$, and as the weight of the added edges in $G^{(i-1)}$ sums up to $\sum_{H \in \mathcal{H}} w^{(i-1)}(\pi_H)$, $T^{(i-1)}$ is an MDST of $G^{(i-1)}$.

Lemma 4 (follows from Lemma 8 in [9]). *Let $G^{(i-1)}$ be a graph with a set of 0-weight components $\mathcal{H}$ in accordance with Lemma 3 after $i - 1 \geq 0$ mega-steps. Let $G^{(i)}$ be the graph obtained by contracting for each $H \in \mathcal{H}$ the ball $B_H(C_H, \beta_H)$, where β_H is the length of a shortest path π_H that has only its first node outside H and ends in C_H. Let $T^{(i)}$ be an MDST of $G^{(i)}$.*

Then setting $T^{(i-1)}$ to the edge set resulting from uncontraction of $T^{(i)}$ and performing the following operation for each $H \in \mathcal{H}$ yields an MDST:

- *uncontract C_H (into a 0-weight cycle),*
- *add the edges of π_H inside H (the first edge of π_H has been selected in the uncontraction of $T^{(i)}$), and*
- *add each 0-weight edge of H and C_H whose endpoint is not a node of π_H.*

We stress that the proof from [9] requires that the paths π_H are shortest paths only to establish that the cost of the weight of the constructed DST is minimal. Thus, we have the following corollary.

Corollary 4. *Assume the same setting as in Lemma 4, except that the paths π_H are not necessarily shortest paths. Then the construction of the lemma yields a DST of weight equal to $w^{(i)}(T^{(i)}) + \sum_{H \in \mathcal{H}} w^{(i-1)}(\pi_H)$.*

In summary, the challenge for obtaining an approximation algorithm lies in relating the weight of Corollary 4 to the weight of an MDST.

4 $(1 + \varepsilon)$-approximate MDST from SSSP Approximation

Throughout this section, we assume that all edge weights are non-negative. The algorithm maintains this invariant when modifying edge weights. Hence, we can rely on SSSP approximation algorithms that assume non-negative edge weights as well. Formally, such an algorithm provides the following output.

Definition 1 $((1 + \varepsilon)$-**approximate SSSP**). *For a given graph G and root r, a $(1 + \varepsilon)$-approximate directed SSSP algorithm returns a DST T of G such that* $\mathrm{dist}_T(r, v) \leq (1 + \varepsilon) \cdot \mathrm{dist}_G(r, v)$ *for all $v \in V(G)$. The output is given by each $v \in V(G) \setminus \{r\}$ learning about its parent and* $\mathrm{dist}_T(r, v)$.

For the remainder of the section, $\mathcal{A}$ denotes an algorithm following the Fischer-Oshman framework [9] for computing an MDST, while $\mathcal{A}'$ denotes our approximate version, which is obtained by replacing the exact directed SSSP solution by a $(1 + \varepsilon)$-approximation and using the distances in the tree(s) instead of the exact ones. Recall that we enforce that the minimum edge weight resulting from a contraction is 0, cf. Sect. 2, so the approximate SSSP algorithm will always operate on graphs with non-negative weights.

In this section, we will establish the following theorem.

Theorem 3. *If $w(u, v) \geq 0$ for all $(u, v) \in E$, $\mathcal{A}'$ computes a $(1+\varepsilon)$-approximate MDST.*

Theorems 1 and 2 readily follow from this theorem and the running time bounds from [9]. In more detail, besides calling the SSSP subroutine, their framework uses $\tilde{O}(\sqrt{n} + D)$ and $\log^{O(1)} n$ rounds per mega-step in Congest and the Congested Clique, respectively, yielding running times of $\tilde{O}(T_{\mathrm{SSSP}}(n, D, \varepsilon) + \sqrt{n} + D)$ in Congest and $\tilde{O}(T_{\mathrm{SSSP}}(n, D, \varepsilon)$ in the Congested Clique. In Congest, the lower bound of $\tilde{\Omega}(\sqrt{n} + D)$ on any polynomial approximation to SSSP [21] implies that $\tilde{O}(T_{\mathrm{SSSP}}(n, D, \varepsilon) + \sqrt{n} + D) = \tilde{O}(T_{\mathrm{SSSP}}(n, D, \varepsilon))$.

Why Analyzing the use of Approximate SSSP is Challenging. We would like to replace the exact SSSP computation in the Fischer-Oshman framework with an approximate one, assuming that the graph has non-negative weights. The trouble with that lies in the analysis of the algorithm. Where Fischer and Oshman argue that they simulate Edmonds steps, we run into the obstacle of relating the computed solution to an optimal one. The sequence of contractions and, accordingly, uncontractions performed can be vastly different even with only minor changes in the outcome of the SSSP computation.

A simple attempt at fixing this issue could be to modify the graph to enforce that the approximately shortest paths found by the subroutine become actual shortest paths in a slightly distorted topology. Unfortunately, simply scaling down the edge weights of such paths (or scaling up the non-path edges' weights) might not achieve this. A tree that approximates distances to the source up to factor $1 + \varepsilon$ can still contain edges (p, c) for which parent p and child c satisfy that $\mathrm{dist}_G(p, c) \ll w(p, c)$ – the local error can be amortized over a much larger distance to the root. This means that we do not have enough information to adjust edge lengths such that (i) the computed paths become shortest paths and (ii) the weight of an MDST changes little.

We overcome the above obstacle by modifying both the topology and, at least on a formal level, also generalizing the solved problem. Intuitively, we still follow the strategy given above, but we accept that we introduce additional edges and nodes into the graph. Fortunately, these modifications are necessary only to create an execution of the Fischer-Oshman algorithm that we can compare to in order to establish the approximation guarantee; no change whatsoever is needed in the actual algorithm beyond the discussed replacement of the SSSP subroutine and performing contractions of the resulting "approximate" balls.

4.1   Shortcuts and Dummy Nodes

The modifications we make to the graph used by the exact algorithm require some bookkeeping. Denote for each node $u \in V$ and each mega-step i by $S_u^{(i)}$ the total amount that node u (or the supernodes resulting from it) would subtract from each of its incoming edges from outside the contracted balls during contractions up to and including mega-step i[5]. In other words, adding $S_u^{(i)}$ to the current weight of an incoming edge restores its weight in the original graph. Similarly, we apply this to the shortcut edges. We only ever need to add edges (u, v) that have residual weight $\beta > 0$ after the first $i-1$ mega-steps. To generate a corresponding edge for $U^{(i)}$, we pick arbitrary nodes $u', v' \in V$ that ultimately get contracted into u and v, respectively, and set the weight of (u', v') in $U^{(i)}$ to $\beta + S_{v'}^{(i-1)}$.

Simply put, our construction first stretches all edges by factor $1 + \varepsilon$ for $\mathcal{A}$ to obtain $U^{(0)}$, so that $\mathrm{opt}(U^{(0)}) = (1 + \varepsilon)\mathrm{opt}(G)$[6]. Then, in mega-step i, we add "shortcuts" to obtain $U^{(i)}$ from $U^{(i-1)}$. These shortcuts satisfy that (i) they do not affect any already performed mega-steps when using $U^{(i)}$ as input rather than $U^{(i-1)}$ and (ii) $\mathcal{A}$ performs the same contractions (i.e., with the same ball centers and radii) on $U^{(i)}$ as $\mathcal{A}'$ on $G^{(i-1)}$ in mega-step i. Thus, after the last iteration $i_{\max}$, we have a one-on-one mapping of the sequence of contractions of both algorithms.

Recall that the ball radii are also the cost the exact algorithm charges to its contractions (cf. Lemma 3), summing up to the weight of the computed MDST (cf. Lemma 4). $\mathcal{A}'$ charges the same cost to its contractions, corresponding to the weights of the *approximately* shortest paths its SSSP subroutine found. As these weights add up to the cost of the computed DST in the same way as for $\mathcal{A}$, the weight of the DST of G computed by $\mathcal{A}'$ equals the weight of an MDST of $U^{(i_{\max})}$. Finally, we show that going from $U^{(i-1)}$ to $U^{(i)}$ can only decrease the weight of an MDST, implying that $\mathrm{opt}(U^{(i_{\max})}) \leq \mathrm{opt}(U^{(0)}) = (1 + \varepsilon)\mathrm{opt}(G)$.

---

[5] "Would" here indicates that nodes might be inside a contracted region without edges to the outside.

[6] While this may result in non-integral edge weights, they can still be easily represented with $O(\log n)$ bits.

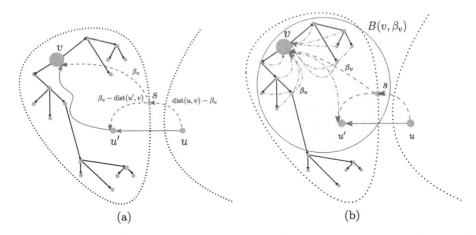

Fig. 1. Dashed red edges represent gadget replacement at a boundary edge and dash dotted blue edges represent shortcut edges. Note that the contraction of $B(v, \beta_v)$ eliminates all the added edges and nodes again; the construction merely ensures that the exact algorithm contracts exactly $B(v, \beta_v)$. Note that to obtain the graph before contractions, the introduced edges will be connected to some nodes inside the contracted supernodes (see Definition 2).

Meeting the requirements (i) and (ii) concurrently is tricky. We achieve this by introducing a gadget that subdivides boundary edges according to our needs, without affecting the weight of an MDST[7]. Together with the right shortcut edges, the resulting gadget shapes $B_{U^{(i)}}(v, \beta_v)$ in the right way without interfering with the algorithm's prior execution or the weight of an MDST.

Definition 2 (Shortcuts with Dummy Nodes). *Consider the graph $G^{(i-1)}$ after $i-1$ mega-steps of the exact algorithm on $U^{(i-1)}$. For each $v \neq r$ without selected incoming edge denote by β_v the ball radius computed using the approximate SSSP algorithm (i.e., the distance for leaving the weakly connected component in the tree computed by the SSSP approximation algorithm). For each edge $(u, u') \in (V(G^{(i-1)}) \setminus B_{G^{(i-1)}}(v, \beta_v)) \times B_{G^{(i-1)}}(v, \beta_v)$, we replace the edge in $G^{(i-1)}$ by the following gadget (see Fig. 1):*

- *A new dummy node s.*
- *An edge (u, s) of weight $\text{dist}_{G^{(i-1)}}(u, v) - \beta_v$.*
- *An edge (s, u') of weight $\beta_v - \text{dist}_{G^{(i-1)}}(u', v)$.*
- *An edge (s, v) of weight β_v.*

We then obtain $U^{(i)}$ from $U^{(i-1)}$ by adding the dummy nodes and changing the edge set of $U^{(i)}$ as follows.

- *Remove all edges from nodes that are contracted into u to nodes that are contracted into u'.*

---

[7] This holds true under the assumptions that the spanning tree needs not contain the added vertices, which is sufficient for our purposes.

- *For each new node s and each of its edges, denote by x the endpoint that is not s and by w its weight. Choose an arbitrary node $y \in V$ that got contracted into x (or x itself if $x \in V$). Add an edge with endpoints s and y of matching orientation and weight $w + S_y^{(i-1)}$ to $U^{(i)}$.*
- *For each $u \in B_{G^{(i-1)}}(v, \beta_v)$, denote by $x, y \in V$ nodes that got contracted into u and v, respectively. Add (x, y) with weight $\beta_v + S_y^{(i-1)}$ to $U^{(i)}$.*

Dummy nodes need not be spanned by a DST, i.e., $\mathrm{opt}(U^{(i)})$ denotes the minimum cost of a tree rooted at r spanning $V(G)$. To match our needs, $\mathcal{A}$ is a slighty different version of the Fischer-Oshman algorithm, where dummy nodes do not seek to select edges "on their own." However, they can take part in the shortest paths the algorithm selects. These changes are exactly those that make the algorithm "behave the same way" on $U^{(i)}$ and $U^{(i-1)}$ until mega-step i.

Corollary 5. *$\mathcal{A}$ computes a lightest tree that is rooted at r and spans $V(G)$.*

Proof (Sketch). A simple check of the arguments in Sect. 3 shows that a tree spanning all non-dummy nodes is computed. To see optimality, note that it still holds that *if* a dummy node takes part in the tree, we need to pay at least the weight of its lightest incoming edge to include it (cf. Lemma 1). Thus, for each 0-degree non-root regular node we must pay at least as much as the weight of the shortest path connecting to it from outside its weakly connected component, as it needs to get connected to the root component in some way (cf. Lemma 3).   ☐

To relate $\mathrm{opt}(U^{(i)})$ to $\mathrm{opt}(G)$, we first show that the replacement of Definition 2 does not introduce negative cycles or otherwise unduly distort the distance structure of the graph.

Lemma 5. *For any $i \geq 0$, in the graph resulting from applying gadgets of Definition 2 to $G^{(i)}$ the following holds:*

1. *no negative-weight cycle exists,*
2. *for each edge $(u, u') \in (V(G^{(i)}) \setminus B_{G^{(i)}}(v, \beta_v)) \times B_{G^{(i)}}(v, \beta_v)$, the distance from u to v does not change,*
3. *for each $u' \in B_{G^{(i)}}(v, \beta_v)$ the distance from u' to v does not change.*

Proof. The proof is by induction on i. Note that initially all edges have non-negative weight, so no negative-weight cycle is present. Let $E_i = \{e_1, \ldots, e_m\}$ be the set of boundary edges that need to be replaced by a gadget according to Definition 2. We perform an induction over the individual replacements, where we maintain the above invariants. For $j \in [m]$, let $\hat{G}_j$ be the graph resulting from replacement of the first j edges of E_i in $G^{(i)}$ (in particular, $\hat{G}_0 = G^{(i)}$).

Observe that, after replacement of $e_j = (u, u')$, any cycle involving s contains (u, s) and either (s, u') or (s, v). By Definition 2, we have that $w_{\hat{G}_j}(u, s) + w_{\hat{G}_j}(s, v) = \mathrm{dist}_{G^{(i)}}(u, v) \geq 0$, so no negative cycle can be formed containing (u, s) and (s, v). By the induction hypothesis, in $\hat{G}_{j-1}$ distances are well-defined (i.e., non-negative and satisfying the triangle inequality). Therefore, any cycle involving (u, s) and (s, u') is of weight at least

$$w_{\hat{G}_j}(u, s) + w_{\hat{G}_j}(s, u') + \text{dist}_{\hat{G}_{j-1}}(u', u)$$
$$= \text{dist}_{G^{(i)}}(u, v) - \text{dist}_{G^{(i)}}(u', v) + \text{dist}_{\hat{G}_{j-1}}(u', u) \qquad \text{Definition 2}$$
$$\geq \text{dist}_{G^{(i)}}(u, v) - \text{dist}_{G^{(i)}}(u', v) + \text{dist}_{\hat{G}_{j-1}}(u', v) - \text{dist}_{\hat{G}_{j-1}}(u, v) \quad \Delta\text{-inequality}$$
$$= 0 \qquad \text{I.H.}$$

This shows the first part of the invariant for index j. In particular, w.l.o.g. we may consider only simple path for the remainder of the proof.

For the second part, it is sufficient to show that the distance from u to v does not change, as then the same follows for all other considered edges by the induction hypothesis. To see that this holds true, observe first that the path (u, s, v) has weight $\text{dist}_{G^{(i)}}(u, v)$ by construction, implying that $\text{dist}_{\hat{G}_j}(u, v) \leq \text{dist}_{G^{(i)}}(u, v)$. To prove that also $\text{dist}_{\hat{G}_j}(u, v) \geq \text{dist}_{G^{(i)}}(u, v)$, consider the simple paths from u to v. If they do not contain s, the induction hypothesis implies that they are not too light. The remaining paths are (u, s, v) (which we considered) and simple paths containing (u, s, u'). Any of the latter has weight at least

$$w_{\hat{G}_j}(u, s) + w_{\hat{G}_j}(s, u') + \text{dist}_{\hat{G}_{j-1}}(u', v)$$
$$= \text{dist}_{G^{(i)}}(u, v) - \text{dist}_{G^{(i)}}(u', v) + \text{dist}_{\hat{G}_{j-1}}(u', v) = \text{dist}_{\hat{G}_{j-1}}(u, v) \qquad \text{I.H.}$$

Thus, the second part of the invariant holds for index j.

It remains to show the third part of the invariant. Since the gadget replacement does not affect paths within $B_{G^{(i)}}(v, \beta_v)$, for each $u' \in B_{G^{(i)}}(v, \beta_v)$ we have that $\text{dist}_{\hat{G}^{(j)}}(u', v) \leq \text{dist}_{G^{(\hat{j}-1)}}(u', v)$. Assuming for contradiction that $\text{dist}_{\hat{G}^{(j)}}(u', v) < \text{dist}_{G^{(\hat{j}-1)}}(u', v)$, this must be due to a (simple) path containing s. By the already established second part of the invariant for index j, such a path cannot contain both u and u', as the subpath from u to u' would have weight at least $\text{dist}_{\hat{G}_{j-1}}(u, u')$, i.e., the invariant would be violated for index $j - 1$. However, by Definition 2 the edge (s, v) has weight β_v, which equals the weight of (s, u') plus $\text{dist}_{G^{(i)}}(u', v)$. Thus, if (u, s, v) would be too light, so would be some path involving both u and u'. The third part of the invariant follows. $\qquad \square$

4.2   Proving Theorem 3

Denote by $G^{(i)'}$ the graph algorithm $\mathcal{A}'$ computed after i mega-steps. Denote by $T_v^{(i)}$ an approximate shortest path tree of $G^{(i-1)'}$ rooted at v returned by approximate SSSP algorithm. For each $v \in V \setminus \{r\}$ with indegree 0, let β_v be the cost of minimum approximate shortest path entering the weakly connected component of v, according to $T_v^{(i)}$. We first prove a one-to-one correspondence between the mega-steps of $\mathcal{A}$ and $\mathcal{A}'$.

Lemma 6. *The gadget construction from Definition 2 ensures that after i mega-steps, $V(G^{(i)}) = V(G^{(i)'})$, $E(G^{(i)}) = E(G^{(i)'})$, and $\text{dist}_{G^{(i)}} \geq (1 + \varepsilon)\text{dist}_{G^{(i)'}}$. Moreover, each contraction uses the same value of β_v in $\mathcal{A}$ and $\mathcal{A}'$.*

Proof. We prove the claim by induction, where the base case of $i = 0$ is trivial. For the step from $i-1$ to i, we first note that (i) changing $U^{(i-1)}$ to $U^{(i)}$ does not affect which balls are contracted during the first $i - 1$ mega-steps and (ii) after $i-1$ megasteps, results in the graph created from $G^{(i-1)}$ by applying the gadget construction and adding for each $r \neq v \in V(G^{(i-1)})$ of indegree 0 and each $u \in B_{T_v^{(i)}}(v, \beta_v)$ an edge (u, v) of weight β_v. This holds true, because the edges that are added due to the gadget construction were not inside any previously contracted balls, and the values $S_x^{(i)}$ are chosen precisely such that they account for any weight loss of the new edges during the first $i - 1$ mega-steps.

Hence, denote the graph resulting from applying the gadget construction and adding the above edges to $G^{(i-1)}$ by $\hat{G}$, and fix some $r \neq v \in V(G^{(i-1)})$ of indegree 0. Observe first that $B_{T_v^{(i)}}(v, \beta_v) \subseteq B_{\hat{G}}(v, \beta_v)$, as each $u \in B_{T_v^{(i)}}(v, \beta_v)$ has an edge (u, v) of weight β_v. In particular, this includes the endpoint of the path of length β_v giving rise to the contraction performed by $\mathcal{A}'$ on $G^{(i-1)'}$, implying that $\mathcal{A}$ will contract a ball of radius at most β_v around v. Moreover, for any dummy node s that has been introduced when replacing an edge (u, u') with $u' \in B_{T_v^{(i)}}(v, \beta_v)$, there is an edge (s, v) of weight β_v. Hence $s \in B_{\hat{G}}(v, \beta_v)$.

By the induction hypothesis, it holds that $\text{dist}_{G^{(i-1)}} \geq (1+\varepsilon)\text{dist}_{G^{(i-1)'}}$, yielding $B_{G^{(i-1)}}(v, \beta_v) \leq B_{G^{(i-1)'}}(v, \beta_v/(1 + \varepsilon))$. Due to the approximation gurantee of the SSSP algorithm, there can be no path shorter than $\beta_v/(1 + \varepsilon)$ reaching v from outside its weakly connected component. By Lemma 5, each node outside $B_{G^{(i-1)}}(v, \beta_v)$ satisfies that its distance to v is not changed by the gadget construction. Thus, $\mathcal{A}$ must contract exactly $B_{G^{(i-1)}}(v, \beta_v) = B_{\hat{G}}(v, \beta_v)$. Moreover, any edge resulting from (u, u') and the contraction of $B_{G^{(i-1)}}(v, \beta_v) \ni u'$ will satisfy that its weight is at least $\text{dist}_{G^{(i-1)}}(u, v) - \beta_v$, implying that distances in the graph after contraction are at least as large as if we performed the contractions in $G^{(i-1)}$. Hence, $\text{dist}_{G^{(i)}} \geq (1 + \varepsilon)\text{dist}_{G^{(i)'}}$ follows from the facts that $\text{dist}_{G^{(i-1)}} \geq (1 + \varepsilon)\text{dist}_{G^{(i-1)'}} \geq \text{dist}_{T_v^{(i)}}$ and that $\mathcal{A}'$ setting a negative edge weight to 0 can only happen for edges at the boundary of the contracted balls, which in $\mathcal{A}$ are assigned a positive weight. □

This establishes the desired relation between the weight of the trees constructed by $\mathcal{A}$ and $\mathcal{A}'$, respectively. Denote by $i_{\max}$ the number of mega-steps $\mathcal{A}'$ performs on G.

Corollary 6. $\mathcal{A}'$ *on G constructs a DST of the same weight as $\mathcal{A}$ on* $U^{(i_{\max})}$.

Proof. By Lemma 6, $\mathcal{A}$ on $U^{(i_{\max})}$ and $\mathcal{A}'$ on G perform the same sequence of contractions with the same ball radii. By inductive application of Corollary 4, they hence compute DSTs of the same weight. □

Hence, it remains to show that the gadget replacements do not increase the weight of a tree spanning all (non-dummy) nodes.

Lemma 7. *For all i, $\text{opt}(U^{(i)}) \leq (1 + \varepsilon)\text{opt}(G)$.*

Proof. As $U^{(0)} = (V, E, (1 + \varepsilon)w_G)$, we have that $\text{opt}(U^{(0)}) = (1 + \varepsilon)\text{opt}(G)$. Thus, it is sufficient to show that $\text{opt}(U^{(i)}) \leq \text{opt}(U^{(i-1)})$ for all $i > 0$. We show first that in the graph $G^{(i-1)}$, the modifications by introducing the gadgets do not increase the weight of the MDST. To see this, consider an MDST T of $G^{(i-1)}$. If a gadget removes an edge (u, u') of T, we replace it by the edges (u, s) and (s, u') of the corresponding gadget. By Lemma 5, distances in $G^{(i-1)}$ are well-defined. Hence, we can apply the triangle inequality to see that the combined weight of these edges satisfies

$$w_{G^{(i-1)}}(u, s) + w_{G^{(i-1)}}(s, u') = \mathrm{dist}_{G^{(i-1)}}(u, v) - \mathrm{dist}_{G^{(i-1)}}(u', v)$$
$$\leq \mathrm{dist}_{G^{(i-1)}}(u, u') \leq w_{G^{(i-1)}}(u, u').$$

Thus, we obtain a tree T' of weight at most $w_{G^{(i-1)}}(T)$ spanning all but possibly some of the dummy nodes introduced by the gadgets. Recalling that we are not required to span dummy nodes, denoting by $\hat{G}$ the graph after gadget replacement we conclude that $\mathrm{opt}(\hat{G}) \leq \mathrm{opt}(G^{(i-1)})$.

To complete the proof, we invoke Lemma 6, showing that $\mathcal{A}$ performs the same sequence of contractions with the same ball radii in both $U^{(i-1)}$ and $U^{(i)}$. By inductively applying Corollary 4, we conclude that

$$\mathrm{opt}(U^{(i-1)}) - \mathrm{opt}(U^{(i)}) = \mathrm{opt}(\hat{G}) - \mathrm{opt}(G^{(i-1)}) \geq 0,$$

i.e., $\mathrm{opt}(U^{(i)}) \leq \mathrm{opt}(U^{(i-1)})$. □

By Lemma 4, the DST computed by $\mathcal{A}$ is actually an MDST of $U^{(i_{\max})}$. Hence, by Lemma 7, its weight is $\mathrm{opt}(U^{(i_{\max})}) \leq (1 + \varepsilon)\mathrm{opt}(G)$. Thus, this completes the proof of Theorem 3.

References

1. Becker, R., Karrenbauer, A., Krinninger, S., Lenzen, C.: Near-optimal approximate shortest paths and transshipment in distributed and streaming models. In: Richa, A.W. (ed.) Symposium on Distributed Computing (DISC), pp. 7:1–7:16 (2017)
2. Bock, F.: An algorithm to construct a minimum directed spanning tree in a directed network. Developments in operations research, pp. 29–44 (1971)
3. Censor-Hillel, K., Kaski, P., Korhonen, J.H., Lenzen, C., Paz, A., Suomela, J.: Algebraic methods in the congested clique. Distrib. Comput. **32**(6), 461–478 (2016). https://doi.org/10.1007/s00446-016-0270-2
4. Chechik, S., Mukhtar, D.: Single-source shortest paths in the CONGEST model with improved bound. In: Emek, Y., Cachin, C. (eds.) Symposium on Principles of Distributed Computing (PODC), pp. 464–473. ACM (2020)
5. Chu, Y., Liu, T.: On the shortest arborescence of a directed graph. Scientia Sinica **14**, 1396–1400 (1965)
6. Drucker, A., Kuhn, F., Oshman, R.: On the power of the congested clique model. In: Halldórsson, M.M., Dolev, S. (eds.) Symposium on Principles of Distributed Computing (PODC), pp. 367–376. ACM (2014)
7. Edmonds, J.: Optimum branchings. J. Res. Nat. Bureau Stand. B **71**(4), 233–240 (1967)
8. Elkin, M.: An unconditional lower bound on the time-approximation trade-off for the distributed minimum spanning tree problem. SIAM J. Comput. **36**(2), 433–456 (2006)

9. Fischer, O., Oshman, R.: A distributed algorithm for directed minimum-weight spanning tree. In: DISC (2019)
10. Gabow, H.N., Galil, Z., Spencer, T., Tarjan, R.E.: Efficient algorithms for finding minimum spanning trees in undirected and directed graphs. Combinatorica **6**(2), 109–122 (1986)
11. Ghaffari, M., Parter, M.: MST in log-star rounds of congested clique. In: Proceedings of the 2016 ACM Symposium on Principles of Distributed Computing, pp. 19–28. PODC 2016 (2016)
12. Hegeman, J.W., Pandurangan, G., Pemmaraju, S.V., Sardeshmukh, V.B., Scquizzato, M.: Toward optimal bounds in the congested clique: Graph connectivity and MST. In: Proceedings of the 2015 ACM Symposium on Principles of Distributed Computing. PODC 2015, pp. 91–100 (2015)
13. Jurdziński, T., Nowicki, K.: MST in $O(1)$ rounds of congested clique. In: Proceedings of the Twenty-Ninth Annual ACM-SIAM Symposium on Discrete Algorithms. SODA 2018, pp. 2620–2632 (2018)
14. Kutten, S., Peleg, D.: Fast distributed construction of small k-dominating sets and applications. J. Algorithms **28**(1), 40–66 (1998)
15. Le Gall, F.: Powers of tensors and fast matrix multiplication. In: Proceedings of the 39th International Symposium on Symbolic and Algebraic Computation. ISSAC 2014, pp. 296–303 (2014)
16. Lotker, Z., Pavlov, E., Patt-Shamir, B., Peleg, D.: MST construction in $O(\log \log n)$ communication rounds. SPAA 2003, pp. 94–100 (2003)
17. Lovasz, L.: Computing ears and branchings in parallel. In: 2013 IEEE 54th Annual Symposium on Foundations of Computer Science, pp. 464–467 (1985)
18. Nowicki, K.: A Deterministic Algorithm for the MST Problem in Constant Rounds of Congested Clique. CoRR abs/1912.04239 (2019)
19. Pandurangan, G., Robinson, P., Scquizzato, M.: The distributed minimum spanning tree problem. Bull. EATCS **125**, 24 (2018)
20. Peleg, D., Rubinovich, V.: A near-tight lower bound on the time complexity of distributed minimum-weight spanning tree construction. SIAM J. Comput. **30**(5), 1427–1442 (2000)
21. Sarma, A.D., et al.: Distributed verification and hardness of distributed approximation. SIAM J. Comput. **30**, 1235–1265 (2012)

Distributed Detection of Clusters of Arbitrary Size

Bogdan-Adrian Manghiuc[✉][iD]

School of Informatics, The University of Edinburgh, Edinburgh, UK
b.a.manghiuc@sms.ed.ac.uk

Abstract. Graph clustering is a fundamental technique in data analysis with a vast number of applications in computer science and statistics. In theoretical computer science, the problem of graph clustering has received significant research attention over the past two decades, which has led to pivotal algorithmic breakthroughs. However, the design of most graph clustering algorithms is based on complicated techniques from computational optimisation, which are not applicable for processing massive data sets stored in physically remote locations.

In this work we present a novel distributed algorithm for graph clustering. Most of the previous algorithms only work for graphs with balanced-sized clusters, which restrict their applications in many practical settings. Our proposed algorithm works for graphs with clusters of *arbitrary size* and its performance is analysed with respect to every *individual* cluster. In addition, our algorithm is easy to implement, and only requires a polylogarithmic number of rounds for many graphs occurring in practice.

Keywords: Distributed computing · Graph clustering · Randomised algorithms

1 Introduction

Graph clustering, also known as community detection, is one of the most fundamental problems in algorithms with applications in distributed computing, machine learning, network analysis, and statistics. Over the past four decades, graph clustering algorithms have been extensively studied from both the theoretical and applied perspectives [10,21]. On the theoretical side, the problem is known as graph partitioning and is one of the most fundamental NP-hard problems. Among the many reasons, we mention its connection to several important topics in theoretical computer science including the Unique Games Conjecture and the Small Set Expansion Conjecture. Because of this, most graph clustering algorithms with better approximation guarantee are based on complicated spectral and convex optimisation techniques [17,22], whose runtime is slow even in the centralised setting. From the practical point of view, graph clustering is a key component in unsupervised learning, and has been widely applied in data mining, analysis of social networks, and statistics. In particular, since many graphs

© Springer Nature Switzerland AG 2021
T. Jurdziński and S. Schmid (Eds.): SIROCCO 2021, LNCS 12810, pp. 370–387, 2021.
https://doi.org/10.1007/978-3-030-79527-6_21

occurring in practice (e.g. social networks) are stored in physically distributed servers (sites), designing simple and more practical distributed algorithms, with better performance, has received a lot attention in recent years [2–4,8,12,23,24].

We study graph clustering algorithms in the distributed setting. We assume that the input $G = (V, E)$ is an unweighted distributed network over a set of $|V| = n$ nodes and $|E| = m$ edges. The set of nodes is always fixed and there are no node failures. Each node is a computational unit communicating only to its neighbours. We consider the synchronous timing model when, in each round, a node can either send the same message to all its neighbours or choose not to communicate. We assume that every node knows the rough size of $|V|$, which is not difficult to approximate, however the global structure of G is unknown to each node. Every node v has a unique[1] identifier $\mathsf{ID}(v)$ of size $O(\log(n))$. We will assume that any message sent by a node v will also contain $\mathsf{ID}(v)$.

In this work we study the clustering problem when the input G consists of k well-defined clusters $S_1, \cdots, S_k$ that form a partition of V, i.e., it holds that $S_i \cap S_j = \emptyset$ for $i \neq j$ and $\bigcup_{1 \leq i \leq k} S_i = V$. We allow the nodes in the network to exchange information with their neighbours over a number of rounds T. At the end of the T rounds, every node v determines a label indicating the cluster in which it belongs. Our objective is to design a distributed algorithm which guarantees that: (1) most nodes within the same cluster would receive the same label, and (2) every cluster would have its own unique label. The performance of our algorithm is measured by (1) the total number of proceeded rounds T, (2) the approximation guarantee, i.e., how many nodes in each cluster receive the correct label, and (3) the total message complexity, i.e., the total number of words exchanged among the nodes.

Structure of Clusters. The performance of a clustering algorithm always depends on the inherent cluster structure of the network: the more significant the cluster structure is, the easier the algorithm could approximate it. To quantify the significance of the cluster structure associated with the underlying graph, we follow the previous reference [18,19] and introduce the gap assumption. For any set $S \subset V$, let the conductance of S be

$$\phi_G(S) \triangleq \frac{|\partial(S)|}{\text{vol}(S)},$$

where $\partial(S) = E(S, V \setminus S)$ is the set of edges crossing S and $V \setminus S$, and $\text{vol}(S)$ is the sum of degrees of nodes in S. We define the k-*way* expansion of G by

$$\rho(k) \triangleq \min_{\text{partitions } S_1, \ldots, S_k} \max_{1 \leq i \leq k} \phi_G(S_i),$$

and we call a partition $\{S_i\}_{i=1}^{k}$ that achieves $\rho(k)$ an optimal partitioning.

One of the basic facts in spectral graph theory is a tight connection between $\rho(k)$ and the eigenvalues of the normalised Laplacian matrix of G. In particular, Lee et al. [14] proved the so-called higher-order Cheeger inequality:

---

[1] Every node v can randomly select a number between $[1, \text{poly}(n)]$, such that, with high probability, those numbers are distinct.

$$\frac{\lambda_k}{2} \leq \rho(k) \leq O(k^3)\sqrt{\lambda_k}, \tag{1}$$

where $0 = \lambda_1 \leq \cdots \leq \lambda_n \leq 2$ are the eigenvalues of the normalised Laplacian of G. By definition, it is easy to see that a small value of $\rho(k)$ ensures the existence of disjoint $S_1, \ldots, S_k$ of low conductance. On the other hand, by (1) we know that a large value of λ_{k+1} implies that no matter how we partition G into $k+1$ subsets $S_1, \ldots, S_{k+1}$, there will be at least one subset S_i for which $\phi_G(S_i) \geq \frac{\lambda_{k+1}}{2}$. To formalise this intuition, we follow the previous reference (e.g., [19,23]) and define

$$\Upsilon_G(k) \triangleq \frac{\lambda_{k+1}}{\rho(k)}.$$

By definition, a large value of $\Upsilon_G(k)$ would ensure that G has k well-defined clusters.

Our Result. Our main result is an improved distributed graph clustering algorithm for inputs with k-well defined clusters. For the ease of presentation, we assume that G is d-regular, however our algorithm works and the analysis follows as long as the maximum degree $d_{\max}$ of G and the minimum degree $d_{\min}$ satisfy $d_{\max}/d_{\min} = O(1)$. Our result is as follows:

Theorem 1 (Main Result). *Let $G = (V, E)$ be a d-regular network with $|V| = n$ nodes, $|E| = m$ edges and k optimal clusters $S_1, \ldots, S_k$. If $\Upsilon_G(k) = \omega\left(k^4 \log^3(n)\right)$, there is a distributed algorithm that finishes in $T = O\left(\frac{\log(n)}{\lambda_{k+1}}\right)$ rounds, such that the following three statements hold:*

1. *For any cluster S_j of size $|S_j| \leq \log(n)$, every node $u \in S_j$ will determine the same label. Moreover, this label is $\mathsf{ID}(v)$ for some $v \in S_j$.*
2. *With probability at least 0.9, for any cluster S_j of size $|S_j| > \log(n)$, all but $o(|S_j|)$ nodes $u \in S_j$ will determine the same label. Moreover, this label is $\mathsf{ID}(v)$ for some $v \in S_j$.*
3. *With probability at least 0.9, the total information exchanged among the n nodes, i.e. the message complexity is $\widetilde{O}\left(\frac{n^2}{\lambda_{k+1}}\right)$, where $\widetilde{O}(\cdot)$ hides poly $\log(n)$ factors.*

Now we discuss the significance of our result. First of all, notice that $\lambda_{k+1} = \Omega(1)$ in many practical settings [16,18], and in this case our algorithm finishes in $T = O(\log n)$ rounds. Secondly, our result significantly improves the previous work with respect to the approximation ratio. As far as we know, the vast majority of the previous algorithms for distributed clustering are analysed with respect to the *total* volume (or number) of misclassified nodes *over all clusters* (e.g., [2–4,23]). However, this form of approximation is unsatisfactory when the underlying graph contains clusters with very unbalanced sizes, since an upper bound on the total volume (or number) of misclassified nodes could still imply that nodes from a smaller cluster are completely misclassified. Our current work successfully overcomes this downside by analysing the approximation guarantee with respect to *every* approximated cluster and its optimal correspondent.

To the best of our knowledge, such a strong approximation guarantee with respect to every optimal cluster is only known in the centralised setting [13,19]. We show that such result can be obtained for distributed algorithms as well.

It is not difficult to image that obtaining this strong approximation guarantee would require a more refined analysis on the *smaller* clusters, since clusters with different size might have different orders of mixing time if random walk based processes are needed when performing the algorithm. Surprisingly, we are able to show that our algorithm is able to *perfectly* recover every small cluster. To the best of our knowledge, such a result of perfectly recovering small clusters is unknown even for centralised algorithms, and our developed subroutine of small cluster recovery might have other applications.

Finally, as a key component of our algorithm, we present a distributed subroutine which allows most nodes to estimate the size of the cluster they belong. This subroutine is based on the power method applied to a number of initial vectors. We show that the information retrieved by each node after this process is sufficient for most nodes to obtain good estimates for the size of their cluster. We believe that our present algorithm and the developed techniques would inspire further applications for many different problems concerning multiple and parallel random walks [11,20] or testing clusters of communities in networks [9,15].

Related Work. There is a large amount of work on graph clustering over the past decades, and here we discuss the ones closely related to ours. First of all, there have been several studies on graph clustering where the presence of the cluster structure is guaranteed by some spectral properties of the Laplacian matrix of an input graph. Von Luxburg [16] studies spectral clustering, and discusses the influence of the eigen-gap on the quality of spectral clustering algorithms. Peng et al. [19] analyse spectral clustering on well-clustered graphs and show that, when there is a gap between λ_{k+1} and $\rho(k)$, the approximation guarantee of spectral clustering can be theoretically analysed. Gharan and Trevisan [18] designed an approximation algorithm that, under some condition on the relationship between λ_k and λ_{k+1}, returns k clusters $S_1, \ldots, S_k$ such that both the inner and outer conductance of each S_i can be theoretically analysed. Allen-Zhu et al. [1] present a local algorithm for finding a cluster with improved approximation guarantee under some gap assumption similar with ours.

For distributed graph clustering, the work most related to ours is the distributed algorithm developed by Sun and Zanetti [23]. In comparison to our algorithm, the algorithm in [23] only holds for graphs that consist of clusters of balanced sizes, and the approximation guarantee (i.e., the number of misclassified nodes) of their algorithm is with respect to the volume of the input graph, while the approximation guarantee of our algorithm is with respect to *every* individual cluster. Becchetti et al. [3] presented a distributed graph clustering algorithm for the case $k = 2$, based on an Averaging dynamics process. However, their analysis holds only for a restricted class of graphs exhibiting sparse cuts. Becchetti et al. [4] extended the results for a more general class of volume regular networks with k clusters. Nonetheless, their results apply to reasonably balanced networks, which is a setting more restricted than ours. Finally, we would like to mention a related sequence of work on decomposing graphs into expanders [6,7]. However, we highlight that these algorithms cannot be applied in our setting for the following reasons: the number of partitioning sets could be much larger than the initial number of clusters k and the decomposition also allows some fraction of nodes not to be in any cluster [7].

Notation. We consider the input network $G = (V, E)$ to be an unweighted d-regular network on $|V| = n$ nodes and $|E| = m$ edges. The $n \times n$ adjacency matrix is denoted A_G and is defined as $A_G(u, v) = 1$ if $\{u, v\} \in E$ and $A_G(u, v) = 0$ otherwise. The normalised Laplacian of G is the $n \times n$ matrix defined as

$$\mathcal{L}_G \triangleq I - \frac{1}{d} \cdot A_G.$$

We denote the eigenvalues of $\mathcal{L}_G$ by $0 = \lambda_1 \leq \cdots \leq \lambda_n \leq 2$. For any subset $S \subseteq V$, we denote the characteristic vector $\mathbf{1}_S \in \mathbb{R}^n$ by $\mathbf{1}_S(v) = 1$ if $v \in S$ and $\mathbf{1}_S(v) = 0$ otherwise. For brevity, we will write $\mathbf{1}_v$ whenever $S = \{v\}$.

We will consider the setting when the input network G contains k disjoint clusters $S_1, \ldots, S_k$, that form a partition of V. For a given node $v \in V$, we will denote by $\mathcal{S}(v)$ the cluster that contains v. We will write $\text{Broadcast}_u(\text{Message})$ whenever a node u sends a Message to its neighbours and we will drop the subscript u whenever that is clear from the context. We will denote the label of a node v by $L(v)$ and we will assume that initially $L(v) = \perp$, for all nodes v. Throughout our algorithm, some nodes $v \in V$ will become *active*. We will use the notation v^* whenever referring to an active node v.

2 Algorithm Description

Our algorithm consists in three major phases: Averaging, Small Detection and Large Detection, which we will describe individually.

Averaging Phase: The Averaging phase (Algorithm 1) consists in the execution of n different diffusion processes, one for every node. To each diffusion process, say corresponding to a node v, we associate a set of vectors $\{x_i^v\}_i$ such that, after every round i, every node u in the network will store the value $x_i^v(u)$. The value $x_i^v(u)$ is the mass value that node u received from node v after i rounds. Initially (round 0) the diffusion process starts from $x_0^v = \frac{1}{\sqrt{d}} \mathbf{1}_v$, i.e. all mass value $\frac{1}{\sqrt{d}}$ is concentrated at node v with 0 mass to the other nodes. For a general round i, the vector x_i^v is constructed iteratively, via the recursive formula

$$x_i^v(u) = \frac{1}{2} x_{i-1}^v(u) + \frac{1}{2d} \sum_{\{u,w\} \in E} x_{i-1}^v(w), \tag{2}$$

for any u. We remark that, the only information a node u needs in round i are the values $x_{i-1}^v(w)$ for all its neighbours w. We note that at any round i, node u

does not need to update the values x_i^v for all nodes v in the network. Instead, u focuses on the diffusion processes started at the nodes which u has already seen throughout the process. To keep track of the already seen nodes, u maintains the set $\mathsf{Seen}(u)$ (See Line 2 of Algorithm 1).

Now let us discuss the intuition behind this phase. The goal of the diffusion process started at node v is that, after $T = \Theta\left(\frac{\log(n)}{\lambda_{k+1}}\right)$ rounds, the entire mass $\frac{1}{\sqrt{d}}$ is split roughly equally among all nodes inside the cluster $\mathcal{S}(v)$, with very few of this mass exiting the cluster. A closer look at Eq. (2) tells us that the diffusion process started at v is nothing but a T-step, $1/2$-lazy random walk process starting from the vector $\frac{1}{\sqrt{d}}\mathbf{1}_v$. It is well known [5] that, assuming G is connected, the vectors x_i^v will converge to the uniform distribution as i goes to infinity. However, if the process runs for merely $T = \Theta\left(\frac{\log(n)}{\lambda_{k+1}}\right)$ iterations, one should expect the vector x_T^v to be close to the (normalised) indicator vector of the cluster $\mathcal{S}(v)$. This is because $\frac{\log(n)}{\lambda_{k+1}}$ corresponds to the local mixing time inside the cluster $\mathcal{S}(v)$. Therefore, after T rounds, we expect for every $u \in \mathcal{S}(v)$, the values $x_T^v(u)$ to be similar and significantly greater than 0, while for nodes $w \notin \mathcal{S}(v)$, we expect the values $x_T^v(w)$ to be close to 0.

At the end of the Averaging phase, based on the values $\{x_T^v(u)\}_v$ each node u computes an estimate ℓ_u for the size of its cluster. We define the estimates as

$$\ell_u \triangleq \frac{3}{d \cdot \sum_v [x_T^v(u)]^2},$$

and we will show that, for most nodes u, the estimates satisfy $\ell_u \in [|\mathcal{S}(u)|, 4|\mathcal{S}(u)|]$ (see Lemma 6).

Algorithm 1. Average (u, T)

Require: A node u, a number of rounds $T = \Theta\left(\frac{\log(n)}{\lambda_{k+1}}\right)$

1: Set $x_0^u(u) = \frac{1}{\sqrt{d}}$ and $x_0^v(u) = 0$ for all $v \neq u$ ▷ Initialisation step
2: $\mathsf{Seen}(u) = \{u\}$.
3: **for** $i = 1 \ldots T$ **do**
4:      Broadcast$\left(\{(x_{i-1}^v(u), \mathsf{ID}(v)) \,|\, v \in \mathsf{Seen}(u)\}\right)$
5:      **for all** $(x_{i-1}^v(w), \mathsf{ID}(v))$ that u receives **do**
6:          Add v to $\mathsf{Seen}(u)$
7:      **for all** $v \in \mathsf{Seen}(u)$ **do**
8:          $x_i^v(u) = \frac{1}{2}x_{i-1}^v(u) + \frac{1}{2d}\sum_{w \sim u} x_{i-1}^v(w)$.   ▷ Update the current status
9: **return** $\{x_T^v(u)\}$.

Small Detection Phase: The purpose of this phase is for every node u in a cluster of small size $|\mathcal{S}(u)| \leq \log(n)$ to determine its label. Again, we focus on the intuition behind this process and we refer the reader to Algorithm 2 for a formal description. From the perspective of a node u, we would like to use the values $\{x_T^v(u)\}_v$ to decide which nodes are in its own cluster. Informally, the values $\{x_T^v(u)\}_{v \in S(u)}$ should be similar and close to $\frac{1}{\sqrt{d}|S(u)|}$ since, for every diffusion process started at $v \in S(u)$ we expect the $\frac{1}{\sqrt{d}}$ mass to be equally distributed among all nodes in the cluster. At the same time, we expect the values $\{x_T^w(u)\}_{w \notin S(u)}$ not to be very large, because they correspond to random walks started in a different clusters. Therefore, if $|S(u)|$ is not too big, we expect to see a clear separation between $x_T^v(u)$ and $x_T^w(u)$, for any $v \in S(u)$ and $w \notin S(u)$.

Since u knows that it is a member of its own cluster, it can use $x_T^u(u)$ as a reference point. Namely u computes the pairwise differences

$$y_v \triangleq |x_T^u(u) - x_T^v(u)|,$$

for all v and sorts them in increasing order. Let us call $y_{v_1} \leq \cdots \leq y_{v_n}$ to be those values. Based on the previous remarks, it should be expected that the first $|S(u)|$ values are small and correspond to nodes $v \in S(u)$. Then, u performs a binary search to find the exact size of its cluster $S(u)$ (lines 4-10 of Algorithm 2). Finally, u sets its label to be the minimum[2] ID among nodes corresponding to the smallest $|S(u)|$ values $\{y_{v_i}\}$.

Algorithm 2. SmallDetection $(u, \ell_u, \mathrm{RW}(u))$

Require: A node u, an estimated cluster size ℓ_u, a list of values $\mathrm{RW}(u) = \{x_T^v(u)\}$
1: **for all** v **do**
2:     Compute $y_v = |x_T^u(u) - x_T^v(u)|$.
3: Sort the values $\{y_v\}$ and call the sorted ones $y_{v_1} \leq \cdots \leq y_{v_n}$
4: Let $i_{\mathrm{low}} = 1$, $i_{\mathrm{high}} = \ell_u$.   ▷ The binary search step
5: **while** $i_{\mathrm{low}} + 1 < i_{\mathrm{high}}$ **do**   ▷ At the end of the loop, we have $i_{\mathrm{low}} = |S(u)|$
6:     $i = \lfloor \frac{i_{\mathrm{low}} + i_{\mathrm{high}}}{2} \rfloor$
7:     **if** $y_{v_i} < \frac{9}{10\sqrt{d} \cdot i}$ **then**
8:         $i_{\mathrm{low}} = i$
9:     **else**
10:         $i_{\mathrm{high}} = i$.
11: $L(u) = \min_{v_i} \{\mathrm{ID}(v_i) | i \leq i_{\mathrm{low}}\}$ ▷ Determining the label
12: **return** $L(u)$.

At the end of this phase we would like to stress two important facts. First of all, it is really crucial that the cluster $S(u)$ has size $|S(u)| \leq \log(n)$. Otherwise, the values $\{x_T^v(u)\}_{v \in S(u)}$ would be too small for u to distinguish them. Therefore, we cannot use this approach to determine the label of all nodes in the network. Secondly, we remark that for the algorithm to work, every node u should be in possession of the value $x_T^u(u)$. This can be ensured only if all nodes start their own diffusion process.

---

[2] The minimum does not play any special role here, it is only used to guarantee consensus among all nodes in the same cluster. The maximum ID works just as fine.

Large Detection Phase: In this phase, the algorithm will detect the remaining clusters of large and medium size, that are clusters S with $|S| > \log(n)$. The formal description of this phase can be found in Algorithm 3. Again, a node u in such a cluster would like to use the values $\{x_T^v(u)\}_v$ to determine the composition of its cluster. Unfortunately, node u cannot trust all values $x_T^v(u)$ because of the error in the diffusion processes caused by some mass exiting the cluster.

To overcome this difficulty, we use a different approach. We want each cluster S_j to select some representatives, which we will refer to as active nodes. The label of the cluster S_j will be the minimum ID among the active nodes in S_j. The purpose of this selection is to avoid the (bad) nodes for which the diffusion process does not behave as expected. To that extent, we let each node u activate itself independently (Line 3 of Algorithm 3), with probability

$$p(u) \triangleq \frac{5 \cdot \log(100k)}{\ell_u}.$$

Since for most nodes $\ell_u \approx |S(u)|$, the probability $p(u)$ is large enough to ensure that: every cluster will have at least one active node and, in expectation, there will not be too many active nodes overall. If a node u becomes active, it will announce this in the network, along with its estimated cluster size ℓ_u. This happens throughout T rounds of communication (Lines 6–14 of Algorithm 3). In such a round j, every node v in the network keeps a list $\mathsf{Act}(v)$ of the active nodes v has seen up to round j. Then, v checks which of those active nodes he has not yet communicated, broadcasts them in a Message (Line 12 of Algorithm 3) and marks them as Sent. This process ensures that every node v announces each active node at most once, which significantly reduces the communication cost.

Coming back to node u, at the end of the T rounds u has seen all active nodes $v^* \in \mathsf{Act}(u)$. Node u considers an active node v^* to be in $\mathcal{S}(u)$, if two conditions are satisfied: 1) its estimated cluster size ℓ_u and ℓ_{v^*} are similar and 2) the value $x_T^{v^*}$ is similar to what u expects to see. More precisely, u sets the threshold

$$t_u \triangleq \frac{1}{2\sqrt{d\ell_u}},$$

and considers its set of candidates

$$\mathsf{Cand}(u) \triangleq \left\{ v^* \middle| v^* \in \mathsf{Act}(u), \frac{\ell_u}{4} \leq \ell_{v^*} \leq 4\ell_u \text{ and } x_T^{v^*}(u) \geq t_u \right\}.$$

The set of candidates $\mathsf{Cand}(u)$ represents the set of active nodes that u believes are in its own cluster. If $\mathsf{Cand}(u) \neq \emptyset$, then u sets its label to be the $\min_{v^* \in \mathsf{Cand}(u)} \mathsf{ID}(v^*)$. Otherwise, if u is unlucky so that $\mathsf{Cand}(u) = \emptyset$, then u randomly chooses an active node $v^* \in \mathsf{Act}(u)$ and selects its label as $L(u) = \mathsf{ID}(v^*)$ (Lines 20–23 of Algorithm 3).

Algorithm 3. LargeDetection $(u, \ell_u, \mathrm{RW}(u), T)$

Require: A node u, an estimated cluster size ℓ_u, a list of values $\mathrm{RW}(u) = \{x_T^v(u)\}$, the number of rounds T

1: Set $\mathsf{Act}(u) = \emptyset$, $\mathsf{Cand}(u) = \emptyset$, $\mathsf{Sent}(v) = $ false, $\forall v$ ▷ Initialisation step
2: **if** $L(u) = \perp$ **then**
3:     Activate u with probability $p(u) = \frac{5\log(100k)}{\ell_u}$.   ▷ Activation step

4: **if** u becomes active **then**
5:     Set $\mathsf{Act}(u) = \{(u, \ell_u)\}$
6: **for** $j = 1 \ldots T$ **do**   ▷ Propagation step
7:     Message $= \emptyset$
8:     **for all** $(v^*, \ell_{v^*}) \in \mathsf{Act}(u)$ and $\mathsf{Sent}(v^*) = $ false **do**
9:        Add (v^*, ℓ_{v^*}) to Message
10:       Set $\mathsf{Sent}(v^*) = $ true
11:     **if** Message $\neq \emptyset$ **then**
12:       Broadcast (Message).
13:     **for all** v^* such that u received (v^*, ℓ_{v^*}) in round j **do**
14:       Add (v^*, ℓ_{v^*}) to $\mathsf{Act}(u)$.
15: Set $t_u = \frac{1}{2\sqrt{d} \cdot \ell_u}$
16: **for all** $(v^*, \ell_{v^*}) \in \mathsf{Act}(u)$ **do**
17:     **if** $\frac{\ell_{v^*}}{4} \leq \ell_u \leq 4\ell_{v^*}$ and $x_T^{v^*}(u) \geq t_u$ **then**
18:       Add v^* to $\mathsf{Cand}(u)$
19: **if** $\mathsf{Cand}(u) \neq \emptyset$ **then**   ▷ Labeling step
20:     Set $L(u) = \min_{v^* \in \mathsf{Act}(u)} \{\mathsf{ID}(v^*)\}$
21: **else**
22:     Choose a random $(v^*, \ell_v^*) \in \mathsf{Act}(u)$
23:     Set $L(u) = \mathsf{ID}(v^*)$
24: **return** $L(u)$.

The Main Algorithm: Now we bring together all three subroutines and present our main Algorithm 4. We note that once a node u has determined their label, that will not change in the future. This is because Algorithm 3 can only change the label if $L(u) = \perp$ initially. Moreover, even if a node has determined their label in the Small Detection phase, they still participate in the Large Detection phase since they are active parts in the Propagation step (Lines 6–14) of Algorithm 3.

3 Analysis of the Algorithm

In this section we analyse our distributed algorithm and prove Theorem 1. Remember that we assume G is a d-regular network with optimal k clusters $S_1, \ldots, S_k$. Moreover, we work in the regime when G satisfies the assumption that

$$\Upsilon_G(k) = \omega \left(k^4 \log^3(n) \right). \tag{3}$$

Algorithm 4. Cluster (u, n)

Require: A node u, the number of nodes in the network n.

1: Set $T = \Theta\left(\frac{\log(n)}{\lambda_{k+1}}\right)$.   ▷ Choose $\lambda_{k+1} = \frac{1}{\text{poly}\log(n)}$ in practice

2: Set $L(u) = \bot$.

3: Let $\text{RW}(u) = \text{Average}(u, T)$.   ▷ Perform the Averaging phase

4: Let $\ell_u = 3/\left(d\sum_v [x_T^v(u)]^2\right)$ be the estimate for $|\mathcal{S}(u)|$.

5: **if** $\ell_u \le 4\log(n)$ **then**

6:     $L(u) = \text{SmallDetection}(u, \ell_u, \text{RW}(u))$ ▷ Perform the Small Detection phase

7: $L(u) = \text{LargeDetection}(u, \ell_u, \text{RW}(u), T)$ ▷ Perform the Large Detection phase

8: **return** $L(u)$.

For brevity, we will use Υ instead of $\Upsilon_G(k)$. We will structure the analysis of our algorithm in five subsections. In Subsect. 3.1 we recap some of the results in [23] and present the guarantees achieved after the Averaging phase of the algorithm. In Subsect. 3.2 we show that most nodes in the network can obtain a good estimate for the size of their cluster. In Subsect. 3.3 we deal with the analysis of the Small Detection phase of the algorithm. We will ultimately show that for all clusters S_j of size $|S_j| \le \log(n)$, all nodes $u \in S_j$ will determine the same label, unique for the cluster S_j. In Subsect. 3.4 we analyse the Large Detection phase of the algorithm. In this phase, most nodes in clusters of size at least $\log(n)$ will decide on a common label that is unique for the cluster. We also show that the number of misclassified nodes for each cluster is small. Finally, we conclude with the proof of Theorem 1 in Subsect. 3.5.

3.1 Analysis of the Averaging Phase

Recall that the Averaging phase consists in performing n diffusion processes for $T = \Theta\left(\frac{\log(n)}{\lambda_{k+1}}\right)$ rounds. For a node v, its own diffusion process can be viewed as a lazy random walk starting at $x_0^v = \frac{1}{\sqrt{d}}\mathbf{1}_v$ and following the recursion

$$x_{i+1}^v = Px_i^v,$$

where

$$P \triangleq \frac{1}{2} \cdot I + \frac{1}{2d} \cdot A_G = I - \frac{1}{2}\mathcal{L}_G$$

is the transition matrix of the process. It is known that, assuming G is connected, the vectors $\{x_i^v\}$ will converge to the stationary distribution as i goes to infinity. However, if the power method runs for $T = \Theta\left(\frac{\log(n)}{\lambda_{k+1}}\right)$ phases, we expect $x_T^v \approx \frac{1}{\sqrt{d} \cdot |\mathcal{S}(v)|} \cdot \mathbf{1}_{\mathcal{S}(v)}$. Sun and Zanetti [23] formalise this intuition and give a concrete version of the above observation (See Lemma 2). The intuition behind their result lies in the fact that, for graphs G with k good clusters, there is a strong connection between the bottom k eigenvectors of $\mathcal{L}_G$ and the normalised indicator vectors of the clusters [19].

We will now introduce the notation required to formalise the above discussion. Let $f_1, \ldots, f_k$ be the bottom k eigenvectors of $\mathcal{L}_G$ and let $\{\chi_{S_1}, \ldots, \chi_{S_k}\}$ be the normalised indicator vectors of the clusters S_i, that is $\chi_{S_i} \triangleq \frac{1}{\sqrt{|S_i|}} \mathbf{1}_{S_i}$, for all i. Let $\tilde{\chi}_i$ be the projection of f_i onto $\text{span}\{\chi_{S_1}, \ldots \chi_{S_k}\}$ and let $\{\widehat{\chi}_i\}$ be the vectors obtained from $\{\tilde{\chi}_i\}$ by applying the Gram-Schmidt orthonormalisation[3]. For any node v, we define the discrepancy parameter

$$\alpha_v \triangleq \sqrt{\frac{1}{d} \sum_{i=1}^{k} (f_i(v) - \widehat{\chi}_i(v))^2}.$$

We are now ready to state the result relating x_T^v to the indicator vector of the cluster $\mathbf{1}_{S(v)}$:

Lemma 2 (Adaptation of Lemma 4.4 in [23]). *For any $v \in V$, if we run the lazy random walk for $T = \Theta\left(\frac{\log n}{\lambda_{k+1}}\right)$ rounds, starting at $x_0^v = \frac{1}{\sqrt{d}} \mathbf{1}_v$, we obtain a vector x_T^v such that*

$$\left\| x_T^v - \frac{1}{\sqrt{d} \cdot |S(v)|} \cdot \mathbf{1}_{S(v)} \right\|^2 = O\left(\frac{k^2}{d \cdot \Upsilon \cdot |S(v)|} + \alpha_v^2\right). \tag{4}$$

One can view the RHS of (4) as an upper bound for the total error of the diffusion process that started at v. To that extent, let us define the set of vectors

$$\varepsilon_v \triangleq x_T^v - \frac{1}{\sqrt{d} \cdot |S(v)|} \cdot \mathbf{1}_{S(v)} \tag{5}$$

and we will use for shortend $\varepsilon_{(v,u)} = \varepsilon_v(u)$. It is important to note that the order of the pair matters, since $\varepsilon_{(v,u)}$ corresponds to a diffusion process started at v, while $\varepsilon_{(u,v)}$ corresponds to a diffusion process started at u.

Under this notation, Eq. (4) becomes

$$\sum_{u \in V} \varepsilon_{(v,u)}^2 \leq C_\varepsilon \left(\frac{k^2}{d \cdot \Upsilon \cdot |S(v)|} + \alpha_v^2\right), \tag{6}$$

for some absolute constant C_ε. While one should expect each individual error $\varepsilon_{(v,u)}$ to be relatively small, i.e. $O\left(\frac{1}{|S(v)|}\right)$, it is not immediately clear why this should be the case. Indeed, the presence of α_v in Eq. (6) can cause significant perturbation. Given the relatively complicated definition of this parameter, the only upper bound we are aware of is the following:

Lemma 3. *It holds that*

$$\sum_{v \in V} \alpha_v^2 = O\left(\frac{k^2}{d \cdot \Upsilon}\right) \leq \frac{C_\alpha \cdot k^2}{d \cdot \Upsilon}, \tag{7}$$

for some absolute constant $C_\alpha > 0$.

---

[3] For a more detailed discussion of the connection between the sets $\{f_i\}$, $\{\chi_{S_i}\}$, $\{\tilde{\chi}_i\}$ we refer the reader to [19].

3.2 Estimating the Cluster Size

In this section we will show that most nodes in every cluster are able to estimate approximately the size of their cluster. Recall that the estimate that each node u computes is

$$\ell_u = \frac{3}{d \sum_v [x_T^v(u)]^2},$$

and we want to show that for most nodes u we have that $|\mathcal{S}(u)| \le \ell_u \le 4 \cdot |\mathcal{S}(u)|$. To that extent, we split the set of (bad) nodes, that do not obey the above condition, into two categories:

$$\mathcal{B}_{\text{big}} \triangleq \left\{ u \,\middle|\, \ell_u > 4 \,|\mathcal{S}(u)| \right\} \qquad \text{and} \qquad \mathcal{B}_{\text{small}} \triangleq \left\{ u \,\middle|\, \ell_u < |\mathcal{S}(u)| \right\}.$$

Moreover we let

$$\mathcal{B}_\ell \triangleq \mathcal{B}_{\text{big}} \cup \mathcal{B}_{\text{small}}$$

and we will show that in each cluster, only a small fraction of nodes can be in $\mathcal{B}_\ell$. We start with set $\mathcal{B}_{\text{big}}$ and here we show that only a small fraction of nodes in each cluster can be in $\mathcal{B}_{\text{big}}$.

Lemma 4. *For every cluster S_j it holds that*

$$|\mathcal{B}_{\text{big}} \cap S_j| \le \frac{|S_j|}{2 \cdot 500k \cdot \log(nk)}.$$

Now we focus on the set $\mathcal{B}_{\text{small}}$. In this case, we will prove something stronger, namely that in each cluster S_j the fraction of nodes estimating some value ℓ is directly proportional to the value of ℓ. In other words, the smaller the value of ℓ, the fewer the number of nodes will estimate it. This result is crucial for the analysis of the Large Detection phase. To that extent, we define the level sets

$$\mathcal{B}_{\text{small}}^i \triangleq \left\{ u \,\middle|\, \ell_u < \frac{|\mathcal{S}(u)|}{2^{i-1}} \right\},$$

for $i = 1, \ldots, \log(n)$. The following result formalises our discussion.

Lemma 5. *For every cluster S_j and every $i = 1, \ldots, \log(n)$ it holds that*

$$|\mathcal{B}_{\text{small}}^i \cap S_j| \le \frac{|S_j|}{2^i \cdot 500k \cdot \log(nk)}.$$

Now we are ready to state and prove the main result of this subsection.

Lemma 6. *Almost all nodes $u \in V$ have a good approximation $\ell_u \approx |\mathcal{S}(u)|$. That is, for every cluster S_j the following conditions hold:*

1. $\frac{|\mathcal{B}_\ell \cap S_j|}{|S_j|} \le \frac{1}{500k \cdot \log nk}$;
2. $\forall u \notin \mathcal{B}_\ell$, it holds that $|\mathcal{S}(u)| \le \ell_u \le 4|\mathcal{S}(u)|$.

Proof. Applying Lemmas 4 and 5 we have that

$$\frac{|\mathcal{B}_\ell \cap S_j|}{|S_j|} \le \frac{|\mathcal{B}_{\text{small}} \cap S_j|}{|S_j|} + \frac{|\mathcal{B}_{\text{big}} \cap S_j|}{|S_j|} \le \frac{1}{500k \cdot \log(nk)}.$$

$\square$

3.3   Analysis of the Small Detection Phase

This subsection is dedicated to the analysis of the Small Detection phase of our clustering algorithm and thus to the analysis of Algorithm 2. In this section we will show that our algorithm will perfectly recover all clusters of small size. We first introduce some notation. Up to a permutation of the indices, without loss of generality we consider the clusters $S_1, \ldots, S_p$ such that

$$|S_i| \le \log(n),$$

for each $1 \le i \le p \le k$. Moreover, we will denote by

$$\mathcal{A} = S_1 \cup \cdots \cup S_p$$

to be the union of these clusters. The proof of our claim lies on the key observation that, for nodes $u \in \mathcal{A}$, there is a large enough gap between the mass values of diffusion processes started in the same cluster and processes started indifferent clusters. This observation is formalised below.

Lemma 7. *For any $u \in \mathcal{A}$ and $v \in V$ the following statements hold.*

1. *If $v \in \mathcal{S}(u)$, then $|x_T^u(u) - x_T^v(u)| \le \frac{1}{100\sqrt{d} \cdot \log(n)}$;*
2. *If $v \notin \mathcal{S}(u)$, then $|x_T^u(u) - x_T^v(u)| \ge \frac{9}{10\sqrt{d} \cdot |\mathcal{S}(u)|}$*

Now we state and prove the main result of this subsection.

Lemma 8. *Let S_j be a cluster such that $|S_j| \le \log(n)$. At the end of the Small Detection phase of the algorithm, all nodes $u \in S_j$ will agree on a unique label. Moreover, this label is $\mathsf{ID}(v)$, for some $v \in S_j$.*

Proof. Let S_j be some cluster of size $|S_j| \le \log(n)$ and let $u \in S_j$ be some node. Applying Lemma 6, we see that all nodes $u \in S_j$ have an approximation $|S_j| \le \ell_u \le 4|S_j| \le 4\log(n)$. Therefore every node $u \in S_j$ will certainly perform the Small Detection phase (Line 6 of Algorithm 4).

Firstly, u sorts the values $y_v = |x_T^u(u) - x_T^v(u)|$, for all $v \in V$. Say the sorted values are $y_{v_1} \le \cdots \le y_{v_n}$. Notice that if $w_1 \in S_j$ and $w_2 \notin S_j$, by Lemma 7 it must be that

$$|x_T^u(u) - x_T^{w_1}(u)| \le \frac{1}{100\sqrt{d} \cdot \log(n)} < \frac{9}{10\sqrt{d} \cdot |S_j|} \le |x_T^u(u) - x_T^{w_2}(u)|.$$

Therefore, u knows that the first $|S_j|$ values, namely $y_{v_1}, \ldots, y_{v_{|S_j|}}$ correspond to nodes in its own cluster and the other values correspond to nodes in different clusters. Thus, u needs to find a pair of consecutive values $y_{v_i} \leq y_{v_{i+1}}$ such that $v_i \in S_j$ and $v_{i+1} \notin S_j$.

To do this, u performs a binary search to find the size of its cluster. At any intermediate phase, say u considers the value y_{v_i}, for some i, and compares this with $\frac{9}{10\sqrt{d}\cdot i}$. If $y_{v_i} < \frac{9}{10\sqrt{d}\cdot i}$ we claim that $i \leq |S_j|$. If not, then $v_i \notin S_j$ and by Lemma 7 we have that

$$y_{v_i} \geq \frac{9}{10\sqrt{d}\cdot|S_j|} \geq \frac{9}{10\sqrt{d}\cdot i},$$

which gives the contradiction. Similarly, we can show that if $y_{v_i} \geq \frac{9}{10\sqrt{d}\cdot i}$ then $i > |S_j|$.

Once the node u finds the exact size of its cluster $|\mathcal{S}(u)|$, he also knows which nodes are in the same cluster, i.e. $v_1, \ldots, v_{|\mathcal{S}(u)|}$. Thus u can set its label to be the smallest ID among nodes in its cluster. This holds for all nodes $u \in S_j$ and all clusters S_j.   □

3.4   Analysis of the Large Detection Phase

At this point, we will assume all n random walks have been completed, i.e. the T rounds have been executed and each node u has a list of values $\{x_T^v(u)\}_v$. From the perspective of u, we would like to use this information to decide which nodes are in the same cluster as u and which are not. Unfortunately, node u cannot trust all values $x_T^v(u)$ because of the error term $\varepsilon_{(v,u)}$. Going back to Eq. (6), we see that these errors are dependent on the parameters α_v. To overcome this issue, we define the notion of a γ-bad node, that is a node v for which the value of α_v is large relative to its cluster size:

Definition 9. *We say that a node u is γ-bad if*

$$\alpha_u \geq \frac{\gamma \cdot C_\alpha \cdot k^2}{d \cdot \Upsilon \cdot |\mathcal{S}(u)|}.$$

The set of γ-bad nodes is denoted by

$$\mathcal{B}_\gamma \triangleq \left\{ u \,\middle|\, \alpha_u \geq \frac{\gamma \cdot C_\alpha \cdot k^2}{d \cdot \Upsilon \cdot |\mathcal{S}(u)|} \right\}.$$

One should think about the γ-bad nodes as nodes for which the diffusion process does not necessarily behave as expected. Hence we want to avoid activating them since they are not good representatives for their own clusters. To put it differently, combining Eq. (6) with the above definition, we have the following remark:

Remark 10. For every node $v \notin \mathcal{B}_\gamma$ it holds that

$$\|\varepsilon_v\|^2 \leq C_\varepsilon (1 + C_\alpha \cdot \gamma) \cdot \left(\frac{k^2}{d \cdot \Upsilon \cdot |\mathcal{S}(v)|} \right) \leq \frac{2 \cdot C_\varepsilon \cdot C_\alpha \cdot \gamma \cdot k^2}{d \cdot \Upsilon \cdot |\mathcal{S}(v)|}.$$

For the rest of the analysis, we will consider the value

$$\gamma \triangleq 500k \cdot \log(100k). \tag{8}$$

As for the question of how many γ-bad nodes are inside each cluster, the answer is not too many and is formalised in the Lemma bellow:

Lemma 11. *Let S_j be some cluster. It holds that*

$$|\mathcal{B}_\gamma \cap S_j| \leq \frac{|S_j|}{\gamma}.$$

The ultimate goal of the activation process is to select representatives for each cluster in such a way that the following conditions hold: (1) Every cluster has at least one active node, (2) The total number of active nodes is small and (3) No γ-bad node becomes active. Recall that each node activates independently with probability

$$p(u) = \frac{5 \log(100k)}{\ell_u}.$$

For most nodes, i.e. $u \in V \setminus \mathcal{B}_\ell$, the probabilities are good enough to ensure the three conditions hold. The tricky part is to deal with nodes $u \in \mathcal{B}_\ell$. More precisely, for nodes u such that $\ell_u \ll |\mathcal{S}(u)|$ and $u \in \mathcal{B}_\gamma$ the activation probability is simply too large to reason directly that no such node becomes active. We overcome this by first showing that, with high constant probability, no node $u \in \mathcal{B}_\ell$ becomes active, and based on this no node in $\mathcal{B}_\gamma$ becomes active as well. We formalise our discussion in Lemma 12, which is the main technical result of this subsection.

Lemma 12. *With probability at least 0.9, the following statements hold:*

A1. No node from $\mathcal{B}_\ell \cup \mathcal{B}_\gamma$ becomes active.
A2. Every cluster S_j contains at least one active node $v_j^* \in S_j \setminus \mathcal{B}_\ell$;
A3. The total number of active nodes is $n_a \leq 500k \cdot \log(100k)$;

Now we are ready to state the main result of this subsection.

Lemma 13. *At the end of the Large Detection phase, with probability at least 0.9, for any cluster S_j of size $|S_j| > \log(n)$, all but $o(|S_j|)$ nodes $u \in S_j$ will determine the same label. Moreover, this label is $\mathsf{ID}(v)$ for some $v \in S_j$.*

Proof (Sketch). We assume the conclusions of Lemma 12 hold. Fix some cluster S_j. We focus on the nodes $u \in S_j' = S_j \setminus \mathcal{B}_\ell$ and assume the other nodes are misclassified. This is sufficient since, by Lemma 6, $|S_j \cap \mathcal{B}_\ell| = o(|S_j|)$. Let s_j^* be the active node in S_j of smallest ID. By (A2) and (A1) we know s_j^* exists and $s_j^* \notin \mathcal{B}_\ell \cup \mathcal{B}_\gamma$. Let $u \in S_j'$ be a misclassified node. By the Algorithm's description we know one of the two conditions must happen:

1. $s_j^* \notin \mathsf{Cand}(u)$
2. $\exists v^* \notin S_j$, but $v^* \in \mathsf{Cand}(u)$

We look at each condition separately. For the first one, since $s_j^*, u \in S_j'$, it must be that $x_T^{s_j^*}(u) < t_u$. This means that the error $\varepsilon_{(s_j^*,u)}$ is large in absolute value: $\varepsilon_{(s_j^*,u)} < -\frac{1}{2\sqrt{d}|S_j|}$. But since $s_j^* \notin \mathcal{B}_\gamma$, by Remark 10 the total error $\left\| \boldsymbol{\varepsilon}_{s_j^*} \right\|$ cannot be too large. This means that the first condition can happen only for a small number $o(|S_j|)$ of nodes. For the second condition the argument is similar. Let v^* be an active node such that $v^* \notin S_j$, but $v^* \in \mathsf{Cand}(u)$. Since $v^* \in \mathsf{Cand}(u)$, we know that $\ell_u \approx \ell_{v^*}$ and that the error $\varepsilon_{(v^*,u)}$ is quite large: $\varepsilon_{(v^*,u)} \geq t_u$. However, by (A1) $v^* \notin \mathcal{B}_\gamma$, so $\left\| \boldsymbol{\varepsilon}_{v^*} \right\|$ cannot be too large. Therefore v^* can be a candidate for a limited number of $u \in S_j'$. Summing over all active nodes and using the upper bound (A3) is sufficient to show that condition 2 can happen only for a small number $o(|S_j|)$ of nodes. □

3.5 Proof of the Main Result

In this section we bring everything together and prove Theorem 1:

Proof (Proof of Theorem 1)
Number of Rounds. Firstly, let us look at the number of rounds of our Algorithm 4. We know that the Averaging phase of the algorithm takes $T = \Theta\left(\frac{\log(n)}{\lambda_{k+1}}\right)$ rounds. The Small Detection phase does not require any extra rounds of communication. For the Large Detection phase, we have again T rounds. This brings the total number of rounds to

$$2 \cdot T = \Theta\left(\frac{\log(n)}{\lambda_{k+1}}\right).$$

Clustering Guarantee. Secondly, we will look at the clustering guarantees of Algorithm 4. Let S_j be some cluster of G. If $|S_j| \leq \log(n)$, then by Lemma 8 we know that all nodes of S_j will choose the same label, that is the minimum ID among nodes in S_j. If $|S_j| > \log(n)$, by Lemma 13 it follows that with probability at least 0.9 all but $o(|S_j|)$ nodes will determine the same label that is the ID(v) for some $v \in S_j$.

Communication Cost. Let us first look at the cost for the Averaging phase. In any round $i \leq T$, every node u has to send to all its neighbours the values $\{x_{i-1}^v(u)\}$. This results in a total communication cost of $\text{cost}_{\text{Avg}} = O(T \cdot n \cdot m)$. Again, for the Small Detection phase there is no cost attached. While for the Large Detection phase, by Lemma 13 we know that, with probability at least 0.9, the total number of active nodes is $n_a = O(k \log(n) \cdot \log(k \log(n)))$. By the design of Algorithm 3, every node u in the network will broadcast each active node at most once. Therefore the total communication cost in the Large Detection phase is $\text{cost}_{\text{LD}} = O(m \cdot n_a) = O(mk \cdot \log(k))$. This gives in total a communication cost of $O(\text{cost}_{\text{Avg}} + \text{cost}_{\text{LD}}) = O(T \cdot n \cdot m)$. We remark that, while in general the number of edges could be $m = \Theta(n^2)$, we can first apply the sampling scheme in [23] to sparsify our network and then run our algorithm. The sparsification ensures that the structure of the clusters, the degree sequence and the parameter $\Upsilon_G(k)$ are preserved up to a small constant factor and the resulting number of edges becomes $m = \widetilde{O}(n)$. Thus the final communication cost can be expressed as $\widetilde{O}(T \cdot n^2)$. □

Acknowledgements. I would like to thank my supervisor Dr. He Sun for helpful discussion and comments on improving the presentation of this paper.

References

1. Allen-Zhu, Z., Lattanzi, S., Mirrokni, V.S.: A local algorithm for finding well-connected clusters. In: 30th International Conference on Machine Learning (ICML 2013), pp. 396–404 (2013)
2. Becchetti, L., Clementi, A.E.F., Manurangsi, P., Natale, E., Pasquale, F., Raghavendra, P., Trevisan, L.: Average whenever you meet: Opportunistic protocols for community detection. In: 26th European Symposium on Algorithms (ESA'18). LIPIcs, vol. 112, pp. 7:1–7:13. Schloss Dagstuhl - Leibniz-Zentrum für Informatik (2018). https://doi.org/10.4230/LIPIcs.ESA.2018.7
3. Becchetti, L., Clementi, A.E.F., Natale, E., Pasquale, F., Trevisan, L.: Find your place: simple distributed algorithms for community detection. SIAM J. Comput. **49**(4), 821–864 (2020). https://doi.org/10.1137/19M1243026
4. Becchetti, L., Cruciani, E., Pasquale, F., Rizzo, S.: Step-by-step community detection in volume-regular graphs. Theoret. Comput. Sci. **847**, 49–67 (2020). https://doi.org/10.1016/j.tcs.2020.09.036
5. Boyd, S.P., Ghosh, A., Prabhakar, B., Shah, D.: Randomized gossip algorithms. IEEE Trans. Inf. Theory **52**(6), 2508–2530 (2006). https://doi.org/10.1109/TIT.2006.874516
6. Chang, Y., Saranurak, T.: Improved distributed expander decomposition and nearly optimal triangle enumeration. In: Robinson, P., Ellen, F. (eds.) Proceedings of the 2019 ACM Symposium on Principles of Distributed Computing, PODC 2019, Toronto, ON, Canada, 29 July–2 August 2019, pp. 66–73. ACM (2019). https://doi.org/10.1145/3293611.3331618
7. Chang, Y., Saranurak, T.: Deterministic distributed expander decomposition and routing with applications in distributed derandomization. In: 61st Annual IEEE Symposium on Foundations of Computer Science (FOCS 2020), pp. 377–388. IEEE (2020). https://doi.org/10.1109/FOCS46700.2020.00043
8. Chen, J., Sun, H., Woodruff, D.P., Zhang, Q.: Communication-optimal distributed clustering. In: Lee, D.D., Sugiyama, M., von Luxburg, U., Guyon, I., Garnett, R. (eds.) 29th Advances in Neural Information Processing Systems (NeurIPS 2016), pp. 3720–3728 (2016)
9. Czumaj, A., Peng, P., Sohler, C.: Testing cluster structure of graphs. In: 47th Annual ACM Symposium on Theory of Computing (STOC 2015), pp. 723–732. ACM (2015). https://doi.org/10.1145/2746539.2746618
10. Fortunato, S.: Community detection in graphs. Phys. Rep. **486**(3–5), 75–174 (2010)
11. Georgakopoulos, A., Haslegrave, J., Sauerwald, T., Sylvester, J.: The power of two choices for random walks. arXiv preprint arXiv:1911.05170 (2019)

12. Hui, P., Yoneki, E., Chan, S.Y., Crowcroft, J.: Distributed community detection in delay tolerant networks. In: Proceedings of 2nd ACM/IEEE International Workshop on Mobility in the Evolving Internet Architecture. Association for Computing Machinery (2007). https://doi.org/10.1145/1366919.1366929

13. Laenen, S., Sun, H.: Higher-order spectral clustering of directed graphs. In: 33rd Advances in Neural Information Processing Systems (NeurIPS 2020) (2020)

14. Lee, J.R., Gharan, S.O., Trevisan, L.: Multiway spectral partitioning and higher-order Cheeger inequalities. J. ACM **61**(6), 37:1–37:30 (2014). https://doi.org/10.1145/2665063

15. Li, A., Peng, P.: Community structures in classical network models. Internet Math. **7**(2), 81–106 (2011). https://doi.org/10.1080/15427951.2011.566458

16. von Luxburg, U.: A tutorial on spectral clustering. Stat. Comput. **17**(4), 395–416 (2007). https://doi.org/10.1007/s11222-007-9033-z

17. Ng, A.Y., Jordan, M.I., Weiss, Y.: On spectral clustering: analysis and an algorithm. In: 14th Advances in Neural Information Processing Systems (NeurIPS 2021), pp. 849–856. MIT Press (2001)

18. Oveis Gharan, S., Trevisan, L.: Partitioning into expanders. In: 25th Annual ACM-SIAM Symposium on Discrete Algorithms (SODA 2014), pp. 1256–1266. SIAM (2014). https://doi.org/10.1137/1.9781611973402.93

19. Peng, R., Sun, H., Zanetti, L.: Partitioning well-clustered graphs: spectral clustering works!. SIAM J. Comput. **46**(2), 710–743 (2017). https://doi.org/10.1137/15M1047209

20. Sauerwald, T., Zanetti, L.: Random walks on dynamic graphs: mixing times, hitting times, and return probabilities. In: 46th International Colloquium on Automata, Languages, and Programming (ICALP 2019). LIPIcs, vol. 132, pp. 93:1–93:15. Schloss Dagstuhl - Leibniz-Zentrum für Informatik (2019). https://doi.org/10.4230/LIPIcs.ICALP.2019.93

21. Schaeffer, S.E.: Graph clustering. Comput. Sci. Rev. **1**(1), 27–64 (2007). https://doi.org/10.1016/j.cosrev.2007.05.001

22. Shi, J., Malik, J.: Normalized cuts and image segmentation. IEEE Trans. Pattern Anal. Mach. Intell. **22**(8), 888–905 (2000). https://doi.org/10.1109/34.868688

23. Sun, H., Zanetti, L.: Distributed graph clustering and sparsification. ACM Trans. Parallel Comput. **6**(3), 17:1–17:23 (2019). https://doi.org/10.1145/3364208

24. Yang, W., Xu, H.: A divide and conquer framework for distributed graph clustering. In: 32nd International Conference on Machine Learning (ICML 2015). JMLR Workshop and Conference Proceedings, vol. 37, pp. 504–513 (2015). JMLR.org

Author Index

Printed in the United States
by Baker & Taylor Publisher Services